Rand McNally
PICTORIAL WORLD ATLAS

Rand McNally

PICTORIAL
WORLD ATLAS

Brian P. Price

Rand McNally & Company
Chicago · New York · San Francisco

CONTENTS

13   EUROPE

57   USSR

67   ASIA

Rand McNally Pictorial World Atlas, Copyright © 1980 by Rand McNally & Company
Map pages, World Political Information Tables and Index pages © Rand McNally & Company from *The International Atlas* © 1969 Rand McNally & Company, re-edited for *The Earth and Man* © 1972
Thematic Maps from Goode's World Atlas © 1978 Rand McNally & Company

 The text Copyright © 1980 by Intercontinental Book Productions Limited and Rand McNally & Company

Designed by Intercontinental Book Productions Limited

SBN 528-83105-4
All rights reserved
Library of Congress Number: 79-50872
Printed in the United States of America

Photographs
All photographs were supplied by Colour Library International Limited except for those listed below.

Picture credits are by page number/picture number.
Australian News and Information Service: 109/1, 109/2, 109/3
British Antarctic Survey: 189/1, 189/2, 189/3
British Petroleum Company: 17/1
Camera Press: 41/2, 41/3, 41/4, 53/1, 79/1, 154/1, 170/2
Bruce Coleman Limited: 188/1
Rosemary Hartill: 138/1, 141/2
Italian State Tourist Office: 19/2
Novosti Press Agency: 58/3, 59/1, 59/2, 59/3, 60/1, 60/2, 61/2, 194/1
Volkswagen UK Limited: 17/3
Ginzy, Atoz/Van Cleve: 176/1

Front end paper: Kleine Scheidegg Jungfrau, Switzerland
Back end paper: Tahiti

87 AFRICA

107 OCEANIA

121 MIDDLE AMERICA

133 SOUTH AMERICA

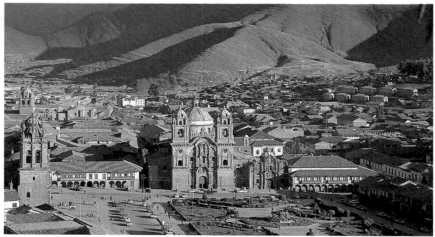

149 NORTH AMERICA

189 POLAR REGIONS

193 WORLD TO VIEW

201 INDEX

INTRODUCTION

At any given moment the minds of most people are concerned primarily with their own immediate world: the farmer with his land, animals and crops, the office worker with his piles of paper, the housewife with her home and family. Think, though, of man in relation to the earth, with its surface area of 500 million km² (nearly 200 million sq mi), which is seemingly large enough to accommodate and provide for all of mankind. The contribution, then, of any one person to world achievement is minute.

Population has accelerated alarmingly in the last 130 years. From 1,200 million in 1850, world population rose to 2,485 million in 1950, 2,982 million in 1960 and 3,635 million in 1970. By 1978, the figure was 4,119 million. The world's population will almost certainly have doubled again in the half century 1930–'80. And by the year 2000, at the present rates of growth, it could be over 6,500 million.

At the same time as man's numbers have increased, so too have his overall demands on the earth. Granted there are great differences between the demands of the developed world and those of the developing world. Yet the living standards of a large proportion of the world's population are now far higher than those of their ancestors. There has been more than a proportionate increase in the demands for food, raw materials and material possessions. Such trends cannot go on forever. Men must become aware of the consequences of their own actions, be it building up population pressure, abusing nature or wasting limited resources.

Water has long been taken from the rivers and seas, but what do we put back? Sewage, poison wastes from industries, fertilizers and pesticides washed from the land, radioactive waste in 'safe' containers – all these are mixed up in the seas. If unchecked, such noxious substances could one day make the water which is essential to life a danger to that life.

Until comparatively recently people have also taken the earth's resources for granted, without much thought for the coming generations. Fossil fuels are the classic case, and it is now likely that the world's oil riches will have been largely squandered during the twentieth century. Where will man turn next for a new source of energy?

Careless use of the land must not go unremarked. In the long history of developing new lands, man has sometimes made his own catastrophes by stripping the natural vegetation. On a large scale, the dust bowl of the southern interior of the USA created in the late 1920s and early '30s was a classic case. But, on many smaller scales, the use of shifting agriculture in many areas of the Third World also leads to a waste of the land.

In the past then, we have tended to be rather rash and careless in our use of the environment. Fortunately, the inventive and enquiring minds of modern scientists have been ever busy. In the field of agriculture, new strains of seeds, new breeds of animals and new techniques of farming have led to increases in the amount of food which can be grown on a given area. In industry, new inventions and techniques have greatly increased the speed of producing many materials and goods and decreased the production costs. In science and technology, the opening up of new areas of knowledge, such as electronics and computing, enable more tasks to be done for more people by fewer.

Thus, more and more should we regard this as the quickening world, thankful for the inventiveness of men's minds, thankful for the apparent riches of the earth yet ever conscious of the fact that man treads a tightrope from which he could so easily fall through his own thoughtlessness and stupidity.

How to Use this Atlas

The conventional continental division of the world is no longer ideal for modern purposes. The USSR, for instance, which straddles two continents, is important and large enough to be given separate treatment. Further, the Americas are increasingly divided into three: the largely English-speaking North, the Spanish/Portuguese heritage of the South, and the patchwork of predominantly Latin mainland states together with the Caribbean and other islands of Middle America. In this atlas, therefore, the world has been divided into nine major areas: Europe and Asia, with the USSR as a separate entity; Africa; Oceania; the three Americas as described and, in addition, the Polar Regions.

Each continental section within the atlas is self-contained, and each section, with the exception of the Polar Regions, contains the following features:

Political maps
Mainly on two scales, the smaller (1:13,200,000) presenting the continents as a whole on one or more maps, the larger (1:3,300,000) showing countries or areas in greater detail. The maps emphasize political features and show the main physical features.

Text
Each continental section begins with a Physical Profile, giving details of world location, size, landscape and climate. Further information covers the continent's history, culture, population, politics, industry, commerce, communications, agriculture, forestry, fishing, natural resources and economy. Rounding off each continent, under the heading '. . . . . . . Countries', is information on the individual countries. There are entries for every country, arranged in alphabetical order.

Travelogs
Interspersed with the 1:3,300,000 maps of Europe, expanded text and picture coverage give lighter, general summaries of selected European countries.

Opposite: Golden Pavilion of the Kinkaku-Ji Temple, Kyoto, Japan

Illustrations
Throughout the book 300 color illustrations (numbered for ease of reference) reveal the great variety of natural environments, and also show aspects of industry, agriculture, architecture, or everyday life. Extended captions complement the pictures.

Diagrams
In measures of world activity, growth and standards, three main criteria have been used. National trade figures (imports and exports) give an impression of the extent to which a country has developed and is involved in the world scene. The average earnings of the population indicate the living standards of the people. Finally, the average amounts of energy used per capita relate to one of the key issues in the world and are also a barometer of levels of development. Using common scales throughout the book for ease of cross reference, three diagrams within each continental section show the ranges within these sets of figures for selected countries. The diagrams are based on the most recent available statistics.

Mineral production tables
Within the main continental sections, under the heading 'Natural Resources', each table gives world production of ores, the continental share per ore and the principal producing countries.

Country reference tables
This table, which is found at the end of the country entries, covers every country within the continent, giving details of political status on the following classification:

A Independent countries.
B Countries with internal independence, yet under the control of another country at least for foreign and defense matters.
C Colonies which are completely dependent on another country. Also component units within certain countries.
D Component states or provinces within selected federal countries.

State capitals are listed, followed by data on national area, population, birth rates, death rates and, finally, the average annual percentage increase in the national populations in recent years. Comparisons of these figures reveal clearly the centers of the world population explosion. When compared with the existing populations and densities of populations, they give an added indication of the parts of the world where sheer population pressure, regardless of the local ability to cater for its needs, is greatest.

Following the continental sections other features are as follows:

Polar Regions
Due to their similarities of climate the Arctic and the Antarctic have been treated as a unit. A general introduction is followed by maps of the Arctic and the Antarctic and detailed information.

Thematic maps
In the 'World to View' section are world maps on the subjects of languages, literacy, predominant economies, population density and climatic regions. Each is accompanied by explanatory text.

Index
Found at the end of the book this is an alphabetical list of the names appearing on the maps, giving a page reference, coordinates and, where applicable, a symbol indicating the nature of the feature.

The above breakdown is a guide to the scope of the atlas's component units. Used in conjunction with the Contents, Index and Major Data page references (opposite) it will provide an invaluable key to the information you need.

For example, you may want to find out about Poland's economy and how this rates in world terms. Turn firstly to the individual entry for Poland (p. 24) under the heading 'European Countries'; this gives general details of the Polish economy. Within the main European section are the diagrams showing imports/exports, per capita income, and energy usage (pp. 17, 18, 19): these provide specific data on key areas of the economy. Polish figures can be readily compared with those for other European countries. Reference to diagrams in other continental sections give worldwide comparisons.

Also within the main European section, under the headings 'Industry, Commerce and Communications', 'Agriculture, Forestry and Fishing', 'Natural Resources', and 'European Economy' (pp. 15–19), is information on aspects of the European economy as a whole, with specific references to Poland. The table of mineral production (p. 16), under 'Natural Resources', shows the principal minerals Poland produces.

The map of Central Europe (pp. 36–37), at a scale of 1:3,300,000, includes Poland, showing something of her physical relief and indicating her position in relation to her neighbors. Following this there is a brief reference to the Polish economy under the travelog heading 'Eastern Europe' (p. 41).

Finally, in the 'World to View' section, the world map of 'Predominant Economies' (pp. 194–195) indicates Poland's principal economic activities.

Important data appears in the diagrams and tables in each continental section. Page references are listed below, continent by continent.

MAJOR DATA: page references

	DIAGRAMS			TABLES	
	Imports/ Exports	Income	Energy	Mineral Production	Country Reference
Europe	17	18	19	16	24
USSR	59	60	60	60	61
Asia	71	72	73	71	78
Africa	89	90	91	90	98
Oceania	109	110	110	110	114
Middle America	123	124	125	123	128
South America	135	136	137	137	142
North America	152	153	154	153	159

Legend to Maps

Inhabited Localities

The symbol represents the number of inhabitants within the locality

1:3,300,000	•	0—10,000	1:13,200,000	·	0—50,000
1:6,600,000	○	10,000—25,000		⊛	50,000—100,000
	⊙	25,000—100,000		⊞	100,000—250,000
	⊡	100,000—250,000		⊠	250,000—1,000,000
	▣	250,000—1,000,000		■	>1,000,000
	■	>1,000,000			

Urban Area (area of continuous industrial, commercial, and residential development)

The size of type indicates the relative economic and political importance of the locality

Écommoy	Lisieux	**Rouen**
Trouville	**Orléans**	**PARIS**

Hollywood □   Section of a City, Neighborhood
Westminster

Bi'r Safâjah °   Oasis

Capitals of Political Units

BUDAPEST   Independent Nation

Cayenne   Dependency (Colony, protectorate, etc.)

GALAPAGOS (Ecuador)   Administering Country

Villarica   State, Province, etc.

White Plains   County, Oblast, etc.

Alternate Names

Basel   **MOSKVA**   English or second official language names are shown
Bâle   MOSCOW   in reduced size lettering

Ventura   Volgograd   Historical or other alternates in the local language
(San Buenaventura)   (Stalingrad)   are shown in parentheses

Political Boundaries

International (First-order political unit)

1:3,300,000
1:6,600,000
1:13,200,000

———·———·———   Demarcated, Undemarcated, and Administrative

——·——·——·——   Disputed de jure

—— —— —— ——   Indefinite or Undefined

—·—·—·—·—·—   Demarcation Line

Internal

State, Province, etc. (Second-order political unit)
GUAIRA

County, Oblast, etc. (Third-order political unit)
WESTCHESTER

ANDALUCIA   Historical Region (No boundaries indicated)

Miscellaneous Cultural Features

PARQUE NACIONAL CANAIMA ▲   National or State Park or Monument

FORT CLATSOP NAT. MEM. ▲   National or State Historic(al) Site, Memorial

BLACKFOOT IND. RES.   Indian Reservation

FORT DIX ■   Military Installation

▲ TANGLEWOOD   Point of Interest (Battlefield, cave, historical site, etc.)

⊥ STEINHAUSEN   Church, Monastery

∴ UXMAL   Ruins

Y WINDSOR CASTLE   Castle

∕ AMISTAD DAM   Dam

World Index Map

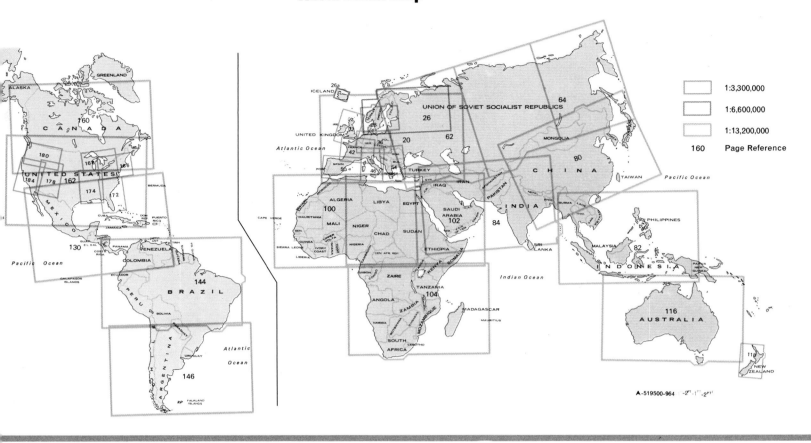

	1:3,300,000
	1:6,600,000
	1:13,200,000
160	Page Reference

A-519500-964

Transportation

1:13,200,000	1:3,300,000 1:6,600,000	
		Primary Road
		Secondary Road
		Minor Road, Trail
		Primary Railway
		Airport

MACKINAC BRIDGE	Bridge
GREAT ST. BERNARD TUNNEL	Tunnel
TO CALAIS	Ferry

	Shipping Channel
Canal du Midi	Navigable Canal
	Intracoastal Waterway

Metric-English Equivalents

Areas represented by one square centimeter at various map scales

1:3,300,000	1:6,600,000	1:13,200,000
1,089 km²	4,356 km²	17,424 km²
421 square miles	1,682 square miles	6,725 square miles

Meter=3.28 feet
Kilometer=0.62 mile

Meter² (m²)=10.76 square feet
Kilometer² (km²)=0.39 square mile

Hydrographic Features

	Shoreline	The Everglades	Swamp
	Undefined or Fluctuating Shoreline	SEWARD GLACIER	Glacier
Amur	River, Stream	L. Victoria	Lake, Reservoir
	Intermittent Stream	Tuz Gölü	Salt Lake
	Rapids, Falls		Intermittent Lake, Reservoir
	Irrigation or Drainage Canal		Dry Lake Bed
	Reef	(395)	Lake Surface Elevation
764 ▽	Depth of Water		

Topographic Features

			Lava
Mt. Kenya △ 5199	Elevation Above Sea Level		Sand Area
76 ▽	Elevation Below Sea Level		Salt Flat
Mount Cook ▲ 3764	Highest Elevation in Country	A N D E S KUNLUNSHANMAI	Mountain Range, Plateau, Valley, etc.
Khyber Pass ⚌ 1067	Mountain Pass		
133 ▼	Lowest Elevation in Country	BAFFIN ISLAND NUNIVAK ISLAND	Island
		POLUOSTROV KAMČATKA CABO DE HORNOS	Peninsula, Cape, Point, etc.

Elevations and depths are given in meters
Highest Elevation and Lowest Elevation of a continent are underlined

ARCTIC OCEAN

More Laptevych

NOVOSIBIRSKIJE OSTROVA

ZEML'A FRANCA-IOSIFA

Barents Sea

Hammerfest

Murmansk

NOVAJA ZEML'A

Karskoje More

Dikson

Nordvik

Chatanga

Tiksi

Arctic Circle

Narvik

Narjan-Mar

Vorkuta

Salechard

Nori'sk

Igarka

Jenisej

Lena

Verchojansk

SWEDEN

FINLAND

Helsinki

Ladožskoje Ozero

Archangel'sk

Ob'

Lensk

Jakutsk

Anadyr

60°

Stockholm

LENINGRAD

Perm'

Sverdlovsk

Čel'abinsk

Omsk

Irkutsk

Krasnojarsk

Magadan

Ochotsk

København

POLAND

MOSKVA

Gor'kij

URALSKIJE

Novosibirsk

Ozero Bajkal

Čita

Nikolajevsk

Sea of Okhotsk

Petropavlovsk-Kamcatskij

Bering Sea

Warszawa

UNION OF SOVIET SOCIALIST REPUBLICS

GORY

Karaganda

Chabarovsk

ALEUTIAN IS. (U.S.)

G.D.R.

Kijev

Kujbyšev

Ural

Ozero Balchaš

Ulaanbaatar

OSTROV SACHALIN

Južno-Sachalinsk

45°

CZECH.

Praha

Volgograd

Astrachan'

Alma-Ata

MONGOLIA

Haerbin

KURIL'SKIJE OSTROVA

HUNG.

Budapest

Gora El'brus

Caspian Sea

Aral'skoje More

Taškent

GOBI

ALTAJ

Vladivostok

Sapporo

ROM.

Beograd

5633

BOL'ŠOJ KAVKAZ

TIEN SHAN

Wulumuqi

N. KOREA

Pyongyang

Sea of Japan

HONSHŪ

JAPAN

Sendai

Bucureşti

Black Sea

Istanbul

Baku

Suoche

BEIJING PEKING

Shenyang

S. KOREA

Pusan

Fukuoka

OSAKA

TŌKYŌ

BUL.

Sofija

Ankara

Tbilisi

Huhehaote

Tianjin

Lüda

Qingdao

Athinai

TURKEY

Tehrān

Kābul

Islāmābād

Hwangho

Lanzhou

Xi'an

Yellow Sea

SHANGHAI

MALTA

CYPRUS

LEB.

SYRIA

Esfahān

AFGHANISTAN

Rawalpindi

HIMALAYAS

Lasa

Chengdu

Nanjing

Wuhan

Changtha

Tarābulus

ISRAEL

Baghdād

IRAN

Lahore

NEPAL

Everest

8848

Chongqing

Changjiang

Fuzhou

LIBYA

AL-QĀHIRAH

CAIRO

JORDAN

IRAQ

Ābādān

KUWAIT

PAKISTAN

DELHI

Kathmandu

CHINA

Kunming

Guangzhou

T'aipei

TAIWAN

EGYPT

Aswān

SAUDI

Ar-Riyād

QATAR

UNITED ARAB EMIRATES

Karāchi

New Delhi

Tropic of Cancer

CALCUTTA

Dacca

BURMA

HONG KONG (U.K.)

Ha-noi

Red Sea

Makkah

Masqat

OMAN

Ahmadābād

INDIA

BNGL.

HAINANDAO

South

PACIFIC

OCEAN

WAKE ISLAND (U.S.)

ARABIA

BOMBAY

Hyderābād

Bay of

THAILAND

VIETNAM

China

Philippine

MARIANA

Sea

NIGER

CHAD

Al-Khurtūm

YEMEN

P.D.R. OF YEMEN (P.D.R. of Yem.)

SUQUTRA (P.D.R. of Yem.)

Arabian

Bangalore

Madras

Bengal

Krung Thep

Bangkok

KAM.

Phnum Pénh

Sea

MANILA

PHILIPPINES

GUAM (U.S.)

PACIFIC ISLANDS

TRUST TERRITORY (U.S.)

MICRONESIA

MARSHALL

ISLANDS

Kano

Ndjamena

SUDAN

DJIBOUTI

Djibouti

RAS ASIR

Sea

Cochin

SRI LANKA

ANDAMAN ISLANDS (India)

Thanh-pho Ho Chi Minh

Davao

CAROLINE ISLANDS

IGERIA

CEN. AFR. REP.

Addis Abeba

MALDIVES

NICOBAR ISLANDS (India)

Colombo

MALAYSIA

BRUNEI

Equator

KIRIBATI (GILBERT ISLANDS)

Yaoundé

Bangui

ETHIOPIA

ROMALIA

Medan

Kuala Lumpur

Singapore

BORNEO

SULAWESI

NAURU

TUVALU

RIAL NEA

reville

GABON

CONGO

ZAIRE

UGANDA

Kampala

KENYA

Nairobi

Lake Rudolf

Mogadisho

SEYCHELLES

CHAGOS ARCHIPELAGO (B.I.O.T.)

SUMATERA

Palembang

JAKARTA

INDONESIA

Banjarmasin

Ujung Pandang

PAPUA NEW GUINEA

Mount Wilhelm 4509

NEW GUINEA

Port Moresby

SOLOMON

ISLANDS

MELANESIA

SOLOMON ISLANDS

Brazzaville

Kinshasa

RWANDA

BURUNDI

Bujumbura

Lake Victoria

Kilimanjaro 5895

Mombasa

JAWA

Surabaya

TIMOR

CAPE YORK

Luanda

Lubumbashi

TANZANIA

Zanzibar

Dar-es-Salaam

CHRISTMAS ISLAND (Austl.)

Darwin

Gulf of Carpentaria

NEW HEBRIDES (Fr.–U.K.)

Lobito

ANGOLA

ZAMBIA

Lilongwe

Lake Nyasa

INDIAN

Alice Springs

Coral

NEW CALEDONIA (Fr.)

Suva

FIJI

Windhoek

NAMIBIA (S. Afr. Admin.)

ZIMBABWE

Salisbury

Lusaka

MOZAMBIQUE

OCEAN

Tropic of Capricorn

MADAGASCAR

MAURITIUS

RÉUNION (Fr.)

Antananarivo

Sea

Cairns

Rockhampton

Nouméa

Walvisbaai (S. Afr.)

Gaborone

BOTSWANA

Johannesburg

Pretoria

Maputo

SWAZILAND

AUSTRALIA

Brisbane

DRAKENSBERG

LESOTHO

Durban

Perth

Darling

SOUTH AFRICA

Cape Town

Port Elizabeth

CAPE OF GOOD HOPE

Adelaide

Canberra

Mount Kosciusko 2228

Melbourne

Sydney

Tasman Sea

NORTH ISLAND

Auckland

NEW ZEALAND

Wellington

TASMANIA

Hobart

SOUTH ISLAND

Christchurch

45°

ÎLES KERGUELEN (F.S.A.T.)

Antarctic Circle

ENDERBY LAND

AMERY ICE SHELF

WILKES LAND

60°

75°

C   T   I   C   A

Kilometers

0   1000   2000   3000   Km.

Statute Miles

0   1000   2000   3000   Mi.

One centimeter represents 825 kilometers.
One inch represents approximately 1320 miles.
Robinson Projection
Scale 1:82,500,000

EUROPE
Physical
Profile

World Location and Size

Europe is joined to the continent of Asia. Its eastern limits can be regarded as the Ural Mountains which run north to south across the Soviet Union at about 60°E. Although the huge country of the USSR is thus divided between Europe and Asia, for the purposes of this atlas the USSR is being treated as a separate geographical unit.

Europe is situated in the Northern Hemisphere. Its north to south extent is some 4,000 km (2,500 mi) from North Cape in Norway within the Arctic Circle at 71°N to the island of Crete in the Mediterranean Sea at 35°N. From west to east, mainland Europe extends from the Portuguese coast immediately west of Lisbon at nearly 10°W to the margins of the Black Sea in Romania at 29°E, a distance of approximately 3,400 km (2,100 mi). Beyond the mainland, Iceland, the Azores and parts of the Irish Republic lie even farther west.

Within the whole bounds of 35° to 71°N and 10°W to 29°E there is also a large area of ocean and sea. The precise outline of Europe is as intricate as that of any continent, and for a land area of its total size it has a long coastline. The Baltic, Adriatic and Aegean Sea coasts, as well as the fjord coastline of Norway, the margins of all the islands and the more regular-shaped coasts of France and Iberia, together make over 48,000 km (30,000 mi) of coast.

Landscape

The three main physical regions of Europe are two areas dominated by uplands, one in the northwest and the other in the south, and one lowland area fanning out from a narrower north-south extent in the west to a wider one in the east. This pattern persists even where the continental area is interrupted by expanses of sea. There are no great open expanses of relatively monotonous landscape such as are found in some other continents. Not even the lowlands surrounding the Baltic Sea are as expansive as, say, the interior lowlands of North America, the Great Siberian Plain or Amazonia.

The uplands of the north and west are mostly of Caledonian age and are the remains of a chain of mountains formed about 350 million years ago. Today these reach heights of 2,472 m (8,104 ft) in Norway and 1,343 m (4,406 ft) in Scotland. Not all parts of the continent which were formed in Caledonian times are similarly mountainous. Parts of Sweden and all Finland, for example, have been

Opposite: The Colosseum, Rome, Italy

Europe's contrasting physical scope: 1 Mojacar, Almeria – Spanish hilltop town; 2 Hammerfest, Norway – the world's northernmost town. The sun never sets from May to August and never rises from November to February

reduced over the ages by erosion to their present lower physique. The mountains of Iceland were mainly produced by more recent volcanic activity, Iceland being one of the few places in Europe which is volcanically active today.

The lowlands which lie east-west across Europe occupy the largest area of the three major regions. Geologically they are younger than the northern uplands, but older than much of the area to the south. The landscape often has a gently rolling appearance, being a succession of low hills, referred to as scarps, with vales between. Such landscapes dominate much of lowland Britain and northern France. For the most part these lowland areas are less than 150 m (500 ft) above sea level.

Geologically, the mountains of the south are among the youngest parts of the continent, being of Alpine age, less than 100 million years old. They are part of the great system of mountains which lies west-east from northern Spain, through Italy, Switzerland, Austria and the Balkan countries and then on into the USSR and Asia. These are the highest mountains within Europe, rising to 4,807 m (15,771 ft) in Mont Blanc.

As well as the high mountains of the Alpine system, other older upland areas are found in southern Europe. The south central parts of France, parts of central and southern Germany and of western Czechoslovakia are eroded mountain systems which were formed about 200 million years ago in the Hercynian age. In the Massif Central of France these rise to 1,885 m (6,188 ft).

In very recent geological times, northern Europe and the higher parts of the southern mountain areas have been covered with ice. Much smaller areas of northern and mountain Europe are glaciated today. At its maximum advance, the ice covered most of the continent north of about 52°N. It eroded the landscape in many places, and today such features

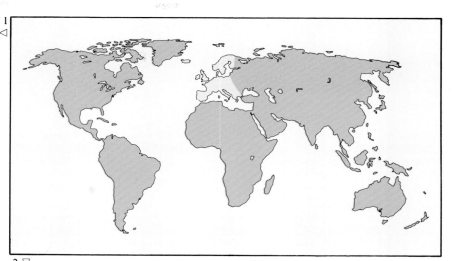

as the Norwegian fjords and the Scottish lochs are evidence of this glaciation. In other places, the ice carried and then deposited much fertile soil which is today the basis of some of the rich farmlands of the central lowlands.

Europe is a continent of comparatively short rivers. No location in the whole continent is more than about 650 km (400 mi) from the sea. The longest river and largest river system is the Danube, rising in southern Germany and flowing eastward to the Black Sea.

Climatic Background

Europe lies on the west side of the world's largest single land mass, Eurasia, almost entirely north of 40°N and south of the Arctic Circle. Since there are no mountain barriers running parallel to the Atlantic coast except in Norway, the warming influences of the west-east moving maritime airs are felt well into the central parts of the continent. Thus most of Europe experiences temperate climates either of the cool or the warm varieties.

Most of western Europe has no month of the year in which the average temperature is less than 0°C (32°F) or above 22°C (72°F). Rainfall is spread fairly evenly throughout the year with no marked 'wet'

and 'dry' seasons. Rainfall totals are almost all above 550 mm (22 in) and in upland areas of the west coast far higher.

Southern Europe also experiences average monthly temperatures always above 0°C (32°F) and in many places always above 6°C (43°F). In some places, particularly in the eastern Mediterranean area, the average monthly temperature in the summer can easily reach as high as 27°C (80°F).

In Eastern Europe and much of Scandinavia, from Bulgaria northward to Finland and much of Sweden, the winters are colder, with the average monthly temperature falling below 0°C (32°F) in midwinter. In the north of this region, the average monthly temperature in the summer months may rise to only 17°C (62°F), while in the south, in Romania and Bulgaria, it rises to above 24°C (75°F), giving the highest temperature range in all of Europe. This pattern is typical, since temperature ranges increase in places which are farther from the moderating effects of an ocean. Northern Europe extends sufficiently far to contain a small area of Polar climates in which no month has an average temperature higher than 10°C (50°F), such conditions being found in the extreme north of Scandinavia and much of Iceland.

EUROPE

Throughout history Europe has been the birthplace of most major developments in Western Civilization, from the democratic principle as originated in Greece, through parliamentary government as developed in the United Kingdom and the evolution of colonial systems as operated by a number of West European countries, to the growth of the industrial and now the technological age. Many of these fundamentals have been adopted by countries in other parts of the world.

Thus, despite being the second smallest of the eight sectors under review, with only Middle America having a smaller total area, there is little doubt that Europe's influence on the whole world has been collectively greater than that of any other continental area. In more recent times, however, other continents have become increasingly important, both politically and economically, due largely to the influence of individual countries, particularly the United States of America and the Soviet Union.

Recent Historical and Political Background

Twice within twenty-five years Europe has been torn apart by wars which subsequently embroiled much of the rest of the world. In the aftermath of both wars, her statesmen struggled to forge a lasting peace – first, in the international arena, through the ill-fated League of Nations. Now Europe is shaping her own destiny with trading links and economic agreements which have joined one-time enemies together as peacetime partners.

Today's unity between British and German politicians, or between governments in Paris and Bonn would have been unthinkable in the high summer of 1914. Then a more powerful Austria and Germany fought Russia, France, Italy, the United Kingdom and the British Empire and, later the USA. The inevitable cost in millions of lives and in the economic impoverishment of virtually the whole continent, left Europe and the rest of the world seeking a way to prevent any similar future catastrophe. Many of the former European kingdoms had been replaced by republics, often controlled by dictators at the head of one-party government systems. Pre-World War I prosperity was not easy to restore, and the world of the 1920s and early '30s was a breeding ground for tension and international anxiety.

The League of Nations was bedevilled by dissent between the major power blocs and its influence was reduced, partly by the severe attitude taken towards their 1914–18 enemies by the western allies, and partly because the USA, for all her help, was not a member, and the Soviet Union did not join until 1934. At the same time, a succession of trade cycles resulted in economic uncertainty and social unrest in many parts of Europe. Germany's share of these problems produced Adolf Hitler and the Nazi party whose nationalist, expansionist policies led the world into a second global war only twenty-one years after the first had ended.

This time, after an initial period in which Germany, Italy and Japan (the Axis powers) together expanded their territory to almost the whole of continental Europe, parts of North Africa, the USSR, the Middle East and much of SE Asia, the Allies (The United Kingdom and the British Commonwealth, the USA, the USSR, China, France and some other European countries) stemmed the Axis tide and, in 1945, were victorious. But again, the resultant economic and social damage was enormous.

Since 1945, Europe has been divided into two broad groups of countries: in the West, those which are essentially democratic and pursue the principles of freely-elected government; in the East, those which are Socialist (Communist) states, with a one-party system of government. Within both groups, the existence of a large number of small political units, compared with the geographically and demographically large units of the new powers in the world, such as the USA, the USSR, and now China, led Europeans to think of various kinds of unification and cooperation. Thus, in Western Europe in the last thirty years a number of supranational organizations with defense, economic and general political links have been established, forming what we know today as the European Community.

In 1948, Belgium, the Netherlands and Luxembourg established an economic union called Benelux. The aims of this union were to establish economic and social uniformity in such matters as prices, wages, taxation and social security, and to remove trade restriction between the three member countries. Then following a lead given in 1945 by the French politician Jean Monet, the European Coal and Steel Community (ECSC) was set up in 1951. In 1958 the European Economic Community (EEC) and the European Atomic Energy Commission (Euratom) were set up. Initially, six countries (Belgium, France, West Germany, Italy, Luxembourg and the Netherlands) were members of these groups.

1 Forth Bridges, Scotland; 2 Life Guards in the Mall, London, England; 3 Greek windmill; 4 Grand Canal Venice, Italy; 5 Memorial to the Discoveries, Lisbon, Portugal; 6 Eiffel Tower, Paris, France; 7 Cheese Market, Gouda, the Netherlands

Switzerland and Sweden, traditionally neutral countries, were not prepared to compromise such a position, and the United Kingdom was understandably concerned about the impact of membership of the European Community on the Commonwealth. These three joined with Austria, Denmark, Norway and Portugal in 1959 to establish what was termed 'little Europe', EFTA (The European Free Trade Association), and later extended it to include Iceland and links with Finland. The objectives of EFTA were purely economic, with the eventual establishment of free trade between all members.

In 1973, the United Kingdom and Denmark transferred to the European Community which, with the admission of Eire, expanded its membership to nine, and began to pursue common aims over wider economic, industrial and agricultural policies. Also, since that time, EFTA and the EEC countries have developed closer economic links.

Since World War II, Western Europe has seen the establishment of other international groups, giving evidence of the new spirit of co-operation in place of the earlier dominance of nationalism. Western Europe also has mutual defense links with the USA and Canada through the North Atlantic Treaty Organization (NATO).

At the same time, the countries of Communist eastern Europe have been establishing their own international organizations, with the USSR playing a dominant role. The Warsaw Pact (the equivalent of NATO) provides for the maintenance of peace through the mutual defense of Albania, Bulgaria, Czechoslovakia, East Germany, Hungary, Poland, Romania and the USSR. The Council for Mutual Economic Assistance (COMECON) is the East European equivalent of the European Community. All Warsaw Pact countries except Albania are members, together with Cuba and Mongolia, two non-European members, and some associate members.

Industry, Commerce and Communications

European industry has developed over the last 250 years so that today the great industrial complexes of West Germany, France, the United Kingdom, the Benelux countries, northern Italy, East Germany, Poland and Czechoslovakia, as well as many other smaller areas within Spain, southern Sweden, Denmark, Austria and Switzerland add up to the largest single industrial concentration in the world. Within this area, the all-important iron and steel industry provides a base for the production of a wide range of metal goods, from heavy engineering and shipbuilding, through vehicle and aircraft construction to a whole range of consumer goods and, at the other end of the scale, intricate precision engineering. Other major European manufacturing industries are textiles, electrical engineering and food processing.

Many Europeans work in what are broadly termed the service industries, some 28 percent of the working population being employed in offices, another 15 percent in the retail and wholesale trades and a further 6 percent in transport and distribution services. Overall then, two out of every five working Europeans are engaged in nonmanufacturing activities, but still play an essential part in both the European and world economy. For example, London, Zurich and other smaller financial centers within Europe conduct a large part of all the world's banking and insurance services.

Europe is made up of many great trading nations. As most countries have a coastline, a series of major sea ports have developed. Rotterdam, London, Antwerp and Marseilles, for example, handle large quantities of imports and exports every year. Within continental Europe large rivers and canal systems also handle much cargo.

Similarly, European road, rail and air networks are as densely developed as anywhere in the world. Today's railroads tend to concentrate on two types of passenger transport, carrying workers (commuters) from their homes to their work, usually within or around the large towns and cities, and inter-city travel, rather than rural as in the past. Freight transport by rail, albeit diminishing, has been modernized and remains viable.

Major road-building programs in the last half-century mean that Europe now has a complex network of high speed roads, known variously as autobahnen in Germany, autostrada in Italy and motorways in the United Kingdom.

Air travel within Europe increases annually. Although still comparatively expensive for distances over 400 km (250 mi) it is quicker, center to center, than either rail or road. Today, European air services are used by a wide range of passengers, from businessmen to tourists.

Europe's complex coastline and many offshore islands necessitate frequent ferry services. Ferries are numerous in Scandinavia and the Mediterranean Sea, as well as being available to reach many continental countries from the UK.

Agriculture, Forestry and Fishing

Before man developed the European landscape, forests dominated the natural scene. In the western parts throughout the British Isles, Denmark, France, the low countries and West Germany, as well as in parts of Scandinavia and the Danube Basin, these forests were largely deciduous. In parts of northern Sweden and the lower mountain areas of south and southeastern Europe, coniferous trees were dominant. Mixed forests covered much of eastern Europe, while in the south there was predominantly Mediterranean vegetation. Upland Norway, Iceland and the highest parts of the Alps were clothed in short Alpine vegetation.

Today, much of this natural cover has been removed in the lowland areas and the land developed, mainly for commercial agriculture. Many of the soils of lowland Europe are either rich loess and limon deposited by the wind in recent glacial times or fertile clays and loams. On the areas of poorer soils of lowland Europe, and many parts of upland Europe, the original forest has often been developed commercially and programs of forest management introduced.

Around the land mass the width of the continental shelf varies greatly. The shallow waters of the shelf provide rich fishing grounds, especially within the North Sea, around Iceland, to the west of the British Isles and in the Mediterranean.

Of all the large temperate regions of the world, Europe has had the longest period of development, and many of the world's great strides forward in terms of agricultural development have been made in the continent. Commercial farming, for the most part highly efficient, has been established and developed in recent times. Broadly, dairying plays a major role throughout much of the British Isles and in a belt through northern France, the low countries, Denmark, northern Germany and Poland as well as southern Sweden and Finland. Crop farming and livestock raising are more important in the areas south of the main dairying belt. In the extreme south, crops suited to the warmer Mediterranean type climate dominate the agricultural scene.

The temperate European lowlands provide some of the richest farmlands in the world. Even so, Europe as a whole needs to import much of its foodstuffs, and within the continent there is much trading of specific crops which are produced abundantly in one area but less so in others.

Remember that the land area of

European retailing has many faces: 1 Sponge seller, Athens, Greece – divers take living sponges from the seas; 2 Basket shop, Dinan, France – a typical French provincial scene; 3 Oxford Street, London, England – the world-famous shopping street is lined with large department stores

EUROPE

Europe is only 3.5 percent of the world total but its population nearly 12 percent of the world total. Thus, in proportional terms, where Europe's share of world production of a given crop or raw material exceeds both these figures she must rate as a significant producer in those fields. The following figures give examples of her role in world production.

The Mediterranean lands of the south, grow about 15 percent of the world's citrus fruits. About 75 percent of world olive oil also comes from these areas. Together with parts of southeast and middle Europe, these lands also produce 30 percent of the world's hemp fiber, 13 percent of its annual corn production of over 330 million tons and 12 percent of its tobacco.

Wheat is by far the most important European cereal, being grown in nearly every country, with France, Italy and West Germany as the leading individual producers. Yet, despite producing over 22 percent of the world total of over 400 million tons per year, the continent still has to import large quantities. Barley is also grown widely in Europe, about 36 percent of the world total of 180 million tons per year being produced here, particularly in France, the United Kingdom, West Germany and Denmark. Of all other crops, Europe is a major producer of oats (33 percent of the world's output of 51 million tons), sugar beets (50 percent of the world's total of 46 million tons), grapes which yield over 70 percent of the world's wine, and apples (49 percent of the world's annual production of over 22 million tons).

Much European farming may be classified as mixed in that crop growing and animal husbandry exist side by side. Cattle farming is most concentrated in the lowlands, for both beef and dairy production. Some 11 percent of all the world's cattle are found in a broad belt from Eire to Poland and the Balkans. Sheep farming, particularly in the upland areas, concentrated in Spain, parts of France, the United Kingdom, Italy and the countries of southeast Europe, accounts for 12 percent of the world's total. As well as lamb and mutton production, these countries supply nearly 10 percent of the world's wool. Pig farming is also concentrated in certain regions, often in association with dairy farming because pigs can be fed on skimmed milk. Southeast England, northern France, the Netherlands, Denmark, both East and West Germany and Poland are the most significant areas.

Much of the continent is still forested, especially in Scandinavia, and middle and eastern Europe. Both softwoods (conifers) and temperate hardwoods are grown and felled. In a typical year Sweden, Finland and Norway provide most of Europe's 41 percent share of the world's total wood pulp and pulp products. Likewise, Sweden, Finland, Austria and Romania lead in sawn timber production; Europe accounts for 20 percent of the world's total.

Many European countries have large fishing fleets and her fishermen account for about 18 percent of the world's total annual catch. In recent years, however, it has become necessary to control fishing and prevent the depletion of stocks.

Natural Resources

For such a relatively small continent, Europe has a wide range of mineral resources and large deposits of some of them. Modern industrial economies are based largely upon supplies of fuel and power. Europe has a number of important coal fields which were among the first ever to be developed. Today, the major coal fields of Silesia, the Ruhr, the United Kingdom and some smaller European fields, account for about 20 percent of the world's hard coal production (bituminous coal and anthracite) which is currently about 2,300 million tons per year. In addition, East Germany is the world's leading producer of soft coal (lignite), and there are other important fields of lignite in West Germany, Czechoslovakia, Poland and southeast Europe.

Until recently, western Europe produced very little fuel oil and natural gas, although eastern Europe fared better with major oil fields in Romania. However, the last twenty years have seen much oil and natural gas exploration under the western parts of the European lowlands. So far the richest fields have been found beneath the North Sea, the lowlands of the Netherlands and North Germany. New fields may soon be found in these and other parts of lowland western Europe.

Only about one-tenth of the world potential for hydroelectric power (HEP) has yet been developed. Europe, a continent of comparatively short rivers, many of which have small discharges when compared with the rivers of the other continents, may only possess about 5 percent of the world's total potential of 3,000 million kilowatts installed capacity. However, some European countries have made great strides to develop HEP, particularly those without large deposits of coal and/or oil. Norway and Sweden lead in this respect and still have more rivers to harness. France and Italy have both developed over 75 percent of their potential, while other alpine countries with a smaller potential have steadily developed this valuable resource.

The second raw material upon which modern industrial economies are based is iron ore. In this, Europe is also reasonably well endowed for a continent of its size, producing about 9 percent of the world's total of approximately 540 million tons (iron content) per year. France accounts for about 35 percent of Europe's output, mainly from the extensive, rich deposits of Lorraine. Sweden has two large deposits, one just north of the Arctic Circle and the other in the Bergslagen district farther south. Between them, these two account for almost 50 percent of Europe's output. Spain, Norway and the United Kingdom are Europe's other leading iron ore producers. That Europe's share of world iron ore production has fallen from over 18 percent to its present figure in the post World War II era is more a reflection of increasing production elsewhere than of the continent's declining output. It is currently estimated that Europe still possesses 9 percent of the world's proven reserves of over 260,000 million tons (iron content).

Other valuable ores are found in Europe in varying quantities, summarized in the table above.

Ore	Average Annual World Production (million tons)	Europe's Share (percent)	Principal European Producing Countries
bauxite	80.3	15	Hungary, Greece, France
chrome	7.2	12	Albania
cobalt	0.03	11	Norway, France, Finland
copper	7.4	10	Poland, Yugoslavia
lead	3.2	20	Yugoslavia, Bulgaria, Sweden, Poland
nickel	0.733	3	Greece
silver	0.01	9	Poland, Sweden, Yugoslavia
tungsten	0.036	5	Portugal, France
vanadium	0.02	12	Finland, Norway
zinc	5.4	18	Poland, West Germany, Sweden

1 Olive groves, Alcaudete, Spain – half a million tons of olive oil are produced yearly by the Spaniards; 2 Burgundy Château and vineyard, *France – one of the great wine regions; 3 Commercial harbor, Rhodes – fishing by traditional methods continues in the Greek Islands*

European industry is highly developed and continues to expand: 1 Production platform in British Petroleum's Forties field – North Sea oil should make Britain self-sufficient in this fuel in the 1980s; 2 Harbor of Gothenburg, Sweden – this major port is famed for its shipbuilding and fishing; 3 Volkswagen assembly line, Wolfsburg, W Germany – the giant car manufacturing company, is representative of this country's industrial and economic resurgence after World War II

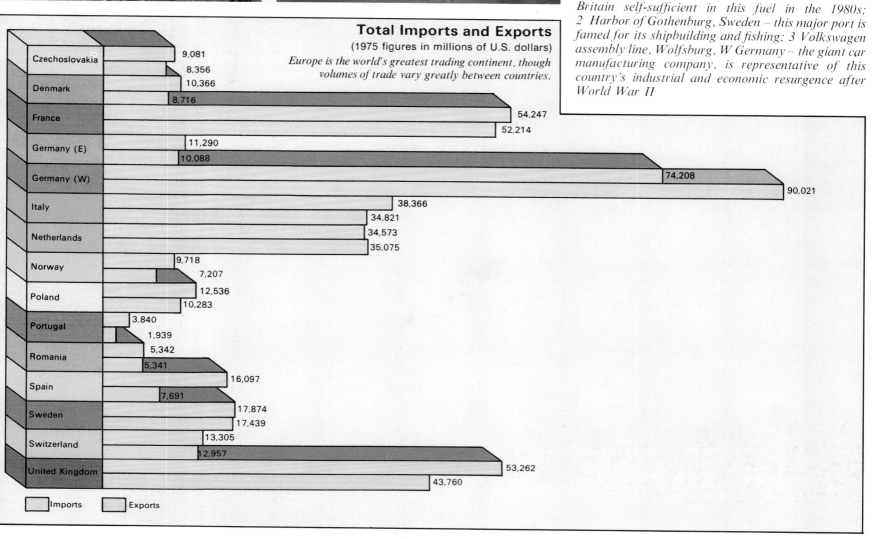

Total Imports and Exports
(1975 figures in millions of U.S. dollars)
Europe is the world's greatest trading continent, though volumes of trade vary greatly between countries.

Country	Imports	Exports
Czechoslovakia	9,081	8,356
Denmark	10,366	8,716
France	54,247	52,214
Germany (E)	11,290	10,088
Germany (W)	74,208	90,021
Italy	38,366	34,821
Netherlands	34,573	35,075
Norway	9,718	7,207
Poland	12,536	10,283
Portugal	3,840	1,939
Romania	5,342	5,341
Spain	16,097	7,691
Sweden	17,874	17,439
Switzerland	13,305	12,957
United Kingdom	53,262	43,760

☐ Imports   ☐ Exports

European Economy

The population map of Europe shows the greatest concentration of people in a broad belt extending from Wales, England and northern France in the west, across the low countries and Germany to southern Poland in the east. Elsewhere, much of Italy, western France and the Rhône-Saône Valleys, and parts of south-east Europe also have an overall density exceeding 150 persons to the square kilometer (390 persons to the square mile). The least heavily peopled parts of the continent are the cooler upland areas of the north and the upland areas of Mediterranean and southeast Europe.

Europe, of course, is highly urbanized in many parts, with more than 30 metropolitan areas of over 1 million population. Of these, London, Paris, Essen–Dortmund–Duisburg and Madrid are the largest, each with over 4 million inhabitants. Rome, Barcelona, Milan and West

Berlin have over 3 million. In some areas, groups of towns and cities close together make up large concentrations of millions of people. The largest conurbations are in midland and northern England, northern France, Belgium and the Netherlands, northern Germany and the industrial cities of southern Poland.

By world standards the population of Europe is currently fairly static. Birth rates in excess of 40 per 1,000 are found in Africa and Asia and, when coupled with lower death rates, combine to make annual increases in population in excess of 4 percent. European birth rates rarely exceed 20 per 1,000 and are often as low as 11 or 12, so that overall the normal increase in European population is less than 1 percent per annum.

Most of the European countries are among the world's leading developed economies either in the free market (democratic) or planned (socialist) world, and many European countries have been and still are

great trading nations. How then does Europe as a whole and its individual member countries stand in comparison to other continental areas today?

Between 1939 and 1958 the world-wide values of both imports and exports rose by 4.5 times; between 1958 and 1975, by nearly 8 times. Such figures demonstrate the considerable growth in world trade during these periods and, despite the confusing effects of inflation on the units of measurement, act as a relevant yardstick against which to measure the trade of a continental area or even an individual country.

European imports in the same two periods rose by only 3.9 times and just over 8.5 times. Her exports rose by 4.7 times and just over 8.5 times. Collectively then, the countries of Europe have performed better than average in the competition tables of world trade.

The performance of individual European countries and groups of trading countries during the periods

1938–'58 and 1958–'75 reveal considerable differences, as shown in the following examples. Compare the figures with those quoted above for the whole continent.

As a group, the nine countries now in the EEC reduced their share of European imports during these periods from 75.8 to 64.9 percent, but their share of exports remained comparatively steady, at 72.0 and 72.5 percent. The EFTA group of countries has fared less well: their share of imports has fallen overall (14.3 to 14.1 percent) but so has their share of exports (15.8 to 13.0 percent). Where figures for individual countries are concerned, those for the UK show the most marked decline both for imports (35.0 to 12.1 percent) and exports (27.3 to 10.8 percent). Other countries which have lost ground, for both imports and exports, include Austria, Denmark, the Irish Republic and Norway.

Some countries, however, have increased their share of both imports

17

Comprising many great trading nations, Europe has excellent communication links, with its many islands relying heavily on sea transport: 1 Hydrofoil at St Helier, Jersey, Channel Islands; 2 Tower Bridge, London, England – up river, the Thames sees few merchant ships; 3 Europe's longest road bridge links the Swedish mainland with Öland island

EUROPE

and exports. The 1945 partition of Germany makes it impossible to compare her performance since 1938, but certainly West Germany has improved her position considerably since 1958; imports have risen from 15.0 to 16.8 percent of the European total, but exports from 19.3 to 22.1 percent. Three others, France, the Netherlands and Switzerland, have fared similarly, increasing their share of exports more than imports.

The trading position of other countries has no single pattern. For some, such as Bulgaria, Poland and Spain, the increasing share of imports has outstripped that of exports. For others, like Belgium, Czechoslovakia, Finland, Hungary, Greece and Sweden, the share of imports has risen but that of exports has declined.

It is also possible to compare the change in the incomes of countries and groups of countries in percentage terms. For example, the overall rise in per capita incomes in the non-Communist world between 1960 and 1974 was 186 percent, as compared to a rise of 290 percent in all Europe.

The rise in European per capita incomes thus outstripped that of all other *continental* areas; only Oceania with a rise of 279 percent came anywhere near it, though the countries of the Middle East, a subregion of Asia, surpassed it with 445 percent.

Marked differences can be seen between individual European countries. For example, Austrian per capita incomes rose by 386 percent, French by 275 percent, Portuguese by 404 percent, Swedish by 267 percent and British by 147 percent. The absolute dollar values must also be taken into account. The Portuguese

for example, have obviously improved their incomes over five times, but are still relatively poor. Within the five selected countries, the United Kingdom, in comparison, has fared badly in both absolute and relative terms, slipping from second to fourth place.

Energy production and consumption figures and, perhaps more significantly, the figures for per capita consumption of energy, are further ways in which the state of the European economy can be compared with other parts of the world. For all its reserves of coal, Europe is well

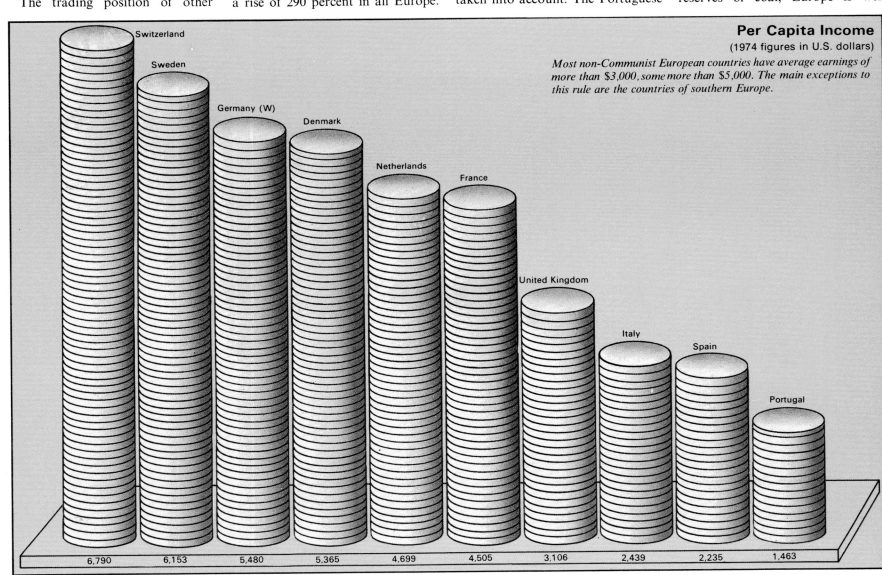

Per Capita Income
(1974 figures in U.S. dollars)
Most non-Communist European countries have average earnings of more than $3,000, some more than $5,000. The main exceptions to this rule are the countries of southern Europe.

Switzerland 6,790
Sweden 6,153
Germany (W) 5,480
Denmark 5,365
Netherlands 4,699
France 4,505
United Kingdom 3,106
Italy 2,439
Spain 2,235
Portugal 1,463

known to be a great energy-deficient area. It has yet to prove and develop its own oil reserves fully, and is still heavily dependent upon the world's oil rich areas.

Overall, when energy figures are reduced to a common unit of million tons coal equivalent, Europe produced 1131.74 mtce in 1975 yet consumed 2021.75 mtce. She thus produced 13.2 percent of the world's energy but consumed 25.3 percent. Among the large energy-consuming countries, Czechoslovakia imported 23 percent, France 77 percent, East Germany 30 percent, West Germany 50 percent, Italy 84 percent and the United Kingdom 38 percent each of their needs. In all Europe, Romania is just self-sufficient while only the Netherlands and Poland are significant exporters of energy.

A final index of Europe's position in a quickening world is the amount of energy consumed per head of population. In the continent as a whole in 1975 the figure was 4,227 kilograms per head (kg/ca), very high by overall world standards, reflecting the area's great industrial activities. Yet there are great differences from country to country. Luxembourg, with its small population and substantial iron and steel industry used the phenomenal amount of 15,504 kg/ca, while at the other end of the scale, Albania used only 741 kg/ca and Portugal 983. In general, southern European countries have a lower energy consumption than northern ones, reflecting both the climate and the lower industrial development.

Many European countries developed their economies early and reached a mature stage by or before the mid-twentieth century. At present, with new political and economic incentives, the continent as a whole is just managing to hold its relative position in the trading world, with an overall slight improvement in the last two decades.

Over the last five years, however, her overall relative position has worsened. Such fluctuations in fortune over a brief time span can also be seen in variations from country to country for the same period, as revealed most significantly in the individual trade and per capita incomes figures.

We have now moved from an era in which energy self-sufficient Europe was the great industrial heart of the world to one in which European industry is heavily dependent upon imported energy. In the short term, as Europe develops her own oil resources this situation may improve. By the end of this century, as global oil resources run down, world technology will need to harness new energy sources. It must be hoped that a significant contribution, as yet an unknown quantity, will be made by Europe.

Many traditional cottage industries are still preserved throughout Europe: 1 Thatcher, Bideford-on-Avon, Warwickshire, England – cottages roofed with varieties of reed are found mainly in the southern parts, but this is one of many country crafts experiencing a modern nationwide revival; 2 Cheese making in the Emilia-Romagna region of Italy – food processing, in particular cheeses for which the country is renowned, is the main occupation of this fertile area which stretches across northern Italy; 3 Lace maker in national dress, Bruges, Belgium – handmade lace, especially from this medieval town, is much prized and a great tourist attraction

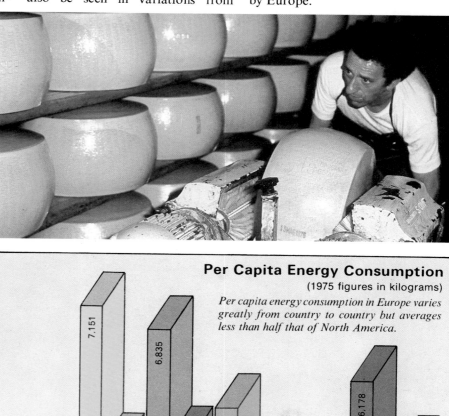

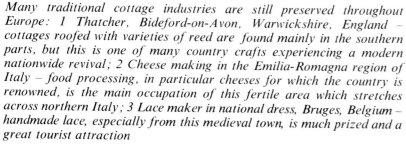

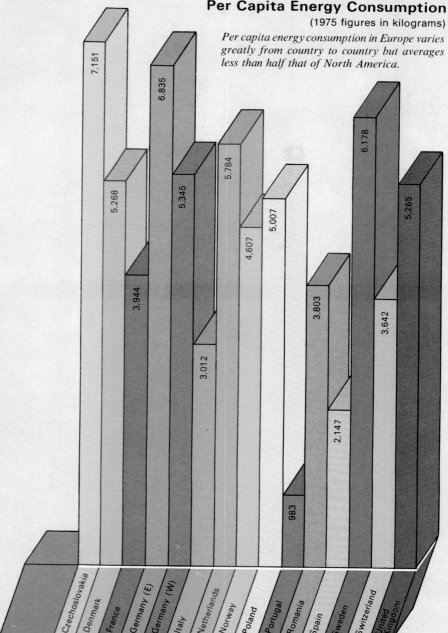

Per Capita Energy Consumption
(1975 figures in kilograms)

Per capita energy consumption in Europe varies greatly from country to country but averages less than half that of North America.

Country	kg/ca
Czechoslovakia	7,151
Denmark	5,268
France	3,944
Germany (E)	6,835
Germany (W)	5,345
Italy	3,012
Netherlands	5,784
Norway	4,607
Poland	5,007
Portugal	983
Romania	3,803
Spain	2,147
Sweden	6,178
Switzerland	3,642
United Kingdom	5,265

Kilometers

Statute Miles

Scale 1:13,200,000

One centimeter represents 132 kilometers.
One inch represents approximately 210 miles.

Miller Oblated Stereographic Projection

European Countries

Albania

A mountainous country, bordering the Adriatic Sea, Albania boasts a language unlike any other, based on ancient Illyrian. Previously predominantly Moslem, the country has been officially atheist since 1967 when all places of worship were closed. This Socialist peoples' republic and member of the Warsaw Pact is unique in the Eastern bloc in that it is not a member of COMECON, but has strong political and economic links with China, 70 percent of all trade being with that country. In recent years, minerals such as chrome ore, copper, lignite and crude oil have been steadily developed. Farming is restricted to the coastal lowlands and the Korçë Basin, with corn, wheat and sugar beet as the main crops grown there.

Andorra

Situated high in the Pyrenees Mountains, Andorra is curiously semi-independent politically, paying taxes to neighbors France and Spain and using the currency of both countries. In recent years tourism has outpaced agriculture as a source of revenue, although many Andorrans still grow a variety of crops and keep sheep and goats.

Austria

Prior to 1914 the Austro-Hungarian state dominated Central Europe. Austria was established as a separate, smaller country between the two world wars, and after World War II its independence was reestablished in 1955. It is now a member of EFTA. Austria today is perhaps best known for its tourist attractions – cities like Vienna and Salzburg and the mountain ski resorts. Many are employed in dairying and cereal farming. Minerals extracted include iron ore, lignite and graphite from one of the world's major deposits.

Belgium

A founder member of the EEC, Belgium now plays host to the Community in its capital, Brussels. Belgians are predominantly Roman Catholic, but are divided culturally between the northern areas where Flemish, a language similar to Dutch, is spoken, and French-speaking Walloonia in the south. The north and west of this small, densely populated kingdom bordering the North Sea, comprises low-lying rich agricultural land, while to the south and southeast are the forest uplands of the Ardennes. Farming in the north is very intensive, with dairying and pig production following close on the heels of major crops such as sugar beet, potatoes and cereals. Although coal and iron ore mining have both declined recently, a wide range of heavy and manufacturing industries still flourishes.

Bulgaria

The Peoples' Republic (Socialist) of Bulgaria is a member of both the Warsaw Pact and COMECON, 80 percent of all her trade being with the European Communist countries. A limited mineral production is on the increase, especially lignite, iron ore and copper outputs. Both arable and dairy farming play a major part in the lives of many Bulgarians, whose language is one of the simplest in the Slavonic group. Most people follow the Eastern Orthodox faith.

Channel Islands

Some 140 km (90 mi) south of the British mainland, the nine inhabited Channel Islands are a British crown possession with internal self-government. English is the main language, though a form of Norman-French is also spoken. Jersey, the largest island, relies heavily on tourism and agriculture. Guernsey, next in size, with seven smaller dependencies, is famed for its cows, greenhouses, tomatoes and flowers.

Czechoslovakia

A landlocked Central European federal Socialist republic, Czechoslovakia is a member of both the Warsaw Pact and COMECON, 67 percent of all her trade being with the European Communist countries. After a period of unrest in 1968, more liberal leaders took control of the country. They were soon deposed, following the occupation of the land by armed forces from other Warsaw Pact countries. Czechoslovakia was established in 1918 following the break up of Austria-Hungary, and both Czech and Slovak languages are spoken today. Czechoslovak agriculture is highly efficient, dairying and pig farming playing a major part, with sugar beet, wheat, potatoes and barley the principal crops. Forestry also contributes greatly to the national economy. Coal and iron ore are the most important of the country's limited mineral resources. In recent years a range of basic manufacturing industries has been successfully established.

Denmark

The kingdom of Denmark comprises a low-lying peninsula and groups of islands separating the North and Baltic Seas. The Danish farming system is highly organized and very efficient. Dairy cattle dominate the green pastures, although some root crops and barley are grown, mainly for animal feeding. Food processing, especially bacon and dairy products, is of prime importance to the economy. In recent years, however, a wide range of manufacturing industries has been established, and today nearly three times as many people work in such industries as on the land. Denmark joined the EEC in 1973.

Faeroe Islands

A group of 21 islands 500 km (310 mi) southeast of Iceland, the, Faeroes belong to Denmark but have had internal self-government since 1948. The name Faeroes is taken from the Danish for 'sheep islands' and sheep farming, along with fishing, is the most important occupation. Fish, fresh and processed, and craft products are exported mainly to Scandinavia and the United Kingdom.

Finland

The most northerly country of mainland Europe, Finland has a low-lying, forested and lake-strewn landscape. Such severe winters grip the land that even the capital, Helsinki, in the south of the country, is icebound. Generally, farming, forestry, mining, especially for copper and iron, and manufacturing industries all play their part in the economy. A democratic republic which steers a careful political course between the Soviet Union and Western Europe, Finland has a treaty of friendship and cooperation with the USSR and is also an associate member of EFTA. Like the other Scandinavian peoples, most Finns are members of the Lutheran National Church.

France

The largest country in Western Europe, France is a democratic republic. It has coastlines facing in three directions (north, west and south), a variety of rich agricultural lowlands and less prosperous upland areas, including parts of the Alps which rise to a maximum height of 4,807 m (15,771 ft) and a wide range of climates. A major tourist country.

1 △　　　2 ▽　　　3 ▽

1 Schröcken, Vorarlberg, Austria – dairying is a major occupation in this picturesque mountain region; 2 East Berlin, E Germany – the modern TV Tower rises alongside the ancient cathedral in this physically divided city; 3 Market day, Split, Yugoslavia – spectacular Roman ruins and the fine harbor attract tourists and commerce to this Dalmatian port

rightly famed for its capital, Paris, France remains predominantly rural. It is the world's largest producer of wines, mainly from the Rhône and Saône river valleys, the Loire valley, Bordeaux and Champagne. In addition to large outputs of cereals and vegetables, cattle and sheep farming both play a major part in French agriculture. Industrially, iron ore production is most important, while coal production is declining; there is a large iron and steel industry. The automobile, aircraft, textile, chemical and food processing industries are all large. France is a founder member of the EEC and most of her trade is with other members of this group.

Germany (Democratic Republic of East)

About a third of the geographical area of the united Germany of the interwar years now forms the Socialist Democratic Republic of East Germany. A member of both the Warsaw Pact and COMECON, some 75 percent of all its trade is with the European Communist countries. East Germany's lignite (soft coal) output is the largest for any single country in the world. Mineral production and a range of industries generate about 70 percent of the national income, although forestry, and crop and animal farming are also important.

Germany (Federal Republic of West)

Occupying over half of the area of the old united Germany, the Federal Republic of West Germany comprises ten main states (Länder) and the western parts of Berlin. West Berlin, with a metro population of about 4 million, is the largest city in the Federal Republic. Bonn, in North Rhine–Westphalia, with over 500,000 population, has been the capital since 1949. Since World War II, West Germany has developed as a leading member of the Western European group of countries, being a founder member of the EEC and trading mainly with fellow members. It is the biggest hard coal producer of West Europe, and has the largest iron and steel industry within the EEC. A range of major manufacturing industries are concentrated in the northern Ruhr area, the port cities of the North Sea coast and the large cities of the south. The northern lowlands form the major agricultural area, followed by the areas of rolling landscapes in the south. Sugar beet, potatoes, barley and wheat are the main crops, pigs and cattle the most numerous farm animals. German wines from the Rhine and Mosel valleys play a valuable part in the economy, as does forestry.

Gibraltar

Guarding the western entrance to the Mediterranean, Gibraltar rises steeply from its base on the south Spanish coast to a height of 429 m (1,408 ft). The Rock of Gibraltar thrives on air and naval activities – its artificial harbor and airfield are of great strategic importance – tourism and commercial ship repairing. Although the Spaniards claim that it is part of their country, Gibraltar has been a British crown colony since 1704. The small, rocky promontory has apparently little wish to become entirely independent, although it has a large degree of self-government, and in 1967 it voted by over 12,000 to 44 to retain British links.

Greece

A mountainous peninsula and island country in the extreme southeast of Europe, Greece relies heavily on the many tourists who annually sample its ancient treasures and modern amenities. Although much of the land is unsuitable for agriculture, cereals, cotton, tobacco, olives, grapes and citrus fruit are grown.

Major industries are food processing, textile and chemical production. A few minerals are produced in modest quantities and some are exported. Greece is currently negotiating to become a member of the EEC.

Hungary

Over 60 percent of all Hungary's trade is with the European Communist countries, as this peoples' republic (Socialist) is a member of both the Warsaw Pact and COMECON. The leading industries are food processing, metal, textile and chemical production. Coal – both hard and soft – and bauxite are the major minerals. Arable farming, especially corn, wheat, sugar beet and potatoes, as well as raising pigs, sheep and cattle, is of prime importance to the economy. The Hungarians speak a language, Magyar, which is most akin to Finnish.

Iceland

A volcanic island in the North Atlantic Ocean just south of the Arctic Circle, Iceland was formerly part of the Danish realm; its language is

related to both Danish and Norwegian. It achieved independence in 1918 and declared itself a democratic republic in 1944. Iceland, whose economy is based on fishing, is a member of EFTA.

Irish Republic

Comprising 26 counties in the southern part of Ireland, the modern independent republic (Eire) was formerly united with Great Britain and Northern Ireland, but finally severed all links with the Commonwealth in 1949. Both English and Gaelic are spoken. Most of the Irish are Roman Catholics. Known as 'the Emerald Isle', from the rich, green landscape, southern Ireland is predominantly agricultural. Food processing and brewing are the leading industries. The Irish Republic has been a member of the EEC since 1973.

Isle of Man

Lying in the middle of the Irish Sea, this attractive island relies heavily on tourists, although sheep and cattle are raised, as are some crops. A member of the Commonwealth, the Isle

European Countries

of Man has internal government by the Court of Tynwald but United Kingdom control of external affairs.

Italy

A democratic republic of Mediterranean Europe, Italy freely elects the members of both houses of parliament. The state religion is Roman Catholicism to which almost everyone adheres. As fountainhead of the ancient Roman Empire, Italy has a great range of cultural and religious treasures which attract many tourists every year to the cities of Rome, Venice and Florence. Other popular holiday areas are the Riviera coast, the isle of Capri and the Italian lakes on the border with Switzerland. The 'boot' of Italy is a long peninsula whose backbone is the Apennine Mountains which extend to the very 'toe' in the south; the southern ranges of the Alps dominate the extreme north. Still primarily agricultural, the richest and most extensive farmlands are within the basin of the Po River. In addition to temperate crops like wheat, sugar beet and potatoes, Italy grows rice, tobacco, olives and citrus fruit. Crude oil production has expanded rapidly in recent years, especially in Sicily, and modest quantities of a range of minerals are also produced. Italian textiles, particularly silk, are world famous. Most industry is concentrated in the north, especially in the large cities. Southern Italy is less developed. Italy was a founder member of the EEC.

Liechtenstein

This small, independent alpine principality is united with Switzerland for diplomatic and customs purposes. Dairying is the most important agricultural activity of this picturesque mountainous area, and in recent years industries such as precision engineering, food processing and ceramics have developed.

Luxembourg

The Grand Duchy of Luxembourg is a small but rich independent state situated between Belgium, France and West Germany. Both at the end of the Franco-Prussian War and World War I its people decided to remain independent of the surrounding larger powers. Since 1948, however, Luxembourg has abandoned its neutral status and has been a member of NATO. French and German are spoken, but most of the people use the Letzeburgesch dialect. A founder member of the EEC, Luxembourg's greatest strengths economically are its iron ore deposits and the iron and steel industry based on them.

Malta

Greeks, Romans, Carthaginians, Phoenicians and Arabs all used Malta at some time. For 268 years it was the base of the Knights of St John, but became a British colony following the Napoleonic Wars. Today it is a small, independent Mediterranean island republic within the Commonwealth. It was of enormous strategic importance during World War II, when the valor of its people in withstanding attacks from the Axis powers led in 1942 to the award of the George Cross, the highest British award for civilian bravery. The subsequent decline of its role as an important air and naval base has led to the development of a number of new industries such as textiles and rubber and food processing to replace the decreasing dock activities.

Monaco

Enclosed on the land side by France, the small, independent Mediterranean principality of Monaco enjoys a special administrative relationship with its powerful neighbor. Next to the Vatican it is the world's smallest sovereign state. Most of the revenue comes from tourism.

Netherlands

Often mistakenly referred to as Holland, the Netherlands is a low-lying kingdom bordering the North Sea. It has one of the highest population densities in Europe. Much of the Netherlands lies below sea level, behind protecting dikes and seawalls, and some of its richest farmlands have been reclaimed from the sea in recent times. Dutch agriculture is highly organized and efficient, as is a wide range of industries close to the great ports of Rotterdam and Amsterdam. The Netherlands was a founder member of the EEC.

Norway

An independent kingdom since 1905, Norway has been closely linked with its neighbors Sweden and Denmark throughout its history. Famed for its mountains and fjords, most Norwegian land is unproductive, only 3 percent being farmed and some 23 percent forested. The economy rests largely on forestry, fishing and mining (especially of high grade iron ore and copper) and their associated processing industries. A member of EFTA, Norway earns much foreign currency from its large oceangoing merchant navy, and from tourism. Its government successfully negotiated entry to the EEC, but the Norwegian people voted against the move in a referendum late in 1972.

Poland

Now over 1,000 years old, the country of Poland has not always enjoyed independence and its precise geographical boundaries have changed frequently. It is today a people's republic (Socialist) which is a member of both the Warsaw Pact and COMECON, although its foreign trade is almost as great with the western world as with the Soviet bloc. Poland possesses the second largest coal field in Europe, upon which the many industries of Silesia are based. Principal farm products are cereals, root crops and dairy products.

Portugal

Together with Spain and Gibraltar, Portugal is situated in the Iberian peninsula. The Atlantic islands of Madeira and the Azores are parts of metropolitan Portugal. Less than half the land is farmed, a quarter forested and the remainder is unproductive. Famed for its vineyards and production of port wine, Portugal also produces more than half of the world's cork. Other leading exports are wood pulp, resins and sardines. Portugal is a member of EFTA.

COUNTRY REFERENCE: EUROPE

European Countries	Political Status	State Capital	Area		Population	Population Density		Births per Thousand Persons	Deaths per Thousand Persons	Mean Annual Percentage Increase in Population
			km²	sq mi		per km²	per sq mi			
Albania	A	Tirane	28,748	11,100	2,655,000	92	239	33.3	8.1	3.1
Andorra	A	Andorra	453	175	28,000	62	160	20.1	4.6	3.7
Austria	A	Vienna	83,849	32,374	7,500,000	89	232	12.3	12.7	0.5
Belgium	A	Brussels	30,513	11,781	10,005,000	328	849	12.3	12.0	0.4
Bulgaria	A	Sofia	110,912	42,823	8,820,000	80	206	16.6	10.3	0.6
Channel Islands	C	St Peter Port (Guernsey)	78	30	54,000	692	1,800	11.5	13.1	1.1
	C	St Helier (Jersey)	116	45	75,000	647	1,667			
Czechoslovakia	A	Prague	127,876	49,373	15,095,000	118	306	19.5	11.5	0.6
Denmark	A	Copenhagen	43,069	16,629	5,090,000	118	306	14.1	10.2	0.6
Faeroe Islands	C	Torshavn	1,399	540	40,000	29	74	19.9	7.3	1.0
Finland	A	Helsinki	337,032	130,129	4,770,000	14	37	14.2	9.4	0.4
France	A	Paris	543,998	210,039	53,208,000	98	253	15.2	10.4	0.8
Germany (E)	A	East Berlin	108,178	41,768	16,695,000	154	400	10.8	14.3	0.2
Germany (W)	A	Bonn	248,533	95,959	61,070,000	246	636	9.7	12.1	0.6
Gibraltar	C	Gibraltar	6	2	30,000	5,000	15,000	19.8	7.0	0.5
Greece	A	Athens	131,944	50,944	9,340,000	71	183	15.6	8.9	0.5
Hungary	A	Budapest	93,032	35,920	10,690,000	115	298	18.4	12.4	0.3
Iceland	A	Reykjavik	103,000	39,800	225,000	2.2	5.7	20.6	6.9	1.3
Irish Republic	A	Dublin	70,285	27,137	3,210,000	46	118	21.6	10.	1.1
Isle of Man	C	Douglas	588	227	64,000	109	282	11.7	16.7	2.9
Italy	A	Rome	301,250	116,313	56,710,000	188	488	14.8	9.9	0.8
Liechtenstein	A	Vaduz	160	62	25,000	156	403	12.6	7.3	0.8
Luxembourg	A	Luxembourg	2,586	998	365,000	141	366	11.2	12.2	0.2
Malta	A	Valletta	316	122	275,000	870	2,254	18.7	9.7	−0.2
Monaco	A	Monaco	1.5	0.6	26,000	17,333	43,333	8.2	12.3	0.9
Netherlands	A	Amsterdam and The Hague	40,844	15,770	13,945,000	341	884	13.0	8.3	1.0
Norway	A	Oslo	323,878	125,050	4,060,000	13	32	14.0	9.9	0.7
Poland	A	Warsaw	312,677	120,725	34,865,000	112	289	19.0	8.7	0.9
Portugal	A	Lisbon	92,082	35,553	9,660,000	105	272	19.6	11.0	0.2
Romania	A	Bucharest	237,500	91,699	21,760,000	92	237	19.7	9.1	0.9
San Marino	A	San Marino	61	24	21,000	344	875	17.4	7.7	0.6
Spain	A	Madrid	504,750	194,885	36,530,000	72	187	18.2	8.1	1.1
Sweden	A	Stockholm	449,750	173,649	8,265,000	18	48	12.6	10.8	0.4
Switzerland	A	Bern	41,288	15,941	6,270,000	152	393	12.4	8.8	1.2
UK	A	London	244,013	94,214	55,890,000	229	593	12.4	11.8	0.3
Vatican	A	Vatican City	0.4	0.2	1,000	2,500	5,000	—	—	—
Yugoslavia	A	Belgrade	255,804	98,766	21,875,000	86	221	18.1	8.6	0.9
EUROPEAN TOTAL (exc. USSR)			4,870,569.9	1,880,566.8	479,207,000	98	255	—	—	—

1 Monte Carlo, Monaco – the yacht harbor and casino of this Riviera capital attract an internationally famous clientele; 2 Iceland – hot springs are found all over this volcanic island; 3 Amsterdam, the Netherlands – the capital's famous canals, running through the city, are home for a floating population of houseboat dwellers, including lots of cats!

Romania

A member of both the Warsaw Pact and COMECON, Romania is a mountainous Socialist republic bordering on the Black Sea. Oil and natural gas are produced in substantial quantities. Coal, iron ore and other minerals are extracted, and a wide range of manufacturing industries has been developed. Tourism is a modern growth industry. Principal exports, mainly to other East European countries, are oil products, cereals, chemicals and machinery. The Danube lowlands of the south and east and other western lowlands are the most important agricultural areas.

San Marino

Founded in the fourth century, San Marino claims to be the world's oldest republic. Tourism and the sale of postage stamps bring in much foreign currency to this small state. It is surrounded entirely by Italy with whom it has a long standing treaty of friendship. Wines, textiles and ceramics are the major exports.

Spain

One of the largest yet least developed countries of Western Europe, Spain, together with Portugal and Gibraltar, occupies the whole of the Iberian peninsula. Following an economically disastrous Civil War in the late 1930s, Spain was ruled as a dictatorship by General Franco until 1975 when it returned to being a monarchy with an elected parliament. With over 30 million visitors each year, the Spanish economy depends a great deal on tourism. Spain is still largely an agricultural country, roots and cereals being the major temperate crops, with grapes, olives and citrus fruit grown widely. A range of mineral deposits is currently being developed, but only iron ore is mined on a large scale. Textiles are the major manufacturing industry.

Sweden

The Scandinavian kingdom of Sweden is one of the most prosperous countries of Western Europe. With a long tradition of neutrality, Sweden is today a member of EFTA, but not of any European political union. Only a small part of the land is farmed, but over half is forested, forming the basis of the country's all-important timber industries. Swedish high quality iron ore deposits are large and provide another major export item, along with smaller amounts of copper, zinc and lead.

Switzerland

Neutral Switzerland is a member of EFTA and provides the headquarters for many international organizations. Tourists are attracted throughout the year to this landlocked alpine federal republic, especially for the scenery and traditional winter sports. Switzerland's agriculture is highly organized, dairying being the main activity. The most successful industries are precision and electrical engineering and toy making.

The United Kingdom

England, Scotland, Wales and Northern Ireland comprise the United Kingdom which occupies most of the British Isles, a group of islands separated from mainland Europe by the North Sea and the English Channel. It is a constitutional monarchy with a two chamber parliament, the House of Commons being freely elected and the House of Lords composed of hereditary and nominated peers. Britain was the mother country of an extensive Empire until the twentieth century. In recent years most of the former dependent countries and dominions have achieved independence. Today, many are members of the Commonwealth of Nations which has no constitution yet exists for mutual cooperation and assistance. The English language is today the most widely spoken in the world and the established Anglican Church is the second largest in the Christian world. Geographically, the southern and eastern parts of the country are lower-lying and agriculturally more productive than the more rugged northern and western areas. Farming is well developed and efficient, but 40 percent of the nation's food still has to be imported. Previously a member of EFTA, the United Kingdom did not join the EEC until 1973.

Vatican City

A tiny sovereign state within the city of Rome, the Vatican provides an independent base for the headquarters of the Roman Catholic Church. Governed by the Pope, it has its own coins and stamps, and a radio station which broadcasts in 31 different languages.

Yugoslavia

Created in 1918 by the union of the south Slavic peoples, Yugoslavia is a Balkan country bordering on the Adriatic Sea. A number of Slavonic languages are spoken, the most widespread being Serbo-Croat. Yugoslavs have religious freedom; the Eastern Orthodox, Roman Catholic and Islamic faiths are the strongest. Although a Socialist federal republic, among the European Communist countries Yugoslavia has always maintained most independence from the Soviet bloc, being neither a member of the Warsaw Pact nor of COMECON. Leading agricultural crops are corn, wheat, potatoes and tobacco. A range of valuable ores are mined in addition to coal and iron. The main industries are metals, chemicals and textiles.

Kilometers 0   100   200   300 Km.

Statute Miles 0   100   200   300 Mi.

Scale 1:6,600,000

One centimeter represents 66 kilometers.
One inch represents approximately 105 miles.

Lambert Conformal Conic Projection

27

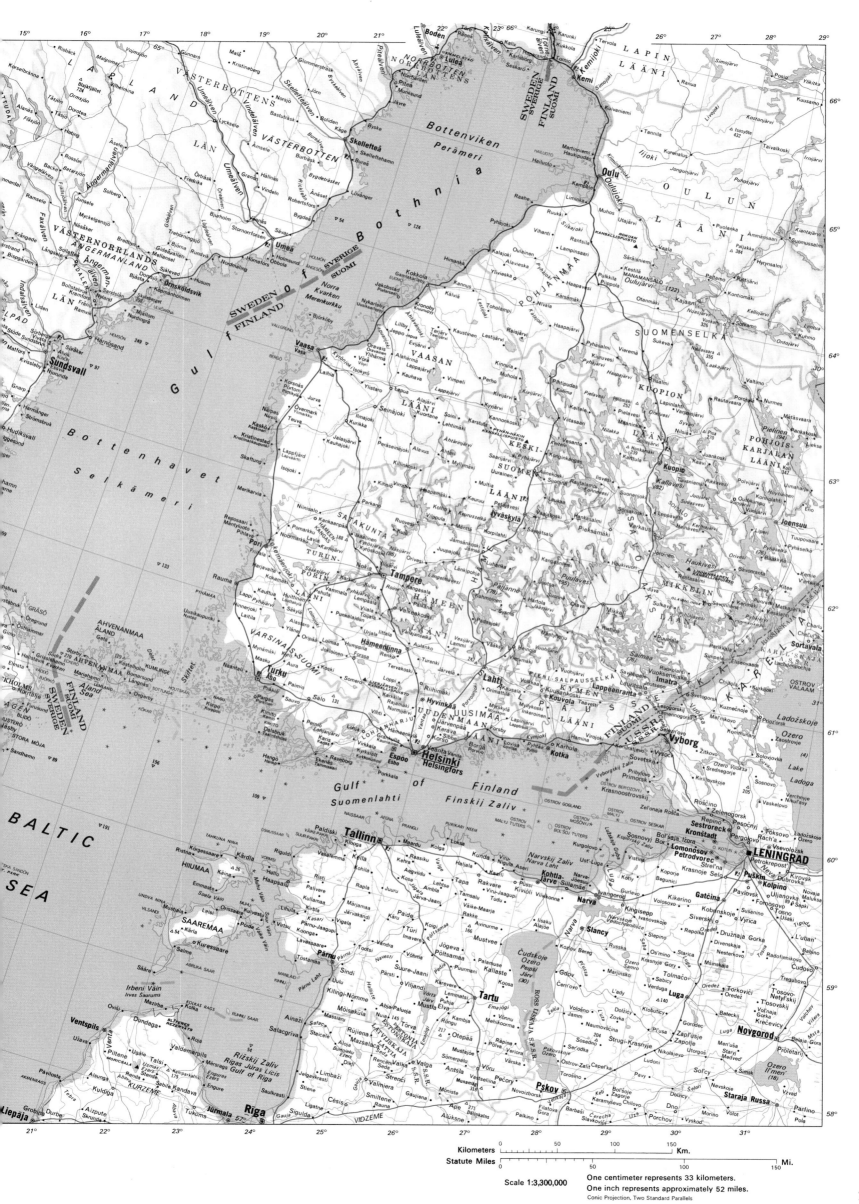

Scandinavia

Alike, yet different; sophisticated but simple; vast open spaces and intimate cities; an advanced economic society, yet one that includes a race of nomadic herdsmen. All these contradictions are to be found in the four countries which make up Europe's northern attic, Scandinavia, a land of wild beauty, friendly peoples and room to move.

Think of Scandinavia and you think of the great outdoors, where mountains, lakes and forests combine in one marvellous year-round winter sports center. Water is ever-present, from Sweden's thousands of lakes, to Norway's spectacular fjords and glaciers, Finland's sailing waters and the sea around Denmark. Trees too stretch away as far as the eye can see, especially in Sweden, the largest country. Here, log cabins are scattered across remote landscapes and many different types of wood products are manufactured, all with the clear-cut lines that are the trademark of Scandinavian design. In northern Norway, 'land of the midnight sun', there are prolonged hours of summer daylight. And farther north, the reindeer herding Lapps cope happily with the extremes of almost continual summer light and winter darkness.

By contrast, the Scandinavian capitals are places of warmth and sophistication. Few can resist the charm of little Denmark's 'wonderful Copenhagen', a cosmopolitan city where, contrary to popular myth, sexual license is not all-pervasive. Here, visitors can relax in the famous Tivoli gardens funfair or eat hearty Smørrebrød – Danish open sandwiches. Stockholm, the 'Venice of the north', epitomizes Swedish style and cleanliness, the old town with its narrow streets and cluttered shops contrasting with the modern business center and spacious lakeside suburbs. Today a major port, Oslo, the Norwegian capital, is as fair as its Viking forefathers while Helsinki, in Scandinavia's most unspoiled country, Finland, mixes modern amenities with a picturesque setting.

1 Romsdal area, Norway; 2 Sergels Torg, Stockholm, Sweden; 3 Olavinlinna Castle, Savonlinna, Finland; 4 Engelsholm Castle, Jutland, Denmark; 5 Log cabins at lakeside, Hjarpesto, Sweden; 6 Norwegian fjord; 7 Little Mermaid, Copenhagen, Denmark; 8 Kornhamnstorg to the south of the Royal Palace, Stockholm, Sweden

6 △

7 ◁

8 ▷

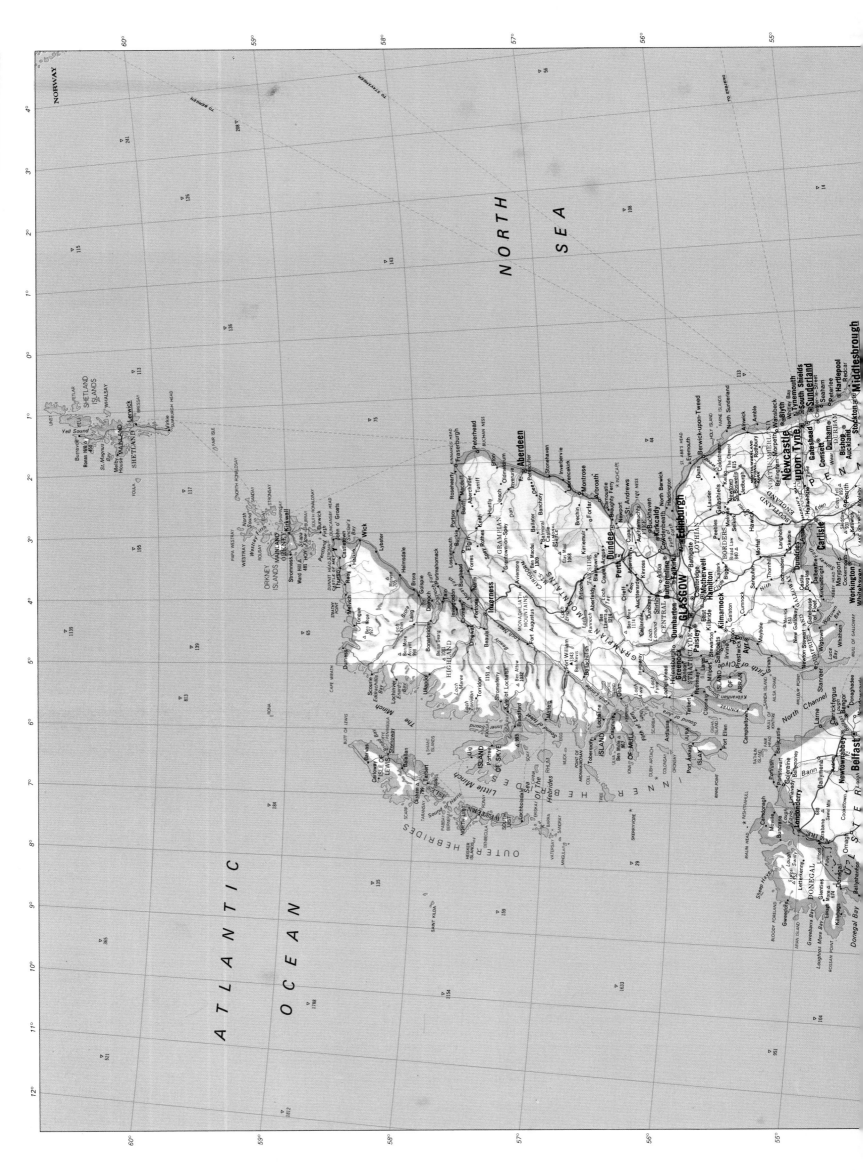

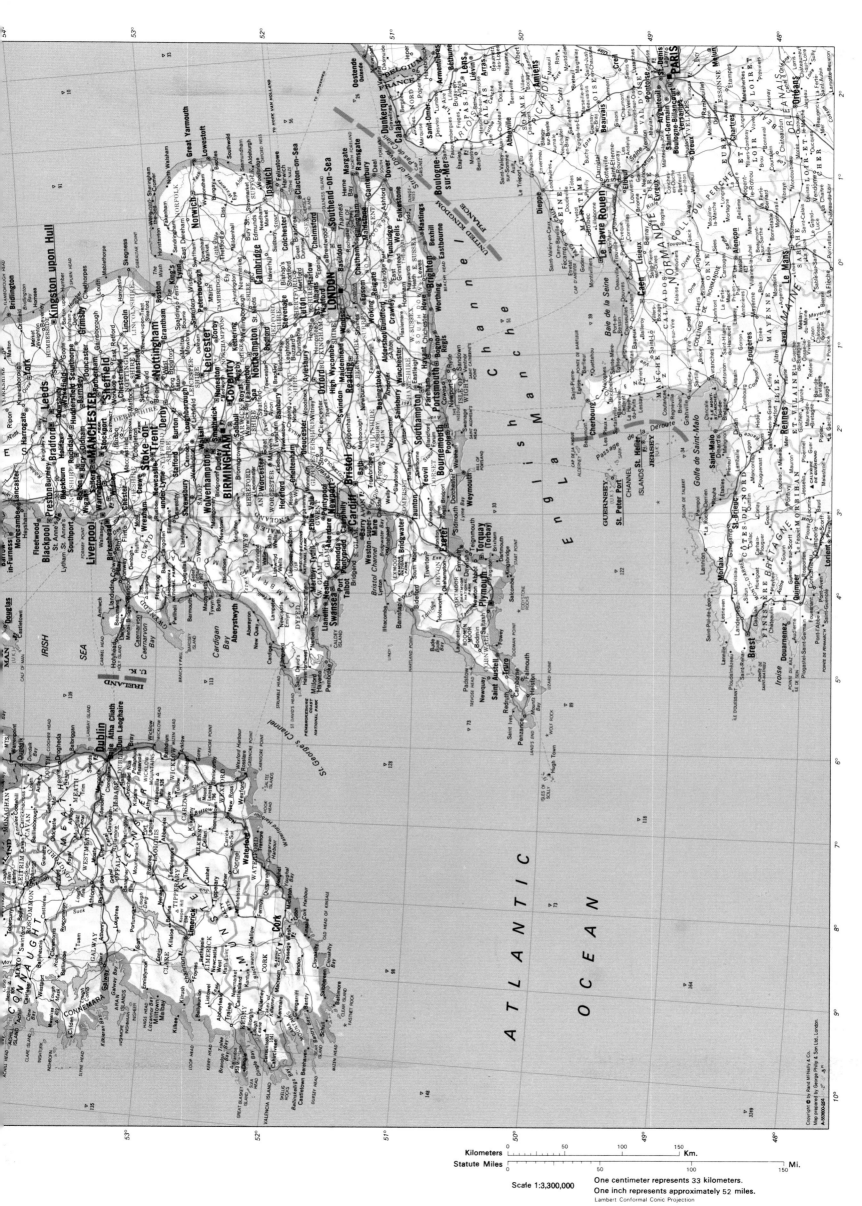

Kilometers

Statute Miles

Scale 1:3,300,000

One centimeter represents 33 kilometers.
One inch represents approximately 52 miles.
Lambert Conformal Conic Projection

33

British Isles

In a changing world, Shakespeare's 'sceptred isle' still retains much of its individuality and tradition. The sunset of Empire, an increased European awareness, dissent in Northern Ireland and demands for a national voice from the Scots and Welsh, have not lessened overall pride in the British heritage. The monarchy is still respected by the mass of the people as representing the values of patriotism and family life. Small wonder then that immigrants, exiles and visitors alike are won over by this liberal society surrounded by a wealth of history.

London still represents England to those who have ventured no farther than Piccadilly Circus and the Tower, Buckingham Palace and Westminster Abbey. Visitors to the ancient university cities of Oxford and Cambridge, or the architectural splendors of Regency Bath, may feel they know more of the country. But England stretches from the glorious West Country coast through soft Cotswold villages and the sweeping landscapes of Constable's Suffolk to the remote splendor of the Northumberland moors. Soccer is the national craze, but more aristocratic sports still reign supreme: Wimbledon tennis, rowing at Henley, racing at Ascot and cricket at Lords.

In the north, Scotland also combines a fierce love of tradition with the modern pace of industrial life as the country benefits from the discovery of offshore oil. The golfer's paradise, the naturalist's delight, this land of lochs and mountains offers the cosmopolitan delights of the capital, Edinburgh, the wild beauty of the highlands and islands as typified by remote crofts and grey fishing villages.

Ireland, too, is a place of beauty and contrasts, made all the more apparent and heartbreaking by the present internal conflict. But everywhere, from the northern loughs to the southern mountains, from urbane Dublin to the comparative poverty of the west, this land of Yeats and Shaw exudes a sense of hospitality and pride. And in Wales, where music and rugby football are equal gods, that same warmth is extended in the Celtic tongue, through Cardiff and the industrial valleys of the south to Snowdonia.

1 Tower of London, England; 2 Canterbury Cathedral, Kent, England; 3 Scarborough harbor, Yorkshire, England; 4 Derwent Water, Cumberland, England; 5 Ruins of Melrose Abbey, Roxburghshire, Scotland; 6 The docks at sunset, River Clyde, Glasgow, Scotland; 7 Menai Suspension Bridge, linking Anglesey, Gwynedd, to mainland Wales; 8 Vale of Clara, County Wicklow, Irish Republic; 9 Thirteenth century Caerphilly Castle, Glamorgan, Wales

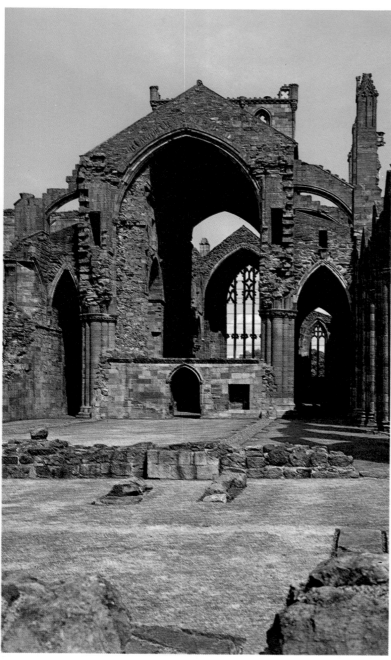

5
◁

6
▷

7
▷

8
◁

9
▷

Kilometers 0 50 100 150 Km.

Statute Miles 0 50 100 150 Mi.

Scale 1:3,300,000

One centimeter represents 33 kilometers.
One inch represents approximately 52 miles.
Conic Projection, Two Standard Parallels.

1 △   2 ▽   3 ▽

West Germany, Austria and Switzerland

West Germany dominates this part of the map as it does the European economy. Yet the industrial landscapes of the Ruhr and Saarland are only as representative of this multifaceted country as the vine-clad slopes of the Rhine and Mosel rivers, the nightlife of Hamburg's famous Reeperbahn, the romance of Heidelberg and the fairy-tale scenic splendors of Bavaria. A cultural giant too, this country can claim to have produced such great writers as Goethe and Schiller, and to have an especially powerful musical inheritance in the works of Beethoven and Brahms. By contrast, East Germany, while containing the manufacturing centers of Leipzig, Magdeburg and Dresden, has not enjoyed a similar economic recovery since World War II. Germany's former traditional capital, Berlin, since 1961 divided by the concrete wall built by the East, retains a particular significance for both countries.

What they lack in size and economic power, the neighboring countries of Austria and Switzerland make up for in outstanding scenery and solid worth. Austria's renowned cultural centers of Vienna, Innsbruck and Salzburg are equalled in appeal by the mountainous Tirol region, winter sports centers and health spas. In Switzerland, home of financial wizards, precision watch making and dairying, the scenery is no less spectacular with beautiful lakes and splendid peaks such as the Matterhorn, and the ski resorts of St Moritz and Davos are world famous.

1 Neuschwanstein Castle, Bavaria, W Germany; 2 The port, Hamburg, W Germany; 3 Heidelberg, W Germany; 4 Belvedere Palace, Vienna, Austria; 5 Castle near Salzburg, Austria; 6 Herd of dairy cows, near Interlaken, Switzerland; 7 Skiing, Switzerland

The Netherlands, Luxembourg and Belgium

No longer banded together as an economic threesome, the 'Benelux' countries of Belgium, Luxembourg and the Netherlands still remain a delightful entity while retaining their individual charm. Situated at the mouth of the Rhine, the Netherlands is rightly called the 'gateway to Europe'. Known the world over as a land of cheese, canals and bulbs, more importantly it houses the world's largest seaport in Europoort, Rotterdam, and Amsterdam, the friendly capital, is the world center for diamond cutting. Belgium, now destined to be home to EEC bureaucrats, is undervalued as a tourist country, except for the capital, Brussels, with its magnificent market place, and the medieval pearl of Bruges. The wooded heights of the Ardennes region, in particular, are a hiker's and a gastronome's delight. These roll on into little Luxembourg, itself a land of magic castles, rivers, forests and enchanting towns.

1 Vianden, Luxembourg; 2 Bruges, Belgium; 3 National Monument in Dam Square, Amsterdam, the Netherlands; 4 Drainage mills, the Netherlands

Eastern Europe

The political map of Central Europe has been changed twice in this century, once in 1919 and again in 1945. In the modern Soviet satellite countries the vast rolling estates and artistic splendors which characterized Central Europe before World War I have disappeared. But the spirit of the peoples remains unquenched. The Hungarian Magyars, once part of two great empires, still mainly work the land, retaining their old traditions and culture.

A land of great scenic attractions, with its extensive Bohemian forests and magnificent Carpathian Mountains, Czechoslovakia too is in many ways outwardly unchanged. Many beautiful buildings, such as the medieval Charles Bridge, are now being restored in the capital, Prague, one of Europe's most charming, relatively 'undiscovered' cities.

Poland, a once mighty nation which was partitioned among Russia, Prussia, and Austria in the 18th century, regained its sovereignty in 1918 only to lose it to Nazi Germany in 1939 during the opening weeks of World War II. After the war, Poland lost much more territory to the USSR and came under its domination but the Poles have been able to regain a degree of individual freedom.

1 Ols Village, East Hungary; 2 Old town square, Prague, Czechoslovakia; 3 Town Hall, Poznan, Poland; 4 Svetla glassworks, Bohemia, Czechoslovakia

1 △

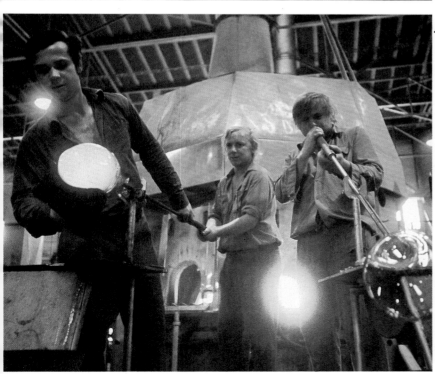

2 ◁

3 ▷

4 ◁

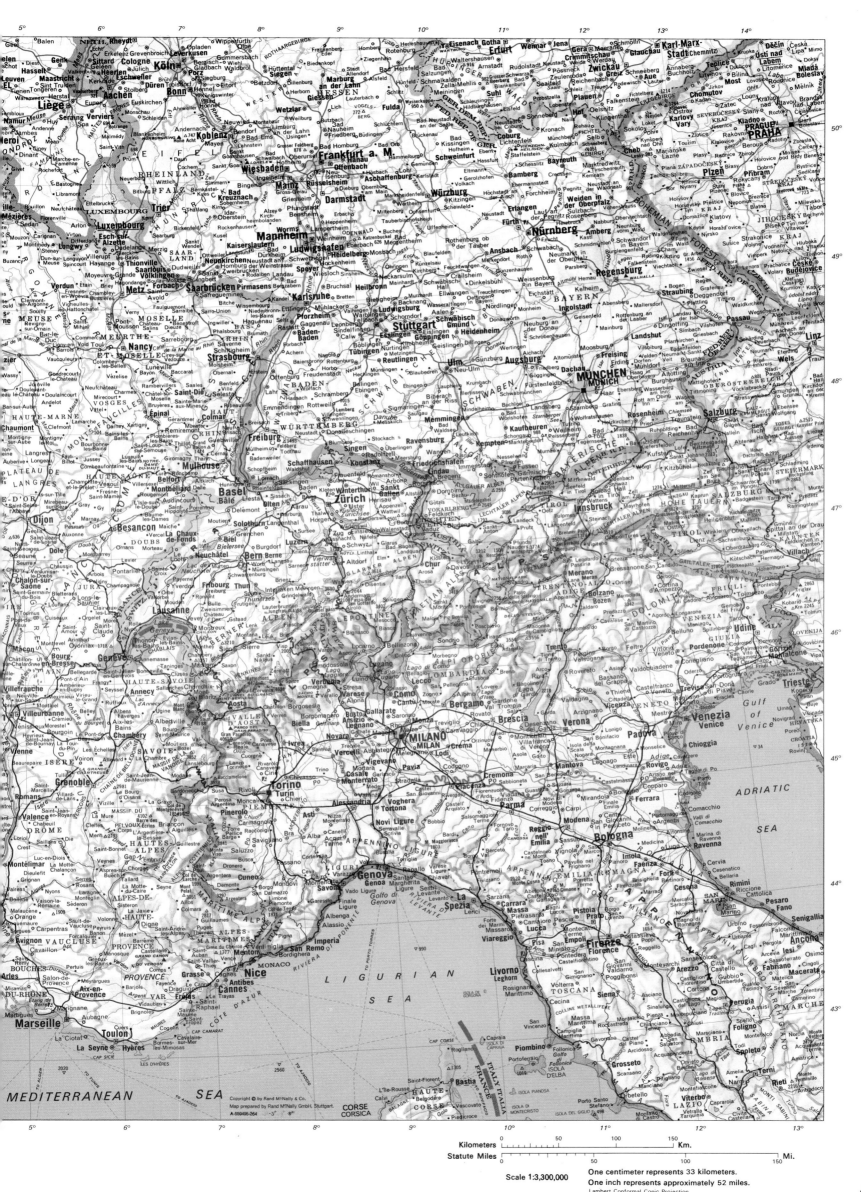

Kilometers

Statute Miles

Scale 1:3,300,000

One centimeter represents 33 kilometers.
One inch represents approximately 52 miles.
Lambert Conformal Conic Projection

43

1 △

2 ▽

France

France has so much in its favor that less well-endowed countries might be forgiven a passing resentment at such good fortune. Rich in natural resources, with a pleasing position and climate, there is small wonder that the inhabitants of this large and lovely country often seem to have little time for the world outside. For, despite its size and wealth, France is predominantly a nation of small towns and villages where home and family, the church and trade rule supreme.

Is it not strange then, that a land so indisputably rural, with a still large and vociferous peasantry, should be renowned the world over for its enviable chic and its undoubted sophistication? Thus the influence of the capital, Paris, is asserted far beyond its own region. Indeed, its dictates in the world of fashion and the arts are followed more slavishly in London and New York than in its own country. France has been in the forefront of true western culture for centuries, and Paris itself has been the cradle of writers and artists too numerous to mention. Look around at the museums, galleries, artistic treasures and monuments, and you can see the past glory of the mighty French Empire, the golden Bourbons and the military might of Napoleon, all part of an historic heritage which continues unbroken to the present day, despite the major upheaval of Revolution in 1789.

France in the 1980s is strongly placed on the economic front with its major manufacturing centers at Lille, Lyons and Paris and the port of Marseille in the south. But it is for its splendid beaches that the Riviera coast is best known; the elegant resorts of Nice and Cannes vying with St Tropez and its starlet strip. Farther west the wild, swampy Camargue region with its roaming horses and wealth of wildlife is a great attraction for naturalists. Inland, the ancient towns of Arles, Avignon and Nîmes are much visited. The southwest also has fine beaches, the forests of the Landes area and, above all, Bordeaux, the greatest wine area in the world. Others may prefer the wilder Brittany coastline, the quiet charm of the Loire region with its magnificent chateaux or the gently pastoral area of the Dordogne. All this, and much, much more, is France.

1 Arc de Triomphe, seen from the Champs Elysées, Paris; 2 Château de Chenonceaux, Loire; 3 Seafood market in Quimper, Brittany; 4 Grape harvest, Bordeaux area; 5 Le Grande Motte, near Montpellier

3 △

4 ◁

5 ▷

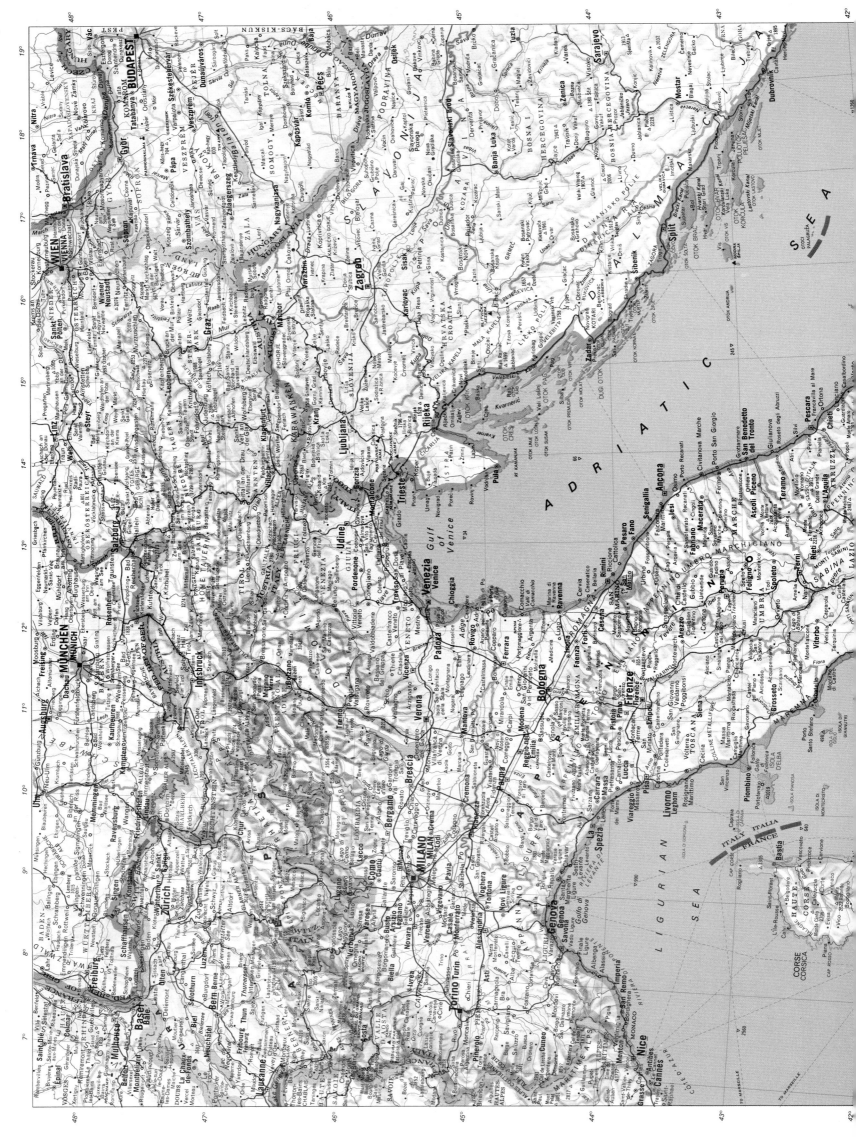

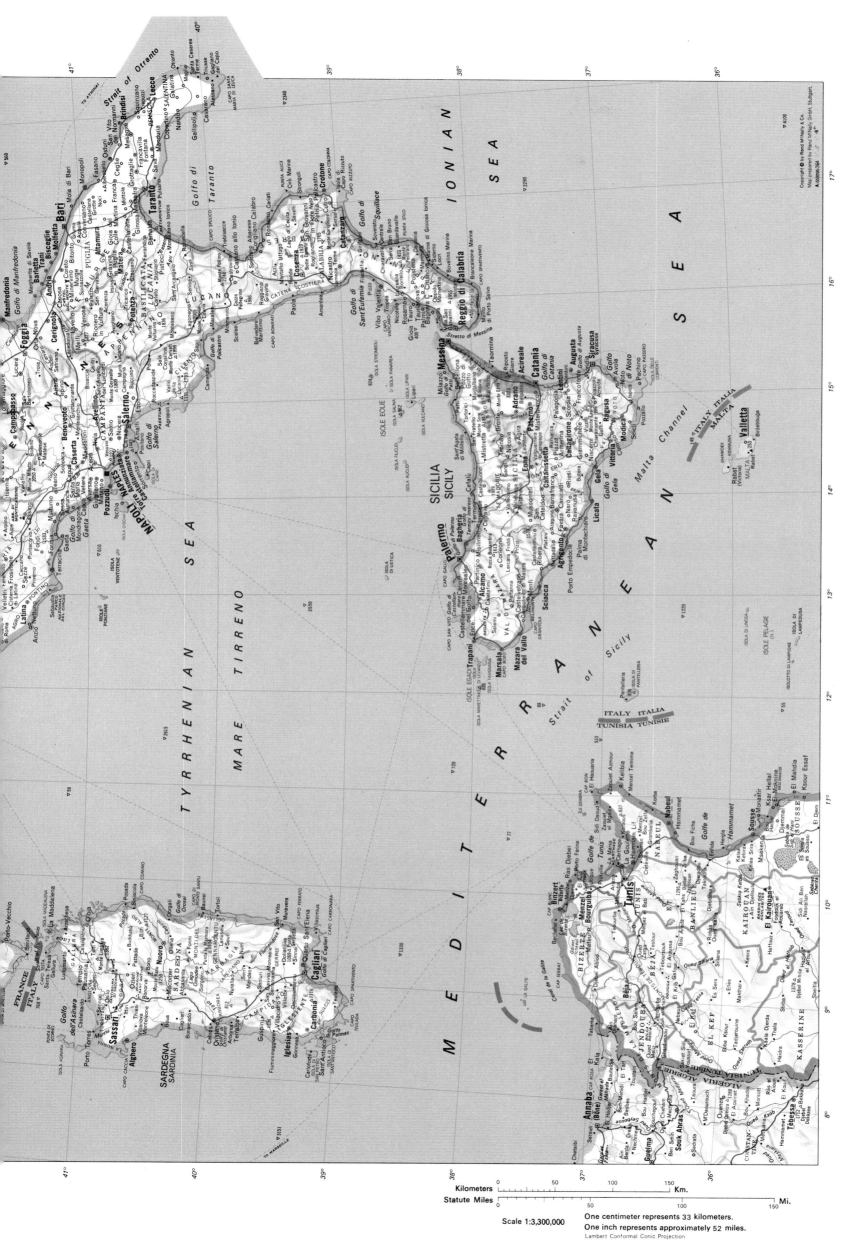

Kilometers

Statute Miles

Scale 1:3,300,000

One centimeter represents 33 kilometers.
One inch represents approximately 52 miles.

Lambert Conformal Conic Projection

Italy

Like its people, Italy can be by turns volatile and subdued, extremely wealthy or gratingly poor, spontaneous and welcoming or difficult to know. It is, above all, a cultural colossus where the influence of the Roman Catholic Church is all-pervasive. Sadly, as in the case of Venice, where little is being done to prevent this unique island city of gondolas, canals, St Mark's Square and the Rialto, from slipping back into the sea, this preeminence is in danger of disappearing under the ravaging hordes of over-enthusiastic sightseers and under-energetic city fathers.

At its peak during the Roman Empire which spread its influence throughout the world, Rome itself, the Eternal City, contains more architectural and artistic masterpieces than any other place in the world. Among these are the Colosseum, first used in AD 80, a year after Pompeii was destroyed by the eruption of Vesuvius, and the Forum, built in the fifth century AD. At Rome's heart is the Basilica of St Peter and the Vatican, home of the Roman Catholic Church. Rome also has such favorite haunts as the Trevi Fountain and the Spanish Steps.

Golden Florence, in Tuscany, birthplace of the Renaissance, combines a wealth of priceless treasures in its buildings and museums with the prosperity of a modern city. Classic monuments, like Michelangelo's David, and historic architecture, such as the sixteenth-century Ponte Vecchio, rub shoulders with students and tourists alike. Then there is Milan, Italy's economic pulse, with its truly awe-inspiring cathedral.

And there is more to this country of hot summers and superb scenery. Positano on the fashionable Costa Amalfitina, the artistic haven of Portofino and the Italian coast resorts all have much to offer. Inland, the Italian Lakes lie serenely at the foot of the Alps, while to the northeast are the dramatic Dolomites with their famous skiing resorts.

1 Cathedral, Baptistry and Leaning Tower, Pisa, Tuscany; 2 Gondolier, Venice, Veneto; 3 Portofino, Liguria; 4 Milan Cathedral, Lombardy; 5 Positano, Campania; 6 Cortina d'Ampezzo, Dolomites; 7 Spanish Steps, Rome, Latium

4 △

5 ◁

6 ▷

7 ◁

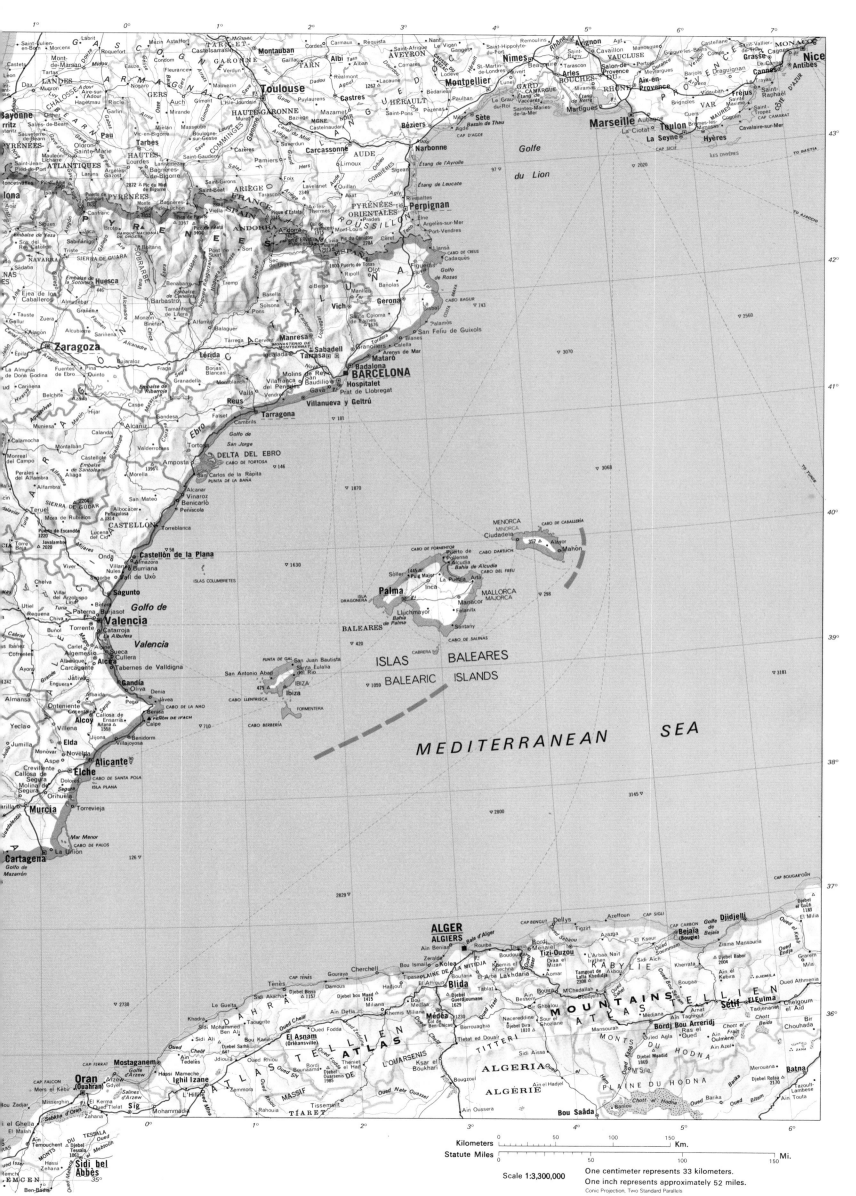

51

Spain and Portugal

Despite their physical togetherness, Spain and Portugal are two very different countries. The traveler may come to appreciate both, but his heart will always belong to the one first visited. Enter Iberia across the hot, arid countryside of Don Quixote's Spain, and you will remain forever in the thrall of this land of fiesta and flamenco, where Moslem palaces vie with endless olive groves, sun-bathed beaches and snow-clad mountains. But Portugal, with its softer landscape, gentle people, white-walled villages and haunting fado music, has a special appeal. Undisturbed by the last two great wars, Lisbon, the capital, retains much of its past glory, the elegant nineteenth-century buildings and boulevards contrasting sharply with the winding alleyways of the old Arab quarter, the Alfama. Close by, the dignified resorts of Estoril and Cascais provided a pleasant exile for many of Europe's deposed ruling families, suitably near to the old royal palaces at Byron's beloved Sintra, and Quelez. Along the coasts, brightly-painted small boats, often crewed by men in traditional garments, still go out to fish in the time-honored way.

If previously best known throughout the world for their fortified wines – Spanish sherry from Jerez and port from Portuguese Oporto – both countries now rely heavily on the benefits of tourism. While Portugal's Algarve area, still comparatively unspoiled, is becoming increasingly popular, Spain, in particular, is recognized as Europe's holiday playground. Here, the vast hotel blocks on the highly commercialized Costas Brava and del Sol contrast starkly with the unchanged lifestyle of the interior where hilltop villages and vast plains give way to thriving, historic cities.

At its heart, Spain remains the land of Hemingway, where bulls still run in the streets of Pamplona, and the land of El Greco, whose magnificent paintings in Toledo are matched by the town's spectacular location. Home to the plundering conquistadors, the civilizing Moors and the feared Spanish Inquisition, Spain continues to be, above all, the land of the *feria* where holy processions and modern celebrations combine in annual outbursts of gaiety and reverence throughout the country.

1 Benidorm, Costa Blanca, Spain; 2 Barcelona Cathedral, Catalonia, Spain; 3 Matador at a Spanish bull fight; 4 Portuguese vineyard; 5 Seville horse fair, Andalusia, Spain; 6 Fishermen, Sesimbra, Portugal

1 Erechtheion, Acropolis, Athens, Greece; 2 Lake Bled, Yugoslavia; 3 Corinth Canal, Greece; 4 Farm houses, Yugoslavia; 5 Monastery at Meteora, Greece; 6 Greek Orthodox priests; 7 Island of Mykonos, Greece

Greece and Yugoslavia

In many ways remarkably different, historically, politically and ethnically, Greece and Yugoslavia jointly epitomize life in southeastern Europe. Greece, home of some of Europe's earliest civilizations, now relies heavily on tourism which is also increasing in the less commercially developed yet spiritually resilient Socialist Yugoslavia.

Today, 'the glory that was Greece' is still seen in breathtaking ancient ruins. Placed atop the rock of the Acropolis, the classical architectural simplicity of the Parthenon (fifth century BC), represents the high point of the great age of Athens, the modern capital.

The largest of the Balkan countries, Yugoslavia remains primarily agricultural, although its Serbian capital, Belgrade, and Zagreb in Croatia, are growing industrial centers. The country is perhaps best known for its beautiful Adriatic coastline.

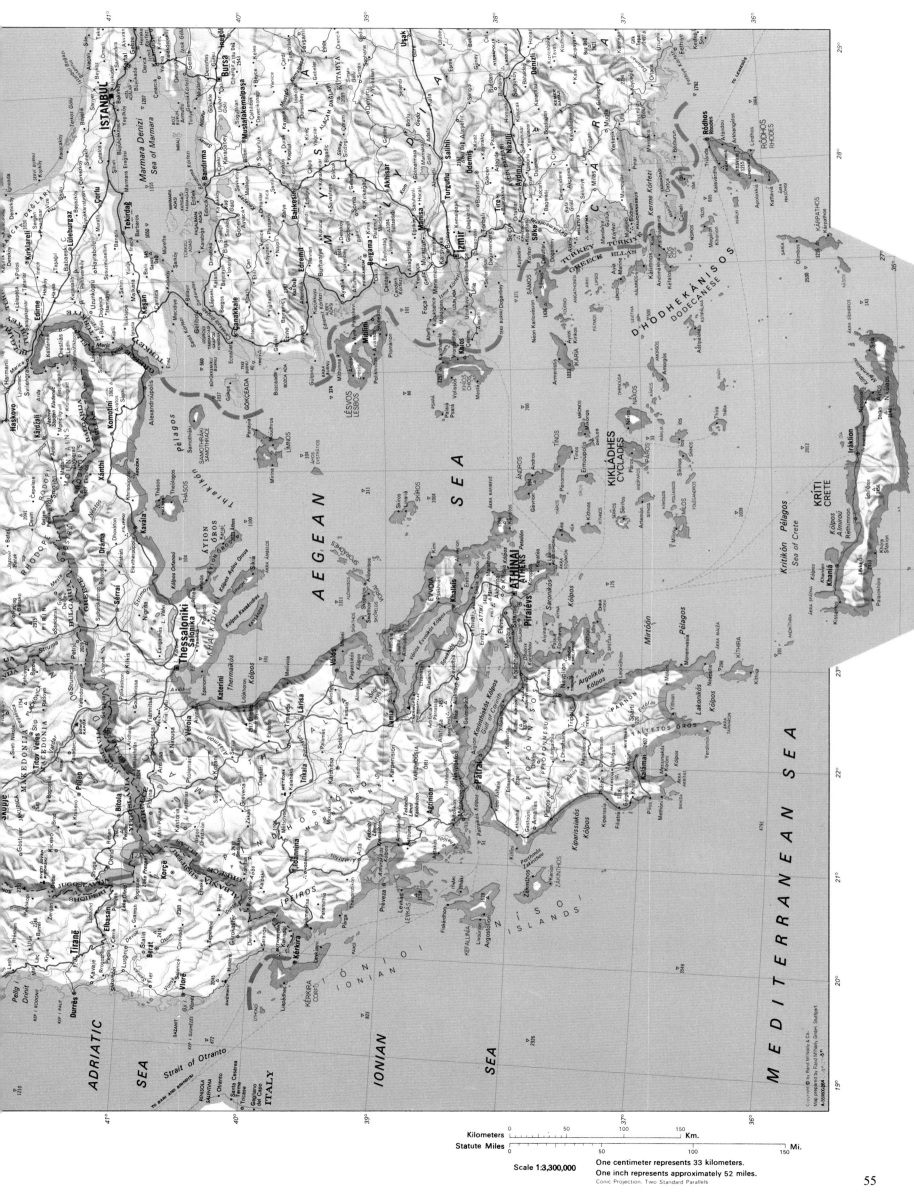

Kilometers
Statute Miles

Scale 1:3,300,000

One centimeter represents 33 kilometers.
One inch represents approximately 52 miles.
Conic Projection, Two Standard Parallels

USSR Physical Profile

World Location and Size

The world's largest country, the USSR straddles the conventional boundaries of two continents, Europe and Asia. Mainland USSR extends from nearly 78°N in the Taymyr Peninsula to almost 35°N on the Afghanistan border, a distance of about 4,800 km (3,000 mi). Beyond the mainland, Soviet islands in the Arctic extend beyond 81°N. From west to east the USSR stretches from the Czechoslovak border at 22°E to the Bering Strait at 170°W, thus extending nearly half way round the globe in the Northern Hemisphere. In time terms, when it is 8 a.m. in Moscow it is 6 p.m. in the Cukotskij Peninsula.

Of a total area of nearly 22,275,000 km² (8,600,350 sq mi), 25 percent is in Europe and 75 percent in Asia. For such a land mass, the USSR has only limited stretches of effective coastline which are ice-free throughout the year. In the northwest only a small part of the Arctic coast is ice-free all year and in the west, parts of the Baltic freeze in winter, but most of the Black Sea coast and its ports remain open all the time. The north-flowing rivers are blocked for up to seven months each year.

Landscape

Most USSR land borders are in mountainous parts of the country. The south and east are the highest areas while the northern, central and western parts are dominated by plains.

European USSR is dominated by the eastern parts of the North European Plain. Only the Central Russian Uplands, the Valdai Hills, rising to 346 m (1,125 ft) northwest of Moscow, and the uplands of the Kola Peninsula rising to 1,191 m (3,907 ft) stand above this. The lower plains continue eastward through the basins of the Rivers Don, Volga and North Dvina to the Ural Mountains which form the only major north-south divide in western USSR.

To the south of this lowland region lies the Black Sea with its outlet to the Mediterranean Sea and the Caspian Sea which is a focus of inland drainage. The Carpathian Mountains on the border with Romania rise to 2,061 m (6,762 ft) and the Caucasus Mountains between the Black and Caspian Seas rise to 5,633 m (18,481 ft). East of the Caspian Sea lies the Turanian Plain and an area of inland drainage focusing on the Aral Sea. Uplands surround this whole region, particularly to the south and east where the boundaries with Afghani-

Opposite: St Isaac's Cathedral in the center of Leningrad, Russia

stan and China lie within the Pamir and the Tien Shan ranges. Here is the highest land in the USSR rising in Communism Peak to 7,495 m (24,590 ft). East and northeast of the Turanian Plain are the Lake Balkash Basin and the Kazakh Uplands.

West of the River Yenisey and east of the Urals is the extensive West Siberian Plain. This has a total area of over 2.5 million km² (1 million sq mi) and constitutes the largest single area of plain land in the world.

The landscape east of the Yenisey is more varied and elevated. The Central Siberian Plateau between the Yenisey and the Lena Rivers is

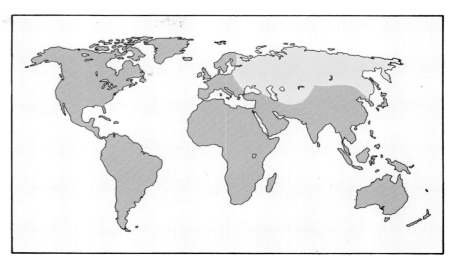

generally above 300 m (1,000 ft) and in the south reaches to above 3,000 m (10,000 ft) in the Sayan and Yablonovy Mountains. The Putoran Mountains of the north rise to a maximum height of 1,701 m (5,581 ft). The remote region east of the Lena River is dominated by a series of mountain ranges, Verkhoyansk, Cherskiy, Chukot and Sredinny which reach a maximum of 4,750 m (15,584 ft) in the Kamchatka Peninsula.

The USSR is a land of great rivers draining in four directions. In the west are comparatively short rivers, like the Don, the Dnepr and the Dvina flowing to the Black or Baltic Seas. In the east, the Amur and many smaller rivers flow eastward to the Pacific. About half the country is drained northward by the Ob, Yenisey and Lena River systems. Finally, the Volga and Ural flow to the Caspian Sea and the Amu-Darya and Syr Darya to the Aral Sea, in the largest inland drainage basin of the world.

Climatic Background

The Soviet Union is the most extensive west-east land mass in the world. It is almost entirely north of the 40°N parallel, is flanked on its southern borders by highland areas and is climatically little influenced by either the Atlantic or Pacific Oceans. Seen overall, the country's climates are characterized by large temperature ranges and low precipitation.

The southern parts of Soviet Central Asia experience a mid-latitude desert climate. Over a large area, the average monthly temperature in January falls to −10°C (14°F) but in July rises to 30°C (86°F). Nowhere does annual precipitation rise above 200 mm (8 in) and it is often far less.

In a broad belt from the southern Ukraine to the Mongolian and Chinese borders lies the area of the dry mid-latitude steppe climate. The temperature range here is higher in the east than in the west, say −30°C (−22°F) to 16°C (61°F) compared

Spassity Tower, Kremlin, Moscow – one of the 18 towers in the wall circling the citadel at the heart of the capital

with −4°C (25°F) to 22°C (72°F). Low annual rainfall, less than 400 mm (16 in), comes mainly in the summer.

In the extreme north of the country, polar climates extend from west to east. Most places in this area have at least one month when the average temperature is above freezing, but no month's average rises above 10°C (50°F).

Between these southern desert/steppe and the northern polar climates, most of the USSR has a more humid climate with a wide annual temperature range. In the west, the July average temperature may approach 22°C (72°F) with the winter average going as low as −10°C (14°F). Precipitation, with a summer maximum, comes throughout the year and may total 700 mm (28 in). This decreases farther east and the temperature range increases.

USSR

The Union of Soviet Socialist Republics did not exist when the twentieth century began. Now it rivals the USA in military might and its potential and economic sphere of influence is larger than that of the British Empire at its zenith. At its heart, Russia – still ruled by the feudal Tsars at the start of World War I – mastered modern technology to put the first man in space. The birthplace of Communism, a major battleground of World War II, Russia created the modern USSR amid the smoke of the uneasy peace of the mid-1940s and '50s.

A decade later, the world held its breath when the Cuban missile crisis brought the USA and the USSR, by now the world's two most powerful nations, to the threshold of war. But later, when Warsaw Pact forces put down the Czech revolt in 1968, the West did not intervene and subsequent confrontations have been confined to the United Nations, strategic arms limitation talks or to the Helsinki conference which served as the trigger for another flashpoint, human rights.

Population Growth

Although dominated by Russia, the Soviet Union comprises more than 100 national groups of which perhaps two dozen each have a population of over one million. Many of these groups are concentrated in particular geographical areas which are thus accorded appropriate administrative status.

Russians (137.1 million), Ukrainians (49.9 million) and White Russians (9.5 million) make up over 75 percent of the population. These peoples are all slav-speaking.

The major Altayan peoples of Soviet Central Asia (the Central Asian Republics) are Uzbeks (9.2 million), Tatars (5.3 million) and Kazakhs (4.4 million). Other peoples with populations in excess of one million include, among the Uralian group, Mordovians, Karelians and Estonians.

Throughout recent times, the peopling of the Soviet Union has taken place in a number of distinct phases. Between 1600 and 1850, within European Russia, the main movements were from the forested northern lands into the more open steppe lands of the south and southeast. From 1800 onward, and particularly after the abolition of serfdom in 1860, the Russians moved eastward to the steppe lands beyond the Urals. In the first decade of the twentieth century Russians were migrating eastward at a rate of 600 per day. Throughout this time there had been a steady trickle of migrants from the west into the Russian Empire. Thus, the imperial population grew by natural increase and immigration to 171 million by 1913.

Then, from 1914 to 1926, years of world war, revolution, civil war and emigration, on average the national population fell by 2 million per year.

The next thirteen years saw a complete reversal of this trend and by 1940 the population of the USSR had risen to its highest ever. During World War II, 20 million Soviet lives were lost, a large proportion being young males. Thus, by the war's end, the total population was still only 173 million and the sex and age structure within that total had suffered a major imbalancing blow. Still, during the next thirty years or so the numbers rose to 260.1 million.

Political Development

The Russian Empire prior to 1917 expanded over a thousand year period. It grew from a relatively small area between the Gulf of Finland in the north and a line well north of the Black Sea in the south, to include most of the present territories of the USSR and also modern Finland, parts of Poland and parts of Turkey. The USSR as we know it today is administratively and politically the product of little over 60 years.

Russia's long history up to 1917 is dominated by certain individuals and families. In the mid-sixteenth century, the first Tsar of all the Russias, Ivan the Terrible, established autocratic control over a much enlarged territory. The Romanov Dynasty was established in the mid-seventeenth century. Peter the Great (1689–1725) introduced new social and industrial ideas from the then advanced countries of Western Europe. Later, in the 1780s under Catherine the Great, Russia's extent was pushed as far west as it was ever to be. During the nineteenth century, the country expanded eastward into Moslem Central Asia and on to the Pacific.

By the beginning of the present century, the empire was not only having difficulties with some neighboring countries, but internally revolutionary pressures were growing against the oppressive regime of the Romanovs. War with Japan led to territorial losses in the east; fighting against Germany in World War I, the Imperial Russian Armies suffered heavy losses. In 1917, the Communist revolution broke out.

From 1918 to 1922 the country was gripped by civil war. Eventually the Bolsheviks defeated the non-Communist White Russians supported by the western allies. They had lost some lands in the west where Finland, Estonia, Latvia, Lithuania and Poland had been reestablished as separate countries.

During World War II, Germany attacked the USSR in June 1941 and the western allies joined forces with the Soviets. After making immense territorial gains, the Germans were eventually forced back, and by 1945 the Soviet armies had overrun Eastern Europe. Since the end of the war, the Soviet Union has had a dominant interest in the maintenance of Communist governments in the eastern bloc of European countries.

Since the creation of the Soviet Union, a system of internal political control has evolved which provides varying degrees of self-government for particular areas. Soviet Socialist Republics (SSRs) are the highest administrative unit, within which smaller units may exist.

Industry, Commerce and Communications

Before the revolution, Russia was predominantly agricultural. Since 1928, a series of five-year plans have been implemented. The early plans sought to establish heavy industries and the rational development of mineral resources. When World War II caused much damage to the industries of the western areas, newer strategically safer locations farther east were developed. Since then more emphasis has been placed on manufactured, consumer goods than on heavy industry.

One of the largest concentrations of the iron and steel industry is in the southern Ukraine; iron ore comes from Krivoy Rog and coking coal from the Donbas area. The largest production centers are Donetsk and Zaporozhye. The Urals contain the next most significant places, with Magnitogorsk and Chelyabinsk being the largest individual centers. Farther east, Temirtau and Novokuznetsk were established in the 1930s and smaller plants have been set up more recently in the far east.

1 △

2 ▽

3 ▽

1 Summer Palace, Leningrad, Russia
2 Interior of GUM, the largest store in the world, Moscow, Russia
3 Harvesting wheat, Dmitrovski state farm, Yakut Autonomous Republic

Large concentrations of the petro-chemical industries, especially in the southern Ukraine, the Greater Moscow Region, the Urals area and the Kuzbas region farther east have developed since the 1930s.

Leningrad, Moscow, Gorki, the Urals and Ukraine towns are variously the main centers of heavy industrial equipment, vehicles, railway and farming equipment manufacture. Lighter engineering is more widely scattered. Textiles and clothing have long been concentrated in the European areas but have more recently been established in Soviet Central Asia and Transcaucasia. Food processing is usually market orientated and is thus predominantly in the west, but is tending to spread eastward.

The USSR is an advanced industrial society, yet 22 percent of the working population, about 25 million workers, are still employed in farming. Some 26 percent are employed in manufacturing industries, 10 percent in transport and communications and 6 percent in trade and commerce.

Communications in the USSR are all state controlled. Railroads provide some 60 percent of the freight mileage and 50 percent of the passenger mileage. The rail network is densest in the west. Beyond the Urals are a number of routes to Soviet Central Asia, two to the Lake Baykal region and one to the Pacific.

By Western standards the Soviet road network is ill-developed. Car ownership and long-distance road haulage are limited. Only in the west is the system truly efficient and well maintained. For long distance passengers and mail, as well as for wider purposes in the remote areas, planes are increasingly used. Today, some 100 million air passengers are carried internally each year. Despite the problems of the winter freeze, many rivers of the west are used for barge and larger ship movements. Links exist between the Baltic, Black, White and Caspian Seas.

Agriculture, Forestry and Fishing

Perhaps 30 percent of the USSR could be used for crop farming, but only about one-third of that is currently so utilized. Twice as much land is given over to pasture and grazing. About half of the national area is forested and the remainder is either tundra of the north, deserts of the south or mountains.

During the 1920s and '30s and following World War II, agriculture took a back seat in the total national economic scene, while industrial development was given higher priority. Since 1953, following the death of Stalin, farming has been made modern and more efficient. All land is nationalized and organized in state farms (Sovzhoz) and collectives (Kolkhoz).

The forest zone extends from the Finnish and Baltic margins in a broad belt to the Pacific. There are over 7.5 million km² (3 million sq mi) of forests, two-thirds in the Asiatic

parts of the country. These, and the European forests are being systematically exploited from the southern margins. In European Russia, sawmills, pulp and paper making plants and wood chemical works are widely scattered. Farther east, so much of the forests are as yet untouched. Currently, timber production stands at about 390 million cubic meters and paper at 4 million tons per year. Nearly 85 percent of the wood produced is soft and only 15 percent hard. In total, the Soviet Union accounts for 16 percent of the world's timber production.

The USSR is the world leader in wheat production, growing as much as 24 percent of the 400 million tons produced each year. It is also the leading producer of barley – 37 percent of the world's 190 million tons, oats – 34 percent of the world's 50 million tons, and rye – 43 percent of the world's 28 million tons. By contrast, only 3 percent of the world's corn comes from the USSR.

Nearly 30 percent of the world's potatoes are grown in the USSR and it is again the world leader. It comes second only to the USA in growing tomatoes, producing 9 percent of the world's total. The USSR also produces a phenomenal major share of the world's sugar beets: 34 percent, nearly four times as much as the second largest producer, the USA. In contrast the USSR figures poorly in world fruit growing, though it does account for 9.5 percent of the world's grapes. Of the beverage crops, the USSR accounts for about 5.5 per-

cent of the global tea production.

The USSR figures prominently in the production of industrial, vegetable fibers, being the leader in cotton lint production, the producer of nearly three-quarters of the world's flax and only marginally second to India in accounting for 25 percent of the world's hemp.

The Soviet Union is also well placed in the world's livestock and animal products standings, having 9 percent of the 1,214 million cattle, 9 percent of the 645 million pigs and 14 percent of the 1,038 million sheep. Nearly one-quarter of the world's cows' milk, one-eighth of its hens' eggs, one-sixth of its greasy wool and one-twelfth of its raw silk also originate here.

Finally, the Soviet Union is currently second only to Japan as a world fishing nation. Its large long-range fleet catches some 14 percent of the world's fish total. In addition, Soviet whalers also gather half of all the world's catch of the diminishing stocks of whales.

Natural Resources

The Soviet economy is based very heavily upon home production of fuel and power. The country has major coal fields in both the developed west and in the developing central and eastern areas. In total, the USSR accounts for about 25 percent of the world's hard coal production (bituminous and anthracite) which is currently about 2,300 million tons per year. The Soviet Union is also the world's second most important

producer of soft coal (lignite). About 175 million tons per year, 20 percent of the world total, comes from the Moscow Basin and recently developed fields farther east.

By 1976 the USSR had become the world's largest single producer of crude oil with 520 million tons, 18 percent of the world total. The Baku oil fields, formerly the major source, have now been overtaken by the Ural-Volga fields. The USSR is thought to have the largest natural gas reserves in the world, producing over 300 million cubic meters per year. This represents some 24 percent of world output, and puts the USSR second in the world production tables. The fields of Soviet Central Asia and the area north of Tyumen are most important.

It is estimated that the Soviet Union's hydroelectric potential is the highest of any single country in the world, over 400 million kilowatts installed capacity. Much of this lies in the valleys of the great north-flowing rivers of the Soviet heartland. Around 10 percent has been installed and the annual HEP production is third in the world, behind the USA and Canada. One-eighth of the Soviet's consumed electricity is derived from hydro sources.

The Soviet Union is by far the world's leading producer of iron ore, contributing about 140 million out of the world's total of about 540 million tons (iron content) per year, 26 percent of the total. The iron ore fields of Krivoy Rog in the Ukraine are the largest, the long-developed fields of the Ural region

Soviet agriculture is generally highly mechanized and is organized on collective lines: 1 Festival of reindeer tenders, Moma state farm, Yakut Autonomous Republic – fishing, trapping and cattle raising are also carried out in this Siberian republic of very cold winters; 2 Piling up cotton at Tedjen state farm, Turkmen – this is the most valuable crop of this primarily desert region; 3 Caviar weigher at the Ust-Kamchatka fish factory, Russia – the part-nomadic people of this remote eastern territory hunt and fish for a livelihood

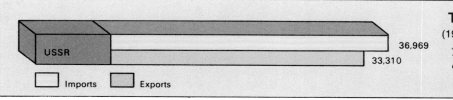

USSR		36,969
		33,310
☐ Imports	■ Exports	

Total Imports and Exports
(1975 figures in millions of U.S. dollars)

The modern trade figures for the USSR are similar to those of Canada, and show remarkable recent growth.

USSR

are the second largest. Ore deposits farther east, particularly those of the Kuznets area, are now being developed systematically. The USSR's estimated iron ore reserves are over 260,000 million tons, 44 percent of the world total.

The USSR contains a wide range of other mineral ores, some of them in significant quantities, as the table right shows.

Soviet Economy

The distribution of population in the USSR is very uneven. The greatest concentrations are in the west, south of the 60th parallel. Here are the richest and most advanced agricultural lands and most of the large urban developments. Other centers of high average population density are found in Soviet Central Asia. In both, densities in excess of 100 per sq km (250 per sq mi) are found over large areas. About two-thirds of the population are living on the plain lands of European USSR, that is on about one-sixth of the national area.

Elsewhere, the line of the Trans-Siberian Railway and the river valleys are at the center of the belt of higher population density. In all other places, population is thinly scattered.

Compared with the USA and the countries of Western Europe, a lower proportion of the population is concentrated in large urban areas, 100.2

Ore	Average Annual World Production (million tons)	USSR Share (percent)	Principal USSR Locations
bauxite	80.3	8	Urals
chrome	7.2	27	Urals
cobalt	0.03	5	Urals
copper	7.4	16	Kazakh, Urals, Central Asian Republics and Transcaucasia
gold	1 million kg	31	East Siberia and the Far East
lead	3.2	16	Central Asian Republics
manganese	22.8	39	Nikopol and Chiatura
molybdenum	0.084	11	The Far East
nickel	0.733	17	Urals and Yenisey Basin
silver	0.01	17	Karelia and the Far East
tungsten	0.036	20	East Siberia
vanadium	0.02	23	Central Asian Republics
zinc	5.4	13	Central Asian Republics, Urals and Salair region

million being classified as rural and 159.9 million as urban. There are 24 metro areas over 1 million in the USSR of which Moscow, Leningrad, Donetsk, Kiev and Tashkent have populations in excess of 2 million. Seventeen of the 24 metropolitan areas are west of the Urals, which is a further indication of the economic dominance of the west in the country as a whole.

Yet, population changes and increases during recent years show how the areas east of the Urals are growing in importance. For example, between 1961 and 1976 percentage increases were 74.1 in Uzbek, 37.6 in Kazakh and only 16.1 in Byelorussia. The overall growth rate is 0.9 percent per annum, though in Asiatic USSR it is more than double that figure. Two distinctive features of the population of the USSR are the imbalance between the sexes and the gap in the age pyramid caused by the large losses of World War II.

Soviet emphasis has been on industrial growth: 1 Bratsk Power Station, Irkutsk, Russia; 2 Temirtau iron and steel plant, Kazakh SSR

When analyzing the USSR's economic progress we must remember that some data may not always be directly comparable with that for non-Communist countries. For instance, where finance figures are concerned, there is the problem of using a meaningful exchange rate.

Available trade figures over the years 1938, '58 and '75 show remarkable growth when compared, for example, with those of the USA or a number of European countries. Imports rose from $273 million to $4,350m (1,493 percent increase) and then to $36,969 million (750 percent increase). The comparable export figures were $255 million to $4,298 million (1,585 percent increase) and then to $33,310 million (675 percent increase). In essence these reflect the lack of trade between the USSR and the outside world before World War II, its rapid growth thereafter, especially through trade with other Communist countries and, in the later period, an increasing volume of trade with the non-Communist world.

The Soviet Union makes no regular return on per capita incomes, and comparisons over a period are thus not possible. However, occasional figures are available for particular years, of which a figure of $2,790 for 1976 can be usefully compared with certain other countries: USA $5,923,

West Germany $5,480, France $4,505 and UK $3,106.

In the mid-1970s the USSR had an energy surplus, 1,650 million tons coal equivalent (mtce) being produced and 1,410 mtce consumed. Coal output stood at 712 million tons, 43 percent of the national energy production, being a higher proportion of the national total than for any other large energy-producing country except China. Oil and oil products are the major energy export, and have increased their share of total national energy production from around 14 percent in 1945 to 45 percent in 1976.

The per capita consumption of energy in 1975 was 5,546 kg, a fraction over half that of the USA. Much of this figure is expended in industrial production and services rather than in direct personal use.

The modern economy of the USSR has shown remarkable growth; in little over half a century it has mushroomed from a revolutionary catastrophe, has been seriously curtailed by world wars and has been centrally planned by governments which have on occasion, brought large changes of emphasis in the development of the country. Since World War II, the Soviet Union has been the dominant power in the Communist world and has, in many respects, narrowed the gap, if not closed it, between itself and the other great world power, the USA.

How will the Soviet Union develop internally and act in the international scene in the coming years? As the present leadership of the USSR will change fairly soon, forecasting is especially difficult. However, some significant points can be noted. Economic growth has been slowing down slightly in recent years, which must cause concern in a country with so many agricultural workers and so much extractive and heavy industry. It is becoming increasingly necessary to exploit the comparatively expensive resources of the eastern frontiers. Although industrial productivity now grows at a little over 3 percent per annum, the maintenance of even this figure seems unlikely. Oil exports, a valuable source of overseas currency, seem bound to decline in the 1980s.

At the same time, the Soviet Union is increasing its defense expenditure by 4.5 percent per annum. If it continues to do this while the national growth rate stagnates, it may be able to hold its present military position vis-a-vis the West only at the expense of a fall in the home living standard. Then, unless trends in productivity take an upturn, the country may lose ground in the constant struggle to maintain military parity with the non-Communist world.

Yet such matters cannot be looked at in isolation. Other considerations, such as the growth rates of the Western economies and the role of Communist China in the next decade or so must also be taken into account. The potential of the USSR is enormous; the way in which it will be harnessed must depend on a balance of internal decisions and the general consensus of other leading world powers.

Per Capita Energy Consumption
(1975 figures in kilograms)

Energy consumption in the USSR is little more than half that of North America.

5,546

USSR

Per Capita Income
(1976 figures in U.S. dollars)

Average earnings in the USSR work out at about half those of the USA.

USSR

2,790

USSR Republics

Russia

More than 75 percent of the whole USSR lies in this uniquely constituted federal republic. Stretching from the Baltic to the Pacific, it has a huge range of landscapes and climates. In value terms it accounts for over two-thirds of the country's agricultural output and about 60 percent of its industrial output. Extensive crop-lands stretch across the south; here, and to the north, pastoral farming is also extensive. The great forest lands lie even farther north. In the Urals area and elsewhere, coal, iron ore and crude oil are all extracted in large quantities. The population is most densely settled in the west, with Moscow (7.6 million) and Leningrad (4.3 million), but a string of medium and large cities has developed in the 'new lands' east of the Urals and to the Pacific. These collectively contain virtually every industrial activity found in the country.

More than any other republic, Russia is sub-divided into smaller political units. There are 16 Autonomous Soviet Socialist Republics (ASSRs), the largest of which is the Yakut ASSR covering over 3 million km² (nearly 1.2 million sq mi). Each ASSR is largely settled by one racial group and now enjoys a great deal of local political control. There are also 5 Autonomous Regions (ARs) in Russia, each of which has less local political control.

The Baltic Republics – Estonia, Latvia and Lithuania

Once part of the Russian Empire, these achieved independence in 1919 but were subsequently admitted to the USSR in 1940. Formerly their economies were firmly based on agriculture, but in recent years a range of industries has become increasingly important. All three, but particularly Estonia, have valuable timber and pulp industries. In Estonia shale is used for gas making and peat for firing electricity stations. In Latvia and Lithuania, textiles, food processing and engineering are other major industries. Agriculturally, rye, oats and vegetable growing as well as some pastoral farming are the main activities.

Three European Republics – Byelorussia, Moldavia and the Ukraine

Some of the richest agricultural and industrial landscapes of the whole USSR are found in Europe. The Ukraine in particular, produces over one-quarter of all the Soviet's grains and three-fifths of its sugar beet. Corn, potatoes, flax, sunflower seeds and fruits are produced widely in the southern parts. Peat cutting and timber production are more signifi-

cant farther north. Industrially, 60 percent of the USSR coal reserves lie beneath Ukrainian soil; today 30 percent of the annual output comes from here, 50 percent of the iron ore and 60 percent of the manganese. Nearly half the Soviet iron and steel production also comes from the Ukraine. Other major industries include food processing, petro-chemicals, engineering including vehicle and farm equipment manufacturing, textiles and leather. Besides individual large cities in each republic, the cluster of major cities in southeast Ukraine is the largest in the whole union.

Soviet Central Asia – Kazakh, Kirghiz, Tadzhik, Turkmen and Uzbek

Kazakh is by far the largest of these republics. Kirghiz and Tadzhik are mountainous, the others mainly dry plain lands. Irrigation plays a large part in agriculture. Nomadic herding

of cattle and sheep is traditional and valuable. Apart from wheat, sugar beet and vegetables, tobacco, cotton, citrus fruit and rice are also grown here. Raw materials extracted include coal, iron ore, crude oil, natural gas, tungsten, copper and lead. The range of industries in the largest cluster of Soviet large towns east of the Urals includes food processing, iron and steel, petrochemicals, engineering, textiles and leather working. Tashkent (1.5 million), capital of Uzbek, is the fourth largest city in the USSR.

Transcaucasia – Armenia, Azerbaidzhan and Georgia

Created out of the former Transcaucasian SSR in 1936, these three SSRs are situated between the Black and Caspian Seas, bordering Iran, Turkey and Russia. Mountains and large river basins dominate the landscapes. Irrigation is employed in some areas to grow a wide range of

1 Eleventh century church, Novgorod, Russia – one of the oldest towns in the Republic; 2 Bridge over the Dnieper, Kiev, Ukraine – the USSR's third largest city is a major communications center; 3 Domes of the Kremlin; 4 Changing guard, Lenin's Tomb, Red Square, Moscow

subtropical and temperate crops, of which wheat, cotton, subtropical fruits, grapes, corn and potatoes are the most valuable. Sheep are more numerous than cattle and goats. A wide range of industries have been established on a modest scale; these include food processing, textiles and leather goods, metal working, light engineering, vehicle and railway construction. The extraction and processing of oil in the Caspian lowlands is of great national importance.

The Transcaucasian republics also contain a number of smaller political divisions: Azerbaidzhan has 1 ASSR and 1 AR; Georgia has 2 ASSRs and 1 AR.

REFERENCE TABLE: USSR

USSR Republics	Political Status	State Capital	Area		Population	Population Density	
			km²	sq mi		per km²	per sq ml
Armenia	D	Jerevan	29,800	11,500	2,887,000	97	251
Azerbaidzhan	D	Baku	86,600	33,450	5,801,000	67	173
Byelorussia	D	Minsk	207,600	80,150	9,520,000	46	119
Estonia	D	Tallinn	45,100	17,400	1,456,000	32	84
Georgia	D	Tbilisi	69,700	26,900	5,046,000	72	188
Kazakh	D	Alma-ata	2,715,000	1,048,300	14,592,000	5.4	14
Kirghiz	D	Frunze	198,500	76,650	3,433,000	17	45
Latvia	D	Riga	63,700	24,600	2,601,000	40	106
Lithuania	D	Vilnius	65,200	25,150	3,381,000	52	134
Moldavia	D	Kisinov	33,700	13,000	3,902,000	116	300
Russian SFSR	D	Moscow	17,075,400	6,592,850	137,053,000	8.0	21
Tadzhik	D	Dusanbe	143,100	55,250	3,538,000	25	64
Turkmen	D	Aschabad	488,100	188,450	2,627,000	5.4	14
Ukraine	D	Kiev	603,700	233,100	49,941,000	83	214
Uzbek	D	Tashkent	449,600	173,600	14,332,000	32	83
USSR TOTAL	A	Moscow	22,274,900	8,600,350	260,110,000	12	30

Note: For the whole USSR, Birth rate per thousand persons 18.2
Death rate per thousand persons 9.3
Mean annual percentage increase in population 0.9

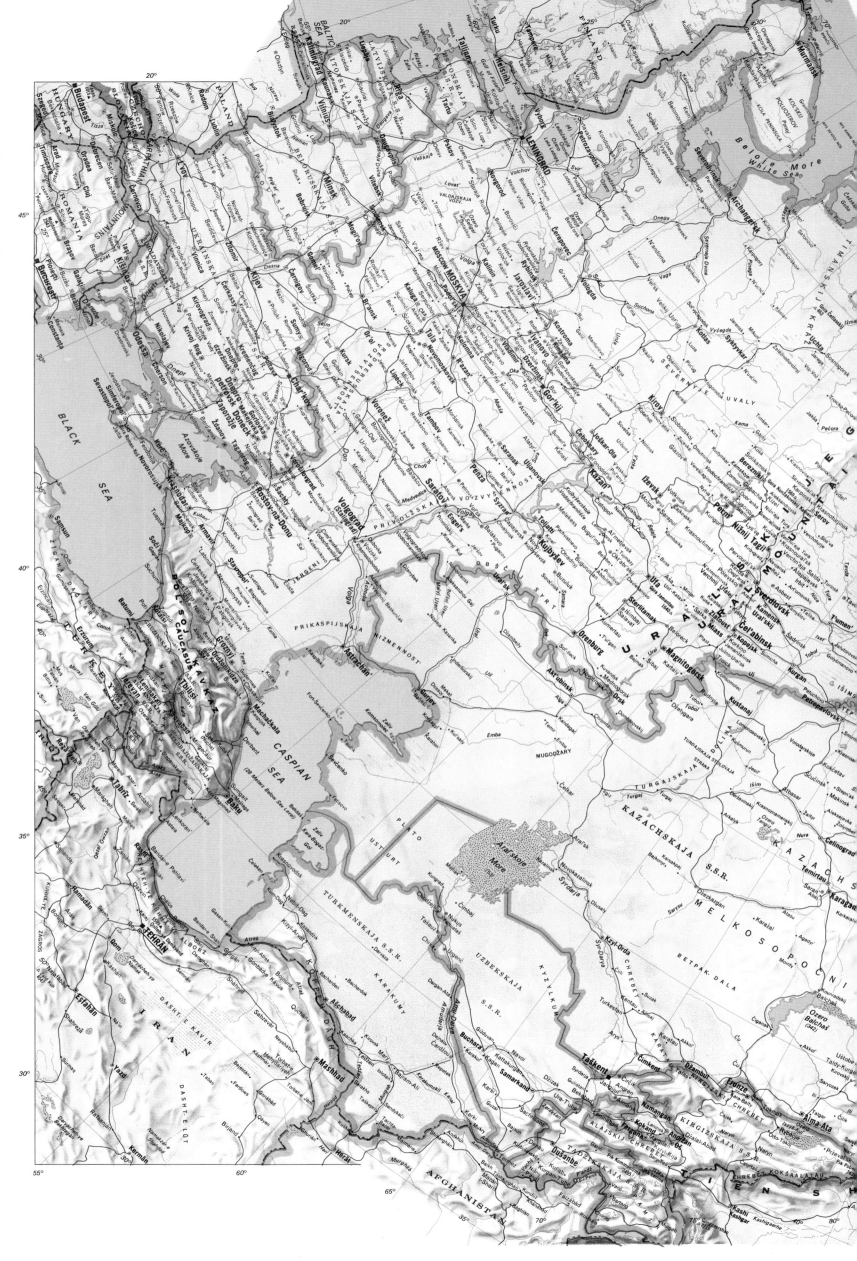

Kilometers

Statute Miles

Scale 1:13,200,000

One centimeter represents 132 kilometers.
One inch represents approximately 210 miles.

Lambert Conformal Conic Projection

Copyright © by Rand McNally & Co.
Map prepared by Esselte Map Service AB, Stockholm.
A-579594-264

BARENTS SEA

KARSKOJE MORE
KARA SEA

MORE LAPTEVY

LAPTEV SE

NOVA JA ZEML'A

SEVERNAJA ZEML'A

OSTROV KOMSOMOLEC

Pečorskoje More

Arctic Circle

Vorkuta

POLUOSTROV JAMAL

GYDANSKIJ POLUOSTROV

POLUOSTROV TAJMYR

GORY BYRRANGA

SEVERO - SIBIRSKAJA NIZMENNOST

Noril'sk

PLATO PUTORANA

SREDNE - SIBIRSKOJE PLOSKOGORJE

SIBERIA

ZAPADNO - SIBIRSKAJA NIZMENNOST'

SOVETSKAJA FEDERATIVNAJA SOCIALISTIČESKAJA

RESPUBLIK

RUSSIAN SOVIET FEDERATED SOCIALIST REPUBLIC

UNION

OF

SOVIET

SOCIA

Omsk

Tomsk

Novosibirsk

Kemerovo

Anžero-Sudžensk

Krasnojarsk

Bratsk

Lena

Leninsk-Kuzneckij

Belovo

Prokopjevsk

Kiselʹovsk

Novokuzneck

Barnaul

Abakan

STANOVOJE NAGORJE

STANOVOY MOUNTAINS

Bijsk

Semipalatinsk

Rubcovsk

ZAPADNYJ SAYAN

VOSTOČNYJ SAJAN

SAJAN MOUNTAINS

Čeremchovo

Angarsk

Irkutsk

Ozero Bajkal
Lake Baykal

Ulan-Ude

Čita

KAZACHSKAJA S.S.R.

Ustʹ-Kamenogorsk

CHREBET TARBAGATAJ

Gora Belucha

CHREBET TANNU-OLA

SAJANY

YABLONOVYJ CHREB

Yining
Kuldja

XINJIANG WEIWUER ZIZHIQU
SINKIANG
ZHUANGAERPENDI

CHINA

MONGOLIA

CHANGAJN NURUU

Ulaanbaatar

Kilometers

Statute Miles

Km.

Mi.

Scale 1:13,200,000

One centimeter represents 132 kilometers.
One inch represents approximately 210 miles.

Lambert Conformal Conic Projection

Copyright © by Rand McNally & Co.
Map prepared by Esselte Map Service AB, Stockholm
A-579395-264

ALASKA
UNITED STATES

Chukchi Sea

EAST SIBERIAN SEA
VOSTOČNO- SIBIRSKOJE MORE

OSTROVA SIBIRSKIJE

OSTROV VRANGELJA

Proliv Longa

Arctic Circle

Bering Strait

SAINT LAWRENCE ISLAND

NUNIVAK ISLAND

Bering Sea

Anadyrskij Zaliv

EKIATAPSKIJ CHREBET

ANADYRSKOJE PLOSKOGORJE

KORJAKSKOJE NAGORJE

KOLYMSKAJA NIZMENNOST

AN'UJSKIJ CHREBET

JUKAGIRSKOJE PLOSKOGORJE

PENŽINSKIJ CHREBET

Zaliv Šelichova

MOMSKIJ CHREBET

CHREBET ČERSKOGO

CHREBET SUNTAR- CHAIATA

CHREBET SETTE-DABAN

SREDINNYJ CHREBET

KOMANDORSKIJE OSTROVA

POLUOSTROV KAMČATKA

Magadan

Petropavlovsk-Kamčatskij

REPUBLICS

Jakutsk

CHREBET DŽUGDŽUR

SEA OF OKHOTSK
OCHOTSKOJE MORE

Lena

STANOVOJ CHREBET
NAGORJE
ALDANSKOJE

ŠANTARSKIJE OSTROVA

KURIL'SKIJE OSTROVA
KURIL ISLANDS

Komsomol'sk-na-Amure

OSTROV SACHALIN SAKHALIN

Blagoveščensk

Chabarovsk

Južno-Sachalinsk

DAXINGANLINGSHANMAI

NEIMENGGU ZIZHIQU

MONGOLIA

Beian

HEILONGJIANG

Yichun

Hegang

Shuangyashan

Habomai, Shikotan, Kunashiri, and Etorofu, occupied by the U.S.S.R. since 1945, are claimed by Japan pending a final peace treaty.

Qiqihaer Tsitsihar

CHINA

MANCHURIA

Haerbin

Jiamusi

Asahikawa

Kushiro

Otaru
Sapporo
Muroran
HOKKAIDO

Mudanjiang

Ussurijsk

Hakodate

Vladivostok

SEA OF JAPAN

JAPAN

HONSHU

Hachinohe

Akita

Morioka

PACIFIC OCEAN

65

ASIA
Physical Profile

World Location and Size

Asia is joined to both Europe and Africa. Its western limits are the Ural Mountains, lying north to south in the USSR at about 60°E, the Caspian Sea, Asia Minor, the eastern Mediterranean coast and the Red Sea. The main land mass is clearly defined to south, east and north by the Indian, Pacific and Arctic Oceans, but Asia also includes a large number of islands, especially off its southeast and east coasts. As we are treating the USSR as a separate geographical unit, the area here under review as Asia is but the southern portion of the whole continent.

Asia is predominantly in the Northern Hemisphere. The continent's west-east extent is from the Aegean Sea at 26°E to the Japanese island of Hokkaido at 146°E, a third of the way around the world at about 40°N latitude. Although the USSR extends north of the Arctic Circle, for our purposes Asia extends from the northernmost part of China, in Manchuria at 53°N to the Indonesian Islands at 10°S; even that is one-third of the distance between the North and South Poles.

Landscape

Asia may be divided into five distinct physical units, each separated from its neighbor by a line of mountains. Southwest Asia includes all countries south of the border with the Soviet Union, from the Mediterranean and Red Seas east to Afghanistan and western Pakistan. Its northern area is rugged and mountainous, reaching 5,604 m (18,387 ft) in the Elburz Mountains of northern Iran. Within the broad mountain region lie some extensive plateaus such as the Plateau of Iran. Turkey and northern Iran are both prone to earthquakes.

South of this general area it is geologically more complex. Its western region is part of the great Rift Valley which extends from East Africa to Syria. The mountains of the Arabian peninsula rise to 3,760 m (12,336 ft). East of these, the land level falls across the great desert expanse of the Arabian Peninsula to the lowland belt occupied by the Persian Gulf and the southeast flowing Tigris and Euphrates rivers.

Central Asia, farther east, is the most remote and physically extreme area of the whole world. Bounded in the north by the Tien Shan and the Sayan Mountains, it extends southward across western China, Mongolia and Tibet to the Himalayas. Within Sinkiang Province, China, the

Opposite: Twelfth century Jagannath temple, Puri, eastern India

Turfan Depression descends to a level of 154 m (505 ft) below sea level. In contrast, Mount Everest in the Himalayas is the world's highest point, some 8,848 m (29,028 ft) above sea level. Though encircled by mountains, the area's heartland is a series of plains, predominantly uninviting dry lands including the Takla Makan and Gobi Deserts, and the Tibetan Plateau.

Still farther east lie the large river valleys of Eastern Asia, flanked by the hills and low tablelands of eastern China. Also within this region lie Korea, the Japanese islands and Taiwan. The islands are essentially the tops of a great mountain ridge rising steeply from the floor of the Pacific Ocean. They are part of the 'Pacific Ring of Fire', a zone of modern active volcanoes and frequent earthquake activity. This is much the smallest of the areas covered so far, yet the most important in population and broad development terms.

South of the mountains of Central Asia lies the Indian subcontinent which is composed of two distinctly different areas. Much of the Deccan, a triangular-shaped tableland which occupies the southern parts of the peninsula, lies at 500 m (1,650 ft) to 700 m (2,300 ft). Its margins rise in the Western and Eastern Ghats to greater heights, 2,695 m (8,842 ft) and 1,680 m (5,512 ft) respectively. Then, between the Deccan and the Himalayas are the great valleys of the Indus, Ganges and Brahmaputra Rivers.

South of China and east of India/Bangladesh lie the intricately shaped peninsulas of Southeast Asia, and the islands beyond. The northern flanks are mountainous, the principal mountain axis being north to south. Lower mountain chains then extend into peninsulas, particularly into Burma, Malaysia, Laos and Vietnam. A number of large rivers flow southward across broad plains in Burma, Thailand and Kampuchea. In the islands farther south, the mountain axis changes to northwest/southeast (Sumatra) and then west/east (Java). The easternmost islands lie in the 'Pacific Ring of Fire'.

Climatic Background

Situated on the east and southeast side of the world's largest single land mass, Asia extends from the equatorial region to temperate mid-latitudes and contains several very high mountain ranges. Consequently, it exhibits a wide range of climatic types, including the unique three season pattern of the monsoon lands. The extreme west, on the littoral of Turkey, in Cyprus, the Levant coast and into parts of lowland Iraq, has a Mediterranean type of climate. The summer is very dry, and total precipitation may be only 500 mm (20 in). Average temperatures in the hottest month may be well into the low

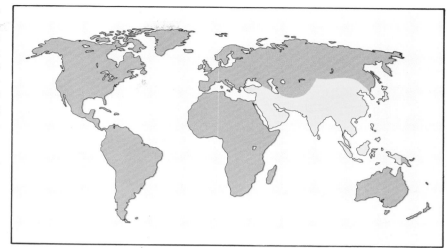

Japan's advanced bullet train passes through snow near Maibara: a mountainous country with active volcanoes and prone to earthquakes, Japan has a monsoonal climate with heavy summer rains and cold winters in parts

20°sC (mid 70°sF) on the fringe of the Mediterranean. Farther east, annual temperature ranges increase, summer monthly averages rise higher and total precipitation decreases.

The transition zone between a humid subtropical climate and the dry climates of desert and steppe lands is thus quickly crossed. So much of Asia falls within these two climatic categories. The Arabian Peninsula, the Plateau of Iran, the Makran coast, much of Pakistan and parts of northwest India experience a true hot desert climate. Average annual precipitation nowhere exceeds 250 mm (10 in) and is often less than half that. Monthly average temperatures are never below freezing and in the high sun season exceed 32°C (90°F).

North of this region, throughout much of interior Iraq, Iran, Afghanistan and, in India, south of the Great Desert and east of the Western Ghats, extends a belt of steppeland climates. Annual rainfall is slightly higher and the range of temperatures lower. Then, within the Anatolian Plateau, in Mongolia and parts of northeast China, lower precipitation with lower temperatures produce the mid-latitude steppe climates. In these the lowest winter average monthly temperature falls below 0°C (32°F), and the summer temperature rises into the low 20°sC (mid 70°sF).

The great upland heart of Asia experiences mountain climates in which altitude is the predominant factor. Precipitation is very variable, but is often low. Average temperatures are surprisingly low for the latitude, with readings below freezing for as many as six months.

In Eastern Asia, most of lowland China, Korea and Japan the annual precipitation is much higher and the

average temperatures lower. To the north, the rains fall throughout the year or, on the mainland, largely in summer. Farther south, in southern Honshu and Kyushu as well as in much of southern China and northern Laos, Vietnam and Thailand, summer average temperatures exceed 27°C (80°F) and annual precipitation exceeds 1,250 mm (50 in).

Much of peninsula India, Burma, Malaysia, southern Thailand, Laos, Vietnam, Kampuchea and the islands of SE Asia experience tropical rainy climates. The average temperature of even the coolest month exceeds 18°C (64°F) and the high summer average temperatures then reach the high 20°sC (low 80°sF). Near the equator the average monthly temperatures stay near 27°C (80°F) all year.

Precipitation is constant throughout the year in many of the islands, but India, Bangladesh and Sri Lanka are subject to the unique monsoons. From mid-December to early March dry, comparatively cool air from central Asia crosses the Himalayas and then blows out into the Indian Ocean. From then to the end of May the heat builds up. In June, when low pressure develops over central Asia, hot wet winds blow onshore bringing with them very heavy rains. The exact amount of rainfall varies but, at its most extreme, the world's highest average annual precipitation of 11,610 mm (457 in) is experienced 1,311 m (4,300 ft) up in the Assam hills, at Cherrapunji.

ASIA

Asia is something of an enigma in the modern world. The contrasting economies found there today, in large measure conceal the great ages in the continent's past. Herein lies the scene of many early civilizations – the Sumerians in Mesopotamia over 5,000 years ago, the great Indus Valley cultural center over 4,000 years ago, the Chinese dynastic developments culminating in the artistic excellence of the Chou some 1,000 years BC, the empire of Alexander the Great 700 years later.

Asia has also been the birthplace of most of the world's great religions – Buddhism founded in India and Confucianism in China in the sixth century BC, Christianity in Palestine, and Mohammedanism in Arabia in the sixth century AD.

More recently, before European intervention, great empires have come and gone and centuries of wars have swept the area – the Byzantine Empire from the fourth century onward, the Mongols led by Genghis and Kubla Khan in the thirteenth century, the sixteenth century Ottomans. Then the British, French and Dutch, in particular, moved into parts of Asia to establish outposts of their recent empires. Today even these connections have mainly crumbled and the continent is made up of independent countries.

Asia's sheer size underlines its conflicting characteristics. It includes the new, rising economic generation of the Middle East and Japan. China and India in particular embrace rich histories yet have unrealized potential in the modern world. Its differences in life-styles, languages, religions and politics are greater than those found in any other single continent – from the Tibetans who never leave their mountain aeries to the Arab teenagers who commute by jet to shop in Europe's capital cities. Here lies the quickening world in perhaps its most dramatic form.

The Peoples and Their Life-Styles

Asia is the most heavily peopled continent. It is also the one whose population is growing most rapidly. Indeed, total population has increased at alarming rates this century. Living standards for so many people are extremely low; life expectancy is also low by modern standards. Birth rates in Asia are high and death rates lower.

In recent times parts of Asia have developed economically along Western lines, especially Japan and Israel. The oilrich Arab countries are also developing fast, though not for the benefit of all their peoples. Generally, despite some large urban centers and growing industries, the rest of Asia is still dominated by subsistence farming. In a continent of territorial and climatic extremes, millions of Asians thus face the almost annual consequences of crop failure and famine, as well as disastrous floods and tropical storms.

Among the great number of racial groups to be found in Asia, the main ones are the Mongoloids, the Caucasoids, and the Negroids. And just as there are many races, so there are many religions, with different areas being dominated by different faiths. India is predominantly Hindu, the Arab world is largely Moslem, China presents a mixture of Buddhism and Confucianism, and Japan a mixture of Buddhism and Shintoism.

Industry, Commerce and Communications

Compared with the leading areas of the developed world, particularly Europe and North America, Asia is, as a whole, industrially ill-developed. Whereas Western Europe accounted for nearly 31 percent of the world's value added in manufacturing industries in 1975, the USA 29 percent and the USSR nearly 16 percent, Asia accounted for only 10.6 percent. Certain individual countries such as Japan, China, and India are, however, comparatively well developed as are Hong Kong, Singapore, Java, Israel and Turkey.

Japan, for instance, is now one of the world's leading industrial nations, noted for such products as ship building (first in the world), cars (world second) and precision engineering, such as optics, electrical and electronics (world first for both radio and TV manufacture). In all Asia, Japan's trade with the outside world is greater than any other. She also currently rates third in world steel production, third also in the production of aluminum and second in pig iron. Such placings all show remarkable progress during the post World War II era.

China too has made great strides forward since the Communist revolution and the establishment of the People's Government in 1949. While agriculture has been given priority over industry in many respects, China is now the world's fourth largest pig iron producer, fifth largest steel producer and fourth tin producer. By contrast, in the same field, India, with its longer history of development, rates consistently lower: tenth for pig iron, fifteenth

1 △

2 ▽   3 ▽

1 China – the Great Wall, 2,400 km (1,500 mi) long, at Zhang Jia Khou.
2 Hong Kong – Typhoon Shelter.
3 Japan – Tokyo's lively Ginza area.

for steel and fourteenth for aluminum. In comparison with Japan, however, both China and India, with their far larger populations, are still striving to satisfy home demands and are not major world traders.

Taking these same two countries, 74 percent of their combined working population is engaged on the land, about 10 percent in manufacturing, 2 percent in extractive industry and 2 percent in building. Only 4 percent are engaged in trade and commerce, 2 percent in transport and communications and 6 percent in the other service industries. Such figures show the extent to which Asian economies are still agriculturally-based, apart from Japan, Hong Kong and Israel, and the very small part of the economies which are within the service industries. Overall, it is doubtful if more than one in twenty of the whole Asiatic population are thus employed.

Asia plays a fragmented role in world trade. As already indicated, Japan is unique. Some Southeast Asian countries trade in specialist products like rubber, tea, hardwoods, rice, jute and cotton textiles. The Arab states of Southwest Asia make a major contribution to world trade in that some 45 percent of all crude oil originates there and the great bulk of this is exported.

Apart from the specialist oil terminals, Asia has few major sea and air ports. Karachi, Bombay, Calcutta, Bangkok, Singapore, Hong Kong, Canton, Shanghai, Tokyo/Yokohama and Osaka/Kobe are the most important coastal cities with large airports. Inland waterways also play a substantial role in China, and to a lesser extent in India.

Considering the nature of the terrain, the population distributions and the average per capita incomes in many countries, it is hardly surprising that much of Asia is ill-provided with road and rail facilities. India, the Malay peninsula, Asia Minor and Japan have the most effective transport networks, unlike China, Southwest and Southeast Asia. On the railroads, steam haulage is still important in India, though improved diesel services are now being introduced. By contrast, Japan has modern rail facilities with heavily congested urban networks within and around the large cities as well as some rapid inter-city travel.

Agriculture, Forestry and Fishing

In its natural state the vegetative cover of Asia was very varied. In the southwest the landscape was dominated by desert. Farther north, along the Levant coast and in Asia Minor, a more luxuriant broadleaf and mixed shrub vegetation was found. To the east of this, in a broad belt extending to the lowlands of eastern China, in an area bounded to the south by the Persian Gulf and the Himalayas, was desert or grassland. Broadleaf deciduous woodland occupied much of central India, eastern China, Korea and inland Burma and Thailand. The hotter,

1 △

2 ◁

3 ▷

4 ▽

The rich tapestry of Asia is shown in contrasts – rich memorials to the dead and squalid living conditions, luxuriant islands and arid deserts, modern industry and folk art: 1 Masad, Iran – dominated by the golden domed tomb of the Imam Riza, the sacred city is also a commercial center; 2 Rice paddy workers, Bali – coffee and copra are also grown in this fertile Indonesian island; 3 Tibetan refugees weaving rugs, Nepal – many Tibetans followed their leader, the Dalai Lama, to India in 1959 when the revolt against the occupying Chinese was put down; 4 Rubber tapping, Malaysia – this quite wealthy country owes its prosperity mainly to rubber

ASIA

wetter environments of Southeast Asia were covered with broadleaf evergreen forests or mixed forest of broadleaf evergreen and deciduous trees.

The economic potential of those areas with a rainfall deficiency is very limited, and the high mountain areas and desert regions are largely void of population and agricultural activity. By contrast, in the great northern areas where grassland takes over from true desert, extensive animal herding dominates the landscape.

Throughout much of the heavily forested areas of the southeast, including most of the islands, primitive agriculture prevails. Much of India and Bangladesh, the Indus valley, parts of Burma, Thailand and the Mekong river system, parts of Malaysia and Indonesia, eastern and southern China, Korea and Japan contain the most attractive farming lands. Here, well over 60 percent of the large population depend upon small holdings, or on state farms in the Communist countries.

The dominant cereal crops are rice and wheat. Rice is particularly demanding where rainfall and temperature are concerned; wheat is less restricted by these particular factors. Rice is grown primarily in the areas influenced by the monsoon winds and rains, but wheat can be grown in the drier places. World rice production now averages some 350 million tons per year, of which China accounts for 33 percent, India 20 percent, Indonesia 6 percent and Bangladesh and Japan 4 percent each. In total, Asia grows over 85 percent of the world's rice. Over 95 percent of this is for home consumption, although over 60 percent of world trade in rice, amounting to about 10 million tons, originates in Asia. In all, Asia produces about 29 percent of the world's wheat. World production now exceeds 400 million tons in an average year. China accounts for about 10 percent of this and India 7 percent, with only the Soviet Union and the USA producing more.

Asia accounts for nearly one-fifth of the world's corn, which comes mainly from China, India, Java, Pakistan and Turkey, and a slightly larger proportion of its barley with some two-thirds of this being grown in China, followed by Turkey, India and Japan. Oats and rye are comparatively unimportant being grown only in the cooler parts of China, Japan and Turkey. By comparison, millet and grain sorghum production in Asia dominate the world output, China growing nearly a half of the world's millet and India over one-sixth of the world's total sorghum production.

Asia is the world leader in tea. Overall some 83 percent of the world's total comes from this continent, and over 70 percent of world tea trade originates here. Individually, India grows 31 percent, China 20 percent, Sri Lanka 12 percent, Japan 6 per cent and Indonesia 4 percent.

More than two-fifths of world sugarcane output also comes from Asia, mainly in the tropical and equatorial parts, with India producing 21 percent of the world total, China, 6.5 percent, Pakistan, 4 percent, the Philippines, 4 percent and Thailand, 2.5 percent. Smaller quantities of sugar beet are grown farther north and west in China, Turkey, Iran and Japan.

Asia dominates world natural rubber production, some 92 percent of the annual 3.4 million tons total coming from Southeast Asia, in particular Malaysia (44 percent of the world total), Indonesia (24 percent) and Thailand (11.5 percent).

Except for flax, vegetable fibers grow readily in the humid parts of Asia. China is second only to the USSR in world cotton production with 19 percent. India is the leading world producer of hemp fiber with 29 percent of the total. Finally, over 95 percent of the world's jute is grown in Asia, especially in China, India and Bangladesh.

Asiatic production contributes greatly to world totals of a number of other tropical and subtropical crops: over four-fifths of the coconuts come from the Philippines, Indonesia and the Indian subcontinent; three-fifths of the peanuts come, especially, from India and China, and nearly a half of the world's tobacco comes from China, India and Turkey.

Asia has more cattle than any other continent, but the sacred significance of the animal in many parts makes this fact somewhat meaningless where food value is concerned. India has more cows than any other country, China is fifth in the world tables and Bangladesh ninth. India, China, Turkey, Iran, Pakistan, Bangladesh, Indonesia and Yemen account for about half the world's goats. China alone has nearly two-fifths of the world's pigs. What is most remarkable is the fact that no other single country in the world has a quarter of this massive total. Pigs are of little significance elsewhere in the continent. China, Turkey, India, Iran, Pakistan, Afghanistan and Mongolia together account for about 28 percent of the world's sheep population.

Asia is rich in a variety of woods. Southeast Asia and the Islands, as well as parts of the Indian subcontinent, have tropical hardwoods, while farther north in China and Japan temperate hardwoods and some softwoods are found. In total, over a quarter of the world's sawn timber comes from these areas, with China, Indonesia, India, Japan and the smaller islands leading. Japan

1 △   2 ▽   3 ▽

Asia is home for the world's great religions: 1 Marble Temple, Bangkok, Thailand – Buddhist monks also act as village school teachers; 2 Bar Mitzvah, Western 'Wailing' Wall, Jerusalem, Israel – in the old part of this ancient city stands one of the Jews' most sacred places; 3 Manikanika Ghat, Varanasi, India – from these steps, thousands of Hindu pilgrims bathe in the Ganges

and China are the major Asiatic exporters.

The seas off eastern and southern Asia are rich in a range of fish. Of an average world catch of about 70 million tons, Japan and China alone account for about one quarter. India, South Korea, Indonesia, Thailand, the Philippines and Vietnam contribute a further sixth of the world total. Japan also accounts for one third of the world's whale catch.

Natural Resources

Asia's natural resource base is not yet fully appreciated as large parts of the interior have not been comprehensively surveyed. Thus, modern developments of fossil fuels and minerals are currently somewhat regionalized, with only vague indications of riches elsewhere.

Major bituminous coal and anthracite fields are found in eastern and southern Asia. In total, Asia produces over a quarter of the world's average annual output of hard coal. China alone accounts for some 450 million tons per year, then India produces about 100 million tons annually, followed by Japan and North Korea. Lignite output in Asia is small, coming mainly from China.

Over 45 percent of the world's annual oil output originates in Asia, particularly the southwestern countries. Saudi Arabia is now second only to the USSR, producing over 420 million tons per year (15 percent of the world total). Iran, Iraq, Kuwait and other small Persian Gulf States account for a further 22 percent of world production, giving the Arab states a very strong position in today's crude oil markets. The remainder of Asia is of minor importance in oil production. Natural gas is also of little significance in Asia, either for local use or export, only Iran and China producing significant amounts.

Although the dry lands of Asia have little HEP potential, the countries of the east and southeast have far more. With the exception of Japan, however, little of this potential has yet been developed. Japan now rates as the world's fourth largest HEP producer, with a total of 86,000 million kwh per year. India, with greater potential, has only installed about 10 percent of it, producing 31,000 million kwh per year. Countries with less development thus far are China, which is estimated to have over 8 percent of the world's potential, Burma, Indonesia and Vietnam.

Asia is somewhat scantily provided with the iron ore upon which modern industry relies heavily. Her proven reserves are more limited than those of any other continent except Africa, standing at little over 6 percent of the world 260,000 million tons (iron content). Chinese reserves are considerable, however, and current annual production, mainly from the fields of Shansi, Hopei, Shantung and Tayeh is about 40 million tons iron content. This is over twice that of India, the second largest Asiatic producer.

Israel and Japan together, the Middle Eastern countries and the remaining Asiatic countries as a group, each account for about one-third of the continent's international trade.

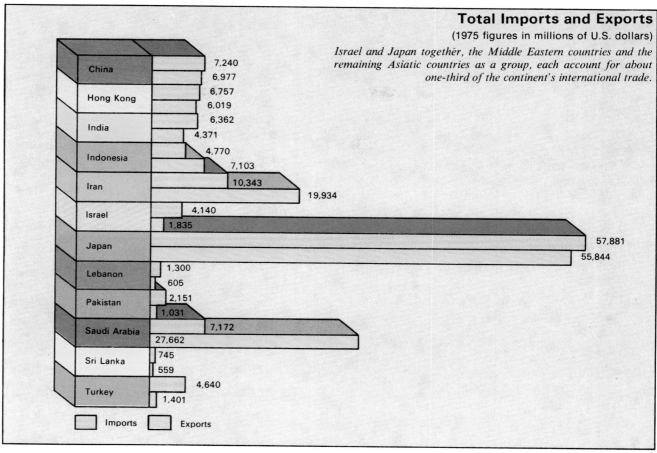

Country	Imports	Exports
China	7,240	6,977
Hong Kong	6,757	6,019
India	6,362	4,371
Indonesia	4,770	7,103
Iran	10,343	19,934
Israel	4,140	1,835
Japan	57,881	55,844
Lebanon	1,300	605
Pakistan	2,151	1,031
Saudi Arabia	7,172	27,662
Sri Lanka	745	559
Turkey	4,640	1,401

☐ Imports ☐ Exports

The Middle East oil bonanza has brought new wealth, amenities and western life-styles: 1 Desalination plant, Abu Dhabi, UAE – in a land where water is at a premium, new agricultural systems use treated sea water; 2 Oil rig, Qatar – crude oil production may be all-important to this barren land, but many tribesmen prefer to rear camels; 3 TV recording session for a 'pop' show, Jedda, Saudi Arabia – oil revenues have introduced some dubious western culture to a primarily desert country

Other mineral ores and precious metals are found in Asia, but apart from tin and tungsten current production of many is very limited, as the table below shows.

Asian Economy

Apart from Europe, including the European parts of the Soviet Union, no other contiguous part of the world is anywhere near as consistently densely peopled as either the Indian subcontinent or the eastern and southern parts of China. Japan too is similar to the British Isles both in size and population. And, beyond these major areas, other smaller regions such as Asia Minor, the Levant coast, the lower river valleys of Southeast Asia and parts of Indonesia and the Philippines are also highly peopled. By contrast, most of the continent is sparsely populated. Southwest and southcentral Asia as well as western China have less than 5 persons per km² (12 per sq mi).

A predominantly agricultural and developing continent, Asia surprisingly contains some 71 metro areas over 1 million. There are 22 in China, of which eight have populations in excess of 2 million, and seven in Japan, where Tokyo, 25.2 million, ranks first in the world.

Ore	Average Annual World Production (million tons)	Asia's Share (percent)	Principal Asiatic Producing Countries
bauxite	80.3	5	Indonesia, India
chrome	7.2	22	Turkey, India, Philippines, Iran
copper	7.4	8	Philippines, China, Japan
gold	1 million kg	4	Japan, Philippines
lead	3.2	8	China, N Korea, Japan
manganese	22.8	8	India, China
molybdenum	0.084	2	China, Japan, S Korea
nickel	0.733	4	Philippines, Indonesia
silver	0.01	3	Japan
tin	0.2	58	Malaysia, Thailand, Indonesia, China
tungsten	0.036	50	China, N & S Korea, Thailand, Japan, Burma
zinc	5.4	11	Japan, N Korea, China, Iran

ASIA

India has 11, four of which have populations between 2 and 10 million. Thereafter, Indonesia and South Korea each have 3, Pakistan, Bangladesh, Taiwan, Turkey and Vietnam have 2 each, and Burma, Hong Kong, Iran, Iraq, North Korea, the Philippines, Singapore and Thailand have 1 each.

Asia's population changes are volatile, in some countries increasing at rates as high as anywhere in the world. Many Asian countries have birth rates in excess of 40 per 1,000, and some of these, like Bangladesh, Indonesia, Thailand and Vietnam, already have large populations. India, the second most populated country, has a birth rate of nearly 35 per 1,000 and China, with over 850 million population, has a birth rate of 27 per 1,000. Death rates, though high by the standards of more advanced countries, are far lower than birth rates, the average is in the high teens and a few countries have developed medical services to a point where death rates have fallen below 8 per 1,000. The combination of these two sets of figures leads to an overall annual population increase of over 2.5 percent. Herein lies the greatest focus of the population explosion which has carried the world total to over 4,000 million in the recent years.

Even by the kindest definitions, few Asian countries can be classified as developed market economies. Most are developing, China as the second largest centrally planned economy, and the oil producing states have uniquely lopsided economies. Compare the performance of Asia in general and some individual countries in world trade during the periods 1938–'58 and 1958–'75 with overall world performances. In imports, Asian totals rose by 2.6 and 8.9 times (compared with world figures of 4.5 and 8.0); in exports Asian totals rose by 2.3 and 11.3 times (compared with world figures of 4.5 and 8.0). Taking into account the impact of inflation, these figures are remarkable in revealing how the continent lagged behind world trends until way into the 1950s but has performed so much better since then.

This is in large measure due to economic growth in particular areas. Japan alone, Asia's largest trading nation by far, increased its imports by 1.8 and then 18 times in the two periods of time, and its exports by 1.6 and then 18.5 times. The oil-producing states increased imports by 5.8 and 13.7 times, and exports by 8.7 and 18.7 times. But the figures for the remainder of free Asia were 2.5 and only 5.7 times for imports, 1.4 and only 6.1 times for exports.

1 △   2 ▽

Asian industry and commerce remain comparatively under-developed in contrast with the west, apart from one or two notable exceptions: 1 Hong Kong and Shanghai Bank, Hong Kong – – banking revenue helps offset an adverse trade balance in this place of thousands of small factories; 2 Industrial pollution, Japan – Asia's major producing and trading country pays the penalty for its industrial success with an unclean atmosphere

Per Capita Income
(1974 figures in U.S. dollars)

The average earnings of most east and southeast Asians are less than $500. Yet the figures for citizens of some oil-producing states, Japan and Israel, are very much higher.

Kuwait	Japan	Israel	Saudi Arabia	Iran	Cyprus	Korea (S)	Sri Lanka	Pakistan	India
11,063	3,546	3,235	2,484	1,295	1,274	452	223	149	136

Available per capita income figures for Asia are not as revealing as in many other continents, since the distribution of wealth is more uneven than in many parts of the world. This is particularly true in the oil-producing states. Worldwide, averages rose by 186 percent between 1960 and 1974; in the oil states they rose by 445 percent, in free southern and eastern Asia by 330 percent, in Japan by 750 percent.

However, such percentage figures must be viewed cautiously and absolutes stressed to illustrate the poverty of much of Asia compared with, say, European and North American countries. In 1974, the per capita income of the USA was $5,923, of West Germany $5,480 and of the UK $3,106. In Asia, Kuwait topped the table with $11,063 (an exceptional case), while Japan was top of the large countries with $3,546, Israel next with $3,235, then Saudi Arabia with $2,484. Among the lowest average incomes recorded were Sri Lanka $223, Pakistan $149 and India $136.

Overall, Asia is a marked energy surplus continent, entirely due to the oil riches of the Middle East. In 1975, 2,470 million tons coal equivalent (mtce) were produced and 1,410 mtce consumed. The Middle East countries accounted for 1,508 mtce of the product but only used 127 mtce, thus providing a phenomenal surplus. The remainder of free Asia had to import large quantities since production was only 317 mtce and consumption 658 mtce. China, North Korea, Vietnam and Mongolia, the planned economies, together had a small surplus. Individually, India needs to import a mere 14 percent of her total needs of 132 mtce, while Japan has to import 90 percent of her total needs of about 400 mtce. Other noteworthy examples of importing and exporting are Indonesia and Brunei with their large oil surpluses, and South Korea which imports about half of its needs of 36 mtce.

Asia's range of energy consumptions (expressed in kilograms per head per year) is as large as any in a single continent. Though total consumption is small, some of the oil-producing states are world leaders in per capita terms. Even the 11,000 kg/ca of the USA looks small compared with the 35,300 kg/ca used by the 280,000 people living in Qatar. But figures of less than 100 kg/ca are often recorded – Bangladesh 28, Burma 51, Kampuchea 16, Laos 63, Nepal 10 – in the least developed countries.

Overall it is difficult to generalize about Asia's economic position in the modern world. However, individual parts and separate countries can be commented on. Japan is the continent's one great example of a developed economy, its phenomenal recovery after the devastation of World War II providing one of the economic miracles of the last quarter century. The oil-producing countries, especially those of the Middle East, currently have the energy-deficient countries of the developed world at

1

Per Capita Energy Consumption
(1975 figures in kilograms)

Apart from high amounts in the oil-producing countries, Asiatic energy consumption per head ranges from Japan's modest figure to the minute ones of many third world countries.

Country	kg
China	693
Hong Kong	1,119
India	221
Indonesia	178
Iran	1,353
Israel	2,806
Japan	3,622
Lebanon	928
Pakistan	183
Saudi Arabia	1,398
Sri Lanka	127
Turkey	630

Everyday life in Asia: 1 Supermarket, Abu Dhabi, UAE – new prosperity, new products; 2 Fish shop near the Galata Bridge, Istanbul, Turkey – ancient Byzantium now relies mainly on trade and tourism; 3 Children welcome guests to a Chinese commune – nearly 75,000 People's Communes now work the land

a disadvantage. Their potential power has yet to be assessed. Nevertheless, at this time, these countries have immense riches and will continue to accumulate foreign currency and overseas investments as long as their liquid gold lasts and they remain politically stable.

China and, to a lesser extent the other Communist states of South east Asia, are currently developing in diverse and often unknown ways. The economic potential of these countries which contain nearly a quarter of the world's population is enormous, but it will be some years before the state plans for industry and agriculture achieve their possible greatness. By contrast, India is something of an enigma. Another heavily peopled land with a lengthy history and connection with Britain, its progress is far more lumbering. Finally, growth and progress in the rest of Southeast Asia appears varied.

Wherein lies the economic future for this continent? How will the oil-rich states utilize the economic strength which their limited resources give them? Can Japan maintain its present remarkable position in world industry and trade? How rapidly can China emerge from its largely isolated position of the last quarter of a century, develop internally and become a leading world trader? These are some of the questions to which the coming decades may provide surprising answers.

2

Asian Countries

Afghanistan

Formerly a kingdom, Afghanistan has been a republic since 1973. Its economy is based largely on the agriculture of the valleys and plains areas, which occupy less than one-tenth of the country, the rest being mountain or desert. Raising Persian lambs, wheat, fruit and cotton farming are important activities, with lamb skins, raw cotton and fruit being the main exports. Less than one-twentieth of the population live in large towns; three times as many are nomadic. In 1980, Afghanistan was invaded and occupied by the USSR.

Bahrain

Composed of a number of low-lying islets near Qatar, off the east coast of Saudi Arabia, Bahrain has a fierce, desert climate. Completely independent since 1971, for the previous 90 years the country was an independent sheikdom enjoying British protection. The ruling family, the Al Khalifa dynasty, have been in control for 200 years. Home-produced crude oil and oil piped from Saudi Arabia is refined locally before being exported. Aluminum smelting, engineering and ship repairing are growing rapidly. Her main trading partners are the USA, the UK, West Germany and other West European countries.

Bangladesh

Formerly the eastern province of Pakistan, since 1971 Bangladesh has been a separate independent republic within the Commonwealth. It is a densely-peopled, lowland country which centers on the deltas of the Ganges and Brahmaputra. Disastrous floods have impeded her economic progress. Agriculture is the base of the economy, with rice, jute, tea and sugarcane the main crops. Textiles, paper making and sugar refining are valuable industries.

Bhutan

This small landlocked Himalayan state is independent, but neighboring India officially guides her foreign affairs. Traditionally, crop and animal farming as well as forestry have provided the economic base. Now mining, hydroelectric power production and tourism are being developed steadily.

British Indian Ocean Territories

Formed in 1965 from a number of scattered islands in the western Indian Ocean, this British colony today comprises the Chagos Archipelago, some 1,700 km (1,000 mi) southwest of Sri Lanka. The small population mainly fish and grow food crops.

Brunei

A member of the Commonwealth, this self-governing sultanate in North Borneo enjoys British protection. Most of the land is untouched forest and the cleared areas are now mainly planted with rubber trees. The oil and natural gas fields of Seria and those offshore provide about 90 percent of the country's exports. Rubber and native crafts account for much of the other foreign earnings, mainly from the UK, her main trading partner, followed by Australia and New Zealand.

Burma

A Socialist republic since 1974, Burma left the then British Commonwealth in 1948 to become an independent federal country. All its borders are mountainous. Agriculture is the leading activity, with rice, wheat, corn, millet, tea, sugarcane and rubber as major crops. Hardwoods, especially teak, are an important source of foreign earnings. Crude oil is produced in modest quantities; lead, tungsten and tin to a lesser extent. International trade is still limited, rubber, cotton and crude oil being the leading items. Burma relies heavily on internal waterways.

China

After the USSR and Canada, the People's Republic of China is the largest country in the world. It contains about 20 percent of the world population. Most Chinese live in small settlements and derive their living from the land, although there are a number of large modern cities in the east. After 3,000 years' rule by a series of powerful dynasties, twentieth-century China has been torn by conflict and revolution culminating in the establishment of the Communist state in 1949. Until about 1970 the country was virtually closed to the outside world. The dominating figure of Chairman Mao-Tse-Tung was responsible for the Great Proletarian Cultural Revolution initiated in 1966. During and after this period China began to develop more contacts with the outside world, a policy continued by Mao's successor, Hua-Kuo-Feng. The ideological conflict between Peking and Moscow also continues.

Agriculture was reorganized after 1949 and today the country is self-sufficient in all needs except cotton. Cereals, root crops, industrial crops and livestock, especially pigs, have priority. The total area of controlled irrigation is the highest for any country in the world. Mineral pro-

1 Phosphate industry, Jordan – this is the chief resource of this desert area; 2 Peking, China – despite slow moves to western ways, bicycles remain the Chinese capital's most common form of transport; 3 Wall of fort, Lahore, Pakistan – the country's second largest city is known mainly for its carpets and textiles

duction is considerable, headed by coal, iron ore, crude oil, tungsten and tin.

Since the Communist state was created, industry has been developed in a series of five-year programs. While the old cottage industries persist, new textile, heavy metallurgical, chemical, vehicle, engineering, cement and paper industries have been established. Today 80 percent of China's international trade is with the non-Communist world, with Japan, Hong Kong, Australia and Canada being her main partners.

Christmas Island

Lying 350 km (210 mi) south of Java in the eastern Indian Ocean, Christmas Island is now under Australian sovereignty. The extraction of phosphates is the island's major industry. Exports are mainly to Australia, New Zealand, Singapore and Malaysia.

*1 Rooftop view of Jerusalem, Israel –
this 4,000 year old city, sacred to
Jews, Moslems and Christians, remains a continuing source of conflct;
2 Nha-Trang, Vietnam – the Communist regime has led to a growing tide of
refugees from the old South; 3 Fishing
boats and nets, Macau, China – fish is
the main export of this Portuguese
territory*

Cocos Islands

These lie 1,000 km (600 mi) west of
Christmas Island. Their control was
passed from Singapore to Australia
by the British government in 1955.
The meteorological station there
provides information for eastern
Indian Ocean weather forecasting.

Cyprus

The eastern Mediterranean island of
Cyprus is an independent republic
within the Commonwealth. Agriculture and mining are its main
activities. Potatoes, wine and grapes,
copper, asbestos and iron pyrites are
its major exports. Fuel oils, cereals
and textiles are the main imports.
The Cypriot population of 80 per
cent Greek orthodox and 20 percent
Turkish Moslem do not coexist
happily.

Hong Kong

This British crown colony comprises
the main island of Hong Kong, some
other islands and a small part of the
Chinese mainland near the mouth of
the Pearl River. There are estimated
to be over 33,000 factories in the
colony, many very small. These
produce a wide range of consumer
goods for the world market, of which
textiles, electronic and electrical
goods, clocks and watches, toys and
plastic goods are major examples.
The adverse balance of visible trade
is offset by earnings from banking,
insurance, tourism and other services.

India

This subcontinental area has a history of civilization which dates back
to about 2500 BC. Modern India, the
largest part of the former British
viceroyalty, is now a republic and has
been an independent member of the
Commonwealth since 1947. It is a
strange mixture of long-standing
traditions and attempts to bring the
country fully into the late twentieth
century. Over 80 percent of the
modern population are Hindus, sub-
divided by the caste system – Priests
and Scholars (Brahmins), Warriors
(Kshatriyas), Merchants (Vaishyas),

Workers (Sudras). Moslems are the
second largest population group.
India, though only about one-third
the size of China, has today Asia's
second largest population equaling
75 percent of the population of
China. The concentrations of people
in the plains of the north are some of
the densest in the world.

Most Indians live off the land,
many deriving a meager existence
from it. Recent attempts have been
made to improve agriculture, and
progress in the introduction of new
strains of seeds, modern equipment
and fertilizers is steady. Rice, wheat,
millet, tea, sugarcane, cotton and
jute are the leading crops. Draft
animals are kept, but the Hindu
religion regards the cow as sacred so
it is not generally eaten. Sheep and
goats are raised for slaughter. Indian
mineral reserves are great but have
yet to be systematically exploited.
Iron ore, coal, manganese, bauxite
and copper are at present extracted.
The leading industries are iron and
steel, cotton and silk textiles and
carpet making. Jute and cotton
manufactures, tea, iron ore and
leather goods are the major exports;
imports are wheat, oil products,
machinery and fertilizers. India's
main trading partners are the USA,
Japan, Iran, the UK and the USSR.

Indonesia

Java, Sumatra, Sulawesi and most of
Borneo are the largest islands in this
independent republic which was a
Dutch colony from 1600 till 1941.
Three-quarters of the people live by
farming, many growing subsistence
crops. Rubber, coffee, tea and sugarcane are the main commercial crops.
Indonesia has rich deposits of oil, tin
and bauxite. Crude oil, tin, rubber,
palm oil and kernels and coffee are
the main exports. Rice, chemicals,
machinery and consumer goods are
the major imports.

Iran

Lying between the Persian Gulf and
the Caspian Sea, Iran (formerly
Persia) has a history which goes
right back to the Persian Empire of
2,500 years ago. Normally, crude oil
production is the main base of the
economy. Other important products
and exports are cotton, carpets, wool
and hides. Wheat, sugar beet, oats
and rice are the most extensively
grown crops. In spite of the country's
great revenue deriving from oil exports, it is a land of stark contrasts
in living standards; most of the population is rural and very poor. In
recent years, civil unrest has grown
so that in 1979 the ruler, the Shah,
reputedly one of the world's richest
men, was forced to leave the country.
An islamic republic has been established, re-introducing all the ancient
laws.

Iraq

This former kingdom became a
republic in 1958. It is centered on the
fertile basin of the Rivers Tigris and
Euphrates. Much land is irrigated
and part of the large revenues of the
national oil companies are used to
introduce still more irrigation
schemes. Apart from oil, dates, wool
and cotton are the major exports.
For home consumption, wheat, barley, rice and livestock products are
important.

Israel

In 1948 the independent country of
Israel was established within much
of the former British mandated territory of Palestine, and proclaimed as
a homeland for the Jews. Since then,
tension has existed between this
young home for Zionism and its
Arab neighbors. This has resulted
in two short wars (in 1967 and 1973)
which have threatened to escalate
into large-scale international conflict. However, in 1979 a peace treaty
between Israel and Egypt was signed,
following mediation by the USA.
There is a new mood of cautious coexistence between the two nations,
though this is not shared by other
Arab states. The country is by far the
most economically developed and
balanced of all in western Asia.
Agriculture, mining and industry are
highly organized. The main exports
are processed diamonds, chemicals,
oil products and citrus fruit.

Asian Countries

Japan

Asia's most advanced country comprises a large series of over 3,000 islands off the east coasts of China, Korea and the USSR. Most of the population live on the four main islands of Honshu, Hokkaido, Kyushu and Shikoku. Japan has been ruled by the same dynasty since being united as one nation nearly 1,800 years ago. During the present century it has been involved in a series of conflicts with Russia, Manchuria and China and then joined forces with Germany and Italy in World War II. Defeat in 1945 came after the only two nuclear bombs ever used in war had destroyed the cities of Hiroshima and Nagasaki. In the last 30 years the Japanese economy has been remarkably reestablished, and the country now enjoys one of the highest living standards in all Asia.

Only one-sixth of the whole country is suitable for farming, and now little more than 10 percent of the labor force works on the land. Crop production has been diversified recently. The demand for rice has fallen and though it is still a major crop, wheat, barley, sugar beet and cane and fruits are of increasing significance. The mountains and steeper slopes are mainly forested, yielding valuable timber. While Japan is no longer the world's leading fishing nation, she still accounts for about 17 percent of the world's annual catch.

The country is ill-endowed with minerals. However, Japanese industry is now well established and organized, highly competitive and very diversified: ship building, vehicle making, textiles, optics and electronics are but a few of her major activities. These depend to a large extent on the importing of raw materials. Japan trades with all parts of the world, but especially with the USA, her Southeast Asia neighbors, Australia and Canada.

Jordan

The modern Arab kingdom of Jordan was established in 1949. Most of the country is desert land, only 10 percent being cultivated. Irrigation plays a vital part in farming. Wheat, water melons, citrus fruit and tomatoes are the most important crops. Phosphate rock production and exporting is an important part of the national economy. To date, the search for oil in Jordan has yielded no commercial return.

Kampuchea

Formerly known as Cambodia and then the Khmer Republic, Kampuchea was part of the former country of French Indochina. Increasing economic problems and the infiltration of Communist guerillas from neighboring Vietnam led to the removal of the ruler Prince Sihanouk in 1970. Following a short period of civil war, the Communist forces of the Khmer Rouge defeated the republicans in 1974. Farming, fishing and forestry are the main occupations. Rice, rubber, corn and freshwater fish are the most important products. A little phosphate, iron ore, limestone and some precious stones are mined.

Korea (North)

The northern part of the Korean peninsula is a people's democratic (Socialist) republic. Here, mineral production is far more important than agriculture. Coal, iron, lead, zinc and copper are the leading minerals. A wide range of industries employ about 40 percent of the national workforce. Rice, corn and other grains are the leading crops, all farms now being collectivized. Most trade is with Russia.

Korea (South)

The southern part of the Korean peninsula is officially known as the Republic of Korea. Its economy is more evenly based than that of the north. Rice, barley, wheat, beans and tobacco are the leading crops. A large oceangoing fishing fleet is kept. The extraction of coal, iron ore, copper and lead is limited; only tungsten, in which Korea is a world leader, is produced in great quantities. A range of manufacturing industries have been developed. Most trade is with the USA and Japan.

Kuwait

This tiny, independent sheikdom on the Persian Gulf is an almost entirely flat desert land, with very little cultivated area. In the last thirty years, since oil was first extracted, it has developed into one of the world's major oil-producing countries. It is estimated that nearly 14 percent of the world's oil reserves lie beneath such a small land.

Laos

Formerly part of French Indochina and then a civil-war torn kingdom, this landlocked country is now an independent people's democratic (Socialist) republic. One of the least developed countries of SE Asia, its agriculture is largely subsistent and primitive. Forest products, sawn timber (especially teak), plywood and matches, are the main export items apart from tin, which is the only exploited mineral from the wide range known to exist.

Lebanon

This small republic bordering the eastern Mediterranean is unique among Arab countries in that the majority of the population are Christian. Less than 40 percent of the country can be cultivated. Citrus and other fruit, tobacco, olives and wool are exported in large quantities to pay for imported foodstuffs and manufactured goods. Iron ore and other minerals exist but to date have been little developed.

Macau

Two islands and part of a Chinese peninsula near the mouth of the Canton River have formed the Portuguese territory of Macau since 1557. Its importance as a trading center is small compared with nearby Hong Kong, but it has a large fishing industry.

Malaysia

An independent federal country within the Commonwealth, Malaysia comprises the Malay Peninsula (West Malaysia) and parts of northern Borneo (East Malaysia). Rubber, tin, timber and palm oil account for about 75 percent of the national exports. Agriculture centers on rice.

1 △

2 △

3 ▽

1 Looking toward the channel, Penang, Malaysia – the state capital and main port, George Town, like the island, is known simply as Penang; 2 Kyrenia, Cyprus – this attractive Mediterranean island relies mainly on farming and tourism; 3 Isa New Town, Bahrain – much oil revenue is being pumped back into new community projects and developing industry

palms, fruits, sugar and tea. The population is 45 percent Malay, 35 percent Chinese and 20 percent Indian, Pakistani and smaller tribal groups.

Maldive Islands

Now an independent republic, this collection of over 2,000 coral atolls lying southwest of Sri Lanka was a British protectorate until 1965. Fishing, especially for bonito, is the main activity. Tourism has been growing in importance in recent years.

Mongolia

The Mongolian People's (Socialist) Republic is a sparsely populated landlocked country lying between the USSR and China. Most Mongols, descendants of Genghis Khan's people, are herdsmen, and animals and their products provide the great majority of the country's exports. Coal, copper, molybdenum and phosphates are the main minerals found. There is little industry. A member of COMECON, Mongolia trades mainly with its Communist neighbors and currently relies on them to support a substantial trade deficit.

Nepal

Landlocked between Tibet and India, Nepal is a Hindu kingdom situated in the Himalayas. Farming is the most important activity, with rice, corn, wheat, millet and jute the chief crops. What small deposits of coal and iron ore are known are not yet exploited. Textiles, sugar milling, leather and shoe making and native crafts are the major industries. Most international trade is with India.

Neutral Zone

From 1922 to 1966 part of the Arabian Desert was declared a neutral zone to be jointly administered by Saudi Arabia and Kuwait. Since 1966 it has been partitioned, but the natural resources extracted from the area, especially oil, are shared by the two countries.

Oman

This independent sultanate is largely desert in the southeastern part of the Arabian peninsula. Dates, fruit and sugarcane are grown on parts of the coastal lowlands, the hills and at oases. Since the mid-1960s oil production has grown steadily, and is now the major source of foreign revenue. Most trade is conducted

with the United Kingdom, India, Australia and Japan.

Pakistan

The independent Moslem republic of Pakistan was established in 1947. Its original eastern province has since become the separate country of Bangladesh. The majority of the population lives by farming. Wheat, corn, cotton, millet, barley and fruits are the main products. Small quantities of a range of minerals are extracted. A large program of water control for irrigation and hydro-electric power production is helping agricultural and industrial development. Food processing and textiles are the main industries.

Philippines

Only one-tenth of the 7,000 islands in the independent republic of the Philippines are inhabited. Most of the population live on 16 of them, about half on Luzon. Crop farming,

forestry and fishing are important activities. The islands have a wide range of mineral resources: gold, silver, iron, copper and chromite are most valuable. Food processing, leather processing and native craft production are the major industries. Most trade, via Manila, is with the USA.

Qatar

This is an independent sheikdom on the Persian Gulf. In the last thirty years oil production has risen steadily. Natural gas is also produced. Some nomadic tribesmen herd livestock and a little fishing is carried out along the coast. Among the uses to which the considerable oil revenues are put is the provision of free social service, education and health.

Saudi Arabia

This largely desert kingdom occupies most of the Arabian peninsula. About half the population are still engaged

in nomadic herding and oasis agriculture. Dates, alfalfa, barley and citrus fruit are the main crops. Since oil was first discovered in the 1930s the country has rapidly become a world leader in crude oil production. Oil refining is now a major industry and other oil is exported unrefined. Her main trading partners are Japan, the USA, West Germany and the United Kingdom.

Singapore

Singapore became an independent republic within the Commonwealth in 1965, having previously been part of the Malaysian federation. This small island country has a mainly Chinese population. Its economic importance derives from commerce, transit trading and processing. Chemicals, timber, rubber, tin and plastic industries are most important. In recent years a major fishing industry has been established. Most trade is with Malaysia, Japan and the USA.

Asian Countries

Sri Lanka

Formerly known as Ceylon, Sri Lanka is an island lying south of the Indian peninsula. It is a democratic republic within the Commonwealth. The majority of the people live by agriculture, mainly producing tea, rice, rubber and coconuts. Tea is the major export. Graphite is the most important mineral extracted and exported; a range of gem stones are also mined. Food processing, chemicals, cement and textile production are the leading industries. Among her trading partners are China, Japan, Australia and United Kingdom.

Syria

This east Mediterranean Arab republic is agriculturally self-sufficient. Wheat, barley, cotton and tobacco are the main crops. Cattle and sheep are also important. Textiles and food processing are the major industries. The mineral wealth of the country is not fully realized, although phosphates are worked, and lead, copper, nickel and chromite have been found. Natural gas has been discovered and the search for oil, present beneath so many parts of the Middle East deserts, continues, though it has so far not met with success.

Taiwan

Formerly called Formosa, Taiwan is a large island 160 km (100 mi) from the Chinese mainland. It became part of China in 1945 but since mainland China became a people's republic, Taiwan has been a separate non-Communist country, receiving support from the USA. About as many people farm as work in industry. Sugarcane, rice, sweet potatoes and tropical fruits are the main crops. Metal manufacture, textiles, chemicals and cement making are the major industries. Coal is the most developed mineral, and reserves of copper, sulphur and oil are also being successfully investigated. Taiwan's main trading partners are Japan, the USA, West Germany and the United Kingdom.

Thailand

This Southeast Asian kingdom used to be known as Siam. Farming and forestry are the main activities. Rice is the most valuable product, followed by rubber. Other leading crops are sugarcane, tapioca, corn and coconuts. Teak, yang and other trees are felled. Of a wide range of minerals, fluorite, gypsum, iron and lignite are most important. Fishing is also a significant activity. Food and rubber processing, as well as handicrafts, are the main industries.

Turkey

Since 1923, Turkey has been an independent republic. It occupies the whole of Asia Minor and a small part of southeast Europe on the opposite side of the Turkish Straits. Based largely on its historic and cultural attractions, such as those in Istanbul, tourism is growing steadily. More than 65 percent of the population live by farming. Cereals, cotton, tobacco, fruits, olives and grapes are the main products. Important minerals include hard and soft coal, iron ore, crude oil and chromite; others have yet to be commercially exploited. Raw materials are exported and manufactured goods imported.

United Arab Emirates

This independent country in Southwest Asia was formed in 1971 from seven sheikdoms formerly known as the Trucial Oman or the Trucial States. The whole area is predominantly desert, with the exception of the Buraimi Oasis in Abu Dhabi which provides a significant area of farmed land. The economy otherwise is entirely based on the oil produced and exported, mainly from Dubai and Abu Dhabi. Oil exploration in the other emirates has been intensified in recent years.

Vietnam

Once part of French Indo-China, Vietnam was partitioned into two states in 1954, the North being Communist and the South non-Communist. During the 1960s, Communist infiltration, supported by the USSR, was a growing problem in the South. Increasingly the USA supported the democratic South, eventually deploying a large army in its defense. The Vietnam war officially ended in 1973; two years later, Communist infiltration led to the fall of Saigon, the southern capital, and the creation of a united Socialist republic. The problem of giving sanctuary to boatloads of refugees fleeing from the present regime occupies neighboring countries.

Most Vietnamese are farmers, producing mainly rice, corn, sugarcane, sweet potatoes and cotton. Rubber is the main export. Coal mining is important. The existence of a range of other minerals including gold, chromite and oil is known, but to date there has been little development of these. Textiles and food processing are the main industries. Since reunification, the USSR and China have been her main trading partners and aid-givers.

Yemen

This Arab republic borders the Red Sea. Where irrigation schemes have been established, agriculture is the main activity. Millet, corn, fruits, dates and coffee are the major crops. Sheep and goats are also kept. Salt extraction and export is important. Other exports include hides, coffee and qat, a narcotic. Japan and China are the main trading partners.

Yemen (People's Democratic Republic)

In 1967 the 17 sultanates of the Federation of South Arabia were overrun by a nationalist organization, and renamed. Today, the country is sometimes distinguished from the neighboring Arab republic (see above) by being called Southern Yemen. Agriculture is the main activity, with sorghum, sesame and millet as the chief crops. Long-staple cotton is now being grown and is a major export. Fishing exports also provide valuable foreign earnings. Aden, a former British colony, is an important oil-bunkering port.

COUNTRY REFERENCE: ASIA

Asian Countries	Political Status	State Capital	Area km²	Area sq mi	Population	Population Density per km²	Population Density per sq mi	Births per Thousand Persons	Deaths per Thousand Persons	Mean Annual Percentage Increase in Population
Afghanistan	A	Kabul	647,500	250,000	20,565,000	32	82	49.2	23.8	2.4
Bahrain	A	Al-Manamah	598	231	268,000	448	1,160	30.0	—	3.1
Bangladesh	B	Dacca	142,775	55,126	84,605,000	593	1,535	49.5	28.1	2.4
Bhutan	B	Paro & Thimbu	47,000	18,200	1,245,000	26	68	43.6	20.5	2.1
British Indian Ocean Territory	C	Victoria, Seychelles	47	18	1,800	38	100	—	—	—
Brunei	B	Bandar Seri, Begawan	5,765	2,226	190,000	33	85	33.4	4.3	2.5
Burma	A	Rangoon	678,033	261,790	31,815,000	47	122	39.5	15.8	2.4
China	A	Peking	9,561,000	3,691,500	855,546,000	89	232	26.9	10.3	1.7
Christmas Island	C	The Settlement	135	52	3,600	27	69	10.1	—	—
Cocos Islands	C	—	14	5	700	50	140	—	—	—
Cyprus	A	Nicosia	9,251	3,572	645,000	70	181	22.2	6.8	0.3
Hong Kong	C	Victoria	1,034	399	4,445,000	4,299	11,140	19.7	5.2	1.8
India	A	New Delhi	3,183,643	1,229,210	627,990,000	197	511	34.6	15.5	2.1
Indonesia	A	Jakarta	1,919,270	741,034	138,180,000	72	186	42.9	16.9	—
Iran	A	Tehran	1,648,000	636,300	34,160,000	21	54	45.3	15.6	2.8
Iraq	A	Baghdad	434,924	167,925	12,069,000	28	72	48.1	14.6	3.3
Israel	A	Jerusalem	20,770	8,019	3,610,000	174	450	28.3	7.2	3.2
Japan	A	Tokyo	372,197	143,706	114,650,000	308	798	17.2	6.4	1.3
Jordan	A	Amman	97,740	37,738	2,900,000	30	77	47.8	14.7	3.5
Kampuchea	A	Phnom Pénh	181,035	69,898	8,712,000	48	125	46.7	19.0	2.8
Korea (N)	A	Pyongyang	120,538	46,540	16,855,000	140	362	35.7	9.4	2.7
Korea (S)	A	Seoul	98,477	38,022	36,735,000	373	966	28.8	8.9	1.7
Kuwait	A	Al-Kuwayt	16,000	6,200	1,091,000	68	176	47.1	5.3	5.6
Laos	A	Vientiane	236,800	91,400	3,485,000	15	38	44.6	22.8	2.4
Lebanon	A	Beirut	10,230	3,950	3,096,000	303	784	39.8	9.9	3.0
Macau	C	Macau	16	6	284,000	17,750	47,333	—	—	1.8
Malaysia	A	Kuala Lumpur	332,633	128,430	12,845,000	39	100	38.7	9.9	3.0
Maldives	A	Male	298	115	141,000	473	1,226	50.1	22.9	2.0
Mongolia	A	Ulan Bator	1,565,000	604,200	1,552,000	1.0	2.6	38.8	9.3	3.0
Nepal	A	Kathmandu	140,797	54,362	13,280,000	94	244	42.9	20.3	2.3
Neutral Zone			5,700	3,560						
Oman	A	Muscat	212,457	82,030	824,000	3.9	10	—	—	3.1
Pakistan	A	Islamabad	895,496	345,753	77,040,000	86	223	36.0	12.0	3.3
Philippines	A	Manila	300,000	115,831	44,505,000	148	384	43.8	10.5	3.0
Qatar	A	Doha	11,000	4,247	100,000	9.1	24	—	—	3.0
Saudi Arabia	A	Riyadh	2,149,690	830,000	9,645,000	4.5	12	49.5	20.2	3.0
Singapore	A	Singapore	581	224	2,320,000	3,993	10,357	17.7	5.1	1.7
Sri Lanka	A	Colombo	65,610	25,332	14,085,000	215	556	29.5	7.7	2.3
Syria	A	Damascus	185,180	71,498	7,968,000	43	111	45.4	15.4	3.3
Taiwan	A	T'Aipei	35,961	13,885	16,770,000	466	1,208	—	—	—
Thailand	A	Bangkok	514,000	198,500	44,600,000	87	225	43.4	10.8	3.2
Turkey	A	Ankara	780,576	301,382	41,605,000	53	138	39.6	14.6	2.4
United Arab Emirates	A	Abu Dhabi	83,600	32,300	239,000	2.9	7.4	—	—	3.1
Vietnam	A	Hanoi	332,559	128,402	48,475,000	146	378	41.9	13.8	2.2
Yemen	A	San'a	195,000	75,300	5,690,000	29	76	49.6	20.6	2.9
Yemen People's Democratic Republic	A	Aden	287,683	111,075	1,825,000	6.3	16	49.6	20.6	3.3
ASIA TOTAL (exc. USSR)			27,526,613	10,629,290	2,346,665,100	85	221	—	—	—

1 △

2 ◁

3 ▷

4 ◁

*1 Troglodyte dwellings, Cappadocian Province, Urchisar, Turkey;
2 Folk dancers, Tehran, Iran – the traditional arts and crafts of Persia
still abound in the modern, oil-producing Moslem nation; 3 Damnoen
Saduak, outside Bangkok, Thailand – this rural floating market has
more to offer than its counterpart in the capital; 4 Oil derrick, UAE –
Abu Dhabi is by far the largest oil-producing emirate, followed by
Dubai, though oil exploration continues in the other emirates*

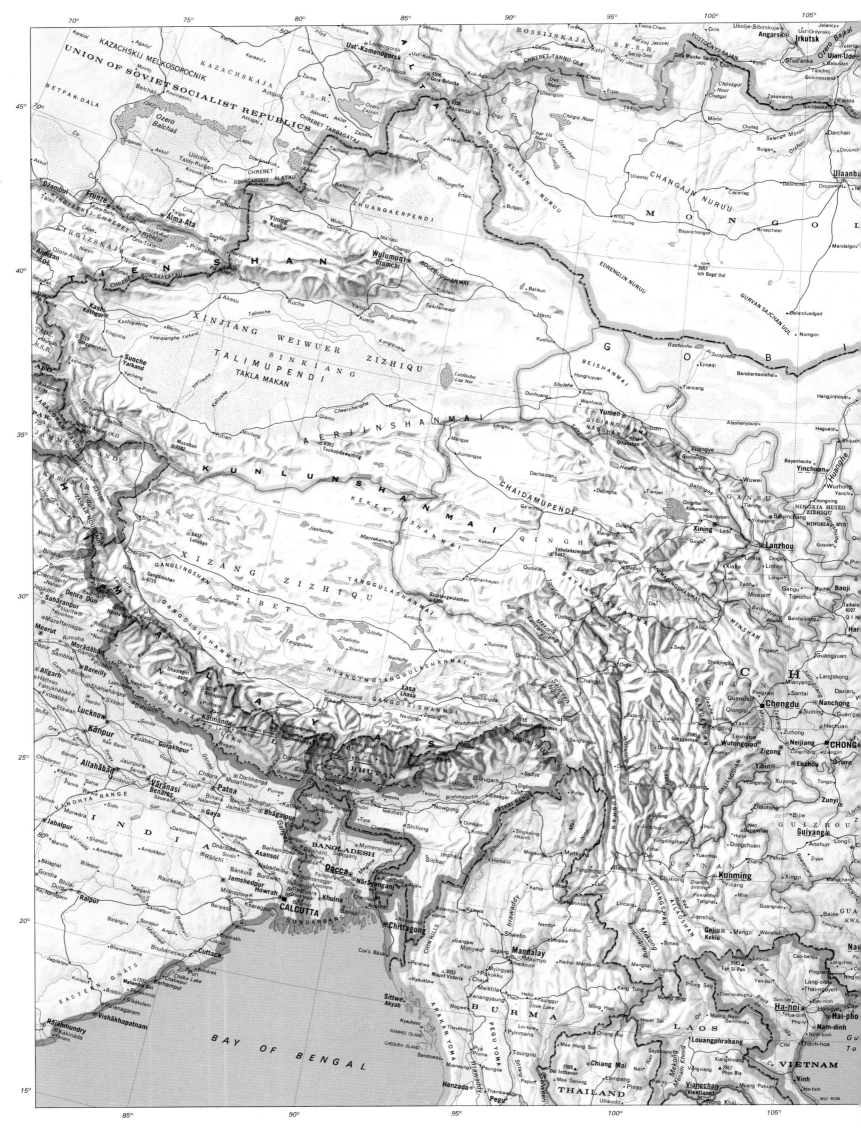

Kilometers
Statute Miles

Scale 1:13,200,000

One centimeter represents 132 kilometers.
One inch represents approximately 210 miles.
Lambert Conformal Conic Projection

81

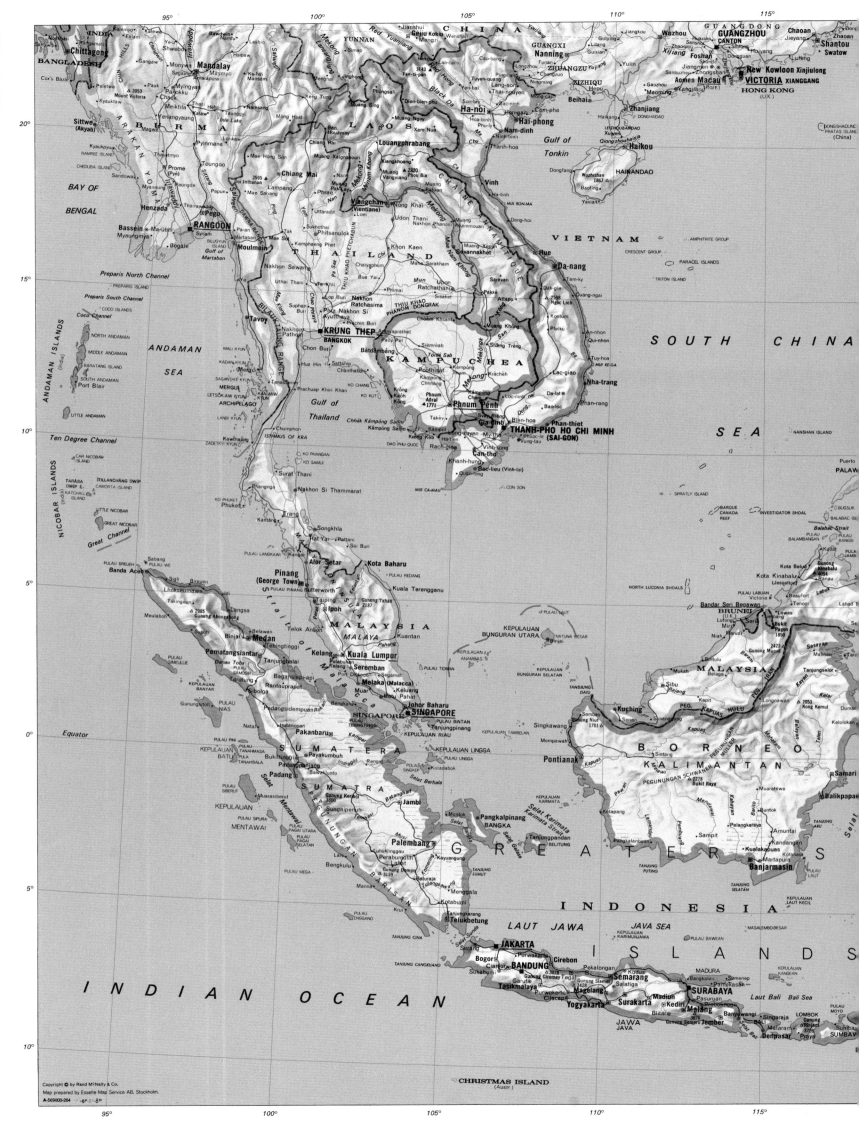

One centimeter represents 132 kilometers.
One inch represents approximately 210 miles.

Scale 1:13,200,000

Lambert Conformal Conic Projection

83

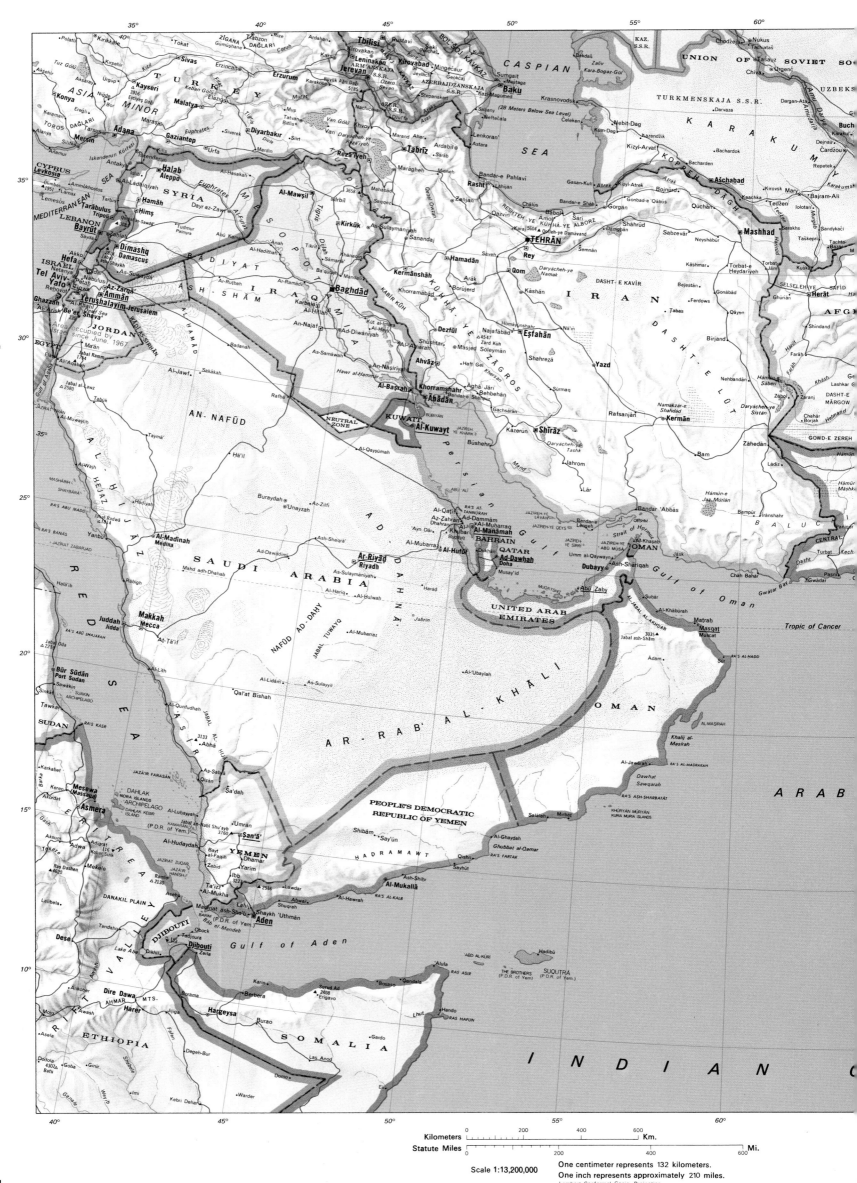

Kilometers |0 200 400 600|
— Km.
Statute Miles |0 200 400 600| Mi.

Scale 1:13,200,000

One centimeter represents 132 kilometers.
One inch represents approximately 210 miles.
Lambert Conformal Conic Projection

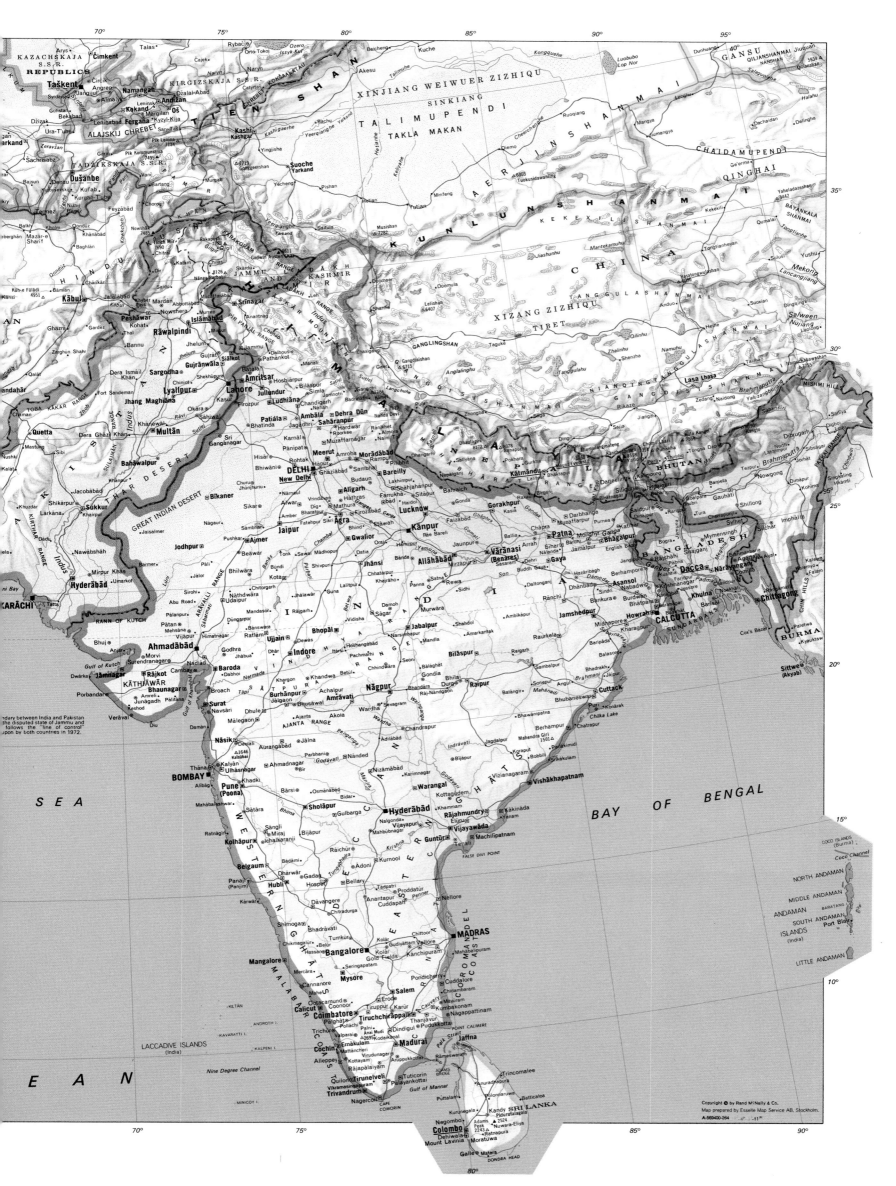

85

AFRICA
Physical Profile

World Location and Size

Africa is geographically separated from Asia by the Suez Canal and from Europe by the Straits of Gibraltar. It is a compact continent which sits uniquely astride the equator, extending from 37°N in Tunisia to almost 35°S in South Africa, a north-south distance of some 7,900 km (4,900 mi). Its west to east extent is greatest in the Northern Hemisphere where it stretches from Dakar in Senegal at 17°W to the Horn of Africa in Somalia at 51°E, some 7,100 km (4,450 mi). Geographically, it includes the large island of Madagascar and a number of smaller island groups in the Indian and Atlantic Oceans.

Landscape

Plateaus dominate the African landscapes, most of the continent being above 180 m (600 ft). These plateaus are found at different heights, usually with a steep edge between them. This is especially so where the lowest plateau falls to the coastal plains which are very narrow in all parts of the continent except the west and northeast coasts of the Sahara region and in Mozambique and Somalia. In general the level of the highest plains is greater in the south – average height 1,000 m (3,300 ft) – than in the north – average height 300 m (1,000 ft).

The eastern third of Africa contains the greatest relief, provided by the spectacular feature of the Great Rift Valley, an enormous belt of faulting in the earth's crust extending from Lake Nyasa in the south to the Red Sea and onward into Asia in the north. This rift system divides in two across the East African Plateau of Kenya, Tanzania and Uganda, and is up to 160 km (100 mi) wide and 5,100 km (3,200 mi) long in Africa alone. Most of the continent's great natural lakes are found within the system. Lake Victoria lying between the two main valleys, has a surface area of nearly 69,500 km² (26,830 sq mi), being second only to Lake Superior as the world's largest fresh water lake.

Close to the Rift Valley are a number of mountainous areas, some still containing active volcanoes, which rise to Africa's highest point at Mount Kilimanjaro, 5,895 m (19,340 ft). The most extensive mountain range, the Ethiopian Highlands, rises to 4,620 m (15,158 ft). In the northwest the barrier of the Atlas Mountains of Morocco and Algeria, rising to 4,167 m (13,665 ft), effectively divides the coastal strip from the Sahara. At the other end of

Opposite: Table Mountain from Cape Town, Republic of South Africa

the continent, the Drakensberg Mountains of South Africa reach 3,660 m (12,008 ft). Only two other mountain regions approach a maximum height of 3,000 m (10,000 ft), the Ahaggar Mountains of southern Algeria and the Tibesti Massif.

Some parts of Africa, such as the Lake Chad Basin and the northern Kalahari Desert area focusing on the Okavango Swamp, are internal drainage basins. Elsewhere, there are many comparatively short rivers flowing to the Atlantic and Indian Oceans. The world's longest river, the Nile, flows northward for 6,700 km (4,160 mi) from the East African lakes to the

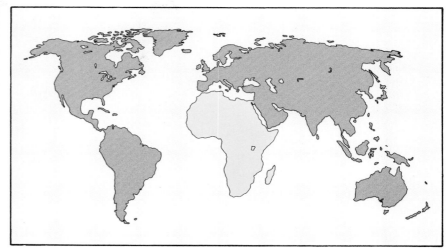

Mediterranean Sea. In West Africa, the Niger follows a circuitous course for 4,190 km (2,595 mi) between the highlands of Sierra Leone and its delta in Nigeria. The Zaire Basin, in equatorial Africa, occupies 12 percent of the continent, with the Zaire River (formerly Congo River) as its main channel. In the southeast, the Zambesi flows for 2,600 km (1,615 mi) from Angola eastward to the Indian Ocean, cascading over the Victoria Falls en route. All African rivers contain similar waterfalls and cataracts, where they drop from one plateau level to a lower one.

Climatic Background

Since the continent sits astride the equator, certain climatic features are mirrored on the opposite sides of the 0° latitude. In the extreme north of Morocco, Algeria and Libya, as well as the southern tip of South Africa, the climate is pleasantly subtropical. Summers here are dry, with the highest monthly average temperature above 22°C (72°F) and no winter average monthly temperature below 10°C (50°F). The South African plateau, farther east, has a cooler subtropical climate with no dry

season and the greater part of its rainfall in summer.

In a belt of central and western Africa within 5° of the equator, and on the east coast of Madagascar, equatorial climates provide rainfall throughout the year with totals in excess of 1,500 mm (60 in) and often more than 2,500 mm (100 in). Monthly average temperatures never fall below 18°C (64°F) and reach 27°C (the low 80°sF) at their maximum.

In a broad area around the equatorial belt shaped like a giant horseshoe lying on its side, precipitation becomes less intense, and, although temperatures never fall below 18°C (64°F) in any month, they show a greater seasonal range. These are the climates of the tropical savanna lands which, due to the effects of altitude in much of east and south central Africa, are markedly cooler than they might be.

North and south of the savanna lands lie the areas of semi arid and true desert climates. In the north, the Sahara constitutes the world's largest single desert area. Average summer temperatures in the arid regions may reach 37°C (98°F) in one month, the winter monthly average temperature falling back only to 15°C (59°F) and

Mount Kilimanjaro in Tanzania, soars above the giraffes in the Amboseli game reserve, Kenya – Africa's highest mountain, at 5,895 m (19,340 ft), is always covered in snow at its peak

the precipitation, often negligible, rarely exceeding an average of 125 mm (5 in). Rain, when it does fall, is brief but torrential.

Overall, two characteristics dominate African climates. Firstly, 75 percent of the continent has a water supply problem. Average rainfalls may appear to be sufficient but, except in the equatorial areas, the variation in rainfall from one year to the next creates great potential difficulties unless enormous water control schemes are introduced. Secondly, for all its intertropical situation, the fact that so much of Africa is mid and high level tableland modifies the heat, so that consistently high temperatures are the exception to the rule outside the desert areas. Thus, while the temperature on the Kenyan coast may be unpleasantly high, on the East African Plateau, still on the equator but 1,500 m (5,000 ft) above sea level, it is lower; for every 100 m (330 ft) of altitude, the temperature falls 1°C (0.55°F).

AFRICA

International observers refer to the world in three distinct divisions: the developed free nations, the developed Communist nations and the remaining developing 'Third World'. With the exception of South Africa, all of the African continent lies within this Third World. Here is the largest single group of newly independent countries which provide one of the great international challenges of our time. Within the developed world, the democratic countries of the West are anxious not to seem to be interfering too much in Africa's struggle for identity and economic advance. Yet they are keeping a keen eye on pro-African moves from the Communist bloc. One of the most fascinating international questions for the rest of this century concerns the development of the African continent and the roles which will be played by the free and the Communist world in that process.

The Peoples and Their Cultures

Africa may well have been the birthplace of mankind. Certainly East Africa has provided the oldest known skeleton of a prehistoric man, thought to be nearly 4 million years old. Today the population of this continent includes every major racial group. The Sahara separates the two main native groups, the Caucasian peoples to the north, and the Negroes to the south.

The Caucasians are similar to those peoples found in Europe and the Indian sub-continent. Though the color of their skin varies they are all swarthy with black hair. The Hamite group includes the nomadic peoples of the Sahara, Tuareg and Fulani, and the Berbers of northwest Africa. Farther east, live the Semite group, thought to have migrated from southwest Asia perhaps as recently as only 1,500 years ago. Together these make up the Arab peoples.

The Sudanese Negroes of West Africa are regarded as the purest of this group. They include the large populations of Yorubas, Ibos, Wolofs and Mandinkas, as well as a number of smaller tribal groups. In southern Africa, the other main group, the Bantu, are not pureblooded Negroes, being of mixed stock.

Intermarriage between peoples has also produced the Nilotes of the Nile Valley and the half-Hamites of East Africa. Diminutive peoples include the Bushmen and Hottentots of the southern desert lands and the Zaire Basin Pygmies. Distinct from both the Arabs and the Negroes are the Madagascar peoples, descended from Polynesians whose forefathers must have arrived here by westward migration across the Indian Ocean.

Within very recent times parts of Africa have been settled by Europeans, some of whom left when their adopted countries became independent. Likewise small populations of southeast Asian settlers in East Africa have recently been reduced, largely through expulsion by the newly-independent African governments. South Africa, however, is still politically controlled by a substantial white minority population, and, until 1979, Zimbabwe-Rhodesia was similarly controlled.

Despite European and eastern influence over two centuries, the new governments of Black Africa are understandably anxious to build their countries in a manner reflecting their ancient cultures. There is much emphasis for instance on the tribe and family where the ties of kinship are preserved through many generations. Individual Africans are conscious of their blood relationships with far more people than are, say, Europeans and Americans. African religion too is still a powerful influence, despite the introduction of Christianity and the Islamic faith.

Prior to the colonial period, little of African development was recorded except in the northern parts. History was largely known through spoken accounts and recall rather than in documentary evidence. Now, the numerous African languages are widely used in both written and spoken form. Swahili and Yoruba dominate literature and writing, though both French and English are widely used, as are other European languages.

Political Development

For a period of over 500 years, from 1415 onward, Africa increasingly attracted the attention of the powerful European nations who were anxious to spread their influence. Portugal, Holland, Britain and France all looked for sources of slave labor for other parts of their expanding empires, and later for raw materials for their own developing industries.

During the nineteenth century, names such as Livingstone, Stanley, Speke, Caillié and Nachtigal became famous for their exploration of the African interior. This led to great rivalry between the European nations in the opening up of this 'dark continent'. By 1900, often regardless of tribal territories, the map had been filled in with claims by the British, French, Portuguese, Germans, Spanish and Italians. Particularly in those colonies with less inviting climates, the imperial powers' objectives were solely exploitation. Where a colony's climate was more suited to the Europeans themselves, they became settlers. For the next half century or so each colony provided materials for the mother country without any real preparation for the ultimate responsibilities of self-government which was to follow.

African nationalism increased greatly after World War II. Whereas in 1951 only three African countries were independent, by now there are few parts of the continent which have not achieved that status. From 1956 to 1968, 38 new independent countries emerged, many changing their colonial names for ones with greater African significance. For example, the Gold Coast became Ghana, the Belgian Congo became the Congo Democratic Republic and later Zaire, Nyasaland became Malawi and Northern Rhodesia became Zambia.

Today, the Arab-dominated north and the white-ruled south apart, the new countries face enormous problems. Since their boundaries are based on fossilized European colonial claims rather than the real African tribal areas, what internal cohesion do some of the countries have? How does each state govern itself; by Western democratic ideas or along one-party lines, by some different tribal system, or does it fall victim to

1 General view of Johannesburg, Republic of South Africa; 2 Tribal dancers in traditional dress, South Africa; 3 Tississat Falls, on the Blue Nile, near Bagar Dar, Ethiopia, northeast Africa

military rule? What form of unity or cooperation should there be between nations whose peoples have much in common? More than any other continent, Africa, in this early phase of independence for such a large proportion of its peoples, faces large political as well as economic problems.

Industry, Commerce and Communications

With a few exceptions, especially South Africa with its extensive range of raw materials and climates which were most appealing to European settlers, the African countries show less development than any other comparable group. If South Africa is excluded, the value of goods manufactured in the whole continent is less than that of such individual countries as the Netherlands, Sweden or Belgium. Raw materials are largely exported to other continents instead of being used for local industry.

On a global map showing the principal locations of manufacturing industries, with its great concentrations in the developed world, only South Africa, Egypt, Ghana and Nigeria show up with marked agglomerations. Elsewhere, in Africa, manufacturing industries, where they exist at all, are comparatively small and scattered.

For most African countries, development at the present time is very difficult. Small-scale local industries, such as food processing, wood, clothing and leather working may be set up with limited capital. But for larger scale developments, it is necessary either to receive financial aid from overseas or to earn large quantities of foreign currency by exporting valuable raw materials. The first alternative is not always easy, as the conditions placed upon international loans are not always attractive to the borrowers. The second is harder for most African countries which lack adequate concentrations of the raw materials. Even when such resources exist, their development also needs overseas investment before they can be exploited on a sufficiently large scale. Herein lies a chicken and egg situation which bedevils so many national aspirations in a continent like Africa. Even the oil- and mineral-rich countries are finding that the road to steady development is not easy.

Communications in Africa are severely hindered by the natural conditions. Dense forests, extensive desert areas, and wide rivers which contain frequent waterfalls, all make travel difficult. Many original roads and railroads were developed only to take raw materials from their sources to the coast. Even now, rail networks are only effectively developed in a few countries, mainly South Africa and parts of the Mediterranean countries. Slowly, new railroads are being developed but, like industry, these are hampered by lack of capital. Outside many African cities and the better developed areas in the south, roads are largely ill-made, being dusty in the hot season and muddy in the wet one. Rivers and lakes are usable in parts. Travel over long distances, from Kenya to Nigeria or Egypt to South Africa, is only really possible now that air routes have been developed.

Agriculture, Forestry and Fishing

When assessing Africa's contribution to world output of given products, remember that the continent's land area is just over one-fifth, and its population just over one-tenth that of the whole world.

Farming is still the sole occupation of most of the population although much of the land is illsuited to agriculture. The people live by subsistence farming, trying to make a meager living by growing enough food for themselves and their families, with perhaps a little extra for use as barter. In many areas shifting cultivation is employed whereby a patch of forest is cleared and worked until the soil is exhausted, then the people move on to clear another area and so on. Simple tools such as hand hoes and machetes are used. The prevalence of the tsetse fly and its accompanying diseases makes large-scale animal raising impossible. The main subsistence crops are yams, corn, cassava and peanuts.

In more developed areas, where the climate will allow, some of these crops and others are grown in a more systematic way. Commercial farming is found in some of the better developed areas. Then it will often be found that one or two crops are most important, and will contribute much to the country's exports. On the savanna lands, corn especially, peanuts, yams, and cassava are the leading crops with cotton, millet and tobacco of lesser importance.

In a west-east belt from Guinea to Nigeria, in the Sudan and Ethiopia, as well as in scattered parts of eastern and southern Africa, millet and sorghum are the major cereal crops. Africa produces 18 percent of the world's combined total of nearly 82 million tons, half of Africa's output coming from Nigeria and the Sudan. Mainly from South Africa, Egypt and Zimbabwe-Rhodesia, Africa contributes nearly 10 percent of the world's sugar cane production. World production of cassava is currently over 105 million tons, of which Africa accounts for about 37 percent.

In equatorial and tropical areas, harvesting tree crops is a major activity. Over 67 percent of the world's output of about 1.4 million tons of cocoa comes from equatorial Africa. 28 percent of the world's coffee production of about 3.6 million tons comes from a wider area.

Africa is second to Asia as the most important rubber-producing continent, with Nigeria, Liberia, Zaire, Ivory Coast and the Cameroon accounting for 7 percent of the world total. Dates are the main cash crop at the Sahara oases which produce nearly 40 percent of the world's output, especially in Egypt, Algeria, the Sudan and Morocco. Vegetables, fruit, and some cotton is also grown at the oases. Cotton is grown in far larger quantities in the Nile valley of Egypt and the Sudan.

In the extremes of the continent, in South Africa and the Mediterranean coastlands, grapes, citrus fruit and temperate cereals, especially wheat and barley are all grown. The areas which are suited to such crops are but a tiny part of the whole continent, so African contribution to world output will be relatively small.

Successful livestock raising is carried out in some tropical parts and the two extremes of the continent. 9 percent of the world's sheep are found in South Africa, Ethiopia, Morocco and the Sudan; they are kept both for wool and meat. South Africa is the world's fifth most important producer of wool. Nearly 7 percent of the world's cattle are herded on the plateaus of Ethiopia, the Sudan, Tanzania, South Africa, Nigeria and Kenya. In the desert, camels provide milk as well as being beasts of burden. Goats are also herded in many semi-arid regions.

Fishing is of minor importance in Africa. South Africa alone in the continent is one of the world's 20 most important fishing nations, accounting for 2 percent of the fish

Ways of earning a living in the world's second largest continent are many and varied: 1 Fishing the river Niger, Nigeria – most of the population live by farming but a wide range of industries is developing; 2 Tea picking, Kenya – this is one of the major crops of the cooler highland areas; 3 Picking coconuts, Casamance, Senegal – the main crop here is peanuts which is one of the country's major exports

Total Imports and Exports
(1975 figures in millions of U.S. dollars)

Few African countries are large traders despite the recent discovery of oil in some areas.

	Imports	Exports
Algeria	5,861	4,442
Egypt	3,751	1,402
Gabon	469	943
Ghana	805	760
Ivory Coast	1,127	1,181
Kenya	938	476
Morocco	2,568	1,543
Nigeria	6,041	7,994
South Africa	7,589	5,315
Sudan	957	437
Zaire	905	827
Zambia	937	809

AFRICA

catch and 6 percent of whales. Recently however, both in the natural and the man-made lakes of the interior, schemes to introduce commercial fishing systematically have been started.

Much of equatorial and tropical Africa is clothed in extensive and valuable hardwood forests which have been developed to a limited extent. Where world production of hardwood is concerned, Nigeria (5 percent), Tanzania (2.5 percent), the Sudan (1.6 percent) and Ethiopia (1.6 percent) are the leading producers.

Natural Resources

Africa's mineral base differs from that of many other continents in that there are no widespread reserves of coal and iron ore. Likewise the other raw materials found widely in other parts of the world are also ill-distributed here. Colonial exploitation and lack of overseas investment may have hindered previous industrial growth, but this lack of raw materials will inevitably continue to limit traditional industrial development.

South Africa, economically the most advanced country, produces about 75 million tons of coal each year (3.8 percent of world output) while the rest of the continent, notably Zimbabwe-Rhodesia and Nigeria, accounts for less than half this figure.

Those few African countries which do have iron ore reserves are largely exploiting it for export. Liberia accounts for some 18 million tons iron content per year, South Africa 9 million, Mauritania 5 million and Angola 3 million tons. Thus, in total the continent produces less than 8 percent of the world's annual output; and her proven reserves are less than 3 percent of the world total.

Africa's contribution to world production of other minerals and precious stones is very variable, but her proven reserves may be conservatively estimated on account of under-exploration. She does make a leading contribution to world outputs of cobalt, vanadium, manganese and chrome, and very especially of gold and diamonds.

Only in the last two decades have the oil reserves of northern and western Africa begun to be realized. Now, the riches beneath the Sahara and the lowlands bordering the Gulf of Guinea are the subject of much

Ore	Average Annual World Production (million tons)	Africa's Share (percent)	Principal African Producing Countries
bauxite	80.3	11	Guinea
chrome	7.2	37	S Africa, Zimbabwe-Rhodesia
cobalt	0.03	69	Zaire, Zambia, Morocco
copper	7.4	19	Zambia, Zaire, S Africa
diamonds	42.7 million carats	66	Zaire, S Africa, Botswana, Ghana, Namibia, Sierra Leone
gold	1 million kg	57	S Africa, Zimbabwe-Rhodesia, Ghana
lead	3.2	4	Morocco, Namibia
manganese	22.8	33	S Africa, Gabon, Ghana, Morocco
nickel	0.733	5	S Africa, Botswana, Zimbabwe-Rhodesia
silver	0.01	3	S Africa, Morocco, Zaire
tin	0.2	6	Zaire, Nigeria, S Africa
vanadium	0.02	43	S Africa, Namibia
zinc	5.4	5	Zaire, S Africa

exploration and exploitation. By 1976 Nigeria had risen to eighth place in the world crude oil production tables, accounting for nearly 103 million tons (3.7 percent of world output); Libya 93 million tons and Algeria 50 million tons are next most important.

In all, just over 10 percent of the world's crude oil comes from Africa, the great bulk of which is exported. For the future, it is estimated that she has about 10.5 percent of known world reserves.

Africa also has about 10 percent of the world's proven natural gas reserves, although currently these are not so well developed, with less than 4 percent of the world's natural gas production coming from Algeria and Libya combined. The continent plays a more significant role in current uranium production and may contribute more in the future as she possesses over a quarter of the world's

reserves. South Africa, Nigeria and Gabon together account for 23 percent of current world production. Algeria and Madagascar have as yet untouched deposits.

Equatorial and tropical Africa have an estimated quarter of the world's HEP potential, mainly in the rivers of the Zaire Basin and East and West Africa, the Nile valley and Madagascar. Yet only a tiny fraction of this has been developed, so that Africa produces less than 3 percent of the world's total. Her main internationally famed HEP installations are at Volta Dam (Ghana), Kariba Dam (Zambia and Zimbabwe-Rhodesia), the Aswan High Dam (Egypt) and Cabora Bassa Dam (Mozambique). Of course, these and other proposed schemes can only be worthwhile when a demand for electricity is there, wherein lies part of the vicious circle ensnaring Africa's development.

African Economy

The population map of Africa shows well over 95 percent of the total area of the continent to have less than 10 persons to the km² (25 per sq ml). Only in limited parts – the Nile valley, the northwest coastal strip, parts of West and East Africa, around Lake Nyasa and in South Africa – are there large areas with populations in excess of 100 per km² (250 per sq mi).

Within these areas of high concentration, Africa has a few large cities which dominate their respective nations. The 11 metro areas over 1 million are: Cairo, Johannesburg, Alexandria, Kinshasa, Lagos, Casablanca, Algiers, Cape Town, Durban, Addis Ababa and Tunis.

African population is currently growing at a considerable rate. Most countries have birth rates in excess of 40 per 1,000, many in excess of 45 and some 50 per 1,000. Death rates are mainly in excess of 20 per 1,000 and sometimes higher. Such figures resemble those of parts of Asia, though there the death rates are often lower. The annual increase in each African country's population is often between 2.5 and 3.0 percent, and only rarely in excess of 3.5 percent, high figures by modern world standards.

Overall, African countries are among the world's least developed economies anywhere. Even excluding the islands and smaller mainland countries, the great majority of African countries have annual imports and exports valued at less than $500 million (contrast France and

Apart from South Africa, the continent is industrially under-developed: 1 Gold mine shaft heads, Johannesburg, S Africa – in the middle of the world's richest gold field, the country's largest city is an important manufacturing center; 2 Ebony carver, Nigeria – local crafts are the main industry of many communities

Per Capita Income
(1974 figures in U.S. dollars)

Overall, the average earnings of Africans are the lowest of all the continental areas, being little over $300. Only South Africans earn more than $1,000.

South Africa	Algeria	Mauritius	Ivory Coast	Tunisia	Zambia	Morocco	Nigeria	Egypt	Kenya
1,146	870	612	600	596	504	370	340	251	197

the United Kingdom with 100 times and the USA with 200 times such a figure). There are however, eight countries whose annual imports and exports are each valued at more than $1,000 million.

The growth of African trade over the years 1938–'58 and 1958–'75 was as follows: imports up by 3.9 and 4.9 times respectively and exports up by 4.6 and 6.0 times respectively. But, the absolute figures show the poor performance as a whole. By 1975 imports were worth only $44,700 million and exports $40,400 million.

The exceptions to the pattern of poor development lie at the north and south extremes of the continent, plus Nigeria and the Ivory Coast. The Mediterranean countries of Africa were more advanced than those of black Africa early in the twentieth century and today some of their trading performances have been enhanced by oil development. Thus, Libya's imports rose from $47 m to $97 m to $3,554 million and her exports from $6 m to $14 m to $6,837 million in the years 1938, '58 and '75. Algeria's advance has been slightly less dramatic. Egypt, Tunisia and Morocco, all in the top eight trading nations of Africa, advanced, but more slowly.

In West Africa, Nigeria ranked as a modest trading nation before World War II, with imports and exports valued at $42 million and $47 million. Now, thanks to comparatively rapid development soon after 1945 and then, in the last decade the development of oil resources, these figures have risen to $5,041 million and $7,994 million respectively. The Ivory Coast has advanced at about the same rate but with consistently lower absolute figures.

South Africa is the trading giant of Africa, but even so is only comparable with, say, Hungary or India. Modern performance is $7,589 million imports and $5,315 million exports.

Where such figures exist, per capita incomes act as a further measure of the lack of development and lower standards of living found in the continent. Remembering that the EEC countries in 1974 had an average per capita figure of $4,000, and that in the USA the figure was $5,923, the overall African figure was $350. Many countries have no accurate measure but may be reckoned to be no higher than $100. In heavily-populated Egypt the 1974 figure was $260, Nigeria with its oil revenues and large population, $320, and Algeria with its growing oil revenues and lower population, $870. Some other countries with different resources have comparatively high average per capita incomes, such as Ivory Coast ($600), Tunisia ($596), Zambia ($504) and Morocco ($370), but this does not necessarily mean a higher overall standard of living. Again, South Africa is the exception to all African patterns. Here over the whole population, average incomes in 1974 were $1,146.

Africa's energy production and consumption figures again demon-

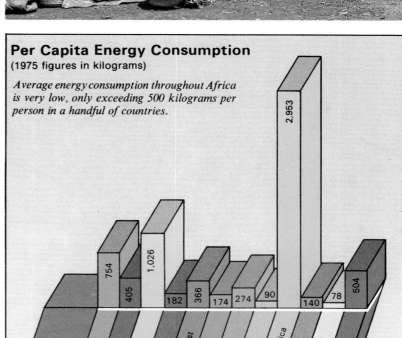

Trading and bartering are an essential part of African life: 1 The Kasbah, Tetúan, Morocco – the souk is an instant tourist trap in all North African countries; 2 Street market, Ghana – a more western life-style characterizes one of the first African countries to become independent. Ghana is the world's leading cocoa producer; 3 Roadside market, Tanzania – the economy here is based on producing crops for home use

Per Capita Energy Consumption
(1975 figures in kilograms)

Average energy consumption throughout Africa is very low, only exceeding 500 kilograms per person in a handful of countries.

Country	kg
Algeria	754
Egypt	405
Gabon	1,026
Ghana	182
Ivory Coast	366
Kenya	174
Morocco	274
Nigeria	90
South Africa	2,953
Sudan	140
Zaïre	78
Zambia	504

strate the lack of development. The following figures need to be viewed remembering the overall lack of coal, the recent discoveries of oil and the largely untapped HEP resources. In 1975 all Africa produced 456 million tons coal equivalent (mtce) and used 157 mtce. The continent is thus a net exporter of energy, largely due to Algeria (83 mtce produced, 13 mtce used), Libya (111 mtce produced, 3 mtce used) and Nigeria (131 mtce produced, 6 mtce used). Elsewhere, few countries consume more than 1 mtce or produce that much. South Africa is again the exception with production of 70 mtce and consumption of 84 mtce.

Energy consumption is only 393 kg/ca overall, and in many countries it is below 100. It is rising so that in the northern oil-rich countries, Algeria (754) and Libya (1,299) are among the continent's leaders. South Africa has the highest use with over 2,950 kg/ca, but even this is low by developed world standards.

In making an overall review of Africa's future prospects it is important to remember the exceptions to the rule. For instance, Africa north of the Sahara is very different from black Africa. It is part of the Arab world with its newly found oil riches.

These will bring in quick though only temporary revenues for use in western style projects. The overall standard of living may be greatly improved by new industries, changes in agricultural methods and the further development of tourism.

South Africa, with its advanced economy and white minority control, is a country apart. The national policy of racial segregation, apartheid, is widely abhorred inside Africa and elsewhere. In the coming years, it may well lead to internal problems far greater than those already experienced. Today Zimbabwe-Rhodesia has a similarly mixed population with more acute political problems, and the outside world, which has taken various initiatives to try to help in their solution, awaits the outcome.

Despite the few nations which have developed specific resources and thus gained a comparative lead over the rest, in general, black Africa is seeking advancement but is having much difficulty in going about it. Since 1963 independent countries have formed the Organisation for African Unity, with headquarters in Addis Ababa, to encourage cooperation and unity between nations and to oppose colonialism in general and European rule in South Africa. There

are now 44 member nations. All black Africa's independent countries are members of UNO. Many were former British colonies and are now members of the Commonwealth and some other countries are members of the French Community. A number have set up special trading agreements with the EEC. Still others which prefer the Socialist to the capitalist model have developed links with China, the USSR and Cuba.

Understandably, after the colonial experiences of their forefathers, modern Africans and their leaders may regard their relationships with the former imperial powers circumspectly. They may view their new alliances with non-African nations in the same light, and some even have reservations about the relationships with other African countries. A period of trust and stability is very much needed so that the development of this large continent can be accelerated soon. Whether the great human and economic potential here can be harnessed in the near future, or whether the whole continent will become embroiled in the black/white confrontations of South Africa and Zimbabwe-Rhodesia is a question which greatly occupies the developed world at the present.

African Countries

Algeria

A French possession until 1962, since when it has been an independent republic, Algeria is the second largest country in Africa, but over 90 percent of its area is part of the Sahara desert. Near the Mediterranean coast, cereal, citrus fruit and grape production are important. Forestry and herding dominate the mountains to the immediate south. Iron ore, phosphates, zinc and lead have, for a long time, been valuable minerals. Since 1957, Algeria has developed oil and natural gas fields beneath the Sahara, and these now provide over 90 percent of foreign earnings. France and other EEC countries are her major trading partners.

Angola

A Portuguese overseas territory until 1975, Angola is now an independent peoples' republic in south-west Africa. Much of the land is very dry and infertile. Most of the population live by subsistence farming, growing corn, peanuts or rice. Coffee, cotton and palms are grown commercially in some parts. There is valuable oyster fishing off the south coast. Coffee, corn, oysters and palm oil are all exported. Diamonds and iron ore have been worked and exported for many years: more recently crude oil extraction and exporting has been started. The chief imports are textiles, foodstuffs and machinery.

Benin

Formerly called Dahomey, Benin was part of French West Africa until 1960, since when it has been an independent republic. It is a small country bordering the Gulf of Guinea. Most of the population live off the land, growing corn and cassava. In the south, palms are the main crop, palm products being the country's leading exports, followed by cocoa. Coffee and cotton production have been steadily stepped up in recent years. Small quantities of chromite, gold and iron ore are mined.

Botswana

This independent, landlocked republic in southern Africa was known as the Bechuanaland protectorate until 1966. It is a member of the Commonwealth. Much of the country is an arid tableland. Most of the Bantu population live by herding cattle and dairying. Crop farming is unreliable on account of the variable rainfall, though it is more reliable where boreholes have been drilled. Animal products are the chief exports but diamonds, copper and nickel exports are rapidly rising. Machinery and metal products, foodstuffs and fuel oils are the main imports. Botswana is a member of the South African

Customs Union and conducts most of her trade with countries in that group and the United Kingdom.

Burundi

Since 1962, the southern part of the former United Nations Trust Territory of Rwanda-Burundi has been the independent republic of Burundi. It is a small, densely-peopled, landlocked country on the highland margins of the East African Plateau. Subsistence agriculture is most important, with beans, cassava, corn, sweet potatoes and peanuts being among the major crops. Cattle are also kept. Coffee is grown for export, as is cotton, but the latter is being superseded by tea. Minerals are little developed though large reserves of nickel have been proved. Textiles, foodstuffs and vehicles are the major imports. The EEC countries and the USA are her main trading partners.

Cameroon

From 1919 till the early 1960s, France and the United Kingdom controlled two trusteeship territories in western Africa. Since then most of these two areas have been the federal republic of the Cameroon. Most of the people live by subsistence farming. The main cash crops are cocoa,

coffee and bananas. Cotton and rubber are of lesser importance. Bauxite is the only exploited mineral and is mainly exported. A range of hardwoods is felled and exported as well. The EEC countries, especially France, and the USA are her main trading partners.

Cape Verde

Formerly a Portuguese overseas territory, these fifteen islands off the west coast of Africa have been independent since 1975. Eventually, union with Guinea-Bissau, another former Portuguese territory on the mainland, is a distinct possibility. The islands are mountainous and volcanic. Coffee, bananas and cassava are grown in the valleys and a range of livestock is kept.

Central African Republic

In 1960 this former part of French Equatorial Africa, known as Ubangi Shari, became the landlocked, independent Central African Republic; for a time it was the Central African Empire. It is mainly savanna with forests in the south. Most of the people live by subsistence farming, with corn, peanuts and sorghum as the main crops. Cotton and coffee are the leading export produce.

Diamonds and gold are also mined and exported.

Chad

Part of French Equatorial Africa until 1960, since when it has been an independent, landlocked country, Chad is desert land in the north and savanna land in the south. It has one of the lowest population densities in all Africa. In the north, nomadic herdsmen roam the dry lands with their animals. Farther south, subsistence farming and commercial cotton, peanut and sugarcane growing are the major activities. Cotton and meats are the only exports; fuel oils, fibers and machinery are the main imports.

Comoro Islands

Four islands in the Mozambique Channel formed the French overseas

1 Viergen de las Nieves, Las Palmas, Canary Islands – although belonging to Spain, this group of North Atlantic islands is only 96 km (60 mi) from Africa; 2 Harar, Ethiopia – this ancient walled city is the country's chief Islamic center; 3 Musicians, Brikama, The Gambia – tourism is being developed to broaden the one-crop economy based on peanuts

1 △

2 ▽

3 ▽

territory of the Comoro Islands from 1960 to 1976. Then, three became the independent country of the Comoro Islands and the other, Mayotte, became an overseas department of France. A range of commercial crops are planted in small areas: copra, sisal, vanilla, perfume plants and coffee are most important. Subsistence farming centers on cassava, sweet potatoes and other vegetables, but much foodstuff has to be imported. France is her main trading partner.

Congo

Formerly part of French Equatorial Africa, under the name of the Middle Congo, the republic became independent in 1960 and is now a member of the French Community. The country sits astride the equator and is largely clothed in equatorial rain forest. Most of the population live near the River Zaire or the coast. Subsistence farming is the main activity. A little lead, zinc and gold are mined and exported. Timber, palm products and peanuts are also exported. Crude oil was discovered in 1969 and production is now rising.

Djibouti

Until 1977, The Afars and Issas was a French overseas territory. Since then, newly named, it has been an independent republic. Lying on the Gulf of Aden in East Africa, the land is mainly a stony desert. Most of the population is nomadic, herding goats, sheep and camels. Some market gardening is found around the main towns and at the Ambouli Oasis. A few minerals have been proved, but none has been developed. Fishing for pearls, sponges and shellfish is conducted in the coastal waters. Foodstuffs and fuel oils are the main imports, hides and cattle the main exports.

Egypt

The Arab republic of Egypt occupies the extreme northeast corner of Africa, and extends into Asia. It is mainly a desert land, but its present population centers and ancient civilizations which developed over 5,000 years ago and lasted for nearly 2,500 years centered around the Nile and its delta. Today such monuments to this golden age may be seen in the Pyramids, the Sphinx and the Temple of Abu Simbel. In recent years Egypt has been one of the main Arab states in conflict with Israel, which she borders. Territory formally recognized as Egyptian is still occupied by Israelis. Yet a new mood of cautious

1 Fishing boats, Monrovia, Liberia – the 'home' port for the world's biggest merchant navy operating under flags of convenience was opened in 1948; 2 Gebel Togo, Aswan, Egypt – a Nubian village which has remained unchanged for centuries; 3 Flocks at Colomb-Béchar, Algeria – the oasis town of Béchar, in the Atlas foothills, is known for its date palms

coexistence is growing up between the two countries, following the signing of a peace treaty in 1979.

For home consumption wheat, corn and millet are the main crops. Cotton, citrus fruit, potatoes, rice and sugar cane are grown for export. The Aswan High Dam in the south has revolutionized irrigation control and provides hydroelectricity for industry and the urban areas generally. Textiles, chemicals, foodstuffs and cement production are the major industries. Leading minerals are iron ore, phosphates and salt: crude oil production is rising again following the regaining of the Sinai field from Israel. The Suez Canal, a major international waterway for conventional shipping, not supertankers, crosses Egypt from the Red Sea to the Mediterranean. Since reopening in 1975, after eight years of closure, following the Arab/Israeli War, it has provided valuable foreign revenue and is now being developed as a tax-free industrial zone.

Equatorial Guinea

Since 1968 the mainland area of Rio Muni, the Corisco Islands and Fernando Póo have been independent. Previously a Spanish colony, they now rely economically upon Spain, the USSR and Cuba. Hardwoods from the rain forests together with cocoa and coffee are the main exports, although political uncertainties since independence have led to a lack of confidence in the economy so that production and exports have fluctuated greatly.

Ethiopia

Formerly known as Abyssinia, Ethiopia has a very long and legendary history. Until 1975 it was a kingdom ruled by a house said to be descendants of King Solomon and the Queen of Sheba. Since then it has had a series of military governments. It is an upland country and most people live on the central tableland. Coffee, sugarcane, corn, barley and tobacco are among the main crops. Sheep and cattle are raised. Food processing and the textiles industries are being steadily developed. Coffee is the major export, foodstuffs, machinery and fuel oils the main imports. The USA, Italy, West Germany and Japan are her main trading partners.

Gabon

Now a member of the French Community, the independent republic of Gabon was formerly part of French Equatorial Africa. Lying close to the equator in West Africa the land is mainly clothed in dense rain forest. Subsistence farming and a little coffee, cocoa and peanuts grown for export are important activities. Mahogany and okoumé are valuable woods felled and exported. Iron ore, manganese, uranium and crude oil are all produced, but overall development is slow. Principal trading partners are the USA and members of the EEC.

African Countries

Gambia

Formerly a British colony, since 1970 this narrow strip of land stretching along either bank of the Gambia River in West Africa, has been an independent republic within the Commonwealth. The economy balances on the growing and exporting of peanuts and their products. Rice production for home consumption is increasing. Foodstuffs, textiles, machinery and fuel oils are the main imports. The United Kingdom and USA are her main trading partners.

Ghana

Formerly known as the Gold Coast, a British colony, and the trusteeship territory of Togoland, Ghana was one of the first African countries to achieve independence in 1957. Predominantly agricultural, it is the world's leading producer and exporter of cocoa. Coffee and rubber production are being increased. Corn, rice, cassava and yams are the main foods grown for home consumption. Gold,

1 Camel handler, Nabeul, Tunisia – these long-suffering camels remain the desert lands' most useful animal; 2 Nairobi, Kenya – the administrative capital also attracts many visitors to the nearby National Park; 3 Fishermen's cottages, Camara de Lobos, Madeira – part of Portugal, this volcanic island group lies 640 km (400 mi) west of the coast of Africa

diamonds, manganese and bauxite are the most valuable minerals. Since independence, the world's largest man-made lake, for irrigation control and the production of HEP, has been created behind the Volta dam. Foodstuffs, fuel oils, chemicals, machinery and manufactured goods are the chief imports. Her chief trading partners are the EEC, the USA and other West African countries.

Guinea

Part of French West Africa until 1958, Guinea then became an independent republic outside the French Community. West Africa's most mountainous country, it is an important mining area. Bauxite accounts for 60 percent of exports, and iron ore and diamonds are also important. The main crops are coffee, rice, cassava, palms, bananas, pineapples and peanuts. Large herds of cattle are raised in the uplands.

Guinea-Bissau

Formerly the Portuguese overseas province of Portuguese Guinea, this Atlantic coast country has been independent since 1974. It aims to unite with the Cape Verde Islands. Subsistence farming and some cash cropping are the main activities; rice, cassava, palms and peanuts are the main crops. Inland, cattle raising is carried out on the plateau country. There are large reserves of bauxite but development has hardly begun.

Ivory Coast

Until 1960 the Ivory Coast was a part of French West Africa, but is now an

independent republic. It is potentially one of the richest countries of West Africa. Coffee and cocoa are the leading crops both by production and as exports. Cotton production is rising steadily. For home consumption yams, cassava and rice are the main crops. Sheep, cattle and goats are herded in the interior. Diamonds, manganese and iron ore are major minerals. Timber is the most valuable export. Main imports are machinery, cement and fuel oils. Her chief trading partners are the EEC countries, especially France, and the USA.

Kenya

Since 1963, the former British East African colony of Kenya has been an independent republic within the Commonwealth. Sitting astride the equator, the land may be divided into two, the cooler western uplands and the hotter eastern lowlands. In the west, wheat, corn, coffee and tea are the main crops and cattle are raised. Coconuts, cotton, corn and sugarcane are important in the east. In the highest areas, forestry is significant; a range of minerals is extracted but together they add less to the economy than timber production. Tourism is a growing activity, with game parks and the highland areas being the major attractions. The United Kingdom, Japan, West Germany and the USA are her main trading partners.

Lesotho

The former British protectorate of Basutoland, a small, upland, landlocked area of southern Africa, became the independent country of

Lesotho within the Commonwealth in 1966. It is primarily agricultural. Corn, wheat and sorghum are the chief crops, and sheep, goats and cattle are raised. There is a small diamond mining industry, but many of the Bantu population now work in the mines of neighboring South Africa. Cattle, wool and mohair are the main exports; foodstuffs, fuel oils and machinery the main imports. Most trade is with the United Kingdom and other African countries.

Liberia

This is the oldest independent country in West Africa, having been established in 1822 as an American settlement for freed slaves and granted independence 25 years later. Iron ore and rubber are the most important exports, and timber, coffee and cocoa are also exported. Rice, cassava and sugarcane are grown as well. The main imports are foodstuffs, machinery and manufactured goods. Most trade is with the EEC countries and the USA.

Libya

A North African republic, Libya was established in 1951 by the United Nations from three provinces which were then under French and British control, following World War II. The land is largely desert, with a fertile coastal belt and a few oases and irrigated areas. Dates, olives, citrus fruit and cereals are the main products. Sheep and goats are the most valuable animals. Leather and food processing and other small industries have been established. More recently, Libya has become a

1 Desert patrol near Gadames, Libya – at the borders with Tunisia and Algeria, this Saharan town is an important stopover for the camel caravans; 2 Sugarcane harvest, Mauritius – this crop is the basis of the economy, accounting for nearly all its exports; 3 Harbor, Mozambique – this country with its long coastline handles trade for neighboring landlocked states

leading world producer of crude oil, and now has a substantial annual trade balance which is being used in part to develop agriculture and industry.

Madagascar (Malagasy)

From 1896 till 1958 this island, lying some 400 km (240 mi) off the southeast African coast, was a French colony. Since independence it has been known variously as the Democratic Republic of Malagasy or Madagascar. Agriculture is the base of the economy. Rice, millet, corn and cassava are the main food crops. Coffee, vanilla and cloves are exported, as are animal products. Chromite is the major mineral, while graphite, phosphates and mica are extracted in smaller amounts. The range of processing industries is being steadily increased. Foodstuffs, metalware and chemicals are the main imports. Most trade is with the EEC.

Malawi

This landlocked independent republic in southern Africa was the British Protectorate of Nyasaland until 1964 and is a member of the Commonwealth. It is predominantly rural and about 80 percent of foreign earnings come from agricultural exports. The most important subsistence crops are corn, millet and cassava. Tobacco, tea, cotton and peanuts are the main cash crops. The few known minerals have yet to be exploited. Major imports are foodstuffs, machinery, vehicles, fuel oils and building materials. Most trade is conducted with the United Kingdom, other EEC countries and the USA.

Mali

Until 1958 this landlocked country of the western Sahara was known as French Sudan. It then federated with Senegal to become the Mali Federation, but less than two years later became a separate republic. In the dry areas, nomadic herding is the main activity. Irrigation schemes elsewhere enable millet, peanuts, rice, corn and cotton to be grown. Iron ore, manganese and phosphates are known but are little exploited. Exports are mainly cotton, rice, peanuts and animal products; foodstuffs, machinery, fuel oil and building materials are the main imports. Most trade is with the EEC, especially France, and the USA.

Mauritania

In 1960 the French protectorate of Mauritania became an independent republic. Its territory was expanded in 1976 when it took in part of the former Spanish Sahara. It is largely a dry desert tableland facing the Atlantic Ocean in West Africa. In the south, near the Senegal river, corn, millet and peanuts are mainly grown. Elsewhere, the population are mostly nomadic herdsmen. Iron ore and copper are both important minerals, accounting for over 90 percent of foreign earnings and giving the country a substantial balance of payments surplus. Much trade is with the EEC, especially France, and the USA.

Mauritius

This group of islands in the Indian Ocean some 800 km (500 mi) east of the Malagasy Republic, has been an independent republic within the Commonwealth since 1968. Prior to being a British colony, it had belonged to first the Dutch and then the French. The republic's economy depends heavily on the production of sugar cane which is sometimes adversely affected by tropical storms. Other crops being developed for export are tea and tobacco. Forestry is also of increasing importance. While agricultural products account for nearly all exports, the country imports a wide range of foodstuffs, oil and consumer goods. Most trade is with Commonwealth countries, especially the United Kingdom, Australia and Canada as well as South Africa.

Mayotte

From 1960 till 1976 Mayotte was part of the French overseas territory of the Comoro Islands, a group of four islands in the Mozambique Channel. Since then, the others have been independent but Mayotte has become an overseas department of France. In part this separation is religion-based, since Mayotte has a predominantly Catholic population while the other islands are predominantly Moslem.

Morocco

Independent since 1956, this northwest African kingdom was previously partly a French and partly a Spanish protectorate. More recently, in 1976, the country has incorporated part of the former Spanish Sahara into its bounds. Most of the population live on the coastal lowlands, and 70 percent of them live off the land. Wheat, barley, vegetables, olives and citrus fruit are the main crops. Stock raising, wine production, fishing and some forestry are also significant. Phosphates are the most valuable mineral; lead, manganese and iron ore are of lesser importance. Fruit and minerals are the main exports, manufactured goods the main imports. France and West Germany are her main trading partners.

Mozambique

This former Portuguese overseas territory has been independent since 1975. With a long coastline on the Indian Ocean, its ports serve not only its own needs but also those of the three neighboring landlocked states of Malawi, Zimbabwe-Rhodesia and Zambia, as well as parts of South Africa. Subsistence farming is practiced widely, but in the more fertile valleys and along the north coast, sugar cane, cashew nuts, cotton, copra, sisal and tea are produced for export. Africa's largest HEP scheme is located at Cabora Bassa and will provide power when completed for Mozambique and her neighbors.

95

African Countries

Namibia

Until World War I this dry corner in the southwest of the continent was a German colony. Since then it has been first a mandated territory and then a United Nations trusteeship territory administered by South Africa. It is now the newest independent country in the continent. Diamonds extracted from the coastal alluvial terraces are the main base of the economy. Livestock herding is widespread, crop farming being largely limited to the northern areas.

Karakul pelts (from a small sheep) are the major agricultural product. Fishing is an important coastal activity, pilchards and lobsters being valuable catches. International trade, except with South Africa, is conducted through Walvis Bay.

Niger

Since 1960 this former part of French West Africa has been an independent republic within the French Community. Landlocked, it is mainly desert and savanna land. In the driest areas nomadic herding is the main activity. Elsewhere, subsistence farming with millet, rice and corn as the main crops is important. Mineral resources include uranium, which has been developed in the last ten years, salt and tin. Peanuts, gum arabic, salt, uranium and animal products are the main exports. Most trade is with France and other EEC countries. Most trade is conducted through Niamey on the main north-south Saharan road.

Nigeria

A federal republic of West Africa and a member of the Commonwealth, Nigeria achieved independence from Britain in 1960. Its population is by far the greatest in all Africa, and the density of population the highest apart from that of some of the smaller countries and islands. The natural vegetation ranges from semi-desert in the north to mangrove swamp on the Gulf of Guinea coast in the south. While most of the population live by farming, the economy is increasingly dependent on mineral production and exports. Palm kernels, cotton, cocoa and peanuts are the main cash crops. Corn, millet, rice and cassava are of lesser importance. Nigeria is one of the few African countries to produce coal. Tin and columbite have also been mined for many years. Since the 1960s, oil and natural gas have developed to provide well over 90 percent of the country's foreign earnings. Among tropical African countries, Nigeria has the widest range of developing and expanding manufacturing industries.

The country takes its name from the river which flows from its northwest corner to the south coast. Together with its tributaries, the Niger River is the largest system in West Africa. The area to the west and south of the river, the former lands of the Yoruba peoples, is today the economic heart of the country. Here lie the Yoruba Highlands at heights between 300 m (1,000 ft) and 500 m (1,700 ft). Elsewhere heights of up to 1,200 m (4,000 ft) are reached, but the levels of development are lower in these remoter regions.

Reunion

This Indian Ocean, volcanic island, some 900 km (560 mi) east of Madagascar, is a French overseas department, and as such sends representatives to the National Assemblies in Paris. Sugarcane is the main crop and export, and feeds a number of processing factories on the island. Rum, corn, essences and tobacco are also produced. Pigs, sheep and cattle are raised. Rice and cement are the main imports. Most trade is with France and other European countries.

1 Pounding corn, Cap Vert-Tiaroye, Senegal – farming is the major occupation here; 2 Termite hill, Tsavo National Park, Kenya – Africa's famous wildlife is protected from big game hunters in such reserves; 3 Cape Town, South Africa – dominated by the flat-topped Table Mountain, the provincial capital is rightly famed for its beauty and climate

Rwanda

The former United Nations trust territory of Rwanda-Burundi divided into two independent nations in 1962. The republic of Rwanda is landlocked, small and one of the most heavily populated parts of all Africa. Most of the people live by subsistence agriculture; beans, cassava, corn and sorghum being among the leading staple food crops. Coffee, tea, cotton and pyrethrum are produced as cash crops. A little tin ore is mined and exported.

St Helena

This small volcanic island 1,900 km (1,200 mi) west of the African mainland is a British colony. A number of other islands are associated with it, particularly Ascension Island 1,100 km (700 mi) to the northwest and Tristan da Cunha 2,400 km (1,500 mi) to the south-southwest. Only small areas are cultivated, flax being the main product feeding a small lace-making industry. Vegetables and fruit are grown for local consumption. Each island group is very remote. At one time they were important centers for shipping and radio communications.

Sao Tome and Principe Islands

Lying some 200 km (130 mi) off the coast of West Africa in the Gulf of Guinea, these islands were formerly a Portuguese overseas territory. Since 1975 they have been a democratic republic. The volcanic soils are very fertile and much land is used for producing cocoa, copra, coconuts, coffee, bananas and palm oil. As well as the natural labor force, migrant workers from the mainland come each year to work on the plantations. The considerable farming exports provide the base for a healthy balance of trade. Most trade is conducted with European countries which sell manufactured goods in return.

Senegal

The oldest French colony in Africa until 1958, when it became a partner with French Sudan in the independent federation of Mali, since 1960 Senegal has been a separate republic. Extensive areas are farmed, peanuts and millet being the major crops. Sheep, goats and cattle are kept in large numbers. Rich fishing grounds lie off the coast. Phosphates are currently the most important mineral produced. Recently large iron ore reserves have been discovered which may be the richest in all Africa. Peanuts, phosphates and fish are the main exports, rice, sugar, fuel oils and textiles the main imports. Most trade is conducted with the EEC countries and the USA.

Seychelles

This group of about 90 volcanic islands in the Indian Ocean some 1,600 km (1,000 mi) east of the

1 △

2 △

3 ▽

Kenyan coast was formerly a British colony, but since 1976 it has been an independent republic within the Commonwealth. At that time, Aldabra, Farquhar and Desroches Islands, which had previously been part of the British Indian Ocean Territories within Asia, joined the new nation. Food crop production is being stepped up, as is fishing for both home consumption and export. Copra and cinnamon bark are the main cash crops and exports. Rice, sugar, fuel oils and manufactured goods are the leading imports. Tourism is becoming increasingly important. Her main trading partners are the United Kingdom, Kenya, Australia and South Africa.

Sierra Leone

In 1961 this former British colony in West Africa became an independent member of the Commonwealth. The coastal lowlands are covered with tropical forest while the interior undulating plateau is a savanna land. Rice is the main staple food crop, cassava, corn and vegetables being of subsidiary importance. Fishing is increasing steadily but still does not provide all the home needs. Cash crops, and the main agricultural exports include cocoa beans, peanuts, coffee, ginger and palm kernels. Diamonds and bauxite are important products, accounting for over 65 percent of the country's foreign earnings. Foodstuffs, manufactured goods and fuel oils are the main imports. The United Kingdom and Japan are her main trading partners.

Somali Republic

Lying in the eastern 'horn' of Africa, this democratic republic was created as an independent country in 1960 from the former British Somaliland protectorate and the Italian trusteeship territory of Somalia. It is essentially a hot, dry country. Most of the population are nomadic herdsmen raising cattle, goats and camels. Near the main rivers of the south, cotton, sugarcane, bananas, other fruit and corn are grown. Tuna and mother of pearl are both taken from the Indian Ocean. The known reserves of iron ore, gypsum, berylium and columbite have yet to be developed. A little uranium is mined. Fruit, livestock and animal products are the main exports.

South Africa

This republic is economically the most advanced country in all Africa. Of the total population of 25.8 million, about 4 million are white. Its internal policy of separate development for the white settlers and the black natives (apartheid) led to its withdrawal from the Commonwealth in 1961. The climate of many parts of the country, both on the coast and the plateau, is particularly attractive to Europeans. Agriculture is well developed commercially, corn and wheat being the leading cereals; deciduous and citrus fruit are also important, as is pastoral farming.

Mineral production is far more significant to the overall economy. South Africa is the world's leading gold producer. Coal production is the highest for any African country; diamonds, copper, manganese, asbestos, iron ore and chrome are all mined in considerable quantities. A wide range of manufacturing industries have been developed, with food processing, heavy industry and engineering, chemicals, textiles and small industries accounting for nearly 23 percent of the national product. Now, more foreign earnings come from manufactured goods than either mineral or agricultural exports. Imports are mainly machinery, vehicles, manufactured goods and fuel oils, plus chemicals. EEC countries, especially the United Kingdom and West Germany; Japan; the USA and other Western Hemispheric countries are her main trading partners.

Sudan

The largest single country in Africa was administered jointly by the United Kingdom and Egypt until 1956, since when it has been an independent republic. The Nile and its tributaries provide the main focus of economic activity, much of the rest of the country being desert. The Sennar Dam provides water for the large irrigated area of the Gezira. Here and elsewhere in lowland Sudan, long staple cotton is the major crop. Besides cotton, peanuts, oil seed and gum arabic are the main exports. Fertilizers, machinery, sugar and

fabrics are the main imports. China, Italy and West Germany take 40 percent of Sudanese exports. The United Kingdom and the USA are the leading sources of imports.

Swaziland

Since 1968, this landlocked country of southern Africa has been an independent member of the Commonwealth. While the majority of Swazis live by subsistence agriculture, the national economy is broadly and firmly based on a range of agricultural products and minerals. Sugar, and wood pulp from the forested mountains are the main exports. Other valuable crops are citrus fruit, rice, cotton, corn and sorghum. Cattle and goats are both widely kept. Iron ore and asbestos are the most important minerals. Swaziland is joined in a customs union with South Africa. It currently enjoys an annual balance of payments surplus with the rest of the world.

Tanzania

The East African mainland country of Tanganyika became independent in 1961, as did the nearby islands of Zanzibar and Pemba in 1963. Together they now form the United Republic of Tanzania. The mainland agricultural economy is currently being diversified. Cotton is the major crop, sisal is of declining importance and the production of other crops like citrus fruit, cocoa, corn and

Pyramids, Egypt – one of the ancient world's great civilizations, Egypt under the Pharaohs employed vast manpower and primitive tools to create architectural wonders such as the tomb of Tutankhamen, the huge temples at Luxor and Karnak and, above all, the magnificent pyramids at Gizeh, 2650–2550 BC, one of the wonders of the ancient world

nuts is being increased. Cattle ranching and dairying are also being developed. Hardwoods are of increasing export importance. Zanzibar and Pemba are the major world source of cloves. Mineral production in Tanzania is dominated by diamonds. Foodstuffs and manufactured goods form the bulk of the country's imports. The United Kingdom, other EEC countries, Japan and China are her main trading partners.

Togo

Since 1960, this former West African United Nations trusteeship territory has been an independent republic within the French Community. The shape of the country is long and narrow with its main axis lying north-south. The coastal strip is low and swampy while the interior is an undulating plateau region. Corn, yams and cassava are the main subsistence crops. Coffee, cocoa, palm products, peanuts and cotton are the main cash crops. Since independence, mining activity has increased. Phosphates are the most important product; reserves of bauxite and iron ore

African Countries

have yet to be exploited on a large scale. Phosphates, coffee and cocoa account for nearly 90 percent of the foreign earnings. Most trade is with EEC countries.

Tunisia

Lying between Algeria and Libya on the north coast of Africa, this independent Arab-speaking republic was a French protectorate from 1881 till 1956. A wide range of crops are produced for both home consumption and export, with citrus fruit, olives, cereals, grapes and dates all being important. Sheep, cattle and goats are the most widely kept animals. Phosphates are the leading mineral, with iron ore, lead and zinc of lesser importance. Tourism is growing. France and the USA are her main trading partners.

Uganda

This landlocked East African independent republic is a member of the Commonwealth. It is mainly a savanna land, set high up on the East African Plateau. Cotton and coffee are the leading commercial crops and exports. Tea, tobacco, peanuts and corn are of lesser importance. Copper is the most valu-

able mineral in terms of both output and exports. Most trade is conducted with the United Kingdom, the USA, Japan and West Germany.

Independent Uganda was controlled by a civil government for more than eight years. Then, in 1971, the eight year rule of General Amin began. Only in early 1979 was this ended with the aid of troops from neighboring Tanzania.

Upper Volta

Formerly part of French West Africa, Upper Volta has been an independent republic since 1960. Subsistence and livestock farming are the main activities of this landlocked country. Cattle, sheep and goats are most numerous animals. Corn, sorghum, millet and peanuts are the main crops. Some cotton is grown for export. Mineral exploitation is limited by remoteness, manganese being the leading product. Her main trading partners lie in the EEC, especially France, and the USA.

Zaire

This central African republic was a large Belgian colony until 1960, called the Belgian Congo. It then became independent as Congo (Kinshasa) and changed its name to Zaire in 1972. The country centers on the extensive equatorial forests of the Congo Basin and has a short Atlantic

coastline. Subsistence and commercial farming have both declined in recent years and are now subject to a 'revival program'. Palm products, coffee, rubber, tea and timber are the main exports from the land. However, the national economy is based more on mining, mainly in the southern area of Shaba, with copper, zinc, gold and cobalt being the leading products. Copper alone accounts for 65 percent of the foreign earnings.

Zambia

Formerly known as Northern Rhodesia, this independent republic was established in 1964. It is a member of the Commonwealth. The national economy of this landlocked country rests heavily on the production of copper ore and products. Other minerals of lesser importance are zinc, cobalt and lead, as well as coal. The country also rates highly in the African development of HEP. Over 70 percent of the population live off the land, but their contribution to the national product is only 10 percent. Corn, tobacco, cotton and peanuts are the principal products. Cattle, sheep and goats are found over a wide area. Copper, copper products and tobacco are the main exports; machinery, vehicles, fuel oils, chemicals and manufactured goods the main imports. EEC and EFTA countries as well as the USA are her main trading partners.

Zimbabwe–Rhodesia

Formerly known as Southern Rhodesia, this landlocked country of southern Africa was once part of the British Empire and then Commonwealth. Currently about 277,000 of the population are white and 6,220,000 black. In 1965 its white minority government made a unilateral declaration of independence, thus effectively severing relations with the United Kingdom and the Commonwealth. Since that time, there have been various initiatives by the UK, the USA and others trying to restore constitutional government, based on some form of revised system of franchise introducing majority rule. Early in 1979 elections were held to establish the first ever parliament with a majority of black members. It remains to be seen if this settlement will be successful.

Among the leading crops grown are corn, tobacco, sugar, cotton, oranges and coffee, but since 1965 when Rhodesian international trade was made subject to United Nations sanctions, production figures have been unpublished.

1 Looking down into Ngorongoro Crater, Tanzania – one of Africa's most memorable landscapes; 2 Pigmy woman and child, Uganda – most Ugandans are of the Bantu tribe and speak Swahili; 3 Beach scene, Seychelles – a profitable tourist industry

COUNTRY REFERENCE: AFRICA

African Countries	Political Status	State Capital	Area km²	Area sq mi	Population	Population Density per km²	Population Density per sq mi	Births per Thousand Persons	Deaths per Thousand Persons	Mean Annual Percentage Increase in Population
Algeria	A	Alger	2,381,741	919,595	18,073,000	7.6	20	47.8	15.4	3.2
Angola	A	Luanda	1,246,700	481,353	7,214,000	5.8	15	47.2	24.5	1.8
Benin	A	Porto Novo	112,622	43,484	3,405,000	30	78	49.9	23.0	3.1
Botswana	A	Gaborone	600,372	231,805	718,000	1.2	3.1	45.6	23.0	3.4
Burundi	A	Bujumbura	27,834	10,747	4,003,000	144	372	48.0	24.7	2.0
Cameroon	A	Yaoundé	475,442	183,569	6,725,000	14	37	40.4	22.0	1.9
Cape Verde	A	Praia	4,033	1,557	314,000	78	202	29.2	8.8	2.1
Central African Republic	A	Bangui	622,984	240,535	1,923,000	3.1	8.0	43.4	22.5	2.2
Chad	A	Ndjamena	1,284,000	495,800	4,255,000	3.3	9.0	44.0	24.0	2.1
Comoro Islands	A	Moroni	2,079	803	314,000	151	391	46.6	21.7	3.1
Congo	A	Brazzaville	342,000	132,000	1,455,000	4.3	11	45.1	20.8	3.1
Djibouti	A	Djibouti	23,000	8,900	152,000	6.6	17	—	—	—
Egypt	A	Al-Qahirah	1,002,000	386,900	39,320,000	39	102	35.5	12.4	2.2
Equatorial Guinea	A	Malabo	28,051	10,830	325,000	12	30	36.8	19.7	1.7
Ethiopia	A	Addis Ababa	1,221,900	471,778	29,775,000	24	63	49.4	25.8	2.5
Gabon	A	Libreville	267,667	103,347	537,000	2.0	5.2	32.2	22.2	1.0
Gambia	A	Banjul	11,295	4,361	559,000	49	128	43.3	24.1	2.5
Ghana	A	Accra	238,537	92,100	10,905,000	46	118	48.9	21.9	2.7
Guinea	A	Conakry	245,857	94,926	4,695,000	19	49	46.6	22.9	2.4
Guinea-Bissau	A	Bissau	36,125	13,948	539,000	15	39	40.1	25.1	1.5
Ivory Coast	A	Abidjan	322,463	124,504	7,095,000	22	57	45.6	20.6	2.5
Kenya	A	Nairobi	582,644	224,960	14,545,000	25	65	48.7	16.0	3.6
Lesotho	A	Maseru	30,355	11,720	1,622,000	53	138	39.0	19.7	2.2
Liberia	A	Monrovia	111,369	43,000	1,810,000	16	42	49.8	20.9	2.3
Libya	A	Tarabulus	1,759,540	679,362	2,678,000	1.5	4.0	45.0	14.7	4.2
Madagascar	A	Antananarivo	587,041	226,658	8,399,000	14	37	46.0	25.0	1.5
Malawi	A	Lilongwe	118,484	45,747	5,385,000	45	118	50.5	26.5	2.5
Mali	A	Bamako	1,239,710	478,655	6,050,000	4.9	13	50.1	25.9	2.5
Mauritania	A	Nouakchott	1,030,700	397,950	1,484,000	1.4	3.7	44.8	24.9	2.7
Mauritius	A	Port Louis	2,045	789	901,000	441	1,142	25.1	8.1	1.0
Mayotte	C	Dzaoudzi	373	144	43,000	115	299	46.4	21.5	3.0
Morocco	A	Rabat	446,550	172,415	18,595,000	42	108	46.2	15.7	—
Mozambique	A	Maputo	783,763	303,771	9,745,000	12	32	43.1	20.1	2.3
Namibia	C	Windhoek	823,168	317,827	910,000	1.1	3.0	45.0	16.7	2.3
Niger	A	Niamey	1,267,000	489,200	4,925,000	3.9	10	52.2	25.5	2.7
Nigeria	A	Lagos	923,768	356,669	66,190,000	72	186	49.3	22.7	2.7
Reunion	C	Saint-Denis	2,510	969	525,000	209	542	28.1	7.1	2.4
Rwanda	A	Kigali	26,338	10,169	4,421,000	168	435	50.0	23.6	2.9
St Helena	C	Jamestown	419	162	8,000	19	49	24.9	8.1	—
Sao Tome & Principe Islands	A	Sao Tome	964	372	83,000	86	223	45.0	11.2	1.8
Senegal	A	Dakar	196,722	75,955	5,295,000	27	70	55.4	23.9	2.4
Seychelles	A	Victoria	404	156	61,000	136	352	32.8	8.8	2.8
Sierra Leone	A	Freetown	71,740	27,699	3,252,000	45	117	44.7	20.7	1.5
Somali Republic	A	Mogadisho	637,657	246,201	3,391,000	5.3	14	47.2	21.7	2.6
South Africa	A	Pretoria & Cape Town	1,222,161	471,879	27,061,000	22	57	42.9	15.5	2.6
Sudan	A	Al-Khurtum	2,505,813	967,500	16,726,000	6.7	17	47.8	17.5	2.5
Swaziland	A	Mbabane	17,366	6,705	515,000	30	77	49.0	21.8	3.1
Tanzania	A	Dar-es-Salaam	945,087	364,900	16,154,000	17	44	47.0	22.0	2.7
Togo	A	Lome	56,000	21,600	2,366,000	42	110	50.6	23.3	2.6
Tunisia	A	Tunis	164,150	63,379	5,875,000	36	93	33.9	13.8	2.4
Uganda	A	Kampala	256,886	91,076	12,521,000	53	137	45.2	15.9	3.3
Upper Volta	A	Ouagadougou	274,200	105,800	6,376,000	23	60	48.5	25.8	2.3
Zaire	A	Kinshasa	2,345,409	905,567	26,705,000	11	29	45.2	20.5	2.8
Zambia	A	Lusaka	752,614	290,586	5,406,000	7.2	19	51.5	20.3	3.3
Zimbabwe-Rhodesia	A/C	Salisbury	390,580	150,804	6,860,000	18	45	47.9	14.4	3.5
AFRICA TOTALS			30,336,232	11,704,988	429,164,000	14	37	—	—	—

2 ▽

3 ▽

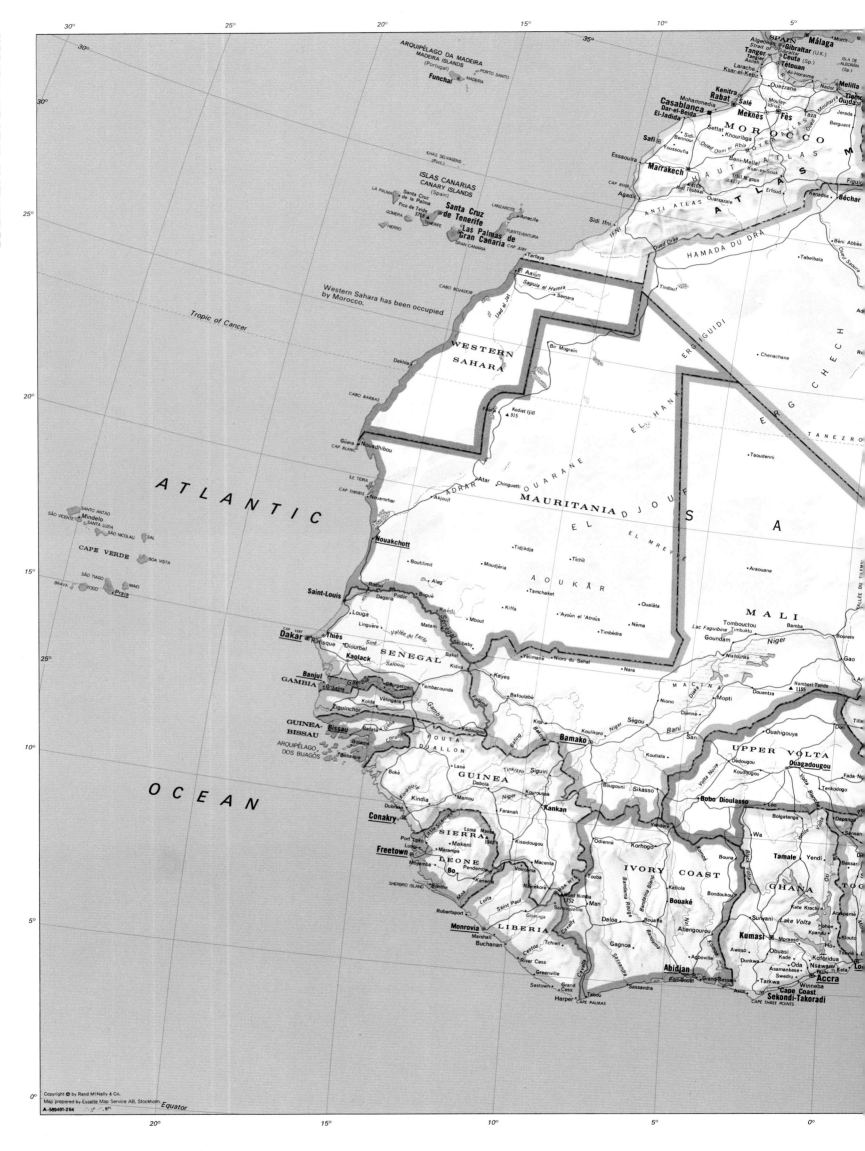

ARQUIPÉLAGO DA MADEIRA
MADEIRA ISLANDS
(Portugal)

Funchal • MADEIRA • PORTO SANTO

SPAIN
Algeciras • Gibraltar • Málaga
Tanger Gibraltar (U.K.) • Motril
Ceuta • ISLA DE ALBORÁN (Sp.)
Tétouan • Melilla
Larache • Al-Hoceima
Ksar-el-Kebir • Ouezzane • Nador • Oujda
Mohammedia • Taza • Berguent
Kenitra • Rabat • Salé • Moulay Idriss
Casablanca • MOROCCO
Dar-el-Beida • Meknès • Fès
El-Jadida • Settat • Khouribga
Safi • Youssoufia • Oued Oum er Rbia • Figuig
Essaouira • Beni-Mellal • Ifrane
Marrakech • HAUT ATLAS • Erfoud
Agadir • Jbel Toubkal • Ouarzazate • Kénadsa • Béchar

ILHAS SELVAGENS
(Port.)

ISLAS CANARIAS
CANARY ISLANDS
(Spain)
LA PALMA • Santa Cruz • LANZAROTE
Santa Cruz de Palma • de Tenerife • Arrecife
GOMERA • Pico de Teide 3718 • FUERTEVENTURA
HIERRO • TENERIFE • Las Palmas de Gran Canaria
GRAN CANARIA • CAP JUBY

ANTI ATLAS • ATLAS
CAP RHIR • Sidi Ifni • Béni Abbès
IFNI • Tabelbala
Oued Drâa
HAMADA DU DRÂA

•Tarfaya

CABO BOJADOR
El Aaiún
Saguia el Hamra
Semara • Tindouf

Western Sahara has been occupied
by Morocco.

Tropic of Cancer

Dakhla • WESTERN • Bir Mogrein • Chenachane • CHECH
SAHARA

ERG IGUIDI
CABO BARBAS

Fdérik • ERG • TANEZROUFT
• Kediet Ijill ▲ 915

Güera • Nouadhibou • EL HANK
CAP BLANC

ÎLE TIDRA
ADRAR • OUARANE
CAP TIMIRIS • Atâr • Chinguetti • DJOUF • SA
Nouâmghâr • Akjoujt • MAURITANIA • EL • A

EL MREYE
Nouakchott
• Boutilimit • EL MREYE
• Tidjikja • Tichît
• Moudjéria • Araouane
AOUKÂR
• Tamchaket
• Kiffa • Oualâta
Saint-Louis • Aleg • Bogué • Kaédi • Mbout
Dagana • Podor • • 'Ayoûn el 'Atroûs • Néma
Louga • Matam • Timbédra
CAP VERT • Linguère • Sélibaby • Lac Faguibine • Tombouctou • Bamba
Dakar • Thiès • Vallée du Ferlo • SENEGAL • Bakel • Yélimané • Timbuktu
Rufisque • Diourbel • Saloum • Kidira • Nioro du Sahel • Goundam • Niger • Gao
Kaolack • SENEGAL • Kayes • Nara • Niafunké
Banjul • Saloum • Tambacounda • Bafoulabé • MACINA • Hombori Tondo
GAMBIA • Brikama • Georgetown • Koulikoro • Niono • Mopti • ▲ 1155 • Douentza
Gambia • Kolda • Vélingara • Kédougou • Djenné • Tilb
Ziguinchor • Gabú • FOUTA • Kita • Bani • Ségou • San • Ouahigouya • Dori
GUINEA- • DJALLON • Bamako • Koutiala • UPPER VOLTA
BISSAU • Bissau • Labé • Laoé • Sikasso • Dédougou • Ouagadougou
ARQUIPÉLAGO • Bolama • Siguiri • Bougouni • Koudougou • Fada N'Gourma
DOS BIJAGÓS • Boké • Dabola • Léo • Tenkodogo
• Boffa • GUINEA • Kankan • Bolgatanga • Dapango
OCEAN • Kindia • Mamou • Kouroussa • Yandéré • Bobo Dioulasso • Wa
Conakry • Dubréka • Faranah • Odienné • Korhogo • TOGO
SIERRA • Loma Mans 1948 • Kissidougou • Bouna • Tamale • Yendi
Port Loko • Makeni • Marampa • Bondoukou • GHANA
Freetown • LEONE • Macenta • Voinama • Touba • IVORY COAST • Sunyani • Kete Krachi
Moyamba • Bo • Pendembu • Nzérékoré • Man • Katiola • Kpandu • Hohoe
SHERBRO ISLAND • Bonthe • Kenema • Mt Nimba • Bouaké • Atakpamé
• Bandama • 1752 • Bouaflé • Abengourou • KUMASI • Koforidua • Keta
Robertsport • Lofa • Sannquellie • Daloa • Gagnoa • Obuasi • Nsawam • Ada
Monrovia • LIBERIA • Gbarnga • Cavally • Bandama • Awaso • Oda • Swedru
Marshall • Buchanan • Tchien • Sassandra • Dunkwa • Asamankese • Winneba
Cestos • River Cess • Abidjan • Tarkwa • Cape Coast
River Cess • Grand Cess • Grand-Bassam • ACCRA
Greenville • Sassandra • Port-Bouet • Sekondi-Takoradi
Sastown • Tabou • CAPE THREE POINTS
Harper • CAPE PALMAS

ATLANTIC

CAPE VERDE
SANTO ANTÃO • Mindelo • SAL
SÃO VICENTE • SANTA LUZIA
SÃO NICOLAU • BOA VISTA
BRAVA • FOGO • SÃO TIAGO • MAIO
Praia

Equator

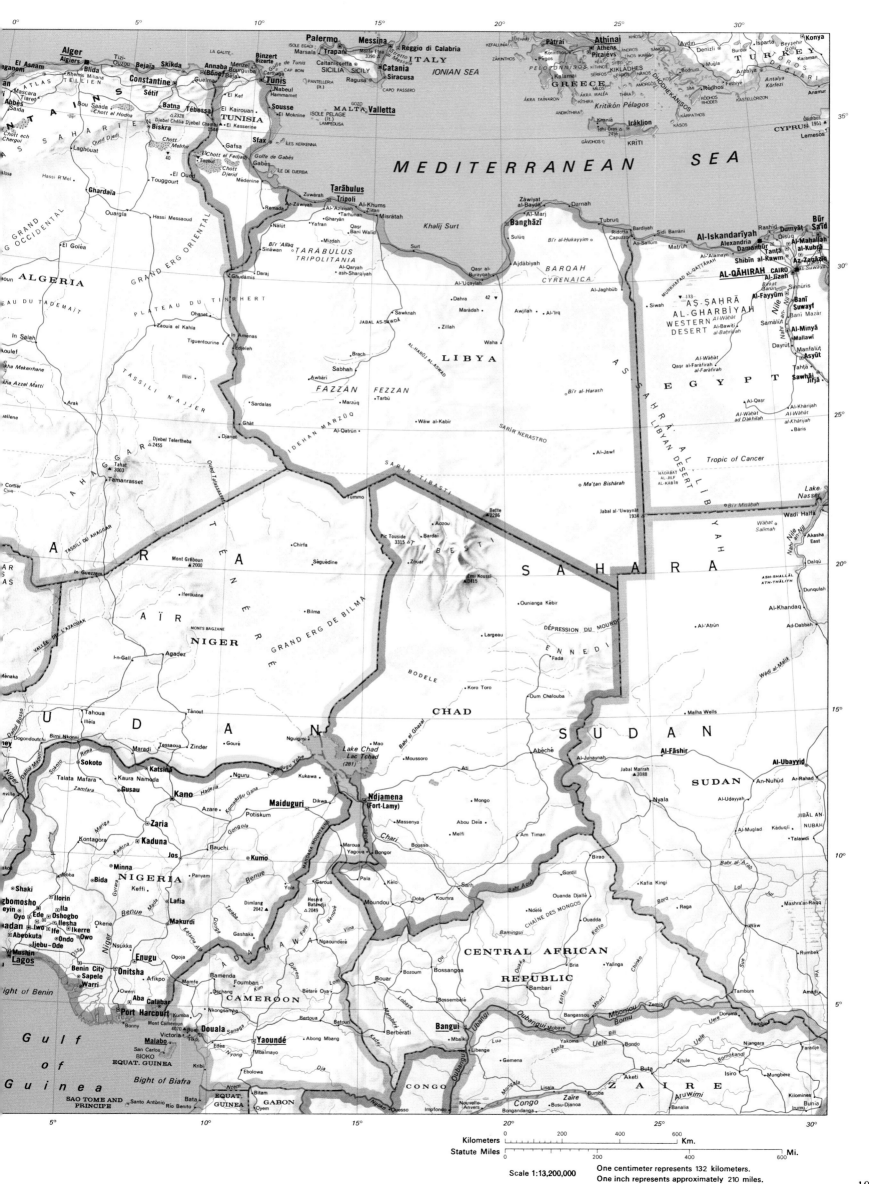

Kilometers 0 200 400 600 Km.
Statute Miles 0 200 400 600 Mi.

Scale 1:13,200,000
One centimeter represents 132 kilometers.
One inch represents approximately 210 miles.
Miller Oblated Stereographic Projection

101

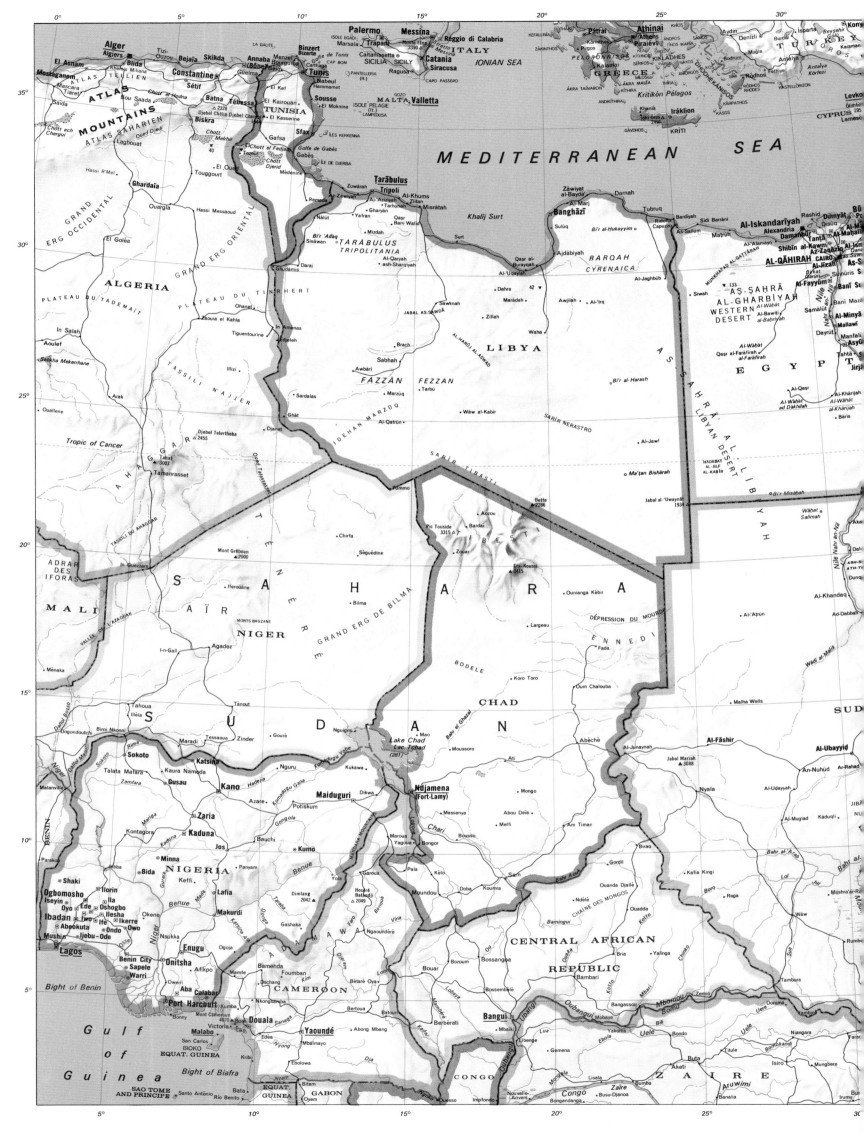

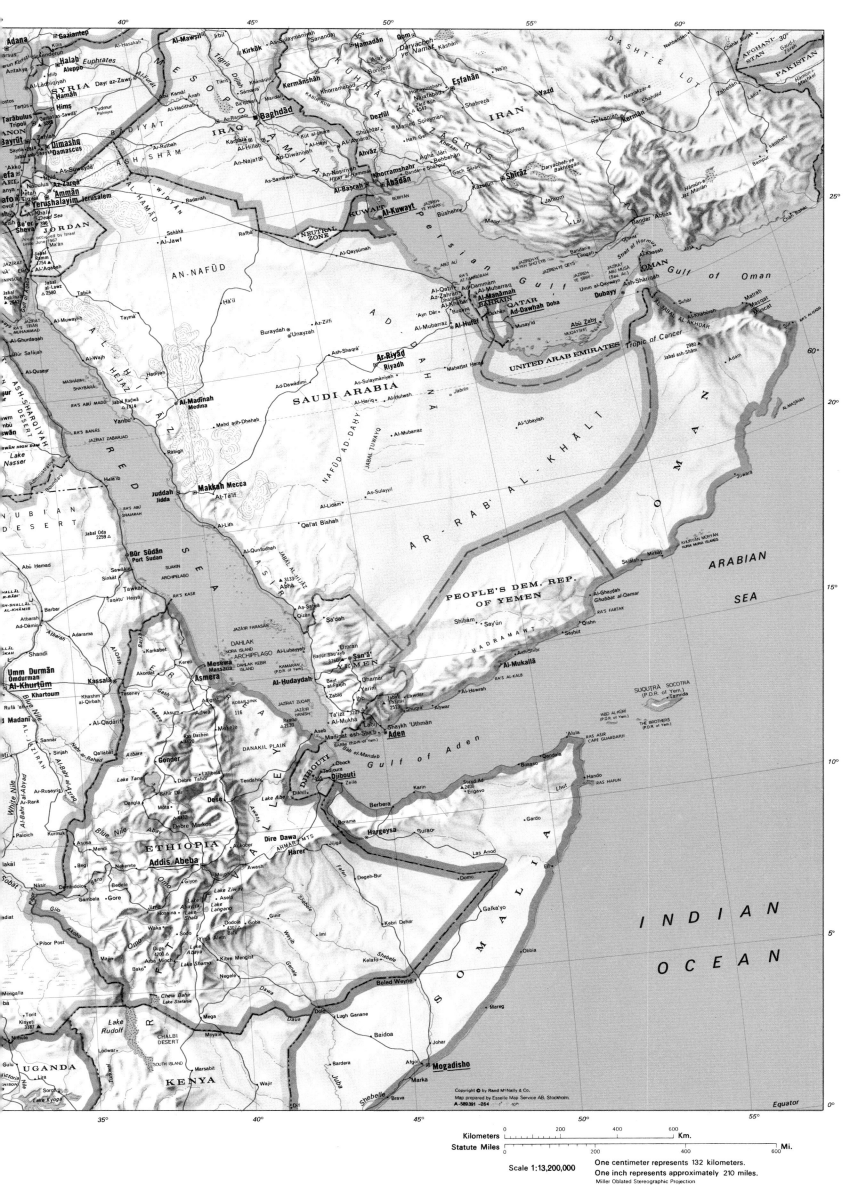

Scale 1:13,200,000

Kilometers |_____|_____|_____| Km.
0   200   400   600

Statute Miles |_____|_____| Mi.
0   200   400   600

One centimeter represents 132 kilometers.
One inch represents approximately 210 miles.
Miller Oblated Stereographic Projection

Copyright © by Rand M°Nally & Co.
Map prepared by Esselte Map Service AB, Stockholm.
A-589391 -264

103

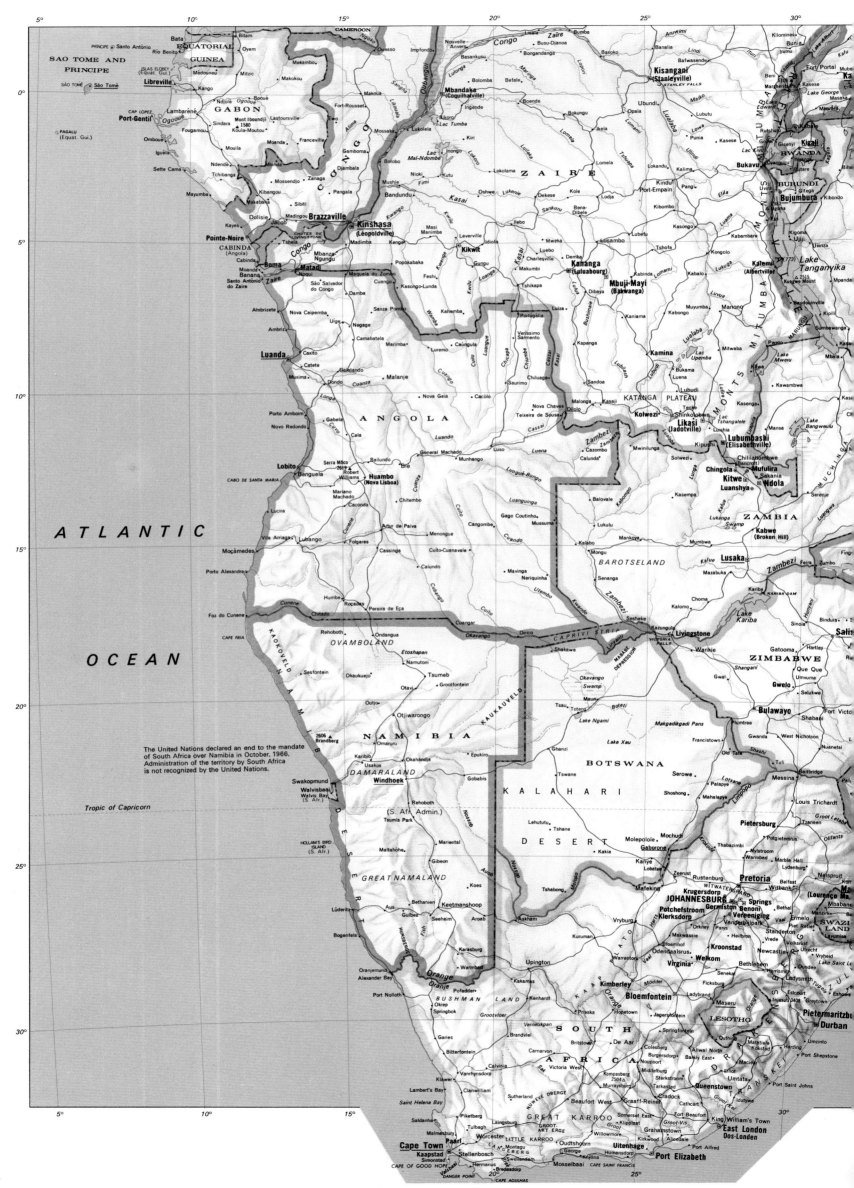

The United Nations declared an end to the mandate of South Africa over Namibia in October, 1966. Administration of the territory by South Africa is not recognized by the United Nations.

INDIAN OCEAN

Equator

SOMALIA

Shebelle Brava

Mado Gashi

Afmadu Jilib Jamame

Kismayu Jumbo

Bur Gavo

Kolbio

Garissa

Bura

KENYA

Nairobi Kitui

YATTA PLATEAU

Galana

Malindi

Kipini

PATE ISLAND Lamu

SEYCHELLES

PRASLIN ISLAND LA DIGUE

SILHOUETTE VICTORIA

MAHÉ ISLAND

Mombasa

MASAI STEPPE

Korogwe Weti PEMBA ISLAND

Tanga Chake Chake

Pangani

AMIRANTE ISLANDS (Sey.) ÎLE DESROCHES (Sey.)

PLATTE ISLAND (Sey.)

Zanzibar ZANZIBAR

Bagamoyo

Dar-es-Salaam

ULUGURU MOUNTAINS

ALPHONSE ISLAND (Sey.)

COETIVY ISLAND (Sey.)

MARIA ISLAND

Kilindoni

PROVIDENCE ISLAND (Sey.)

Kilwa Kivinje

Kilwa Kisiwani

ALDABRA ISLANDS (Sey.)

SAINT PIERRE ISLAND (Sey.)

COSMOLEDO GROUP (Sey.)

CERF ISLAND (Sey.)

Lindi

ASSUMPTION ISLAND (Sey.)

ASTOVE ISLAND (Sey.)

Mikindani

Mwara

FARQUHAR GROUP (Sey.)

CABO DELGADO Palma

AGALEGA ISLANDS (Mauritius)

Mocímboa da Praia

Ibo Quissanga

GRANDE COMORE

Moroni COMOROS

ÎLES GLORIEUSES (Fr.)

CAP D'AMBRE

Porto Amélia

Fomboni ANJOUAN

Mutsamudu

MOHÉLI

SAINT-SÉBASTIEN

CAP SAINT-SÉBASTIEN

Diégo-Suarez

Montepuez

BANC DU GEYSER

NOSY MITSIO

Namapa

MAYOTTE (Fr.)

Dzaoudzi

Ambilobe Vohémar

NOSSI-BÉ

Moçambique

Hell-Ville Ambanja

MASSIF DU TSARATANANA Maromokotro 2876

Nacala-Velha

NOSY LAVA

Analalava

Bealanana Doany Sambava

MOZAMBIQUE

Antsohihy Andapa Antalaha

Baie de Narinda

Belandriana

Baie de la Mahajamba

Majunga

Port-Bergé Sofia Maroantsetra CAP EST

Lac Kinkony PRESQU'ÎLE MASOALA

CAP SAINT-ANDRÉ

Marovoay Mampikony Mandritsara Mananara

ÎLE CHESTERFIELD

Soalala

TROMELIN (Fr.)

Besalampy

ÎLE JUAN DE NOVA (Fr.)

Tsaratanana

Maevatanana

Maintirano ÎLE SAINTE-MARIE

Tamborohano

Ambodifototra

Morafenobe

Andriamena ÎLE SAINTE-MARIE

Lac Alaotra Fénérive

ÎLES BARREN

Betsiboka

Ambatondrazaka

MADAGASCAR

Maintirano

Ankazobe

Tamatave

Tsiroanomandidy

Brickaville

Ankavandra Antananarivo

Beld

ANKARATRA

Miandrivazo Ambatolampy Vatomandry

Antsirabe

Tsiribihina Mahabo

Ambositra Mahanoro

Morondava Malaimbandy

Mandabe Ambositra Nosy Varika

Mananjary

MADAGASCAR

Mangoky Manja

Fianarantsoa

Morombe Beroroha

Ambalavao Manakara

CAP SAINT-VINCENT Ankazoabo

Port Louis Mahébourg

Curepipe MAURITIUS

Pic Boby 2658

Ihosy Manakara

Le Port Saint-Denis

Saint-Paul RÉUNION

Saint-Pierre (Fr.)

ÎLE EUROPA (Fr.)

Farafangana

MASCARENE ISLANDS

Tuléar

Betroka Vangaindrano

Betioky

Midongy Sud

Tropic of Capricorn

Bekily

Ampanihy

Androka Fort-Dauphin

Tsihombe Ambovombe

CAP SAINTE-MARIE

INDIAN OCEAN

Kilometers

0 200 400 600 Km.

Statute Miles

0 200 400 600 Mi.

Scale 1:13,200,000

One centimeter represents 132 kilometers.

One inch represents approximately 210 miles.

Miller Oblated Stereographic Projection

OCEANIA

Australia, New Zealand, Papua New Guinea and a number of island countries scattered over the south and central Pacific Ocean comprise Oceania. Together, the three named countries make up nearly 99 percent of the total land area and contain nearly 92 percent of the total population. Australia alone has over 90 percent of the land area and nearly two-thirds of the total population.

The principal Pacific islands and island groups within Oceania may be regarded in three areas, Melanesia, Micronesia and Polynesia. Occupy-ing the smallest area, Melanesia lies closest to Australia. It extends north-west to southeast from New Guinea to the Solomon Islands, New Cale-donia, New Hebrides and Fiji. Melanesia means the black isles, and these are inhabited by darkskinned peoples with short frizzy hair.

Micronesia, meaning the little isles, contains no islands as large as the main ones of Melanesia. Farther to the north, it covers a larger area of ocean. Lying more west-east, it extends from the Caroline Islands and Guam in the west to the Gilbert Islands in the east. Micronesian peoples have a dark brown skin and long straight black hair.

Polynesia covers the largest area of the three, extending from 25°N to 40°S and from 160°E to 100°W. Some of its islands are associated politically with either the USA or Chile and are described in the appropriate con-tinental sections. Polynesians are generally tall with light brown skin and black hair.

Mainly because of Oceania's frag-mented nature it is difficult to identify any unifying character. The islands comprise such a small part of the whole and, for all their wide variety of longitudinal and climatic posi-tions, have mainly simple economies. In contrast, the largest land masses had strong ties with the United Kingdom for a long time. Although Australia and New Zealand are still members of the Commonwealth, their geographical remoteness, Bri-tain's reorientated position vis-a-vis Europe and the Common Market, and the development of new resources and markets around the Pacific mean that these two countries are now reducing the proportion of their trade conducted with Europe and increasing that conducted elsewhere.

Australian Physical Profile

World Location and Size

Australia extends through nearly 3,700 km (2,300 mi) north to south, from Cape York in Queensland to South East Cape in Tasmania. Its west-east distance is similar from the Western Australia coast at 113°E near Carnarvon to the Pacific mar-gins of Queensland and New South Wales at nearly 154°E. Situated entirely in the Southern Hemisphere, it straddles the Tropic of Capricorn.

Landscape

For the most part the country is a vast undulating plateau. The great exceptions are: the eastern mountains extending from Cape York in the north to Victoria in the south, which are rarely more than 160 km (100 mi) inland from the coast and reach 2,230 m (7,316 ft) in Mount Kos-ciusko, New South Wales; the low-land area of the Central Basin extending from eastern South Aus-tralia to the Gulf of Carpentaria; and the plains which are found around most of the coast, wide in some parts like the central southern area and narrow in the extreme southeast.

Water resources are a great prob-lem in much of Australia whose rivers fall into two main types. Many comparatively short rivers flow to-ward the east coast from the divide of the Eastern Highlands, and a few in the north and the southwest are reliable in their flow. Also, parts of the interior are crossed by major river systems of which the Murray and its tributaries is the largest example. These rivers have a large discharge in their headwaters but lose much of this as they flow west-ward across the drier interior lands of the Central Basin. Parts of this area are drained by rivers which dry up in the hot season and/or only

Opposite: Expressways near the har-bor, Sydney, N S W, Australia

reach lakes whose surface areas vary greatly throughout the year.

A distinctive water feature of Australia is the series of artesian basins. In these, rainfall in the sur-rounding areas percolates under-ground and is then brought back to the surface through man-made bore-holes. The Great Artesian Basin underlies much of western Queens-land, northeast South Australia and northwest New South Wales, extend-ing for 1,554,000 km² (600,000 sq mi). Farther south the Murray River Basin occupies a smaller area. West-ern Australia also has four smaller basins around its coastal margins.

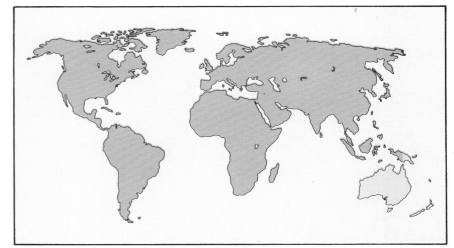

Climatic Background

There are three main groups of climate present in Australia. Only the temperate humid climate is at all attractive to white settlers who are found only in limited parts of the country. Nowhere in the temperate areas does the average temperature of the coldest winter month, July, fall below freezing, and in summer the averages rise above 18°C (64°F), reaching above 22°C (72°F) in places. The extreme southwest of Western Australia has a Mediterranean type of climate with summer temperatures reaching the higher levels and a marked lack of summer rain.

Farther east, in southern South Australia and parts of western Vic-toria, similar summer temperatures are experienced and the rainfall, mainly in the winter, is greater. Still in the temperate group, the east coast climate, from Tasmania to the central Queensland area, shows more even distribution of rainfall in the south to a summer maximum north of the tropic. In the south, the highest monthly average temperatures are below 20°C (68°F) but in the north they are well above 22°C (72°F).

The northern coastal areas of the country experience tropical climates in which even the coolest month has an average temperature above 18°C (64°F) and there is a marked summer maximum in the rainfall, totals exceeding 2,000 mm (80 in) in places.

The great heartland of Australia,

Rain forest village, Malekula, New Hebrides – like many of the Pacific islands, this group is of volcanic ori-gins. Most places have over 2,250 mm (90 in) of rain a year, with high tem-peratures giving humid conditions

from the Indian Ocean in the west, eastward to the interior slopes of the Highlands of the Pacific border-ing states, is an area of marked rain-fall deficiency with higher average temperatures than elsewhere in the continent. In the most arid central parts, precipitation rarely exceeds 250 mm (10 in), the summer tempera-ture may reach 27°C (80°F), and in the winter drops only to 12°C (54°F). Around the margins, less extreme climates may be found.

OCEANIA

Historical and Political Background

Situated on the opposite side of the globe from Europe, this part of the world was among the last places to be visited by the 'Old World' explorers. In 1606 Dutch navigators landed on the north coast and the Cape York Peninsula. Little impressed by the hot lands, the Dutch took no further interest in this area which they called New Holland. Some 82 years later, the English explorer William Dampier reached the barren wastes of the northwest coast, and reported unenthusiastically of his finds on his return home.

Only in 1770 were the more inviting parts of southeast Australia discovered by Captain Cook who first sailed to Tahiti and New Zealand before reaching the coasts of what are now New South Wales and Queensland. Cook laid formal claim to this land for the British crown and reported enthusiastically on its potential when he returned home.

However, interest in this distant land did not grow until after Britain had lost her American colonies a few years later. The earliest settlement centered on Port Jackson, which has subsequently developed into the large city of Sydney. For the first thirty years or so the Blue Mountains presented an impenetrable barrier to westward expansion. Then, in 1813, a route was pioneered to the rich plains of the interior, and very soon development of the plain around Bathurst and the Darling Downs country farther north began.

During the first half of the nineteenth century many new settlements were established: Tasmania in 1803, Brisbane in 1824, the Swan River colony in the distant southwest in 1829, Melbourne in 1835 and Adelaide in 1836. At about the same time, despite domination by the original settlement in New South Wales, separate provinces or colonies were being established; Tasmania (1825), Western Australia (1831), South Australia (1834), Victoria (1851), Queensland (1859). By 1850 the population had risen to just over 400,000. But it was not until the early 1860s, when the population had risen to over 1 million, that the first south-north crossing of the country was made.

The initial attraction of the new lands was for farming. Merino sheep from Spain soon flourished there and produced the world's finest wool. Also, in 1851, mineral prospecting received a great lift with the discovery of gold at Bathurst, and nearly ten years later in Western Australia.

By the end of the century, when the separate colonies federated to become the Commonwealth of Australia under the British crown, the population had risen to 3.7 million. From that time it grew steadily by natural increase and further immigration; in 1940 it was 7 million, in 1960 it was 10.2 million and now it is over 13.6 million.

The indigenous population of Australia are the Aborigines, who came originally by sea from southeast Asia. Their forebears probably arrived about 16,000 years ago. They now number about 40,000 and live mainly on special reserves.

Today the six original colonies have been added to by the creation of the Northern Territory and the Australian Capital Territory of Canberra. These eight constitute an independent federal country which is a member of the Commonwealth. As one of the most developed countries in its area it also plays a leading part in a number of organizations for collective development and security, such as the Colombo Plan Countries and SEATO.

Industry, Commerce and Communications

Prior to World War II Australia was essentially a primary producer, exporting agricultural products and some raw materials, largely to countries within the then British Empire and Commonwealth, and importing most of her manufactured needs. Since then a wide range of manufacturing industries have been developed so that today the Australian economy is far more balanced. The main centers of these industries are near to the coasts especially around the major cities and towns of the southeast, from Adelaide to Brisbane, and in the extreme southwest of the country.

The present labor force, excluding those in agriculture, is about 4.75 million. Of these, 1.2 million are employed in manufacturing, 0.95 million in wholesale and retail trade, 1.6 million in public services such as administration, community service, health and education and 0.35 million in transport industries.

Australia's communications networks are best developed in the east and the southwest. Roads have been developed right around the coasts; Victoria, New South Wales and Queensland are well served but south-north routes across the heart of the country are few. Likewise, railroads link Western Australia across the Nullarbor Plain with South Australia then on into Victoria, New South Wales and Queensland, but the line from Adelaide to Darwin has never been completed. In recent years isolated lines serving the rich iron ore fields of the northwest have been constructed to the nearest harbors. Aircraft are of considerable use in Australia, both city to city and city to 'the outback' – the remote areas, popularly exemplified by the Flying Doctor Service. Remote parts also find the radio a great boon for communication. For example, Australia

1 Sheepshearing, Australia; 2 The Southern Alps, South Island, New Zealand; 3 Native dancers, Suva, Fiji, southwest Pacific; 4 Herd of cattle crossing the Davidson river, Tully, Queensland, Australia

uses the radio as an educational aid for families in the outback.

Agriculture, Forestry and Fishing

In their natural state the Australian native forests are principally hardwoods. Over 90 percent of those forests are comprised of the distinctive Eucalypts, popularly known as 'gum trees'. These range in form from the 100 m (330 ft) tall giant trees of the dense forests of the southeast to the shrublike form of the mallee extending across south central Australia. Broadly, the natural vegetation of the country is densest in the southwest, the east and the north. Farther inland, grass becomes increasingly important as the mulga and other acacias grow ever more thinly over the ground. Ultimately the arid heart of the country is true sand desert.

First and foremost, Australian farming is based on animals. There are nearly 150 million sheep here, more than in any other country, being some 15 percent of the total world population. These produce over 750 thousand tons of greasy wool each year, about 30 percent of the world total. This represents the best yield per animal anywhere in the world. Individually, only the USSR and China produce more mutton and lamb. Australia also has over 33 million head of cattle, nearly 3 per-

cent of the world total. Beef raising is more important than dairying, and the country is the world's seventh largest beef producer.

Today the richest areas for crop farming are in the best watered parts of the interior eastern plains, the lower parts of the great Murray-Darling river basin and the southern parts of South Australia, most of Victoria and parts of southwest Western Australia. Australia ranks highly in the production of cereals. Wheat, grown in the better watered parts of the temperate south, is the foremost example. In all some 12 million tons are produced each year, that is about three-quarters of the French output and more than twice that of the United Kingdom. Barley and oats are also grown in the temperate parts. In each of these crops, Australia ranks among the top fifteen world producers.

Tropical Queensland is a major producer of sugarcane, Australia being ninth in this world table. Nearly 24 million tons, 3.5 percent of the world's output, is grown here. However, Australia plays a very limited part in the growing of other tropical crops. By contrast, temperate fruits and grape growing have been fairly extensively developed. Australia, especially Tasmania, produces 1.5 percent of the world's apples (324,000 tons). Over 2 percent of the world's pears and 1.3 percent of the

world's grapes are grown in the south-east.

Australia does not rank highly in fishing, though it is the world's fifth largest whaling nation. A range of timber is also produced in modest quantities, particularly in the southeast and Tasmania.

Natural Resources

Modern Australian expansion has grown outward from the temperate lands of the south. Initially, the land resources and farming potential were most valued in the east as well as southwest, but then the gold, coal and iron ore resources were realized. More recently as the land has been more extensively surveyed and explored, far richer reserves of iron ore have been proven in the drier areas and the tropical north, as well as a large range of other minerals.

In world terms, Australia is a comparatively modest bituminous coal producer. From the fields of eastern New South Wales, annual output is now approaching 75 million tons per year. Assessing this figure in terms of population rather than area, it places Australia quite high in the world tables. The same applies to lignite production, with Victoria's rich deposits now yielding over 31 million tons per year.

Australian crude oil production is now increasing steadily, with the

fields off the southeast coast being most significant. The annual output of 20 million tons is less than 0.75 percent of the world total but puts Australia eighteenth in the world table. Natural gas production, currently around 6,000 million cubic meters per year is also increasing. Perhaps more interestingly, uranium production is as yet very small but it is estimated that over one-fifth of the world's reserves lie in the extreme Northern Territory and in the west of Queensland. Southeast Australia is also an area of considerable HEP potential, exemplified by the Snowy Mountains scheme. As yet less than a fifth of this has been harnessed, but that alone provides more than one-fifth of the country's total electricity needs.

Within the last two decades Australia's iron ore production has been dramatically increased by opening up the resources of arid Western Australia. The fields of South Australia and southern Western Australia once supplied only Australia's needs, but now the country is the world's second largest producer, mining about 60 million tons (iron content) per year, much of which is exported to Japan. Present known reserves are only 6.4 percent of the world total but it is likely that further fields will be discovered in the drier areas.

One of the world's richest deposits

Agriculture, particularly raising sheep, is the prime Australian occupation, but important mineral deposits have created industry and a large urban population: 1 Harvesting sugarcane, Rocky Point, Queensland – this is the main crop of the eastern region of the second largest state; 2 Boning meat, Rockhampton, Queensland – like the state capital, Brisbane, this large port has important packing houses and exports meat products; 3 Blast furnaces at the AIS plant, Port Kembla, New South Wales – iron and steel works predominate in this industrial center; 4 Zinc and phosphate works, Derwent river, Tasmania – the island has large mineral resources, including zinc and copper, and metals are its leading exports, ahead of newsprint and paper products from its forestry industry

Total Imports and Exports
(1975 figures in millions of U.S. dollars)

Australia and New Zealand dominate Oceania's world trade. The islands' figures are all low. Overall there is a visible balance of payments deficit.

	Imports	Exports
Australia	9,811	11,575
Fiji	268	159
New Caledonia	348	289
New Zealand	3,152	2,152
Papua New Guinea	483	475

OCEANIA

of bauxite has been developed in the Cape York Peninsula within the last twenty years. Smaller fields in the Northern Territory and southwest Western Australia have also been opened up. Collectively these make Australia the world's most important producer of this ore with 21 million tons, over 29 percent of the world's annual output.

Australia contributes variously to the world production of other mineral ores. She is the third largest producer of lead, mining 391 thousand tons (lead content) per year, i.e. 12 percent of the world total, largely from the Broken Hill area of New South Wales and from western Queensland. Largely from the same two areas comes nearly 8 percent of the world's zinc, of which Australia is again the third most important world producer. Nickel production of 75 thousand tons nickel content, just under 10

percent of the world total, puts Australia in fourth position in this world table. The country's output of some other resources is summarized in the table below:

The Australian Economy

Taken as a single unit the population density of Australia is extremely low, being only 1.8 per km² (4.6 per sq mi) No other large country in the world which includes areas developed along western industrial lines has so low an average figure. Well over 80 percent of the country has fewer than 1 person per km² (2.5 per sq mi) while only a few very limited areas around the state capitals have densities in excess of 100 per km² (250 per sq mi).

By far the largest state capitals are Sydney (3,155,200) and Melbourne (2,717,600). These are the only two million-plus metro areas in the land, though Brisbane, Adelaide and Perth now have populations in excess of three-quarters of a million people.

Ore	Average Annual World Production (million tons)	Australia's Share (percent)
cobalt	0.03	3
copper	7.4	3
gold	1 million kg	2
manganese	22.8	7
silver	0.01	8
tin	0.2	4
tungsten	0.036	3

Taken as a whole, Australia's population is growing at a rapid rate by most western standards. This is partly due to the continuing policy of attracting new settlers, mainly from Europe. Each year some 120–140,000 new migrants are attracted to the country and perhaps 100–115,000 earlier arrivals and others leave. But Australia also has a higher birth rate than many western countries, 17.2 per 1,000 overall, which is far higher than the typical death rate for a 'developed' country of 8.1 per 1,000. There are some marked regional and state differences lying behind the overall growth rate which currently runs at about 1.6 percent per year; Queensland's and Western Australia's populations are rising at much faster rates than any other parts of Australia.

With the growth of her agricultural, mining and other industrial activities in the last twenty years, Australia has moved from a position of deficit in her visible trade to one of surplus. Whereas in 1938 imports and exports were $517 million and $518 million respectively, by 1958 they were $1,776 million and $1,660 million, and by 1975, $9,811 million and $11,575 million. Imports had risen by 2.43 and 4.52 times and exports by 2.20 and 5.97 times. Clearly the last figure, though not as high as some seen in other parts of the world, is the most remarkable

index of the country's growth within the last twenty years.

Over the period 1960–'74 Australia's per capita incomes rose from $1,438 to $5,884, a rise of 309 percent. This very high figure is marginally better than that for Europe as a whole and far better than that for the whole non-Communist world for the same period.

Australia had an agreeable energy surplus in 1975 with 111.05 million tons coal equivalent (mtce) produced and only 87.56 mtce consumed. The latter figure indicates a per capita consumption of 6,485 kg/ca, comparable with the highest figure for individual European countries, but far lower than those for the USA and Canada.

Australia, which in certain parts displays many characteristics of a well developed country, has an expanding economy. As a country with net immigration it is attracting young people with growing families, and its age pyramid is thus weighted in the younger age groups. In more than one sense this is a country with plenty of youthful energy.

With its wide natural resource base, its growing contacts with other transpacific countries and its traditional links with the Commonwealth, Australia is well set to play an increasingly important part in the world's market and political meeting places.

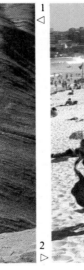

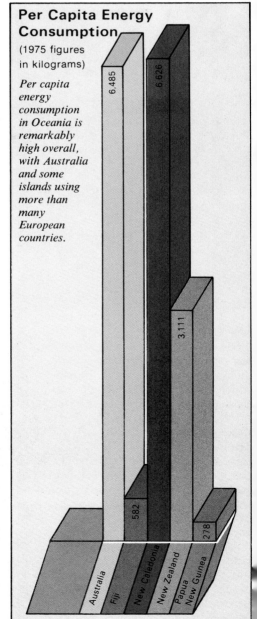

Per Capita Energy Consumption
(1975 figures in kilograms)

Per capita energy consumption in Oceania is remarkably high overall, with Australia and some islands using more than many European countries.

6,485		6,626		
			3,111	
Australia	Fiji 582	New Caledonia	New Zealand	Papua New Guinea 278

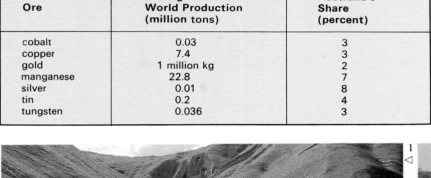

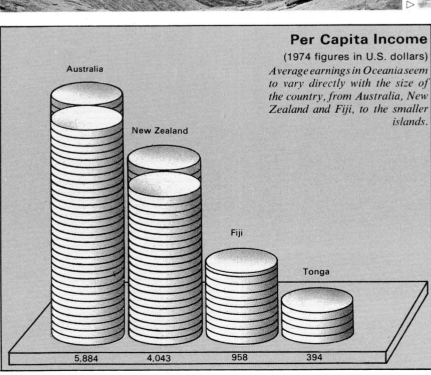

Per Capita Income
(1974 figures in U.S. dollars)

Average earnings in Oceania seem to vary directly with the size of the country, from Australia, New Zealand and Fiji, to the smaller islands.

Australia — 5,884
New Zealand — 4,043
Fiji — 958
Tonga — 394

With such a large land mass, extending through a range of latitudes, Australia is a land of extremes in terrain and climate: 1 Ayers Rock, Northern Territory – part monsoon area with grasslands, forests and swamps, and part desert, these central and northern regions are inhabited by the country's largest number of native aborigines who are mainly nomadic herdsmen, many preferring to resettle their old tribal homelands instead of living in the special reserves set aside for them with health and educational facilities; 2 Bondi Beach, Sydney, New South Wales – perhaps the most famous worldwide, this is just one of the fine beaches and vacation areas to the east of the state capital

Oceanian Countries

Australia

Australian Capital Territory

An area of federal territory within New South Wales was demarcated in 1911 and the federal capital of Canberra established. The city with its provision for central government and administration was developed in the 1920s after World War I. Today the area is almost entirely devoted to government and tertiary services.

New South Wales

Today only the fifth largest Australian state, New South Wales has the highest population of any in the federation. Economically it has a broad base. The most important crops are wheat, barley, hay, rice and oats, while the numbers of sheep, lambs and pigs are the highest, and the cattle population the second highest, for any state. Most of Australia's coal is mined here. Silver, lead and zinc are the other leading minerals. One of Australia's most established centers of iron and steel production is located in New South Wales, and a wide range of manufacturing industries are to be found in the Sydney area. The Blue Mountains have developed as a major tourist area.

Northern Territory

The third largest constituent part of modern Australia is largely desert waste with a northern belt of tropical lands. Overall it is the most inhospitable part of the whole country. Its development is so limited that it still rates only as a territory, not a state. Agricultural research and development is slow. Mineral resources offer a brighter economic prospect, all extracted products being shipped either to other parts of Australia or abroad. Bauxite is currently most valuable, followed by manganese. Iron, lead, zinc and rich deposits of uranium have yet to be effectively developed. This is the area in which most of the Aborigine Reserves have been established.

Queensland

Now the second largest state in the federation, Queensland today has the third largest population, most of which is found on the coastal fringes, especially in the southeast corner. As the northernmost of the tier of states, in the climatically appealing east of the country, Queensland extends to tropical latitudes. It has a distinctive range of crops. Wheat, barley, hay and potatoes are the major temperate crops, and sugar cane, sorghum, pineapples, corn, citrus fruit, peanuts and cotton are important tropical crops. Queensland has more cattle than any other state, and the second highest number of pigs but comparatively few sheep. Bauxite mining in the extreme north is a most valuable part of the economy; coal, copper, silver and lead are also important. Tourism centers on its expansive beaches and the Great Barrier Reef with its attractive coral features and tropical fish.

South Australia

With the bulk of its population clustered in the southeast corner, this is both the fourth largest and the fourth most heavily populated state. Economically it has a broad though somewhat limited base. Farming in the comparatively dry areas depends on careful soil conservation and irrigation. Wheat and barley are the major cereals; temperate and citrus fruit farming is a distinctive activity, as is grape growing and wine making. South Australia's mineral output includes iron ore, lead, copper and gypsum. Metal processing, car manufacturing, ship building and food processing are the most important industries.

Tasmania

This smallest Australian state also has the lowest population total. Its agricultural activities are varied, with hay, potatoes and barley as the major crops. Sheep, cattle and pigs are all found throughout the island. Iron ore, coal, zinc and copper as well as silver and gold are all mined. This state of fast-flowing rivers has large HEP installations, most valuable for the refining of aluminium. Forestry is of especial importance, newsprint and other paper products being second only to metals as exports.

Victoria

This is next to the smallest of the six original colonies which federated in 1901, yet it has the second highest population today. Together with parts of New South Wales, South Australia and the island of Tasmania, it is climatically most akin to the home countries of the European settlers. Economically, agriculture is the most important activity. Wheat, hay and barley are the leading crops. Vegetables and fruit farming are also important. The numbers of sheep, cattle and pigs are each third largest for any Australian state and, for the area of this state, very large indeed. Victoria has modest reserves of gold and lignite, and is now the country's leading producer of both crude oil and natural gas. There are also large valuable forests. The Greater Melbourne area is a major focus for industries, especially textiles, petrochemicals, aluminum refining, car manufacturing and food processing.

Western Australia

Australia's largest state comprises so much arid land that the country's fifth highest state population is mainly clustered in the southwest corner, some 2,000 km (1,300 mi) from the nearest large concentration of people around Adelaide in South Australia. Farming is of great importance in the southwest where wheat is the major crop, with hay, barley and oats of lesser significance. Temperate fruit farming and, farther north, orange growing are also important. Only New South Wales has more sheep and lambs. Cattle and pigs play a smaller part. Traditionally, Western Australia mining was dominated by gold but in recent years iron ore, bauxite and now crude oil and natural gas production have assumed far greater significance. New processing plants for these raw materials have developed quickly.

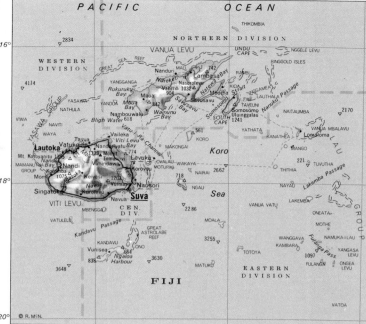

New Zealand: 1 Mt Egmont, 2,518 m (8,260 ft) and farmlands from Tariki, Taranaki, North Island – some 90 percent of the country's all-important dairy cattle graze on the island's lowlands; 2 Aerial view of Queenstown, South Island – on the shores of the beautiful Lake Wakatipu this tourist town is well placed for exploring the area; 3 Bora Bora, Tahiti Viti Levu and Vanua Levu are the two largest islands of Fiji, Oceania's fourth largest country. They lie on the Pacific Ring of Fire

Oceanian Countries

American Samoa

The Samoan Islands are a Polynesian group approximately midway between Australia and Hawaii. The eastern islands have been an unincorporated territory of the USA since 1900. A wide range of tropical crops are grown but little is exported. Fishing, especially for tuna, is more important, providing the major export item. Other exports include pet foods and native crafts. Major imports include building materials, rice, sugar and fuel oils.

Cook Islands

Lying fairly widely scattered some 3,000 km (1,900 mi) northeast of New Zealand in the Polynesian islands of the southwest Pacific, the Cook Islands are mainly of volcanic origin. First discovered in 1773 by

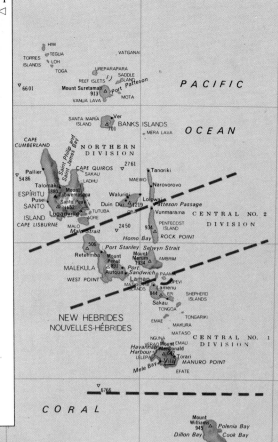

activity and sugar exports produce over 60 percent of foreign earnings. Copra, ginger and gold are the other main exports. Fiji's animal farming is expanding rapidly, and forestry and tourism are being developed systematically.

French Polynesia

Scattered over a wide area in the eastern Pacific, since 1958 the islands of French Polynesia have enjoyed the status of an overseas territory within the French Community. Local

Australia: 1 Aborigine, Wessel Islands – Stone Age arts are practiced by the country's oldest inhabitants; 2 Todd River, Alice Springs, Northern Territory, situated in the remote dry heart of Australia

New Caledonia and New Hebrides: both these groups of islands within Melanesia, are of volcanic origins

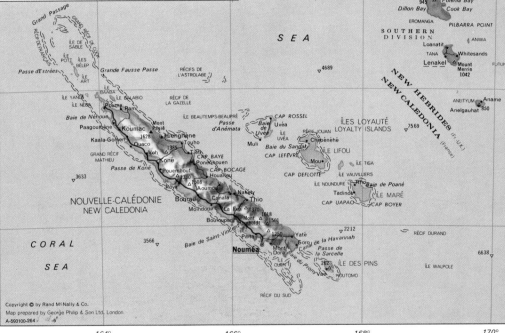

Captain Cook, they were made a British protectorate in 1888 and a New Zealand territory in 1901. Since 1965 they have enjoyed internal self-government. Well over half the population live on the island of Rarotonga (see map p.114); 13 other islands are peopled, the most important being those in the south of the group. Major exports are citrus fruits, bananas, copra and pearl shells.

Fiji

Comprising nearly 850 Melanesian islands in the southwest Pacific, Fiji is the fourth most heavily populated country in Oceania, and the most populated of all the island groups. Today only about 42 percent of the people are of Melanesian descent, with over 50 percent being of Indian origin. A British colony for nearly 100 years, Fiji became independent in 1970, and remains a member of the Commonwealth. Sugarcane growing is the prime

government is thus in the hands of an island-elected assembly under the presidency of an appointed governor. The islands also send representatives to the French Assemblies in Paris. The five groups in the political unit are the Pacific Windward Islands and Leeward Islands (together called the Society Islands), the Tuamotu, the Tubuai Islands and the Marquesas Islands. The economies are essentially agricultural and tourist based. Chief exports are copra, coffee, citrus fruit, vanilla and mother of pearl.

The Gilbert Islands

This larger part of the former British colony of the Gilbert and Ellice Islands also includes Phoenix and Line Islands. They achieved internal self-government in 1976 and full independence nearly three years later, remaining within the Commonwealth. Most of the islands are atolls – Christmas Island is the world's largest atoll – and have very little soil. Only coconuts grow read-

ily; copra and the highly valuable deposits of phosphates form the bases of the national economy.

Guam

This largest and most southerly island in the Marianas Archipelago of Micronesia, is an outlying yet unincorporated territory of the USA, ceded from Spain in 1898. It is the USA's most westerly Pacific outpost and is of major strategic importance both as a naval and air base. About a quarter of the present population are US service personnel and their families. The native population is mainly of Malay origin. Agriculture concentrates on corn, sweet potatoes, cassava, bananas, citrus fruit and vegetable growing, as well as pig and cattle raising and poultry farming.

Nauru

A tiny Micronesian coral island approximately 20 km (12 mi) in cir-

cumference, Nauru's core contains extensive deposits of high grade phosphates, the country's sole export. Foodstuffs and raw materials for the phosphate industry are the main imports. The island was a German colony from 1888–1914, a British colony from 1920–1947, a joint (Australia, New Zealand, United Kingdom) trusteeship territory till 1968, and is now an independent republic which has a special relationship with the Commonwealth.

New Caledonia

The largest volcanic island in Melanesia with a number of small dependencies, New Caledonia is a French overseas territory. Local government is in the hands of an appointed High Commissioner and an island-elected council and territorial assembly. Representatives are also sent to the French Assemblies in Paris. The chief crops produced are coffee, copra, corn and vegetables. The main island is far more important for its mineral production, especially a rich nickel deposit.

New Hebrides

This group of Melanesian islands between New Caledonia and Fiji is politically unique in that, since 1906, it has been an Anglo-French condominium. The islands are a dependent territory whose external administration is shared between London and Paris. Copra, cocoa and coffee are exported. Rich manganese deposits have been developed recently and are now the major export item.

New Zealand

First discovered by Tasman in 1642, New Zealand comprises two main islands plus a number of smaller ones. In 1840, after a period in which Australians had used some of the anchorages for whaling and trading, a treaty was signed with the native Maoris whereby the country became a British colony. The next 30 years were punctuated with misunderstanding and occasional conflict between the British settlers and the Maoris, but peace has reigned for the past 100 years and more. Since 1907 New Zealand has been independent and is a member of the Commonwealth. It is today one of the most successful plural societies in the world.

The two main islands extend from 34°S to 47°S, a distance of nearly 1,500 km (930 mi) and are separated by the Cook Strait. Both islands are mountainous, the South Island having the Southern Alps running northeast to southwest through its whole length, and rising to 3,764 m (12,349 ft) in Mount Cook. The North Island is volcanic, having both active and extinct cones as well as the famous hot springs and geysers. Mount Ruapehu, still active, rises to 2,797 m (9,175 ft). The most extensive lowland area of the country is the Canterbury Plains on the east side of the South Island.

New Zealand's climates are humid temperate and in many respects are similar to those of the British Isles, especially in the South Island. North Island is a fraction warmer with no single monthly average temperature being below 6°C (43°F). Precipitation totals, which are higher in the mountains, reach 625–1,000 mm (25–40 in) in the eastern parts of South Island and up to 1,250 mm (50 in) in the lowlands of North Island.

The New Zealand economy has been dominated by agriculture, especially pastoral farming, throughout this century. Yet, in recent years, the imbalance of the economy has improved as a range of manufacturing industries have been developed. In a country of nearly 10 million cattle and over 56 million sheep, animal farming is still the backbone of the economy. New Zealand is fourth in the world sheep table with 5.4 percent. She produces 12 percent of the world's wool, too.

Food processing is still the most valuable manufacturing industry; for example, 41 percent of the world's butter and 7 percent of its lamb/mutton comes from here. Textiles, metal fabrication, transport equipment, wood and cork processing, paper making, chemical production and boot and shoe making are the leaders in the growing list of other manufacturing industries. New Zealand is ill-endowed with minerals; there is some coal in both islands and natural gas is extracted in North Island. Both islands have developed a considerable capacity for HEP.

Something like 80 percent of all New Zealand exports are related to agriculture with wool, lamb, beef and butter being the four most valuable items. The list of imports is headed by fuel oils, machinery, transport equipment, textiles, chemicals and raw materials. Australia, the UK, the USA and Japan are the main trading partners.

Niue

Geographically within the Cook Islands, Niue's area is more than that of all the other islands in that group together, but its population is far smaller. It achieved separate internal self-government within the New Zealand overseas territories in 1974 but its economy depends heavily upon aid from the mother country. Copra, sweet potatoes and bananas are the main products.

Norfolk Island

An Australian territory 1,400 km (900 mi) east of the New South Wales coast and 700 km (450 mi) northwest of New Zealand, this was originally used as a penal settlement when, in 1856, the 194 *Bounty* descendants moved from Pitcairn at their own request. Today the attractions of the scenery, beaches and climate have led to the development of a large tourist industry. Most foodstuffs have to be imported.

Pacific Island Trust Territory (US)

Following World War II the USA was appointed by the United Nations to act as trustee of all former Japanese mandated islands in the Pacific between 1° and 22°N, and 130° and 172°E. These Micronesian islands, over 2,100 atolls and smaller islands of which only 96 are inhabited, are mainly in the Caroline, Marshall and Marianas Groups. Some 1,857 km² (717 sq mi) of land are scattered over 8 million km² (3 million sq mi) of ocean. Each district has its own elected local government, while an elected Congress of Micronesia exercises 'federal' control.

Papua New Guinea

For nearly a hundred years the territories of Papua and New Guinea (other than the Netherlands western part which is regarded as part of Asia) were administered variously by Australia and the United Kingdom. Since 1975 the combined areas have been a fully independent state within the Commonwealth. A consistent trading deficit has been converted to a large surplus each year since 1970 by the rapid development of rich copper deposits. Copra and coffee are the next most important exports. Foodstuffs, machinery and manufactured goods are the major imports.

Pitcairn Island

Pitcairn lies approximately midway between New Zealand and Panama, in Polynesia. Its original inhabitants in 1767 were 9 mutineers from the *Bounty* and 18 Tahitians. In 1856 the population of 194 moved to Norfolk Island, but 43 returned soon afterward. Today the population is about 100 and is declining. Since 1898 the island has been an official British dependency; currently the British High Commissioner in New Zealand is the Governor.

Solomon Islands

Comprising one of the largest island groups in Melanesia in the southwest Pacific, to the east of New Guinea, the Solomons became a British Protectorate in the 1890s and achieved independence in 1977. The larger islands are mountainous and heavily forested. Coconuts, copra and rice are the most important crops and forestry is of growing importance.

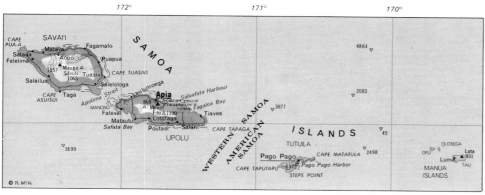

1 Growing copra in the Cook Islands – this crop is the coral islands' main export; 2 Ngauruhoe volcano, North Island, New Zealand – one of three active volcanoes in the Tongariro National Park; 3 Band playing during a carnival on Tutuila – the largest island of Pago Pago, American Samoa

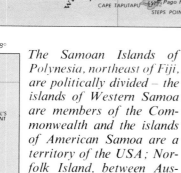

The Samoan Islands of Polynesia, northeast of Fiji, are politically divided – the islands of Western Samoa are members of the Commonwealth and the islands of American Samoa are a territory of the USA; Norfolk Island, between Australia and New Zealand, is a popular vacation spot

Oceanian Countries

Copra, timber, fish products and cocoa are the leading exports. The major imports are machinery, fuels and nontropical foodstuffs.

Tokelau Islands

These are three Polynesian atolls some 480 km (300 mi) north of Western Samoa. Once part of the Gilbert and Ellice Islands, they have been directly associated with New Zealand since 1926. The economic base of the islands is very insecure and the population rely heavily on that country's aid. Since 1965 there has been a government scheme to resettle many of the population on the New Zealand mainland.

Tonga

About 150 coral and volcanic islands due east of Fiji comprise Tonga. The 'Friendly Islands' are distinctive in that they are a long-standing monarchy, the present monarch being King Taufa'ahau Tupou IV, son of Queen Salote Tupou III. A British protectorate from 1900 to 1970, it has since been an independent member of the Commonwealth. Local agriculture concentrates almost entirely on copra and banana production, two important export items. Pig and cattle farming are also important. In recent years the government has pursued development plans in an attempt to broaden the base of the islands' economy.

Tuvalu

Nine Polynesian islands, south of the Gilbert Islands with whom they were formerly associated as the Ellice Islands, have formed a separate British protectorate since 1975. The colony depends heavily on British aid. There is little cultivable soil. Fishing is the major activity.

Wallis and Futuna

The Wallis Islands with Futuna and Alofi are grouped 600 km (380 mi) northwest of Fiji within Polynesia. From 1842 till 1961 they were a French protectorate associated with New Caledonia. Since then they have been an overseas territory of France enjoying local self government and sending representatives to the French Assemblies in Paris. Farming is important with some fishing as well. Coffee, copra and vegetables are the main crops.

Western Samoa

Four inhabited Polynesian islands and a number of smaller ones northeast of Fiji and west of American Samoa make up Western Samoa. The islands are mountainous, being volcanic with coral fringes. Before World War I they belonged to Germany, were administered by New Zealand from 1920 to 1962 and since that time have been an independent country within the Commonwealth. Tropical crops, mainly bananas, cocoa and copra are grown on the coastal strips.

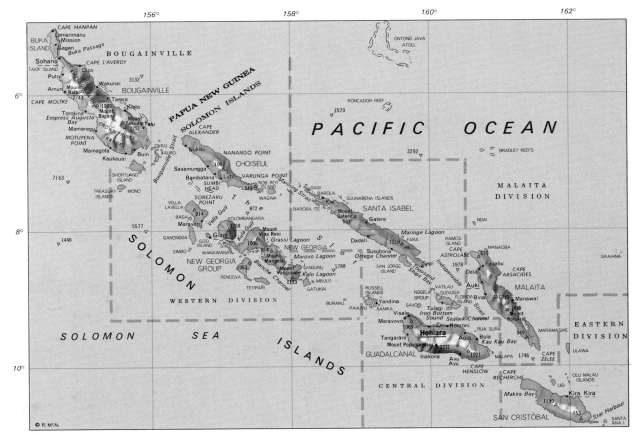

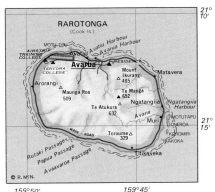

Opposite: 1 Pokutu Geyser, Rotorua, N Island, NZ – hot springs abound here; 2 Village, Western Samoa – food crops are the leading exports; 3 Native musicians, Fiji; 4 Basket-makers, Vavau Islands, Tonga

The Solomon Islands are among the most mountainous of Melanesia; Rarotonga is the most important member of the Cook Islands

COUNTRY REFERENCE: OCEANIA

Oceania Countries	Political Status	State Capital	Area		Population	Population Density		Births per Thousand Persons	Deaths per Thousand Persons	Mean Annual Percentage Increase in Population
			km²	sq mi		per km²	per sq mi			
American Samoa	C	Pago Pago	197	76	33,000	168	434	—	—	—
Australia	A	Canberra	7,686,849	2,967,909	13,858,000	1.8	4.7	17.2	8.1	1.6
NSW	D	Sydney	801,428	309,433	4,886,000	6.1	16	18.5	8.7	1.5
Victoria	D	Melbourne	227,618	87,884	3,730,000	16	42	18.7	8.5	1.6
Queensland	D	Brisbane	1,727,522	667,000	2,084,000	1.2	3.1	19.8	8.7	2.7
S. Australia	D	Adelaide	984,377	380,070	1,273,000	1.3	3.3	17.0	8.2	1.5
W. Australia	D	Perth	2,527,621	975,920	1,171,000	0.5	1.2	19.1	7.3	2.9
N. Territory	D	Darwin	1,347,519	520,280	100,000	0.07	0.2	29.3	6.1	7.3
Tasmania	D	Hobart	68,332	26,383	412,000	6	16	18.5	8.4	0.9
ACT	D	Canberra	2,432	939	202,000	83	215	24.2	3.9	10.0
Cook Islands	C	Avarua	241	93	18,000	75	194	32.8	5.7	−2.6
Fiji	A	Suva	18,272	7,055	595,000	33	84	28.8	4.3	1.9
French Polynesia	C	Papeete	4,000	1,550	138,000	35	89	33.7	7.2	3.5
Gilbert Islands	C	Bairiki	857	331	58,000	68	175	22.3	6.5	3.5
Guam	C	Agana	549	212	96,000	175	453	30.4	4.2	2.1
Nauru	A	—	21	8	7,300	348	913	32.2	8.3	—
New Caledonia	C	Noumea	19,058	7,358	141,000	7.4	19	32.2	7.9	3.6
New Hebrides	C	Vila	14,760	5,700	100,000	6.8	18	—	—	2.9
New Zealand	A	Wellington	268,675	103,736	3,245,000	12	31	18.4	8.1	1.9
Niue	C	Alofi	259	100	3,000	12	30	19.0	4.8	−3.2
Norfolk Island	C	Kingston	36	14	2,000	56	143	9.5	5.3	8.2
Pacific Islands (US Trust Territory)	C	Saipan	1,857	717	129,000	69	180	40.0	4.5	2.8
Papua New Guinea	A	Port Moresby	461,691	178,260	2,950,000	6.4	17	40.6	17.1	1.6
Pitcairn Island	C	Adamstown	5	2	70	14	35	—	—	—
Solomon Islands	A	Honiara	29,785	11,500	215,000	7.2	19	36.1	13.0	3.1
Tokelau Islands	C	—	10	4	1,600	160	400	24.5	—	—
Tonga	A	Nukualofa	699	270	92,000	132	341	28.3	3.2	2.9
Tuvalu	C	Funafuti	23	9	7,000	304	769	—	—	—
Wallis & Futuna	C	Matu-utu	255	98	9,500	37	97	43.3	10.6	2.5
Western Samoa	A	Apia	2,842	1,097	170,000	60	155	34.9	7.0	2.1
OCEANIA TOTALS			**8,510,941**	**3,286,099**	**21,868,470**	**2.6**	**6.7**	**—**	**—**	**—**

N.B. There are a number of other small islands, island groups and reefs in the Pacific Ocean which are associated with the USA, the UK and New Zealand but are not separately listed here.

1 △

2 ◁

3 ▷

4 ◁

Inset map (top left)

PACIFIC OCEAN

PULAU WAIGEO
Selat Dampier Equator
SALAWATI
Sorong Manokwari
PULAU MISOOL JAZIRAH DOBERAI
Teluk Berau KEPULAUAN SCHOUTEN
Fakfak BIAK
PULAU BANDA NUMFOOR PULAU YAPEN
Bula Kaimana
SERAM PEGUNUNGAN VAN REES
KEPULAUAN KAI PEGUNUNGAN MAOKE
KAI KECIL Dobo Puncak Jaya 5030m
INDONESIA Puncak Trikora 4750m
KEPULAUAN ARU PULAU WOKAM
PULAU KOBROOR NEW GUINEA
KEPULAUAN YAMDENA PULAU TRANGAN
TANIMBAR PULAU YOS SUDARSA
PULAU SELARU Merauke
Digul
Fly

Tanjung Perkam
NINIGO GROUP HERMIT ISLANDS
Jayapura (Sukarnapura)
Aitape Wewak
Sepik KARKAR ISLAND
Madang LONG ISLAND
Mt. Giluwe 4368m Mt. Wilhelm 4509m
PAPUA Lae
NEW GUINEA Huon Gulf
Morobe
Gulf of Papua
Popondetta
OWEN STANLEY RANGE
Port Moresby

ADMIRALTY ISLANDS MUSSAU ISLAND
MANUS ISLAND EMIRA ISLAND
NEW HANOVER Kavieng
NEW IRELAND Namatanai
BISMARCK ARCHIPELAGO Rabaul
WITU ISLANDS Kakopo
Talasea The Father △ 2300m
NEW BRITAIN
TROBRIAND ISLANDS
WOODLARK ISLAND
D'ENTRECASTEAUX ISLAND
GREAT SOUTH CAPE
CAPE YORK Samarai
MOA ISLAND BARRIER REEF
CAPE YORK PEN. Coral Sea
Gulf of Carpentaria

MELVILLE ISLAND COBOURG PEN. CROKER ISLAND
BATHURST ISLAND Van Diemen Gulf
Darwin WESSEL ISLANDS
AUSTRALIA
Torres Strait
©1979 R.M⁽ᴺ
A-592200-264

Main map

INDIAN

OCEAN

Laut Sawu
Savu Sea TIMOR
PULAU SEMAU Soe
PULAU ROTI Kupang

Timor Sea

HIBERNIA REEF
ASHMORE ISLANDS CARTIER ISLAND (Austl.)

BROWSE ISLAND
BONAPARTE ARCHIPELAGO
ADÈLE ISLAND BEAGLE REEF
BUCCANEER ARCHIPELAGO Collier Bay
CAPE LEVEQUE Yampi Sound
King Sound
Derby

MELVILLE ISLAND
BATHURST ISLAND CAPE CROKER
COBOURG PEN.
Van Diemen Gulf CROKER ISLAND
Beagle Gulf Clarence Strait
Darwin ARNHEM
POINT BLAZE Rum Jungle
Pine Creek
CAPE LONDONDERRY Daly
CAPE Katherine
Joseph Bonaparte Gulf
York Sound Wyndham
Kununurra Victoria River Downs
Lake Argyle Victoria
KIMBERLEY PLATEAU NORTHERN
Halls Creek Wave Hill Newcas...
Gordon Downs Water...
Fitzroy Crossing
Mount Ord Lan... Woo...
KING LEOPOLD RANGES
DURACK RANGE
Ord
TANAMI
TERRITO...
DESERT
Barro...

ROWLEY SHOALS
CAPE LATOUCHE TREVILLE
Broome
La Grange
Fitzroy
EIGHTY MILE BEACH

Shay Gap GREAT SANDY DESERT
De Grey
Port Hedland
Marble Bar
Nullagine
Gregory Lake
Lake Wills
Lake White (Dry)
Lake Mackay (Dry Salt Lake)
Mount Leisler △ 901 Mount Ze...
△ 1511

DAMPIER ARCHIPELAGO
MONTEBELLO ISLANDS Dampier
Roebourne
BARROW ISLAND
MURON ISLANDS
NORTH WEST CAPE Onslow
Exmouth Gulf Pannawonica
HAMERSLEY RANGE Wittenoom
Mount Brockman 1129 △ △ 1235
Tom Price △ Mount Bruce
Ashburton Paraburdoo Newman
Fortescue
Lyons
POINT CLOATES
Lake Dora Lake Auld (Dry)
Lake Disappointment (Dry Salt Lake)
Savory
WESTERN
GIBSON DESERT
Lake Macdonald (Dry)
Lake Neale (Dry) Lake Amadeus (Dry)
Mount Olga 1069 △ △ 936.6
△ Mount Essendon Mount Aloysius △ 1085
Ayers Rock 867 △
MACDONN...

Tropic of Capricorn
CAPE CUVIER
Geographe Channel Lake Macleod
Carnarvon Mount Augustus △ 1105
Gascoyne
BERNIER ISLAND Woorramel
DORRE ISLAND Shark Bay
DIRK HARTOG ISLAND Woorramel
Naturaliste Channel
STEEP POINT
Murchison
Peak Hill
ROBINSON RANGES
Meekatharra
Nannine
Wiluna
Lake Carnegie (Dry)
△ 906
Lake Wells (Dry)
AUST...
△ 1439 Mount Woodroffe

Cue Lake Austin (Dry)
Sandstone
Boogardie Mount Magnet
Agnew Mount Redcliffe △ 576
Leonora Malcolm
Lake Carey (Dry Salt Lake)
Laverton
Yeo Lake (Dry)
GREAT VICTORIA DESERT
Lake Maurice (Dry) SOU...
Maralinga
Ooldea

HOUTMAN ABROLHOS
Northampton Mullewa Yalgoo
Geraldton
Dongara Three Springs
GREEN HEAD
Mongers Lake (Dry Salt Lake)
Lake Barlee (Dry Salt Lake)
Lake Moore (Dry)
Menzies
Lake Raeside Lake Ballard
Lake Minigwal (Dry)
Kanowna
Kalgoorlie Coolgardie Boulder
Zanthus
Rawlinna
Haig Forrest Deakin
NULLARBOR PLAIN
Eucla
CAPE ADIEU
SAINT PETER ISL

Moora
Dalwallinu Bonnie Rock
Bencubbin
Bullfinch Southern Cross
Lake Lefroy (Dry)
Lake Cowan (Dry Salt Lake)
Norseman
Lake Dundas (Dry)
Eyre

Moora
DARLING RANGE
Mocket Northam Merredin
Stirling York Kellerberrin
Perth Beverley
Fremantle Brookton Hyden
Pinjarra Narrogin
Bunbury Wagin
Collie Newdegate
Geographe Bay Nyabing
CAPE NATURALISTE Katanning
Busselton Gnowangerup
Bridgetown Ravensthorpe
Augusta Manjimup Hopetoun
CAPE LEEUWIN Pemberton Bluff Knoll 1096 △
Denmark Mount Barker
POINT D'ENTRECASTEAUX Albany
WEST CAPE HOWE King George Sound
HOOD POINT
Esperance Bay CAPE ARID
ARCHIPELAGO OF THE RECHERCHE
CAPE KNOB CAPE VANCOUVER
POINT CULVER
Great Australian Bight
INV...

INDIAN OCE...

135° 140° 145° 150° 155°

ra **Sea**

BOGU
ISLAND
WARRIOR REEFS

Daru
SABAI ISLAND

Kokoda
Mount Victoria
4036
OWEN STANLEY RANGE
Kumusi
Gona
Popondetta

Losuia
D'ENTRECASTEAUX ISLANDS

TROBRIAND ISLANDS
WOODLARK ISLAND

VELLA LAVELLA
RANONGGA Gizo
KOLOMBANGARA
RUSSELL ISLANDS
CHOISEUL
SANTA ISABEL

Wanigela

CAPE WESSEL
WESSEL ISLANDS

Torres
MOA ISLAND
Strait
Port Moresby
PAPUA
NEW GUINEA
NEW GUINEA

Esa-Ala

SOLOMON ISLANDS

Tulaghi
GUADALCANAL

PRINCE OF WALES ISLAND
Endeavour Strait
CAPE YORK

Gulf of
Papua

Rigo
Abau

Samarai
Milne Bay

MISIMA I.
LOUISIADE ARCHIPELAGO

Solomon Sea

Honiara 160°
Mt. Popomanaseu 2331

Buckingham Bay

CAPE GREY

THE ENGLISH COMPANYS ISLANDS

CAPE ARNHEM

CAPE YORK

Wenlock
CAPE GRENVILLE

Iron Range

LONG REEF

RENNELL

INDISPENSABLE REEFS

GROOTE EYLANDT

CAPE BEATRICE

DUIFKEN POINT
Albatross Bay
Weipa
YORK

Archer Bay
Aurukun Mission

PENINSULA

OSPREY REEF

C o r a l   S e a

Limmen Bight
MARIA ISLAND
SIR EDWARD PELLEW GROUP
VANDERLIN ISLAND

Gulf
of
Carpentaria

CAPE KEER-WEER

Coen

Coleman

Musgrave

Borroloola

MORNINGTON ISLAND
WELLESLEY ISLANDS
BENTINCK ISLAND

Mitchell
Staaten

Laura
Cooktown

BOUGAINVILLE REEFS

WILLIS GROUP
(Austl.)

HOLMES REEFS

BARKLY TABLELAND

Nicholson
Burketown

Normanton

CAPE GRAFTON
Mareeba
Atherton
Cairns
Ravenshoe
Bartle Frere 1611
Innisfail

CHILCOTT ISLAND
(Austl.)

DIAMOND ISLETS
(Austl.)

LIHOU REEFS AND CAYS

15°

Chillagoe

Leichhardt

Croydon

Forsayth
Einasleigh

GREAT

HINCHINBROOK ISLAND
Ingham

Halifax Bay
Greenvale

FLINDERS REEFS

MALAY REEF

TREGOSSE ISLETS
(Austl.)

ABINGTON REEFS

MELLISH REEF

Ranken Store

Camooweal
Dobbyn

Gilbert
Norman

DIVIDING

Townsville
CAPE CLEVELAND

Ayr
Home Hill

Mount Isa
Cloncurry

Richmond
Hughenden

Flinders
Charters Towers
Pentland

Burdekin
Bowen
Proserpine
Collinsville

CUMBERLAND ISLANDS

BARRIER

ILES CHESTERFIELD
(N. Cal.)

ILE DE SABLE
(N. Cal.)

Duchess
SELWYN RANGE
Selwyn

Dajarra

Winton

Netherdale

Mackay
Sarina

NORTHUMBERLAND ISLES
CAPE PALMERSTON
Broad Sound

MARION REEF

20°

Boulia
Hamilton
Burke

RANGE

Aramac

Blair Athol
Clermont

SWAIN REEFS

TOWNSHEND ISLAND

SAUMAREZ REEF

KENN REEF

WRECK REEF
(Austl.)

SIMPSON
DESERT

QUEENSLAND
Longreach
Ilfracombe
Barcaldine

Emerald
Rockhampton
Mount Morgan
Yeppoon
Keppel Bay
CAPE CURTIS
Gladstone
Port Curtis

CAPRICORN GROUP
BLINKER GROUP

BIRD ISLET

CAYE DE L'OBSERVATOIRE
(N. Cal.)

BELLONA REEFS

G R E A T   A R T E S I A N

Aramac
Alpha

Springsure

Biloela

CATO ISLAND

Tropic of Capricorn

Windorah

RANGE

Adavale
Yaraka
Blackall

Theodore
Monto

Bundaberg
Hervey
Childers

SANDY CAPE

FRASER ISLAND

P A C I F I C

25°

Eromanga
Charleville
Augathella

Injune
Taroom

Wondai
Gayndah
Plainland

Birdsville

Thargomindah

Mitchell
Roma

Murgon
Maryborough

BASIN

GREY

Quilpie

Wyandra

Miles

Wonbah
Kingaroy
Nanango
Kilcoy

Gympie

Cunnamulla

Saint George
Moonie

Mount Kangaroo
Dalby
Toowoomba
Ipswich

MORETON ISLAND

Brisbane
Southport

Birdie
Dirranbandi
Macintyre
Goondiwindi
Warwick
Boonah

O C E A N

AUSTRALIA

Cooper
Creek
Innamincka

RANGE

Mungindi
Stanthorpe
Tenterfield

Murwillumbah
CAPE BYRON
Ballina

NORTH STRADBROKE ISLAND

Lake Yamma Yamma

Moree
Warialda
Inverell
Glen Innes

Casino
Lismore

Lake Eyre
North
(Dry Salt Lake)

STURT
DESERT

Sturts Stony Desert

Lake Blanche
(Dry)

Tilpa

Bourke
Walgett

Namoi
Narrabri

Maclean
Grafton

Coffs Harbour

30°

Lake Eyre
South

Marree

Lake Callabonna
(Dry)

Milparinka

Wilcannia

Round Mountain 1608
Armidale

Kempsey

Smoky Cape

MIDDLETON REEF

ELIZABETH REEF

Lake
Torrens

Copley

Lake
Frome
(Dry Salt Lake)

Menindee

Coonamble
Gilgandra

Gunnedah

Werris Creek
Tamworth

Port Macquarie

Broken Hill

NEW SOUTH WALES

Nyngan
Dubbo

Taree

Sugarloaf Point

LORD HOWE ISLAND
(N.S.W.)

Olary

Narromine

Wellington
Mudgee

Singleton
Maitland

BALLS PYRAMID
(N.S.W.)

Lake
Gairdner
(Dry Salt
Lake)

FLINDERS RANGE
Saint Mary Peak
1165
Hawker

Peterborough
Jamestown

Cobar

Condobolin
Lake Cargelligo
Forbes
Orange
Bathurst
Katoomba

Cessnock
Newcastle
Woy Woy

GAWLER RANGES

Iron Knob

Burra

Ivanhoe
Roto

Parkes

SYDNEY
Parramatta

EYRE PENINSULA

Kimba
Whyalla
Quorn
Port
Augusta

Renmark
Loxton

Hay
Hillston

Young
Cowra

Goulburn
Campbelltown

Wollongong
Shellharbour

Wallaroo
Kadina

Balranald

West Wyalong
Griffith

Bowral

Nowra
JERVIS BAY

Wentworth
Mildura

Narrandera
Cootamundra

Yass

Port Lincoln

Spencer
Gulf

Swan Hill
Deniliquin

Leeton
Junee

Tumut

Queanbeyan

INVESTIGATOR STRAIT

Elizabeth
Adelaide

Murray Bridge
Pinnaroo

Wagga Wagga

Canberra
A.C.T.

KANGAROO ISLAND

Victor Harbor
Lake Alexandrina

Kerang

RIVERINA

Billabong Creek

Albury
Wodonga
Lake Hume
Tumbarumba

Bega

35°

Encounter
Bay

Bordertown

Echuca
Shepparton
Benalla

Wangaratta
2229
Mount Kosciusko

Bombala

CAPE HOWE

Naracoorte

Horsham

Bendigo
Maryborough
Castlemaine

Cooma

Orbost

Kingston Southeast

Penola
Ararat
Stawell

Whittlesea

Bairnsdale

T a s m a n

CAPE JAFFA

Millicent

Hamilton

VICTORIA

GREAT

Ballarat
MELBOURNE

Sale
Moe
Traralgon
Morwell

NINETY MILE BEACH

S e a

Mount Gambier

Portland
Port Fairy
Warrnambool

Geelong

DIVIDING

Wonthaggi
Foster

POINT HICKS

CAPE NELSON

CAPE OTWAY

PHILLIP ISLAND

WILSONS PROMONTORY

SOUTH POINT

KING ISLAND

KENT GROUP

Bass Strait

HUNTER GROUP
CAPE GRIM

FLINDERS ISLAND
FURNEAUX GROUP
CAPE BARREN ISLAND

40°

Smithton
Burnie
Devonport
Ulverstone
Beaconsfield
Scottsdale

Saint Marys

SANDY CAPE

Zeehan

Mount Ossa
1617

Launceston

FREYCINET PENINSULA

CAPE SORELL

Strahan

TASMANIA

MARIA ISLAND

LOW ROCKY POINT

TASMANIA
New Norfolk
Huonville
Geeveston

New Norton
Hobart
Port Arthur

SOUTH WEST CAPE
SOUTH CAPE
SOUTH EAST CAPE

Storm Bay

140° 145° 150° 155° 160° 165°

Kilometers 0   200   400   600 Km.

Statute Miles 0   200   400   600 Mi.

Scale 1:13,200,000

One centimeter represents 132 kilometers.
One inch represents approximately 210 miles.

Lambert Conformal Conic Projection

117

PACIFIC

OCEAN

TASMAN

SEA

NORTH

ISLAND

Selected place and feature names

THREE KINGS ISLANDS
CAPE MARIA VAN DIEMEN
CAPE RENGA
NORTH CAPE
Te Hapua
Te Kao
Awanui
Ahipara Bay
Kaitaia
Mangonui
Parengarenga Harbour
Doubtless Bay
CAPE KARIKARI
Herekino
NINETY MILE BEACH
TAUROA POINT
Broadwood
Kohukohu
Rawene
Kaikohe
Kerikeri
Okaihau
Russell
Opua
BAY OF ISLANDS
CAPE BRETT
Kaeo
Waimate
Kawakawa
Moerewa
Towai
Hikurangi
Kamo
Whangarei
Portland
BREAM HEAD
HEN AND CHICKENS
BREAM BAY
Waipu
Maungaturoto
Paparoa
Ruawai
Dargaville
Hoteo
Kaukapakapa
Helensville
Donnellys Crossing
Tangowahine
Kaihu
Waimamaku
Hokianga Harbour
Kaipara Harbour
NORTH HEAD
POOR KNIGHTS ISLANDS
Whangaruru Harbour
Mangawhai
Wellsford
Warkworth
Leigh
Matakana
KAWAU ISLAND
LITTLE BARRIER ISLAND
GREAT BARRIER ISLAND
Port Fitzroy
CAPE BARRIER
MOKOHINAU ISLANDS
TARANGA ISLAND
BREAM TAIL
Orewa
Albany
Devonport
Auckland
Takapuna
Mount Roskill
Mount Wellington
Manukau
Waitemata
Papatoetoe
Panmure
Manukau Harbour
Port Waikato
Waiuku
Tuakau
Pukekohe
Papakura
Drury
Waiheke Island
WAIHEKE ISLAND
Hauraki Gulf
East Coast Bays
Clevedon
COROMANDEL PENINSULA
Colville
Coromandel
Whitianga
MERCURY ISLANDS
GREAT MERCURY ISLAND
THE ALDERMEN ISLANDS
CAPE COLVILLE
CAPE RODNEY
Coville Channel
Cradock Channel
Firth of Thames
Thames
Waihi
Paeroa
Te Aroha
Waihou
Katikati
Tauranga
Te Puke
Maketu
MAYOR ISLAND
MATAKANA ISLAND
MOTITI ISLAND
Bay of Plenty
Whakatane
Opotiki
WHITE ISLAND
CAPE RUNAWAY
Hicks Bay
EAST CAPE
Te Araroa
Tikitiki
Ruatoria
Tokomaru Bay
Tolaga Bay
Gisborne
Poverty Bay
Huntly
Ngaruawahia
Raglan
Hamilton
Cambridge
Morrinsville
Matamata
Waharoa
Putaruru
Tokoroa
Te Awamutu
Otorohanga
Kawhia
KAWHIA HARBOUR
ALBATROSS POINT
Te Kuiti
Mangakino
Taumarunui
Ohura
Lake Taupo
Taupo
Turangi
Mokai
Rotorua
Lake Rotorua
Lake Rotoiti
KAIMAI RANGE
HAUHUNGAROA RANGE
KAWEKA RA
AHIMANAWA RANGE
RUAHINE RANGE
KAIMANAWA MTS
Murupara
Wairoa
Frasertown
MAHIA PENINSULA
PORTLAND ISLAND
Hawke Bay
CAPE KIDNAPPERS
Napier
Hastings
Havelock North
Clive
Taradale
Waipukurau
Waipawa
Dannevirke
Woodville
Pahiatua
Eketahuna
Masterton
Carterton
Featherston
Greytown
Martinborough
PUKETOI RANGE
TARARUA RANGE
Palmerston North
Feilding
Ashhurst
Foxton
Foxton Beach
Shannon
Levin
Otaki
Wanganui
Waverley
Patea
Hawera
Eltham
Stratford
Normanby
Manaia
Opunake
New Plymouth
Inglewood
Waitara
MOUNT EGMONT
Kaponga
Oakura
Okato
CAPE EGMONT
Taranaki Bight
North Taranaki Bight
South Taranaki Bight
Patea
Waiouru
Raetihi
Ohakune
National Park
Pipiriki
Taihape
Hunterville
Marton
Bulls
Sanson
Waikanae
Paraparaumu
Paekakariki
CAPE FAREWELL
FAREWELL SPIT
Golden Bay
Collingwood
COOK STRAIT

35° 36° 37° 38° 39° 40°

168° 169° 170° 171° 172° 173° 174° 175° 176° 177°

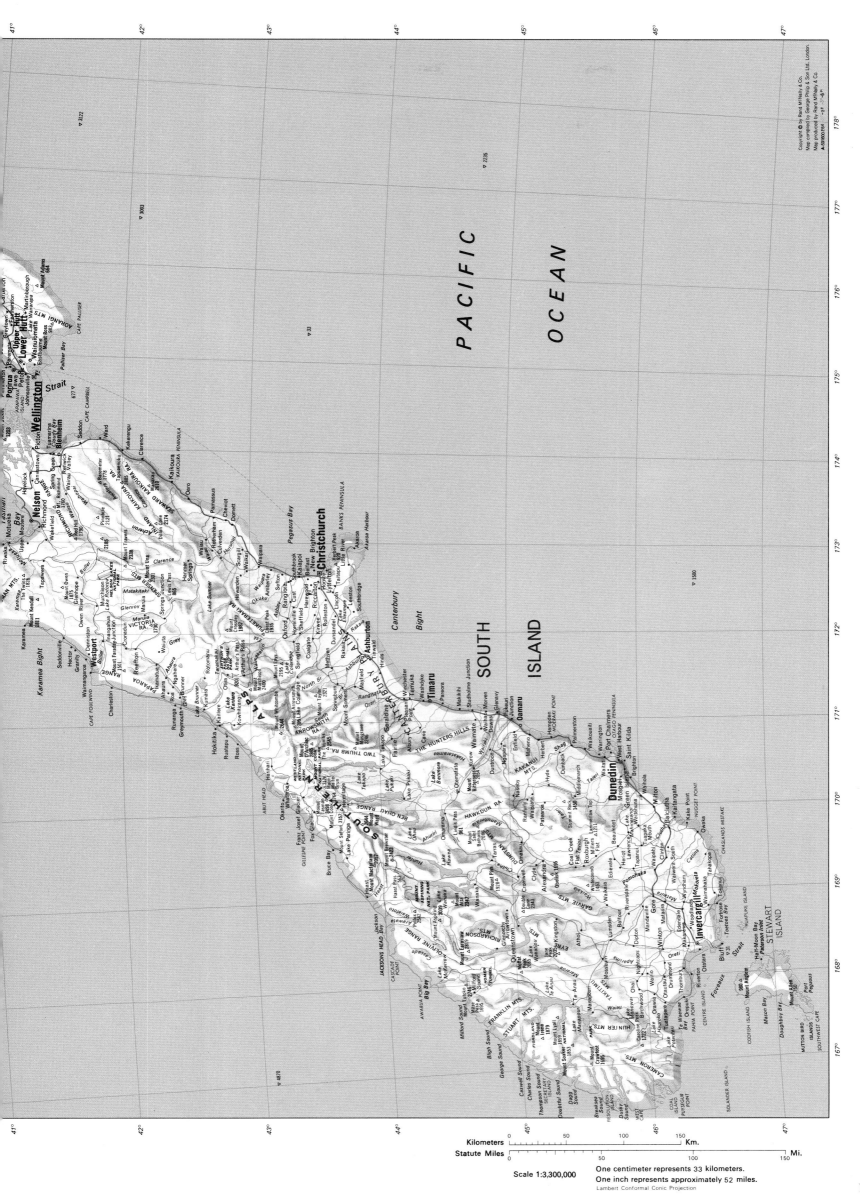

PACIFIC

OCEAN

SOUTH

ISLAND

STEWART
ISLAND

Kilometers
Statute Miles

Scale 1:3,300,000

One centimeter represents 33 kilometers.
One inch represents approximately 52 miles.
Lambert Conformal Conic Projection

MIDDLE AMERICA
Physical Profile

World Location and Size

Although it is the smallest of our nine 'continental' areas, Middle America is scattered over a wide area. On the mainland, the Mexico/USA boundary lies at about 33°N, while the Panama/Colombian boundary is at nearly 7°N. The northwest to southeast extent of the mainland is thus some 4,800 km (3,000 mi). Yet this part of the continent is never more than 1,200 km (750 mi) in west-east extent in Mexico and is often far narrower.

Middle America also includes the islands of the Greater and Lesser Antilles and others lying in the seas between the mainland of the three Americas. Many of these are collectively called the West Indies, lying principally within a belt bounded by 17°N and 22°N, and extending as far into the Atlantic as 59°W.

Landscape

Middle America may be divided into three main physical areas. In the north, in much of Mexico as far south as the Isthmus of Tehuantepec, the great mountain system of North America's Western Cordillera continues. The Sierra Madre Occidental runs parallel to the Pacific coast and rises to a maximum of 4,265 m (13,994 ft). The Sierra Madre Oriental runs parallel to the Gulf of Mexico coast and rises to greater heights in some of the volcanic peaks, such as Popocatepetl, 5,452 m (17,887 ft). Between these two ranges, a complex plateau lies at heights of between 1,200 m (4,000 ft) and 2,400 m (8,000 ft). To the west of all these three lies the great depression occupied by the Gulf of California and the elongated Baja California Peninsula, an extension of the Coast Ranges of the USA.

The southern mainland section of Middle America is physically far more complex. In its northern province, between Tehuantepec and Nicaragua, a series of mainly west-east mountain ridges lie across the isthmus from a high volcanic plateau on the Pacific fringe. Each line of mountains is highest in the west. There are limited coastal lowlands in this area, except in the great Yucatan Peninsula which is an extensive low limestone plain. The mountains of southern Nicaragua, Costa Rica and Panama are separated from the others by the depression containing Lakes Nicaragua and Managua. These mountains present a formidable barrier to movement across the isthmus, running northwest to southeast, then west to east. Through the whole of the second area, there are

Opposite: Market fruit stalls, San Miguel de Allende, Mexico

only four clear routes from Pacific to Caribbean: Tehuantepec, the Motagua River, Lake Nicaragua and the vital line of the Panama Canal.

The third physical province is that of the islands, which is itself in need of subdivision. To the north lies the line of coral reefs making up the Bahamas. Then the islands, often large, of the Greater Antilles are an eastern continuation of the mountains of southern Mexico, Guatemala and Honduras. Finally the Lesser Antilles are mainly a volcanic arc. They are a northeastern extension of the South American Andes. There are also a number of coral islands in

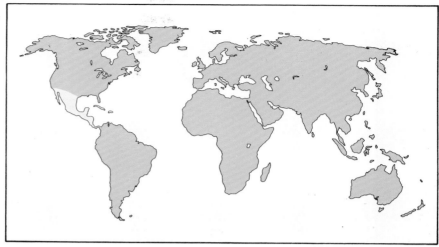

this last area. Thus, the West Indian islands show a great variety of physical features – active volcanoes, extinct volcanoes, coral islands, mountainous islands.

Climatic Background

Virtually all Middle America lies within the tropics. The close proximity to the seas, and the fact that it contains a range of altitudes, accounts for the variety of climates.

Mexico, north of the Tropic of Cancer, experiences dry climates. In the northwest and northcentral

parts lies a subtropical desert area where the monthly average temperature never drops below 0°C (32°F) but rainfall is below 250 mm (10 in). More extensively, central and northeastern Mexico has a subtropical steppe climate in which similar temperatures are accompanied by higher rainfalls, up to 600 mm (24 in).

Except in the high mountain areas, the remainder of the mainland experiences tropical rainy climates, being wetter on the east coast, except in the Yucatan Peninsula, than on the west. Here is the rain forest area where average monthly temperatures

The Pitons, St Lucia, West Indies – the mountainous, wooded Windward Island of volcanic origins

may be around 25°C (77°F) for much of the year and rainfall exceeds 2,500 mm (100 in). In the drier savanna areas of the west, rainfall is only around one-third of this amount.

Many of the islands experience a similar tropical savanna type of climate, though parts, such as the northern coastal strip of Hispaniola and Puerto Rico, have far higher rainfalls. In much of the Caribbean, hurricanes are an occasional menace.

MIDDLE AMERICA

The known history of Middle America dates back to the early settlements of 'Indians' who penetrated from north to south through the Americas about 10,000 BC. Their descendants, the Maya, developed their own civilization.

Population Growth and Political Development

When European settlers first moved to Middle America toward the end of the fifteenth century, there were probably no more than 2 million American Indians. During the early period of European penetration, the American Indian population of the islands was largely wiped out by disease and the effects of enslavement. Far more survived on the mainland, so that today there are very few purebred Amerinds on the islands, and they are now most strongly represented in the mainland countries. Nearly half the population of Guatemala, for instance, is of pure Amerind stock.

In contrast, the population of European descent in most Middle American countries is today low. African Negroes, originally introduced as slaves to the plantations, now form a substantial part of the Caribbean population. It is estimated that over four-fifths of the population of Haiti is of Negro stock, for example. Only in Puerto Rico, the Dominican Republic and Cuba, among the islands, are Negroes in a minority. The present total population of the region is over 112 million, three-fifths of whom live in Mexico.

European influence in Middle America from 1500 onward was essentially by two groups. The mainland was part of the area allocated to Spain under the 1493 agreements between Spain, Portugal and the Pope; the Caribbean islands were part of the area largely left to the Dutch, French and British. Independence movements developed early in the nineteenth century. Mexico was the first country to experience revolution, leading to independence in 1821. Soon, all Spanish territories had established their independence, though the initial Federation of Central American States lasted for only 14 years until it broke up in 1838. Since then there have been few major political changes. The two largest modern developments have been the granting of independence to most of her West Indian colonies by the United Kingdom since World War II, and the development of a Communist regime in Cuba.

Industry, Commerce and Communications

Industrialization in Middle America is a comparatively recent development. Even today on a world scale, it must rank with all Africa as being one of the two least industrially developed regions. However individual Middle American countries have seen the advantages of broadening their economies, being less dependent upon the production and exporting of primary products and the importing of others, including manufactured needs. Industrialization also provides one alternative activity for the rapidly expanding population who cannot be absorbed on the land. Not surprisingly, Mexico has led the way: El Salvador, Costa Rica and now Cuba have followed.

Consumer goods are the first group of industries to have been developed. The home market for textiles and footwear, household goods and foodstuffs is large. While all these consumer industries are found in the leading countries, only some of them exist in the smaller countries. They have been followed by the setting up of heavy industry, iron and steel, petrochemicals and cement production in Mexico, refining Venezuelan

1 Maya ruins, Uxmal, Yucatan, Mexico; 2 Sugar plantation workers, Cuba; 3 Market square, St George's, capital of Grenada, West Indies

oil and fertilizer production in El Salvador, and light engineering in Costa Rica.

Transport networks in mainland Middle America are rather fragmentary. In Mexico, the road and rail networks both focus on Mexico City and have been developed outward to all corners of the country. The road link to the countries of the southeast is complete to Panama, though the Pan American Highway has yet to be completed from here into Colombia. In the other mainland countries rail development has been difficult and costly. Isolated lines serve the more populated parts of most countries. On the islands, rail and road networks are best developed in Cuba and Hispaniola. Throughout the whole of Middle America, air and sea links are also important.

Agriculture, Forestry and Fishing

Farming throughout Middle America was, for a long time, characterized by large estates with much wealth being in the hands of a small fraction of the total population, while the majority of the people were poor, landless peasants, mainly non-Europeans. Changes slowly started to take place in the early twentieth century. The Mexican revolution in 1910 brought about a move to introduce communal ownership and working of the land, but so far this has been applied to less than half the land. More recently in Cuba, the Communist regime has tried to make farming more efficient by establishing state farms. However, overall, land reform has proved difficult to implement speedily.

Within Middle America, pastoral, subsistence and commercial farming are all found where the environmental hazards of too much or too little rainfall and/or altitude and steep slopes do not rule them out. So much of the dense forests remain untouched, except at their margins. Similarly, the arid areas of the north are hardly touched except where irrigation schemes have been introduced, as in northeastern Mexico.

As in the natural grasslands of South America, settlers here soon introduced cattle and sheep, the Mexican plateau being the most inviting environment. Today, Mexico ranks seventh in the world for pigs, with 12 million, eighth for cattle, with nearly 29 million and eleventh for goats with 9,000. Smaller numbers of cattle and pigs are found in many of the other mainland countries and the larger Caribbean islands. Sheep too are found in smaller numbers in some of the mainland countries.

The continent's commercial crop growing is also concentrated in Mexico. It ranks in the world's top ten producers for twelve important crops and has greatest importance for oranges and lemons, third in each; coffee and sorghum, fourth in each; sugar, fifth; pineapples, coconuts and copra, sixth in each. Other Middle American countries mainly appear in

Much of the Caribbean islands' revenue comes from tourism, although some tropical crop production is also important: 1 Cutting bananas in the Bahamas, WI – the poor soil of these coral islands is not generally suited to agriculture; 2 Bridgetown, Barbados, WI – the capital is also the island's only harbor, from which rum is a major export; 3 Going through the Panama Canal – the passage from the Atlantic to the Pacific takes about 8 hours

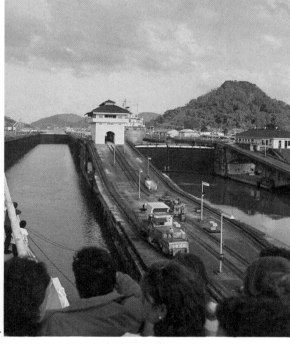

Total Imports and Exports

(1975 figures in millions of U.S. dollars)

Few Middle American countries rank at all highly as trading nations and most import more than they export.

	Imports	Exports
Bahama Islands	1,565	3,416
Costa Rica	643	454
Cuba	4,001	3,680
Dominican Republic	773	894
El Salvador	601	515
Guatemala	733	624
Jamaica	1,113	732
Mexico	6,580	2,859
Netherlands Antilles	2,790	2,393
Nicaragua	517	375
Panama	870	272
Virgin Islands	2,198	1,933

the world tables only for one or two crops, showing an economically dangerous dependence upon them. For example, Cuba is the world's third largest sugarcane producer, yet its second largest product, tobacco, ranks only twenty-fourth; Honduras, Costa Rica and Panama are major banana producers; Guatemala is heavily dependent upon coffee production.

Natural Resources

Middle America is very poorly endowed with mineral resources, having few significant deposits of specific minerals. It lacks coal, even more than South America. Mexico has reserves of over 10,000 million tons of coal but produces only about 5 million tons each year. Yet, Mexican oil reserves and production are such that she now ranks fifteenth in the world, producing over 40 million tons per year, and is of increasing importance to the western world. This may be less than a tenth of the output of the world leaders, but is a third of that of Venezuela, Latin America's leading oil producer. Oil is also produced in Costa Rica and Cuba, and the Caribbean is regarded as one of the world's greatest prospects for future oil exploration. For

Ore	Average Annual World Production (million tons)	Middle America's Share (percent)	Principal Middle American Producing Countries
bauxite	80.3	19	Jamaica
cobalt	0.03	6	Cuba, Honduras
copper	7.4	1	Mexico
lead	3.2	5	Mexico
manganese	22.8	2	Mexico
nickel	0.733	11	Cuba, Dominican Rep.
silver	0.01	16	Mexico, Honduras
tin	0.2	2	Mexico
zinc	5.4	5	Mexico

MIDDLE AMERICA

all its selected areas of high rainfall, Middle America is neither potentially nor actually a great continent for the production of hydroelectric power.

Iron ore is found only in limited quantities in Middle America. Once again Mexico is the leading producer with about 3.6 million tons each year, which places it eighteenth in the world tables.

Middle America's contribution to world output of other minerals is very limited as the table on page 123 demonstrates. Mexico's position as the second largest silver producer and the sixth largest lead producer, Jamaica's as the third largest bauxite producer, Cuba's and the Dominican Republic's as fifth and sixth largest producers of nickel are by far the most significant features.

Middle American Economy

The most extensive area of high average population density in Middle America is the plateau area of southern central Mexico where over 50 per km² (125 per sq mi) are found. Over a wider area in Mexico there are more than 25 persons per km² (60 per sq mi). Elsewhere on the mainland, such figures are only reached in limited areas of the Pacific coast lands of Guatemala, El Salvador and Costa Rica, and in parts of northeast Mexico.

Some Caribbean islands, however, show densities equal to and well above these figures, as can be seen in the table on page 128. In particular, Puerto Rico, Jamaica and the western parts of Cuba among the large islands all have average densities above 150 per km² (375 per sq mi), At the other end of the scale, the least densely populated parts of the continent are the east side of the Yucatan Peninsula, east Honduras and Nicaragua, the Baja California Peninsula and parts of northern central Mexico.

Parts of Middle America are urbanized, though there are only five metro areas of over 1 million. Three of these are in Mexico, where Mexico City with 12.5 million people is one of the world's largest. Guadalajara (2.1 million), Monterrey (1.7 million),

Havana, Cuba (1.9 million) and San Juan, P.R. are the other four metro areas over one million. The capital cities of the Dominican Republic, Guatemala, Haiti, and Jamaica have populations of between half a million and one million, as do three more Mexican cities.

Birth rates in Middle America vary from over 45 per 1,000, as in the mainland countries of Honduras and Nicaragua, as well as the Dominican Republic, to below 20 per 1,000, as in some of the smaller, more advanced islands. Death rates are far lower, most being below 12 per 1,000 and many being single figures. Such figures in combination indicate age pyramids with a wide base in a situation where improving health facilities have increased life expectancy. The overall increase in population in some countries is now over 3 percent. Mexico, the country which so dominates the continent, has a birth rate of over 40 per 1,000, a death rate of only 7.2 per 1,000 – a figure which is lower than those of both the USA and the UK – and a population growth rate of 3.5 percent per annum.

In comparison with the major trading areas, like Europe and North America, this continent plays a minor role in world trade. The value of its imports and exports are about one-twentieth those of all Europe and one-sixth those of North America.

Overall the value of Middle American imports rose by 569 percent and 496 percent, and exports rose by 391 percent and 486 percent between 1938–'58 and 1958–'75 respectively. Together these figures show an unhealthy trend during the first period but improvement in the latter. Although the continent still has a marked balance of payments deficit on visible trade, the position seems to be improving. Some individual countries show a divergence from this norm. For example, Mexico, the largest trader in the continent has a large deficit, and Cuba, Netherlands Antilles and Virgin Islands (US), the next largest traders, smaller deficits each. The Bahama Islands with a substantial trading surplus are unique. Most other Middle American countries are comparatively small traders with deficits on their visible trading.

During the period 1960–'74, per

1 △ 2 ▽

Mexico, Middle America's largest country, is industrially the most highly developed, with vast oil reserves, but there is still much poverty outside the modern major city centers. As a result, regular streams of illegal immigrants to the neighboring United States are frequently apprehended. 1 Cathedral and National Palace, Mexico City – the capital boasts the continent's oldest Christian building as well as fine colonial and modern architecture; 2 Acapulco beach – the world-famous Pacific coast resort, with its warm seas and sandy beaches, is especially popular with US visitors

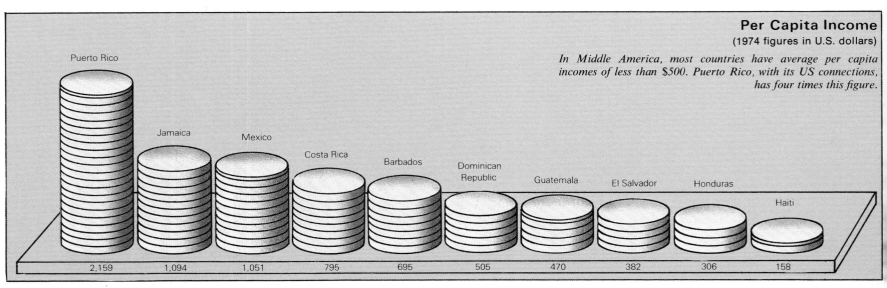

Per Capita Income
(1974 figures in U.S. dollars)

In Middle America, most countries have average per capita incomes of less than $500. Puerto Rico, with its US connections, has four times this figure.

Puerto Rico	Jamaica	Mexico	Costa Rica	Barbados	Dominican Republic	Guatemala	El Salvador	Honduras	Haiti
2,159	1,094	1,051	795	695	505	470	382	306	158

capita income in Middle and South America rose by 220 percent, from $300 to $960. This was slightly better than the overall percentage performance for the non-Communist world. Individually, Middle American countries showed considerable differences. Mexico, on 236 percent, fared better than the average and with its large population dominated the whole scene. Most other countries did worse or far worse. Puerto Rico's per capita income rose by 201 percent, Nicaragua's by 187 percent, Costa Rica's by 123 percent, Guatemala's by 82 percent and El Salvador's by only 71 percent. Absolute values for 1974 make poor comparison with the rest of the world; Puerto Rico had the highest value of $2,159, Mexico had $1,094 but smaller countries had incomes less than $500 per capita.

Middle America is overall a small energy producer and consumer. In 1975, 85.22 million tons coal equivalent (mtce) were produced and 115.60 mtce consumed. Mexico's share of these figures was high, 84.44 and 73.43 mtce respectively, showing this to be the only energy surplus country in the continent. All other countries are net importers of energy, Cuba and Puerto Rico each importing about 10 mtce per year. The remaining countries import small amounts, usually far less than one million tons, except the Dominican Republic, Jamaica, Netherlands Antilles and the Virgin Islands (US).

When energy consumption per capita is considered, three countries which are either connected with the USA or have oil processing industries have high energy uses: Virgin Islands (US) 50,157, Panama Canal Zone 14,150 and Netherlands Antilles 12,231 kg/ca. Some of the small developed islands have comparatively high consumptions per capita, such as Bahama Islands 6,279 and Bermuda 3,090. Many of the islands have figures between 1,500 and 3,000, while most of the mainland countries consume less than 500kg/ca per year.

There are such large differences in the sizes of individual Middle American countries; some areas still await effective development, while others have been selectively exploited for specific products over the years. A possible way to more effective and concerted development in the future may be shown by two recent instances of international cooperation. In 1960 El Salvador, Guatemala, Honduras and Nicaragua created the Central American Common Market (ODECA), which was joined in 1962 by Costa Rica. These five have now established free trade in most commodities between themselves and have increased their trade with each other fivefold since the market was created. More recently, between 1973 and 1974, the Caribbean Common Market was established. This now has thirteen member states and aims at economic cooperation and growth. Mexico is outside both groups though it is associated with South American countries through its membership in the Latin American Free Trade Association.

1 △

2 △　　　　　　　　　　3 ▽

1 Aruba, Netherlands Antilles – despite idyllic scenes like this, the island's economy, like the other two in the southern part of this Dutch group, depends largely on refining oil imported from nearby Venezuela, South America; 2 Bermuda – the near-perfect subtropical climate with warm winters and trade winds cooling the hot summers, makes the Bermudas fine vacation islands and tourism is the main source of revenue; 3 St Vincent, Windward Islands – the delights of the carnival are enjoyed by the inhabitants as much as the visitors. The 1979 eruption of the volcano, Soufrière, has greatly harmed the island's crop-growing and tourism economy

Per Capita Energy Consumption

(1975 figures in kilograms)

Average energy consumption in Middle America ranges from the extraordinary for the Panama Canal Zone, through comparatively high figures for some developed islands, to the more normal levels of most mainland countries and less advanced islands.

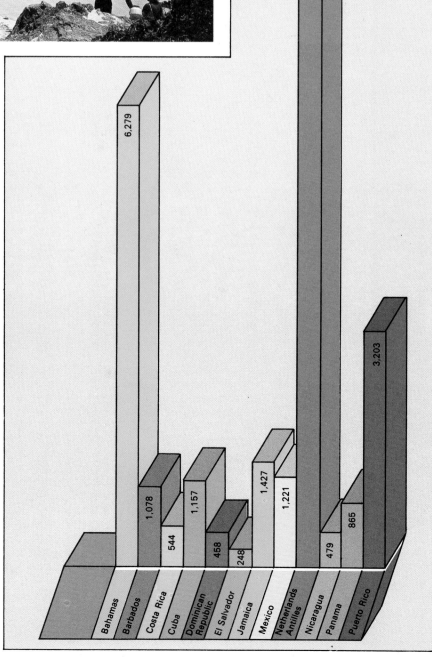

Bahamas 6,279
Barbados 1,078
Costa Rica 544
Cuba 1,157
Dominican Republic 458
El Salvador 248
Jamaica 1,427
Mexico 1,221
Netherlands Antilles 12,231
Nicaragua 479
Panama 865
Puerto Rico 3,203

Middle American Countries

Anguilla

A member of the West Indies Associated States (WIAS), Anguilla was associated with St Kitts-Nevis until 1976. The smallest of the Leeward Islands, it is a member of the Commonwealth with internal self-government, while the UK is responsible for defense and foreign affairs. It is a low coral island with poor soils. Sea salt and fruits are the main products.

Antigua

Together with its dependent islands of Barbuda and Redonda, Antigua is a member of the WIAS. The largest of the Leeward Islands, it has internal self-government. It is a member of the Commonwealth and the UK is responsible for defense and foreign affairs. Mainly a coral island, the remains of an extinct volcano rise to 402 m (1,319 ft) in the south. Sugar and cotton are the main products and exports. The tourist industry is being developed.

Bahama Islands

The Bahamas comprise some 1,700 coral islands and cays north of Cuba and east of Florida. Watling's Island, the first land sighted by Columbus in 1492, is among them. Most are uninhabited. Only New Providence has more than 100,000, and Grand Bahama more than 10,000 inhabitants. Now a member of the Commonwealth, the former British colony achieved complete independence in 1973. The islands' major products and exports are cement, petroleum products, rum, chemicals and fish. A range of small light industries is being developed on the two islands with the largest populations. Tourism is a most important industry.

Barbados

Lying about 170 km (105 mi) east of the Windward Islands, the island of Barbados became an independent country within the Commonwealth in 1966. A British possession for over 350 years, its character earned it the title 'Little England'. Barbados is largely a coral island with a very high population density. Sugar is the dominant crop and the economy is largely dependent upon this, molasses, rum and tourism. Other subsistence crops like yams and cassava are grown.

Belize

Formerly known as British Honduras, this is the only Commonwealth country on the mainland of Middle America. A self-governing colony since 1964, the UK is responsible for its defense, foreign affairs and internal security. It is subject to earthquakes and hurricanes, and in 1961, much of the old capital of Belize City was severely damaged. The building of the new capital city of Belmopan was started in 1967 and the government moved there in 1970. About half the country is forested. Citrus fruit, fruit products, sugar and fish are important to the national economy.

Bermuda

A British island colony within the Commonwealth, some 920 km (570 mi) east of the United States mainland, Bermuda has internal self-government. Of the 150 islands in the group only 20 are inhabited. The attractive climate has led to a great tourist industry, and today one and a half million people visit the islands each year. In 1975 visible exports, of which pharmaceutical products were the major item, brought in about 55 percent of the country's foreign earnings. Tourism and financial services were responsible for the other 45 percent.

British Virgin Islands

East of Puerto Rico and west of the Leeward Islands lies a group known collectively as the Virgin Islands. Those to the west are an unincorporated territory of the USA; the 36 to the east are a British colony which has some measure of internal self-government. The two groups have close social and economic links. Tortola, with a population of just over 8,000, is the largest British island. Farming and fishing are important activities but the developing tourist industry is the biggest source of foreign earnings.

Cayman Islands

Grand Cayman is the most important of the three coral islands which comprise this British colony some 320 km (200 mi) northwest of Jamaica. The main productive activities are fishing, particularly for turtles, boat building and ropemaking. However, the country earns far more foreign currency by its flourishing tourist industry and through its international financial services.

Costa Rica

Except for Panama, this independent republic occupies the narrowest parts of the isthmus joining North and South America. Geographically it is divisible into three broad regions; the comparatively wide Caribbean coastal lowlands, the narrower Pacific coast lowlands and the northwest to southeast chain of volcanic mountains rising to heights of up to 3,819 m (12,530 ft). The main centers of population are in the valleys of the central mountain chain and on the Pacific side of them. Farming dominates the Costa Rican economy. Bananas, corn, sugar, coffee, rice and tobacco are all widely grown. Dairying and stock raising are also important, with marked increases in cattle and pig numbers in recent years.

Costa Rica's mineral reserves are limited. Currently a little gold is produced each year. Deposits of iron ore and sulphur have recently been discovered but have yet to be developed. Bananas, coffee and sugar are her main exports. Manufactured goods, transport equipment, chemicals and petroleum products are the main imports.

Cuba

The republic of Cuba comprises the largest Caribbean island, the smaller Isle of Pines and many smaller islets. It is comparatively flat, apart from the east-west mountain ridge of the extreme east which rises to a maximum height of 1,994 m (6,542 ft), and some hills in the central province of Las Villas and in the extreme west. Formerly a Spanish possession, Cuba became independent in 1898, but was economically tied to the USA until 1959. Since then it has severed relationships with the West and established links with the Soviet bloc. The great bulk of Cuba's international trade is with the USSR and other countries of eastern Europe. The economy is centrally planned. It is the world's third largest producer of sugar. Rice, tobacco, coffee

1 Martinique – devastated by a volcanic eruption at the start of the century, this French island is also hurricane-prone; 2 St Thomas, US Virgin Islands – the main island of this group which attracts more vacation visitors yearly; 3 Grand Cayman – the largest of three coral islands in this British colony where fishing, tourism and banking are the main activities

holdings. Production of sugar, cocoa, coffee, tobacco and rice is, however, concentrated on large estates. Bauxite and iron ore are the most important minerals. Industries have developed a great deal in recent years, particularly sugar processing and textile production. The chief exports are sugar, minerals, cocoa and coffee. Manufactured goods, fuel oil, vehicles and raw materials are the major imports.

El Salvador

The smallest and the most densely populated of the Middle American republics, El Salvador has been independent since 1841. Physically, the lie of the land is from east to west with a main volcanic mountain ridge near the south coast, limited tropical lowlands to the south of this and a wider belt of undulating terrain to the north. The largest centers of population are in the valleys of the central upland area and the south. The country's economy is based mainly on crop and livestock farming. Coffee, rice, corn and sugar growing, and sheep and cattle raising are most important. The forests of El Salvador produce the world's largest quantity of the medicinal gum, balsam. Food processing, textile and footwear production are the leading industries. Over half the country's foreign earnings come from coffee exports. The chief imports are temperate foodstuffs, fuel oil, machinery and manufactured goods.

Grenada

The smallest of the Windward Islands, Grenada was the first to be granted full independence in 1974. A number of tiny islands, the Grenadines, are dependent on her; others are dependent upon St Vincent. Grenada is of volcanic origins and rises to a maximum height of 840 m (2,756 ft) above sea level. On the extensive lower areas a wide range of crops, such as cocoa, nutmegs, bananas, coconuts and citrus fruit are grown.

Guadeloupe

One of the four overseas departments of France, Guadeloupe is a group of two main and five smaller islands. The main western island is dominated by the active volcano, Soufrière; the eastern island is much flatter. They are all situated between the British Leeward Islands and Dominica. Bananas, sugar, rum and pineapples are the principal products and export items. Trade is mainly with France.

Guatemala

This independent mainland republic is physically divided by the mountainous areas of the south and west rising to a height of 4,220 m (13,846 ft) above sea level. Agriculture is vital to the national economy. The Pacific facing coastlands are most important in this respect; the broader lowlands of the north and northeast are less fertile. About two-thirds of the working population are in farming, either subsistence or on the commercial plantations. Coffee, cotton, sugar and beef are the main export items. Large areas of the north and extreme south have valuable hardwood forests which have yet to be developed commercially. Rubber production is being encouraged. Mineral production is very limited. Most industries are connected with food processing, cotton textiles and clothing. Chemicals and foodstuffs are the major imports.

Haiti

The only French-speaking republic in Middle America, Haiti comprises the western third of the island of Hispaniola. It has a large population for its size, over 90 percent of the inhabitants being classified as rural. The standard of living of most Haitians is low when compared with other countries of Middle America. The main commercial crops are coffee, sugar and sisal. Bauxite and copper are both mined by North American companies. Light industries are being developed, and now contribute as much to the country's export earnings as any other single item except coffee. Foodstuffs and fuel oils are the most costly imports.

Honduras

One of the larger Middle American republics, Honduras has an extensive upland interior, a long Caribbean-facing coastal zone and a shorter Pacific coastline. Less than 25 percent of the country is cultivated, though two-thirds of the work force is employed in agriculture. Bananas, coffee, beef cattle and cotton are the principal products and agricultural exports. Some 45 percent of the country is forested with both hard- and softwoods. Forest exports are almost as valuable as coffee. A number of industries have been developed but these employ less than 10 percent of the work force.

Jamaica

The largest and most important Commonwealth country in Middle America, Jamaica became fully independent in 1962 after a period of eighteen years with internal self-government. It is an attractive, mountainous island rising to a maximum height of 2,256 m (7,402 ft). For a long time agriculture was the mainstay of the economy, particularly sugarcane, coconuts, bananas, coffee and citrus fruit production. However, Jamaica has now developed a

and corn are the next most widely produced crops. The forests contain a wide variety of hardwoods which are, as yet, little utilized. Cuban mineral reserves are considerable, with large deposits of nickel, production of which is being rapidly expanded. Iron ore and chromite are also important. A range of industries has been developed, such as textile, cigar and cigarette making and food processing.

Dominica

The largest of the Windward Islands, Dominica is a member of the WIAS. It is of volcanic origins and is by far the highest of the Windward group, rising to 1,447 m (4,748 ft) above sea level. A member of the Commonwealth, it is internally self-governing, but the UK is responsible for defense and foreign affairs. Tropical fruits are most important, especially bananas, limes and cocoa.

Dominican Republic

The independent Dominican Republic forms the eastern two-thirds of the island of Hispaniola. Physically the grain of the country is from east to west, with a central highland ridge rising to 3,175 m (10,417 ft), lowland belts on either side of this followed by coastal ranges and coastal lowlands. Economically, the island is heavily dependent upon agriculture. Half the cultivated area is in small

Middle American Countries

range of industries other than agricultural processing. Textiles, engineering, pharmaceuticals and building construction are all important. The country is also the world's second largest source of bauxite. This and processed alumina now account for two-thirds of Jamaica's foreign earnings. Sugar is the next most valuable export. Raw materials are the main imports. Tourism is of growing importance.

Martinique

Situated between Dominica and the British Windward Islands, this island is one of the four overseas departments of France. The north is dominated by Mount Pelée rising to 1,340 m (4,397 ft), the volcano responsible for one of the worst natural disasters of modern times; on May 8, 1902 its eruption killed 40,000 people. Today, bananas, sugar and rum are the main products and exports of the island. Foodstuffs and manufactured goods are the main imports.

Mexico

By far the largest Middle American country, Mexico is the most northerly. Physically dominated by the Sierra Madre mountains, it has far less forest and far more grassland and desert areas than the others, and ranks among the most developed overall. The population is concentrated in the high plains of the south, the eastern foothills and in the lower valley of the Rio Grande. Mexican agriculture produces a wide range of crops, the major ones by output being sugarcane, corn, coffee, sorghum, wheat, oranges and bananas. Of these, only sugar and coffee are exported in large quantities. Mexican forests, some of which were felled indiscriminately earlier in this century, are now exploited more systematically. Production of a wide range of woods and wood products is now rising steadily. A variety of fish is landed from both the Pacific and the Caribbean.

Mexican mineral reserves are large in a wide range of ores. Crude oil is most valuable to the national economy. One-fifth of the world's silver is mined in Mexico; large uranium deposits are being developed steadily. Manufactured goods, petroleum, coffee, sugar and cotton are the leading exports. Cereals, metal products, electrical goods and vehicles are the main imports. Mexico's chief trading partners are the USA, the EEC countries and Japan.

Montserrat

This scenically attractive island is a British colony situated southwest of Antigua and northwest of Guadeloupe within the Leeward Islands. The economy is heavily dependent on British aid. Sea island cotton, limes, tomatoes and other vegetables are the main products.

Netherlands Antilles

Collectively an internally self-governing Dutch overseas possession, the Netherlands Antilles are found in two groups: the three islands of Aruba, Curaçao and Bonaire lie close to the Venezuelan coast; St Martin, St Eustatius and Saba lie within the Leeward Islands. Over 92 percent of the population live on Aruba and Curaçao. Oil refining is the main activity, with crude oil being imported from Venezuela and refined products being exported to North America and Europe. Phosphates are mined in Curaçao and exported. In the Leeward Islands, fishing, sugar and rum production are the main activities, though they are of far lower value than those of the other islands.

Nicaragua

Middle America's second largest country, this independent republic is quite sparsely populated. Physically it extends from the Pacific to the Caribbean coast where the mountainous backbone of the Middle American isthmus is at its lowest (max height 2,107 m, 6,913 ft). It is also distinctive, physically, for the presence of two large lakes, Nicaragua and Managua. Agriculture is the main occupation with much scope for improved production using irrigation. Cotton, tropical fruits, rice and sweet potatoes are the leading crops grown in the east. Sugar cane, cotton and corn are grown in the west where beef cattle are also raised. Cotton, coffee and meat products are the main exports; manufactured goods, chemicals and fuel oils are the major imports.

Panama

Part of Colombia until 1903, this is the youngest independent republic on the Middle American mainland. Divided in two by the Panama Canal Zone, it occupies the narrowest parts of the Middle American mainland. The land nearest to the canal zone is most heavily populated. Agriculture is not well developed, though it is the mainstay of the national economy. Over 60 percent of the country's foodstuffs is imported. The most important crops grown for local consumption are rice and corn, with only bananas and sugar as significant exports. Mineral developments are just beginning, with the emphasis on three large copper deposits. The economy is, however, largely dependent upon the Panama Canal. The country has a large registered merchant fleet, many of its inhabitants work on the canal, and foreign personnel passing through spend money in the main country.

Panama Canal Zone

Between 1904 and 1914 the USA constructed a most important 58 km (36 mi) long canal across the isthmus of Panama, connecting the Caribbean Sea to the Pacific Ocean. By a treaty with the country of Panama at that time, the USA leased in perpetuity a strip of land about 16 km (10 mi) wide in which they possess full sovereign rights. In 1978, new treaties were signed to give the zone back to Panama by the year 2000 and to maintain its neutrality. The canal is open to shipping of all nations on payment of tolls. In an average year 13,000 oceangoing vessels pass through, carrying about 150 million tons of cargo. Since the canal's opening the amount of oceangoing traffic in the Caribbean area has grown enormously, and Europe's trading relations with the Pacific coasts of all the Americas, Australia and New Zealand have changed radically.

Puerto Rico

Save two smaller islands, Puerto Rico is the most densely populated country in Middle America. An island outlying territory of the USA, it is internally self-governing but dependent upon the US in international affairs. Sugarcane, which is refined into sugar and distilled into rum, is the leading crop but tobacco, cotton,

COUNTRY REFERENCE: MIDDLE AMERICA

Middle American Countries	Political Status	State Capital	Area km²	Area sq mi	Population	Population Density per km²	Population Density per sq mi	Births per Thousand Persons	Deaths per Thousand Persons	Mean Annual Percentage Increase in Population
Anguilla	C	The Valley	91	35	6,000	66	171	—	—	—
Antigua	B	Saint Johns	442	171	75,000	170	439	18.3	7.1	1.4
Bahama Islands	A	Nassau	13,935	5,380	222,000	16	41	18.1	3.9	3.9
Barbados	A	Bridgetown	430	166	250,000	581	1,506	19.5	8.4	0.7
Belize	C	Belmopan	22,965	8,867	150,000	7.0	17	38.7	5.3	3.2
Bermuda	C	Hamilton	54	21	59,000	1,093	2,810	16.3	6.4	1.6
British Virgin Islands	C	Road Town	153	59	10,000	65	170	24.5	7.5	2.4
Cayman Islands	C	Georgetown	260	100	12,000	46	120	24.7	6.0	—
Costa Rica	A	San José	50,900	19,650	2,079,000	41	106	29.5	5.0	2.7
Cuba	A	La Habana	114,524	44,218	9,678,000	85	219	22.3	5.7	1.8
Dominica	B	Roseau	751	290	77,000	103	266	36.4	10.1	1.0
Dominican Republic	A	Santo Domingo	48,734	18,816	5,041,000	103	268	45.8	11.0	2.9
El Salvador	A	San Salvador	21,393	8,260	4,290,000	201	519	40.1	8.0	3.0
Grenada	A	Saint George's	344	133	114,000	331	857	26.2	7.5	0.5
Guadeloupe	C	Basse-Terre	1,780	687	371,000	208	540	28.0	7.3	1.7
Guatemala	A	Guatemala	108,889	42,042	6,525,000	60	155	43.1	12.5	2.5
Haiti	A	Port-au-Prince	27,750	10,714	4,800,000	173	448	35.8	16.3	1.6
Honduras	A	Tegucigalpa	112,088	43,277	2,946,000	26	68	49.3	14.6	4.0
Jamaica	A	Kingston	10,962	4,232	2,080,000	190	491	30.8	7.2	1.7
Martinique	C	Fort-de-France	1,100	425	378,000	344	889	22.4	6.8	1.6
Mexico	A	Ciudad-de-Mexico	1,972,546	761,604	65,555,000	33	86	43.4	7.2	3.5
Montserrat	C	Plymouth	101	39	14,000	139	359	24.3	10.5	—
Netherlands Antilles	C	Willemstad	961	371	242,000	252	652	—	—	1.8
Nicaragua	A	Managua	130,000	50,200	2,347,000	18	47	48.3	13.9	3.3
Panama	A	Panama	75,651	29,209	1,795,000	24	61	31.7	7.1	3.3
Panama Canal Zone	C	Balboa Heights	1,445	558	40,000	28	72	13.2	—	—
Puerto Rico	C	San Juan	8,897	3,435	3,345,000	376	974	23.3	6.5	2.8
St Kitts-Nevis	B	Basseterre	267	103	48,000	178	466	24.1	10.8	0.4
St Lucia	A	Castries	616	238	117,000	190	492	40.9	9.3	1.5
St Vincent	B	Kingstown	388	150	117,000	302	780	34.4	10.0	0.7
Turks and Caicos Islands	C	Grand Turk	430	166	5,000	12	30	34.3	10.4	2.7
Virgin Islands (US)	C	Charlotte Amalie	344	133	102,000	297	766	27.7	5.2	0.5
MIDDLE AMERICA TOTALS			2,729,191	1,053,749	112,890,000	39	101	—	—	—

1 △

2 △   3 ▽

coffee and tropical fruits are also grown. Dairying is more valuable and provides the leading export products. Since World War II, a large number of industries have been established, particularly the manufacture of metal goods, cement, glass and wood products.

St Kitts-Nevis

These two Leeward Islands are members of the WIAS. Until 1976 they were associated with Anguilla. Members of the Commonwealth, they are internally self-governing though the UK is responsible for their defense and foreign affairs. Both are mountainous islands of volcanic origins. St Kitts is the larger and more densely populated. Its most important products are sugar, molasses and salt, while those of Nevis are sugar and cotton.

St Lucia

Fully independent only since February 1979, St Lucia is a member of the Commonwealth and the WIAS. It is the second largest and scenically the most attractive of the Windward Islands, rising to 950 m (3,117 ft). There is still much evidence of its former state as a French possession. Today bananas, cocoa, copra and coconuts are the main exports. Tourism is growing.

St Vincent

The second smallest of the Windward Islands, a member of the Commonwealth and the WIAS, St Vincent is internally self-governing but has its defense and foreign affairs controlled by the UK. It is the most British of the Windward Islands. Physically it is a volcanic island which rises to

1,074 m (3,524 ft) above sea level. A group of tiny islands, some of the Grenadines, are dependent upon it; others are dependent upon Grenada. Arrowroot is the main product; tropical fruits, vegetables and spices are the other main crops.

Turks and Caicos Islands

These two groups of islands are a British colony lying southeast of the Bahamas. Only six are inhabited. Until 1976 they were associated with the Cayman Islands. Fishing is the most important activity, accounting for over 95 percent of the islands' exports. Imports are mainly foodstuffs and manufactured goods.

Virgin Islands (US)

In 1917 the United States purchased the western group of the Virgin

1 Dominican Republic – US aid has helped develop this troubled state which suffered over 50 revolutions; 2 Looking south from Tortola, British Virgin Islands – sailing and fishing can be enjoyed in these mild, sheltered waters; 3 Antigua, Leeward Islands – this attractive island relies increasingly on tourism

Islands from Denmark, the others being a British colony. They are constitutionally an unincorporated territory of the USA. The islanders elect their own governor and legislative representatives, do not vote in the US presidential elections, but send one nonvoting member to the US congress. Tourism is now the base of the islands' economy, with about 1.5 million visitors each year. Manufacturing industries, fruit and vegetable production and building are also important.

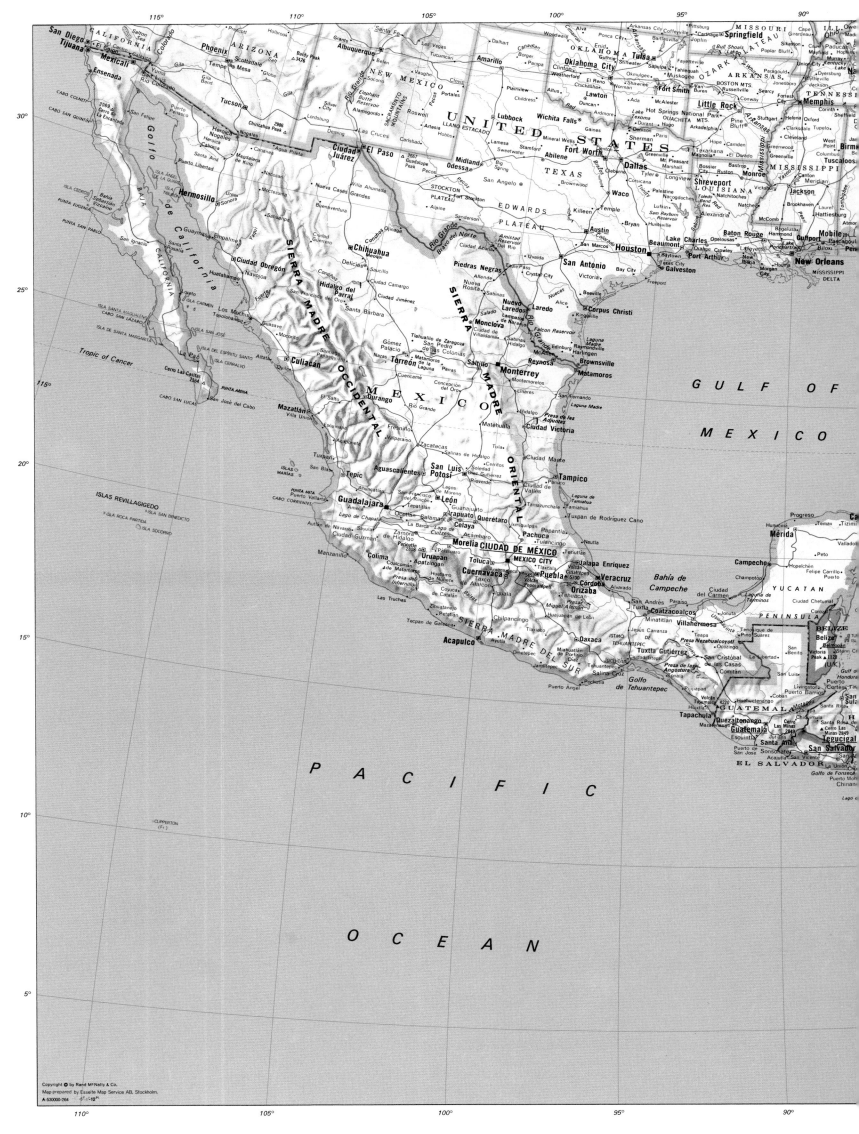

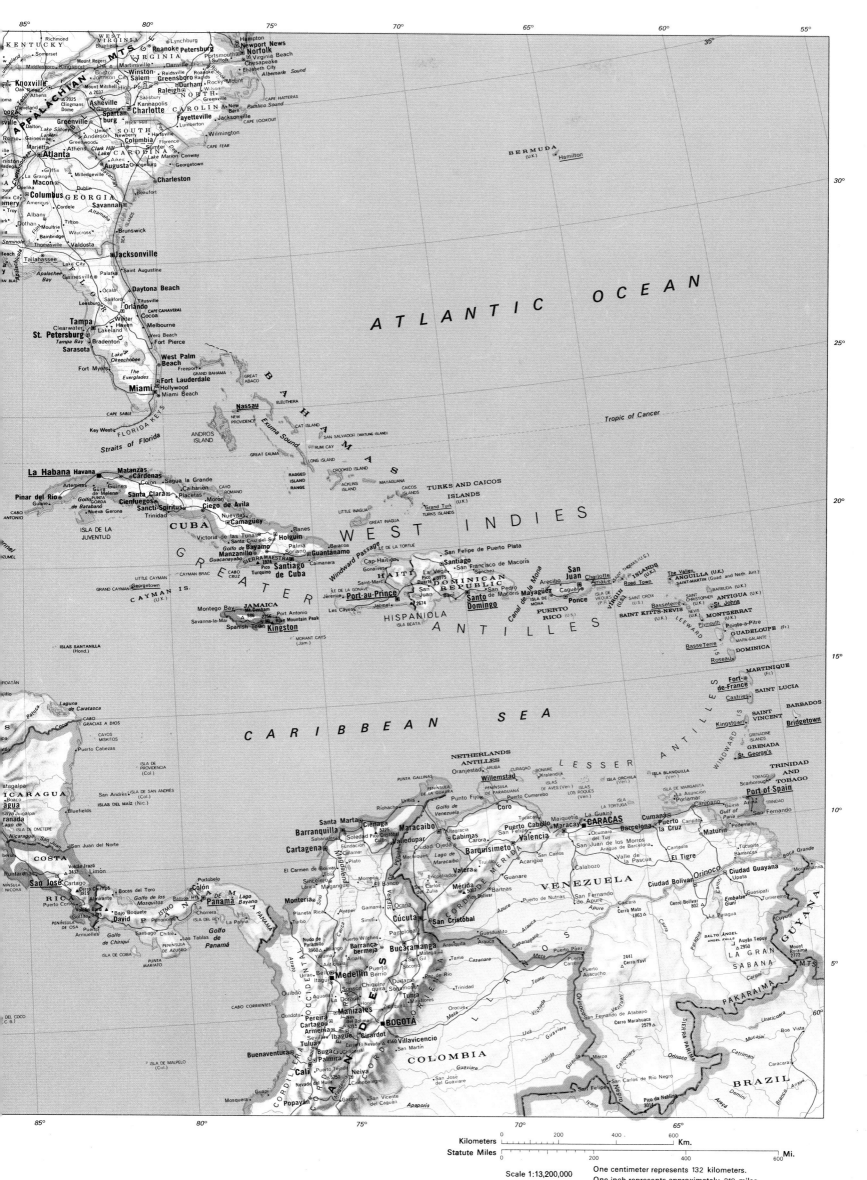

Kilometers
Statute Miles

Scale 1:13,200,000

One centimeter represents 132 kilometers.
One inch represents approximately 210 miles.

Oblique Conic Conformal Projection

131

SOUTH AMERICA
Physical Profile

World Location and Size

The dividing line between Middle and South America lies at the Colombian/Panamanian border, the narrowest land bridge dividing the Pacific Ocean from the Caribbean Sea. The northern coast of the continent extends to 12°N. The southernmost point, Cape Horn, lies at 56°S. Thus, the north-south extent of the continent is 7,450 km (4,600 mi). The west to east extent varies greatly, but in the central equatorial parts it extends from 82°W in northern Peru to 35°W in eastern Brazil, an overall distance of some 5,150 km (3,200 mi).

South America is essentially triangular in shape; the north and east coasts are comparatively straight, but the west coast has a straight southern part and then a convex northern part. The continent also includes a number of offshore islands, including Trinidad and Tobago to the north, the Falkland Islands to the southeast, the Galapagos Islands to the west, the Chonos Archipelago to the southwest and Tierra del Fuego to the south. Apart from the latter two islands, the coastline of the continent is largely physically uncomplicated.

Landscape

The continent may be divided into eight distinct physical areas, four of which are essentially lowlands and the rest uplands. Within each of these two groups is a dominant member: the Amazon Basin is by far the most extensive lowland area and the Andes Mountains the most extensive upland area.

The Amazon Basin is an extremely low-lying area dominated by dense tropical rain forest. It covers a part of central and eastern South America which is almost as large as the whole USA. The main rivers discharge more water than any other single system in the world. The Amazon itself is some 6,275 km (3,900 mi) long.

The continent's second largest river system is dominated by the Parana, Paraguay and Uruguay Rivers. These reach the sea in the Rio de la Plata, an inlet of the Atlantic which extends some 330 km (205 mi) inland. The dominant lie of the land here is gently sloping from north to south.

The third, but far smaller river basin is that of the Orinoco in the north which drains a smaller area than the Amazon, from which it is divided by an extremely low water-

Opposite: Forming part of the border between Brazil and Argentina, the spectacular Iguassu Falls would provide great power if harnessed

shed. These rivers drain the eastern and northern flanks of the Andes as well as the Guiana Highlands. Most of the area is known as the *Llanos*, and is dominated by swamplands.

The last area of lowland, along the Pacific coastal fringes, is the most fragmented. The coastal plains are widest in the extreme north and parts of Chile, where they may reach 80 km (50 mi) at their maximum, but elsewhere the mountains are as little as one-tenth that distance from the ocean. The lowlands are crossed in their humid parts by a number of short rivers which plunge steeply westward from the Andes.

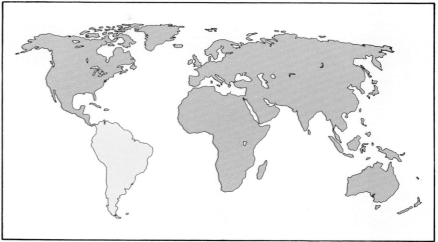

The Andes mountains run parallel to the Pacific coast. In the south there is one main ridge but there are two or three ridges in the north with large valleys between. At its widest, the whole range stretches for about 500 km (310 mi) from west to east. The western slopes are more precipitous than those of the east. The Andes contains a number of active and extinct volcanoes and is still a belt of earthquake activity. It is part of the 'Pacific ring of fire'. Mount Aconcagua in Argentina rises to 6,959 m (22,831 ft), the highest point in the Western Hemisphere.

South and east of the Amazon lies the second largest upland area, the triangular-shaped Brazilian Highlands. These rise quite steeply from the Atlantic fringe and then slope gently into the interior. Their general levels in the southeast average 1,400 m (4,600 ft), and the highest point is 2,890 m (9,482 ft). Geologically, these are far older than the Andes.

The smaller Guiana Highlands of the north, between the Amazon and Orinoco Basins, rise steeply from the former to their highest parts which are over 2,600 m (8,600 ft) up, and then slope gently toward the north.

In the extreme south, the Patagonian Plateau is a lower, irregular, wind-swept tableland rising to a little over 760 m (2,500 ft).

Climatic Background

Extending from the world's largest equatorial basin to the most southerly point in the Southern Hemisphere outside the Antarctic, South America exhibits a wide range of climates. East of the Andes and north of 20°S, is a large area which experiences equatorial and tropical climates which provide for the dense rain forests within 5° to 8° of the equator and the savanna landscapes of parts of the Guianas, Venezuela and much of the Brazilian interior. Average monthly temperatures never fall below 18°C (64°F). Rainfall at its maximum exceeds 2,500 mm (100 in). Similar humid tropical climates are also found on some Brazilian coastal fringes between 12°S and 28°S and on the Colombian coastlands between 9°W and 8°S.

Hot or warm climates are found along the Pacific coastal lowlands from 4°S to 32°S and in a small area east of the Andes around 30°S. Here,

View of the Andes from near Cuzco, Peru; the Inca civilization was centered on this region in an area of magnificent scenery provided by the extensive mountain chain

rainfall is mainly below 125 mm (5 in) per year, and average monthly temperatures reach the high 20°sC (low 80°sF) in the north and the mid 20°sC (mid 70°sF) in the south. The Patagonian Plateau area is one of mid-latitude desert, where rainfall rarely reaches 250 mm (10 in) and average temperatures range between 19°C (66°F) and 0°C (32°F). Steppeland climates are found in a north-south belt east of the Andes and south of 22°S, in northeast Brazil and in a small coastal area of Venezuela.

Warm and cool temperate climates dominate the Pacific coastlines south of 32°S and a triangular area south of 20°S and east of 65°W. In the Pacific strip the north experiences a Mediterranean climate while farther south it becomes cooler and far wetter. The climate in the larger Atlantic-facing area has higher temperatures, with a greater temperature range, and rainfall totals of between 550 mm (22 in) and 1,000 mm (40 in).

SOUTH AMERICA

This, the fifth largest continent, has a well documented history dating back to before the days of the Inca Empire which was at its peak in the second half of the fifteenth century. From about 1500, it attracted European explorers, prospectors and settlers at much the same time as North America, but thereafter the two sister continents developed in entirely different ways. Unlike the north, South America did not unite into large independent countries, but instead a number of separate countries, some of them comparatively small, emerged by the early nineteenth century. Most of these had no ties with European mother countries. In any case, by that time, Spain and Portugal were far from powerful. So, the continent has tended to stagnate during the last 170 years. There is a great potential but it needs harnessing. Well may South America be called 'The Sleeping Giant'.

Population Growth

When Spanish explorers first reached South America in the late fifteenth century, it is estimated that there were some 10–12 million people in the continent. These were all American Indians (Amerinds) whose forefathers had crossed from Asia into North America before those two land masses were divided by the creation of the Bering Strait at the end of the ice age. They then penetrated into the South American continent. It is likely that these people arrived 12,000–15,000 years ago.

From the sixteenth century onward, European settlers mainly from Spain and Portugal, but also a few from France, the Netherlands and the United Kingdom arrived in this new continent. Eastern South America was settled mainly by the Portuguese and elsewhere by the Spanish migrants. By the early years of the nineteenth century when the Spanish Empire disintegrated, it is estimated that there were nearly 10 million European settlers here.

During the second half of the nineteenth century and the first three decades of this, South America saw a steady stream of arrivals from a number of European countries. Italians, British and Germans emigrated there, as well as more from Iberia, especially into the southern temperate parts. By 1900, nearly 40 million of the continent's inhabitants were either European migrants or their descendants.

The third group of people to arrive in South America were the African Negroes who were initially introduced by the Europeans as slaves. They came mainly to the hotter parts and are most numerous in northern Brazil and Colombia.

Today the Europeans dominate with far smaller numbers of Negroes and Amerinds. Yet, all told these three 'pure' groups make up less than half the total population. In addition, there are large numbers of people descended from mixed marriages, an arrangement never resisted by the Roman Catholic Church, and indeed established from the early settlement days when Spanish and Portuguese men took Amerind wives. Today, the offspring of a European and Amerind marriage are known as mestizos; the children of Europeans and Negroes are mulattos; where Amerind and Negro marry the offspring are called zambos. Intermarriage between these three has led to a further blurring of the racial groups which, in time, will become even harder to distinguish.

The present population of the continent is about 227 million which, as we shall see, is very unevenly distributed. Even the proportions of the different racial groups found in individual countries vary greatly. Brazil has about 75 percent of its 113 million directly descended from European stock, 5 percent from Amerind or Negro stock and the remaining 20 percent from mixed marriages, predominantly mestizo. By contrast, only 20 percent of Venezuelans are of European extraction, 10 percent are of Negro stock and the remaining 70 percent are of mixed marriages, again mainly mestizo.

Political Development

The Inca civilization was centered on the Andes mountains. One of its interests then, and for us today, lies in the great technical skills of these peoples, who yet remained completely ignorant of some things which we would regard as vital. They had built huge palaces and temples and evolved a technique of suspension bridge engineering which amazed the European. An elaborate system of roads stretched from one end of the empire to the other. The Incas were also highly skilled craftsmen working in precious metals. Yet, they knew nothing of iron and had not stumbled upon the wheel, a technical wonder known in Europe for over 1,500 years. Further, they had no written language but depended upon quipu, an intricate system of knotted cords, for keeping records.

In 1531 the Inca Empire was effectively overthrown by Pizarro and the Spanish conquistadors. Today a number of its great landmarks, such as the Machu Picchu ruins high in the mountains of Peru, remain as a symbol of this once grand and powerful system, and are a modern tourist attraction.

The sixteenth to the early nineteenth centuries were characterized by the arrival of Spaniards in the west and south and Portuguese in the east, attracted by the precious metals, especially gold, as described in the legend of El Dorado, and the development of new farming lands. Such crops as tobacco and sugarcane, neither of which could be cultivated in Europe, were important initially. The mineral wealth of the interior was slowly realized in the nineteenth century. Then, at a later stage than in North America, a series of wars of independence was waged, out of which emerged nine separate Spanish-speaking countries and one Portuguese-speaking country. This internal division has subsequently been a great hindrance to the continent's development.

Within the present century some countries have been able to establish reasonably sound economies based on locally strong activities and resources: Argentina is the greatest temperate farming land in the continent, Brazil has developed tropical farming plus a range of mining and industrial ventures, and Venezuela is the greatest oil and mineral producing country. But, many of the rest are still comparatively poor. Today, South American politics tend to be predominantly volatile. The overthrowing of presidents and governments by civil revolution or military uprising is a common, almost everyday, feature.

Both the Communist and the democratic world try to influence the directions in which South American countries develop. For example, the present Brazilian constitution set up in 1967 is essentially democratic, with a two-chamber elected congress, president and vice-president. There is a ban on political parties which work against democratic ideals and fundamental human rights. Likewise, Chile adopted a democratic constitution in 1925. In the presidential elections in 1970 the incoming president, on a minority vote, took the country along completely new lines with a Marxist coalition government. This became unpopular both inside Chile and in the outside world. In 1973 the government was overthrown by the military, who have since established a military government, dissolved the National Congress and banned all Communist parties and all other political activities.

Industry, Commerce and Communications

Prior to World War I, most South American countries exported their agricultural and mined raw materials, mainly to the Northern Hemisphere, and there was very little industrial development. In the sixty-plus years since then, some countries have attempted to broaden their economies, establish a range of industries and thus be less dependent on imports of manufactured goods from North America, Europe and elsewhere. During the two periods of world war and throughout the great inter-war economic slump, those countries dependent upon one or two staple exports suffered severe econ-

1 Incas going to church, Pisco, Peru.
2 Bogota, capital of Colombia

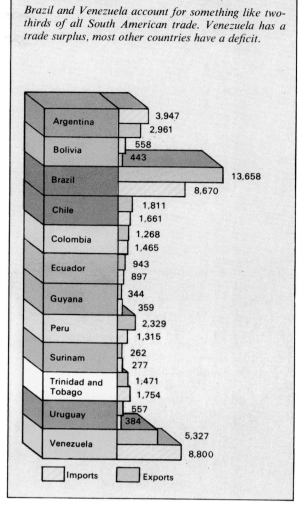

Brazil and Argentina tower above other S American countries as developed economies: 1 Caracas, Venezuela – as with the country, oil is the mainspring of this capital's prosperity; 2 Modern road network, Rio de Janeiro, Brazil – this city and nearby Sao Paulo are the largest urban developments in the whole of the continent; 3 Buenos Aires harbor, Argentina – large meat processing plants surround the capital's busy port, preparing meat for worldwide export

Total Imports and Exports

(1975 figures in millions of U.S. dollars)

Brazil and Venezuela account for something like two-thirds of all South American trade. Venezuela has a trade surplus, most other countries have a deficit.

Country	Imports	Exports
Argentina	3,947	2,961
Bolivia	558	443
Brazil	13,658	8,670
Chile	1,811	1,661
Colombia	1,268	1,465
Ecuador	943	897
Guyana	344	359
Peru	2,329	1,315
Surinam	262	277
Trinidad and Tobago	1,471	1,754
Uruguay	557	384
Venezuela	5,327	8,800

□ Imports   ▨ Exports

omic difficulties, so that diversification in their internal economies became essential.

South American industry is based on a wide range of raw materials, both farm products and mineral resources. Yet the minimal coal deposits hampered development for a long time, and today other energy sources, such as oil, natural gas and HEP have been developed to varying degrees. A second great problem for South American industrialization lies in the limited local markets; if the great majority of the population are poor, demand is limited, industrialization is thus unwarranted so there is little opportunity for the local population to become richer. Yet there is internal pressure to become more independent economically; thus far Brazil, Argentina, Chile and Uruguay have demonstrated most effectively how this can be done. Venezuela, Peru and Colombia are following.

The employment structure of Brazil, which has the largest population and probably the most advanced economy in the continent, provides an interesting contrast with those of developing countries in other continents. More than 2 out of every 5 working persons are employed in farming, about 1 in 6 in manufacturing industries, 1 in 10 in trade and commerce, 1 in 20 in transport and communications and the rest in a range of service industries and other activities.

The physical character of the continent and the way in which population has tended to cluster along the Atlantic seaboard and, to a lesser extent, in the Andean valleys and some Pacific fringe locations, have markedly affected the development of the transport networks. The great river systems are beset by rapids, silting and seasonal flow and, for the most part, traverse the least settled parts of the continent. Yet one day they could play a major part in the development of the interior.

Except in the Pampas area of Argentina and in parts of Brazil's Atlantic fringe, the railroads are ill-developed. They consist largely of isolated lines for specific purposes or radial routes feeding into a single large city. A problem which has only recently been faced is that presented by the existence of so many different gauges. Air transport, both international and movements between the core region of a country and its remoter areas, was developed initially between the two world wars. It has expanded since World War II and is without doubt the most successful mode of transport for the terrain.

Road networks, like rail networks, are inconsistently developed. In their first phase of development, the interwar era, the Pampas and southeast Brazil were the most rapidly developed areas, with a few main routes penetrating into the interior of the temperate southern parts and across the Andes to Chile. Since World War II, the often dreamed of Pan American Highway has been developed from Alaska to Argentina, though it is not yet complete. However, within South America it does provide through communications from Colombia southward to Chile, then eastward to Buenos Aires and northeastward to Rio and Brasilia. Further developments, like the Amazonian Highway, are envisaged, which will aid in the development of the interior.

Agriculture, Forestry and Fishing

Equatorial South America contains the world's largest expanse of broadleaf forest. While some of this has been cleared, the greater part of the Amazon Basin remains agriculturally unproductive. Much of the Pacific coastal strip from 5°S southward and the Andes Mountains are also unsuitable for farming, as is the Gran Chaco area of the interior.

Beyond these negative areas, grazing lands cover the next largest parts of the continent, dominating the farming landscapes south of about 15°S to southern Argentina. However, more intensive and often far more mixed farming is found on the Atlantic coastal fringes of Brazil, Uruguay and Argentina. Grazing and stock raising are also found in the valleys of the Andes, the Llanos and coastal Venezuela.

Livestock was introduced into South America during the sixteenth century. It was not until nearly 300 years later, however, that technological advances, such as refrigeration, made it possible to develop the great grasslands of the south and east, raising stock to be shipped back to the large markets of the Northern Hemisphere. The tropical grasslands and areas as far as 35°S are mainly cattle territory while sheep dominate the cooler areas from there to Cape Horn and also the Andean valleys.

South American grasslands are more reliable than those of South Africa and Australia, and are as yet nowhere near fully exploited. There is much scope for further development here. In all, the continent has nearly 18 percent of the world's 1,210 million cattle. Brazil, with 95 million, Argentina with 60 million, Colombia with 24 million and Uruguay with 11 million, have the largest numbers. Some 12 percent of the world's 1,040 million sheep can be found in South America. Argentina with 25 million, Peru with 17 million and Uruguay with 16 million have the largest numbers. The Argentine is the world's fourth largest wool producer; 167 thousand tons or 7 percent of the world total. Brazil alone has significant numbers of other farm animals, with 36 million pigs and 16,000 goats; 6 and 4 percent of the world totals respectively.

Arable farming in South America is markedly concentrated, crop by crop, in particular areas, with the subtropical and temperate regions of the south again being more important than the hotter parts of the north. Around 3 percent of the world's wheat production comes from this continent, almost entirely from extensive areas of Argentina, where 11 million tons are grown each year. Chile, Uruguay and southern Brazil produce far smaller quantities. Some 9 percent of the world's corn is grown in southern Brazil. Brazil, with 18 million tons, is the world's third largest producer. The only other cereal to be grown in quantity

SOUTH AMERICA

is sorghum. The Argentine contributes 10 percent of the world output, being second only to India in sorghum production.

Within the tropical areas, a few distinctive products loom large. In a typical year, 45 percent of the world's coffee is grown in Brazil, Colombia, Venezuela, Peru and Bolivia, with Brazil alone accounting for nearly 30 percent of the world total. Brazil again, with Ecuador and to a lesser extent Colombia and Venezuela, also produce a quarter of the world's cocoa. Nearly a quarter of the world's sugarcane comes from Brazil, Colombia, Argentina and Peru.

Brazil is also the world's second largest orange producer. Other citrus fruits are grown there in substantial quantities and in Argentina. Finally, Brazil produces more than twice as many bananas as any other single country in the world. Ecuador, Colombia and Venezuela also contribute to South America's share of just over one-third of the global total, making it the undoubted leader in this field.

The continent's vast forest reserves are little developed. Less than 9 percent of the world's sawn timber comes from here. More than two-thirds of that is produced by Brazil, the world leader for sawn broadleaf timber. Colombia is a poor second in the continent.

The Pacific Ocean is rich in fish and comparatively underexploited. Peru, once the world's most important fishing nation, is now fourth in the world with 3.5 million tons (5 percent world total), and Chile fifteenth with 1.1 million tons. Peru is also a leading whaling nation.

Over and above commercial pastoral and arable farming, large areas are still farmed by Amerinds and mixed racial groups on a subsistence basis. Land is held communally or individually, or as a smallholding granted by the plantation owners. Here families grow such crops as corn, cassava, yucca and vegetables for their personal needs. Some of this farming is of a shifting kind, a wasteful practice which it may take a long time to eliminate.

Natural Resources

The power base of this continent goes part way to explain the lack of industrial development. Only Middle America has smaller reserves of coal. Modern outputs are derisory, standing at less than 10 million tons per year, of which Colombia and Brazil each contribute around 3 million tons. Indeed, South America's coal resources are considerably less than Africa's.

Since 1917, South America has become increasingly important as a crude oil producer. Venezuela, in particular, has rich resources, and is today one of the leading producers of the western world. This country is thought to possess 3 percent of the world's crude oil total. Smaller sources of crude oil are found along the Pacific fringes of Ecuador and Peru and in the extreme south of Chile. Some other small fields have been found and exploited east of the Andes, where further exploration is likely to reveal other reserves. Venezuela and Argentina are the only two significant producers of natural gas.

It is estimated that South America has about 12 percent of the world's HEP potential but only a very small part of this has been harnessed. Many of the finest locations are remote, development and transmission costs would be high and, in many cases, the countries with their comparatively backward economies simply do not have the demand for the electricity. Much of the potential is thus unexploited. As in so many fields, Brazil leads in HEP development, with a number of schemes in the highlands providing the great bulk of the nation's electricity needs.

Both in terms of reserves and modern outputs, the continent is well endowed with iron ore. As an individual country, Brazil has the third richest reserves in the world, and is the fourth largest producer with over 7.5 percent of the world's annual output. Venezuela, Chile and Peru are also in the top 15 producers, placing South America overall as the world's third most important continent in this respect.

The table opposite summarizes South America's production of other ores and precious resources.

South American Economy

More than any other continent, the population map of South America shows the main concentrations to be on the coasts and in the lower river valleys. There are also mountain valley concentrations in the tropical northwest. Around the main towns and cities are limited areas in which over 100 people per km^2 (250 per sq mi) live, but, outside these, population densities fall off rapidly. In lowland Argentina, Uruguay and Brazil large areas with more than 25 per km^2 (60 per sq mi) are found. But so much of Amazonia, Patagonia and the mountain areas have less than 1 per km^2 (2 per sq mi).

South American capitals dominate their countries, along with a few other major cities. Known as primate cities, they present a considerable problem to effective, widespread development. Thus, in Argentina, Buenos Aires has a population of 9.3 million; no other metro area has a population one-tenth of that. In Brazil, Sao Paulo has 9.9 million and Rio de Janeiro 8.2 million, with the next largest city, Recife, having only 2.1 million. Santiago in Chile has 2.9 million, the next largest being one-fifth that size. Other million plus cities of the continent are Lima

Many S American Indians live only at subsistence level: 1 Peasants at the market, La Paz, Bolivia – the world's highest sizeable city is at 3,600 m (11,800 ft); 2 Amazonian hunters, Brazil – tribes have been wiped out as areas of rainforest have been cleared; 3 Llama flock, Sacsahuamán, Peru – the ancient Inca rock fortress is a good shelter.

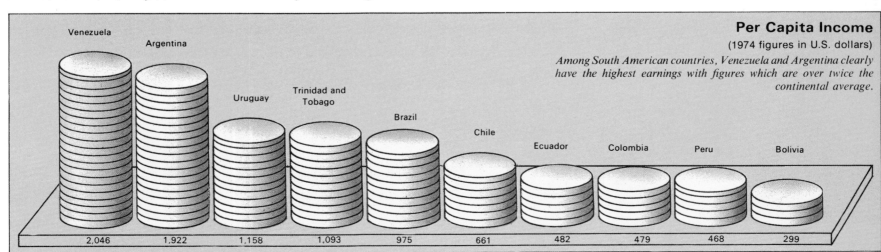

Per Capita Income
(1974 figures in U.S. dollars)

Among South American countries, Venezuela and Argentina clearly have the highest earnings with figures which are over twice the continental average.

Venezuela	Argentina	Uruguay	Trinidad and Tobago	Brazil	Chile	Ecuador	Colombia	Peru	Bolivia
2,046	1,922	1,158	1,093	975	661	482	479	468	299

(Peru) (3.3 million), Montevideo (Uruguay) (1.3 million), Caracas (Venezuela) (2.5 million), Bogota (Colombia) (2.9 million), Medellin (Colombia) (1.5 million).

South American birth rates are mainly far higher than world averages. In some countries they exceed 40 per 1,000 though 25–39 per 1,000 is the norm. Uruguay, with 20.9 per 1,000 has the lowest birth rate. Death rates are mainly below 10 per 1,000. Thus, in the majority of South American countries, population grows by more than 2.5 percent each year, and in six by more than 3 percent annually.

Overall the growth of international trade conducted by South American countries in the past forty years has not kept up with world trends. Although world imports and exports grew by 4.5 and 8 times between 1938–'58 and 1958–'75, South America's import figures grew by only 3.2 and 4.5 times, and exports 3.7 and 3.7 times respectively. Obviously some countries are trading giants compared with others and individual performances have varied greatly. In 1938, Argentina, Brazil and Chile were the three leading countries. By 1975 the order had changed and Brazil, Venezuela and Argentina were the leaders. Between them, these three accounted for over two-thirds of the total international trade of the continent.

South American changes in per capita incomes in the period 1960 to 1974 have outstripped the non-Communist world growth of 186 percent; they have grown by 210 percent, though inflation has been more marked here than in other parts of the world. Some countries have growth figures above, others below this average. The largest growth has been in Brazil, with 390 percent. Other growth figures are Argentina 227 percent, Chile 190 percent and Venezuela 138 percent.

South America's energy production and consumption strikingly demonstrate the continent's deficiency in this field. As a whole, in 1975 the continent produced 334 million tons coal equivalent (mtce) and used 195 mtce. The export surplus of 139 mtce is due entirely to oil from Venezuela which produced 201 mtce and used only 32 mtce, exporting 169 mtce. Seen another way, the rest of the continent produced 133 mtce and used 168 mtce, showing that they had to import over one-fifth of their meager energy needs. In this, Brazil played a major part, its production

1 La Compañia Jesuit church, Quito, Ecuador – one of many architectural gems in this old capital; 2 Rio de Janeiro, Brazil – the splendid bay with its famous Sugar Loaf mountain is a fitting setting for this lively capital

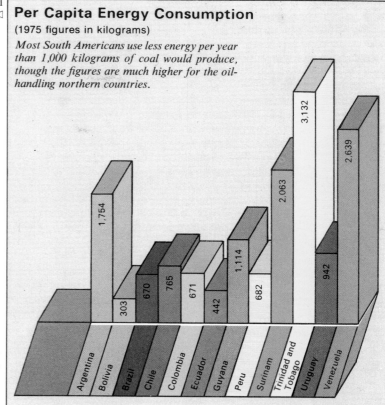

Per Capita Energy Consumption
(1975 figures in kilograms)

Most South Americans use less energy per year than 1,000 kilograms of coal would produce, though the figures are much higher for the oil-handling northern countries.

Country	kg
Argentina	1,754
Bolivia	303
Brazil	670
Chile	765
Colombia	671
Ecuador	442
Guyana	1,114
Peru	682
Surinam	2,063
Trinidad and Tobago	3,132
Uruguay	942
Venezuela	2,639

being nearly 26 mtce but its consumption almost 72 mtce. Argentina has a fine balance of energy production and consumption of just over 42 mtce. In the rest of the continent, only Colombia produces and consumes more than 10 mtce.

Per capita energy consumption figures range from over 3,000 kg/ca in Trinidad and Tobago, 2,640 in Venezuela, to 303 in Bolivia and 153 in Paraguay. The overall continental average in 1975 was 813 kg/ca. Only Africa, with its average of a little less than 400, and Asia with just over 600 kg/ca, have lower figures.

The expression 'The Sleeping Giant' was used earlier to characterize South America. Experts have suggested that, given an appropriate stimulus or lead, the continent would stir. We have seen some of the problems which it faces, both economic and political. Yet there are signs that it is rousing itself, and will continue to do so in coming decades. South America's natural resources are becoming increasingly attractive as alternative supplies in the developed world are being rapidly used up. Some countries which were heavily dependent upon one or two staple exports, realize how dangerous this

is and are making attempts to diversify their economies. Most South American countries have been politically independent for a long time but have made little economic progress. There is now a growing impatience for economic growth and more economic independence.

Internally the problems of inflation are greater here than in other parts of the world, though these should be checked soon. More hopefully, in the last few years some countries, especially Brazil, have shown growths in their national products which have been well placed in the world tables. Things could go wrong, but given effective government of any sort and a little economic good fortune, the remainder of this century could be the time for comparatively rapid progress of many parts of this relatively undeveloped American continent.

Ore	Average Annual World Production (million tons)	South America's Share (percent)	Principal South American Producing Countries
bauxite	80.3	10	Surinam, Guyana
chrome	7.2	2	Brazil
copper	7.4	13	Chile, Peru
lead	3.2	7	Peru, Argentina
manganese	22.8	10	Brazil
molybdenum	0.084	12	Chile, Peru
silver	0.01	18	Peru, Chile, Bolivia
tin	0.2	15	Bolivia, Brazil
tungsten	0.036	9	Bolivia, Brazil, Peru
vanadium	0.02	3	Chile
zinc	5.4	8	Peru

South American Countries

Argentina

The lands around the River Plate were first discovered by Spanish explorers in 1515. They remained under Spanish control until 1816 when Argentina broke away from European rule and became independent. Since 1976 it has been under a military government.

Much of the western part is taken up by the Andes Mountains, rising to 6,959 m (22,831 ft) in Mount Aconcagua. The east of the country is largely plain land. Here, the lush Pampas, one of the world's richest farming regions for both beef and wheat production, is most important to the economy. The Argentinian population is most heavily concentrated in the Plate valley. In the southern area of Patagonia and in the Gran Chaco of the north, as well as in the mountainous west, the population is far smaller.

Argentina is a major trading nation. Her meat exports are the second largest in the world. Wheat, wool, vegetable oils, hides and skins are other leading exports. Among the most valuable imports are chemicals, machinery and electrical equipment and mineral oil. Her main trading partners are the USA, Brazil and West Germany.

Bolivia

Up to one hundred years ago Bolivia extended to the Pacific coast but at that time Chile defeated Bolivia in one of a series of South American wars, and extended her territory northward to the present border with Peru. The area of Bolivia is now little more than one-third of the independent republic of Bolivia which was originally created in 1826. Parts of the original area which extended to the Pacific coast were lost to Chile, Peru, Brazil, Paraguay and Argentina, throughout the nineteenth and early in the twentieth centuries. One of South America's two landlocked countries, Bolivia today largely depends on special arrangements with Peru and Chile for trading through their Pacific coast ports.

Bolivia may be divided into three broad geographical regions: the eastern and northern plains (the *Oriente*), occupying nearly 75 percent of the country; the main eastern ranges of the Andes Mountains running northwest to southeast; the high plains within the Andes (the *Altiplano*), in the west and southwest.

For such a large country, Bolivia is comparatively thinly populated. The greatest centers of population are in the cities and towns in the valleys of the central mountain region and the surrounding farming areas.

Overall, it is a poor agricultural country, though in recent years schemes have been set up to develop the *Oriente* for sugarcane, rice and cotton growing as well as for cattle raising.

Economically, Bolivia depends very largely on the extraction and export of minerals. Some 60 percent of her total foreign earnings come from the sale of tin, zinc, silver, antimony and other minerals. These are mined in difficult conditions high up in the mountains, mainly by Amerinds. Recently, oil and natural gas have been discovered in the south and east of the country; Bolivia is now self-sufficient in both. The chief imports are foodstuffs, machinery, vehicles and other metal manufactures. Most trade is conducted with the USA, Argentina, Japan and West Germany.

Brazil

First discovered in 1500 by the Portuguese, Brazil remained under European influence until it was declared an independent kingdom in 1822. After 67 years and two kings, a republic was established in 1889. Today it is by far the largest single country in South America, occupies nearly 50 percent of the continental area and has just over half of the total population. Unique among the South American republics, the official language of Brazil is Portuguese.

The northern, widest parts contain most of the Amazon Basin. The southern parts are dominated by the Brazilian Highlands. Most of the population is found in the coastal regions and the neighboring highland fringes, especially around the Tropic of Capricorn. Sao Paulo and Rio de Janeiro between them have a population of over 15 million. In an attempt to open up the heart of the

South American landscape is varied and its features frequently breathtaking: 1 Fernando de Noronha, off Brazil – this wild island, with its dramatic coastline, is part of Brazil's smallest state; 2 Machu Picchu, Peru – the ruins of this Inca city, near Cuzco, on a mountainous terraced site, are a major tourist attraction since their discovery in 1911

1 △

2 ▽

country, a new capital, Brasilia, was created some 1,000 km (620 mi) northwest of Rio in 1960. It grew to a city of over 600,000 within fifteen years.

Over 40 percent of the population is classified as rural. Agricultural and forestry exports are three times as valuable as other commodities: sugar, coffee, cotton and pinewood are the most important exports. Other major crops are corn, bananas, oranges and rice.

Much of the potential of Brazil's wide range of minerals has yet to be developed. So many of the riches lie inland where there are no real communication networks. This country has some of the richest iron ore deposits in the whole world, and also large deposits of rarer minerals such as chrome, mica, graphite, manganese and tungsten.

Brazil's most important industries are textiles, HEP, wood processing and paper manufacture. Her main imports are fuels, wheat and a wide range of mechanical goods including vehicles and chemicals. Principal trading partners are the USA, the Netherlands, West Germany, Japan and the United Kingdom.

Chile

When South America's west coast was discovered by Spanish explorers in the early sixteenth century, the narrow strip of land west of the Andes was established as a single colony and Santiago was settled in 1541. Chile freed itself from Spanish rule in 1818, becoming an independent republic. Since 1973 the country has been run by a military government.

Chile extends through nearly 50° of latitude and has a coastline some 4,120 km (2,560 mi) long; yet its east-west extent is rarely more than 200 km (125 mi). From north to south it may be divided into four areas – the inhospitable arid zone of the Atacama Desert, a Mediterranean region, a wetter, windswept forested region and finally a small grassland area.

The natural difficulties in north Chile have been overcome to develop the rich mineral deposits of the arid region. Copper is the most important single mineral and brings in 80 percent of Chile's foreign earnings. About 14 percent of the world's copper is mined in Chile. Iron ore production is increasing and has now overtaken nitrates to become the second most valuable mineral produced by weight.

Well over 60 percent of Chileans are classified as rural, but farm and forest products account for less than 10 percent of the national wealth. Recent efforts have been made to increase agricultural output and reduce the need to import foodstuffs. Wheat, corn and potatoes are the leading crops. Olives, grapes and citrus fruit are also important. Forestry is valuable both for sawn timber and paper products.

Chilean industry has developed steadily in recent years. Iron and steel production is growing at a new plant near Concepcion. The output

of cellulose and wood pulp now increases each year as does textile production. Chile's principal imports are industrial equipment, foodstuffs, fuels, vehicles and chemicals. West Germany, the USA and Japan are her main trading partners.

Colombia

As seen on the modern map, Colombia has only been in existence since 1886. When the northwestern parts of Spanish America, then known as New Granada gained independence in 1819, the state of Greater Colombia included those areas now comprising Panama, Venezuela and Ecuador. Colombia was created from within those areas 67 years later. It is a democratic republic.

The country has both an Atlantic and a Pacific coastline. It may be divided into three broad geographical regions; the southeastern interior lowlands which are scantily populated and underdeveloped; the central mountain region where the main concentrations of population are found, and the coastal lowlands which are more extensive and more developed in the northern, Atlantic-facing parts.

With most of the population living at heights of between 1,200–3,000 m (4,000–10,000 ft) above sea level, where the range of climates varies greatly with altitude, it is not surprising that Colombian agriculture produces a wide range of crops. Tropical crops include coffee, cotton, rice and sugarcane. Temperate crops

1 Quito, Ecuador – the picturesque capital is situated below the Pichincha volcano in a basin of the Andes; 2 Panteon National, Plaza de los Heroes, Asuncion, Paraguay – the capital has strong links with near neighbors Brazil and Argentina; 3 Carnival, Trinidad, W Indies – this Caribbean island relies on tourism and refining oil from nearby Venezuela

include barley, potatoes and wheat. Cattle are the most numerous farm animals. Much agricultural potential has yet to be developed.

Colombia is rich in minerals. Her output of gold is the highest in South America, and her deposits of platinum are thought to be the largest in the world. Emeralds, silver, copper, lead and crude oil play a leading part

South American Countries

in the economy. Colombian exports are dominated by coffee, followed by cotton, emeralds and animal products. Machinery and manufactured goods, rubber, chemicals and fertilizers head the list of imports.

Ecuador

The Spanish colony of Ecuador was established in 1532. Following unrest early in the nineteenth century it threw off European rule in 1819 and joined in a federation with Colombia. It became an independent republic in 1830. Since 1972 it has had a military government.

Ecuador may be divided into three distinct geographical regions. In the east lies the tropical jungle of the Upper Amazon Basin (the *Oriente*).

The Andes, rising in Mount Chimborazo to 6,267 m (20,561 ft) dominate central Ecuador. Here are many valleys which are heavily populated, and which produce temperate crops and animal products. Western Ecuador (the *Costa*), has some of South America's widest coastal plains. Tropical crops are grown here, especially bananas, coffee and cocoa. Much of Ecuador is covered by untouched, inaccessible forest lands. The only wood which is sawn and exported in quantity is balsa.

Ecuador is not well endowed with minerals. There is a little working of copper, gold, silver, lead and zinc. In the last few years, oil exploration has been stepped up and production is rising steadily. Some of this is now exported, but food exports are more important, most trade being conducted with the USA and Europe.

Falkland Islands

A British crown colony whose connection with the United Kingdom is the subject of a dispute with Argentina, the Falkland Islands comprise two large islands, East Falkland with the capital of Stanley, West Falkland, and a number of smaller islands. The whole group lies some 770 km (480 mi) northeast of Cape Horn. Half the population live in Stanley, the rest being scattered over both the main islands. Almost all of the population is descended from British settlers. There are some 650,000 sheep on the islands, providing wool as the main export item. Communication with the outside world is maintained by a weekly air service to Argentina and by an occasional vessel direct to and from the United Kingdom.

A number of other nearby islands in the South Atlantic form the Falkland Island dependencies. South Georgia was once an important whaling and sealing base but is now inhabited only by a small party of scientists of the British Antarctic Survey. No one lives on the South Sandwich Islands.

French Guiana

The Guiana coastlands were originally settled by the Dutch. Following a number of changes involving the French, Portuguese and British, in 1815 the Congress of Vienna created separate colonies, including French Guiana. The smallest of the mainland countries of South America, this is the only one which is not now independent, being one of France's four overseas departments. It has its own local government but also sends representatives to the French National Assemblies in Paris.

The southern boundary of French

1 Montevideo, Uruguay – set in a bay on the shore of the Rio de la Plata, the capital is the main port and industrial city; 2 Shanty town, Buenos Aires, Argentina – much poverty remains away from the heart of the spacious modern city; 3 Indians farming the Altiplano, Bolivia – all agricultural pursuits are difficult on this barren tableland high up in the Andes

1 △

2 ▽

3 ▽

Guiana is the low watershed between the short rivers flowing northward to the Atlantic and the lower left-bank tributaries of the Amazon. Most of the interior is undeveloped forest land. Small areas of the coastal strip have been developed for agriculture, with cassava, sugarcane, bananas and corn being most widely grown. Little livestock is kept.

Guyana

In 1796 the British seized control of the Guiana coast from the original Dutch settlers, and in 1815 the separate colony of British Guiana was established. This became an independent country with the name Guyana in 1966. It is a member of the Commonwealth.

The main centers of population are along the coast and in the lower valleys of the rivers Demerara, Essequibo and Berbïce. The country may be divided into three main geographical regions. The low coastal strip contains the main agricultural areas producing sugarcane, rice, coconuts and citrus fruit. The slightly higher, forested, undulating country contains proven mineral reserves of bauxite, gold, manganese and diamonds. The interior, forested parts of the Guiana Highlands and the tall grasslands extend into Northern Brazil and Venezuela.

For its size, Guyana is an important trading nation, mainly selling to and buying from the USA, the United Kingdom and other countries in the Caribbean area. Sugar, alumina, bauxite, rice, rum and timber products are most important. Imports are headed by vehicles and machinery for the mines and factories, fuels, especially petroleum products, and fertilizers.

There is much scope for expansion and development in Guyana. The forests of the interior are still largely untouched and production could be increased greatly if a road network were developed. In the lower coastal regions, large areas of unimproved land could be settled and developed for tropical crops and grazing land.

Paraguay

The Spanish colony of Paraguay was established in 1535. It became independent in 1811, then suffered heavily in wars against Brazil, Argentina and Uruguay between 1865 and 1870, and against Bolivia between 1932 and 1935. Like Bolivia, it is a landlocked country, depending largely on special arrangements with Argentina to trade with the outside world, using the Rivers Paraguay and Parana and the port of Buenos Aires.

Paraguay is far more thinly populated than the other South American republics, the main centers of population being in the south and southeast. It is also probably the least developed. Much of western and central Paraguay comprises the economically unproductive Gran Chaco.

1 Santiago, Chile – this Andean capital is responsible for the major share of the country's industrial output of such goods as textiles and footwear; 2 Marine iguanas, Galapagos Islands, Ecuador – now a nature reserve, these islands are home for several wildlife species which cannot be found elsewhere, including the large tortoises after which the Galapagos were named. Darwin obtained crucial material here when forming his ideas on evolution in the 1830s; 3 A colorful shopping street scene in La Paz, which is the capital city of Bolivia. La Paz is set high up in the magnificent Andes mountains

South American Countries

In the east and south, soybeans, cotton and wheat are produced. Here, also, some 6 million head of cattle and smaller numbers of pigs and sheep are raised. Large areas of hardwood forest are found in the extreme east, but these have so far been little developed. Paraguay has virtually no commercially exploitable minerals.

By South American standards, Paraguay's foreign trade is very limited. Her main exports are meat products, timber, vegetable oils, tobacco and cotton. Foodstuffs, vehicles, machinery, chemicals and fertilizers are the main imports. The USA, Argentina, Brazil, West Germany and the UK are the main trading partners.

Peru

In precolonial days, Peru was the center of the Inca civilization. It became the most important Spanish colony, achieving independence in 1824. Since 1968 it has been controlled by a military government.

Peru may be divided into four broad geographical regions. From southwest to northeast they are: the Pacific coastal strip averaging about 80 km (50 mi) in width, the coast ranges and the Andes rising to 6,768 m (22,205 ft) with valleys between the main ranges, the high wooded region of the *Montana*, and finally the dense jungle of the Upper Amazon Basin. The main concentrations of population are on the coast and in the Andean valleys.

About 50 percent of the population is classified as rural, but farm products account for only about 16 percent of the value of the national production. Sugarcane, cotton, coffee and wool are the principal items. Sheep, llamas and alpacas are all kept for their wool. Peru is a major world fishing nation in terms of its catch. Anchovies are the most important single fish and are processed into fish meal and exported as an animal feedstuff. Other important fish are tuna and bonito. Peru's fishing industry is now turning to supply the domestic market.

Peru is also an important mineral producer and exporter, especially of lead, copper, iron, silver, zinc and crude oil. Minerals, metals and fish products account for 80 percent of the exports, and agricultural products only 15 percent. Imports are mainly machinery, foodstuffs, chemicals and vehicles. The USA, Japan, West Germany, the Netherlands and the United Kingdom are Peru's main trading partners.

Surinam

Geographically the central country of the three Guiana coast ones, Surinam has always had close ties with the Netherlands, and was a Dutch colony from 1815–1957 known first as Dutch Guiana. In 1975 it gained full independence. Like French Guiana and Guyana, Surinam comprises a settled coastal strip and central valley, beyond which lie expansive forested areas. The latter cover rising ground which reaches the highest parts of the Guiana/Brazil watershed.

Commercial agriculture is limited to the coastal zone and the lower parts of the main valleys. Rice, sugarcane and tropical fruits are the main crops. Livestock numbers are small. The forest reserves are being developed steadily both for sawn timber and wood products like plywood and wood particle board. Far more important are the rich deposits of bauxite and the alumina and aluminum plants which are fed by these, to account for about two-thirds of Surinam's foreign earnings. Foodstuffs and forest products account for most of the rest. Raw materials and machinery are the main imports.

Trinidad and Tobago

The island of Trinidad, just north of the Venezuelan coast, was discovered by Columbus in 1498 and became a Spanish colony in 1532. In 1802 it became a British colony. Tobago, 30 km (19 mi) to the northeast, became a British colony in 1814. The two islands were united administratively in 1889 and became an independent member of the Commonwealth in 1962.

Trinidad's northern margin comprises a highland ridge rising to 940 m (3,084 ft). The central and southern parts present a lower undulating landscape. Tobago is about one-twentieth the size, and is made of a broad southwest to northeast hilly ridge. The population, mainly of African and true Asiatic Indian descent, is just over 1 million in Trinidad and about 50,000 in Tobago.

Both islands are covered with dense natural forest, large parts of which have now been cleared. The most important planted crops are now sugarcane, cocoa, coconuts and citrus fruit. Trinidad also has considerable oil reserves and the natural 'Pitch Lake', covering nearly half a square kilometer from which asphalt is recovered. There are metal processing plants and three oil refineries which process both local and imported crude oil.

Crude oil imports and refined product exports are the main items of international trade. Besides refined oil products, sugar, cocoa and tropical fruits are the main exports. Many nontropical foodstuffs, particularly flour, dairy products, meat and rice, chemicals and a range of manufactured goods have to be imported.

Uruguay

South America's second smallest republic, Uruguay was part of the Spanish territory around the River Plate, and then a province of Brazil. It became an independent country, a buffer state between Argentina and Brazil, in 1828.

Uruguay is low-lying, the highest ground rising to no more than 500 m (1,600 ft) above sea level. The population is fairly evenly spread with the main centers being along the southern coastlands. Agriculture is the base of the national economy with 16.5 million hectares of land farmed. Over 20 million sheep and 8 million cattle are kept on 90 percent of this land and, on the rest, wheat, corn and rice are the three major crops grown. Many factories process agricultural products; meat packing and processing and textiles are most important.

For a country of its size and population, Uruguay has a large foreign trade. Meat products, wool and textiles account for nearly two-thirds of her foreign earnings. Raw materials, fuel oils, chemicals and machinery are the largest imports. Trade is mainly with Brazil and the EEC.

Venezuela

Following the South American Wars of Independence, Venezuela became part of Simon Bolivar's Greater Columbia in 1819. It has been an independent republic since 1830. One of the middle-sized South American republics, it is today the richest of them, largely because of its oil reserves.

First discovered in Venezuela in 1917, oil production rose steadily to just over 2 million barrels per day by the early 1970s. Three-quarters of this output comes from the Maracaibo area. The reserves of the Orinoco region where production has been increasing recently are not yet fully realized.

South of the Orinoco, rich deposits of iron ore are found. These are currently mined and either used in Venezuela or exported, mainly to the USA. Other mined products include gold and diamonds. Rich reserves of manganese, phosphates, nickel and sulphur are also known. With such a broad base of raw materials, Venezuela is in a strong position to establish a wide range of industries. So far, oil refineries, an iron and steel plant and a range of smaller manufacturing industries have already been established.

Venezuela's main farming products are corn, rice, sugarcane, coffee and cocoa. Beef cattle and pigs are the most numerous livestock. Over 40 percent of the population are classified as rural, and a large proportion of them enjoy a low standard of living in a country which is, by South American standards, rich.

Venezuela has a large surplus in her balance of payments created in part by the export of oil, iron ore and coffee which are the three leading commodities; imports of raw materials, machinery, foodstuffs and chemicals come mainly from the USA, Japan and the EEC countries.

1 Caracas, Venezuela – the modern Centro Simon Bolivar presents a sharp contrast to some of the capital's suburbs; 2 Carnival dancer, Rio de Janeiro, Brazil – in a superb setting, with the famous Copacabana beach, Rio attracts the international 'jet set'; 3 Cuzco, Peru – the attractive Inca capital contains many splendid relics of the ancient civilization

COUNTRY REFERENCE: SOUTH AMERICA

South American Countries	Political Status	State Capital	Area km²	Area sq mi	Population	Population Density per km²	Population Density per sq mi	Births per Thousand Persons	Deaths per Thousand Persons	Mean Annual Percentage Increase in Population
Argentina	A	Buenos Aires	2,776,889	1,072,162	26,075,000	9.4	24	22.7	9.4	1.3
Bolivia	A	Sucre and La Paz	1,098,581	424,164	4,887,000	4.4	12	43.7	18.0	2.6
Brazil	A	Brasilia	8,511,965	3,286,487	113,815,000	13	35	37.1	8.8	2.8
Chile	A	Santiago	756,945	292,258	10,740,000	14	37	26.3	9.0	1.7
Colombia	A	Bogota	1,138,914	439,737	25,460,000	22	58	40.6	8.8	3.2
Ecuador	A	Quito	283,561	109,483	8,180,000	29	75	41.8	9.5	3.4
Falkland Islands	C	Stanley	11,961	4,618	1,900	0.2	0.4	21.5	13.8	0.8
French Guiana	C	Cayenne	91,000	35,100	66,000	0.7	1.9	28.3	7.8	3.5
Guyana	A	Georgetown	214,969	83,000	781,000	3.6	9.4	31.6	7.2	2.2
Paraguay	A	Asuncion	406,752	157,048	2,839,000	7.0	18	39.8	8.9	3.0
Peru	A	Lima	1,285,216	496,224	16,795,000	13	34	41.0	11.9	3.2
Surinam	A	Paramaribo	163,265	63,037	454,000	2.8	7.2	36.9	7.2	2.6
Trinidad & Tobago	A	Port of Spain	5,128	1,980	1,118,000	218	565	24.0	6.5	1.2
Uruguay	A	Montevideo	177,508	68,536	2,826,000	16	41	20.9	9.5	1.2
Venezuela	A	Caracas	912,050	352,144	13,047,000	14	37	36.1	7.0	3.1
SOUTH AMERICA TOTALS			17,834,704	6,885,978	227,084,900	13	33	—	—	—

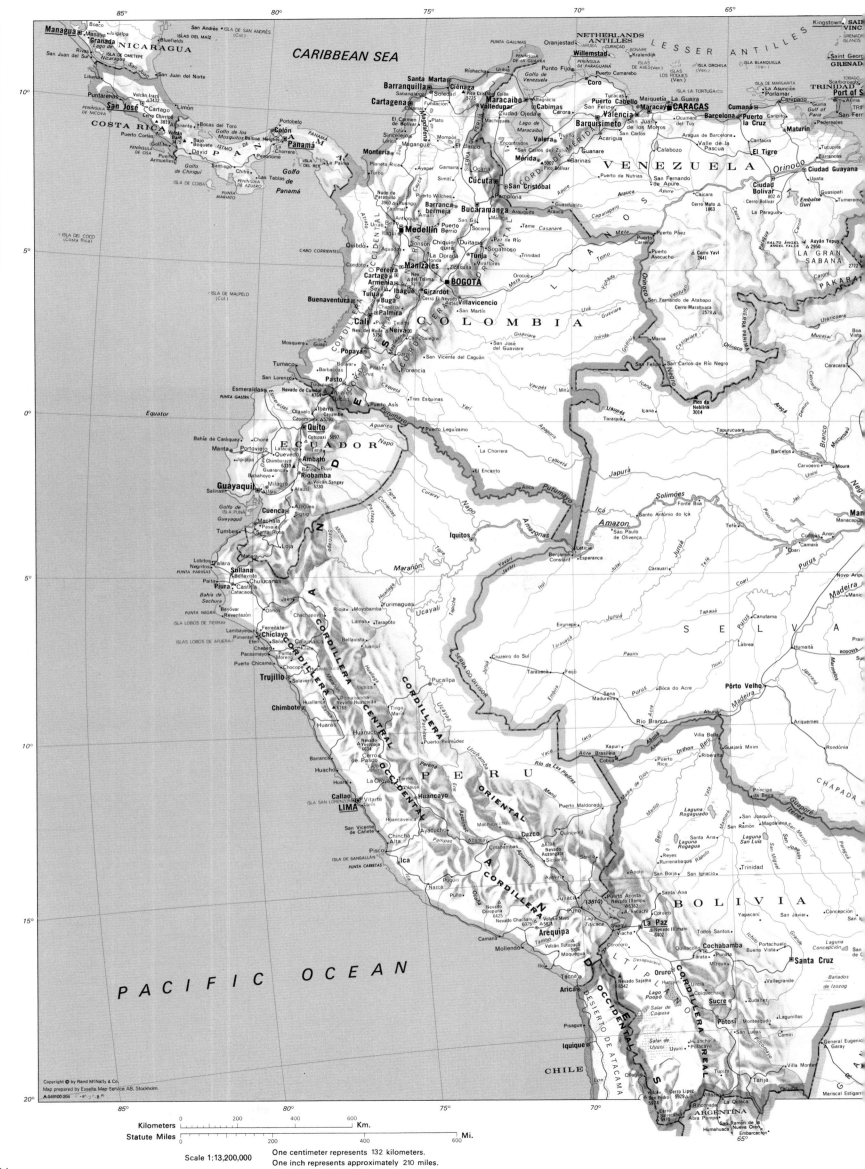

CARIBBEAN SEA

NICARAGUA

COSTA RICA

PACIFIC OCEAN

PANAMA

COLOMBIA

VENEZUELA

NETHERLANDS ANTILLES

LESSER ANTILLES

TRINIDAD

ECUADOR

PERU

BOLIVIA

CHILE

ARGENTINA

SELVA

BOGOTÁ

CARACAS

Quito

LIMA

La Paz

Guayaquil

Medellín

Cali

Maracaibo

Cartagena

Barranquilla

Managua

San José

Trujillo

Arequipa

Cuzco

Amazon

Orinoco

Marañón

Napo

Equator

Kilometers

Statute Miles

Km.

Mi.

Scale 1:13,200,000

One centimeter represents 132 kilometers.
One inch represents approximately 210 miles.

Oblique Conic Conformal Projection

145

PACIFIC

OCEAN

CHILE

ARGENTINA

BOLIVIA

PARA

Tropic of Capricorn

Antofagasta

San Miguel de Tucumán

Santiago del Estero

Catamarca

La Rioja

Córdoba

San Juan

Mendoza

SANTIAGO

Valparaíso

Viña del Mar

Rancagua

Rosario

Junín BUENOS AIRES

Talca

Concepción

Talcahuano

Temuco

Valdivia

Osorno

Puerto Montt

Bahía Blanca

Comodoro Rivadavia

ARCHIPIÉLAGO
JUAN FERNÁNDEZ
(Chile)

ISLA SAN FÉLIX
(Chile)

ISLA SAN AMBROSIO
(Chile)

ISLA WELLINGTON

FALKLAN
ISLAND
ISLAS MALVI
(U.K.)

Punta Arenas

TIERRA DEL FUEGO

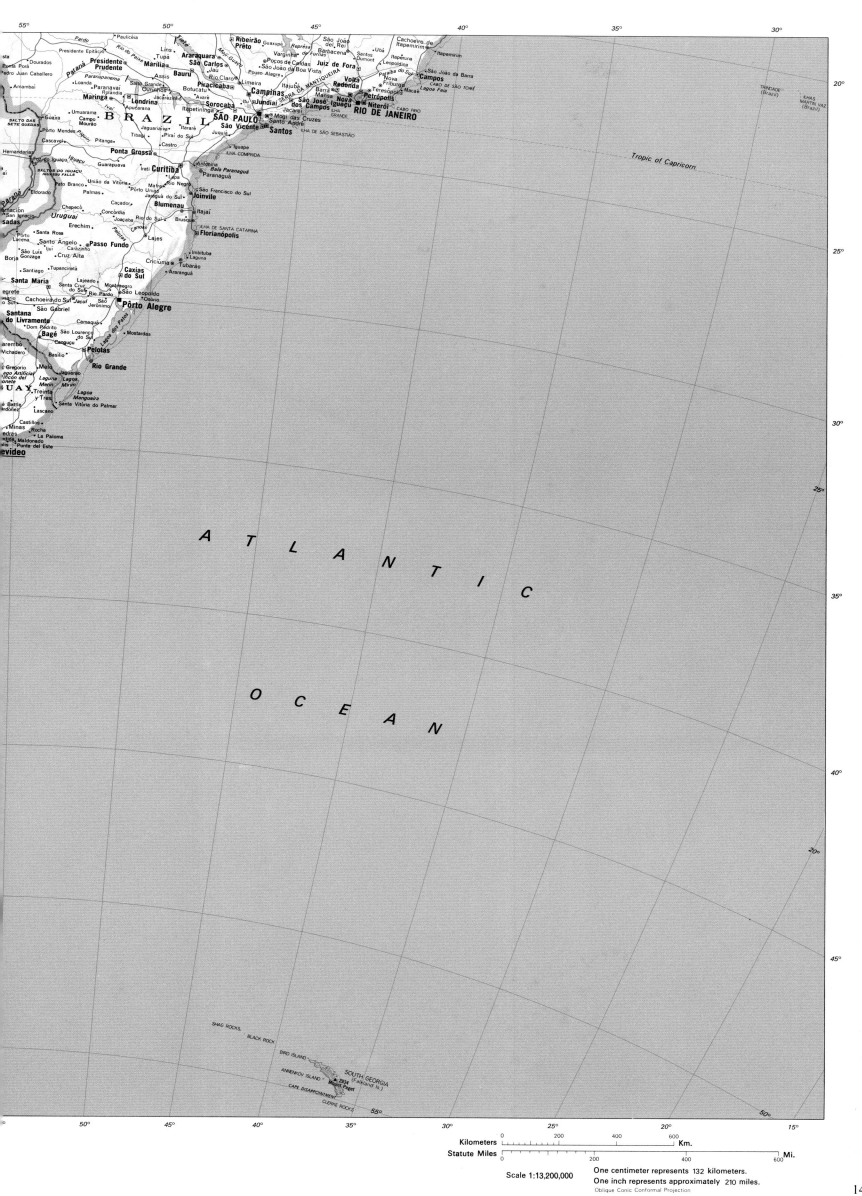

B R A Z I L

Ribeirão Prêto
São Paulo
RIO DE JANEIRO
Curitiba
Florianópolis
Pôrto Alegre
Pelotas
Rio Grande

Tropic of Capricorn

A T L A N T I C

O C E A N

TRINDADE (Brazil)
ILHAS MARTIN VAZ (Brazil)

20°
25°
30°
35°
40°
45°
50°

SHAG ROCKS
BLACK ROCK
BIRD ISLAND
ANNENKOV ISLAND
SOUTH GEORGIA (Falkland Is.)
Mount Paget
CAPE DISAPPOINTMENT
CLERKE ROCKS

Kilometers
Statute Miles

Scale 1:13,200,000

One centimeter represents 132 kilometers.
One inch represents approximately 210 miles.
Oblique Conic Conformal Projection

NORTH AMERICA
Physical Profile

World Location and Size

The Americas stretch from well north of 80°N in the islands of Canada and Greenland to 56°S at Cape Horn. What we define as North America extends from the northern tips of the Canadian Islands to those of Florida Keys at 24°N, a distance of some 6,250 km (3,900 mi). The most westerly point on the mainland of the continent is at 167°W in Alaska. On the Atlantic coast, Labrador lies at 56°W, but Newfoundland and Greenland extend even farther to the east.

Mainland North America is remarkably compact, being essentially rectangular with appendages in the northwest and southeast. Beyond the mainland lie many islands, especially in the north. Within the main rectangle are hundreds of lakes, with the open sea of Hudson Bay in the north.

The North American coastline shows a number of contrasting features. Parts, such as British Columbia and Maine, have a complex, fretted outline with a number of offshore islands. Elsewhere, the outline is far more simple, as in Oregon and California. In places like Texas and Louisiana the coast is one of bars and lagoons.

Landscape

North America can be broadly divided into four major physical regions. In the north, surrounding Hudson Bay in a great crescent-shaped area, lies the Canadian or Laurentian Shield. It has been stripped of most of its soil during recent glaciations, has hundreds of lakes dotted on its surface and has little agricultural potential. The main interest lies in the mineral resources of the old rocks, and in forestry.

Along the east side of the continent lie ranges of mountains with a maximum height of 2,037 m (6,684 ft) in the Blue Ridge area of the Appalachians. Extending from Alabama in the south to the Canadian border in the north, the Appalachians continue into the mainland Maritime Provinces and Newfoundland.

In the west, the Western Cordillera are far more complex and extensive. The Rocky Mountains are in the east of this belt while farther west lie the Sierra Nevada, the Cascades, the Coast Ranges and the Alaska Range. Between and within these lie a number of plateaus, desert basins, including the notorious Death Valley, and such fertile areas as the Central Valley of California and the Willamette Valley/Puget Sound lowlands

Opposite: Dramatic landscape of the Grand Canyon, Arizona, USA

farther north. These mountains today form the highest areas of the continent, rising to 6,194 m (20,320 ft) in Mount McKinley, Alaska. In this most unstable region of the continent lie the famous geysers of Yellowstone National Park, and the much feared San Andreas Fault which threatens many of the urban areas of California.

A wide lowland area stretches from the Arctic Ocean in the north to the Gulf of Mexico in the south. Part of this is very low, as in the floor of the Mississippi and Mackenzie valleys, but the high plains reach to some 1,600 m (5,000 ft) above sea

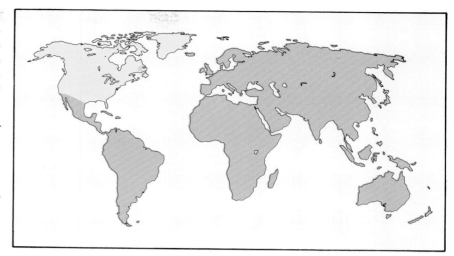

level at the front ranges of the Rocky Mountains.

North America is a land of great rivers and river basins, most of which drain toward the Atlantic and Arctic Oceans, Hudson Bay and the Gulf of Mexico. The central lowlands are drained southward by the 'big-muddy' Mississippi/Missouri Rivers system, and northward by the Mackenzie River and the Saskatchewan/Nelson system. Rivers flowing to the Pacific are mainly shorter, though a few, especially the Colorado, the Columbia/Snake system and the Frazer have developed impressive scenic courses through the mountains to the coast. The Great Lakes comprise another distinctive water feature of the continent.

Climatic Background

Climatically, the North American continent extends from the tropics to the polar wastes, and has a full west-east range from one ocean to the other. Parts of mainland Canada, Greenland and other islands lie well inside the Arctic Circle. In the west of the continent lies the great mountain region which acts as a major barrier to the movement of air from west to east. In the east, the Appalachians have a similar barrier effect to air movements. Thus the interior of

the continent is effectively sealed from oceanic influences, though the unimpeded passage for air moving northward and southward from the Gulf or the Arctic does mean that, at times, warm air may penetrate well north or cold air well south.

In the extreme west, limited areas experience warm and cool temperate climates of an oceanic type. In parts, California enjoys a climate akin to that of some Mediterranean areas, but the coast ranges ensure that the Central Valley, for example, has great temperature extremes and, in the south, an acute water shortage. Farther north, in the coastal strip of Oregon, Washington and British Columbia, the average temperature of the coldest month stays above freezing level, but the summer average monthly temperatures never exceed 22°C (72°F).

East of this coastal area, and south of approximately 55°N, the climates of the mountain ranges are largely inhospitable. Then, those of the basins and ranges and the area as far east as about 102°W can be classified as dry, in that annual precipitation is below 250 mm (10 in) and, with the heat of most areas, this moisture has little useful effect. Temperatures are more extreme here than on the coast, the monthly average being below freezing for parts of the year.

Palos Verdes headland – breathtaking coastline lying south of Los Angeles, near Hermosa and Redondo beaches

Such semi arid areas can be referred to as Steppe lands. In the extreme southwest, in Arizona, Utah and New Mexico, the more extreme conditions of hot deserts prevail, with July temperatures of 33°C (91°F), and 13°C (55°F) in January.

East of 102°W in southeast North America and across the whole continent north of 55°N, the climates may be broadly classified in west-east belts. Except for the tropical tip of Florida, the US south of Kansas, Kentucky and the Virginias enjoys a subtropical climate with rainfall throughout the year and distinctly warm summers. North of this area are progressively cooler and mainly drier zones. Thus the southern parts of the prairie provinces and much of the Great Lakes region enjoy a cool temperature climate, with rainfall increasing to the east.

Still farther north the climates become less and less inviting. Moving through a broad belt of sub arctic climates, in the Tundra margins of northern Canada no month has an average temperature in excess of 10°C (50°F). Ultimately, there is Greenland, an area mostly covered by permanent ice.

NORTH AMERICA

European consciousness of the 'New World' dates from only about 1,000 years ago, and it was not until the 'discovery' voyages of Christopher Columbus (1492) and others that any real interest was focused on the vast North American continent.

The early seventeenth century saw small settlements of pioneers from France, Spain, the Netherlands and, above all, Britain, whose Pilgrim Fathers from that historic *Mayflower* voyage of 1620 laid the foundations for early British dominance. Despite an eighteenth-century influx of immigrants from Ireland and Germany, in 1776 when the colonies established an independent Union of the 13 existing states, four out of five of the new Americans still had English or Scots ancestry. The USA is now one of the two great political and economic world powers, a position it has achieved following a relatively short period of development.

The huge and sparsely peopled land of Canada was first settled permanently by the French but always with a strong British presence. Ceded to the English by the Treaty of Paris in 1763, Canada remained loyal during the War of Independence and was established as a dominion in 1867.

Population Growth

The North American population has grown continuously over the past two centuries, increasing more rapidly in the climatically more attractive USA than in Canada. Throughout this time, natural increase has been boosted by periods of mass migration, particularly from Europe. From the end of the Napoleonic Wars to the outbreak of World War I, about 30 million people crossed the Atlantic to start a new life in this inviting continent. At the peak, nearly 1,300,000 settlers entered the USA alone in 1907, and 400,000 entered Canada in 1913. In the 1920s, restrictions on new immigrants were imposed, and since that time far smaller numbers of new settlers have been able to enter the continent.

Today, when most modern 'Americans' come from European stock, it is necessary to remember that they are not the descendants of the original settlers of this large land mass, nor the only modern group of any significance. The American Indians are thought to have crossed from Siberia to North America some 20,000 years ago, at a time when the Bering Strait had not been established. Their modern descendants are thus recognized as Mongoloid stock, being related to the Japanese and Chinese. When first encountered by Europeans, in a land originally thought to be India, these people with reddish-brown skins came to be known as 'Red Indians'.

At that time, there may have been about a million Indians in North America, with more in Mexico and the lands farther south. During the great European drive westward, the US Indians suffered greatly, being driven from their lands, but they fared better in Canada, due to a peaceful proclamation in 1763. By the end of the nineteenth century, the total population of North American Indians was very low but has now recovered to over 1 million. Almost half live on Indian Reservations covering nearly 25 million hectares (over 61 million acres) across the continent, and many traditional tribal customs are retained. Overall the modern Indians' standard of living is still below that of the white population.

Other Mongoloid groups whose settlement of the cold, northern margins of North America dates back thousands of years are the Eskimos of Alaska, Northern Canada and Greenland and the people of the Aleutian Islands. While retaining their traditional forms of life based on hunting, fishing and some primitive cultivation, both groups have adopted western habits as settlers have penetrated into the subpolar areas. The trading post and the mail-order catalogue have aided this integration into the main streams of modern American life.

European settlers remained with their fellow countrymen, concentrating on specific parts of the continent. The Spaniards, for instance, who settled mainly in the south, in Mexico and the West Indies, then moved northward into what is now the southwest USA. The English and smaller groups of Germans, Dutch and Scandinavians settled the main Atlantic coastal strip from Georgia to the Atlantic provinces, while the French penetrated the St Lawrence lowlands and later the Mississippi Valley to the Gulf coast.

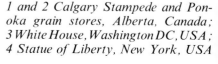

1 and 2 Calgary Stampede and Ponoka grain stores, Alberta, Canada; 3 White House, Washington DC, USA; 4 Statue of Liberty, New York, USA

Finally, North America today has a substantial black population descended from West African slaves transported in vast numbers in the period 1619 to 1865. These were originally brought over to work on the plantations of the southeastern states where the climate was far hotter and wetter than the European settlers were accustomed to. With the abolition of slavery at the end of the Civil War between the Federal north and the Confederate south in 1865, some 4.5 million blacks became free yet remained tied to the plantation area. Since then they have spread out over the rest of America, particularly to northern cities, but more than half of the modern total of over 22 million still live in the southeastern states.

Today, then, no one national group has dominance in the USA. Canada, by contrast has a far higher proportion of its population descended from the English and French, probably over 80 percent. Thus, what may be termed the two 'melting pots' of North American population have produced two very different amalgams: the Canadians have preserved many English and French associations; the US citizens have a strong affection for, and some affinities with, many European countries, but the nation has established its own strong national identity.

Political Development

In 1776 the US consisted of that tier of states stretching from New England in the north to Georgia in the south. When peace was established, following the War of Independence, the border was moved westward to the line of the Mississippi River. Twenty years later, the extent of the country was almost doubled by the Louisiana Purchase, whereby the area extending into modern Montana, Wyoming, Kansas, Oklahoma and Louisiana was bought from the French. By 1819, Florida and a small strip of land which now constitutes southern Alabama and Mississippi had been gained from the Spanish.

Next, Texas, then larger than the modern state, seceded from Mexico and joined the USA in 1845. A year later, the Pacific northwest Oregon Territory between 42°N and 49°N entered the union. California and the southwest were added in 1848. In 1853, the Gadsden Purchase added the Gila Valley, thus effectively completing mainland USA excluding Alaska. Since then, Alaska has been purchased from Russia in 1867 and sovereignty was assumed over Hawaii in 1898.

Within each of these broad geographical areas individual states were only declared when a specified population level had been reached. Thus, within the Louisiana Purchase area, Louisiana itself became a state in 1812 and Arkansas in 1836, but Wyoming was only recognized in 1890 and, finally, Oklahoma in 1907. The last of the conterminous states to be declared were Arizona and New Mexico in 1912.

The eastern US/Canadian border was fixed by treaty after the War of Independence, and thereafter by agreement as the frontier of settlement moved west. North of the 49th parallel, agreed from Lake of the Woods to the Pacific in 1818, Canada grew more slowly. After the dominion was established in 1867 new provinces were added in succession: Manitoba in 1870, British Columbia in '71, Prince Edward Island in '73, Alberta and Saskatchewan in 1905.

Canada became an independent country within the then British Empire and Commonwealth in 1931, and was united with Newfoundland in 1949.

Thus, the internal political organization of most of North America can be seen to be one of rapid change over a period of little more than a century and a half. During that time, the continent developed rapidly in economic terms, so that by the inter-war period of the 1920s–'30s, the whole fortune of the western world was very closely allied to that of the United States in particular.

Since World War II the USA has been the most powerful country within the western world. At a time when the capitalist/Communist rivalry is foremost in all world affairs, the USA has endeavored to contain the area of the world dominated by the eastern bloc. The Charter of the Organization of American States, designed to establish peace and

1 △

2 ▽

3 ▽

USA: Home for many diverse peoples, the United States is a varied nation of energy and exuberance: 1 Chinatown, Manhattan, New York City – reflecting just one aspect of this cosmopolitan city which contains more large communities of ethnic minorities than any other world city; 2 San Francisco, California – the unique cable cars which serve this hilly and lovely city are a great tourist attraction; 3 Football game – football is the most popular sport at US high schools and colleges, followed closely by basketball, with soccer growing rapidly in recent years.

NORTH AMERICA

justice, solidarity and collaboration, territorial integrity and independence for its members, was drawn up in 1948. A year later both the USA and Canada were original signatories to NATO, the military treaty to provide a collective shield for Western Europe against the eastern Communist bloc. The USA has also established military links and alliances westward across the Pacific.

Industry, Commerce and Communications

The North American Manufacturing Belt, the main area of industry and commerce, has no rigid boundaries but, in broad terms, extends from southern New England west to Chicago and Milwaukee. It encompasses many large towns and cities of the northeastern US, the St Lawrence lowlands and lake shores of Canada. Within this area lie the coalfields and iron and steel industries of Pennsylvania, Ohio, Indiana and Illinois as well as the lake-side towns and the Atlantic seaboard. Many manufacturing companies are associated with these basic industries. A prime example is the automobile industry, around Detroit, Michigan.

This great complex had a virtual stranglehold on North American industry until World War I, but the last half century has seen other centers of manufacturing established within the continent. New industrial foci have developed along the western seaboard, in and around Los Angeles, San Francisco, Seattle and Vancouver. Other centers have developed in the interior, e.g. Dallas, Denver, St Louis, Kansas City and Minneapolis-St Paul.

Despite North America's importance as a major agricultural area, only 4 percent of the work force is engaged in farming. By contrast, 23 percent are employed in manufacturing industry, 36 percent in trade and commerce, 25 percent in services and 6 percent in transport and communications. Only a very advanced economy can sustain so many of the working population engaged in non-manufacturing work.

Both the USA and Canada are great trading nations. While the St Lawrence and the Great Lakes freeze in winter, their ports nevertheless handle much internal and international traffic in summer. The

Atlantic seaboard from Halifax southward contains a series of large seaports now well geared to handle the world's largest container ships and bulk carriers. On the west coast newer ports have developed primarily to handle trade with Japan, Australia and other trans-Pacific destinations.

Road, rail and air networks are all densely developed in the most settled parts of the continent, east of the Rockies and south of the climatic hazards of mid and northern Canada. North America is the archetypal home of the automobile. Personalized transport is more developed here than anywhere else in the world. Interstate highways, other state and national routes, and transcontinental roads like the Trans-Canada Highway, provide for rapid travel over long distances. At the same time, city centers handle large volumes of daily traffic, suffer from crippling jams and often lack adequate mass transport.

The American rail network has been severely pruned in recent years as distance travellers have taken to the air. Intercity air travel is as highly developed here as anywhere in the world, and distances between major cities in excess of 450 km (300 mi) almost invariably have rapid jet links. Smaller centers, particularly in the less populated parts, are usually linked by regular air services using slower aircraft.

Agriculture, Forestry and Fishing

With the exception of the true tropical and equatorial, nearly all the world's natural environments existed within the North American continent. Today, many of these have been modified by man, but much of the natural cover remains.

Forests are thought to have covered about half of North America prior to European settlement. Virtually the whole of the Atlantic fringe was clothed in woodland, from coniferous in the north, through mixed areas of deciduous to subtropical in the extreme south. Such forests also existed well to the west. In the western parts of the interior plains, however, first tall grass prairie and, in the drier west, the short grass prairie replaced trees. Together these two areas of valuable rich soil extended from the Texas coast northward to the southern parts of the Canadian prairie provinces, and as far west as the Western Cordillera.

Today, about two-thirds of the area of the old forests still remain. Three important areas of forest are found in the mountains of the west: on the middle slopes of the Rockies, on the lower 2,500 m (8,000 ft) of the British Columbian and Pacific northwest states and on the lower sections of the coast ranges. Especially in the west, these provide some of the most valuable stands of hardwood in the whole world.

North America's forest industries play a major part in modern world supplies. An average of 350 million cubic meters of coniferous wood is felled each year, about twice as much in the US as in Canada. In total, this amounts to about 32 percent of the world total. In the hardwood world table, the contribution is less significant, the US providing less than 6 percent. However, Canada ranks first in the world and the USA second in both wood pulp and newsprint production.

Except in the mountains and desert areas, all of the US has now been adapted to some form of commercial farming. In comparison, much of Canada remains nonagricultural.

Overall, North America is a land of great agricultural surplus. The continent covers some 14.5 percent of the world's surface, and its population is only about 5.9 percent of the world total. Compared with these figures, North America's share of

Canada: 1 Mount Royal, Montreal – 213 km (700 ft) above sea level, this park on volcanic soil overlooks the world's second largest French speaking metropolis; 2 International Nickel's copper cliff plant Sudbury, Ontario – the town is a major world nickel producing center; 3 Alaska Highway – a primarily tourist road from British Columbia to the Yukon

Total Imports and Exports
(1975 figures in millions of U.S. dollars)

The USA is the world's largest trading nation. Remembering that Canada has about one-tenth the population, its trading performance is impressive.

Canada Imports	34,306
Canada Exports	31,881
USA Imports	102,984
USA Exports	106,157

☐ Imports   ▨ Exports

world farming production is remarkably high.

Where cereal production is concerned, North America is among the world leaders for most temperate varieties. Currently, each year's world output of wheat exceeds 400 million tons. The US accounts for some 15 percent of this and Canada for a further 5 percent. Of corn, the world's second cereal, the USA alone accounts for nearly 48 percent of total production. North America features less significantly in barley production, 5 percent coming from Canada and a fraction less from USA. World production of oats is only about one-eighth that of wheat and of this 22 percent is grown in North America.

North America is also a major area for the production of many fruits and vegetables. The US alone is the world leader for apples (13 percent), oranges (28 percent), grapefruit (65 percent) and tomatoes (17 percent). It is also a world leader in growing soybeans, sugar beets, potatoes, a range of other fruits, tobacco, cotton and peanuts.

Where livestock are concerned, the USA ranks second to India, with 11 percent of the total population of cattle, and third to China and the USSR with 8 percent of the pigs.

North America as a whole accounts for 15 percent of the world's milk production, 16 percent of its hen eggs and 5 percent of its fish.

Natural Resources

North America is well endowed with the supplies of fuel and power upon which modern industrial economies depend. The continent has, in addition, rich reserves of a wide range of minerals.

After a period in which coal production declined, North American output has again risen in the last decade. Now, only the USSR individually produces more than the USA, and Canada rates twelfth in world production. Over one-third of the world's hard coal is mined in the continent, but lignite (soft coal) is of little importance. On current estimates, over 26 percent of the world's coal reserves lie within North America.

North America again ranks second to the USSR in the production of crude oil, accounting for about one-sixth of world production. Proven reserves are less impressive, however, only 8 percent lying beneath the continent. Reserves of natural gas are also less impressive, standing at only 14 percent, although North

Ore	Average Annual World Production (million tons)	North America's Share (percent)	Principal North American Locations
bauxite	80.3	3	Arkansas
cobalt	0.03	6	Margins of the Shield
copper	7.4	27	W Cordillera and Canadian Shield (USA world leader)
gold	1 million kg	6	W Cordillera in both Canada and USA
lead	3.2	28	W Cordillera in both Canada and USA
molybdenum	0.084	75	Colorado
nickel	0.733	34	Canadian Shield (Canada world leader)
silver	0.01	26	W Cordillera
tungsten	0.036	13	USA W Cordillera
vanadium	0.02	19	USA W Cordillera
zinc	5.4	32	W Cordillera, Appalachia and Canadian Shield (Canada world leader)

America accounts for about half of the world's production of natural gas each year. With an eye to the possible future potential of nuclear energy, it should be noted that currently the USA produces 44 percent and Canada 25 percent of the world output of uranium, and their proven respective reserves are 30 and 13 percent of the world total.

As with crude oil, so with iron ore. The US has proven reserves of 7,500 million tons, but these represent only 3 percent of world reserves. Canada has far greater reserves, 33,700 million tons. Currently the two countries produce 46 million and 34 million tons respectively each year, representing together about 15 percent of the world total. Much of the Canadian ore is exported to the USA and Europe. The US also imports from Venezuela.

North America's share of world outputs of other minerals is, in many cases, considerable, as the table shows.

Electricity production and consumption play a relatively minor part in total energy figures, but the absolute totals for North America are at the head of the world league tables. As an industrial country, the US consumes twice as much electricity as any other world power, over 2 trillion kilowatt-hours per year. Of this, 15 percent is hydro, 9 percent nuclear and 76 percent thermal. Canada consumes about one-tenth that total, indicating a similar per capita consumption, but no less than 74 percent of this is hydroelectric-power (HEP), 4 percent nuclear and only 22 percent thermal. Of all the continental areas, North America has made the greatest progress in harnessing water power, over half the potential capacity having been installed.

North American Economy

Within the continent, population is most concentrated in the great belt which encompasses the megalopolis from Boston, through New York and Philadelphia to Baltimore and Washington, in the industrial cities of the Great Lakes area and St Lawrence lowlands and in the three large urban concentrations of the Pacific fringes. In all these areas, the average density of population exceeds 200 persons per km² (500 per sq mi).

These concentrations apart, the population east of about 98°W is greater than 20 per km² (50 per sq mi) in all but the less hospitable areas. West of that line, it is mainly less than 10 per km² (25 per sq mi). In Canada, outside the main cities of the east, the prairie provinces and the Vancouver area, it is very thinly spread. There are within the USA 29

Canada: 1 Sawmill, shore of Lake Slocan, British Columbia – lumbering is a major industry in this westerly mountainous province; 2 Horses grazing on the Great Plains, South Saskatchewan – nearly 70 percent of Canada's wheat output comes from the rolling 'big sky' country of the prairie provinces, much of it going for export

1 △   2 ▽

Per Capita Income

(1974 figures in U.S. dollars)

There is little difference between the average earnings of Americans and Canadians. At just under $6,000 their average incomes are among the highest in the world.

Canada   USA

| 5,840 | 5,923 |

NORTH AMERICA

metro areas over 1 million, of which 15 contain more than 2 million people. New York with 16.6 million, Los Angeles with 9.4 million and Chicago with 7.8 million are the three largest. Canada has three cities whose metro areas have over 1 million inhabitants: Toronto and Montreal each with 2.8 million and Vancouver with 1.2 million.

Although world population is currently rising at a little over 4 percent per annum, this figure is nowhere near reached in North America. In the continent as a whole, the birth rate is running at 14.8 per thousand while the death rate is 8.9 per thousand. Thus, the net increase is some 0.8 percent per annum.

Remembering that inflation distorts figures which are compared over the years, there is no denying that the value of all North American imports rose 6.3 times from 1938 to 1958 and 7 times between 1958 and 1975. The corresponding figures for all North American exports were 5.8 and 6.1 times. All four figures are well above the corresponding world averages, giving a clear indication of both the major part played by the US and Canada in world trade and the growth of their contribution during the last 40 years.

The trading performance of the North American countries over the period 1938–'58 and 1958–'75 has advanced as much as that of almost any country in the developed world. Canadian imports rose from $691 million to $5,205 million and then to $34,306 million. As such figures reflect not only genuine growth but also inflation, they represent actual percentage increases of 653 and 559 respectively. Exports rose from $865 million to $5,045 million (483 percent increase) and then to $31,881 million (532 percent increase). The comparable figures for the US were, imports, $2,180 million, $13,298 million and $102,984 million (510 and 675 percent increases) and exports, $3,064 million, $17,775 million and $106,157 million (479 and 498 percent increases).

Thus, over the selected periods, Canada's imports have risen more rapidly than exports, but the recent trends are hopeful for a return to a balance of visible trade. Yet, in the USA where there has always been a surplus on visible trade, growth rates overall are a fraction lower and a little worrying in that imports are growing more rapidly than exports.

As for incomes, in the period 1960 –'74 these rose by 186 percent in the non-Communist world and by 290 percent in Europe. In Canada the rise has been 206 percent and in the USA 137 percent. Clearly, with the population of the USA approximately ten times that of Canada, the average figure for the continent is not surprisingly only 142 percent.

North America ranks as the world's greatest energy consuming continent on a per capita basis and the absolute figures for consumption are also very high. Canada is a net exporter of energy; 268.42 million tons coal equivalent (mtce) were produced in 1975 and 225.57 mtce consumed. In the US, the corresponding figures were 2,036 mtce and 2,349 mtce. For a continent which contains less than 6 percent of the world's total population, that North America produces nearly 27 percent of the world's energy in an average year yet consumes about 32 percent of it, is indeed remarkable. In large measure this reflects the high degree of development in both Canada and the US. But, as was clearly recognizable in the attempt of the US federal government to reduce energy consumption during and after the 'oil crisis' of 1973, these figures also reflect a somewhat extravagant attitude to energy consumption in the area. Indeed, in 1975 the USA was still consuming energy at the rate of 11,000 kg/ca and Canada 9,880 kg/ca. Compare this with elsewhere in the world – except for a few very small Middle Eastern countries where per capita figures do not add up to large *total* amounts – where the highest figures are 7,151 in Czechoslovakia, 6,485 in Australia and 6,178 in Sweden.

Although North America is still looked upon as the 'New World', it should be noted that its countries developed their economies only a short time behind those of Europe, the world leaders in industrial and commercial growth. While the US and Canada participated in both twentieth-century world wars which rocked Europe, the North American continent was not physically involved in either. The North American economies continue to grow, though they now face new challenges. There is the rivalry between the USA and the USSR as the leaders of the western and eastern blocs. There is the resurgence of such countries as Japan and the European recovery, including the remarkable economic growth of West Germany. There is the as yet unmeasured growth of China.

The US has been a world leader for more than half a century, at times with hardly a competitor in sight in economic fields. But the age of that unchallenged supremacy is past. As new technologies develop, the economically most advanced countries will be in intense competition. American attitudes to world competition and world change may themselves be subject to considerable adjustment. Remember that the USSR put the first artificial satellite into orbit around the earth but that the US put the first man on the moon. International brinkmanship reached its zenith at the time of the Cuban crisis when America forced the Soviet Union to retract. Later, however, in Vietnam the US had to concede that there could be no 'victory'.

In the Third World where neo-colonialism is replacing the old colonial systems after a short period of independence for the 'new nations', the US pursues policies apparently designed not to upset the global objectives of detente. Problems at home like the political shock of Watergate, a less stable economy and a weakened dollar, and the growth of the environmental and other lobbies must have their effect.

Doubtless North America will continue to have an important influence on the rest of the world, but there can be no denying that the US no longer is in the unchallenged position it held previously.

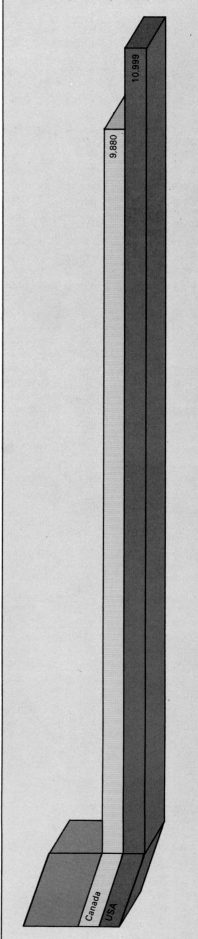

Per Capita Energy Consumption
(1975 figures in kilograms)

In North America, energy used per person is considerably higher than for almost anywhere else in the world. Even the USSR and Europe, the next most energy-hungry continental areas, use only 55 and 42 percent of the North American figures respectively.

10.999

9.880

Canada

USA

1 △   2 ▽

USA: Industrial and agricultural development throughout the country is as varied as the landscape of the 50 states: 1 Ford River Rouge Plant, Detroit, Michigan – part of the world's biggest automobile manufacturing complex; 2 Sugar refinery, Hawaii – the last state to join the union has fertile farmland for production of the islands' main crops, which are pineapples and sugarcane

North American Countries

Canada

The second largest country in the world, Canada is by far the least populated of all the world's giant states in total and density terms. This is a measure of both its youthful development and its northerly latitude. It is a federal state with ten constituent provinces and two territories, and it is a member of the British Commonwealth. The population is now predominantly of English descent but that of Quebec province is predominantly French. In recent times particularly, a separatist movement has received considerable support in French Canada. Some predict that Quebec might well secede from the union, which was first created from the four provinces of Ontario, Quebec, New Brunswick and Nova Scotia in 1867. This would leave Anglo-Canada in two parts, the Atlantic provinces in the east, and the larger and economically far more significant portion, in the center and west.

A land of great potential, Canada is also a land of contrasts. Its range of raw materials is vast; extensive softwood forests and smaller but considerable hardwood forests; a wide range of minerals; rich fishing grounds off both east and west coasts; areas of great agricultural potential. Yet much of it is physically remote and climatically uninviting.

The Atlantic Provinces

New Brunswick, Newfoundland/ Labrador, Nova Scotia and Prince Edward Island in the extreme east of Canada are remote from the main population centers. Newfoundland may have been the first part of North America ever discovered by European adventurers as early as AD 1000. All four provinces have important lumbering and fishing industries. Specialist farming is important in some areas, such as the major potato growing provinces of Prince Edward Island and New Brunswick, and fruit production, especially apples, in Nova Scotia. Labrador has an important range of minerals; about half of Canada's iron ore is extracted from a belt which straddles the border with Quebec, and uranium has been discovered. The ports of the Atlantic provinces play a major role in Canadian and US Atlantic trade, especially in winter when the St Lawrence freezes.

Quebec

As with all Canadian provinces, most of the developed and populous parts are found in the south, here straddling the St Lawrence River. Quebec farming, with its distinctive French origins and layout, is dominated by pasture, hay growing and dairy cattle. About 25 percent of Canada's butter and cheese come from this area. Mineral production, from the same belt as that found across the border in Labrador, is very important; iron, copper and zinc being the major ores extracted. Elsewhere, asbestos production is particularly significant, some 70 percent of Canada's total output coming from the Eastern Townships. Quebec also accounts for about 40 percent of Canada's hydroelectric power production. Forestry products – pulp, paper and cardboard – are another major industrial group, the extensive forests of the north accounting for half of Canada's pulp production in a typical year. Montreal, one of Canada's largest and most cosmopolitan cities, has a metropolitan area population equal to that of Toronto, and has a wide range of industries – clothing and textiles, shoe making, food processing, transport equipment and other manufactured goods.

Ontario

Most of the population is clustered along the northern shores of Lakes Ontario and Erie and, to a lesser extent, in an east-west belt along the Ottawa River. This is Canada's leading industrial province, with major centers of iron and steel making, oil refining and chemical industries, automobile assembly, pulp and paper production and food processing being found here. Prior to the opening of the St Lawrence Seaway in 1959, oceangoing vessels could navigate the great river only as far as Montreal, Quebec, which thus developed as the major manufacturing center. Ports and cities farther west were served only by smaller lake vessels. Now that Toronto and other cities are equally accessible to the ocean, when the St Lawrence is not frozen over, their importance has increased. Ontario's agricultural heart is in the southwest peninsula, between Lakes Erie and Huron. Here, soils, climate and markets combine to create a prosperous arable and dairying area. In addition, large amounts of fruit are grown in the Niagara peninsula. Farther north within the Shield area, Ontario, too, has rich mineral resources, nickel, copper, iron and gold being the leader.

The Prairie Provinces

West from Ontario, the three provinces of Manitoba, Saskatchewan and Alberta present an expansive landscape which rises in a series of steps toward the Western Cordillera. The archetypal prairie farm scene, however, exists only in a semi-elliptical area in the south. Here, wheat farming dominates – though it is often mixed with stock raising – with Saskatchewan accounting for 65 percent of Canada's sown area and 60 percent of her annual output. Most wheat is marketed via the great cities of the prairies, and much is exported, mainly to Europe. Farther north and west, livestock raising,

1 Las Vegas, Nevada, USA – a name synonymous with gambling and lavish entertainment; 2 Pacific Rim National Park, Vancouver Island, British Columbia; 3 Oil well, Condor, Alberta, Canada – 85 percent of the country's crude oil comes from this mineral-rich prairie province

dairying and mixed farming become increasingly important, especially with the modern rapid growth of the large prairie towns, like Edmonton and Calgary. The prairie provinces also account for the bulk of Canada's fossil fuel production. Coal reserves have long been exploited, and today Alberta's annual output is approximately 10 million tons. However, crude oil, oil sands and natural gas discoveries and development during the last 30 years have been rapid. Alberta produces 85 percent of Canada's crude oil and 90 percent of her natural gas. Saskatchewan also possesses the world's largest potash deposits.

British Columbia

The great mountain province of Canada is, in some ways, remote from the rest of the federation. Little of its land is suited to farming, although there are important specialist activities like apple growing in Okanagan Valley and dairying in the lower Frazer Valley. Fishing, though significant, plays a smaller part in the economy of the province than is sometimes thought. Forestry is far more vital. Copper, zinc, lead and to a lesser extent coal, crude oil and natural gas are the leading mineral products.

The population of the metropolitan area of Vancouver is the third highest in all Canada, and is now twice as large as either Edmonton or Winnipeg. It is the largest urban area west of Toronto and is Canada's major outlet to the Pacific.

The Northern Tier

North of the 60th parallel, except for the area east of Hudson Bay, lie the mountain Territory of the Yukon and the more extensive mainland and island parts of the Northwest Territories. Best known to the public from the pioneer days of the Klondike Gold rush, the Yukon is still most important for its mineral wealth. However, the scope of its mineral base is now recognized, with zinc, lead, silver, copper and gold rating most highly in value terms. Forestry has great potential, but has yet to be systematically developed. The Northwest Territories are far more extensive. Here, zinc, lead, gold, silver and copper are the main products. Yellowknife is the largest town and center of gold production. Furs yield almost as much revenue as gold. A modest production of crude oil from the Mackenzie Basin has been maintained for nearly 60 years. Today

North American Countries

larger areas are being searched for further fields. Facing directly across the Polar ice to the north coast of the USSR, this attic of North America has increasing strategic importance for the whole continent.

Greenland

Popularly regarded as the world's largest island, 85 percent of this land is covered by a permanent ice cap. The western coastal strip contains 90 percent of the population who are mainly Eskimo. As Greenland is still part of the Danish realm, the few citizens of European descent are mostly from that country and most trade is with Denmark, although Greenland's defense is controlled by a Danish/American agreement. The USA maintain air bases here. Fishing and processing are the most significant activities, though mineral prospecting and extraction is of growing importance. Coal mining ceased recently; cryolite, a rare mineral important in the production of aluminium, has been mined for some time; lead and zinc mining started in 1973; the search for oil is intensifying off the west coast.

St Pierre and Miquelon

This group of eight islands to the immediate south of Newfoundland is an overseas territory of France. As the name suggests, they lie in two distinct sections. Oddly, the far smaller St Pierre group contains 90

percent of the total population. Largely bare rock, the islands are useless for farming. Cod fishing on the Grand Banks is the main occupation; fish processing industries are obviously important.

The United States of America

Created in 1776 when the 3 million inhabitants of the 13 original states on the Atlantic seaboard declared their independence from Britain, the present area of the USA makes it the fourth largest country in the world. In those 200 years the federation of states has grown to a modern total of 50; the country extends from Atlantic to Pacific coasts of the North American continent and has two non-contiguous states, Alaska and Hawaii, as well as a number of outlying territories (classified separately within this atlas). As of the 1970 census the country contained over 203 million, and in 1980 the population was estimated to be approximately 220 million.

In the late nineteenth and twentieth centuries, the USA developed economically into the free world's most powerful country. It is a land of great physical contrasts. Agriculturally it produces a wide range of crops: citrus fruit, sugarcane and cotton from the subtropical south and southwest; great quantities of cereals, especially corn and wheat, as well as tobacco and soybeans, from the mid-latitude continental interior, and truck farming crops from the densely populated areas of the northeast. Stock raising, pig rearing, dairying and, to a lesser extent sheep farming, are also important.

The US economy is also based on a wide range of minerals. Coal,

natural gas and crude oil are all produced in large quantities, although the latter is now imported from Venezuela and the Middle East. Precious minerals and metal ores are extracted over a wide area. Based on its rich agricultural and mineral resources, the range of industries is such that it would almost be possible for the USA to isolate itself economically from the outside world. However, this would take much time and require drastic reductions in fuel requirements of US autos.

The very size of the USA makes it unrealistic to attempt overall descriptions of its modern geography and economy. Although parts of the country which have a popular image go under such titles as the 'Great Plains', the 'Midwest' and the 'Manufacturing Belt', such areas do not account for the whole nation, sometimes overlap and are inevitably subject to rather vague notions about their precise extent. We are therefore for the sake of convenience using nine geographical divisions based on state boundaries.

New England

Comprising six comparatively small states in the extreme northeast of the country, in overall terms this is the smallest division, yet it is the second most densely populated. Maine covers nearly half of the area yet has less than ten percent of the inhabitants, and Vermont too is thinly populated. The great economic heart then is in Massachusetts, Connecticut, Rhode Island and the southern part of New Hampshire.

Much of New England lies within the original area of colonial America and thus has a long history of development. Agriculture today is

very specialized, and large areas which were once cleared and farmed have now reverted to forest. Truck farming and dairying are the leading activities. Timber production and fishing, two long-standing occupations, are still significant.

Overall, the division is singularly deficient in minerals. Most important is the manufacturing industry of the many towns lying in a broad belt from Boston in the east toward New York in the southwest. The traditional market leaders of textiles and leather manufacturing have now been surpassed by electrical and electronics industries, instrument making and other metal industries.

One of the increasingly appreciated resources of New England is its tourist potential. In the summer its southern shores provide readily accessible inlets and beaches for the nearby urban population. The coast of Long Island Sound is now dotted with marinas at which many of the population of the region moor their craft. Farther east, Cape Cod is a retreat from the nearby cities. Farther north, the beaches and rocky coast of Maine offer a cooler attractive environment, not only for US citizens but also for Canadians from Quebec and Ontario.

The mountains, rivers and lakes of Vermont, New Hampshire and Maine attract both summer and winter tourists. State Parks on the coast and inland at places like Mount Monadnock provide camping, picnicking and hiking facilities. The dramatic colors of the forest in the fall attract many visitors. Winter sports are also popular throughout this region.

Middle Atlantic

To the immediate west and southwest of New England lies the slightly larger but equally compact division of the Middle Atlantic. This includes the states of New Jersey, New York and Pennsylvania and extends across the northern Appalachians from the Atlantic seaboard to the two easternmost Great Lakes. The mountains extending northeast to southwest through the region constitute something of a divide and include little cropland. It was across this area that so many of the stream of migrants who have entered the USA in the last 200 years and more have passed. Today, the Middle Atlantic as a whole is of enormous importance in the US economy. Herein lies one of the world's largest conurbations and other large centers of population.

Early colonial settlement developed a more broadly based agriculture than that of neighboring divisions. Today, the demands of the large urban areas have led the farmers to concentrate on two main activities: dairying, largely for milk, not butter and cheese, extending throughout the division, and truck farming on the Atlantic seaboard and the southern shores of Lakes Ontario and Erie. Specialist farming still continues; for example, poultry, tobacco, apples and mushrooms are

1 Greenland – Eskimo hunting walrus, an occupation which, like sealing and whaling, has been replaced by fishing for the majority of the population of these ice-covered parts; 2 Houston, Texas USA – the largest city in the state is at the center of a wealthy industrial area, as well as being the headquarters of NASA, which is the United States National Aeronautics and Space Administration

1 △   2 ▽

all of great significance in Lancaster County, Pennsylvania, where dairying is the staple activity.

America's earliest iron and steel industry was based here, using the iron of eastern Pennsylvania, charcoal from the Appalachian forests and later coal from the same state. Today, Pennsylvania is the main American focus for both iron and steel production. It also accounts for about 15 percent of the US coal output as well as being the original and a continuing producer of crude oil and natural gas.

New Jersey and New York States have a broader manufacturing base. Food processing, clothing and some textiles, chemical and metal manufacturing are most valuable. Commerce and service industries also dominate many of the cities.

Perhaps, above all, the Middle Atlantic is known for its large urban areas focusing on some of the original colonial settlement ports, New York and Philadelphia, the original capital city of the independent USA of 1776, being the most famous. New York has the advantages of both easy access to the Atlantic and routes to the interior. These are somewhat offset by the disadvantage of its physical site, centering on Manhattan Island between two large rivers, which today manifests itself in the chronic congestion of the central areas of the city. The New York metropolitan area now has more people in it than any other single world city, and as a trading, commercial and manufacturing center it dominates the whole North American continent.

East North Central

North of the Ohio River, east of the Mississippi and primarily south of the westernmost Great Lakes lies a group of five states, Ohio, Indiana, Illinois, Michigan and Wisconsin. Collectively these contain some of the richest US farmland, parts of two of her most important coal fields and three major industrial centers, Chicago, Detroit and Cleveland.

From east to west the land slopes gently, somewhat monotonously, toward the upper valley of the Mississippi. Much of the area is clothed with rich glacial deposits and the climate is moist enough to maintain the extensive areas of corn in Illinois, Iowa and Indiana at the center of the 'Corn Belt'. This is largely used as animal fodder, feeding locally raised pigs and cattle brought in from the plains. Farther west and north, wheat growing, hay and dairying are more common. To the east, the poorer soils on the margins of the Appalachians and the demands of the urban dwellers have resulted in an emphasis on dairying and truck farming.

The division comprises the western parts of the US 'Manufacturing Belt'. Heavy industry – iron and steel production, chemicals, glass, rubber etc – is found in Ohio, and particularly in the towns close to Lake Erie, such as Cleveland, Toledo and Youngstown. To the north, the

Detroit area of Michigan contains the world's largest concentration of automobile making, an assembly industry which is dependent upon the sheet steel, rubber and other components provided largely from the nearby cities.

Farther west, on the shore of Lake Michigan is Chicago, the third largest single city of the US. It is at the main head of navigation on the Great Lakes, and is but a short canal journey from a major tributary of the Mississippi system, the Illinois river. It is a great industrial center known particularly for its heavy industry, steel production and as the effective 'capital' of the 'Middle West'. It is the largest railroad focus in the whole of the US. The vast metropolitan area sprawls over the flat Illinois landscape. By contrast, Chicago's central business district or 'Loop' soars upward, with skyscrapers ranging up to the Sears Tower, world's tallest.

The towns and cities of the south and west of this division are mainly geared to the needs of the surrounding agricultural areas. Food processing, particularly flour milling and meat packing, are the main activities, though some cities have developed agricultural industries.

West North Central

West of the Mississippi, south of the Canadian border and east of the Western Cordillera lie two tiers of states. The seven most northern states, Minnesota, Iowa, Missouri, North and South Dakota, Nebraska and Kansas – constitute this division. In the east, the extensive landscape of the 'Middle West' continues into Missouri, Iowa and Minnesota. Then the landscape rises up to the different levels of the Great Plains, so that

when the foothills of the Rocky Mountains are reached the level of the plains is about 1,600 m (5,000 ft).

Farming in this area depends on the total rainfall. The farther west, the lower the rainfall, so that corn growing diminishes and wheat and sorghum increase in importance. In Missouri, Iowa and Minnesota, these alternative grains are grown mainly for fodder, but in the west cashcrop growing of wheat is most important.

This, and the modern equivalent of traditional ranching, provide a far more extensive agricultural pattern than that seen farther east. Farm units become larger and the farming activities are such that a smaller population is needed. Much of this area centers on the Missouri River valley; for more than 30 years this has been the subject of federal aid development, though not with the same enthusiasm as is seen in the Tennessee Valley (page 158).

The settlement and industrial development of this area has been understandably less dynamic than that of the Manufacturing Belt to the east. Today the two large urban centers of the southern part, St Louis and Kansas City, have developed from their former roles of agricultural market and transportation centers into more broadly based industrial centers. Farther north, the dynamic twin cities of Minneapolis and St. Paul, situated on the upper Mississippi, dominate the commercial and industrial activity of their region and are a gateway to the vast vacationland of northern Minnesota. Overall, the area is not well endowed with minerals, though in the extreme north, the Mesabi, Vermilion and Cuyuna Ranges in Minnesota are the major US source of iron ore.

1 Toronto, Ontario, Canada – the CN Tower, the world's tallest freestanding structure, dominates the capital of the province as seen from Ontario Place; 2 Indian, New Mexico, USA – many of North America's original inhabitants still live in this southern state, bordering Mexico; 3 Livermore Falls, Maine, USA – the largest of the New England states is, like its northeastern neighbors, especially beautiful in the 'fall'

South Atlantic

Between Pennsylvania in the north and Florida in the south lies a line of Atlantic seaboard states which are nearly all sandwiched between the ocean and the Appalachian watershed: Maryland, Delaware, the District of Columbia, West Virginia, Virginia, North and South Carolina, Georgia and Florida. The northern tier were part of the original group of 13 which declared their independence from Britain in 1776; five of the states in the division were on the side of the South in the Civil War. Along with the states of the lower Mississippi Valley these comprise the area known as the 'South', with its popular image of cotton and tobacco plantations, the land of the American Negro slaves in the pre-Civil War days and, in some ways, the poor relation states. Today, such outmoded, if historically accurate concepts, have been replaced by a more realistic factual assessment.

Physically the South Atlantic states contain a largely infertile coastal belt of sands, swamps and forests, and a western mountain belt. Between these lie the main agricultural areas where the principal crops vary with the latitude. In Georgia, cotton still dominates. Farther north, tobacco is the most important crop. Timber is

North American Countries

also valuable, North Carolina being the fifth most important state of the union for forestry products.

The Virginias are also important for tobacco production, but derive far more of their economic prosperity from their fossil fuel reserves. West Virginia produces more coal than any other single state, while Virginia is seventh in this category.

Food processing apart, textiles are the area's most important manufacturing industry. The southern states gained steadily on the previous major producer, New England, in the first half of this century and now have the lead.

Near to the extremes of this division are two areas of different distinction. In the north, Washington, the nation's capital, lies within the District of Columbia. Formerly part of Maryland and Virginia, this small area has been the seat of the national government and administration since 1790. Spaciously laid out on the banks of the Potomac River, the capital now attracts many home and overseas visitors, not only to the government buildings and national monuments but also to the cultural centers such as the National Gallery and the Smithsonian Institution.

In the south, Florida extends farther south than any other continental part of the union. This subtropical state has developed rapidly in the last 30 years. It is now most significant as a major US source of citrus fruit, as well as producing sugarcane, melons and winter vegetables for the northern states.

East South Central

Traditionally regarded as part of the 'South', Kentucky, Tennessee, Alabama and Mississippi lie between the Appalachians and the Mississippi south of the Ohio River. Within these lies the Tennessee River, the subject of a federal development program which has been a major boost to the economy and morale of the area – the creation of the Tennessee Valley Authority (TVA).

Prior to 1933, the Tennessee River was a menace; its flow fluctuated from season to season, it was of little navigational value, and it was a flood hazard. Agriculture in its whole basin was at a low ebb. By constructing a series of dams, many with bypassing canals, the river is now controlled, navigable and is the source of much hydroelectric power. Within the river basin, schemes to prevent soil erosion have been pursued and the quality of farming has thus improved. Long and bitter political arguments through the years concerning the TVA have tended to breathe caution on similar programs elsewhere, such as in the valleys of the Missouri and the Columbia rivers.

The Gulf states of Mississippi and

Alabama lie largely south of the TVA area. Save in the extreme northeast where the Appalachians extend into Alabama, both are largely flat with subtropical agriculture dominating their economies. Soybeans are the most valuable field crop and cotton second. Poultry, pigs and cattle account for slightly more farm income than do crops. In Alabama, the coal and iron deposits associated with the Appalachians farther north are once again found. These were a major factor in the growth of Birmingham as a major iron and steel center.

West South Central

Between the Mississippi and the Western Cordillera south of about 37°N lie Arkansas, Louisiana, Oklahoma and Texas. Texas alone amounts to over 7 percent of the total area of the US. In the west is the archetypal Great Plains landscape with its cattle ranges; in the east, Arkansas and Louisiana are the western extremities of the old 'Deep South'; in the south lies the modern, prosperous Gulf coastal strip.

Arkansas and Louisiana are still major cotton producing states today, with a yield per hectare (acre) among the highest for any state. In Texas, where modern irrigation

programs have greatly enlarged the crop area, the area of cotton growing is very large but yields are lower. Among a wide range of other crops grown throughout the area, subtropical citrus fruit, rice and peanuts are most noteworthy. Texas is a major beef stock state but also contains the greatest single concentration of sheep in the whole of the US.

The farther west, the lower the rainfall. In this area of the region, where parts of the great dust bowl of the 1920s and '30s can still be seen, the threat of soil erosion persists and conservation measures are applied rigorously. In Oklahoma, the greatest farming trend of the last forty years has been the conversion of arable land to grazing.

In the extreme east, New Orleans on the Mississippi delta is an old-established port at the focus of the river, rail and road network, with seagoing traffic for Middle and South America as well as Africa and Europe. Its French character, revealed in streets, squares, buildings and names, and its connections with the origin of jazz music, make it a most distinctive city. Other ports on the Gulf coastlands have now overtaken it in terms of the volume of traffic handled each year.

Farther west on the Gulf coast and

inland, modern prosperity rests predominantly on mineral wealth and the associated industrial development; in particular, the production of crude oil and natural gas. Here is the largest concentration of these resources in the US. Oil refining and the petrochemical industries have developed rapidly.

Mountain

The physical features present in the inland states west of about 105°W, Montana, Idaho, Wyoming, Utah, Nevada, Colorado, Arizona and New Mexico, are awesome. Here lies the great complex of mountains stretching north-south from the Canadian to the Mexican borders; to the east, the various local ranges which collectively make up the Rocky Mountains; then such ranges as the Bitterroots and the Wasatch and, still farther west, on the Californian border, the Sierra Nevada. Between many of the ranges lie the great plateaus and desert basins. The finest index to the inhospitable nature of the area lies in the average population density of the eight states, 4.3 per km² (11.0 per sq mi). Without such large cities as Denver, Phoenix and Salt Lake City, these figures would be even lower.

1 Dallas, Texas, USA – a center of the oil industry – with other industries such as aircraft, machinery and cotton textiles – this second biggest city in the 'lone star' state. Dallas, an important industrial and commercial city, is also a prime financial and insurance center. 2 Niagara Falls, USA/Canada – about half way down the river which forms part of the North American border, the Falls attract thousands of tourists who don waterproofs to view the torrent up close. The Canadian Horseshoe Falls shown here – at over 670 m (2,210 ft) wide and 54 m (178 ft) high – are bigger than the American Rainbow Falls.

1 △

2 ▽

Lack of water is the farmers greatest problem. In the Great Salt Lake depression, the Snake River area of south Idaho and the Gila Basin in Arizona, however, such aridity has been countered by irrigation and a wide range of crops is now grown. Ranching and lumbering are still the main activities, on a far more extensive scale than anywhere else in the continental part of the union.

The mountain states also contain a wide range of minerals, many discovered by the early pioneers as they moved west along the trails. These 'strikes' gave rise to the mining settlements which enjoyed a limited period of intense activity before becoming ghost towns. Today, copper is the most valuable single ore, a number of mines in Arizona, the open pit mine at Bingham, Utah and the deeper deposits of Butte, Montana, being the largest sources. Southwest Montana and north Idaho have valuable deposits of zinc. Silver is still a major resource of Idaho.

In the summer, the scenic variety of all but the hottest desert areas attract many visitors from both east and west. Winter tourism is based on sports areas like Sun Valley, Idaho and Aspen, Colorado; this is the time of the year to visit the Arizona desert and Death Valley.

Pacific

Of all the regions discussed only the Pacific is noncontiguous. Three of its states in main, continental USA, Washington, Oregon and California, are bounded by the Pacific coast; Alaska, the largest state in the union, is detached from the rest by Canada, and Hawaii is set in midocean. As the US has developed from east to west, these westernmost outposts of the union have shown their most dramatic developments recently.

Much of Washington state, Oregon and California are mountain and plateau country, but the lowland areas and parts of the coastal belt have given rise to great centers of population where large industrial complexes have developed. In Washington state, where the economy was previously based on farming, forestry, fishing and mining, each of which still has its part to play, aircraft and aerospace industries now dominate the manufacturing sector which has become the most valuable activity. Oregon's economy is, however, still based on primary products like timber from the extensive forests.

Today, California, with the highest state population in the union, has a popular image of being the great boom state of the post World War II era. It certainly has a range of activities and products greater than that of any other single state. Crude oil and natural gas production and the petrochemical industries are second only in value to those of the western Gulf states. A range of minerals is extracted from the mountains, in particular around 4 million troy ounces of gold per year. A wide range of modern manufacturing industries has developed.

The value of fish landed is the highest for any US state; farming products range from cotton, sugar beet and rice through all the temperate cereals, temperate and subtropical fruits, including grapes which generate the largest US production of wine. Irrigation is vital for many of the farming activities. Cattle, sheep and pigs are all raised.

The Los Angeles urban area, a group of individual cities which have been dubbed as being centerless, is arguably the largest in the world and certainly the most famous complex of highways in the world, generating, in the still atmosphere of this southwest corner of the country, the equally famous smog. By comparison, San Francisco, confined to the end of a peninsula, is small indeed.

Alaska, at the opposite end of the US climatic spectrum, only joined the union in January 1959. By far the largest state, it is the least densely populated. Originally prized for its strategic importance, and its forestry and fishing resources, it is now most valued for its proven and potential oil reserves.

Hawaii, whose economy is based mainly on tourism, is the most recent state to join the union (March 1959.)

COUNTRY REFERENCE: NORTH AMERICA

North American Countries	Political Status	State Capital	Area km²	Area sq mi	Population	Population Density per km²	Population Density per sq mi
CANADA	A	Ottawa	9,976,139	3,851,809	23,625,000	2.4	6.0
Alberta	D	Edmonton	661,185	255,285	1,889,000	2.9	7.4
British Columbia	D	Victoria	948,596	366,255	2,534,000	2.7	6.9
Manitoba	D	Winnipeg	650,087	251,000	1,050,000	1.6	4.2
New Brunswick	D	Fredericton	73,437	28,354	696,000	9.5	25
Newfoundland	D	St John's	404,517	156,185	573,000	1.4	3.7
NW Territories	D	Yellowknife	3,379,683	1,304,903	44,000	0.01	0.03
Nova Scotia	D	Halifax	55,491	21,425	851,000	15	40
Ontario	D	Toronto	1,068,582	412,582	8,492,000	7.9	21
PEI	D	Charlottetown	5,657	2,184	121,000	21	55
Quebec	D	Quebec	1,540,680	594,860	6,406,000	4.2	11
Saskatchewan	D	Regina	651,900	251,700	947,000	1.5	3.8
Yukon	D	Whitehorse	536,324	207,076	22,000	0.04	0.1
GREENLAND	C	Godthåb	2,175,600	840,000	50,000	0.02	0.06
ST PIERRE AND MIQUELON	C	Saint Pierre	242	93	6,000	25	65
USA	A	Washington DC	9,363,125	3,615,123	217,264,300	23	60
New England							
Connecticut	D	Hartford	12,973	5,009	3,142,500	242	627
Maine	D	Augusta	86,026	33,215	1,086,800	13	33
Massachusetts	D	Boston	21,386	8,257	5,832,600	273	705
New Hampshire	D	Concord	24,097	9,304	838,000	35	90
Rhode Island	D	Providence	3,144	1,214	922,400	293	760
Vermont	D	Montpelier	24,887	9,609	483,300	19	50
NE TOTAL			172,513	66,608	12,305,600	71	185
Middle Atlantic							
New Jersey	D	Trenton	20,295	7,836	7,358,700	363	939
New York	D	Albany	128,401	49,576	18,102,300	141	365
Pennsylvania	D	Harrisburg	117,412	45,333	11,896,700	101	262
MA TOTAL			266,108	102,745	37,357,700	140	364
East North Central							
Illinois	D	Springfield	146,075	56,400	11,277,200	77	200
Indiana	D	Indianapolis	93,993	36,291	5,306,000	56	146
Michigan	D	Lansing	150,779	58,216	9,121,800	60	157
Ohio	D	Columbus	106,764	41,222	10,669,100	100	259
Wisconsin	D	Madison	145,438	56,154	4,616,500	32	82
ENC TOTAL			643,049	248,283	40,990,600	64	165
West North Central							
Iowa	D	Des Moines	145,790	56,290	2,880,900	20	51
Kansas	D	Topeka	213,063	82,264	2,337,200	11	28
Minnesota	D	St Paul	217,735	84,068	4,026,900	18	48
Missouri	D	Jefferson City	180,486	69,686	4,800,800	27	69
Nebraska	D	Lincoln	200,017	77,227	1,564,900	7.8	20
North Dakota	D	Bismark	183,022	70,665	650,500	3.6	9.2
South Dakota	D	Pierre	199,551	77,047	688,400	3.4	8.9
WNC TOTAL			1,339,664	517,247	16,949,600	13	33
South Atlantic							
Delaware	D	Dover	5,328	2,057	587,600	110	286
District of Columbia	D	Washington	174	67	689,000	3,960	10,284
Florida	D	Tallahassee	151,670	58,560	8,651,000	57	148
Georgia	D	Atlanta	152,488	58,876	5,032,400	33	85
Maryland	D	Annapolis	27,394	10,577	4,190,000	153	396
North Carolina	D	Raleigh	136,197	52,586	5,538,600	41	105
South Carolina	D	Columbia	80,432	31,055	2,900,500	36	93
Virginia	D	Richmond	105,716	40,817	5,114,200	48	125
West Virginia	D	Charleston	62,628	24,181	1,846,100	29	76
SA TOTAL			722,027	278,776	34,549,400	48	124
East South Central							
Alabama	D	Montgomery	133,667	51,609	3,725,300	28	72
Kentucky	D	Frankfort	104,623	40,395	3,482,400	33	86
Mississippi	D	Jackson	123,584	47,716	2,379,200	19	50
Tennessee	D	Nashville	109,411	42,244	4,276,400	39	101
ESC TOTAL			471,285	181,964	13,863,300	29	76
West South Central							
Arkansas	D	Little Rock	137,539	53,104	2,143,700	16	40
Louisiana	D	Baton Rouge	125,674	48,523	3,905,500	31	80
Oklahoma	D	Oklahoma City	181,089	69,919	2,823,100	16	40
Texas	D	Austin	692,405	267,339	12,834,700	19	48
WSC TOTAL			1,136,707	438,885	21,707,000	19	49
Mountain							
Arizona	D	Phoenix	295,023	113,909	2,359,600	8.0	21
Colorado	D	Denver	269,998	104,247	2,644,400	9.8	25
Idaho	D	Boise	216,412	83,557	854,900	4.0	10
Montana	D	Helena	381,086	147,138	763,800	2.0	5.2
Nevada	D	Carson City	286,297	110,540	637,000	2.2	5.8
New Mexico	D	Santa Fe	315,113	121,666	1,201,600	3.8	9.9
Utah	D	Salt Lake City	219,931	84,916	1,263,800	5.7	15
Wyoming	D	Cheyenne	253,596	97,914	406,900	1.6	4.2
M TOTAL			2,237,456	863,887	10,132,000	4.5	12
Pacific							
Alaska	D	Juneau	1,518,800	586,412	407,500	0.3	0.7
California	D	Sacramento	411,013	158,693	22,017,500	54	139
Hawaii	D	Honolulu	16,705	6,450	914,200	55	142
Oregon	D	Salem	251,180	96,981	2,372,700	9.4	24
Washington	D	Olympia	176,616	68,192	3,697,200	21	54
P TOTAL			2,374,314	916,728	29,409,100	12	32
NORTH AMERICA TOTALS			21,515,106	8,307,025	240,945,300	11.2	29.0

	Canada	Greenland	St Pierre & Miquelon	USA
NOTE: Birth rate per thousand persons	15.4	19.2	16.6	14.8
Death rate per thousand persons	7.4	6.9	9.1	9.0
Mean annual percentage increase in population	1.3	1.6	0.9	0.8

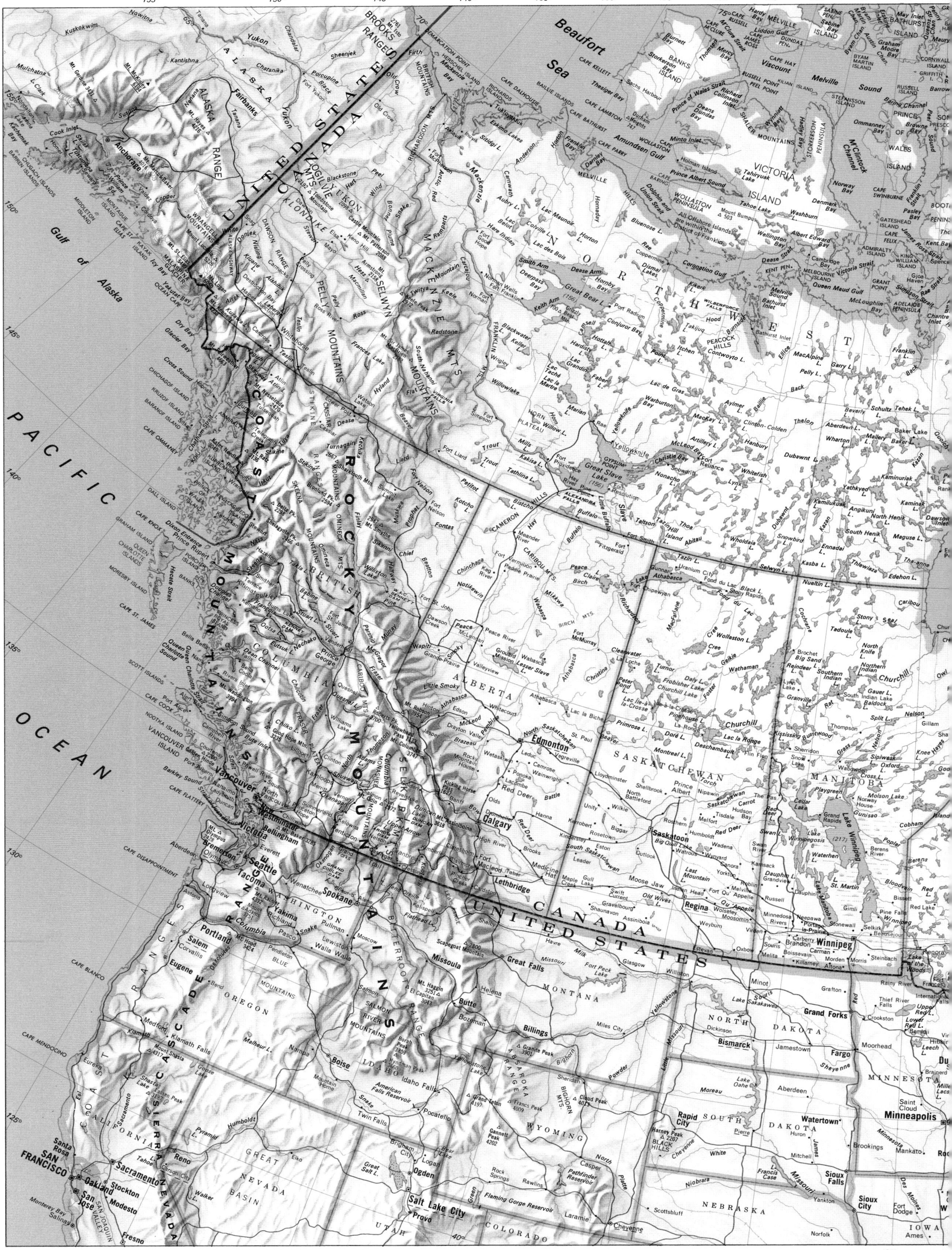

Canada

PACIFIC OCEAN

Gulf of Alaska

Beaufort Sea

ALASKA

UNITED STATES

CANADA

YUKON

NORTHWEST

BRITISH COLUMBIA

ALBERTA

SASKATCHEWAN

MANITOBA

ROCKY MOUNTAINS

COAST MOUNTAINS

MACKENZIE MOUNTAINS

SELWYN MOUNTAINS

BROOKS RANGE

ALASKA RANGE

VICTORIA ISLAND

MELVILLE ISLAND

BANKS ISLAND

WASHINGTON

OREGON

IDAHO

MONTANA

WYOMING

NEVADA

UTAH

COLORADO

NEBRASKA

NORTH DAKOTA

SOUTH DAKOTA

MINNESOTA

IOWA

CASCADE RANGE

SIERRA NEVADA

GREAT BASIN

Anchorage

Fairbanks

Edmonton

Calgary

Saskatoon

Regina

Winnipeg

Vancouver

Victoria

Seattle

Tacoma

Portland

Salem

Eugene

Spokane

Boise

Helena

Butte

Billings

Great Falls

Missoula

Bozeman

Rapid City

Bismarck

Fargo

Grand Forks

Watertown

Sioux Falls

Sioux City

Minneapolis

San Francisco

Oakland

San Jose

Sacramento

Stockton

Modesto

Fresno

Reno

Salt Lake City

Provo

Ogden

Cheyenne

Casper

Great Slave Lake

Great Bear Lake

Lake Athabasca

Lake Winnipeg

Great Salt Lake

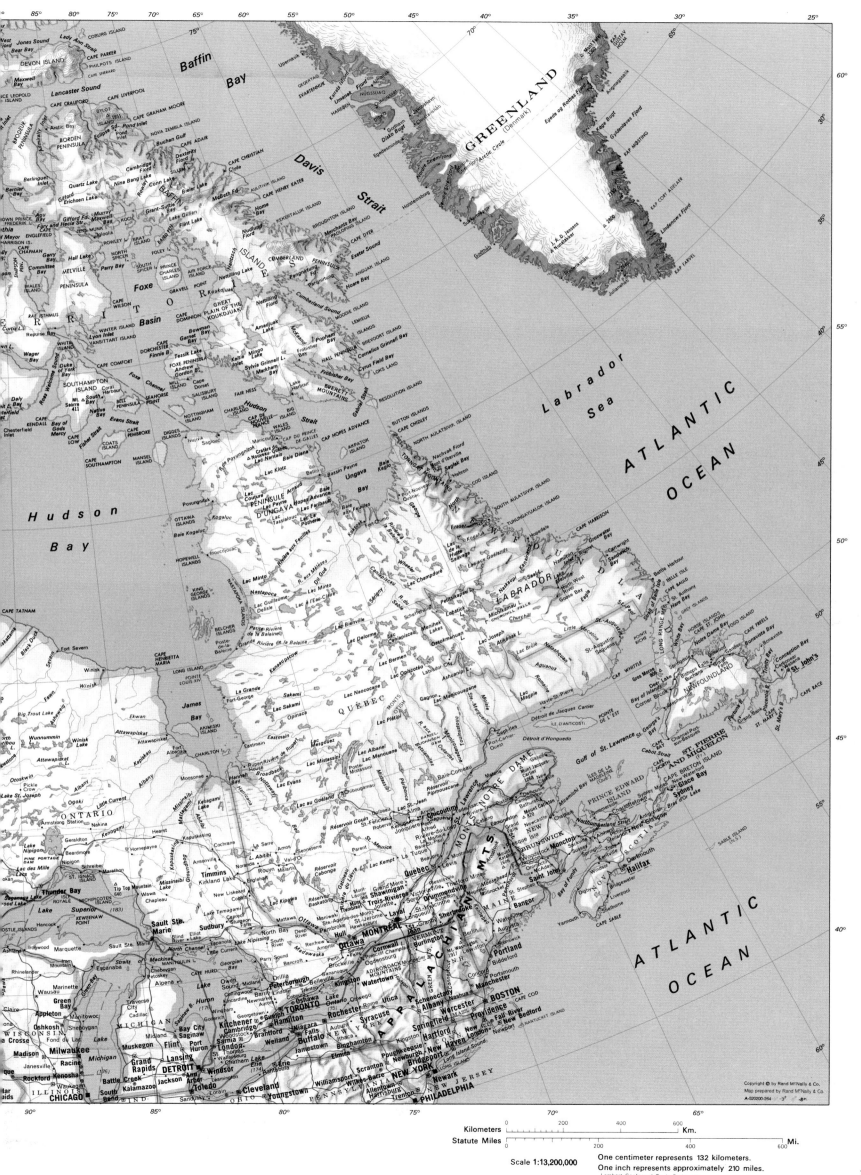

Kilometers
Statute Miles

Scale 1:13,200,000

One centimeter represents 132 kilometers.
One inch represents approximately 210 miles.
Lambert Conformal Conic Projection

161

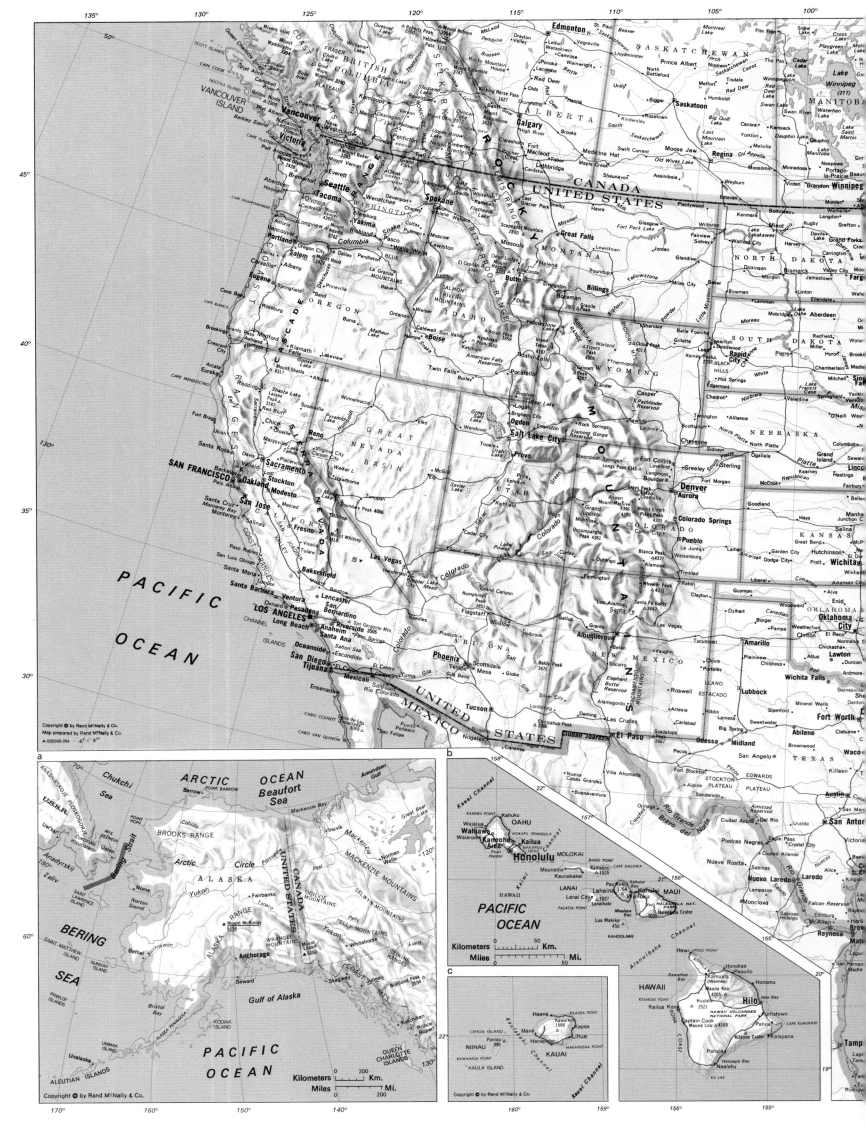

Kilometers
Statute Miles

Scale 1:13,200,000

One centimeter represents 132 kilometers.
One inch represents approximately 210 miles.

Albers Conical Equal-Area Projection

163

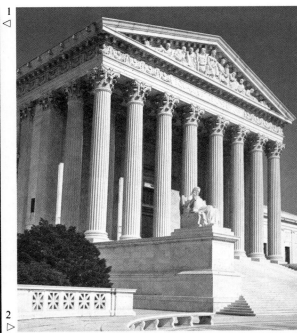

Northeastern U.S.

The great natural ports of America's Atlantic coast have welcomed world travelers since 1620, when the Pilgrims anchored at Plymouth, Massachusetts. From Boston to Baltimore, whalers, traders and fishermen sailed into the harbors that became thriving cities during the nation's first decades of independence. In New York City, the Statue of Liberty stands before the crowded skyline, a symbol and a reminder that thousands of people still seek refuge in the land of liberty.

You can trace more than two hundred years of history in the great cities of the Northeast. Boston's Freedom Trail will lead you to Faneuil Hall, where the American Revolution was born; nearby, you can visit 'Old Ironsides' in the Boston Navy Yard. The Declaration of Independence and the Constitution were conceived in Philadelphia's Independence Hall, with its famous Liberty Bell. In New York, the lofty Empire State Building and the twin World Trade Towers overlook the older center of commerce on Wall Street. In Washington D. C., the domed Capitol, columned Supreme Court building and gracious White House bespeak a still-vital form of government.

Beyond the Northeast's major cities, you'll find the calm beauty of fishing towns, farms and mountain resorts – none of them very far from the commercial centers, but all of them a world apart!

1 Washington, D.C.; 2 Washington, D.C.; 3 West Point, New York; 4 New York City, New York; 5 New Harbor, Maine; 6 Orange, Vermont; 7 Pittsburgh, Pennsylvania; 8 Mystic, Connecticut; 9 JFK Birthplace, Boston, Massachusetts; 10 Queensboro Bridge, New York City, New York

6 △

7 ◁

8 ▷

9 ◁

10 ▷

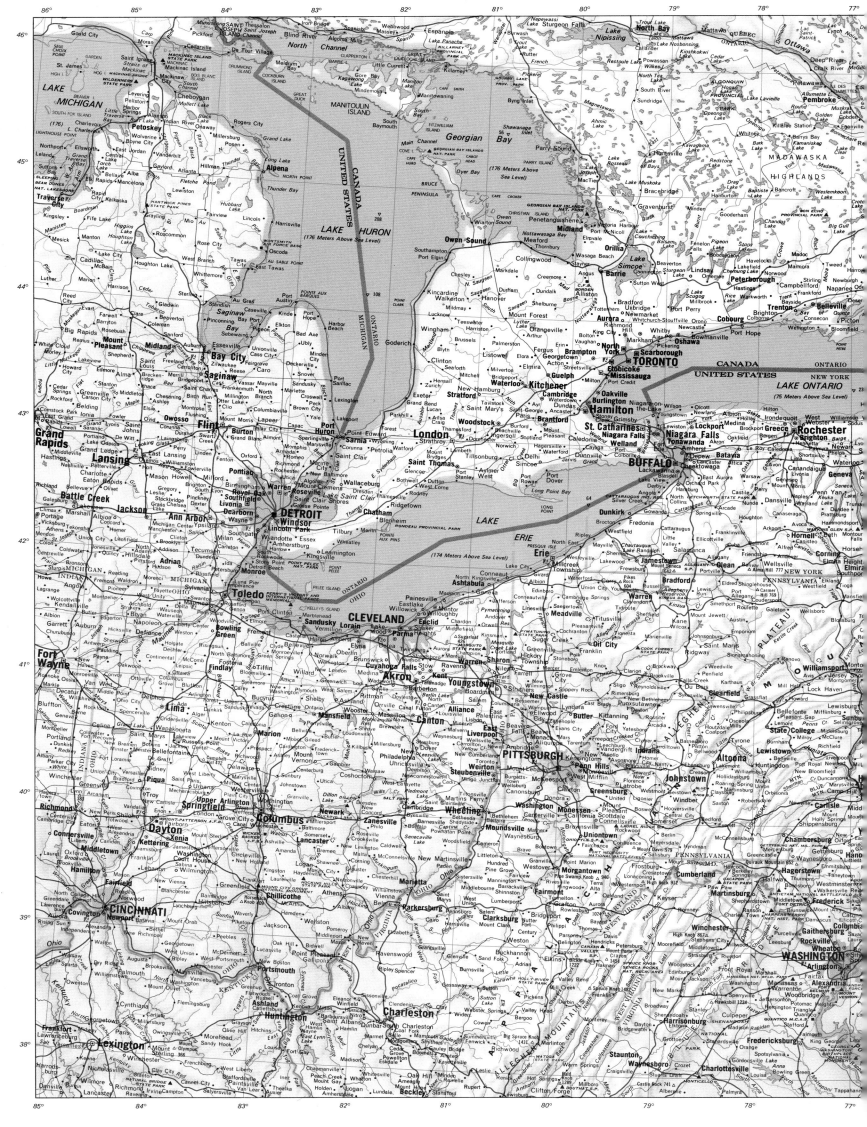

Scale 1:3,300,000
One centimeter represents 33 kilometers.
One inch represents approximately 52 miles.
Albers Conical Equal-Area Projection

Kilometers
Statute Miles

167

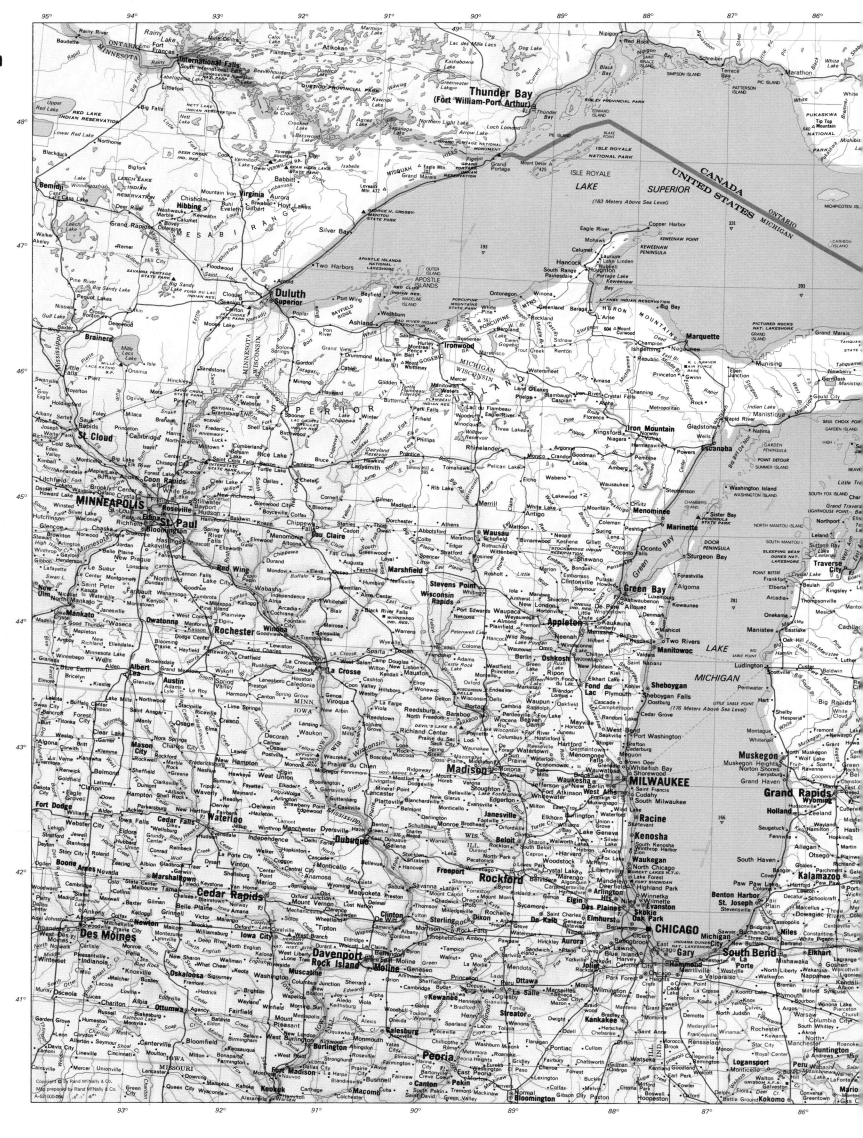

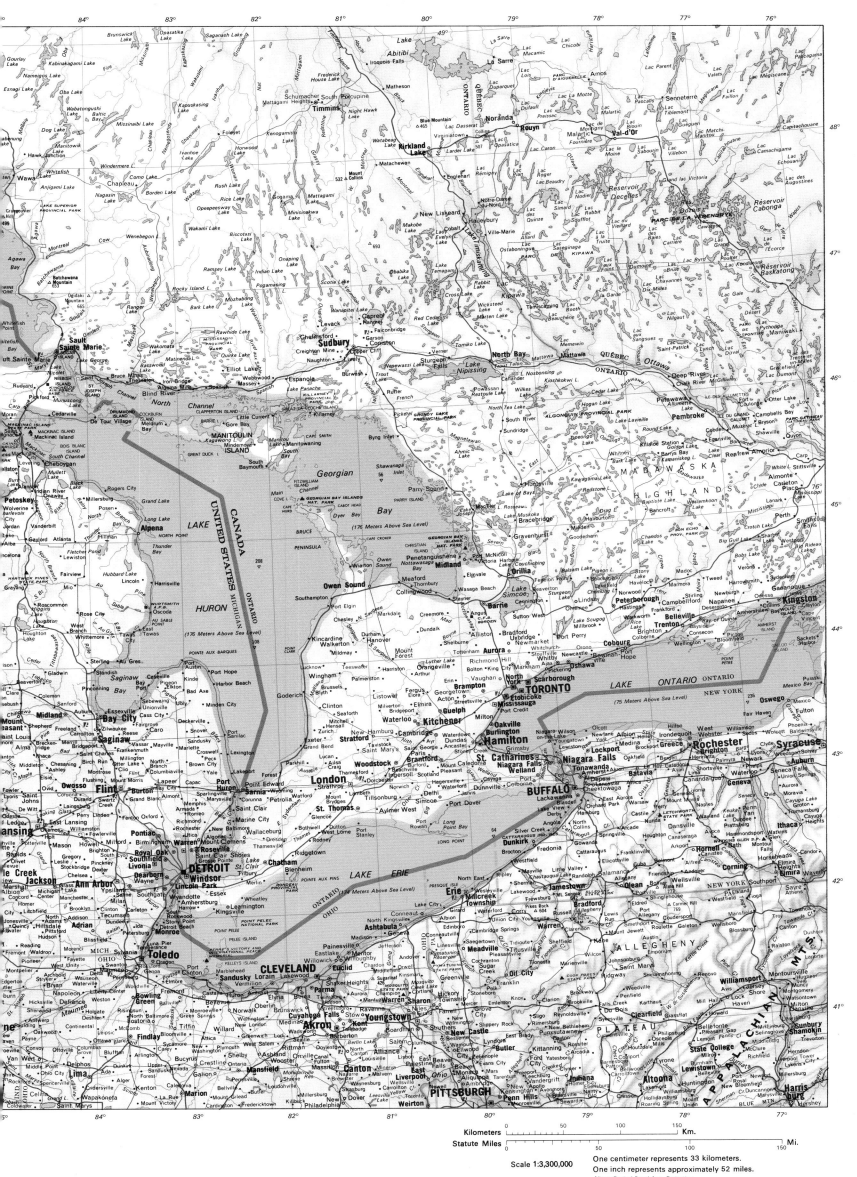

Kilometers
Statute Miles

Scale 1:3,300,000

One centimeter represents 33 kilometers.
One inch represents approximately 52 miles.

Albers Conical Equal-Area Projection

Great Lakes Region

The five Great Lakes formed a natural, navigable route for Indians and early American explorers long before trains sped across the continent. But once the railroads were built, great cities grew up along the shores of the lakes, each one a connecting point for ship and railroad cargoes. During the 19th century, grain and beef from the plains, iron ore from Minnesota, cotton from the South and manufactured goods from the East, all met in Chicago. As technology advanced, the raw materials were turned into steel, refined oil and automobiles, and shipped from the mills and factories of Detroit, Gary and Cleveland. People from all over found work in the Great Lakes cities.

An industrial phenomenon, the Great Lakes are also a great recreation resource. Chicagoans enjoy fine city beaches only blocks away from skyscrapers. Campers and fishermen retreat to the wilderness-ringed bays of Minnesota, Wisconsin and Michigan.

1 St. Urbain Farm, Charlevoix, Michigan; 2 Irrigated Farmland; 3 Aerial view, Chicago, Illinois (foreground) Sear's Tower and Chicago River, (background) Lake Michigan and John Hancock Center; 4 Buckingham fountain, Grant Park, Chicago, Illinois, (constantly changing its colors)

1 △

2 ◁

3 ▷

4 ▽

4 ▽

170

Southeastern U.S.

Sunshine and palm trees, antebellum mansions and Spanish moss, Southern cooking and hospitality are the unchanging and old-fashioned hall marks that still draw visitors to the Southeast – even though they may come to see such modern wonders as Walt Disney World in Orlando, rocket launchers at Cape Kennedy, or the world's tallest hotel in Atlanta.

This region offers the most fascinating contrast of old and new. Founded by Spanish settlers in 1565, St. Augustine, Florida, is the oldest city in the United States. The fabulous restoration at Williamsburg offers tourists a rare opportunity to experience the life-style of colonial Virginians. Savannah's historical seaport and Charleston's lovely gardens recall the serene dignity of another era. Those who enjoy modern playgrounds might head for Miami Beach, Palm Beach, South Carolina's Hilton Head or North Carolina's Pinehurst. The Southeast's natural landmarks are just as varied, ranging from Florida's swampy Everglades to the glorious elevation of the Blue Ridge mountains and the spectacular sand dunes of the Outer Banks.

1 Sunset at Cypress Gardens, Winter Haven, Florida; 2 Palm Beach, Florida; 3 Capitol Building, Atlanta, Georgia; 4 Fairy Castle in Walt Disney World, Lake Buena Vista, Florida

1 △

2 △

3 ▽

4 ▷

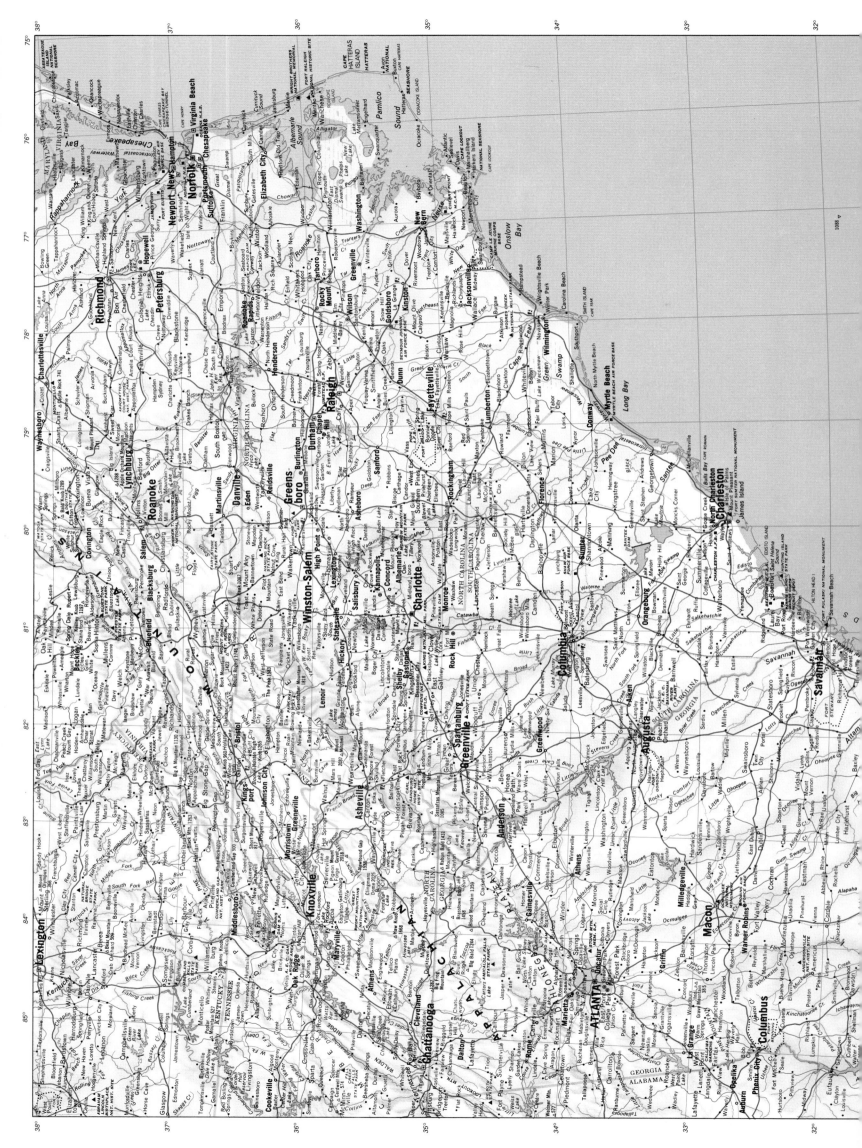

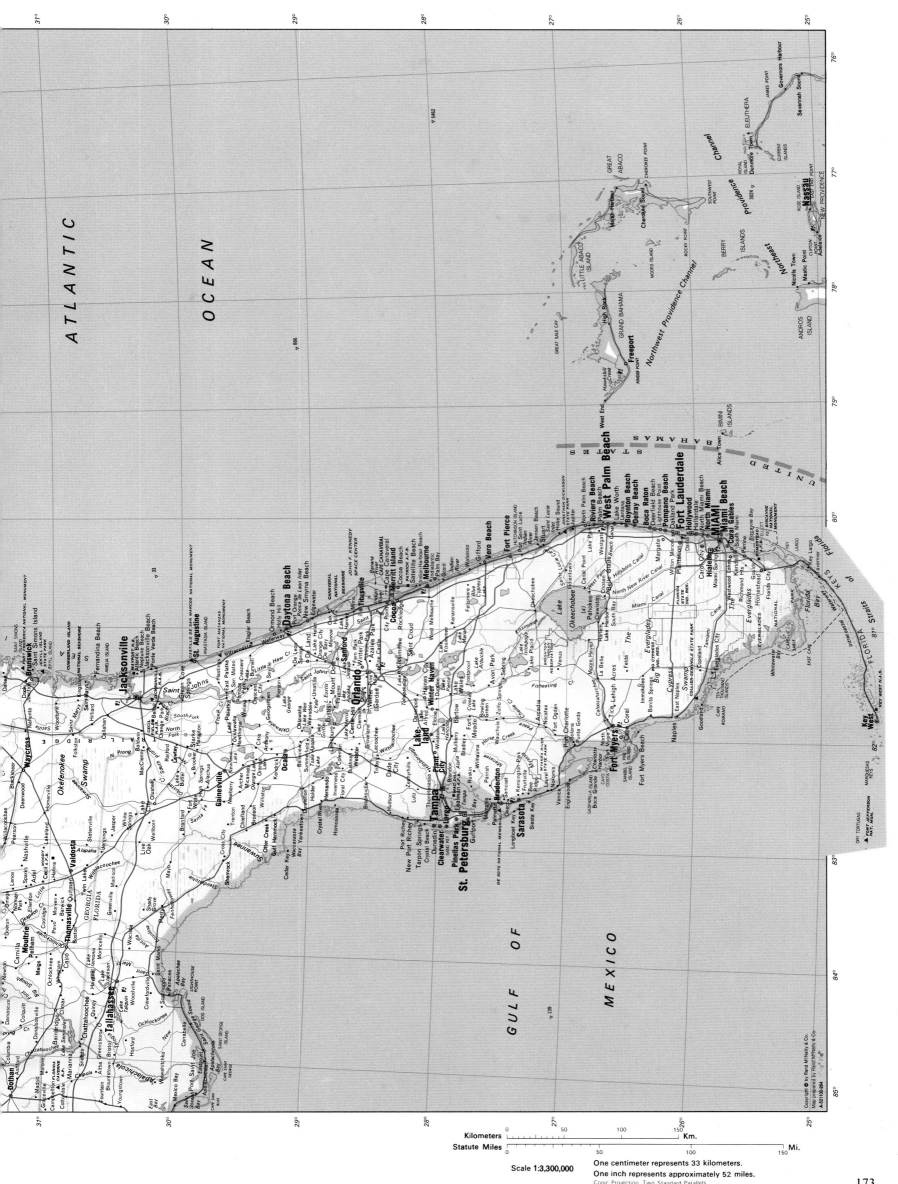

Kilometers

Statute Miles

Scale 1:3,300,000

One centimeter represents 33 kilometers.

One inch represents approximately 52 miles.

Conic Projection, Two Standard Parallels

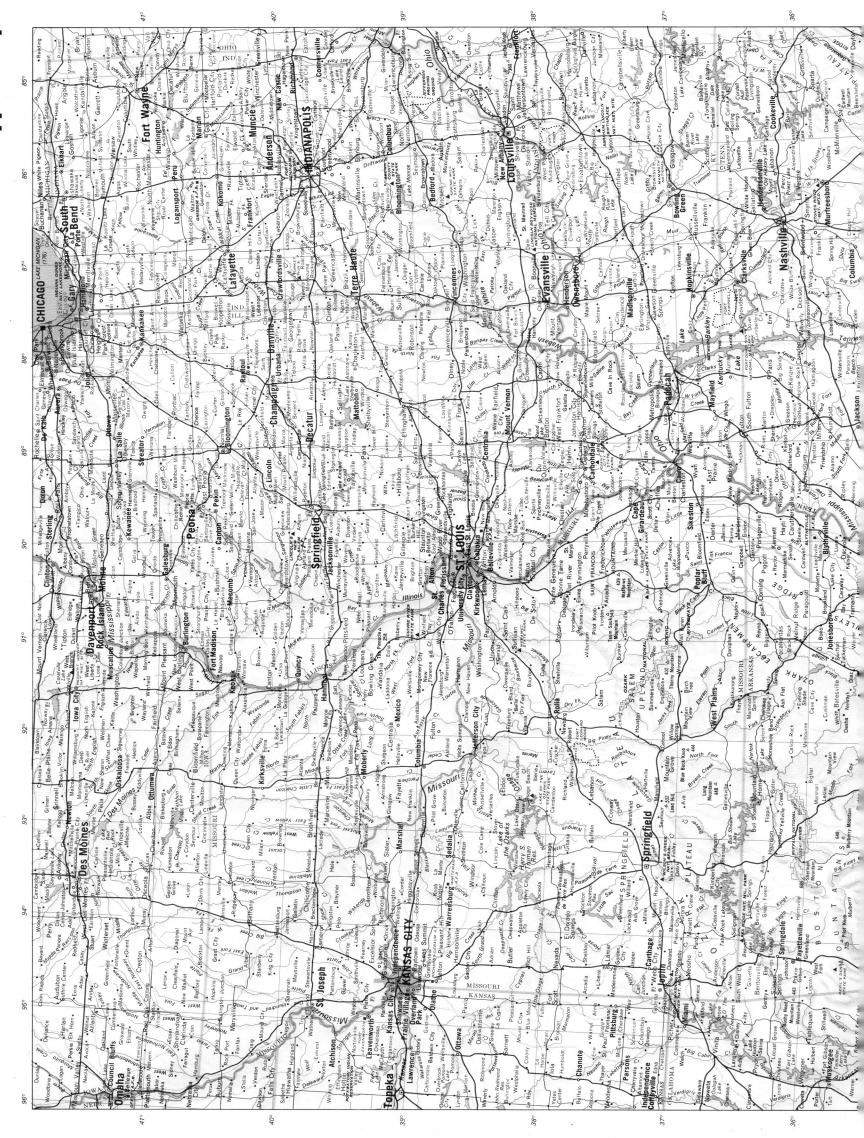

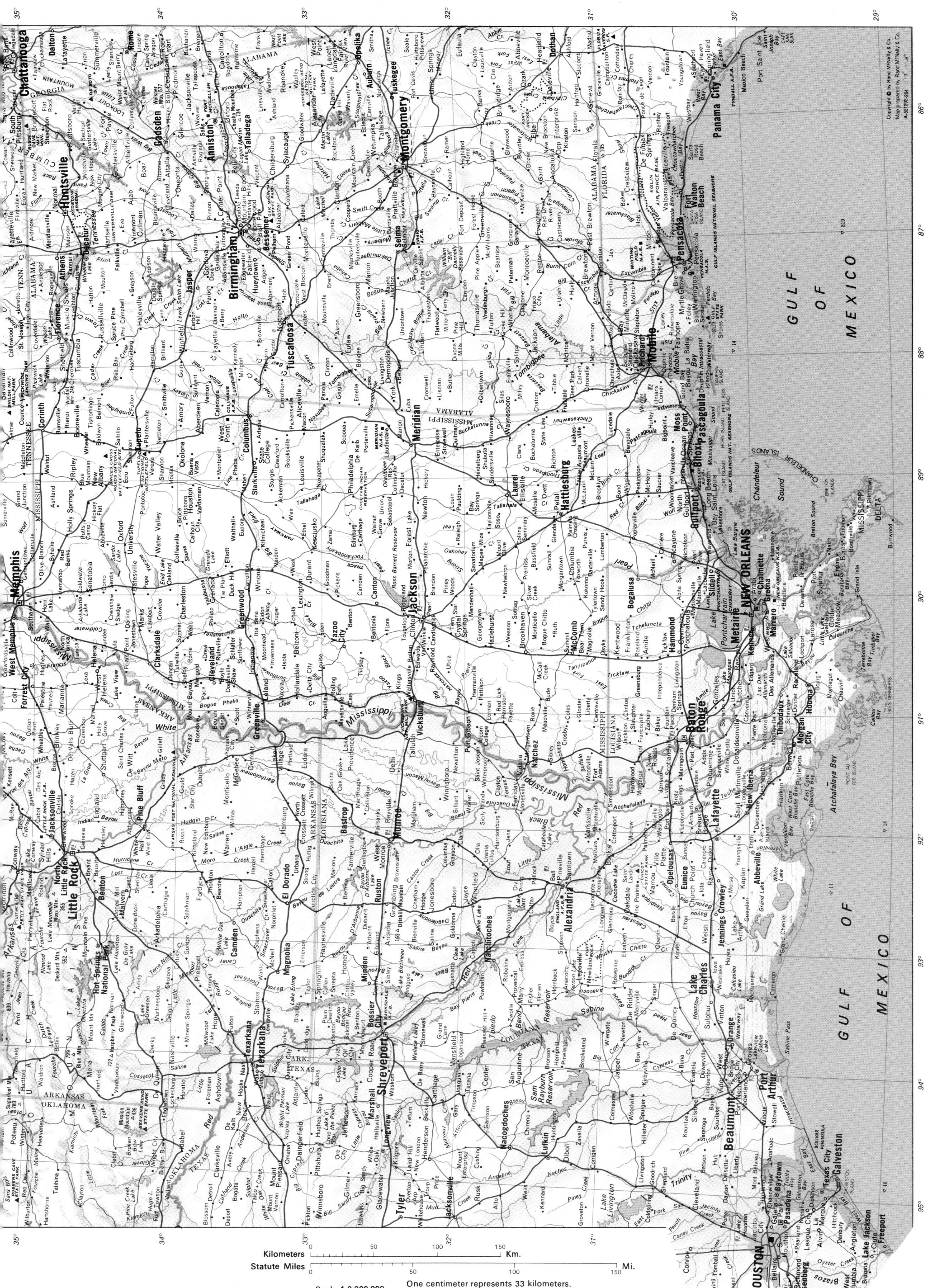

Kilometers 0 50 100 150 Km.
Statute Miles 0 50 100 150 Mi.
Scale 1:3,300,000
One centimeter represents 33 kilometers.
One inch represents approximately 52 miles.
Albers Conical Equal-Area Projection

1 Stockyards, Kansas City, Missouri; 2 Mississippi River Steamer; 3 Country Music Hall of Fame and Museum, Nashville, Tennessee; 4 'Gateway to the West,' St. Louis, Missouri; 5 Maison Bourbon Jazz Club, New Orleans, Louisiana

Mississippi Valley

The rousing strains of Dixieland jazz, the foot-stomping twang of bluegrass and the soulful ballads of country music are as much a part of the Mississippi Valley as the stockyards of Kansas City and the breweries of St. Louis. On the farms, in the hills and in the back quarters of rowdy river towns. America's native music was born and nurtured. Today, the sounds beckon listeners at Nashville's Country Music Hall of Fame, and the nightclubs of New Orleans' French Quarter.

The Mississippi's most famous character is Huck Finn, the raft-roving runaway who has charmed every adult and child since Mark Twain created him in 1876. If you visit the author's family home in Hannibal, Missouri you'll find that it remains true to the famous humorist's writings.

But what would Mark Twain make of modern St. Louis, with its grand amusement park and its towering Gateway Arch? He would undoubtedly recognize the old mansions of Natchez and the thriving commerce of Memphis. But he probably would be surprised by New Orleans' riverfront, now that it has been refurbished for the folks who love to drink chicory-rich coffee as they watch the great Mississippi flow by.

Southern Rocky Mountains

Vistas rise to the heights of Pike's Peak and Mount Evans and fall to the depths of the Grand Canyon and Bryce Canyon in the breathtakingly beautiful Southern Rockies. Outdoorsmen cherish the ski slopes of Vail and Aspen, the extraordinary rock monuments of Utah's Arches National Park, the open skies of the cattle ranches and the crystalline splendor of the mountain lakes.

The man-made attractions of the region span the ages, from the ancient Pueblo ruins at Chaco Canyon, New Mexico to the ultra-modern, multi-spired chapel at the U.S. Air Force Academy near Colorado Springs. People come to Salt Lake City to gaze on the sparkling white buildings as well as the Great Salt Lake and its surrounding desert. Those who visit Denver enjoy both the city's restaurants and shopping and a detour to Rocky Mountain National Park, where Trail Ridge Road climbs above the clouds and mountain peaks. Some of America's oldest civilizations – Hopi, Navajo and Pueblo – flourished beneath the Southern Rockies and their descendants still give the region a unique identity.

1 'Molar Rock' and 'Angel Arch,' Canyonlands National Park, Utah; 2 American Indian; 3 Havasu Creek Falls, Grand Canyon National Park, Arizona; 4 Bryce Canyon National Park, Utah; 5 A rodeo at Gallup, New Mexico; 6 Oak Creek Canyon at Red Rock Crossing, Sedora, Arizona

177

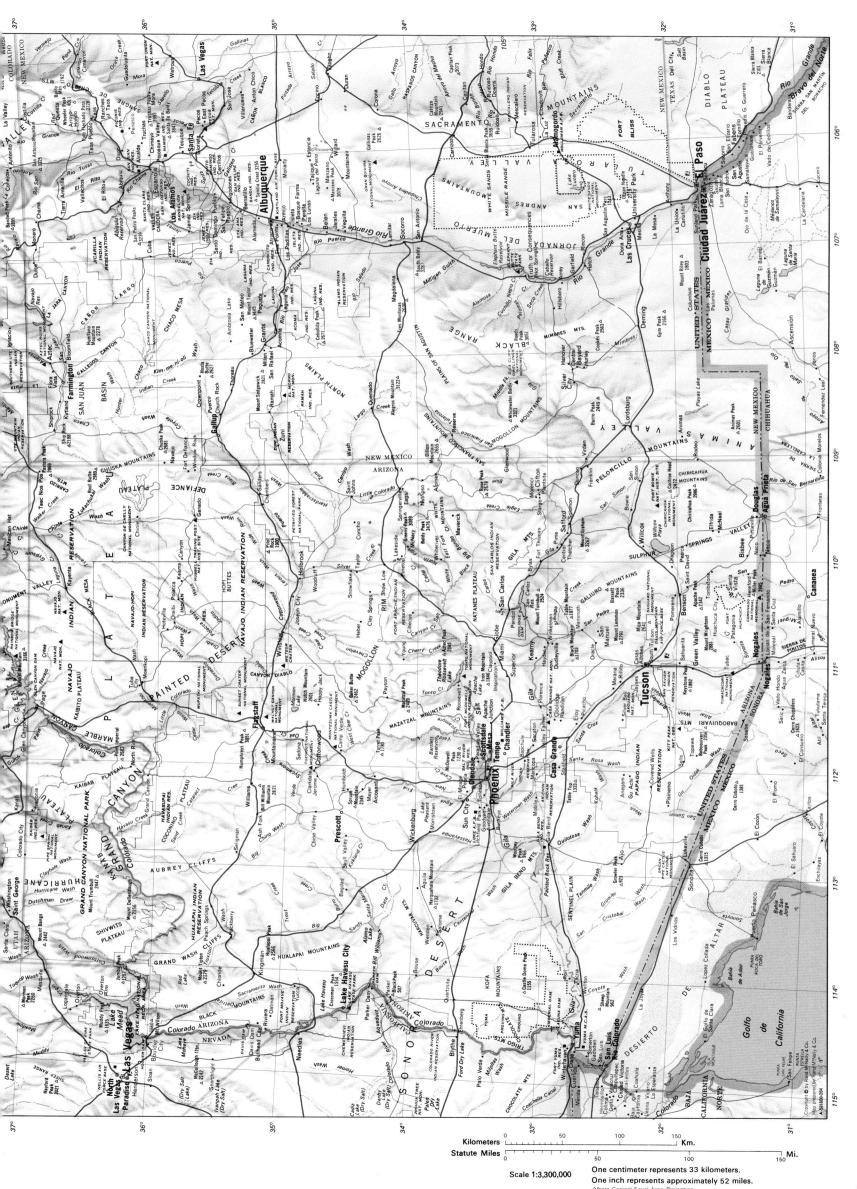

Kilometers
Statute Miles

Scale 1:3,300,000

One centimeter represents 33 kilometers.
One inch represents approximately 52 miles.
Albers Conical Equal-Area Projection

179

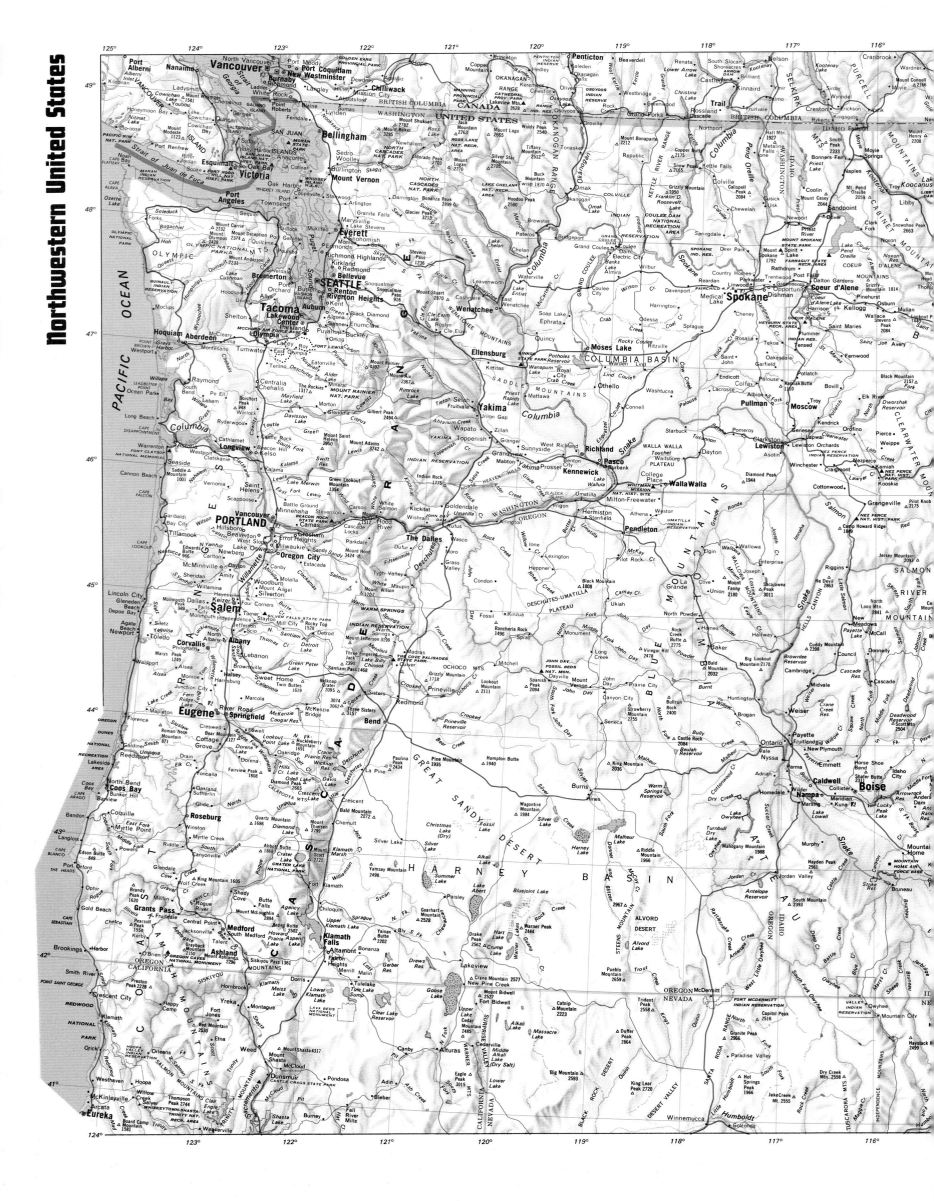

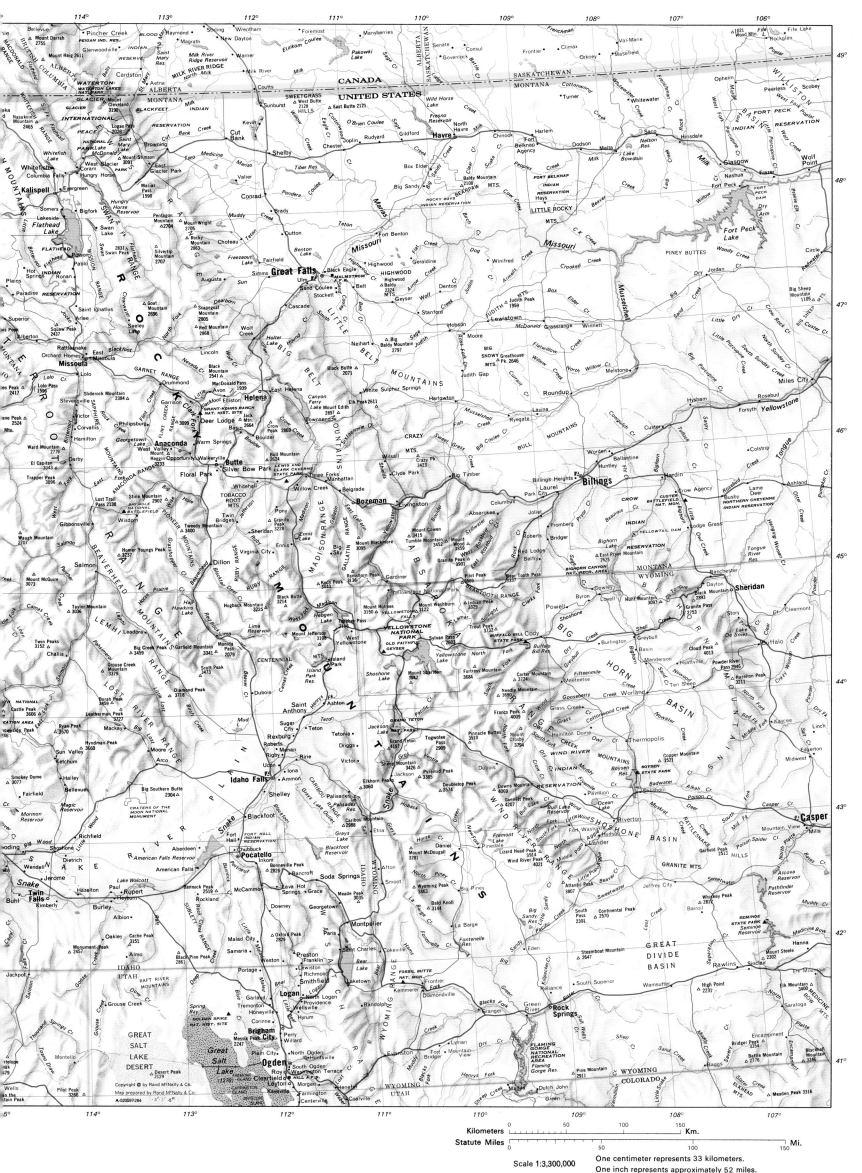

Kilometers

Statute Miles

Scale 1:3,300,000

One centimeter represents 33 kilometers.
One inch represents approximately 52 miles.

Albers Conical Equal-Area Projection

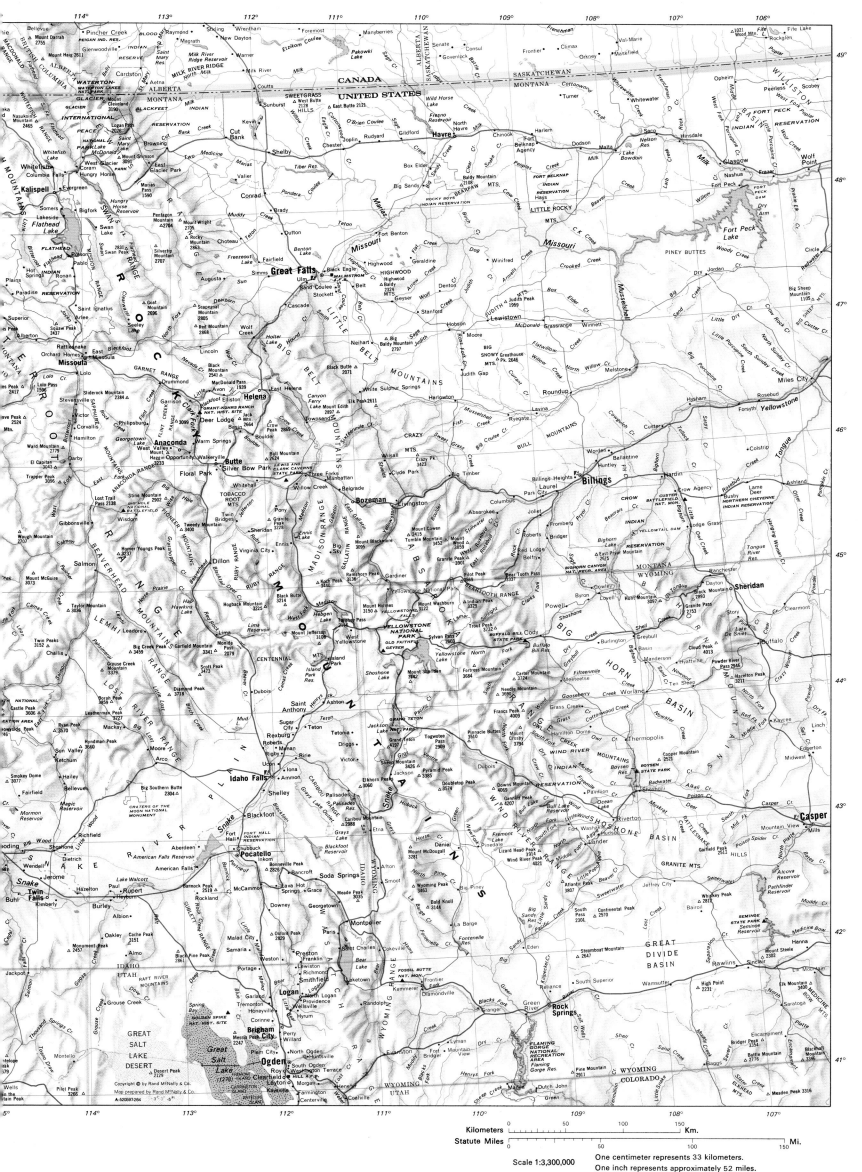

Kilometers
Statute Miles

Scale 1:3,300,000
One centimeter represents 33 kilometers.
One inch represents approximately 52 miles.
Albers Conical Equal-Area Projection

Northwestern U.S.

Residents of the Northwest often boast that their region is America's paradise – it has everything! There's much truth to this claim, for Washington's timberlands, the Willamette valley farms and orchards, the inland cattle ranges and the coastal fishing industry contribute to a diverse bounty. The cities of Portland and Seattle are known for their peaceful prosperity and cultural sophistication. This is also the land of the Snake River, with its spectacular Hells Canyon; the jagged Grand Teton Range; Old Faithful and grizzly bears in Yellowstone National Park; the 'Big Sky' country of Montana; and the glaciers of North Cascades National Park.

Those who want to 'get away from it all' can feel right at home in the primitive mountain areas of Idaho, with their icy, trout-filled streams and herds of wild game. Futuristic-minded people can ride a monorail to Seattle Center and view the Space Needle. Portland, city of roses, charms everyone with its parks, interesting museums and beautiful annual June Rose Festival.

1 Cattle ranch in valley of the Rocky Mountains, Montana; 2 Historic Oregon Trail near Scottsbluff, Nebraska; 3 Sunshine Peak, over 14,000 ft. high in the San Juan Mountains, S.W. Colorado; 4 Lower falls of the Yellowstone River, Yellowstone National Park, Wyoming

1 ▷

2 ◁

3 ◁

4 ▷

1 △

2 △

1 Canoeing on a quiet lake in Idaho; 2 Cattle in a verdant valley between Rocky Mountains; 3 Old Conestoga wagon used by the settlers of Oregon Territory; 4 Abandoned mill on Crystal River, near Marble, Elk Mountains, Colorado

3 ▽

4 ▷

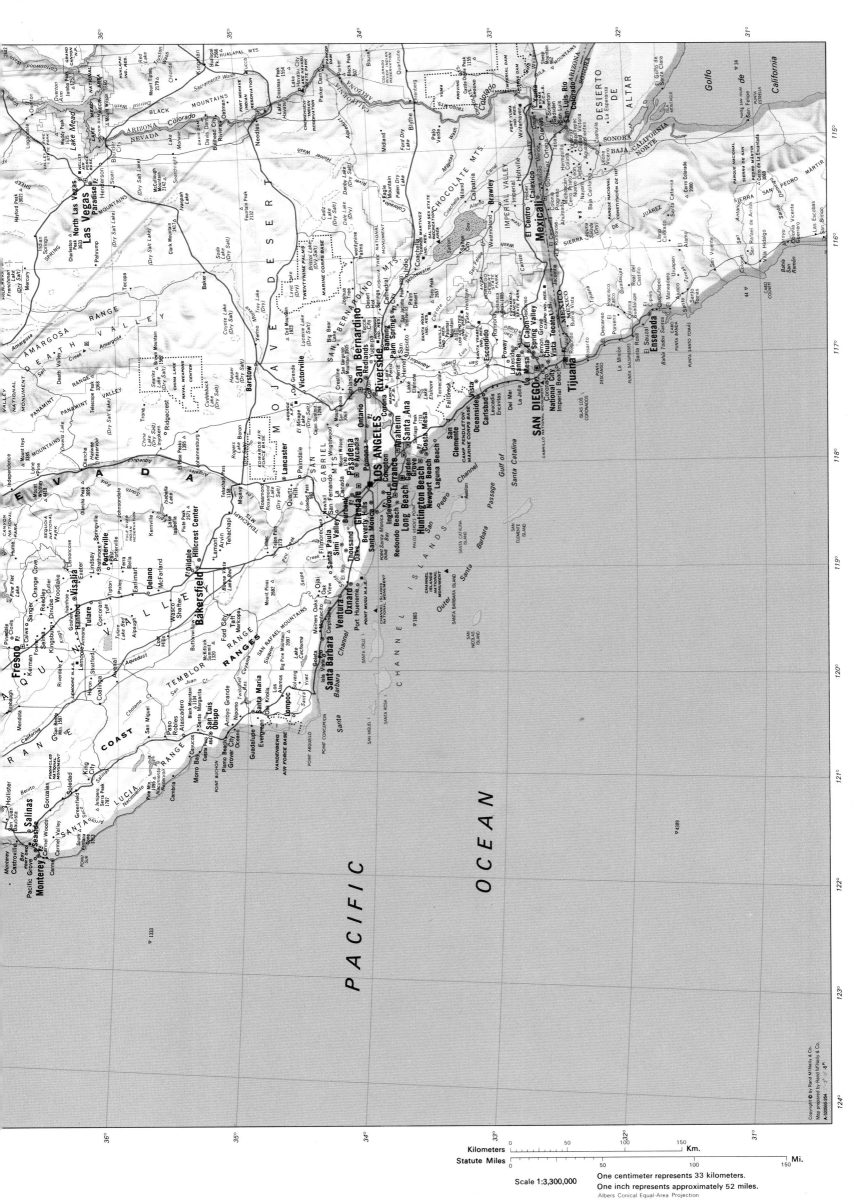

Copyright by Rand McNally & Co.
Map prepared by Rand McNally & Co.
A.202056-204

Kilometers
Statute Miles

Scale 1:3,300,000

One centimeter represents 33 kilometers.
One inch represents approximately 52 miles.
Albers Conical Equal-Area Projection

California and Nevada

Dreams of wealth and glamour have lured travelers to California and Nevada ever since miners saw the glint of gold and silver there. Nowadays, aspiring entertainers move to Los Angeles with their sights set on breaking into 'show biz'; tourists visit Hollywood and Beverly Hills, hoping to catch a glimpse of movie and TV stars; and gamblers eye the roulette wheels of Las Vegas, Reno and Lake Tahoe.

But the most fabulous riches of the region are to be found in its near-perfect climate and stunning scenery. The winding road that hugs California's Pacific coastline reveals a treasury of citrus groves, truck farms and vineyards. The redwood forests, the stark desert and the Sierra Nevada mountains compete in grandeur. The sparkling waters of Lake Mead invite boaters and waterskiers; the glacier-cut cliffs of Yosemite thrill hikers and campers.

Children delight in San Diego's zoo and Wild Animal Park as well as the enchanting world of Disneyland. Adults find endless fascination in San Francisco's Chinatown and Fisherman's Wharf, William Hearst's castle of San Simeon and the great art museums around Los Angeles, including the renowned collections of J. Paul Getty and Norton Simon.

1 The Strip at night, Las Vegas, Nevada; 2 Golden Gate Bridge, San Francisco, California; 3 Dunes in Death Valley National Monument, California; 4 Palm Springs Tramway, Riverside County, California; 5 Downtown Reno, Nevada; 6 Giant redwood trees, Yosemite National Park, California; 7 Harbor, San Diego, California; 8 Dodger Stadium, Los Angeles, California

1 △

2 ▽

POLAR REGIONS

The Arctic and Antarctic each presents some of the harshest conditions found on earth. Other places have the intense winter cold, the lack of plant growth, the snow and ice for parts of the year. But nowhere else are these features so persistently experienced. Add to them the eerie yet beautiful long winter nights, with the sun always below the horizon, and contrasting period when the sun is always above.

Early polar travelers described these scenes most vividly. The Norwegian explorer and humanitarian, Fridtjof Nansen, in his book *Farthest North* (1898), described the long polar night over the Arctic ice sheet:

The sky is like an enormous cupola, blue at the zenith, shading down into green and then into lilac and violet at the edges. Over the ice fields there are cold violet-blue shadows, with lighter pink tints where a ridge here and there catches the last reflection of the vanished day.... Presently the aurora borealis shakes over the vault of heaven its veil of glittering silver, changing now to yellow, now to green, now to red.... And all the time this utter stillness, impressive as the symphony of infinitude.

Then Captain Scott and members of his party recorded their experiences of the often savage Antarctic 'summer', at the other end of the earth. Thus wrote Admiral Edward Evans in *South with Scott*:

The blizzard on the second day pursued its course with unabated violence, the temperature increased however and we experienced driving sleet. The tent floor cloths had pools of water on them and water dripped on our faces as we lay in our sleeping bags. Outside the scene was miserable enough, the poor ponies cowering behind their snow walls the picture of misery.

Yet, apart from the seasonal similarities and the trying weather conditions, the Polar Regions are of very differing character. One comprises the extremities of the great land masses of the Northern Hemisphere, Eurasia and North America, and a deep ocean basin across which they face. The other comprises the extremities of the great oceans of the Southern Hemisphere and the bleak, frozen wastes, which they encircle.

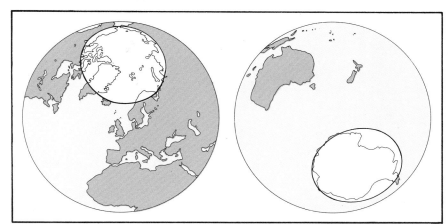

1 ▽

2 ◁

3 ▷

Opposite: Antarctic peninsula; 1 Weddell seal, Graham Land, Antarctic; 2 British Antarctic Survey relief ship landing field party in northern Marguerite Bay – research stations have been set up to chart the wilderness; 3 Tromsö, Norway – the largest town north of the Arctic Circle; 4 Adélie penguins – most penguin species are found in Antarctica;

4 ◁

The Arctic

This is an area of extreme cold surrounding the North Pole. Here, due to the fact that the earth's axis of rotation is not at right angles to an imaginary line joining the earth to the sun, latitude 66° 32′N marks the limits of the polar region within which the sun may be seen in the sky for 24 hours on at least one day in the year, the northern summer solstice, about June 21. By contrast, at the northern winter solstice, about December 22, the sun does not rise above the horizon at all. At the North Pole itself, the sun rises above the horizon at the spring equinox, about March 21, and does not set again until the autumnal equinox, about September 22, Thus, the area within the Arctic Circle, north of 66° 32′N is called the land of the midnight sun. However, within the Arctic Circle the sun, when seen, is always low in the sky.

At the heart of the region lies the huge Arctic Ocean which has an area of about 14 million km² (5.4 million sq mi). This is largely covered by an extensive ice sheet. Around the margins of the polar area, the northern extremities of a number of countries lie within the Arctic Circle: Norway, Sweden, Finland, the USSR, the USA (Alaska), Canada, Greenland and Iceland, as well as a large number of islands. Each of these countries, except Norway, whose coasts are washed by the warm North Atlantic Drift, has some of its coasts ice-bound for part, if not all the year.

Monthly average temperatures in the Arctic range from −40°C (−40°F) in the winter to as high as 15°C (59°F) in the summer. Surprisingly, in many places annual snowfall is low, being as little as 250 mm (10 in), equivalent to only 25 mm (1 in) of rainfall. Much of this becomes compacted into ice which, over the ages, has built up into the great ice sheet over the Arctic Ocean, and the ice caps and valley glaciers of Greenland, the other islands and parts of the mainlands.

At the North Pole the ice sheet is not exceptionally thick, so that an atomic submarine has been able to pass beneath it and then break through to the surface at the Pole itself. Just as the ice builds up in the coldest parts, so it must disperse at the margins, either by melting in situ, or by the breaking away of icebergs which float southward in the Atlantic and Pacific Oceans, there to melt slowly away. In contrast, the Greenland ice cap is as much as 3,000 m (10,000 ft) thick in places.

Where it is not permanently covered by ice, land in the Arctic has a tundra type of vegetation. Mosses, lichens, stunted grass and even dwarf trees cover the ground, as do bright flowers which bloom each spring. The area is also rich in wild life, including seals, walruses, foxes, wolves, reindeer, polar and grizzly bears, as well as a great variety of birds and fishes. These provide a livelihood for such peoples as the Lapps, Chukchees, Samoyeds and the Eskimos who herd, hunt, trap and trade.

The Arctic is also rich in mineral resources. Within the Soviet Arctic, coal, oil, uranium, nickel, copper and tin are all being developed. Norway and Sweden both have rich iron ore deposits. Silver, lead and cryolite are all found and mined in Greenland, while a great variety of resources in North America, especially oil in Alaska and northwest Canada are being exploited. These have attracted developers from the warmer parts of the respective countries who have established new towns.

The exploration of the Arctic has attracted less attention and romance than that of the Antarctic. In the late nineteenth and early decades of the twentieth centuries, attempts were made to explore on foot, to cross the Greenland ice cap, to lodge a ship in the ice and then see where it would be carried and to overfly the pole in a simple aircraft. In these ventures names like Nansen, Amundsen, Peary, Byrd and Watkins stand out.

Many and varied are the methods of transport in and over the Arctic. Walking with the aid of snow shoes and skis, sledding with dog teams and paddling through open water in kayaks are still practiced by the native peoples. Mechanized transport on a local scale now includes light aircraft, helicopters and snowmobiles. For large-scale developments, the coastal ice may be broken through by ice-breakers so that large ships may reach the northern coasts of Siberia, Alaska and Canada. More strangely, the Arctic silence is frequently broken by the distant roar of high-flying jet aircraft, for which the shortest route between many European, North American and Pacific centers lies across these cold lands.

Many world maps distort the spatial relationships of places surrounding the Arctic. Thus, the shortest distance between Archangel'sk and Fairbanks is not along the 65th parallel; it is along a line almost passing over the North Pole. Great Circle positions and distances, so important in strategic and political studies, are only shown on gnomonic map projections as seen below.

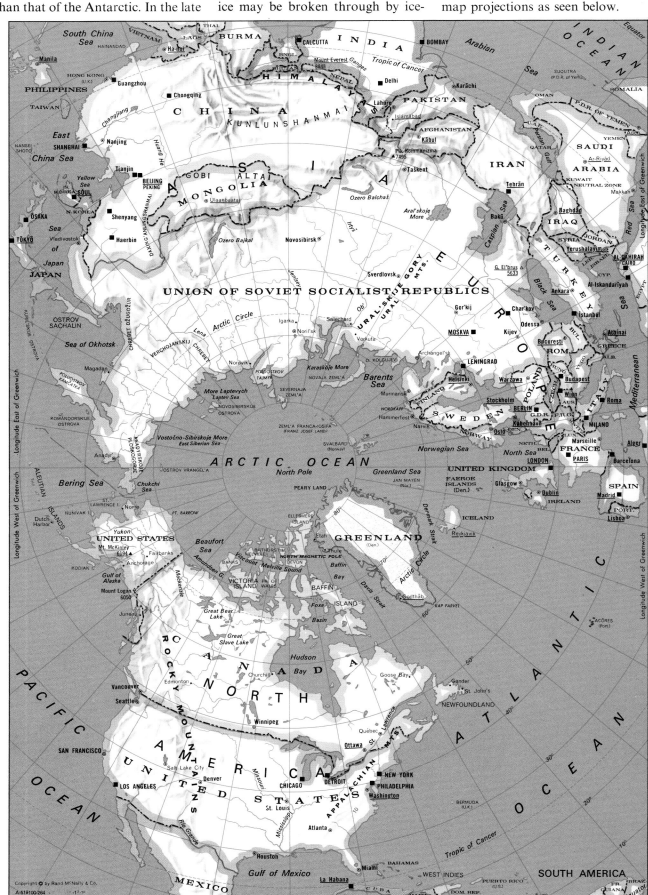

Antarctica

This is predominantly an ice-covered land which rises to considerable heights. Were all the ice to be removed, a very rugged landscape would be revealed; relieved of the weight of ice, the land would rise and the highest peaks would probably match those of the Himalayas.

Latitude 66° 32'S limits the geographical area within which, at the southern summer solstice, about December 22, the sun may be seen in the sky for 24 hours. At the southern winter solstice, about June 21, the sun does not rise above the horizon at all. At the South Pole, high up in the center of the ice-covered land mass, the sun is above the horizon continuously from about September 22 till about March 21, though it is usually low in the sky.

The Antarctic land mass is almost as big as the Arctic Ocean, covering some 13.2 million km² (5.1 million sq mi). Thus, it is larger than either Europe or Australia. In places the land extends north of the Antarctic Circle, as in the peninsula of Graham Land around 65°W and along the coast of Wilkes Land, between 90°E and 140°E. In other places, such as the head of the Ross Sea, the land margin is as near to the Pole as 85°S latitude.

The whole land is covered with ice and snow, except where high mountains project through the frozen surface. The highest point in the Vinson Massif is 5,140 m (16,864 ft) above sea level. Sea ice surrounds the continent, often way beyond the Antarctic Circle.

The climate of Antarctica is far more severe than even that of the Arctic. From the center of this mass representing about 90 percent of the world's permanent ice and snow, bitter winds blow outward. Winter average temperatures, as far as they are known, drop as low as −60°C (−76°F), and even in summer only rise to −20°C (−3°F) in the interior of the continent. Only at the land margins do summer monthly average temperatures rise above freezing.

The two largest seas, the Weddell and Ross, are covered by ice sheets fed from the land by great glaciers. From their margins, as well as the rest of the continent, the sea ice breaks away in icebergs to float northward into the Pacific, Atlantic and Indian Oceans. But these seas, being farther from other continents than their Arctic equivalents, never presented the same iceberg hazards to mariners as did the waters of the North Atlantic.

The Antarctic is almost completely without vegetation, and wild life is very limited. A few tiny invertebrates live on the margins of the land. There are two permanent residents, skuas and the emperor penguins. In addition, the Adélie penguin breeds on the land but lives mainly in the surrounding seas.

This continent has obviously never been appealing for permanent settlement, though its exploration has attracted much attention. When Captain Cook crossed the Antarctic Circle in 1773, he did not sight land. Then, in 1830, John Biscoe, one of the first English explorers to be backed by the newly established Royal Geographical Society, first sighted this continent.

Early in this century, three intrepid explorers were drawn to this virtually unknown continent. Of three expeditions which set out to reach the Pole, Shackleton's just failed but returned safely, and Amundsen's just beat Scott's to return triumphantly. Though successful in its objective, Scott's attempt resulted in the death of all five members of his polar party on their return journey, in an adventure which ranks among the greatest human dramas recalled to this day.

In 1957, International Geophysical Year, twelve nations conducted scientific studies in the continent. About 60 bases were built on the mainland and nearby islands. Studies of the ice, the underlying rocks, the ocean currents and the weather were made. In 1957/58, an ambitious expedition to cross the continent from one side to the other using modern tracked vehicles was successfully led by Sir Vivian Fuchs and Sir Edmund Hillary. At that time a number of countries including the UK, France, Australia and Norway had laid claim to territories in the Antarctic. However, following the International Geophysical Year, in 1959, a 30-year treaty was signed between all nations interested in polar research. All territorial claims have been suspended and the whole area is now free for scientific research, excluding nuclear experiments.

The mineral reserves of the continent are not really known. Coal was brought back by the explorers over 60 years ago, showing that far warmer climates were once enjoyed. Other minerals suspected include copper, nickel and, almost certainly, crude oil. Exploitation of these is, as yet, economically impossible. Except for the scientists and their supply links, by ship and transport aircraft which land on the ice, Antarctica remains a silent continent.

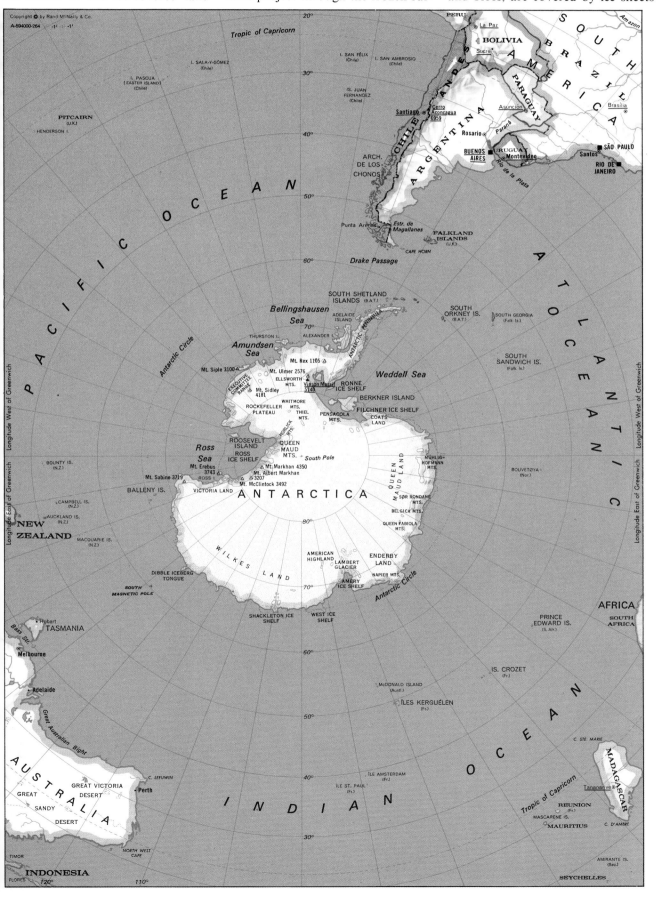

WORLD TO VIEW

The main value of thematic maps is to clarify the immensely varied patterns and distributions of world phenomena. Using appropriate symbols to show one class of geographical information at a time, maps can highlight such topics as the locations of mineral deposits, the distributions of farm animals, etc.

The simplest thematic maps are those which show where particular phenomena are found, with no quantification. For example, the Languages map below uses a series of colors to show where particular languages dominate. It does not show what proportions of the population or how many people speak that language. In the following pages the map of predominant economies also has no mathematical base. It shows

Opposite: Tibetan priests

areas of the world where particular types of economic activity dominate, though it does not show the extent to which other activities, though less important, are also found.

Other types of thematic maps may use a precisely calculated measure. On the Literacy map below, for instance, a percentage scale has been adopted to show the proportions of the population throughout the world who are literate. The average literacy rate for each whole country has been calculated and then plotted according to the selected scale and color scheme. Only for those areas which are essentially uninhabited has the map been left uncolored.

Two other maps on the following pages also have a mathematical base, but in neither are whole countries regarded as the essential units of area. Population densities can be calculated for individual parts of each

country, and then a general picture of world distributions plotted on a selected scale. Using a carefully graded color scheme, with deepest colors for the greatest densities and vice versa, a clear impression of the greatest population pressure points can be given. Finally, using a combination of mathematical measures, a map such as that of climatic regions can be constructed.

Considering the two maps below: the areas of the world with the highest literacy rates are those with the most advanced economies, mainly in the temperate regions. State run services, including education, only come fully into their own with economic development. Thus, on the literacy map, much of Europe, the USSR, North America, Australia, New Zealand and Argentina appear as the countries with over 90 percent of their populations able to read. At

the other end of the scale, it is the countries of the Third World, particularly in Africa, southern and Southeast Asia that have less than a third of their peoples thus qualified.

In recent historic times, languages have been carried around the globe by migrations, thus changing the original language distributions. Today some of the original native tongues have been displaced. Thus the Americas, at one time dominated by Indian languages, are now mainly using Germanic and Romance tongues – English and some French in the North, mainly Spanish and Portuguese in the Middle and South. English has also taken over from the native aboriginal and Polynesian languages in Australia and New Zealand. Likewise, in South Africa, the Bantu and other native tongues are still used, but the introduced languages are English and Afrikaans.

LANGUAGES

Bogdan Zaborski

1 Germanic
2 Romance, 3 Celtic
4 Slavic, 5 Baltic
6 Greek, 7 Albanian
8 Iranian, 9 Armenian
10 Indo-Aryan
URALIAN: 11 Finno-Ugric, 12 Samoyed
13 Turkic
14 Mongolic
15 Tungus-Manchu
16 Korean
17 Japanese
18 Tibetan, 19 Burmese
20 Thai, 21 Chinese
22 Vietnamese
23 Mon-Khmer, 24 Mundar
25 Dravidian
26 Paleosiberian

27 Ket
ASIANITIC: 28 Basque, 29 Caucasian, 30 Burushaski
SEMITIC: 31 Arabic, 32 Hebrew, 33 Amharic

HAMITIC: 34 Berberic, 35 Tuareg, 36 Kyshitic
AUSTRONESIAN: 37 Indonesian, 38 Polynesian, 39 Melanesian
40 Eskimo, 41 Aleut

42 American Indian
43 Australian Aborigine
44 Papua, 45 Negrito, 46 Andaman

47 Bantu
48 Language of intermediate zone between Bantu and Hamit-Semit
49 Hottentot, 50 Bushmen

POLYNESIAN 38

MELANESIAN

POLYNESIAN

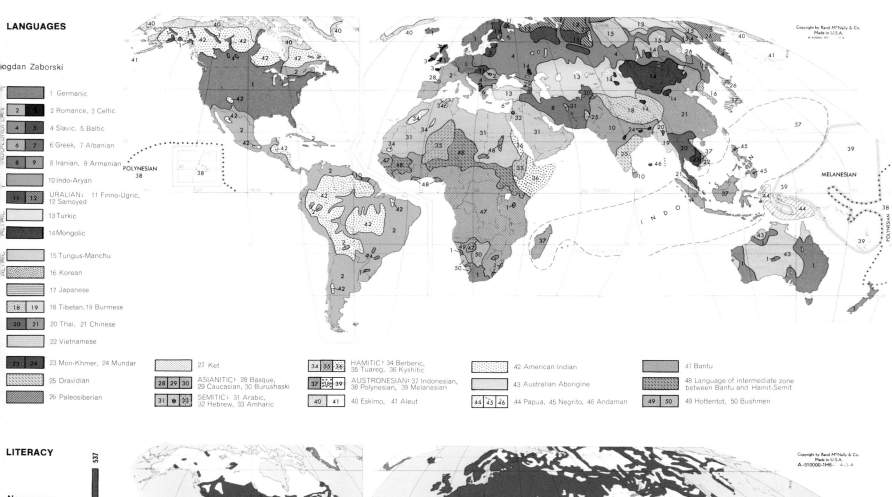

LITERACY

Newspaper Circulation
per 1,000 population

537 JAPAN
373 UNITED STATES
300 SOVIET UNION
231 FRANCE
40 BRAZIL
16 INDIA

>90%
70-90
50-70
World Av. 52% →
30-50
<30
Uninhabited or sparsely populated

Based on Population 15 years and over who can read and write

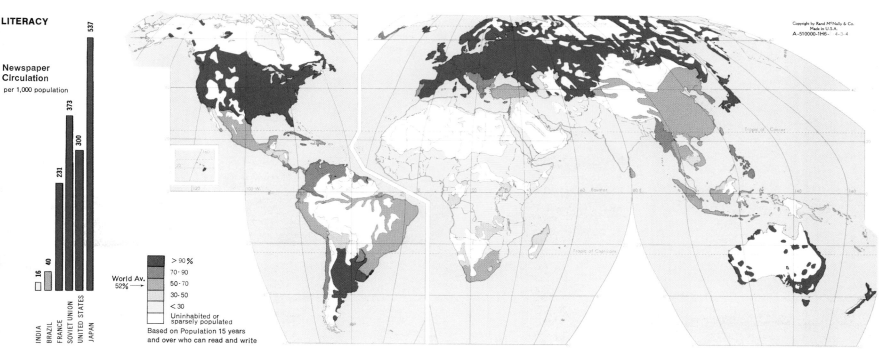

Predominant Economies

Man is neither the master nor the plaything of his environment. His activities are not determined by it, but he is not entirely free to do what he likes where he likes. A modern world map of the patterns of man's economic activities shows every stage, from the simplest forms of making a living from the natural environment, to the most advanced economies of industrial societies. These locations and occupations show a considerable response to the environment, climate and landscape.

Earliest man lived by hunting wild animals and gathering the fruits of the earth. Today such simple activities are still found in some equatorial and tropical areas, both within the dense forest regions and in the dry areas. Many more of the world's dry areas are today used for extensive animal herding, the nomadic herds wandering from one place to another in search of fresh pasture.

Subtropical and temperate regions of the world have been most suited to the development of more intensive forms of farming, whether for growing crops or raising animals. Large-scale ranging of animals, cattle and sheep, dominates the economies of Soviet Central Asia, southeastern South America, some western parts of North America and much of Australia. Elsewhere in North America and Europe as well as on the margins of the southern continents, the most prosperous crop farming and intensive animal farming has been developed.

The establishment of commercial farming in many parts of the world involved clearing the forests. Today forestry is concentrated in those parts which are often less inviting for other activities. Thus, on the northern margins of the developed lands of the Northern Hemisphere, softwood lumbering is a major activity. Hardwoods are felled quite widely in the world's warmer areas.

It is not in the vast farmed areas that man produces his greatest wealth. Extracting the world's mineral resources, producing the enormous array of manufactured goods, and providing the great range of commercial services for today's advanced societies, together form the greatest generators of wealth. Mineral resources may be very unevenly distributed throughout the world but the raw materials are easily transported. The great centers of manufacturing industry and commerce are located in the temperate climate areas most attractive to industrially-minded man. These are mainly in the Northern Hemisphere, particularly in Western and Central Europe, North America, the Soviet Union and Japan. Developments in China, India, Australia, South Africa and South America, though of importance in their own areas are not as significant in the world scene.

1 △

Apart from South Africa, Japan, Australia, New Zealand and the Argentine, the most advanced countries are in Europe and North America. The Soviet Union has made exceptional progress since World War II and must now rank with the USA as a world political and economic force. 1 The new trading center in the Chilanzar district of Tashkent is the largest of its kind in central Asia; 2 Such commercial buildings are common in the United States where most development has been upward, as shown in the modern buildings of Atlanta, Georgia; 3 There is very little comparable development in the Third World countries and much of Asia where subsistence farming predominates

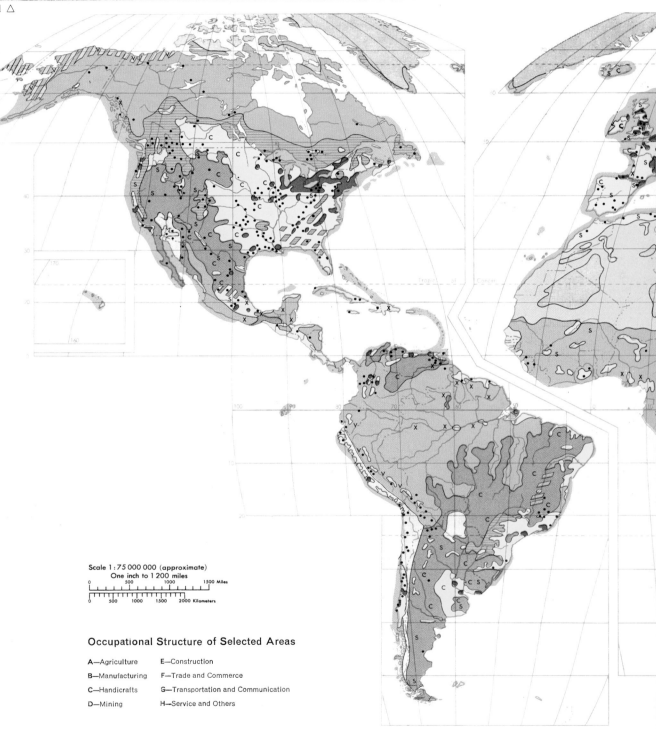

Scale 1 : 75 000 000 (approximate)
One inch to 1 200 miles
0   500   1000   1500 Miles

0   500   1000   1500   2000 Kilometers

Occupational Structure of Selected Areas

A—Agriculture   E—Construction

B—Manufacturing   F—Trade and Commerce

C—Handicrafts   G—Transportation and Communication

D—Mining   H—Service and Others

UNITED KINGDOM
24,709,000 gainfully employed—1975

A 3 · B 32 · D 2 · E 7 · F 13 · G 8 · H 35%

UNITED STATES
84,783,000 gainfully employed—1975

A 4 · B 23 · D 1 · E 4 · F 38% · G 6 · H 24

CANADA
9,364,000 gainfully employed—1975

A 6 · B 20 · D 2 · E 6 · F 23 · G 8 · H 35%

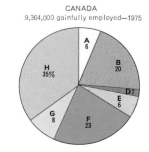

76,41

2 △

3 △

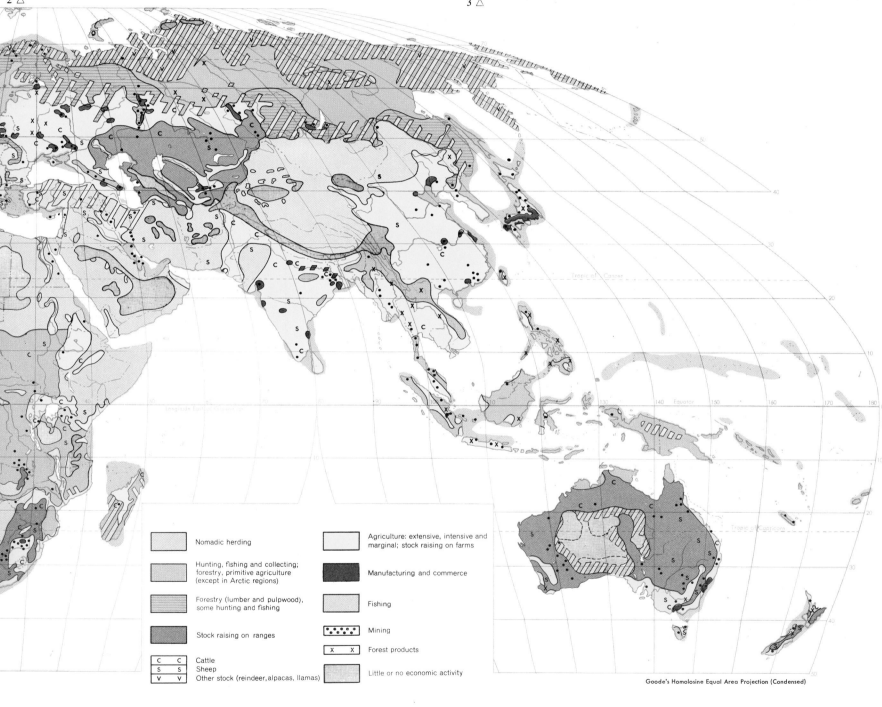

Nomadic herding

Hunting, fishing and collecting;
forestry, primitive agriculture
(except in Arctic regions)

Forestry (lumber and pulpwood),
some hunting and fishing

Stock raising on ranges

C	C	Cattle
S	S	Sheep
V	V	Other stock (reindeer, alpacas, llamas)

Agriculture: extensive, intensive and
marginal; stock raising on farms

Manufacturing and commerce

Fishing

Mining

Forest products

Little or no economic activity

Goode's Homolosine Equal Area Projection (Condensed)

ROPE
loyed—1975

SOVIET UNION
117,094,000 gainfully employed—1975

BRAZIL
29,545,400 gainfully employed—1970

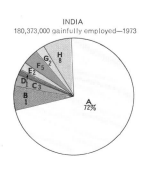
INDIA
180,373,000 gainfully employed—1973

CHINA
270,000,000 gainfully employed—Est. 1970

Population Density

Today the term 'population explosion' prompts varied reactions from the general public, from alarm to apathy. Total world population is growing at an ever increasing rate, yet individual areas have very different growth rates. World population grows at approximately 1.8 percent per annum. Some countries, however, presently have negative growth, while others exceed 4 percent per annum. Most of the high growth rates are in the Third World countries, some of which already have the highest total populations. Most countries of the developed world have growth rates well below the global average. Their total populations at present constitute less than a quarter of the world total.

Each country's average population density has been included in the country reference tables throughout the book. In many cases the distribution within a country is very uneven. Within Europe, where many of the countries have high average densities, local variations are great. In modern commercial and industrial cities densities can exceed 10,000 per km². In rural areas densities may be less than 10 per km². Such variations apply to UK, France and Germany.

Population densities in relation to a whole country may be very different from figures which relate total population to the area of land actually under cultivation. Australia has an average population density of 1.8 per km² (over 4 per sq mi) but with only six percent of the land area cultivated, there are nearly 30 people per square kilometer of cultivated land (76 per sq mi). Likewise Japan's average density of nearly 300 per km² (about 775 per sq mi) converts to a figure of nearly 2,000 per km² (over 5,000 per sq mi) in relation to cultivated land. Corresponding figures for the United Kingdom are 236 (630) and nearly 800 (nearly 2,000), and for the USA, 23 (58) and 104 (269).

A world map of population densities shows the great concentrations not only in the developed countries of Europe and parts of North America, but also in China, India and other developing countries of Southeast Asia. Within these two groups, it is interesting to consider the urban/rural balance. Countries seem to fall into three broad groups. Established industrial countries have the greater proportion of their populations in the towns – the United Kingdom 78 percent, Canada 76 percent, the USA 74 percent, France 70 percent. The developing countries have a much smaller proportion in the urban areas – China 29 percent, India 20 percent. Between these two extremes lie the mid-development countries which now have a near even split between urban and rural populations, the urban figures for them being – Japan 57 percent, Brazil 56 percent, and the USSR 56 percent.

1 △

Asia accounts for much of the world population explosion. 1 Intense overcrowding in cities such as Tokyo, Japan has led to a predominance of high-rise buildings and traffic chaos which the modern rail and expressways shown here do little to alleviate; 2 Hong Kong with its permanent boat dwellers, shanty town and influx of refugees from mainland China, reveals another heavily congested part of the continent; 3 In contrast, Canada, the world's second largest country, has only about one-tenth of the population of its neighbor, the USA, most of which is concentrated in manufacturing towns near the US border. Small planes ferry people and supplies across vast uninhabited areas, especially in the far north.

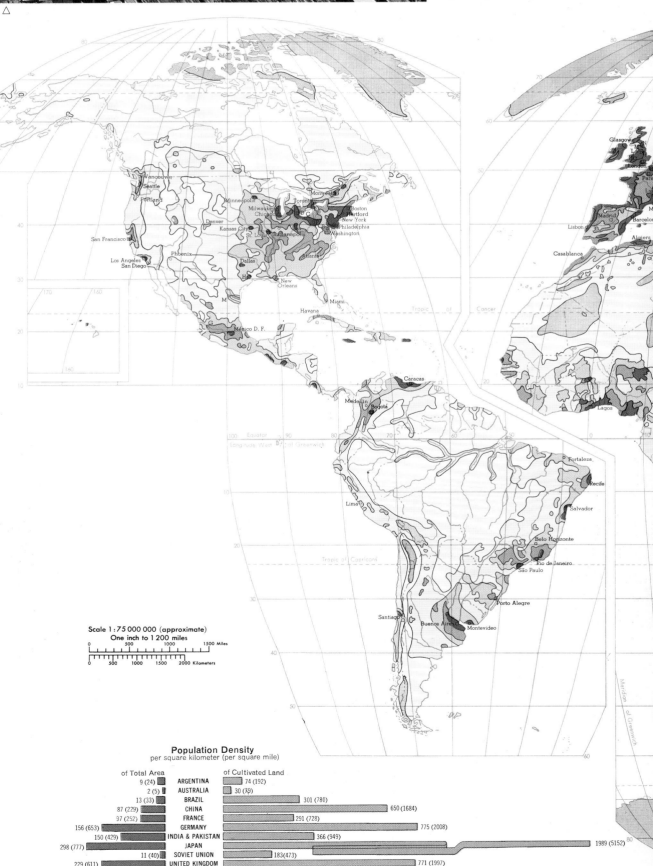

Scale 1:75 000 000 (approximate)
One inch to 1 200 miles

0   500   1000   1500 Miles

0   500   1000   1500   2000 Kilometers

Population Density
per square kilometer (per square mile)

	of Total Area		of Cultivated Land
ARGENTINA	9 (24)		74 (192)
AUSTRALIA	2 (5)		30 (79)
BRAZIL	13 (33)		301 (780)
CHINA	87 (229)		650 (1684)
FRANCE	97 (252)		291 (728)
GERMANY	156 (653)		775 (2008)
INDIA & PAKISTAN	150 (429)		366 (949)
JAPAN	298 (777)		1989 (5152)
SOVIET UNION	11 (40)		183 (473)
UNITED KINGDOM	229 (611)		771 (1997)
UNITED STATES	23 (58)		104 (269)

2 △

3 △

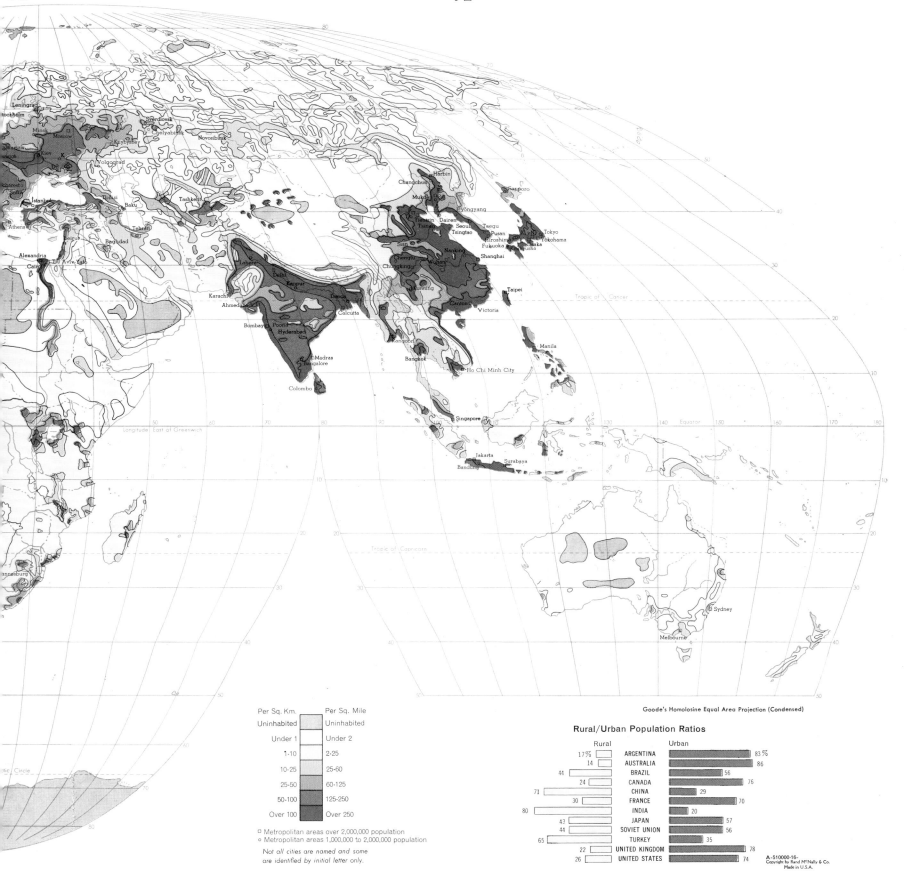

Per Sq. Km.	Per Sq. Mile
Uninhabited	Uninhabited
Under 1	Under 2
1-10	2-25
10-25	25-60
25-50	60-125
50-100	125-250
Over 100	Over 250

▫ Metropolitan areas over 2,000,000 population
○ Metropolitan areas 1,000,000 to 2,000,000 population

*Not all cities are named and some
are identified by initial letter only.*

Goode's Homolosine Equal Area Projection (Condensed)

Rural/Urban Population Ratios

Rural		Urban
17%	ARGENTINA	83%
14	AUSTRALIA	86
44	BRAZIL	56
24	CANADA	76
71	CHINA	29
30	FRANCE	70
80	INDIA	20
43	JAPAN	57
44	SOVIET UNION	56
65	TURKEY	35
22	UNITED KINGDOM	78
26	UNITED STATES	74

A-510000-16-
Copyright by Rand M°Nally & Co.
Made in U.S.A.

Climatic Regions

Each year, every place on the earth experiences a unique sequence of weather. Over a period of time a composite picture of the weather for each area can be worked out by taking the average of the individual years' records; such is a description of the local climate. Similar climates are, of course, experienced in different places. Scientists have noted these similarities and drawn up classifications for world climates.

Variable factors over the earth's surface influence climates. Latitude affects the amount of heat received, due to the differences in the height of the sun in the sky and the length of time it is there. Altitude must also be considered. Whatever the latitude, the higher the place the lower the temperature. Climate is also affected by the relative position of the nearest ocean or sea, the predominant wind direction, ocean currents, and large physical features such as mountains.

The simplest climatic classification relied solely on temperatures, resulting in the very general three-fold division of the world into frigid, temperate and torrid zones. The boundaries of these zones coincided with the Arctic and Antarctic Circles and the Tropics of Cancer and Capricorn. However, those lines do not coincide with the positions of the isotherms, lines joining places which have the same average temperatures. So, more accurate classifications, relying on the actual positions of the isotherms, have been devised.

According to the American scientist, Glenn T. Trewartha, the first critical average monthly temperature is the 18°C (64.4°F) isotherm, below which most tropical plants will not grow. The next critical temperature is the 10°C (50°F) isotherm; many subtropical plants grow in places which have eight months above this level; places with less than four months are of limited use for farming. The most extreme locations have no month with the average temperature above 10°C (50°F).

Following such reasoning, broad zones far more meaningful than 'frigid', 'temperate' and 'torrid' are defined. Subdivisions have been made to allow for other particularly significant climatic features. Is the distribution of rainfall throughout the year even or uneven? Is there a monsoon pattern?

In large parts of the world evaporation is greater than precipitation. This results in semi-arid or steppe climates. Where evaporation is twice precipitation, true desert climates are found. Each of these two climatic groups cuts across the other main ones, and thus may possess tropical, subtropical or temperate characteristics. Finally, upland areas have very distinctive climates, in that temperatures are lower than might be expected and the annual precipitation, is comparatively high.

1 △

The range of climates throughout the world has an overriding effect on the varied lifestyles within each continental area. Africa possesses the world's largest desert, the Sahara. Similar conditions prevail in other parts of the world, as in southeast California, USA, where the main vegetation is cacti such as this Ocotillo in the Anzo-Borrego Desert State Park; Many deserts are now being made fertile in parts by irrigation schemes. 2 Water is continually being harnessed, too, to provide hydro-electric power, as at the famous Victoria Falls, Zambia; 3 In the Himalayas of Asia, the world's most physically extreme part, stands the magnificent Mount Everest, the highest point of our world.

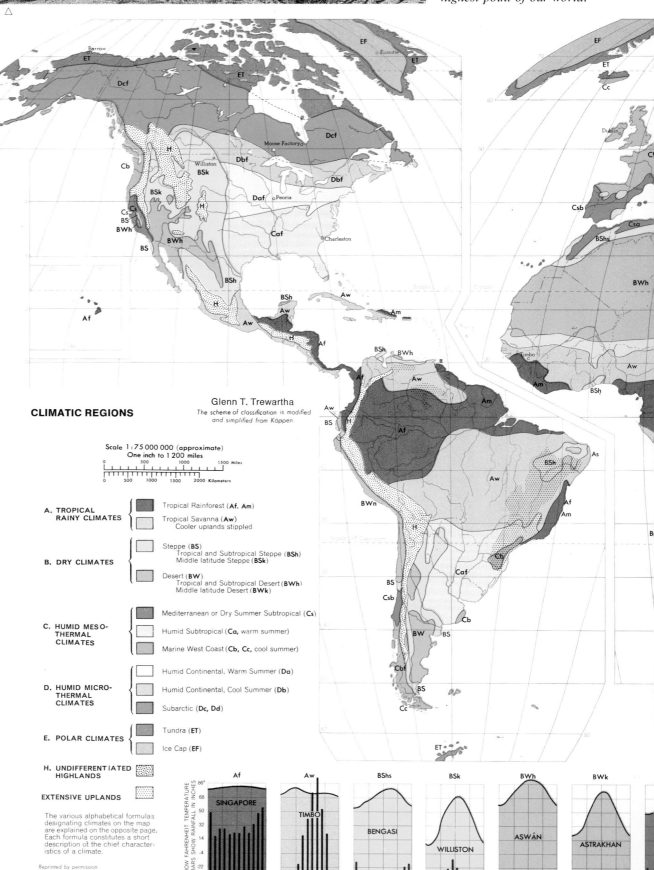

CLIMATIC REGIONS

Glenn T. Trewartha
The scheme of classification is modified and simplified from Köppen.

Scale 1:75 000 000 (approximate)
One inch to 1 200 miles

A. TROPICAL RAINY CLIMATES	Tropical Rainforest (**Af, Am**)
	Tropical Savanna (**Aw**) Cooler uplands stippled
B. DRY CLIMATES	Steppe (**BS**) Tropical and Subtropical Steppe (**BSh**) Middle latitude Steppe (**BSk**)
	Desert (**BW**) Tropical and Subtropical Desert (**BWh**) Middle latitude Desert (**BWk**)
C. HUMID MESO-THERMAL CLIMATES	Mediterranean or Dry Summer Subtropical (**Cs**)
	Humid Subtropical (**Ca**, warm summer)
	Marine West Coast (**Cb, Cc**, cool summer)
D. HUMID MICRO-THERMAL CLIMATES	Humid Continental, Warm Summer (**Da**)
	Humid Continental, Cool Summer (**Db**)
	Subarctic (**Dc, Dd**)
E. POLAR CLIMATES	Tundra (**ET**)
	Ice Cap (**EF**)
H. UNDIFFERENTIATED HIGHLANDS	
EXTENSIVE UPLANDS	

The various alphabetical formulas designating climates on the map are explained on the opposite page. Each formula constitutes a short description of the chief characteristics of a climate.

Reprinted by permission
"Elements of Physical Geography"
Copyrighted 1957 by Glenn T. Trewartha.
Published by the McGraw-Hill Book Company, Inc.

A-515800-00
Copyright by Rand McNally & Co.
Made in U.S.A.

CURVES SHOW FAHRENHEIT TEMPERATURE
VERTICAL BARS SHOW RAINFALL IN INCHES

Af	Aw	BShs	BSk	BWh	BWk
SINGAPORE	TIMBO	BENGASI	WILLISTON	ASWÂN	ASTRAKHAN
Tropical rainforest climate	Tropical savanna climate; with wet and dry seasons	Tropical and subtropical steppe climate	Middle latitude steppe climate	Tropical and subtropical desert climate	Middle latitude desert climate

198

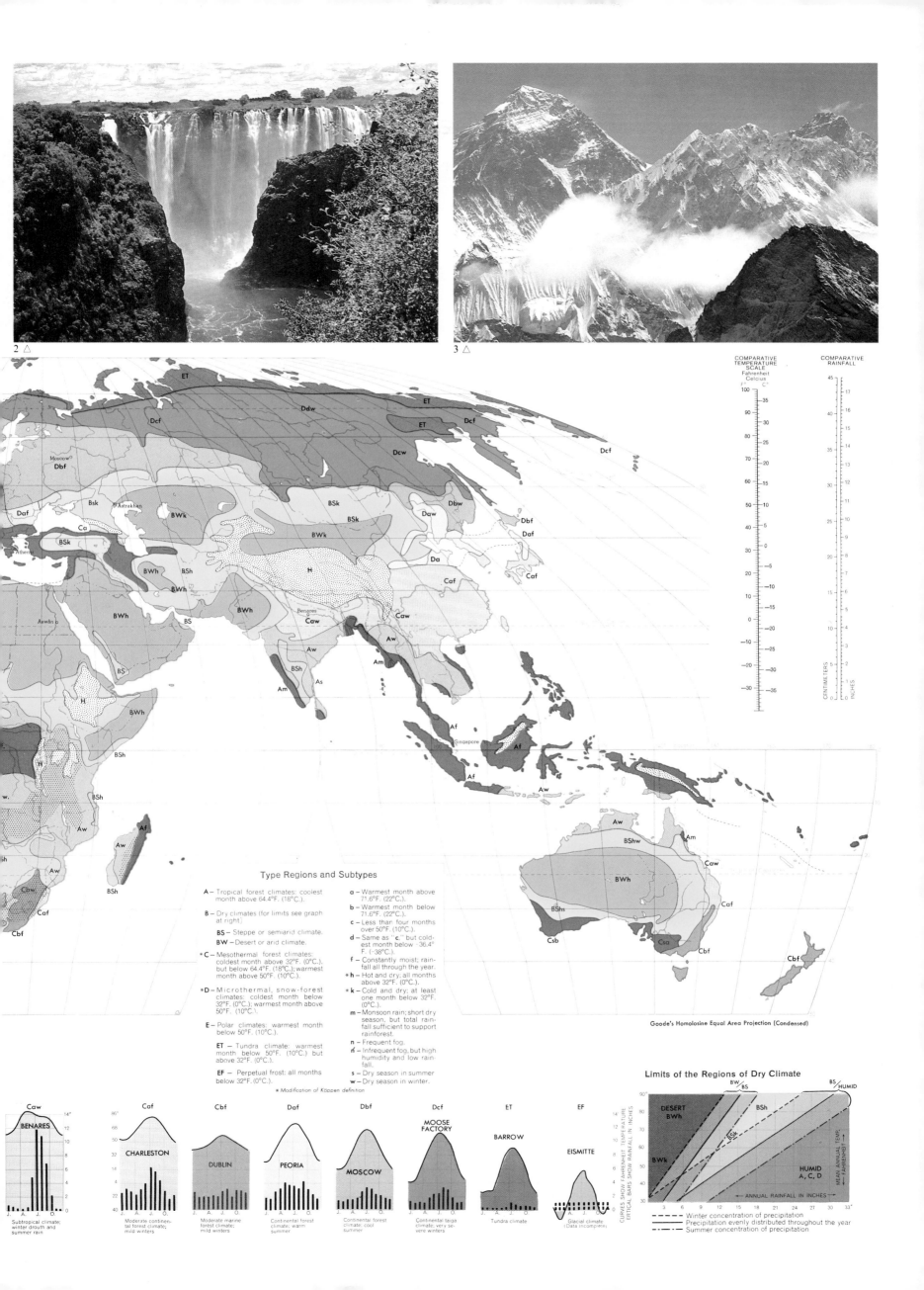

2 △   3 △

COMPARATIVE
TEMPERATURE
SCALE
Fahrenheit
Celsius

COMPARATIVE
RAINFALL

Type Regions and Subtypes

A – Tropical forest climates: coolest month above 64.4°F. (18°C.).

B – Dry climates (for limits see graph at right)

  BS – Steppe or semiarid climate.

  BW – Desert or arid climate.

*C – Mesothermal forest climates: coldest month above 32°F. (0°C.), but below 64.4°F. (18°C.); warmest month above 50°F. (10°C.).

*D – Microthermal, snow-forest climates: coldest month below 32°F. (0°C.); warmest month above 50°F. (10°C.).

E – Polar climates: warmest month below 50°F. (10°C.).

  ET – Tundra climate: warmest month below 50°F. (10°C.) but above 32°F. (0°C.).

  EF – Perpetual frost: all months below 32°F. (0°C.).

a – Warmest month above 71.6°F. (22°C.).

b – Warmest month below 71.6°F. (22°C.).

c – Less than four months over 50°F. (10°C.).

d – Same as "c," but coldest month below -36.4° F. (-38°C.).

f – Constantly moist; rainfall all through the year.

*h – Hot and dry; all months above 32°F. (0°C.).

*k – Cold and dry; at least one month below 32°F. (0°C.).

m – Monsoon rain; short dry season, but total rainfall sufficient to support rainforest.

n – Frequent fog.

ń – Infrequent fog, but high humidity and low rainfall.

s – Dry season in summer.

w – Dry season in winter.

*Modification of Köppen definition

Goode's Homolosine Equal Area Projection (Condensed)

Limits of the Regions of Dry Climate

DESERT
BWh

BWk

BSh

BSk

HUMID
A, C, D

CURVES SHOW FAHRENHEIT TEMPERATURE
VERTICAL BARS SHOW RAINFALL IN INCHES

MEAN ANNUAL TEMP. FAHRENHEIT

ANNUAL RAINFALL IN INCHES

- - - - Winter concentration of precipitation
———— Precipitation evenly distributed throughout the year
-··-··- Summer concentration of precipitation

Caw
BENARES
Subtropical climate; winter drouth and summer rain

Caf
CHARLESTON
Moderate continental forest climate; mild winters

Cbf
DUBLIN
Moderate marine forest climate; mild winters

Daf
PEORIA
Continental forest climate; warm summer

Dbf
MOSCOW
Continental forest climate; cool summer

Dcf
MOOSE FACTORY
Continental taiga climate; very severe winters

ET
BARROW
Tundra climate

EF
EISMITTE
Glacial climate (Data incomplete)

INDEX

Introduction to the Index

The index includes in a single alphabetical list some 16,000 names appearing on the maps. Each name is followed by a page reference and by the location of the feature on the map. The map location is designated by latitude and longitude coordinates. If a page contains several maps, a lowercase letter identifies the inset map. The page reference for two-page maps is always to the left hand page.

Most map features are indexed to the largest-scale map on which they appear. Countries, mountain ranges, and other extensive features are generally indexed to the map that shows them in their entirety.

The features indexed are of three types: *point*, *areal*, and *linear*. For *point* features (for example, cities, mountain peaks, dams), latitude and longitude coordinates give the location of the point on the map. For *areal* features (countries, mountain ranges, etc.), the coordinates generally indicate the approximate center of the feature. For *linear* features (rivers, canals, aqueducts), the coordinates locate a terminating point—for example, the mouth of a river, or the point at which a feature reaches the map margin.

NAME FORMS Names in the Index, as on the maps, are generally in the local language and insofar as possible are spelled according to official practice. Diacritical marks are included, except that those used to indicate tone, as in Vietnamese, are usually not shown. Most features that extend beyond the boundaries of one country have no single official name, and these are usually named in English. Many conventional English names and former names are cross referenced to the primary map name. All cross references are indicated by the symbol→. A name that appears in a shortened version on the map due to space limitations is given in full in the Index, with the portion that is omitted on the map enclosed in brackets, for example, Acapulco [de Juárez].

TRANSLITERATION For names in languages not written in the Roman alphabet, the locally official transliteration system has been used where one exists. Thus, names in the Soviet Union and Bulgaria have been transliterated according to the systems adopted by the academies of science of these countries. Similarly, the transliteration for mainland Chinese names follows the Pinyin system, which has been officially adopted in mainland China. For languages with no one locally accepted transliteration system, notably Arabic, transliteration in general follows closely a system adopted by the United States Board on Geographic Names.

ALPHABETIZATION Names are alphabetized in the order of the letters of the English alphabet. Spanish *ll* and *ch*, for example, are not treated as distinct letters. Furthermore, diacritical marks are disregarded in alphabetization—German or Scandinavian *ä* or *ö* are treated as *a* or *o*.

The names of physical features may appear inverted, since they are always alphabetized under the proper, not the generic, part of the name, thus: "Gibraltar, Strait of ㅂ". Otherwise every entry, whether consisting of one word or more, is alphabetized as a single continuous entity. "Lakeland," for example, appears after "La Crosse" and before "La Salle." Names beginning with articles (Le Havre, Den Helder, Al-Qāhirah, As-Suways) are not inverted. Names beginning "Mc" are alphabetized as though spelled "Mac," and names beginning "St." and "Sainte" as though spelled "Saint."

In the case of identical names, towns are listed first, then political divisions, then physical features. Entries that are completely identical (including symbols, discussed below) are distinguished by abbreviations of their official country names and are sequenced alphabetically by country name. The many duplicate names in Canada, the United Kingdom, and the United States are further distinguished by abbreviations of the names of their primary subdivisions. (See list of abbreviations on pages 201 and 202.)

ABBREVIATION AND CAPITALIZATION Abbreviation and styling have been standardized for all languages. A period is used after every abbreviation even when this may not be the local practice. The abbreviation "St." is used only for "Saint." "Sankt" and other forms of the term are spelled out.

All names are written with an initial capital letter except for a few Dutch names, such as 's-Gravenhage. Capitalization of noninitial words in a name generally follows local practice.

SYMBOL The symbols that appear in the Index graphically represent the broad categories of the features named, for example, ∧ for mountain (Everest, Mount ∧). Superior numbers following some symbols in the Index indicate finer distinctions, for example, $\wedge^{1}$ for volcano (Fuji-san $\wedge^{1}$). A complete list of the symbols and those with superior numbers is given on page 202.

LIST OF ABBREVIATIONS

	LOCAL NAME	ENGLISH
Afg.	Afghānestān	Afghanistan
Afr.	—	Africa
Ala., U.S.	Alabama	Alabama
Alaska, U.S.	Alaska	Alaska
Alg.	Algérie	Algeria
Alta., Can.	Alberta	Alberta
Am. Sam.	American Samoa	American Samoa
And.	Andorra	Andorra
Ang.	Angola	Angola
Anguilla	Anguilla	Anguilla
Ant.	—	Antarctica
Antig.	Antigua	Antigua
Arc. O.	—	Arctic Ocean
Arg.	Argentina	Argentina
Ariz., U.S.	Arizona	Arizona
Ark., U.S.	Arkansas	Arkansas
Ar. Sa.	Al-'Arabīyah as-Sa'ūdīyah	Saudi Arabia
As.	—	Asia
Atl. O.	—	Atlantic Ocean
Austl.	Australia	Australia
Ba.	Bahamas	Bahamas
Baḥr.	Al-Baḥrayn	Bahrain
Barb.	Barbados	Barbados
B.A.T.	British Antarctic Territory	British Antarctic Territory
B.C., Can.	British Columbia	British Columbia
Bdi.	Burundi	Burundi
Bel.	Belgique België	Belgium
Belize	Belize	Belize
Benin	Benin	Benin
Ber.	Bermuda	Bermuda
Ber. S.	—	Bering Sea
Bhārat	Bhārat	India
B.I.O.T.	British Indian Ocean Territory	British Indian Ocean Territory
Blg.	Bâlgarija	Bulgaria
Bngl.	Bangladesh	Bangladesh
Bol.	Bolivia	Bolivia
Bots.	Botswana	Botswana
Bra.	Brasil	Brazil
B.R.D.	Bundesrepublik Deutschland	Federal Republic of Germany
Bru.	Brunei	Brunei
Br. Vir. Is.	British Virgin Islands	British Virgin Islands
Calif., U.S.	California	California
Cam.	Cameroun	Cameroon
Can.	Canada	Canada
Can./End.	Canton and Enderbury	Canton and Enderbury
Carib. S.	—	Caribbean Sea
Cay. Is.	Cayman Islands	Cayman Islands
Centraf.	République centrafricaine	Central African Republic
Česko.	Československo	Czechoslovakia
Chile	Chile	Chile
Christ. I.	Christmas Island	Christmas Island
C. Iv.	Côte d'Ivoire	Ivory Coast
C.M.I.K.	Chosŏn Minjujuŭi In'min Konghwaguk	North Korea
Cocos Is.	Cocos (Keeling) Islands	Cocos (Keeling) Islands
Col.	Colombia	Colombia
Colo., U.S.	Colorado	Colorado
Comores	Comores	Comoros
Congo	Congo	Congo
Conn., U.S.	Connecticut	Connecticut
Cook Is.	Cook Islands	Cook Islands
C.R.	Costa Rica	Costa Rica
Cuba	Cuba	Cuba
C.V.	Cabo Verde	Cape Verde
Dan.	Danmark	Denmark
D.C., U.S.	District of Columbia	District of Columbia
D.D.R.	Deutsche Demokratische Republik	German Democratic Republic
Del., U.S.	Delaware	Delaware
Den.	Danmark	Denmark
Djibouti	Djibouti	Djibouti
Dom.	Dominica	Dominica
D.Y.	Druk-Yul	Bhutan
Ec.	Ecuador	Ecuador
Eire	Eire	Ireland
Ellás	Ellás	Greece
El Sal.	El Salvador	El Salvador
Eng., U.K.	England	England
Esp.	España	Spain
Eur.	—	Europe
Falk. Is.	Falkland Islands	Falkland Islands (Islas Malvinas)
Fiji	Fiji	Fiji
Fla., U.S.	Florida	Florida
Før.	Føroyar	Faeroe Islands
Fr.	France	France
Ga., U.S.	Georgia	Georgia
Gabon	Gabon	Gabon
Gam.	Gambia	Gambia
Gaza	—	Gaza Strip
Ghana	Ghana	Ghana
Gib.	Gibraltar	Gibraltar
Gren.	Grenada	Grenada
Grn.	Grønland	Greenland
Guad.	Guadeloupe	Guadeloupe
Guam.	Guam	Guam
Guat.	Guatemala	Guatemala
Guer.	Guernsey	Guernsey
Gui.-B.	Guinea-Bissau	Guinea-Bissau
Gui. Ecu.	Guinea Ecuatorial	Equatorial Guinea
Guinée	Guinée	Guinea
Guy.	Guyana	Guyana
Guy. fr.	Guyane française	French Guiana
Haï.	Haïti	Haiti
Haw., U.S.	Hawaii	Hawaii
H.K.	Hong Kong	Hong Kong
Hond.	Honduras	Honduras
H. Vol.	Haute-Volta	Upper Volta
Idaho, U.S.	Idaho	Idaho
I.I.A.	Ittiḥād al-Imārāt al-'Arabīyah	United Arab Emirates
Ill., U.S.	Illinois	Illinois
Ind., U.S.	Indiana	Indiana
Ind. O.	—	Indian Ocean
Indon.	Indonesia	Indonesia
I. of Man	Isle of Man	Isle of Man
Iowa, U.S.	Iowa	Iowa
Īrān	Īrān	Iran
'Irāq	Al-'Irāq	Iraq
Ísland	Ísland	Iceland
It.	Italia	Italy
Jam.	Jamaica	Jamaica
Jersey	Jersey	Jersey
Jugo.	Jugoslavija	Yugoslavia
Kam.	Kampuchea	Cambodia
Kans., U.S.	Kansas	Kansas
Kenya	Kenya	Kenya
Kípros	Kípros Kıbrıs	Cyprus
Kiribati	Kiribati	Kiribati
Kuwayt	Al-Kuwayt	Kuwait
Ky., U.S.	Kentucky	Kentucky
La., U.S.	Louisiana	Louisiana
Lao	Lao	Laos
Leso.	Lesotho	Lesotho
Liber.	Liberia	Liberia
Lībiyā	Lībiyā	Libya
Liech.	Liechtenstein	Liechtenstein
Lubnān	Al-Lubnān	Lebanon
Lux.	Luxembourg	Luxembourg
Macau	Macau	Macau
Madag.	Madagasikara	Madagascar
Magreb	Al-Magreb	Morocco
Magy.	Magyarország	Hungary
Maine, U.S.	Maine	Maine
Malawi	Malawi	Malawi
Malay.	Malaysia	Malaysia
Mald.	Maldives	Maldives
Mali	Mali	Mali
Malta	Malta	Malta
Man., Can.	Manitoba	Manitoba
Mart.	Martinique	Martinique
Mass., U.S.	Massachusetts	Massachusetts
Maur.	Mauritanie	Mauritania
Maus.	Mauritius	Mauritius
Md., U.S.	Maryland	Maryland
Medit. S.	—	Mediterranean Sea
Méx.	México	Mexico
Mich., U.S.	Michigan	Michigan
Mid. Is.	Midway Islands	Midway Islands
Minn., U.S.	Minnesota	Minnesota
Miṣr	Miṣr	Egypt
Miss., U.S.	Mississippi	Mississippi
Mo., U.S.	Missouri	Missouri
Moç.	Moçambique	Mozambique
Monaco	Monaco	Monaco
Mong.	Mongol Ard Uls	Mongolia
Mont., U.S.	Montana	Montana
Monts.	Montserrat	Montserrat
Mya.	Myanma	Burma
N.A.	—	North America
Namibia	Namibia	Namibia
Nauru	Nauru	Nauru
N.B., Can.	New Brunswick	New Brunswick
N.C., U.S.	North Carolina	North Carolina
N. Cal.	Nouvelle-Calédonie	New Caledonia
N. Dak., U.S.	North Dakota	North Dakota
Nebr., U.S.	Nebraska	Nebraska
Ned.	Nederland	Netherlands
Ned. Ant.	Nederlandse Antillen	Netherlands Antilles
Nepāl	Nepāl	Nepal
Nev., U.S.	Nevada	Nevada
Newf., Can.	Newfoundland	Newfoundland
N.H., U.S.	New Hampshire	New Hampshire
N. Heb.	New Hebrides Nouvelles-Hébrides	New Hebrides
Nic.	Nicaragua	Nicaragua
Nig.	Nigeria	Nigeria
Niger	Niger	Niger
Nihon	Nihon	Japan
N. Ire., U.K.	Northern Ireland	Northern Ireland
Niue	Niue	Niue
N.J., U.S.	New Jersey	New Jersey
N. Mex., U.S.	New Mexico	New Mexico
Nor.	Norge	Norway
Norf. I.	Norfolk Island	Norfolk Island
N.S., Can.	Nova Scotia	Nova Scotia
N.W. Ter., Can.	Northwest Territories	Northwest Territories
N.Y., U.S.	New York	New York
N.Z.	New Zealand	New Zealand
Oc.	—	Oceania
Ohio, U.S.	Ohio	Ohio
Okla., U.S.	Oklahoma	Oklahoma
Ont., Can.	Ontario	Ontario
Oreg., U.S.	Oregon	Oregon
Öst.	Österreich	Austria
Pa., U.S.	Pennsylvania	Pennsylvania
Pac. O.	—	Pacific Ocean
Pāk.	Pākistān	Pakistan
Pan.	Panamá	Panama
Pap. N. Gui.	Papua New Guinea	Papua New Guinea
Para.	Paraguay	Paraguay
P.E.I., Can.	Prince Edward Island	Prince Edward Island
Perú	Perú	Peru
Pil.	Pilipinas	Philippines
Pit.	Pitcairn	Pitcairn
P.I.T.T.	Pacific Islands Trust Territory	Pacific Islands Trust Territory
Pol.	Polska	Poland
Poly. fr.	Polynésie française	French Polynesia
Port.	Portugal	Portugal
P.R.	Puerto Rico	Puerto Rico
P.S.N.Á.	Plazas de Soberanía en el Norte de África	Spanish North Africa
Qaṭar	Qaṭar	Qatar
Que., Can.	Québec	Quebec
Rep. Dom.	República Dominicana	Dominican Republic
Réu.	Réunion	Reunion
R.I., U.S.	Rhode Island	Rhode Island
Rom.	România	Romania
Rw.	Rwanda	Rwanda
S.A.	—	South America
S. Afr.	South Africa Suid-Afrika	South Africa
Sah. Occ.	Sahara Occidentale	Western Sahara
Sask., Can.	Saskatchewan	Saskatchewan
S.C., U.S.	South Carolina	South Carolina
S. Ch. S.	—	South China Sea
Schw.	Schweiz; Suisse; Svizzera	Switzerland
Scot., U.K.	Scotland	Scotland
S. Dak., U.S.	South Dakota	South Dakota
Sén.	Sénégal	Senegal
Sey.	Seychelles	Seychelles
Shq.	Shqipëri	Albania
Sing.	Singapore	Singapore
S.L.	Sierra Leone	Sierra Leone
S. Lan.	Sri Lanka	Sri Lanka
S. Mar.	San Marino	San Marino
Sol. Is.	Solomon Islands	Solomon Islands
Som.	Somaliya	Somalia
Sp.	España	Spain
S.S.R.	Sovetskaja Socialističeskaja Respublika	Soviet Socialist Republic
S.S.S.R.	Sojuz Sovetskich Socialističeskich Respublik	Union of Soviet Socialist Republics
St. Hel.	St. Helena	St. Helena
St. K.-N.	St. Kitts-Nevis	St. Kitts-Nevis
St. Luc.	St. Lucia	St. Lucia
S. Tom./P.	São Tomé e Príncipe	Sao Tome and Principe
St. P./M.	St.-Pierre-et-Miquelon	St. Pierre and Miquelon
St. Vin.	St. Vincent	St. Vincent
Sūd.	As-Sūdān	Sudan
Suomi	Suomi	Finland
Sur.	Suriname	Suriname
Sūriy.	As-Sūrīyah	Syria
Sval.	Svalbard og Jan Mayen	Svalbard and Jan Mayen
Sve.	Sverige	Sweden
Swaz.	Swaziland	Swaziland
T.a.a.f.	Terres australes et antarctiques françaises	French Southern and Antarctic Territories
Taehan	Taehan-Min'guk	South Korea
T'aiwan	T'aiwan	Taiwan
Tan.	Tanzania	Tanzania
Tchad	Tchad	Chad
T./C. Is.	Turks and Caicos Islands	Turks and Caicos Islands
Tenn., U.S.	Tennessee	Tennessee
Tex., U.S.	Texas	Texas
Thai.	Prathet Thai	Thailand
Togo	Togo	Togo
Tok. Is.	Tokelau Islands	Tokelau Islands
Tonga	Tonga	Tonga
Trin.	Trinidad and Tobago	Trinidad and Tobago
Tun.	Tunisie	Tunisia
Tür.	Türkiye	Turkey
Tuvalu	Tuvalu	Tuvalu
Ug.	Uganda	Uganda
U.K.	United Kingdom	United Kingdom
'Umān	'Umān	Oman
Ur.	Uruguay	Uruguay
Urd.	Al-Urdunn	Jordan
U.S.	United States	United States

Opposite: Antigua Bay, West Indies

Introduction to the Index

LIST OF ABBREVIATIONS CON'T.

KEY TO SYMBOLS

- ⋀ Mountain
- ⋀¹ Volcano
- ⋀² Hill
- ⋊ Mountains
- ⋊¹ Plateau
- ⋊² Hills
-)(Pass
- ⋁ Valley, Canyon
- ≏ Plain
- ≏¹ Basin
- ≏² Delta

- ⪢ Cape
- ⪢¹ Peninsula
- ⪢² Spit, Sand Bar
- I Island
- I¹ Atoll
- I² Rock
- II Islands
- II¹ Rocks
- ⪤ Other Topographic Features
- ⪤¹ Continent
- ⪤² Coast, Beach

- ⪥³ Isthmus
- ⪥⁴ Cliff
- ⪥⁵ Cave, Caves
- ⪥⁶ Crater
- ⪥⁷ Depression
- ⪥⁸ Dunes
- ⪥⁹ Lava Flow
- ≈ River
- ≈¹ River Channel
- ≍ Canal
- ≍¹ Aqueduct

- ↳ Waterfall, Rapids
- ⨆ Strait
- C Bay, Gulf
- C¹ Estuary
- C² Fjord
- C³ Bight
- ⊜ Lake, Lakes
- ⊜¹ Reservoir
- ≋ Swamp
- ⊠ Ice Features, Glacier

- ⊤ Other Hydrographic Features
- ⊤¹ Ocean
- ⊤² Sea
- ⊤³ Anchorage
- ⊤⁴ Oasis, Well, Spring
- ⊹ Submarine Features
- ⊹¹ Depression
- ⊹² Reef, Shoal
- ⊹³ Mountain, Mountains
- ⊹⁴ Slope, Shelf

- □ Political Unit
- □¹ Independent Nation
- □² Dependency
- □³ State, Canton, Republic
- □⁴ Province, Region, Oblast
- □⁵ Department, District, Prefecture
- □⁶ County
- □⁷ City, Municipality
- □⁸ Miscellaneous
- □⁹ Historical

- ✠ Cultural Institution
- ✠¹ Religious Institution
- ✠² Educational Institution
- ✠³ Scientific, Industrial Facility
- ⊥ Historical Site
- ♦ Recreational Site
- ⊠ Airport
- ■ Military Installation

- Miscellaneous
- ⬩¹ Region
- ⬩² Desert
- ⬩³ Forest, Moor
- ⬩⁴ Reserve, Reservation
- ⬩⁵ Transportation
- ⬩⁶ Dam
- ⬩⁷ Mine, Quarry
- ⬩⁸ Neighborhood
- ⬩⁹ Shopping Center

Index

Ande—Barn

Name	Page	Lat °′	Long °′
Anderson, Ind., U.S.	174	40.10 N	85.41 W
Anderson, S.C., U.S.	172	34.31 N	82.39 W
Anderson ≃	160	69.43 N	128.58 W
Andes ⋀	144	17.00 S	70.00 W
Andikíthira I	54	35.52 N	23.18 E
Andižan	62	40.45 N	72.22 E
Andong, Taehan	80	36.35 N	128.44 E
Andong, Zhg.	80	40.08 N	124.20 E
Andorra	50	42.30 N	1.31 E
Andorra □[1]	20	42.30 N	1.30 E
Andover, Eng., U.K.	32	51.13 N	1.28 W
Andover, Mass., U.S.	166	42.39 N	71.08 W
Andøya I	26	69.08 N	15.54 E
Andradina	144	20.54 S	51.23 W
Andrews	172	33.27 N	79.34 W
Andria	46	41.13 N	16.18 E
Ándros I	54	37.45 N	24.42 E
Androscoggin ≃	166	43.55 N	69.55 W
Andros Island I	130	24.26 N	77.57 W
Androth Island I	84	10.49 N	73.40 E
Andrychów	36	49.52 N	19.21 E
Andújar	50	38.03 N	4.04 W
Anelgauhat	112	20.14 S	169.44 E
Aneto, Pico de ∧	50	42.38 N	0.40 E
Angamos, Punta ≻	146	23.01 S	70.32 W
Angara ≃	64	58.06 N	93.00 E
Angarsk	64	52.34 N	103.54 E
Ángel, Salto (Angel Falls) ⌊	144	5.57 N	62.30 W
Ángel de la Guarda, Isla I	130	29.20 N	113.25 W
Angeles	82	15.09 N	120.35 E
Angel Falls → Ángel, Salto ⌊	144	5.57 N	62.30 W
Ängelholm	28	56.15 N	12.51 E
Ångermanälven ≃	28	62.48 N	17.56 E
Angermünde	36	53.01 N	14.00 E
Angers	42	47.28 N	0.33 W
Angleton	174	29.10 N	95.26 W
Anglona ◆[1]	46	40.50 N	8.45 E
Angmagssalik	160	65.36 N	37.41 W
Angoche, Ilha I	104	16.20 S	39.50 E
Angola	174	41.38 N	85.00 W
Angola □[1]	104	12.30 S	18.30 E
Angoulême	42	45.39 N	0.09 E
Anguilla □[2]	130	18.15 N	63.05 W
Anie, Pic d' ∧	42	42.57 N	0.43 W
Anina	54	45.05 N	21.51 E
Aniva, Zaliv C	64	46.16 N	142.48 E
Anjouan I	104	12.15 S	44.25 E
Ankara	20	39.56 N	32.52 E
Ankaratra ⋀	104	19.25 S	47.12 E
Ankeny	168	41.44 N	93.36 W
Anklam	36	53.51 N	13.41 E
Anna	174	37.28 N	89.15 W
Anna, Lake ⊜[1]	166	38.04 N	77.45 W
Annaba (Bône)	100	36.54 N	7.46 E
Annaberg-Buchholz	36	50.35 N	13.00 E
An-Nafūd ◆[2]	84	28.30 N	41.00 E
An-Najaf	84	31.59 N	44.20 E
Annandale, Minn., U.S.	168	45.16 N	94.08 W
Annandale, Va., U.S.	166	38.49 N	77.09 W
Annapolis	166	38.59 N	76.30 W
Annapurna ∧	84	28.34 N	83.50 E
Ann Arbor	168	42.18 N	83.45 W
An-Nāṣirīyah	84	31.02 N	46.16 E
Annecy	42	45.54 N	6.07 E
Annenkov Island I	146	54.29 S	37.05 W
Anniston	174	33.40 N	85.50 W
Annonay	42	45.14 N	4.40 E
An-Nuhūd	102	12.42 N	28.26 E
Annville	166	40.19 N	76.31 W
Anoka	168	45.11 N	93.23 W
Anqing	80	30.31 N	117.02 E
Ansbach	36	49.17 N	10.34 E
Anshan	80	41.08 N	122.59 E
Anson Bay C	113	29.01 S	167.55 E
Antakya	20	36.14 N	36.07 E
Antalaha	104	14.53 S	50.16 E
Antalya	20	36.53 N	30.42 E
Antalya Körfezi C	20	36.30 N	31.00 E
Antananarivo	104	18.55 S	47.31 E
Antarctica •[1]	191	90.00 S	0.00
Antarctic Peninsula ≻[1]	191	69.30 S	65.00 W
Antela, Laguna de ⊜	50	42.07 N	7.41 W
Antelope Island I	178	40.57 N	112.12 W
Antequera	50	37.01 N	4.33 W
Anti Atlas ⋀	100	30.00 N	8.30 W
Antibes	42	43.35 N	7.07 E
Anticosti, Île d' I	160	49.30 N	63.00 W
Antigo	168	45.09 N	89.09 W
Antigua □[1]	130	17.03 N	61.48 W
Antioch	168	42.29 N	88.06 W
Antofagasta	146	23.39 S	70.24 W
Antongil, Baie d' C	104	15.45 S	49.50 E
António Enes	104	16.14 S	39.54 E
Antonito	178	37.05 N	106.00 W
Antsirabe	104	19.51 S	47.02 E
Antwerp → Antwerpen	36	51.13 N	4.25 E
Antwerpen (Anvers)	36	51.13 N	4.25 E
An'ujskij Chrebet ⋀	64	67.30 N	166.00 E
Anvers → Antwerpen	36	51.13 N	4.25 E
Anyang	80	36.06 N	114.21 E
Anžero-Sudžensk	64	56.07 N	86.00 E
Anzin	42	50.22 N	3.30 E
Anzio	46	41.27 N	12.37 E
Aola	114	9.32 S	160.29 E
Aomen → Macau	80	22.14 N	113.35 E
Aomori	80	40.49 N	140.45 E
Aóös (Vijosë) ≃	54	40.37 N	19.20 E
Aôral, Phnum ∧	82	12.02 N	104.10 E
Aosta	46	45.44 N	7.20 E
Aosta, Val d' ∨	42	45.46 N	7.25 E
Aouk, Bahr ≃	102	8.51 N	18.53 E
Aoukâr ◆[1]	100	18.00 N	9.30 W
Aoulef	100	26.58 N	1.05 E
Apa ≃	146	22.06 S	58.00 W
Apache Junction	178	33.25 N	111.33 W
Apalachicola ≃	172	29.44 N	84.59 W
Apaporis ≃	144	1.23 S	69.25 W
Apatin	54	45.40 N	18.59 E
Apatity	26	67.34 N	33.18 E
Apeldoorn	36	52.13 N	5.58 E
Apex	172	35.44 N	78.51 W
Apia	113	13.50 S	171.44 W
Apo, Mount ∧	82	6.59 N	125.16 E
Apolda	36	51.01 N	11.31 E
Apolima Strait ⋃	113	14.50 S	172.10 W
Apopka, Lake ⊜	172	28.37 N	81.38 W
Apostle Islands II	168	46.50 N	90.30 W
Appalachian Mountains ⋀	162	41.00 N	77.00 W
Appennines → Appennino ⋀	46	43.00 N	13.00 E
Appennino (Appennines) ⋀	46	43.00 N	13.00 E
Appennino Abruzzese ⋀	46	42.00 N	14.00 E
Appennino Calabrese ⋀	46	39.00 N	16.30 E
Appennino Ligure ⋀	46	44.30 N	9.00 E
Appennino Lucano ⋀	46	40.30 N	16.00 E
Appennino Napoletano ⋀	46	41.30 N	15.00 E
Appennino Tosco-Emiliano ⋀	46	44.00 N	11.30 E
Appleton	168	44.16 N	88.25 W
Apure ≃	144	7.37 N	66.25 W
Aqaba, Gulf of C	102	29.00 N	34.40 E
Arab	174	34.19 N	86.29 W
'Arab, Baḥr al- ≃	102	9.02 N	29.28 E
Arabi	174	29.57 N	90.02 W
Arabian Sea ≂[2]	84	15.00 N	65.00 E
Aracaju	144	10.55 S	37.04 W
Araçatuba	144	21.12 S	50.25 W
Arad	54	46.11 N	21.20 E
Arafura Sea ≂[2]	82	11.00 S	135.00 E
Aragón □[9]	50	41.00 N	1.00 W
Araguaia ≃	144	5.21 S	48.41 W
Araguari	144	18.38 S	48.11 W
Arakan Yoma ⋀	82	19.00 N	94.40 E
Araks (Aras) ≃	62	40.01 N	48.28 E
Aral'skoje More ≂[2]	62	45.00 N	60.00 E
Arana, Sierra ⋀	50	37.20 N	3.30 W
Aranda de Duero	50	41.41 N	3.41 W
Aran Islands II	32	53.07 N	9.43 W
Aranjuez	50	40.02 N	3.36 W
Araraquara	144	21.47 S	48.10 W
Aras (Araks) ≃	62	40.01 N	48.28 E
Arauca ≃	144	7.24 N	66.35 W
Arāvalli Range ⋀	84	25.00 N	73.30 E
Araxá	144	19.35 S	46.55 W
Arbagia ◆[1]	46	40.00 N	9.10 E
Arbaoua	50	34.54 N	5.56 W
Arboga	28	59.24 N	15.50 E
Arbon	42	47.31 N	9.26 E
Arborea ◆[1]	46	39.55 N	8.50 E
Arbroath	32	56.34 N	2.35 W
Arcachon	42	44.37 N	1.12 W
Arcachon, Bassin d' C	42	44.40 N	1.10 W
Arcade	184	34.02 N	118.15 W
Arcadia, Calif., U.S.	184	34.08 N	118.01 W
Arcadia, Fla., U.S.	172	27.14 N	81.52 W
Arcadia, Kans., U.S.	174	37.38 N	94.37 W
Arcadia, La., U.S.	174	32.33 N	92.55 W
Arcadia, Wis., U.S.	168	44.15 N	91.30 W
Arcata	184	40.52 N	124.05 W
Archangel'sk	26	64.34 N	40.32 E
Archdale	172	35.56 N	79.57 W
Arcos de la Frontera	50	36.45 N	5.48 W
Arda ≃	54	41.39 N	26.29 E
Arden	184	38.36 N	121.23 W
Ardennes ◆[1]	36	50.10 N	5.45 E
Ardila ≃	50	38.12 N	7.28 W
Ardmore, Okla., U.S.	162	34.10 N	97.08 W
Ardmore, Pa., U.S.	166	40.01 N	75.18 W
Arecibo	130	18.28 N	66.43 W
Arena, Point ≻	184	38.57 N	123.44 W
Arendal	28	58.27 N	8.48 E
Areq, Sebkha Bou C	50	35.10 N	2.45 W
Arequipa	144	16.24 S	71.33 W
Arezzo	46	43.25 N	11.53 E
Argenta	46	44.37 N	11.50 E
Argentan	42	48.45 N	0.01 W
Argentera ∧	46	44.10 N	7.18 E
Argentina □[1]	146	34.00 S	64.00 W
Argentino, Lago ⊜	146	50.13 S	72.25 W
Arghandāb ≃	84	31.27 N	64.23 E
Argolikós Kólpos C	54	37.33 N	22.45 E
Argonne ◆[1]	42	49.30 N	5.00 E
Árgos	54	37.39 N	22.44 E
Argostólion	54	38.10 N	20.30 E
Arguello, Point ≻	184	34.35 N	120.39 W
Argun' (Eergu'nahe) ≃	64	53.20 N	121.28 E
Århus	28	56.09 N	10.13 E
Ariano Irpino	46	41.09 N	15.05 E
Ariège ≃	42	43.31 N	1.25 E
Arieș ≃	54	46.26 N	23.59 E
Arima	130	10.38 N	61.17 W
Arizaro, Salar de ≚	146	24.42 S	67.45 W
Arizgoiti	50	43.01 N	2.24 W
Arizona □[3]	162	34.00 N	112.00 W
Arkadelphia	174	34.07 N	93.04 W
Arkansas □[3]	162	34.50 N	93.40 W
Arkansas ≃	162	33.48 N	91.04 W
Arkansas City	162	37.04 N	97.02 W
Arkoma	174	35.21 N	94.26 W
Arkona, Kap ≻	36	54.41 N	13.26 E
Arktičeskij, Mys ≻	62	81.15 N	95.45 E
Arles	42	43.40 N	4.38 E
Arlington, Minn., U.S.	168	44.36 N	94.05 W
Arlington, Va., U.S.	166	38.52 N	77.05 W
Arlington, Wash., U.S.	180	48.12 N	122.08 W
Arlington Heights	168	42.05 N	87.59 W
Arlon	36	49.41 N	5.49 E
Arma	174	37.33 N	94.42 W
Armagh	32	54.21 N	6.39 W
Armavir	62	45.00 N	41.08 E
Armenia	144	4.31 N	75.41 W
Armentières	42	50.41 N	2.53 E
Armidale	116	30.31 S	151.39 E
Armijo	178	35.03 N	106.41 W
Armstrong, Mount ∧	160	63.12 N	133.16 W
Arnaud ≃	160	59.59 N	69.46 W
Arnhem	36	51.59 N	5.55 E
Arnhem Land ◆[1]	116	13.10 S	134.30 E
Árnissa	54	40.48 N	21.50 E
Arno ≃	46	43.41 N	10.17 E
Arnold	174	38.26 N	90.23 W
Arnsberg	36	51.24 N	8.03 E
Arnstadt	36	50.50 N	10.57 E
Arona	46	45.46 N	8.34 E
Arorangi	114	21.13 S	159.49 W
Arosa, Ría de C[1]	50	42.28 N	8.57 W
Arp	184	32.13 N	95.04 W
Ar-Rab' al-Khālī ◆[2]	84	20.00 N	51.00 E
Arran, Island of I	32	55.35 N	5.15 W
Arras	42	50.17 N	2.47 E
Arrats ≃	42	44.06 N	0.52 E
Arrée, Montagnes d' ⋀	42	48.26 N	3.55 W
Ar-Riyāḍ (Riyadh)	84	24.38 N	46.43 E
Arros ≃	42	43.40 N	0.02 W
Arroux ≃	42	46.29 N	3.58 E
Arroyo Grande	184	35.07 N	120.34 W
Árta	54	39.09 N	20.59 E
Artemisa	130	22.49 N	82.46 W
Artesia	162	32.51 N	104.24 W
Artigas	146	30.24 S	56.28 W
Aru, Kepulauan II	82	6.00 S	134.30 E
Arua	102	3.01 N	30.55 E
Aruba I	130	12.30 N	69.58 W
Arun ≃	32	50.48 N	0.33 W
Arusha	104	3.22 S	36.41 E
Aruwimi ≃	104	1.13 N	23.36 E
Arvada	178	39.50 N	105.05 W
Arvika	28	59.39 N	12.36 E
Arvin	184	35.12 N	118.50 W
Arzamas	26	55.23 N	43.50 E
Arzew	50	35.51 N	0.19 W
Arzew, Golfe d' C	50	35.50 N	0.10 W
Arzew, Salines d' ⊜	50	35.40 N	0.15 W
Arzignano	46	45.31 N	11.20 E
Aš	36	50.10 N	12.10 E
Asahikawa	80	43.46 N	142.22 E
Asansol	84	23.41 N	86.58 E
Asbury Park	166	40.13 N	74.01 W
Aščhabad	62	37.57 N	58.23 E
Aschaffenburg	36	49.59 N	9.09 E
Aschersleben	36	51.45 N	11.27 E
Ascoli Piceno	46	42.51 N	13.34 E
Asenovgrad	54	42.01 N	24.52 E
Ashburn	172	31.43 N	83.39 W
Ashburton	118	43.55 S	171.45 E
Ashburton ≃, Austl.	116	21.40 S	114.56 E
Ashburton ≃, N.Z.	118	44.04 S	171.48 E
Ashdown	174	33.41 N	94.08 W
Asheboro	172	35.42 N	79.49 W
Asheville	172	35.34 N	82.33 W
Ashford	32	51.26 N	0.27 W
Ashikaga	80	36.20 N	139.27 E
Ashland, Ky., U.S.	166	38.28 N	82.38 W
Ashland, Ohio, U.S.	166	40.52 N	82.19 W
Ashland, Oreg., U.S.	180	42.12 N	122.42 W
Ashland, Pa., U.S.	166	40.47 N	76.21 W
Ashland, Va., U.S.	172	37.45 N	77.29 W
Ashland, Wis., U.S.	168	46.35 N	90.53 W
Ashland City	174	36.16 N	87.04 W
Ashley, Ill., U.S.	174	38.20 N	89.11 W
Ash-Shāriqah	84	25.22 N	55.23 E
Ashtabula	166	41.52 N	80.48 W
Ashwaubenon	168	44.29 N	88.03 W
Asia Minor ◆[1]	84	39.00 N	32.00 E
Asilah	50	35.32 N	6.00 W
Asinara, Golfo dell' C	46	41.00 N	8.30 E
Asinara, Isola I	46	41.05 N	8.18 E
'Asīr ◆[1]	84	19.00 N	42.00 E
Asmera	102	15.20 N	38.53 E
Åsnen ⊜	28	56.38 N	14.42 E
Aso ≃	46	43.06 N	13.51 E
Aspe	50	38.21 N	0.46 W
Aspen	178	39.11 N	106.49 W
Aspromonte ⋀	46	38.10 N	15.55 E
Assad, Buḥayrat al- ⊜[1]	20	36.00 N	38.00 E
Aṣ-Ṣaḥrā' al-Gharbīyah (Western Desert) ◆[2]	102	27.00 N	27.00 E
Aṣ-Ṣaḥrā' al-Lībīyah (Libyan Desert) ◆[2]	102	24.00 N	25.00 E
Aṣ-Ṣaḥrā' ash-Sharqīyah (Eastern Desert) ◆[2]	102	28.00 N	32.00 E
Assateague Island I	166	38.05 N	75.10 W
Asse	36	50.55 N	4.12 E
Assen	36	52.59 N	6.34 E
Assiniboine, Mount ∧	160	50.52 N	115.39 W
Assisi	46	43.04 N	12.37 E
As-Sulaymānīyah	84	35.33 N	45.26 E
As-Suwaydā'	84	32.42 N	36.34 E
As-Suways (Suez)	102	29.58 N	32.33 E
Asti	46	44.54 N	8.12 E
Astorga	50	42.27 N	6.03 W
Astoria	180	46.11 N	123.80 W
Astrachan'	62	46.21 N	48.03 E
Asturias □[9]	50	43.20 N	6.00 W
Asuisui, Cape ≻	113	13.47 S	172.29 W
Asunción	146	25.16 S	57.40 W
Aswān	102	24.05 N	32.53 E
Asyūṭ	102	27.11 N	31.11 E
Atacama, Desierto de ◆[2]	146	24.30 S	69.15 W
Atacama, Salar de ≚	146	23.30 S	68.15 W
Atar	100	20.31 N	13.03 W
Atascadero	184	35.29 N	120.40 W
'Aṭbarah	102	17.42 N	33.59 E
'Aṭbarah (Atbara) ≃	102	17.40 N	33.56 E
Atchafalaya ≃	174	29.53 N	91.28 W
Atchafalaya Bay C	174	29.25 N	91.20 W
Atchison	174	39.34 N	95.07 W
Athabasca ≃	160	58.40 N	110.50 W
Athabasca, Lake ⊜	160	59.07 N	110.00 W
Athens → Athínai, Ellás	54	37.58 N	23.43 E
Athens, Ala., U.S.	174	34.48 N	86.58 W
Athens, Ga., U.S.	172	33.57 N	83.23 W
Athens, Ohio, U.S.	166	39.20 N	82.06 W
Athens, Pa., U.S.	166	41.57 N	76.31 W
Athens, Tenn., U.S.	172	35.27 N	84.36 W
Atherton	116	17.16 S	145.29 E
Athínai (Athens)	54	37.58 N	23.43 E
Athol	166	42.36 N	72.14 W
Áthos ∧	54	40.09 N	24.19 E
Ath-Thālith, Ash-Shallāl ⌊	102	19.49 N	30.19 E
Atkins	174	35.14 N	92.56 W
Atlanta, Ga., U.S.	172	33.45 N	84.23 W
Atlanta, Tex., U.S.	174	33.07 N	94.10 W
Atlantic	174	41.24 N	95.01 W
Atlantic City	166	39.22 N	74.26 W
Atlas Mountains ⋀	100	33.00 N	2.00 W
Atlas Saharien ⋀	100	33.25 N	1.20 E
Atlas Tellien ⋀	100	36.00 N	3.00 E
Atmore	174	31.02 N	87.29 W
Atrak (Atrek) ≃	84	37.28 N	53.57 E
Ätran ≃	28	56.53 N	12.30 E
Atrato ≃	144	8.17 N	76.58 W
Atrek (Atrak) ≃	84	37.28 N	53.57 E
Aṭ-Ṭā'if	84	21.16 N	40.24 E
Attalla	174	34.01 N	86.05 W
Attawapiskat ≃	160	52.57 N	82.18 W
Attica	174	40.17 N	87.15 W
Attikí ◆[1]	54	38.00 N	23.30 E
Attleboro	166	41.56 N	71.17 W
Attow, Ben ∧	32	57.14 N	5.17 W
Atuel ≃	146	36.17 S	66.50 W
Atwater	184	37.21 N	120.36 W
Auasberge ⋀	104	22.45 S	17.22 E
Aubagne	42	43.17 N	5.34 E
Aubrac ⋀	42	44.40 N	3.00 E
Auburn, Ala., U.S.	174	32.36 N	85.29 W
Auburn, Calif., U.S.	184	38.54 N	121.04 W
Auburn, Ind., U.S.	174	41.22 N	85.04 W
Auburn, Maine, U.S.	166	44.06 N	70.14 W
Auburn, Mass., U.S.	166	42.12 N	71.50 W
Auburn, Nebr., U.S.	174	40.23 N	95.51 W
Auburn, N.Y., U.S.	166	42.56 N	76.34 W
Auburn, Wash., U.S.	180	47.18 N	122.13 W
Auburn Heights	166	42.41 N	83.15 W
Aubusson	42	45.57 N	2.11 E
Auch	42	43.39 N	0.35 E
Auckland	118	36.52 S	174.46 E
Aude ≃	42	43.13 N	3.14 E
Audincourt	42	47.29 N	6.50 E
Audubon	174	41.43 N	94.55 W
Aue	36	50.35 N	12.42 E
Auerbach	36	50.41 N	12.54 E
Augsburg	36	48.23 N	10.53 E
Augusta, It.	46	37.13 N	15.13 E
Augusta, Ark., U.S.	174	35.17 N	91.22 W
Augusta, Ga., U.S.	172	33.29 N	81.57 W
Augusta, Maine, U.S.	166	44.19 N	69.47 W
Augusta, Golfo di C	46	37.10 N	15.20 E
Augustów	36	53.51 N	22.59 E
Auki	114	8.46 S	160.42 E
Aulne ≃	42	48.17 N	4.16 W
Auob ≃	104	26.25 S	20.35 E
Aurich	36	53.28 N	7.29 E
Aurillac	42	44.56 N	2.26 E
Aurora, Colo., U.S.	178	39.44 N	104.52 W
Aurora, Ill., U.S.	168	42.46 N	88.19 W
Aurora, Ind., U.S.	174	39.04 N	84.54 W
Aurora, Minn., U.S.	168	47.31 N	92.14 W
Aurora, Mo., U.S.	174	36.58 N	93.43 W
Aurora, Ohio, U.S.	166	41.19 N	81.21 W
Austin, Ind., U.S.	174	38.45 N	85.48 W
Austin, Minn., U.S.	168	43.40 N	92.59 W
Austin, Tex., U.S.	162	30.16 N	97.45 W
Austintown	166	41.06 N	80.46 W
Australia □[1]	116	25.00 S	135.00 E
Austria (Österreich) □[1]	36	47.20 N	13.20 E
Austvågøya I	26	68.20 N	14.36 E
Autoua	112	16.21 S	167.45 E
Autun	42	46.57 N	4.18 E
Auvézère ≃	42	45.12 N	0.51 E
Aux Barques, Pointe ≻	168	44.04 N	82.58 W
Auxerre	42	47.48 N	3.34 E
Auyán Tepuy ∧	144	5.55 N	62.32 W
Auzangate, Nevado ∧	144	13.48 S	71.14 W
Ava	174	36.57 N	92.40 W
Avaloirs, Les ∧[2]	42	48.28 N	0.07 W
Avana ≃	114	21.14 S	159.43 W
Avarua	114	21.12 S	159.46 W
Avatiu	114	21.12 S	159.47 W
Avatiu Harbour C	114	21.11 S	159.47 W
Ave ≃	50	41.20 N	8.45 W
Aveiro	50	40.38 N	8.39 W
Avellaneda	146	34.39 S	58.23 W
Avellino	46	40.54 N	14.47 E
Aven Armand •[5]	42	44.15 N	3.22 E
Aversa	46	40.58 N	14.12 E
Avery	184	33.33 N	94.47 W
Aves, Islas de II	144	12.00 N	67.30 W
Avesta	28	60.09 N	16.12 E
Aveyron ≃	42	44.05 N	1.16 E
Avezzano	46	42.02 N	13.25 E
Avignon	42	43.57 N	4.49 E
Ávila	50	40.39 N	4.42 W
Avilés	50	43.33 N	5.55 W
Avola	46	36.54 N	15.09 E
Avon	166	42.55 N	77.45 W
Avon □[6]	32	51.30 N	2.40 W
Avon ≃	32	50.43 N	1.46 W
Avondale	178	33.26 N	112.21 W
Avon Lake	166	41.30 N	82.01 W
Avon Park	172	27.36 N	81.31 W
Avranches	42	48.41 N	1.22 W
Awash ≃	102	11.45 N	41.05 E
Awe, Loch ⊜	32	56.15 N	5.15 W
Axiós (Vardar) ≃	54	40.31 N	22.43 E
Ayacucho	144	13.07 S	74.13 W
Ayamonte	50	37.13 N	7.24 W
Ayden	172	35.25 N	77.20 W
Aydın	54	37.51 N	27.51 E
Aydın Dağları ⋀	54	38.00 N	28.00 E
Ayer	166	42.34 N	71.35 W
Ayers Rock ∧	116	25.23 S	131.05 E
Áyion Óros ≻[1]	54	40.15 N	24.15 E
Áyios Nikólaos	54	35.11 N	25.42 E
Ayíou Órous, Kólpos C	54	40.12 N	24.03 E
Aylesbury	32	51.18 N	0.29 E
'Ayoûn el 'Atroûs	100	16.40 N	9.37 W
Ayr	32	55.28 N	4.38 W
Ayre, Point of ≻	32	54.26 N	4.22 W
Ayrolle, Étang de l' ⊜	42	43.05 N	3.03 E
Ayvalık	54	39.18 N	26.41 E
Azalea Park	172	28.32 N	81.15 W
Azaouak, Vallée de l' ∨	100	15.30 N	3.18 E
Azovskoje More ≂[2]	62	46.00 N	36.00 E
Aztec	178	36.49 N	107.59 W
Azuaga	50	38.16 N	5.41 W
Azuer ≃	50	39.08 N	3.36 W
Azuero, Península de ≻[1]	130	7.40 N	80.35 W
Azul	146	36.47 S	59.51 W
Azur, Côte d' •[2]	42	43.30 N	7.00 E
Aẓ-Ẓahrān (Dhahran)	84	26.18 N	50.08 E
Az-Zaqāzīq	102	30.35 N	31.31 E
Az-Zarqā'	84	32.05 N	36.06 E
Azzel Matti, Sebkha ≚	100	25.55 N	0.56 E
B			
Ba ≃	82	13.02 N	109.03 E
Baarn	36	52.13 N	5.16 E
Babaeski	54	41.26 N	27.06 E
Babbitt, Minn., U.S.	168	47.43 N	91.57 W
Babbitt, Nev., U.S.	184	38.39 N	118.37 W
Babelthuap I	82	7.30 N	134.36 E
Babine Lake ⊜	160	54.45 N	126.00 W
Babuyan Islands II	82	19.10 N	121.40 E
Bacabal	144	4.14 S	44.47 W
Bacău	54	46.34 N	26.55 E
Bačka ◆[1]	54	45.50 N	19.30 E
Bačka Palanka	54	45.15 N	19.24 E
Bačka Topola	54	45.49 N	19.38 E
Backnang	36	48.56 N	9.25 E
Bac-lieu (Vinh-loi)	82	9.17 N	105.44 E
Bacolod	82	10.40 N	122.57 E
Badajoz	50	38.53 N	6.58 W
Badalona	50	41.27 N	2.15 E
Bad Axe	168	43.48 N	83.00 W
Bad Doberan	36	54.06 N	11.53 E
Bad Dürkheim	36	49.28 N	8.10 E
Bad Ems	36	50.20 N	7.43 E
Baden, Öst.	36	48.00 N	16.14 E
Baden, Schw.	42	47.29 N	8.18 E
Baden-Baden	36	48.46 N	8.14 E
Bad Freienwalde	36	52.47 N	14.01 E
Bad Harzburg	36	51.53 N	10.33 E
Bad Hersfeld	36	50.52 N	9.42 E
Bad Homburg [vor der Höhe]	36	50.13 N	8.37 E
Bad Honnef	36	50.39 N	7.13 E
Bad Ischl	36	47.43 N	13.37 E
Bad Kissingen	36	50.12 N	10.04 E
Bad Kreuznach	36	49.52 N	7.51 E
Bad Langensalza	36	51.06 N	10.38 E
Bad Mergentheim	36	49.30 N	9.46 E
Bad Nauheim	36	50.22 N	8.44 E
Bad Oeynhausen	36	52.12 N	8.48 E
Bad Oldesloe	36	53.48 N	10.22 E
Bad Pyrmont	36	51.59 N	9.15 E
Bad Reichenhall	36	47.43 N	12.52 E
Bad Salzuflen	36	52.05 N	8.44 E
Bad Salzungen	36	50.48 N	10.13 E
Bad Schwartau	36	53.55 N	10.40 E
Bad Segeberg	36	53.56 N	10.17 E
Bad Tölz	36	47.46 N	11.34 E
Baena	50	37.37 N	4.19 W
Bafa Gölü ⊜	54	37.30 N	27.25 E
Bafatá	100	12.10 N	14.40 W
Baffin Bay C	160	73.00 N	66.00 W
Baffin Island I	160	68.00 N	70.00 W
Bafing ≃	100	13.49 N	10.50 W
Bagdad	178	34.34 N	113.11 W
Baghdād	84	33.21 N	44.25 E
Bagheria	46	38.05 N	13.30 E
Bagnara Cálabra	46	38.18 N	15.49 E
Bagnères-de-Bigorre	42	43.04 N	0.09 E
Bagnols-sur-Cèze	42	44.10 N	4.37 E
Baguio	82	16.25 N	120.36 E
Bagzane, Monts ⋀	100	17.43 N	8.45 E
Bahamas □[1]	130	24.15 N	76.00 W
Bahāwalpur	84	29.24 N	71.41 E
Bahía, Islas de la II	130	16.20 N	86.30 W
Bahía Blanca	146	38.43 S	62.17 W
Bahrain □[1]	84	26.00 N	50.30 E
Baia-Mare	54	47.40 N	23.35 E
Baidoa	102	3.04 N	43.48 E
Baie-Comeau	160	49.13 N	68.10 W
Baile Átha Cliath → Dublin	32	53.20 N	6.15 W
Bailén	50	38.06 N	3.46 W
Băilești	54	44.02 N	23.21 E
Bainbridge	172	30.54 N	84.34 W
Bairoil	180	42.15 N	107.33 W
Baïse ≃	42	44.07 N	0.17 E
Baja	36	46.11 N	18.57 E
Baja California ≻[1]	130	28.00 N	113.30 W
Bajdarackaja Guba C	62	69.00 N	67.30 E
Bajkal, Ozero (Lake Baykal) ⊜	64	53.00 N	107.40 E
Bajo Boquete	130	8.47 N	82.26 W
Baker, La., U.S.	174	30.35 N	91.10 W
Baker, Mont., U.S.	162	46.22 N	104.17 W
Baker, Oreg., U.S.	180	44.47 N	117.50 W
Baker, Mount ∧	180	48.47 N	121.49 W
Baker Lake	160	64.15 N	96.00 W
Baker Lake ⊜	160	64.10 N	95.30 W
Bakersfield	184	35.23 N	119.01 W
Bakony ⋀	36	46.55 N	17.40 E
Bakoye ≃	100	13.49 N	10.50 W
Baku	62	40.23 N	49.51 E
Bakwanga → Mbuji-Mayi	104	6.09 S	23.38 E
Balabac Strait ⋃	82	7.35 N	117.00 E
Balakovo	62	52.02 N	47.47 E
Balambangan, Pulau I	82	7.15 N	116.55 E
Balassagyarmat	36	48.05 N	19.18 E
Balaton ⊜	36	46.50 N	17.45 E
Balboa Heights	130	8.57 N	79.33 W
Balchaš, Ozero ⊜	62	46.00 N	74.00 E
Bald Knob	174	35.19 N	91.34 W
Bald Knob ∧	172	37.56 N	79.51 W
Baldwin, La., U.S.	174	29.51 N	91.33 W
Baldwin, Wis., U.S.	168	44.58 N	92.22 W
Baldwin City	174	38.47 N	95.11 W
Baldwinsville	166	43.09 N	76.20 W
Baldwyn	174	34.31 N	88.38 W
Baldy Peak ∧	178	33.55 N	109.35 W
Baleares □[4]	50	39.30 N	3.00 E
Baleares, Islas (Balearic Islands) II	50	39.30 N	3.00 E
Balearic Islands → Baleares, Islas II	50	39.30 N	3.00 E
Balen	36	51.10 N	5.09 E
Balfate	130	15.48 N	86.25 W
Bali I	82	8.20 S	115.00 E
Balıkesir	54	39.39 N	27.53 E
Balikpapan	82	1.17 S	116.50 E
Balingen	36	48.16 N	8.51 E
Balintang Channel ⋃	82	19.49 N	121.40 E
Balkan Mountains → Stara Planina ⋀	54	43.15 N	25.00 E
Ballarat	116	37.34 S	143.52 E
Ballston Spa	166	43.00 N	73.51 W
Ballymena	32	54.52 N	6.17 W
Balsas ≃	130	17.55 N	102.10 W
Baltic Sea ≂[2]	26	57.00 N	19.00 E
Baltijsk	26	54.39 N	19.55 E
Baltijskaja Kosa ≻[2]	36	54.25 N	19.35 E
Baltimore	166	39.17 N	76.37 W
Baluchistan □[9]	84	28.00 N	63.00 E
Bamako	100	12.39 N	8.00 W
Bambari	102	5.45 N	20.40 E
Bambatana	114	7.02 S	156.48 E
Bamberg, B.R.D.	36	49.53 N	10.53 E
Bamberg, S.C., U.S.	172	33.17 N	81.02 W
Bamenda	100	5.56 N	10.10 E
Bamingui ≃	102	8.33 N	19.05 E
Banana	104	6.01 S	12.24 E
Banana River C	172	28.25 N	80.38 W
Banās, Ra's ≻	102	23.54 N	35.48 E
Banat ◆[1]	54	45.20 N	20.40 E
Banbury	32	52.04 N	1.20 W
Bancroft → Chililabombwe	104	12.18 S	27.43 E
Banda, Laut (Banda Sea) ≂[2]	82	5.00 S	128.00 E
Bandama ≃	100	5.10 N	5.00 W
Bandama Blanc ≃	100	6.54 N	5.31 W
Bandama Rouge ≃	100	6.54 N	5.31 W
Bandar Seri Begawan	82	4.56 N	114.55 E
Bandeira, Pico da ∧	144	20.26 S	41.47 W
Bandırma	54	40.20 N	27.58 E
Bandundu	104	3.18 S	17.20 E
Bandung	82	6.54 S	107.36 E
Banes	130	20.58 N	75.43 W
Bangalore	84	12.58 N	77.36 E
Bangbu	80	32.58 N	117.24 E
Banggi, Pulau I	82	7.17 N	117.12 E
Banghāzī	102	32.07 N	20.04 E
Bangka I	82	2.15 S	106.00 E
Bangkok → Krung Thep	82	13.45 N	100.31 E
Bangladesh □[1]	84	24.00 N	90.00 E
Bangor, N. Ire., U.K.	32	54.40 N	5.40 W
Bangor, Wales, U.K.	32	53.13 N	4.08 W
Bangor, Maine, U.S.	166	44.49 N	68.47 W
Bangor, Mich., U.S.	168	42.18 N	86.07 W
Bangui	102	4.22 N	18.35 E
Bangweulu, Lake ⊜	104	11.05 S	29.45 E
Baní	130	18.17 N	70.20 W
Bani ≃	100	14.30 N	4.12 W
Banī Mazār	102	28.30 N	30.48 E
Banī Suwayf	102	29.05 N	31.05 E
Banja Luka	46	44.46 N	17.11 E
Banjarmasin	82	3.20 S	114.35 E
Banjul	100	13.28 N	16.39 W
Banks Island I, B.C., Can.	160	53.25 N	130.10 W
Banks Island I, N.W. Ter., Can.	160	73.15 N	121.30 W
Banks Islands II	112	13.50 S	167.30 E
Banks Lake ⊜[1]	180	47.45 N	119.15 W
Bann ≃	32	55.10 N	6.46 W
Banning	184	33.56 N	116.52 W
Bannu	84	32.59 N	70.36 E
Banská Bystrica	36	48.44 N	19.07 E
Banská Štiavnica	36	48.28 N	18.56 E
Baoding	80	38.52 N	115.29 E
Baoji	80	34.22 N	107.14 E
Baotou	80	40.40 N	109.59 E
Barabinskaja Step' ≚	64	55.00 N	79.00 E
Baraboo	168	43.28 N	89.45 W
Baracoa	130	20.21 N	74.30 W
Baram ≃	82	4.36 N	113.59 E
Barania Góra ∧	36	49.37 N	19.00 E
Baranoviči	62	53.08 N	26.02 E
Baraoltului, Munții ⋀	54	46.15 N	25.45 E
Baraque de Fraiture ∧	36	50.15 N	5.44 E
Baratang Island I	84	12.13 N	92.45 E
Barataria Bay C	174	29.22 N	89.57 W
Barat Daya, Kepulauan II	82	7.25 S	128.00 E
Barbacena	144	21.14 S	43.46 W
Barbados □[1]	130	13.10 N	59.32 W
Barbas, Cabo ≻	100	22.18 N	16.41 W
Barbastro	50	42.02 N	0.08 E
Barbate de Franco	50	36.12 N	5.55 W
Barberton	166	41.01 N	81.36 W
Barboursville	166	38.24 N	82.18 W
Barbourville	172	36.52 N	83.53 W
Barbuda I	130	17.38 N	61.48 W
Barcellona Pozzo di Gotto	46	38.09 N	15.13 E
Barcelona, Esp.	50	41.23 N	2.11 E
Barcelona, Ven.	144	10.08 N	64.42 W
Bardejov	36	49.18 N	21.16 E
Bárdenas Reales ⋀[1]	50	42.10 N	1.25 W
Bardsey Island I	32	52.45 N	4.45 W
Bardstown	174	37.49 N	85.28 W
Bareilly	84	28.20 N	79.25 E
Barents Sea (Barenc'ovo More) ≂[2]	26	69.00 N	40.00 E
Bar Harbor	166	44.23 N	68.13 W
Bari	46	41.07 N	16.52 E
Barīm I	84	12.40 N	43.25 E
Barinas	144	8.38 N	70.12 W
Barisāl	84	22.42 N	90.22 E
Barito ≃	82	3.32 S	114.29 E
Barka ∨	102	18.13 N	37.35 E
Barkley, Lake ⊜[1]	174	36.40 N	87.55 W
Barkley Sound ⋃	160	48.53 N	125.20 W
Bar-le-Duc	42	48.47 N	5.10 E
Barletta	46	41.19 N	16.17 E
Barnaul	64	53.22 N	83.45 E
Barnegat Bay C	166	39.52 N	74.07 W
Barnesville, Ga., U.S.	172	33.04 N	84.09 W
Barnesville, Ohio, U.S.	166	39.59 N	81.11 W

Name	Page	Lat	Long
Barnsley	32	53.34 N	1.28 W
Barnstaple	32	51.05 N	4.04 W
Barnwell	172	33.15 N	81.23 W
Baro	102	8.26 N	33.13 E
Baroda	84	25.30 N	76.40 E
Barotseland □⁹	104	16.00 S	24.00 E
Barqah (Cyrenaica) ◄¹	102	31.00 N	22.30 E
Barquisimeto	144	10.04 N	69.19 W
Barra, Ponta da ➤	104	23.47 S	35.32 E
Barra Falsa, Ponta da ➤	104	22.55 S	35.37 E
Barrafranca	46	37.23 N	14.13 E
Barra Mansa	144	22.32 S	44.11 W
Barrancabermeja	144	7.03 N	73.52 W
Barranquilla	144	10.59 N	74.48 W
Barre	104	19.49 S	34.52 E
Barre des Écrins ∧	42	44.55 N	6.22 E
Barreiro	50	38.40 N	9.04 W
Barren River Lake @¹	174	36.45 N	86.02 W
Barretos	144	20.33 S	48.33 W
Barron	168	45.24 N	91.51 W
Barrow	162a	71.17 N	156.47 W
Barrow, Point ➤	162a	71.23 N	156.30 W
Barrow-in-Furness	32	54.07 N	3.14 W
Barry	32	51.24 N	3.18 W
Barstow	184	34.54 N	117.01 W
Barth	36	54.22 N	12.43 E
Bartholomew, Bayou ≃	174	32.43 N	92.04 W
Bartlesville	162	36.45 N	95.59 W
Barton	166	44.45 N	72.11 W
Bartonville	168	40.39 N	89.39 W
Bartoszyce	36	54.16 N	20.49 E
Bartow	172	27.54 N	81.50 W
Barú, Volcán ∧¹	130	8.48 N	82.33 W
Barwon ≃	116	30.00 S	148.05 E
Barycz ≃	36	51.42 N	16.15 E
Basatongwulashan ∧	80	33.05 N	91.30 E
Bascuñán, Cabo ➤	146	28.51 S	71.30 W
Basel (Bâle)	42	47.33 N	7.35 E
Basento ≃	46	40.21 N	16.50 E
Başeu ≃	54	47.44 N	27.15 E
Bashi Channel ⋃	82	22.00 N	121.00 E
Basilan	82	6.42 N	121.58 E
Basildon	32	51.35 N	0.25 E
Basin	180	44.23 N	108.02 W
Basingstoke	32	51.15 N	1.05 W
Bassano del Grappa	46	45.46 N	11.44 E
Bassas da India ☊²	104	21.25 S	39.42 E
Bassein	84	16.47 N	94.44 E
Basse-Terre, Guad.	130	16.00 N	61.44 W
Basseterre, St. K.-N.	130	17.18 N	62.43 W
Bassett	172	36.46 N	79.59 W
Bass Strait ⋃	116	39.20 S	145.30 E
Bastia	42	42.42 N	9.27 E
Bastrop	100	32.47 N	91.55 W
Bata	100	1.51 N	9.45 E
Batabanó, Golfo de C	130	22.15 N	82.30 W
Batajsk	62	47.10 N	39.44 E
Batak, Jazovir @¹	54	41.59 N	24.11 E
Batangas	82	13.45 N	121.03 E
Batanghari ≃	82	1.16 S	104.05 E
Batavia, Ill., U.S.	168	41.51 N	88.19 W
Batavia, N.Y., U.S.	166	43.00 N	78.11 W
Bătdâmbâng	82	13.06 N	103.12 E
Bates, Mount ∧	113	29.01 S	167.56 E
Batesburg	172	33.54 N	81.33 W
Batesville, Ark., U.S.	174	35.46 N	91.39 W
Batesville, Ind., U.S.	174	39.18 N	85.13 W
Batesville, Miss., U.S.	174	34.18 N	90.00 W
Bath, Eng., U.K.	32	51.23 N	2.22 W
Bath, Maine, U.S.	166	43.55 N	69.49 W
Bath, N.Y., U.S.	166	42.20 N	77.19 W
Bathgate	32	55.55 N	3.39 W
Bathurst	116	33.25 S	149.35 E
Bathurst Inlet	160	66.50 N	108.01 W
Bathurst Island I, Austl.	116	11.37 S	130.27 E
Bathurst Island I, N.W. Ter., Can.	160	76.00 N	100.30 W
Batna	100	35.34 N	6.11 E
Baton Rouge	174	30.23 N	91.11 W
Batson	184	30.15 N	94.37 W
Battle	160	52.42 N	108.15 W
Battle Creek	168	42.19 N	85.11 W
Battle Ground	180	45.47 N	122.32 W
Battle Mountain	184	40.38 N	116.56 W
Batu ∧	102	6.55 N	39.46 E
Batu Pahat	82	1.51 N	102.56 E
Bauchi	100	10.19 N	9.50 E
Baudette	168	48.43 N	94.36 W
Bauru	144	22.19 S	49.04 W
Bautzen	36	51.11 N	14.26 E
Baxley	172	31.47 N	82.21 W
Baxter Springs	174	37.02 N	94.44 W
Bayamo	130	20.23 N	76.39 W
Bayard	172	32.46 N	108.08 W
Bay City, Mich., U.S.	168	43.36 N	83.53 W
Bay City, Tex., U.S.	174	28.59 N	95.58 W
Bayeux	42	49.16 N	0.42 W
Bayfield	172	37.14 N	107.36 W
Bayındır	54	38.13 N	27.40 E
Bay Minette	174	30.53 N	87.47 W
Bayonne	42	43.29 N	1.29 W
Bayou D'Arbonne Lake @¹	174	32.45 N	92.25 W
Bayou La Batre	174	30.24 N	88.15 W
Bayport	168	45.01 N	92.47 W
Bayreuth	36	49.57 N	11.35 E
Bayrūt	84	33.53 N	35.30 E
Bay Saint Louis	174	30.19 N	89.20 W
Bay Shore	166	40.43 N	73.15 W
Baytown	174	29.44 N	94.58 W
Baza	50	37.29 N	2.46 W
Bazaruto, Ilha do I	104	21.40 S	35.28 E
Beachy Head ➤	32	50.44 N	0.16 E
Beacon	166	41.30 N	73.58 W
Beacon Hill ∧	180	46.08 N	122.57 W
Bear ≃	178	40.11 N	112.08 W
Beardstown	174	40.01 N	90.26 W
Bear Lake @	178	42.00 N	111.20 W
Béarn □⁹	42	43.20 N	0.45 W
Bear Tooth Pass)(	180	44.58 N	109.28 W
Beata, Isla I	130	17.35 N	71.31 W
Beatrice	162	40.16 N	96.44 W
Beaucaire	42	43.48 N	4.38 E
Beauce ◄¹	42	48.22 N	1.50 E
Beaufort, N.C., U.S.	172	34.43 N	76.40 W
Beaufort, S.C., U.S.	172	32.26 N	80.40 W
Beaufort Sea ▽²	162	73.00 N	140.00 W
Beaufort West	104	32.18 S	22.36 E
Beaujolais, Monts du ∧	42	46.00 N	4.30 E
Beaumont	174	30.05 N	94.06 W
Beaune	42	47.02 N	4.50 E
Beauvais	42	49.26 N	2.05 E
Beaver ≃	166	40.42 N	80.18 W
Beaver ≃	160	59.43 N	124.16 W
Beaver Creek ≃	160	59.43 N	103.59 W
Beaver Dam, Ky., U.S.	174	37.24 N	86.52 W
Beaver Dam, Wis., U.S.	168	43.28 N	88.50 W
Beaver Falls	166	40.46 N	80.19 W
Beaverhead ≃	180	45.31 N	112.21 W
Beaverhead Mountains ∧	180	45.00 N	113.20 W
Beaver Island I	168	45.40 N	85.31 W
Beaver Lake @¹	174	36.20 N	93.55 W
Beaverton	180	45.29 N	122.48 W
Bečej	54	45.37 N	20.03 E
Béchar	100	31.37 N	2.13 W
Beckley	166	37.46 N	81.13 W
Beckum	36	51.45 N	8.02 E
Beckville	184	32.14 N	94.27 W
Bedford, Eng., U.K.	32	52.08 N	0.29 W
Bedford, Ind., U.S.	174	38.52 N	86.29 W
Bedford, Iowa, U.S.	174	40.40 N	94.44 W
Bedford, Pa., U.S.	166	40.01 N	78.30 W
Bedford, Va., U.S.	172	37.20 N	79.31 W
Bedfordshire □⁶	32	52.05 N	0.30 W
Beebe	174	35.04 N	91.53 W
Beech Grove	174	39.43 N	86.03 W
Be'er Sheva'	84	31.15 N	34.47 E
Beeville	162	28.24 N	97.45 W
Bega (Begej) ≃	54	45.13 N	20.19 E
Begej (Bega) ≃	54	45.13 N	20.19 E
Beian	80	48.15 N	126.30 E
Beihai	80	21.29 N	109.05 E
Beijing (Peking)	80	39.55 N	116.25 E
Beira	104	19.49 S	34.52 E
Beira Baixa □⁹	50	39.45 N	7.30 W
Beira Litoral □⁹	50	40.15 N	8.25 W
Beirut → Bayrūt	84	33.53 N	35.30 E
Beja, Port.	50	38.01 N	7.52 W
Beja, Tun.	100	36.44 N	9.11 E
Bejaïa	100	36.45 N	5.05 E
Bejaïa, Golfe de C	50	36.45 N	5.25 E
Béjar	50	40.23 N	5.46 W
Békés	54	46.46 N	21.08 E
Békéscsaba	36	46.41 N	21.06 E
Bela Crkva	54	44.54 N	21.26 E
Bel Air	166	39.32 N	76.21 W
Belaja ≃	62	56.00 N	54.32 E
Belaja Cerkov'	62	49.49 N	30.07 E
Belcher Islands II	160	56.20 N	79.30 W
Bel'cy	62	47.46 N	27.56 E
Belding	168	43.06 N	85.14 W
Beled Weyne	102	4.47 N	45.12 E
Belém	144	1.27 S	48.29 W
Belen	178	34.40 N	106.46 W
Belfast, N. Ire., U.K.	32	54.35 N	5.55 W
Belfast, Maine, U.S.	166	44.27 N	69.01 W
Belfast Lough C	32	54.40 N	5.50 W
Belfort	42	47.38 N	6.52 E
Belgaum	84	15.52 N	74.31 E
Belgium □¹	36	50.50 N	4.00 E
Belgorod	62	50.36 N	36.35 E
Belgrade → Beograd	54	44.50 N	20.30 E
Belhaven	172	35.33 N	76.37 W
Beli Drim ≃	54	42.06 N	20.25 E
Belize	130	17.30 N	88.12 W
Belize □²	130	17.15 N	88.45 W
Bell ≃	160	49.48 N	77.38 W
Bellaire	166	40.02 N	80.45 W
Bellaire, Tex., U.S.	174	29.43 N	95.03 W
Belledonne, Chaîne de ∧	42	45.18 N	6.08 E
Bellefontaine	166	40.22 N	83.46 W
Bellefonte	166	40.55 N	77.46 W
Belle Fourche	162	44.40 N	103.51 W
Belle Glade	172	26.41 N	80.40 W
Belle-Île I	42	47.20 N	3.10 W
Belle Isle I	160	51.55 N	55.20 W
Belle Plaine, Iowa, U.S.	168	41.54 N	92.17 W
Belle Plaine, Minn., U.S.	168	44.37 N	93.46 W
Belleview	172	29.04 N	82.03 W
Belleville, Ill., U.S.	174	38.31 N	90.00 W
Belleville, Kans., U.S.	162	39.49 N	97.38 W
Bellevue, Iowa, U.S.	168	42.16 N	90.26 W
Bellevue, Nebr., U.S.	174	41.09 N	95.54 W
Bellevue, Ohio, U.S.	166	41.17 N	82.50 W
Bellevue, Wash., U.S.	180	47.37 N	122.12 W
Bellingham	168	48.49 N	122.29 W
Bellingshausen Sea ▽²	191	71.00 S	85.00 W
Bellinzona	46	46.11 N	9.02 E
Bello	144	6.20 N	75.33 W
Bellows Falls	166	43.08 N	72.27 W
Belluno	46	46.09 N	12.13 E
Belmond	168	42.51 N	93.37 W
Belmont	172	34.02 N	81.01 W
Belmopan	130	17.15 N	88.46 W
Belo Horizonte	144	19.55 S	43.56 W
Beloit	168	42.31 N	89.02 W
Beloje, Ozero @	62	60.11 N	37.37 E
Beloje More (White Sea) ▽²	62	65.30 N	38.00 E
Belomorsko-Baltijskij Kanal ☰	62	62.48 N	34.48 E
Belovo	64	54.25 N	86.18 E
Belper	32	53.01 N	1.29 W
Belton, Mo., U.S.	166	38.49 N	94.32 W
Belton, S.C., U.S.	172	34.31 N	82.30 W
Belucha, Gora ∧	64	49.48 N	86.40 E
Belvidere	168	42.15 N	88.50 W
Belzoni	174	33.11 N	90.29 W
Bemidji	168	47.29 N	94.53 W
Benares → Vārānasi	84	25.20 N	83.00 E
Benavente	50	42.00 N	5.41 W
Bend	180	44.03 N	121.19 W
Bendigo	116	36.46 S	144.17 E
Bendorf	36	50.25 N	7.34 E
Benevento	46	41.08 N	14.45 E
Benguela	104	12.35 S	13.25 E
Benguérua, Ilha I	104	21.58 S	35.28 E
Beni ≃	144	10.23 S	65.24 W
Benicarló	50	40.25 N	0.26 E
Beni-Mellal	100	32.22 N	6.29 W
Benin □¹	100	9.30 N	2.15 E
Benin, Bight of C³	100	5.30 N	3.00 E
Benin City	100	6.19 N	5.41 E
Beni Saf	100	35.19 N	1.23 W
Benmore, Lake @¹	118	44.25 S	170.15 E
Bennettsville	172	34.37 N	79.41 W
Bennington	166	42.53 N	73.12 W
Benoni	104	26.19 S	28.27 E
Bensheim	36	49.41 N	8.37 E
Benson, Ariz., U.S.	178	31.58 N	110.18 W
Benson, N.C., U.S.	172	35.23 N	78.33 W
Benton	174	34.34 N	92.35 W
Benton City	180	46.16 N	119.29 W
Benton Harbor	168	42.06 N	86.27 W
Bentonville	174	36.22 N	94.13 W
Benue (Bénoué) ≃	100	7.48 N	6.46 E
Benxi	80	41.18 N	123.45 E
Beograd (Belgrade)	54	44.50 N	20.30 E
Beppu	80	33.17 N	131.30 E
Berat	54	40.42 N	19.57 E
Berbera	102	10.25 N	45.02 E
Berbérati	100	4.16 N	15.47 E
Berbice ≃	144	6.17 N	57.32 W
Berd'ansk	62	46.45 N	36.49 E
Berea, Ky., U.S.	174	37.34 N	84.17 W
Berea, Ohio, U.S.	166	41.22 N	81.52 W
Berea, S.C., U.S.	172	34.53 N	82.28 W
Berens ≃	160	52.21 N	97.02 W
Beretău ≃	54	47.10 N	21.07 E
Berettyó (Beretţyó) ≃	54	46.59 N	21.07 E
Berettyóújfalu	36	47.14 N	21.32 E
Berezniki	62	59.24 N	56.46 E
Bergama	54	39.07 N	27.11 E
Bergamo	46	45.41 N	9.43 E
Bergen	28	60.23 N	5.20 E
Bergen [auf Rügen]	36	54.25 N	13.26 E
Bergen op Zoom	36	51.30 N	4.17 E
Bergerac	42	44.51 N	0.29 E
Bergisch Gladbach	36	50.59 N	7.07 E
Bergslagen ◄¹	28	59.55 N	15.00 E
Bering Sea ▽²	162a	59.00 N	174.00 W
Bering Strait ⋃	162a	65.30 N	169.00 W
Berkane	50	34.59 N	2.20 W
Berkeley	184	37.57 N	122.18 W
Berkner Island I	191	79.30 S	49.30 W
Berkshire □⁶	32	51.30 N	1.20 W
Berkshire Hills ∧²	166	42.20 N	73.10 W
Berlenga I	50	39.25 N	9.30 W
Berlin (West), B.R.D.	36	52.31 N	13.24 E
Berlin (Ost), D.D.R.	36	52.30 N	13.25 E
Berlin, Md., U.S.	166	38.19 N	75.13 W
Berlin, N.H., U.S.	166	44.29 N	71.10 W
Berlin, N.J., U.S.	166	39.47 N	74.57 W
Berlin, Wis., U.S.	168	43.58 N	88.55 W
Bermejo ≃, Arg.	146	31.52 S	67.22 W
Bermejo ≃, S.A.	146	26.51 S	58.23 W
Bermen, Lac @	160	53.35 N	68.55 W
Bermeo	50	43.26 N	2.43 W
Bermuda □²	130	32.20 N	64.45 W
Bern (Berne)	42	46.57 N	7.26 E
Berne → Bern	42	46.57 N	7.26 E
Bernalda	46	40.24 N	16.41 E
Bernau bei Berlin	36	52.40 N	13.35 E
Bernay	42	49.06 N	0.36 E
Bernburg	36	51.48 N	11.44 E
Berne	174	40.39 N	84.57 W
Berner Alpen ∧	42	46.30 N	7.30 E
Bernie	174	36.40 N	89.58 W
Bernina, Piz ∧	42	46.21 N	9.51 E
Beroun	36	49.58 N	14.04 E
Berounka ≃	36	50.00 N	14.24 E
Berre, Étang de C	42	43.27 N	5.08 E
Berryessa, Lake @¹	184	38.37 N	122.14 W
Berryville	174	36.22 N	93.34 W
Berthoud	178	40.18 N	105.05 W
Berthoud Pass)(	178	39.45 N	105.45 W
Bertrand	174	41.46 N	86.16 W
Berwick, La., U.S.	174	29.42 N	91.13 W
Berwick, Maine, U.S.	166	43.16 N	70.51 W
Berwick, Pa., U.S.	166	41.03 N	76.15 W
Berwick-upon-Tweed	32	55.46 N	2.00 W
Berwyn	168	41.50 N	87.47 W
Besançon	42	47.15 N	6.02 E
Beskid Mountains ∧	36	49.40 N	20.00 E
Bessemer, Ala., U.S.	174	33.25 N	86.57 W
Bessemer, Mich., U.S.	168	46.27 N	90.02 W
Bessemer City	172	35.17 N	81.17 W
Bethalto	174	38.55 N	90.03 W
Bethany, Mo., U.S.	174	40.16 N	94.02 W
Bethel, Alaska, U.S.	162a	60.48 N	161.46 W
Bethel, Conn., U.S.	166	41.22 N	73.25 W
Bethesda	166	38.59 N	77.06 W
Bethlehem, S. Afr.	104	28.15 S	28.15 E
Bethlehem, Pa., U.S.	166	40.37 N	75.25 W
Bethlehem, W. Va., U.S.	166	40.02 N	80.40 W
Béthune	42	50.32 N	2.38 E
Beticos, Sistemas ∧	50	37.00 N	4.00 W
Betpak-Dala ◄²	64	46.00 N	70.00 E
Betsiboka ≃	104	16.03 S	46.36 E
Bette ∧	102	22.00 N	19.12 E
Bettendorf	168	41.32 N	90.30 W
Betzdorf	36	50.47 N	7.53 E
B. Everett Jordan Lake @¹	172	35.45 N	79.00 W
Beverley	32	53.52 N	0.26 W
Beverly	166	42.33 N	70.53 W
Beverly Hills	184	34.03 N	118.26 W
Beverwijk	36	52.28 N	4.40 E
Bexhill	32	50.50 N	0.29 E
Bexley	166	39.58 N	82.56 W
Beykoz	54	41.08 N	29.05 E
Béziers	42	43.21 N	3.15 E
Bhāgalpur	84	25.15 N	86.58 E
Bhaunagar	84	21.47 N	72.09 E
Bhopāl	84	23.15 N	77.25 E
Bhutan □¹	84	27.30 N	90.30 E
Bia, Phou ∧	82	18.59 N	103.09 E
Biafra, Bight of C³	100	4.00 N	8.00 E
Biała ≃	36	50.03 N	20.55 E
Biała Podlaska	36	52.02 N	23.06 E
Białogard	36	54.01 N	16.00 E
Białystok	36	53.09 N	23.09 E
Biarritz	42	43.29 N	1.34 W
Biberach an der Riss	36	48.06 N	9.47 E
Bicaz	54	46.54 N	26.05 E
Bicknell	174	38.47 N	87.19 W
Bida	100	9.05 N	6.01 E
Biddeford	166	43.30 N	70.26 W
Bideford	32	51.01 N	4.13 W
Bié	104	12.22 S	16.56 E
Biebrza ≃	36	53.37 N	22.56 E
Biel (Bienne)	42	47.10 N	7.12 E
Bielawa	36	50.41 N	16.38 E
Bielefeld	36	52.01 N	8.31 E
Bielersee @	42	47.05 N	7.10 E
Biella	46	45.34 N	8.03 E
Bielsko-Biała	36	49.49 N	19.02 E
Bielsk Podlaski	36	52.47 N	23.12 E
Bien-hoa	82	10.57 N	106.49 E
Bienne → Biel	42	47.10 N	7.12 E
Bietigheim	36	48.58 N	9.07 E
Biga	54	40.13 N	27.14 E
Big Bay De Noc C	168	45.46 N	86.43 W
Big Black ≃	174	32.00 N	91.05 W
Big Cypress Swamp ⌶	172	26.10 N	81.38 W
Big Falls	168	48.12 N	93.48 W
Big Fork ≃	168	48.31 N	93.43 W
Bighorn ≃	180	46.09 N	107.28 W
Big Horn Lake @¹	180	45.06 N	108.08 W
Bighorn Mountains ∧	180	44.00 N	107.30 W
Big Lake	178	31.12 N	101.28 W
Big Rapids	168	43.42 N	85.29 W
Big Spring	162	32.15 N	101.28 W
Big Spruce Knob ∧	166	38.16 N	80.12 W
Big Stone Gap	172	36.52 N	82.47 W
Big Sunflower ≃	174	32.40 N	90.40 W
Big Timber	180	45.50 N	109.57 W
Bihać	46	44.49 N	15.52 E
Bijagós, Arquipélago dos II	100	11.25 N	16.20 W
Bijeljina	54	44.45 N	19.13 E
Bijsk	64	52.34 N	85.15 E
Bīkaner	84	28.01 N	73.18 E
Bilāspur	84	22.05 N	82.08 E
Bilbao	50	43.15 N	2.58 W
Bilecik	54	40.09 N	29.59 E
Bili ≃	102	4.16 N	15.47 E
Bilina ≃	36	50.35 N	13.45 E
Billings	180	45.47 N	108.27 W
Billings Heights	180	45.50 N	108.33 W
Biloela	116	24.24 S	150.30 E
Biloxi	174	30.24 N	88.53 W
Biluguun Island I	82	16.24 N	97.32 E
Binche	36	50.25 N	4.10 E
Binga, Monte ∧	104	19.45 S	33.04 E
Bingen	36	49.58 N	7.54 E
Binghamton	166	42.06 N	75.54 W
Bingöl	84	38.53 N	40.30 E
Binzert (Bizerte)	100	37.17 N	9.52 E
Biobío ≃	146	36.49 S	73.10 W
Bioko I	100	3.30 N	8.40 E
Birao	102	10.17 N	22.47 E
Birch Mountains ∧²	160	57.30 N	112.15 W
Bird Island I	172	35.00 N	80.05 W
Birkenhead	32	53.24 N	3.02 W
Bīrlad	54	46.14 N	27.40 E
Bīrlad ≃	54	45.36 N	27.31 E
Birmingham, Eng., U.K.	32	52.30 N	1.50 W
Birmingham, Ala., U.S.	174	33.31 N	86.49 W
Birmingham, Mich., U.S.	168	42.33 N	83.15 W
Bîrzava ≃	54	45.16 N	20.49 E
Birżebbuġa	46	35.49 N	14.32 E
Bisbee	178	31.27 N	109.55 W
Biscarosse, Étang de @	42	44.20 N	1.10 E
Biscay, Bay of C	42	44.00 N	4.00 W
Biscayne Bay C	172	25.33 N	80.15 W
Bisceglie	46	41.14 N	16.31 E
Bischofswerda	36	51.07 N	14.10 E
Bishārah, Ma'tan ▼⁴	102	22.58 N	22.39 E
Bishop Auckland	32	54.40 N	1.40 W
Bishop's Stortford	32	51.53 N	0.09 E
Bishopville	172	34.13 N	80.15 W
Biskra	100	34.51 N	5.44 E
Bismarck	162	46.48 N	100.47 W
Bismarck Archipelago II	116a	5.00 S	150.00 E
Bismarck Range ∧	116a	5.30 S	144.45 E
Bissau	100	11.51 N	15.35 W
Bistcho Lake @	160	59.40 N	118.40 W
Bistriţa	54	47.08 N	24.30 E
Bitola	54	41.01 N	21.20 E
Bitonto	46	41.06 N	16.42 E
Bitterfeld	36	51.37 N	12.20 E
Bitterroot Range ∧	180	47.06 N	115.10 W
Bivins	184	33.01 N	94.12 W
Biwa-ko @	80	35.15 N	136.05 E
Bizerte, Lac de @	46	37.12 N	9.52 E
Bjala Slatina	54	43.28 N	23.56 E
Bjelovar	46	45.54 N	16.51 E
Black (Da) ≃, As.	82	21.15 N	105.20 E
Black ≃, La., U.S.	174	31.16 N	91.50 W
Black ≃, N.Y., U.S.	166	43.59 N	76.04 W
Black ≃, Wis., U.S.	168	43.57 N	91.22 W
Blackburn	32	53.45 N	2.29 W
Black Diamond	180	47.18 N	122.00 W
Blackfoot	180	43.11 N	112.20 W
Blackfoot Reservoir @¹	180	42.55 N	111.35 W
Black Hills ∧	162	44.00 N	104.00 W
Black Lake @	166	44.31 N	75.35 W
Black Mountain	172	35.37 N	82.19 W
Black Mountain ∧	172	36.54 N	82.54 W
Blackpool	32	53.50 N	3.03 W
Black River Falls	168	44.23 N	90.52 W
Black Rock II¹	146	53.39 S	41.48 W
Black Rock Desert ▼²	184	41.10 N	119.00 W
Blacksburg	172	37.14 N	80.25 W
Black Sea ▽²	20	43.00 N	35.00 E
Blacks Fork ≃	178	41.24 N	109.38 W
Blackshear	172	31.18 N	82.14 W
Blackstone	172	37.04 N	78.00 W
Blackstone ≃	166	41.51 N	71.22 W
Blackville	172	33.22 N	81.16 W
Black Volta (Volta Noire) ≃	100	8.41 N	1.33 W
Blagoevgrad	54	42.01 N	23.06 E
Blagoveščensk	64	50.17 N	127.32 E
Blaine, Minn., U.S.	168	45.11 N	93.14 W
Blaine, Wash., U.S.	180	48.59 N	122.44 W
Blairsville	166	40.26 N	79.16 W
Blakely	172	31.23 N	84.56 W
Blanc, Cap ➤, Afr.	100	20.46 N	17.03 W
Blanc, Cap ➤, Tun.	46	37.20 N	9.51 E
Blanc, Mont (Monte Bianco) ∧	42	45.50 N	6.52 E
Blanca	178	37.27 N	105.31 W
Blanca, Bahía C	146	38.55 S	62.10 W
Blanca Peak ∧	178	37.35 N	105.29 W
Blanco, Cape ➤	180	42.50 N	124.34 W
Blanding	178	37.37 N	109.29 W
Blankenburg	36	51.48 N	10.58 E
Blanquilla, Isla I	144	11.51 N	64.37 W
Blansko	36	49.22 N	16.39 E
Blantyre	104	15.47 S	35.00 E
Blasdell	166	42.47 N	78.49 W
Blenheim	118	41.31 S	173.57 E
Bletchley	32	52.00 N	0.46 W
Bleus, Monts ∧, Afr.	102	1.30 N	30.30 E
Bleus, Monts ∧, Zaïre	104	4.31 S	21.02 E
Blida	100	36.28 N	2.50 E
Blissfield	168	41.50 N	83.52 W
Block Island I	166	41.11 N	71.35 W
Bloemfontein	104	29.12 S	26.07 E
Blois	42	47.35 N	1.20 E
Bloody Foreland ➤	32	55.09 N	8.17 W
Bloomer	168	45.07 N	91.29 W
Bloomfield, Ind., U.S.	174	39.01 N	86.56 W
Bloomfield, Iowa, U.S.	168	40.45 N	92.25 W
Bloomfield, Mo., U.S.	174	36.53 N	89.56 W
Bloomfield, N. Mex., U.S.	178	36.43 N	107.59 W
Blooming Prairie	168	43.52 N	93.03 W
Bloomington, Ill., U.S.	168	40.28 N	88.60 W
Bloomington, Ind., U.S.	174	39.10 N	86.32 W
Bloomington, Minn., U.S.	168	44.50 N	93.17 W
Bloomsburg	166	41.00 N	76.27 W
Blossom	184	33.40 N	95.23 W
Blouberg ∧	104	23.01 S	28.59 E
Bludenz	36	47.09 N	9.49 E
Blue Earth	168	43.38 N	94.06 W
Bluefield, Va., U.S.	172	37.15 N	81.17 W
Bluefield, W. Va., U.S.	172	37.16 N	81.13 W
Bluefields	130	12.00 N	83.45 W
Blue Island	168	41.40 N	87.41 W
Blue Mesa Reservoir @¹	178	38.27 N	107.10 W
Blue Mound	184	32.51 N	97.20 W
Blue Mountain ∧	174	34.41 N	94.03 W
Blue Mountain Peak ∧	130	18.03 N	76.35 W
Blue Mountains ∧	180	45.30 N	118.15 W
Blue Nile (Abay) ≃	102	15.38 N	32.31 E
Blue Ridge ∧	162	37.00 N	82.00 W
Bluff Park	174	33.27 N	86.47 W
Bluffton, Ind., U.S.	174	40.44 N	85.11 W
Bluffton, Ohio, U.S.	166	40.54 N	83.54 W
Blyth	32	55.07 N	1.30 W
Blythe	178	33.37 N	114.36 W
Blytheville	174	35.56 N	89.55 W
Bo	100	7.56 N	11.21 W
Boardman	166	41.02 N	80.40 W
Boa Vista I	144	2.49 N	60.40 W
Boaz	174	34.12 N	86.10 W
Böblingen	36	48.41 N	9.01 E
Bobo Dioulasso	100	11.12 N	4.18 W
Bóbr ≃	36	52.04 N	15.04 E
Bobruisk	62	53.09 N	29.14 E
Boby, Pic ∧	104	22.12 S	46.55 E
Boca Raton	172	26.21 N	80.05 W
Bocas del Toro	130	9.20 N	82.15 W
Bochnia	36	49.58 N	20.26 E
Bocholt	36	51.50 N	6.36 E
Bochum	36	51.29 N	7.13 E
Bodega Bay C	184	38.15 N	123.00 W
Bodélé ◄¹	102	16.30 N	17.00 E
Boden	26	65.50 N	21.42 E
Bodensee @	36	47.35 N	9.25 E
Bodmin	32	50.29 N	4.43 W
Bodmin Moor ◄³	32	50.33 N	4.36 W
Bodø	26	67.17 N	14.23 E
Bodrog ≃	36	48.07 N	21.25 E
Boende	104	0.13 S	20.52 E
Boerne	184	29.47 N	98.44 W
Bogalusa	174	30.47 N	89.52 W
Boger City	172	35.29 N	81.13 W
Bognor Regis	32	50.47 N	0.41 W
Bogor	82	6.35 S	106.47 E
Bogotá	144	4.36 N	74.05 W
Bohemian Forest ∧	36	49.15 N	12.45 E
Boiling Springs	172	35.16 N	81.40 W
Bois Blanc Island I	168	45.45 N	84.28 W
Bois du Roi ∧	42	47.00 N	4.02 E
Boise	180	43.37 N	116.13 W
Boizenburg	36	53.22 N	10.43 E
Bojeador, Cabo ➤	82	18.30 N	120.34 E
Boknafjorden C²	28	59.10 N	5.35 E
Bolama	100	11.35 N	15.28 W
Bolbec	42	49.34 N	0.29 E
Bolesławiec	36	51.16 N	15.34 E
Bolingbrook	168	41.42 N	88.03 W
Bolívar, Col.	144	4.21 N	76.10 W
Bolívar, Mo., U.S.	174	37.37 N	93.25 W
Bolívar, Tenn., U.S.	174	35.16 N	88.59 W
Bolívar, Cerro ∧	144	7.28 N	63.25 W
Bolívar, Pico ∧	144	8.30 N	71.02 W
Bolívar Peninsula ➤¹	174	29.27 N	94.39 W
Bolivia □¹	144	17.00 S	65.00 W
Bollnäs	28	61.21 N	16.25 E
Bollullos par del Condado	50	37.20 N	6.32 W
Bolmen @	28	56.55 N	13.40 E
Bologna	46	44.29 N	11.20 E
Bolsena, Lago di @	46	42.36 N	11.56 E
Bol'šezemel'skaja Tundra ◄¹	62	67.30 N	56.00 E
Bol'šoj Kavkaz (Caucasus) ∧	62	42.30 N	45.00 E
Bolton	32	53.35 N	2.26 W
Bolzano (Bozen)	46	46.31 N	11.22 E
Boma	104	5.51 S	13.03 E
Bombay	84	18.58 N	72.50 E
Bomberai, Jazirah ➤¹	82	3.00 S	133.00 E
Bomokandi ≃	102	3.39 N	26.08 E
Bomu (Mbomou) ≃	102	4.08 N	22.26 E
Bon, Cap ➤	100	37.05 N	11.03 E
Bon Air	172	37.32 N	77.34 W
Bonaire I	130	12.10 N	68.15 W
Bonavista Bay C	160	48.45 N	53.20 W
Bondeno	46	44.53 N	11.25 E
Bône → Annaba	100	36.54 N	7.46 E
Bone, Teluk C	82	4.00 S	120.40 E
Bonifacio, Strait of ⋃	46	41.20 N	9.15 E
Bonifati, Capo ➤	46	39.35 N	15.52 E
Bonn	36	50.44 N	7.05 E
Bonners Ferry	180	48.41 N	116.18 W
Bonne Terre	174	37.55 N	90.33 W
Bonnet Plume ≃	160	65.55 N	134.58 W
Bonneville Salt Flats ≃	178	40.45 N	113.52 W
Bonnie Doone	172	35.05 N	78.58 W
Bon Weir	184	30.44 N	93.39 W
Boom	36	51.05 N	4.22 E
Boone, Iowa, U.S.	168	42.04 N	93.53 W
Boone, N.C., U.S.	172	36.13 N	81.41 W
Booneville, Ark., U.S.	174	35.08 N	93.55 W
Booneville, Miss., U.S.	174	34.39 N	88.34 W
Boonville, Ind., U.S.	174	38.03 N	87.16 W
Boonville, Mo., U.S.	174	38.58 N	92.44 W
Boothbay Harbor	166	43.51 N	69.38 W
Boothia, Gulf of C	160	71.00 N	91.00 W
Boothia Peninsula ➤¹	160	70.30 N	95.00 W
Bor, Jugo.	54	44.05 N	22.07 E
Bor, S.S.S.R.	26	56.22 N	44.05 E
Borah Peak ∧	180	44.08 N	113.48 W
Borås	28	57.43 N	12.55 E
Borcea ≃	54	44.40 N	27.53 E
Bordeaux	42	44.50 N	0.34 W
Bordighera	46	43.46 N	7.39 E
Bordj Bou Arreridj	50	36.04 N	4.46 E
Bordj Menaïel	50	36.44 N	3.43 E
Borgå (Porvoo)	28	60.24 N	25.40 E
Borger	162	35.39 N	101.24 W
Borghorst	36	52.07 N	7.23 E
Borgne, Lake C	174	30.05 N	89.40 W
Borgomanero	46	45.42 N	8.28 E
Borgosesia	46	45.43 N	8.16 E
Borisov	62	54.15 N	28.30 E
Borken	36	51.51 N	6.51 E
Borkum I	36	53.35 N	6.41 E
Borlänge	28	60.29 N	15.25 E
Borneo (Kalimantan) I	82	0.30 N	114.00 E
Bornholm I	28	55.10 N	15.00 E
Bornova	54	38.27 N	27.14 E
Boro ≃	102	8.52 N	26.11 E
Borovici	26	58.24 N	33.55 E
Borşa	54	47.39 N	24.40 E
Borščovočnyj Chrebet ∧	64	52.00 N	117.00 E
Bosanski Novi	46	45.03 N	16.23 E
Boscobel	168	43.08 N	90.42 W
Boshan	80	36.29 N	117.50 E
Bositenghu @	80	42.00 N	87.00 E
Bosna ≃	54	45.04 N	18.29 E
Bosporus → İstanbul Boğazı ⋃	54	41.06 N	29.04 E
Bosque Farms	178	34.53 N	106.40 W
Bossangoa	100	6.29 N	17.27 E
Bossier City	174	32.31 N	93.43 W
Bosso, Dallol V	100	12.25 N	2.50 E
Boston, Eng., U.K.	32	52.59 N	0.01 W
Boston, Mass., U.S.	166	42.21 N	71.04 W
Boston Mountains ∧²	174	35.50 N	93.20 W
Bosut ≃	54	44.57 N	19.22 E
Boteti ≃	104	20.08 S	23.23 E
Botev ∧	54	42.43 N	24.55 E
Bothnia, Gulf of C	28	63.00 N	20.00 E
Botoşani	54	47.45 N	26.40 E
Botrange ∧	36	50.30 N	6.08 E
Botswana □¹	104	22.00 S	24.00 E
Botte Donato ∧	46	39.17 N	16.26 E
Bottenhavet (Selkämeri) C	28	62.00 N	20.00 E
Bottineau	162	48.50 N	100.27 W
Bottrop	36	51.31 N	6.55 E
Botucatu	144	22.52 S	48.26 W
Bouaké	100	7.41 N	5.02 W
Bouar	102	5.57 N	15.36 E
Bouârfa	100	32.32 N	1.59 W
Bougainville I	114	6.00 S	155.00 E
Bougainville Strait ⋃	114	6.40 S	156.10 E
Bougaroûn, Cap ➤	50	37.06 N	6.28 E
Boujad	50	32.46 N	3.54 E
Boulder	178	40.01 N	105.17 W
Boulder City	184	35.59 N	114.50 W
Boulogne-Billancourt	42	48.50 N	2.15 E
Boulogne-sur-Mer	42	50.43 N	1.37 E
Boundary Peak ∧	184	37.51 N	118.21 W
Boundary Ranges ∧	162a	56.00 N	130.00 W
Bountiful	178	40.53 N	111.53 W
Bourail	113b	21.34 S	165.30 E
Bourbon	174	41.18 N	86.07 W
Bourg-en-Bresse	42	46.12 N	5.13 E
Bourges	42	47.05 N	2.24 E
Bourgogne □⁹	42	47.00 N	4.30 E
Bournemouth	32	50.43 N	1.54 W
Bou Saâda	100	35.12 N	4.11 E
Bøverdal	28	61.43 N	8.21 E
Bow ≃	160	49.56 N	111.42 W
Bowie	184	39.00 N	76.47 W
Bowling Green, Ky., U.S.	174	37.00 N	86.27 W
Bowling Green, Mo., U.S.	174	39.20 N	91.12 W

Name	Page	Lat	Long
Bowling Green, Ohio, U.S.	166	41.22 N	83.39 W
Bowman	162	46.11 N	103.24 W
Boyer, Cap ⟩	112	21.37 S	168.06 E
Boyertown	166	40.20 N	75.38 W
Boyne City	168	45.13 N	85.01 W
Boynton Beach	172	26.32 N	80.03 W
Boysen Reservoir ⊜¹	180	43.19 N	108.11 W
Boz Burun ⟩	54	40.24 N	26.54 E
Boz Dağ ⋀	54	37.18 N	29.12 E
Bozeman	180	45.41 N	111.02 W
Bra	46	44.42 N	7.51 E
Brač, Otok ‖	46	43.20 N	16.40 E
Bracciano, Lago di	46	42.07 N	12.14 E
Brad	54	46.08 N	22.47 E
Bradano ≈	46	40.23 N	16.51 E
Bradenton	172	27.29 N	82.34 W
Bradford, Eng., U.K.	32	53.48 N	1.45 W
Bradford, Pa., U.S.	166	41.58 N	78.39 W
Bradley	168	41.09 N	87.52 W
Braga	50	41.33 N	8.26 W
Bragança	50	41.49 N	6.45 W
Brāhmani ≈	84	20.45 N	87.00 E
Brahmaputra (Yaluzangbujiang) ≈	84	24.02 N	90.55 E
Braich y Pwll ⟩	32	52.48 N	4.36 W
Brăila	54	45.16 N	27.58 E
Brăilei, Balta ☷	54	45.00 N	28.00 E
Braine-l'Alleud	36	50.41 N	4.22 E
Brainerd	168	46.21 N	94.12 W
Braintree	32	51.53 N	0.32 E
Brake	36	53.19 N	8.28 E
Bran, Pasul)(	54	45.26 N	25.17 E
Branchville	172	33.15 N	80.49 W
Brandberg ⋀	104	21.10 S	14.33 E
Brandenburg	36	52.24 N	12.32 E
Brandon, Man., Can.	160	49.50 N	99.57 W
Brandon, Fla., U.S.	172	27.56 N	82.17 W
Brandon, Miss., U.S.	174	32.16 N	89.59 W
Brandon, Vt., U.S.	166	43.48 N	73.05 W
Brandýs nad Labem	36	50.10 N	14.41 E
Braniewo	36	54.24 N	19.50 E
Branson	174	36.39 N	93.13 W
Brantford	160	43.08 N	80.16 W
Bras d'Or Lake	160	45.52 N	60.50 W
Brasília	144	15.47 S	47.55 W
Braşov	54	45.39 N	25.37 E
Brasstown Bald ⋀	172	34.52 N	83.48 W
Brateş, Lacul ⊜	54	45.30 N	28.05 E
Bratislava	36	48.09 N	17.07 E
Bratsk	62	56.05 N	101.48 E
Bratskoje Vodochranilišče ⊜¹	64	56.10 N	102.10 E
Brattleboro	166	42.51 N	72.34 W
Braunau [am Inn]	36	48.15 N	13.02 E
Braunschweig	36	52.16 N	10.31 E
Brava, Costa ⟩²	50	41.45 N	3.04 E
Bravo del Norte (Rio Grande) ≈	162	25.55 N	97.09 W
Brawley	184	32.59 N	115.31 W
Bray	32	53.12 N	6.06 W
Brazeau ≈	160	52.55 N	115.15 W
Brazil	174	39.32 N	87.08 W
Brazil □¹	144	10.00 S	55.00 W
Brazoria	174	29.03 N	95.34 W
Brazos ≈	174	28.53 N	95.23 W
Brazzaville	104	4.16 S	15.17 E
Brčko	54	44.53 N	18.48 E
Brda ≈	36	53.07 N	18.08 E
Brea	184	33.55 N	117.54 W
Breaux Bridge	174	30.16 N	91.54 W
Breckenridge	162	32.45 N	98.54 W
Břeclav	36	48.46 N	16.53 E
Breda	36	51.35 N	4.46 E
Breë ≈	104	34.24 S	20.50 E
Bregalnica ≈	54	41.43 N	22.09 E
Bregenz	36	47.30 N	9.46 E
Bremen, B.R.D.	36	53.04 N	8.49 E
Bremen, Ga., U.S.	172	33.43 N	85.09 W
Bremen, Ind., U.S.	174	41.27 N	86.09 W
Bremerhaven	36	53.33 N	8.34 E
Bremerton	180	47.34 N	122.38 W
Brenne ⟩¹	42	46.45 N	1.10 E
Brenner Pass)(	36	47.00 N	11.30 E
Brent	174	30.27 N	87.15 W
Brenta ≈	46	45.11 N	12.18 E
Brentwood, Eng., U.K.	32	51.38 N	0.18 E
Brentwood, N.Y., U.S.	166	40.47 N	73.14 W
Brentwood, Tenn., U.S.	174	36.01 N	86.47 W
Brescia	46	45.33 N	13.15 E
Bressanone	46	46.43 N	11.39 E
Bresse ⟩¹	42	46.30 N	5.15 E
Brest, Fr.	42	48.24 N	4.29 W
Brest, S.S.S.R.	62	52.06 N	23.42 E
Breton, Pertuis ⋃	42	46.25 N	1.20 W
Breton Sound ⋃	174	29.30 N	89.09 W
Brevard	172	35.09 N	82.44 W
Brewer	166	44.48 N	68.46 W
Brewster	180	48.06 N	119.47 W
Brewton	174	31.07 N	87.04 W
Brezno	36	48.50 N	19.39 E
Briançon	42	44.54 N	6.39 E
Bridge City	174	30.01 N	93.51 W
Bridgend	32	51.31 N	3.35 W
Bridgeport, Ala., U.S.	174	34.57 N	85.43 W
Bridgeport, Conn., U.S.	166	41.11 N	73.11 W
Bridgeport, Mich., U.S.	168	43.22 N	83.53 W
Bridgeport, W. Va., U.S.	166	39.17 N	80.15 W
Bridgeton	166	39.26 N	75.14 W
Bridgetown	130	13.06 N	59.37 W
Bridgeville	166	38.45 N	75.36 W
Bridgewater, Mass., U.S.	166	41.59 N	70.58 W
Bridgewater, Va., U.S.	166	38.18 N	78.59 W
Bridgwater	32	51.08 N	3.00 W
Bridgwater Bay ⊂	32	51.16 N	3.12 W
Bridlington	32	54.05 N	0.12 W
Bridlington Bay ⊂	32	54.04 N	0.08 W
Brienzer See ⊜	42	46.43 N	7.57 E
Brigham City	178	41.31 N	112.01 W
Brighton, Eng., U.K.	32	50.50 N	0.08 W
Brighton, Colo., U.S.	178	39.59 N	104.49 W
Brighton, Mich., U.S.	168	42.32 N	83.47 W
Brighton, N.Y., U.S.	166	43.08 N	77.34 W
Brilon	36	51.23 N	8.34 E
Brindisi	46	40.38 N	17.56 E
Brinkley	174	34.53 N	91.12 W
Brisbane	116	27.28 S	153.02 E
Bristol, Eng., U.K.	32	51.27 N	2.35 W
Bristol, Conn., U.S.	166	41.41 N	72.57 W
Bristol, Pa., U.S.	166	40.06 N	74.52 W
Bristol, R.I., U.S.	166	41.40 N	71.16 W
Bristol, Tenn., U.S.	172	36.36 N	82.11 W
Bristol, Vt., U.S.	172	44.08 N	73.05 W
Bristol Bay ⊂	162a	58.00 N	159.00 W
Bristol Channel ⋃	32	51.20 N	4.00 W
Bristol Lake ⊜	184	34.28 N	115.41 W
British Antarctic Territory □²	191	60.00 S	45.00 W
British Columbia □⁴	160	54.00 N	125.00 W
British Mountains ⋀	162a	69.00 N	140.00 W
Britt	168	43.06 N	93.48 W
Brive-la-Gaillarde	42	45.10 N	1.32 E
Brixham	32	50.24 N	3.30 W
Brno	36	49.12 N	16.37 E
Broad ≈	172	34.00 N	81.04 W
Brockport	166	43.13 N	77.56 W
Brockton¹	166	42.05 N	71.01 W
Brodhead	168	42.37 N	89.22 W
Brodnica	36	53.16 N	19.23 E
Broken Bow	174	34.02 N	94.44 W
Broken Hill, Austl.	116	31.57 S	141.27 E
Broken Hill → Kabwe, Zam.	104	14.27 S	28.27 E
Bromsgrove	32	52.20 N	2.03 W
Bronlund Peak ⋀	160	57.26 N	126.38 W
Bronson, Kans., U.S.	174	37.54 N	95.04 W
Bronson, Tex., U.S.	184	31.21 N	94.01 W
Bronte	46	37.48 N	14.50 E
Brookfield, Mo., U.S.	174	39.47 N	93.04 W
Brookfield, Wis., U.S.	168	43.04 N	88.09 W
Brookhaven	174	31.35 N	90.26 W
Brookings	162	44.19 N	96.48 W
Brooklyn Center	168	45.05 N	93.20 W
Brooks Range ⋀	162a	68.00 N	154.00 W
Brooksville	172	28.33 N	82.23 W
Brookville, Ind., U.S.	174	39.25 N	85.01 W
Brookville, Pa., U.S.	166	41.09 N	79.05 W
Broomfield	178	39.56 N	105.04 W
Brown Deer	168	43.10 N	87.59 W
Browning	180	48.34 N	113.01 W
Brownsburg	174	39.51 N	86.24 W
Brownsdale	168	43.44 N	92.52 W
Brownstown	174	38.53 N	86.03 W
Brownsville, La., U.S.	174	32.30 N	92.10 W
Brownsville, Tenn., U.S.	174	35.36 N	89.15 W
Brownsville, Tex., U.S.	162	25.54 N	97.30 W
Brownwood	162	31.43 N	98.59 W
Bruay-en-Artois	42	50.29 N	2.33 E
Bruce	174	33.59 N	89.21 W
Bruchsal	36	49.07 N	8.35 E
Bruck an der Mur	36	47.25 N	15.16 E
Brugge	36	51.13 N	3.14 E
Bruneau ≈	180	42.57 N	115.58 W
Brunei □¹	82	4.30 N	114.40 E
Brunsbüttel	36	53.54 N	9.07 E
Brunswick → Braunschweig	36	52.16 N	10.31 E
Brunswick, Ga., U.S.	172	31.10 N	81.29 W
Brunswick, Maine, U.S.	166	43.55 N	69.58 W
Brunswick, Md., U.S.	166	39.19 N	77.37 W
Brunswick, Ohio, U.S.	166	41.14 N	81.50 W
Brunswick, Península ⟩¹	146	53.30 S	71.25 W
Bruntál	36	49.59 N	17.28 E
Brussels → Bruxelles	36	50.50 N	4.20 E
Bruxelles (Brussel)	36	50.50 N	4.20 E
Bryan, Ohio, U.S.	166	41.28 N	84.33 W
Bryan, Tex., U.S.	174	30.40 N	96.22 W
Brzeg	36	50.52 N	17.27 E
Brzesko	36	49.59 N	20.36 E
Bubaque	100	11.17 N	15.50 W
Bübiyān¹	84	29.47 N	48.10 E
Bucaramanga	144	7.08 N	73.09 W
Buchanan, Liber.	100	5.57 N	10.02 W
Buchanan, Mich., U.S.	168	41.50 N	86.22 W
Buchara	62	39.48 N	64.25 E
Bucharest → Bucureşti	54	44.26 N	26.06 E
Bückeburg	36	52.16 N	9.02 E
Buckeye	178	33.22 N	112.35 W
Buckhannon	166	38.59 N	80.14 W
Buckhaven	32	56.11 N	3.03 W
Buckinghamshire □⁶	32	51.45 N	0.48 W
Buckley	180	47.10 N	122.02 W
Buck Mountain ⋀	172	36.40 N	81.15 W
Bucksport	166	44.34 N	68.48 W
Bucureşti	54	44.26 N	26.06 E
Bucyrus	166	40.48 N	82.58 W
Budapest	36	47.30 N	19.05 E
Bude Bay ⊂	32	50.50 N	4.37 W
Buenaventura	144	3.53 N	77.04 W
Buena Vista, Colo., U.S.	178	38.50 N	106.08 W
Buena Vista, Va., U.S.	172	37.44 N	79.21 W
Buendía, Embalse de ⊜¹	50	40.25 N	2.43 W
Buenos Aires	146	34.36 S	58.27 W
Buffalo, Kans., U.S.	174	37.42 N	95.42 W
Buffalo, Minn., U.S.	168	45.10 N	93.53 W
Buffalo, Mo., U.S.	174	37.39 N	93.06 W
Buffalo, N.Y., U.S.	166	42.54 N	78.53 W
Buffalo, Wyo., U.S.	180	44.21 N	106.42 W
Buford	172	34.07 N	84.00 W
Bug ≈	20	52.31 N	21.05 E
Buga	144	3.54 N	76.17 W
Bugul'ma	26	54.33 N	52.48 E
Buhl	180	42.36 N	114.46 W
Buhuşi	54	46.43 N	26.41 E
Buies Creek	172	35.24 N	78.45 W
Bujalance	50	37.54 N	4.22 W
Bujumbura	104	3.23 S	29.22 E
Buka Island ‖	114	5.15 S	154.35 E
Buka Passage ⋃	114	5.25 S	154.41 E
Bukavu	104	2.30 S	28.52 E
Bükk ⋀	36	48.05 N	20.30 E
Bukovica ⟩¹	46	44.10 N	15.40 E
Bulawayo	104	20.09 S	28.36 E
Buldan	54	38.03 N	28.51 E
Bulgaria □¹	54	43.00 N	25.00 E
Bullhead City	178	35.09 N	114.34 W
Bull Shoals Lake ⊜¹	174	36.30 N	92.50 W
Buna	100	2.40 N	39.58 E
Bunbury	116	33.19 S	115.38 E
Bundaberg	116	24.52 S	152.21 E
Bungo-suidō ⋃	80	33.00 N	132.13 E
Bunia	104	1.34 N	30.15 E
Bunkie	174	30.57 N	92.11 W
Burao	102	9.30 N	45.30 E
Buras	174	29.21 N	89.32 W
Burbank	184	34.12 N	118.18 W
Buraydah	84	26.20 N	43.59 E
Burgas	54	42.30 N	27.28 E
Burgaski zaliv ⊂	54	42.30 N	27.33 E
Burg [bei Magdeburg]	36	52.16 N	11.51 E
Burgdorf, B.R.D.	36	52.27 N	10.00 E
Burgdorf, Schw.	42	47.04 N	7.37 E
Burghausen	36	48.09 N	12.49 E
Burgos	50	42.21 N	3.42 W
Burgos □⁴	50	42.20 N	3.40 W
Burgstädt	36	50.55 N	12.49 E
Burgsteinfurt	36	52.08 N	7.20 E
Burhaniye	54	39.30 N	26.58 E
Burhānpur	84	21.19 N	76.14 E
Burien	180	47.29 N	122.21 W
Burjasot	50	39.31 N	0.25 W
Burkesville	174	36.48 N	85.22 W
Burley	180	42.32 N	113.48 W
Burlingame	184	37.35 N	122.22 W
Burlington, Iowa, U.S.	168	40.49 N	91.14 W
Burlington, Kans., U.S.	174	38.12 N	95.45 W
Burlington, N.J., U.S.	166	40.04 N	74.49 W
Burlington, N.C., U.S.	172	36.06 N	79.26 W
Burlington, Vt., U.S.	166	44.29 N	73.13 W
Burlington, Wash., U.S.	180	48.28 N	122.20 W
Burlington, Wis., U.S.	168	42.41 N	88.17 W
Burma □¹	82	22.00 N	98.00 E
Burnie	116	41.04 S	145.54 E
Burnley	32	53.48 N	2.14 W
Burns	180	43.35 N	119.03 W
Burntwood ≈	160	56.08 N	96.30 W
Burriana	50	39.53 N	0.05 W
Bursa	54	40.11 N	29.04 E
Bür Sa'īd (Port Said)	102	31.16 N	32.18 E
Bür Südān (Port Sudan)	102	19.37 N	37.14 E
Burt Lake ⊜	168	45.27 N	84.40 W
Burton	174	43.02 N	83.36 W
Burton-upon-Trent	32	52.49 N	1.36 W
Burundi □¹	104	3.15 S	30.00 E
Bury	32	53.36 N	2.17 W
Bury Saint Edmunds	32	52.15 N	0.43 E
Busambra, Rocca ⋀	46	37.51 N	13.24 E
Bushimaie ≈	104	6.02 S	23.45 E
Bushman Land □⁹	104	29.15 S	20.00 E
Bushnell	168	40.33 N	90.30 W
Busko Zdrój	36	50.28 N	20.44 E
Bussum	36	52.16 N	5.10 E
Busto Arsizio	46	45.37 N	8.51 E
Buta	100	2.48 N	24.44 E
Butare	104	2.36 S	29.44 E
Bute Inlet ⊂	160	50.37 N	124.53 W
Butler, Ind., U.S.	174	41.26 N	84.52 W
Butler, Mo., U.S.	174	38.16 N	94.20 W
Butler, Pa., U.S.	166	40.52 N	79.54 W
Butner	172	36.08 N	78.49 W
Butte	180	46.00 N	112.32 W
Butterworth	82	5.25 N	100.24 E
Butuan	82	8.57 N	125.33 E
Bützow	36	53.50 N	11.59 E
Buxtehude	36	53.28 N	9.41 E
Buxton	32	53.15 N	1.55 W
Büyük Ağrı Dağı (Mount Ararat) ⋀	20	39.42 N	44.18 E
Büyükmenderes ≈	54	37.37 N	27.11 E
Buzău	54	45.09 N	26.49 E
Buzău ≈	54	45.26 N	27.44 E
Buzi ≈	104	19.50 S	34.43 E
Bydgoski, Kanał ☷	36	53.08 N	17.36 E
Bydgoszcz	36	53.08 N	18.00 E
Byron	180	44.48 N	108.30 W
Byrranga, Gory ⋀	64	75.00 N	104.00 E
Bystrzyca ≈	36	51.13 N	16.54 E
Bytom (Beuthen)	36	50.22 N	18.54 E
Bytów	36	54.11 N	17.30 E
Bzura ≈	36	52.23 N	20.09 E

C

Name	Page	Lat	Long
Caballería, Cabo de ⟩	50	40.05 N	4.05 E
Cabanatuan	82	15.29 N	120.58 E
Cabeza del Buey	50	38.43 N	5.13 W
Cabimas	144	10.23 N	71.28 W
Cabool	174	37.07 N	92.06 W
Cabot	174	34.58 N	92.01 W
Cabot Strait ⋃	160	47.20 N	59.30 W
Cabra	50	37.28 N	4.27 W
Çabrera ‖	50	39.09 N	2.56 E
Čačak	54	43.53 N	20.21 E
Caccia, Capo ⟩	46	40.34 N	8.09 E
Cáceres	50	39.29 N	6.22 W
Cache ≈	174	34.42 N	91.20 W
Cachimbo, Serra do ⋀	144	8.30 S	55.50 W
Cachoeiro de Itapemirim	144	20.51 S	41.06 W
Čadca	36	49.26 N	18.48 E
Caddo Lake ⊜¹	174	32.42 N	94.01 W
Cader Idris ⋀	32	52.42 N	3.54 W
Cadillac	168	44.15 N	85.24 W
Cádiz	50	36.32 N	6.18 W
Cádiz, Bahía de ⊂	50	36.32 N	6.16 W
Cádiz, Golfo de ⊂	50	36.50 N	7.10 W
Cadiz Lake ⊜	184	34.18 N	115.24 W
Caen	42	49.11 N	0.21 W
Caernarvon Bay ⊂	32	53.05 N	4.30 W
Caerphilly	32	51.35 N	3.14 W
Cagayan ≈	82	18.22 N	121.37 E
Cagayan de Oro	82	8.29 N	124.39 E
Cagliari	46	39.20 N	9.00 E
Cagliari, Golfo di ⊂	46	39.05 N	9.10 E
Cagnes	42	43.40 N	7.09 E
Caguas	130	18.14 N	66.02 W
Caha Mountains ⋀	32	51.45 N	9.45 W
Cahokia	174	38.33 N	90.10 W
Cahors	42	44.27 N	1.26 E
Caiapó, Serra ⋀	144	17.00 S	52.00 W
Caibarién	130	22.31 N	79.28 W
Caicos Islands ‖	130	21.56 N	71.58 W
Caimanero ≈	130	19.59 N	75.09 W
Cairns	116	16.55 S	145.46 E
Cairo → Al-Qāhirah, Miṣr	102	30.03 N	31.15 E
Cairo, Ga., U.S.	172	30.53 N	84.12 W
Cairo, Ill., U.S.	174	37.00 N	89.11 W
Cairo Montenotte	46	44.24 N	8.16 E
Cajamarca	144	7.10 S	78.31 W
Cajàzeiras	144	6.54 S	38.34 W
Cakovec	46	46.23 N	16.26 E
Calabar	100	4.57 N	8.19 E
Calabozo	144	8.56 N	67.26 W
Calahorra	50	42.18 N	1.58 W
Calais, Fr.	42	50.57 N	1.50 E
Calais, Maine, U.S.	166	45.11 N	67.17 W
Calais, Pas de (Strait of Dover) ⋃	32	51.00 N	1.30 E
Calama	146	22.28 S	68.56 W
Calaraşi	54	44.11 N	27.20 E
Calatayud	50	41.21 N	1.38 W
Calbe	36	51.54 N	11.46 E
Calcasieu ≈	174	30.05 N	93.20 W
Calcasieu Lake ⊜	174	29.50 N	93.17 W
Calcutta	84	22.34 N	88.20 E
Caldas da Rainha	50	39.24 N	9.08 W
Caldeirão, Serra do ⋀	50	37.42 N	8.21 W
Caldey Island ‖	32	51.38 N	4.41 W
Caldwell, Idaho, U.S.	180	43.40 N	116.41 W
Caledonia	166	43.38 N	91.29 W
Calexico	184	32.40 N	115.30 W
Calf of Man ‖	32	54.03 N	4.48 W
Calgary	160	51.03 N	114.05 W
Calhoun	172	34.30 N	84.57 W
Cali	144	3.27 N	76.31 W
Calicut	84	11.15 N	75.46 E
California, Mo., U.S.	174	38.38 N	92.34 W
California, Pa., U.S.	166	40.04 N	79.53 W
California □³	162	37.30 N	119.30 W
California, Golfo de ⊂	130	28.00 N	112.00 W
California Aqueduct ☷	184	35.52 N	117.12 W
Calimani, Munţii ⋀	54	47.07 N	25.03 E
Callao	144	12.04 S	77.09 W
Callosa de Segura	50	38.08 N	0.52 W
Cālmāţui ≈	54	44.50 N	27.50 E
Caltagirone	46	37.14 N	14.31 E
Caltanissetta	46	37.29 N	14.04 E
Calumet	168	47.14 N	88.27 W
Calumet City	174	41.37 N	87.31 W
Calw	36	48.43 N	8.44 E
Cam ≈	32	52.21 N	0.15 E
Camagüey	130	21.23 N	77.55 W
Camanche	174	41.47 N	90.15 W
Camargue ⟩¹	42	43.34 N	4.34 E
Camas	180	45.35 N	122.24 W
Ca-mau, Mui ⟩	82	8.38 N	104.44 E
Camborne	32	50.12 N	5.19 W
Cambrai	42	50.10 N	3.14 E
Cambrian Mountains ⋀	32	52.35 N	3.35 W
Cambridge, Ont., Can.	160	43.22 N	80.19 W
Cambridge, Eng., U.K.	32	52.13 N	0.08 E
Cambridge, Md., U.S.	166	38.34 N	76.04 W
Cambridge, Mass., U.S.	166	42.22 N	71.06 W
Cambridge, Ohio, U.S.	166	40.02 N	81.35 W
Cambridge Bay	160	69.03 N	105.05 W
Cambridgeshire □⁶	32	52.20 N	0.05 E
Camden, Ark., U.S.	174	33.35 N	92.50 W
Camden, Del., U.S.	166	39.07 N	75.33 W
Camden, Maine, U.S.	166	44.12 N	69.04 W
Camden, S.C., U.S.	172	34.16 N	80.36 W
Camden, Tenn., U.S.	174	36.04 N	88.06 W
Camdenton	174	38.00 N	92.45 W
Cameron, Mo., U.S.	174	39.44 N	94.14 W
Cameron, W. Va., U.S.	166	39.50 N	80.34 W
Cameron Hills ⋀²	160	59.48 N	118.00 W
Cameroon □¹	100	6.00 N	12.00 E
Cameroun, Mont ⋀	100	4.12 N	9.11 E
Camilla	172	31.14 N	84.12 W
Campagna di Roma ⟩¹	46	41.50 N	12.35 E
Campbell, Calif., U.S.	184	37.17 N	121.57 W
Campbell, Mo., U.S.	174	36.30 N	90.04 W
Campbell Hill ⋀²	166	40.22 N	83.43 W
Campbellsport	168	43.36 N	88.17 W
Campbellsville	174	37.21 N	85.20 W
Campbellton	160	48.00 N	66.40 W
Campeche	130	19.51 N	90.32 W
Campeche, Bahía de ⊂	130	20.00 N	94.00 W
Camp Hill	166	40.14 N	76.55 W
Campidano ⟩¹	46	39.30 N	8.50 E
Campina	50	37.45 N	4.45 W
Campina Grande	144	7.13 S	35.53 W
Campinas	144	22.54 S	47.05 W
Campobasso	46	41.34 N	14.39 E
Campo de Criptana	50	39.24 N	3.07 W
Campo Grande	144	20.27 S	54.37 W
Campos	144	21.45 S	41.18 W
Canaan	166	42.02 N	73.20 W
Canada □¹	160	60.00 N	95.00 W
Canadian ≈	162	35.27 N	95.03 W
Çanakkale	54	40.09 N	26.24 E
Çanakkale Boğazı (Dardanelles) ⋃	54	40.15 N	26.25 E
Canandaigua	166	42.54 N	77.17 W
Cananea	130	30.57 N	110.18 W
Canarias, Islas (Canary Islands) ‖	100	28.00 N	15.30 W
Canary Islands → Canarias, Islas ‖	100	28.00 N	15.30 W
Canastota	166	43.10 N	75.45 W
Canaveral, Cape ⟩	172	28.27 N	80.32 W
Canavese ⟩¹	46	45.20 N	7.40 E
Canberra	116	35.17 S	149.08 E
Canby	180	45.16 N	122.42 W
Candlestick	174	32.15 N	90.20 W
Cangkuang, Tanjung ⟩	82	6.51 S	105.15 E
Caniapiscau ≈	160	57.40 N	69.30 W
Canicattì	46	37.21 N	13.51 E
Cannelton	174	37.55 N	86.45 W
Cannes	42	43.33 N	7.01 E
Cannock	32	52.42 N	2.09 W
Cannon Falls	168	44.31 N	92.54 W
Canon City	178	38.27 N	105.14 W
Canonsburg	166	40.16 N	80.11 W
Canosa [di Puglia]	46	41.13 N	16.04 E
Cantábrica, Cordillera ⋀	50	43.00 N	5.00 W
Cantal ⋀	42	45.10 N	2.40 E
Canterbury	32	51.17 N	1.05 E
Canterbury Bight ⊂³	118	44.15 S	171.38 E
Canterbury Plains ≊	118	44.00 S	171.45 E
Can-tho	82	10.02 N	105.47 E
Canton, Ga., U.S.	172	34.14 N	84.29 W
Canton, Ill., U.S.	168	40.33 N	90.02 W
Canton, Miss., U.S.	174	32.37 N	90.02 W
Canton, N.C., U.S.	172	35.32 N	82.50 W
Canton, N.Y., U.S.	166	44.36 N	75.10 W
Canton, Ohio, U.S.	166	40.48 N	81.22 W
Canton → Guangzhou, Zhg.	80	23.06 N	113.16 E
Canton and Enderbury □²	10	2.50 S	171.43 W
Cantù	46	45.44 N	9.08 E
Čapajevsk	26	52.58 N	49.41 E
Capanaparo ≈	144	7.01 N	67.07 W
Cape Breton Island ‖	160	46.00 N	60.30 W
Cape Canaveral	172	28.24 N	80.37 W
Cape Coast	100	5.05 N	1.15 W
Cape Cod Bay ⊂	166	41.52 N	70.22 W
Cape Coral	172	26.33 N	81.57 W
Cape Elizabeth	166	43.34 N	70.12 W
Cape Fear ≈	172	33.53 N	78.00 W
Cape May	166	38.56 N	74.55 W
Cape Town (Kaapstad)	104	33.55 S	18.22 E
Cape Verde □¹	100	16.00 N	24.00 W
Cape York Peninsula ⟩¹	116	14.00 S	142.30 E
Cap-Haïtien	130	19.45 N	72.12 W
Capitol View	172	33.57 N	80.56 W
Capiz → Roxas	82	11.35 N	122.45 E
Capraia, Isola di ‖	46	43.02 N	9.49 E
Capri, Isola di ‖	46	40.33 N	14.13 E
Captain Cook	162b	19.30 N	155.55 W
Capua	46	41.06 N	14.12 E
Caracal	54	44.07 N	24.21 E
Caracas	144	10.30 N	66.56 W
Caransebeş	54	45.25 N	22.13 E
Caratasca, Laguna de ⊂	130	15.23 N	83.55 W
Caratinga	144	19.47 S	42.08 W
Caravaca	50	38.06 N	1.51 W
Caravaggio	46	45.30 N	9.38 E
Carballo	50	36.47 N	5.06 E
Carbon, Cap ⟩	50	36.47 N	5.06 E
Carbonara, Capo ⟩	46	39.06 N	9.31 E
Carbondale, Ill., U.S.	174	37.44 N	89.13 W
Carbondale, Kans., U.S.	174	38.49 N	95.41 W
Carbondale, Pa., U.S.	166	41.35 N	75.30 W
Carbonia	46	39.11 N	8.32 E
Carcagente	50	39.08 N	0.27 W
Carcans, Étang de ⊜	42	45.08 N	1.08 W
Carcassonne	42	43.13 N	2.21 E
Carcross	160	60.10 N	134.42 W
Cárdenas	130	23.02 N	81.12 W
Cardiff	32	51.29 N	3.13 W
Cardigan	32	52.05 N	4.40 W
Cardigan Bay ⊂	32	52.30 N	4.30 W
Cardington	166	40.30 N	82.53 W
Cardston	160	49.12 N	113.18 W
Cardzou	62	39.06 N	63.34 E
Carei	54	47.42 N	22.28 E
Carencro	174	30.19 N	92.03 W
Carentan	42	49.19 N	1.14 W
Cares ≈	50	43.19 N	4.36 W
Carey	166	40.57 N	83.23 W
Caribbean Sea ▽²	130	15.00 N	73.00 W
Cariboo Mountains ⋀	160	53.00 N	121.00 W
Caribou	162	46.52 N	68.01 W
Caribou Mountains ⋀	160	59.12 N	115.40 W
Carini	46	38.08 N	13.11 E
Carinhanha	144	14.18 S	43.46 W
Carleton, Mount ⋀	160	47.23 N	66.53 W
Carlin	180	40.43 N	116.07 W
Carlinville	174	39.17 N	89.53 W
Carlisle, Eng., U.K.	32	54.54 N	2.55 W
Carlisle, Ark., U.S.	174	34.47 N	91.45 W
Carlisle, Iowa, U.S.	168	41.30 N	93.29 W
Carlisle, Pa., U.S.	166	40.12 N	77.11 W
Carl Junction	174	37.11 N	94.34 W
Carlsbad, Calif., U.S.	184	33.10 N	117.21 W
Carlsbad, N. Mex., U.S.	162	32.25 N	104.14 W
Carlyle	174	38.37 N	89.22 W
Carlyle Lake ⊜¹	174	38.40 N	89.18 W
Carmacks	160	62.05 N	136.18 W
Carmagnola	46	44.51 N	7.43 E
Carmarthen	32	51.52 N	4.19 W
Carmel, Ind., U.S.	174	39.59 N	86.08 W
Carmel, N.Y., U.S.	166	41.26 N	73.41 W
Carmel Head ⟩	32	53.24 N	4.34 W
Carmi	174	38.05 N	88.10 W
Carmichael	184	38.38 N	121.19 W
Carmona	50	37.28 N	5.38 W
Carnatic ⟩¹	84	12.30 N	78.15 E
Caro	168	43.29 N	83.24 W
Carol City	184	25.56 N	80.16 W
Caroline Islands ‖	82	8.00 N	140.00 E
Carpathian Mountains ⋀	20	48.00 N	24.00 E
Carpaţii Meridionali ⋀	54	45.30 N	24.15 E
Carpentaria, Gulf of ⊂	116	14.00 S	139.00 E
Carpentersville	168	42.07 N	88.17 W
Carpentras	42	44.03 N	5.03 E
Carpi	46	44.47 N	10.53 E
Carpinteria	184	34.24 N	119.31 W
Carranza, Cabo ⟩	146	35.36 S	72.38 W
Carrara	46	44.05 N	10.06 E
Carrauntoohill ⋀	32	52.00 N	9.45 W
Carrboro	172	35.54 N	79.04 W
Carretas, Punta ⟩	144	14.13 S	76.18 W
Carrickfergus	32	54.43 N	5.49 W
Carrington	162	47.27 N	99.08 W
Carrión ≈	50	41.53 N	4.32 W
Carrizozo	178	33.38 N	105.53 W
Carrollton, Ga., U.S.	172	33.35 N	85.05 W
Carrollton, Ky., U.S.	174	38.41 N	85.11 W
Carrollton, Mich., U.S.	168	43.27 N	83.54 W
Carrollton, Mo., U.S.	174	39.22 N	93.30 W
Carson ≈	184	39.45 N	118.40 W
Carson City	184	39.10 N	119.46 W
Carson Sink ≈	184	39.45 N	118.30 W
Cartagena, Col.	144	10.25 N	75.32 W
Cartagena, Esp.	50	37.36 N	0.59 W
Cartago, Col.	144	4.45 N	75.55 W
Cartago, C.R.	130	9.52 N	83.55 W
Carter Lake	174	41.18 N	95.54 W
Cartersville	172	34.10 N	84.48 W
Carterville	174	37.46 N	89.05 W
Carthage, Ill., U.S.	174	40.25 N	91.08 W
Carthage, Miss., U.S.	174	32.46 N	89.32 W
Carthage, Mo., U.S.	174	37.11 N	94.19 W
Carthage, N.Y., U.S.	166	43.59 N	75.37 W
Carthage, Tenn., U.S.	174	36.15 N	85.57 W
Carthage, Tex., U.S.	174	32.09 N	94.20 W
Caruaru	144	8.17 S	35.58 W
Carúpano	144	10.40 N	63.14 W
Caruthersville	174	36.11 N	89.39 W
Carvin	42	50.29 N	2.58 E
Carvoeiro, Cabo ⟩	50	39.21 N	9.24 W
Cary	172	35.47 N	78.46 W
Casablanca (Dar-el-Beida)	100	33.39 N	7.35 W
Casa Grande	178	32.53 N	111.45 W
Casale Monferrato	46	45.08 N	8.27 E
Casarano	46	40.00 N	18.10 E
Casas Adobes	178	32.19 N	110.59 W
Cascade	180	44.31 N	116.02 W
Cascade Bay ⊂	113	29.01 S	167.58 E
Cascade Range ⋀	162	49.00 N	120.00 W
Cascade Reservoir ⊜¹	180	44.35 N	116.06 W
Cascais	50	38.42 N	9.25 W
Cascina	46	43.41 N	10.33 E
Casco Bay ⊂	166	43.45 N	70.00 W
Caserta	46	41.04 N	14.20 E
Casey	174	39.18 N	87.59 W
Cashmere	180	47.31 N	120.28 W
Casiquiare ≈	144	2.01 N	67.07 W
Čáslav	36	49.54 N	15.23 E
Casper	180	42.15 N	106.19 W
Caspian Sea ▽²	20	42.00 N	50.30 E
Cassai (Kasai) ≈	104	3.06 S	16.57 E
Cassano allo Ionio	46	39.47 N	16.20 E
Cassiar Mountains ⋀	160	59.00 N	129.00 W
Cassino	46	41.30 N	13.49 E
Cassville	174	36.41 N	93.52 W
Castelfranco Veneto	46	45.40 N	11.55 E
Castellammare del Golfo	46	38.01 N	12.53 E
Castellammare, Golfo di ⊂	46	38.10 N	12.55 E
Castellammare [di Stabia]	46	40.42 N	14.29 E
Castellaneta	46	40.37 N	16.57 E
Castellón □⁴	50	40.00 N	0.02 W
Castellón de la Plana	50	39.59 N	0.02 W
Castelo Branco	50	39.49 N	7.30 W
Castelsarrasin	42	44.02 N	1.06 E
Castelvetrano	46	37.41 N	12.47 E
Castilla ⟩¹	144	5.12 S	80.38 W
Castilla, Playa de ⟩²	50	37.00 N	6.33 W
Castilla la Nueva □⁹	50	40.00 N	3.45 W
Castle Mountain ⋀	160	64.35 N	135.55 W
Castle Peak ⋀, Colo., U.S.	178	39.00 N	106.55 W
Castle Peak ⋀, Idaho, U.S.	180	44.02 N	114.35 W
Castle Rock, Colo., U.S.	178	39.22 N	104.51 W
Castle Rock, Wash., U.S.	180	46.17 N	122.54 W
Castle Rock Lake ⊜¹	168	43.50 N	89.58 W
Castletown	32	54.04 N	4.40 W
Castres	42	43.36 N	2.15 E
Castries	130	14.01 N	61.00 W
Castro del Río	50	37.41 N	4.28 W
Castuera	50	38.43 N	5.33 W
Cataguases	144	21.23 S	42.42 W
Catahoula Lake ⊜	174	31.30 N	92.06 W
Cataluña □⁹	50	42.00 N	2.00 E
Catamarca	146	28.28 S	65.47 W
Catanduva	144	21.08 S	48.58 W
Catania	46	37.30 N	15.06 E
Catania, Golfo di ⊂	46	37.25 N	15.15 E
Catanzaro	46	38.54 N	16.36 E
Catarroja	50	39.24 N	0.24 W
Catbalogan	82	11.46 N	124.53 E
Cat Island ‖	130	24.27 N	75.30 W
Catlettsburg	166	38.25 N	82.36 W
Catoche, Cabo ⟩	130	21.35 N	87.05 W
Catonsville	166	39.16 N	76.44 W
Catskill	166	42.13 N	73.52 W
Catskill Mountains ⋀	166	42.10 N	74.30 W
Cattolica	46	43.58 N	12.44 E
Caucasus → Bol'šoj Kavkaz ⋀	62	42.30 N	45.00 E
Čaunskaja Guba ⊂	144	69.20 N	170.00 E
Caura ≈	144	7.38 N	64.53 W
Caux, Pays de ⟩¹	42	49.40 N	0.40 E
Cavaillon	42	43.50 N	5.02 E
Cave City	174	37.08 N	85.58 W
Caviana, Ilha ‖	144	0.10 N	50.10 W
Cavite	82	14.29 N	120.55 E
Caxias	144	4.50 S	43.21 W
Cayambe ⋀¹	144	0.02 N	77.59 W
Cayce	172	33.59 N	81.04 W
Cayenne	144	4.56 N	52.20 W
Cayman Brac ‖	130	19.43 N	79.49 W
Cayman Islands □²	130	19.30 N	80.40 W
Cayuga Heights	166	42.28 N	76.30 W
Cayuga Lake ⊜	166	42.45 N	76.45 W
Cazaux, Étang de ⊂	42	44.30 N	1.10 W
Cazorla, Sierra de ⋀	50	37.55 N	2.55 W
Čeboksary	62	56.09 N	47.15 E
Cebu	82	10.18 N	123.54 E
Cecina	46	43.19 N	10.31 E
Cedarburg	168	43.17 N	87.59 W
Cedar City	178	37.41 N	113.04 W

Name Page Lat° ' Long° '

Coromandel Coast •2 84 13.30 N 80.30 E
Coromandel Peninsula ➤1 118 36.50 S 175.35 E
Coromandel Range ✲ 118 37.00 S 175.40 E
Corona 184 33.52 N 117.34 W
Coronado 184 32.41 N 117.11 W
Coronation Island ❙ 191 60.37 S 45.30 W
Coronel 146 37.01 S 73.08 W
Coropuna, Nevado ▲ 144 15.31 S 72.42 W
Corozal 130 18.24 N 88.24 W
Corpus Christi 162 27.48 N 97.24 W
Correggio 46 44.46 N 10.47 E
Correnti, Isola delle ❙ 46 36.38 N 15.05 E
Corrib, Lough ⊜ 32 53.05 N 9.10 W
Corrientes 146 27.28 S 58.50 W
Corrientes, Cabo ➤, Col. 144 5.30 N 77.34 W
Corrientes, Cabo ➤, Méx. 130 20.25 N 105.42 W
Corry 166 41.56 N 73.39 W
Corse (Corsica) ❙ 42 42.00 N 9.05 E
Corse, Cap ➤ 42 43.00 N 9.25 E
Corsicana 162 32.06 N 96.28 W
Cort Adelaer, Kap ➤ 160 62.00 N 42.00 W
Cortez 178 37.21 N 108.35 W
Cortina d'Ampezzo 46 46.32 N 12.08 E
Cortland 166 42.36 N 76.11 W
Cortona 46 43.16 N 11.59 E
Corubal ≃ 100 11.57 N 15.06 W
Çorum 54 39.14 N 28.27 E
Corumbá 144 19.01 S 57.39 W
Corunna 168 42.59 N 84.07 W
Corvallis 180 44.34 N 123.16 W
Corydon, Ind., U.S. 174 38.13 N 86.07 W
Corydon, Iowa, U.S. 168 40.45 N 93.19 W
Cosenza 46 39.17 N 16.15 E
Coshocton 166 40.16 N 81.51 W
Cosmoledo Group ❙❙ 104 9.43 S 47.35 E
Cosne-sur-Loire 42 47.24 N 2.55 E
Costa Mesa 184 33.39 N 117.55 W
Costa Rica □1 130 10.00 N 84.00 W
Costiera, Catena ✲ 46 39.20 N 16.05 E
Costilla 178 36.59 N 105.32 W
Coswig 36 51.53 N 12.26 E
Cotabato 82 7.13 N 124.15 E
Cotentin ➤1 42 49.30 N 1.30 W
Cotmeana ≃ 54 44.24 N 24.45 E
Cotonou 100 6.21 N 2.26 E
Cotopaxi ▲1 144 0.40 S 78.26 W
Cotswold Hills ✲2 32 51.45 N 2.10 W
Cottage Grove 180 43.48 N 123.03 W
Cottbus 36 51.45 N 14.19 E
Cottiennes, Alpes (Alpi Cozie) ✲ 46 44.45 N 7.00 E
Cottondale 174 33.11 N 87.27 W
Cottonport 174 30.59 N 92.03 W
Cottonwood 178 34.45 N 112.01 W
Coubre, Pointe de la ➤ 42 45.41 N 1.13 W
Coulee Dam 180 47.58 N 118.59 W
Coulommiers 42 48.49 N 3.05 E
Council Bluffs 174 41.16 N 95.52 W
Country Homes 180 47.45 N 117.24 W
Courcelles 36 50.28 N 4.22 E
Coventry 32 52.25 N 1.30 W
Covilhã 50 40.17 N 7.30 W
Covington, Ga., U.S. 172 33.35 N 83.53 W
Covington, Ind., U.S. 174 40.09 N 87.24 W
Covington, Ky., U.S. 166 39.05 N 84.30 W
Covington, La., U.S. 174 30.29 N 90.06 W
Covington, Tenn., U.S. 174 35.34 N 89.38 W
Covington, Va., U.S. 172 37.47 N 79.59 W
Cowan 174 35.10 N 86.01 W
Cowdenbeath 32 56.07 N 3.21 W
Cowes 32 50.45 N 1.18 W
Coweta 174 35.57 N 95.39 W
Cowlitz ≃ 180 46.05 N 122.53 W
Cozumel, Isla de ❙ 130 20.25 N 86.55 W
Cradock 104 32.08 S 25.36 E
Craig 178 40.31 N 107.33 W
Crailsheim 36 49.08 N 10.04 E
Craiova 54 44.19 N 23.48 E
Cranbrook 160 49.31 N 115.46 W
Crandon 168 45.34 N 88.54 W
Crane 178 32.42 N 114.40 W
Cranston 166 41.47 N 71.26 W
Crasna (Kraszna) ≃ 54 48.09 N 22.20 E
Crater Lake ⊜ 180 42.56 N 122.06 W
Crateús 144 5.10 S 40.40 W
Crato 144 7.14 S 39.23 W
Crawford 178 38.42 N 107.37 W
Crawfordsville 174 40.02 N 86.54 W
Crawley 32 51.07 N 0.12 W
Crazy Peak ▲ 180 46.01 N 110.16 W
Cree ≃ 160 59.00 N 105.47 W
Cree Lake ⊜ 160 57.30 N 106.30 W
Creede 178 37.51 N 106.56 W
Creil 42 49.16 N 2.29 E
Crema 46 45.22 N 9.41 E
Cremona 46 45.07 N 10.02 E
Cres, Otok ❙ 46 44.50 N 14.25 E
Cresaptown 166 39.36 N 78.50 W
Crescent Group ❙❙ 82 16.31 N 111.38 E
Crescent Lake ⊜ 172 29.28 N 81.30 W
Cresco 168 43.22 N 92.07 W
Crestline 166 40.47 N 82.44 W
Creston 174 41.04 N 94.22 W
Crestone Peak ▲ 178 37.58 N 105.36 W
Crestview 174 30.46 N 86.34 W
Crete 168 41.27 N 87.38 W
Creuse ≃ 42 47.00 N 0.34 E
Creve Coeur 168 40.39 N 89.35 W
Crevillente 50 38.15 N 0.48 W
Crewe 32 53.05 N 2.27 W
Crimmitschau 36 50.49 N 12.23 E
Crisfield 166 37.59 N 75.51 W
Cristóbal Colón, Pico ▲ 144 10.50 N 73.41 W
Crişu Alb ≃ 54 46.42 N 21.17 E
Crişu Negru ≃ 54 46.42 N 21.16 E
Crişu Repede (Sebes Körös) ≃ 54 46.55 N 20.59 E
Crooked Island ❙ 130 22.45 N 74.13 W
Crookston 162 47.47 N 96.37 W
Crooksville 166 39.46 N 82.06 W
Crosby 168 46.28 N 93.57 W
Crosby, Mount ▲ 180 43.53 N 109.20 W
Crossett 174 33.08 N 91.58 W
Cross Fell ▲ 32 54.42 N 2.29 W
Cross Plains 168 43.07 N 89.39 W
Crossville 174 35.58 N 85.02 W
Crotone 46 39.05 N 17.07 E
Crowley 174 30.13 N 92.22 W
Crowleys Ridge ▲ 174 35.45 N 90.45 W
Crown Point 174 41.25 N 87.22 W
Cruz, Cabo ➤ 130 19.51 N 77.44 W
Cruz del Eje 146 30.44 S 64.48 W
Crystal 168 45.00 N 93.25 W
Crystal City, Mo., U.S. 174 38.13 N 90.23 W
Crystal City, Tex., U.S. 162 28.41 N 99.50 W
Crystal Lake 168 42.14 N 88.19 W
Crystal Springs 174 31.59 N 90.21 W
Cserhát ✲ 36 47.55 N 19.30 E
Csongrád 36 46.43 N 20.09 E
Cuando (Kwando) ≃ 104 18.27 S 23.32 E
Cuango (Kwango) ≃ 104 3.14 S 17.23 E
Cuanza ≃ 104 9.19 S 13.08 E
Cuba 174 38.04 N 91.24 W
Cuba □1 130 21.30 N 80.00 W
Cubango (Okavango) ≃ 104 18.50 S 22.25 E
Cúcuta 144 7.54 N 72.31 W
Cudahy 168 42.57 N 87.52 W
Čudskoje Ozero ⊜ 62 58.40 N 27.25 E
Cuenca, Ec. 144 2.53 S 78.59 W
Cuenca, Esp. 50 40.04 N 2.08 W
Cuernavaca 130 18.55 N 99.15 W
Cugir 54 45.50 N 23.22 E
Cuiabá 144 15.35 S 56.05 W
Cuilo (Kwilu) ≃ 104 3.22 S 17.22 E
Cuito ≃ 104 18.01 S 20.48 E
Cuitzeo, Lago de ⊜ 130 19.55 N 101.05 W
Čukotskij Poluostrov ➤1 64 66.00 N 175.00 W
Culebra, Sierra de la ✲ 50 41.54 N 6.20 W
Culebra Peak ▲ 178 37.07 N 105.11 W
Culiacán 130 24.48 N 107.24 W
Cullera 50 39.10 N 0.15 W
Cullman 174 34.11 N 86.51 W
Cullowhee 172 35.19 N 83.11 W
Culpeper 166 38.28 N 77.53 W
Cumaná 144 10.28 N 64.10 W
Cumbal, Nevado de ▲ 144 0.57 N 77.52 W
Cumberland, Ky., U.S. 172 36.59 N 82.59 W
Cumberland, Md., U.S. 166 39.39 N 78.46 W
Cumberland, Wis., U.S. 168 45.32 N 92.01 W
Cumberland ≃ 162 37.09 N 88.25 W
Cumberland, Lake ⊜1 172 36.57 N 84.55 W
Cumberland Gap)(172 36.36 N 83.41 W
Cumberland Sound ⋃ 160 65.10 N 65.30 W
Cumbria □6 32 54.30 N 3.00 W
Cumerna ▲ 54 42.47 N 25.58 E
Cumming 172 34.13 N 84.08 W
Cunene ≃ 104 17.20 S 11.50 E
Cuneo 46 44.23 N 7.32 E
Curaçao ❙ 130 12.11 N 69.00 W
Curepipe 104 20.19 S 57.31 E
Curicó 146 34.59 S 71.14 W
Currituck Sound ⋃ 172 36.20 N 75.52 W
Curtea-de-Argeș 54 45.08 N 24.41 E
Curvelo 144 18.45 S 44.25 W
Curwood, Mount ▲2 168 46.42 N 88.14 W
Cut Bank 180 48.38 N 112.20 W
Cuthbert 172 31.46 N 84.48 W
Cutlerville 168 42.51 N 85.40 W
Cutro 46 39.02 N 16.59 E
Cuttack 84 20.26 N 85.53 E
Cuxhaven 36 53.52 N 8.42 E
Cuyahoga Falls 166 41.08 N 81.29 W
Cuyuni ≃ 144 6.23 N 58.41 W
Cuzco 144 13.31 S 71.59 W
Cyangugu 104 2.29 S 28.54 E
Cynthiana 166 38.23 N 84.18 W
Cyprus □1 20 35.00 N 33.00 E
Cyrenaica → Barqah ◆1 102 31.00 N 22.30 E
Czechoslovakia □1 36 49.30 N 17.00 E
Czechowice-Dziedzice 36 49.54 N 19.00 E
Częstochowa 36 50.49 N 19.06 E

D

Dacca 84 23.43 N 90.25 E
Dachau 36 48.15 N 11.27 E
Dade City 172 28.22 N 82.12 W
Dadeville 174 32.50 N 85.46 W
Dagupan 82 16.03 N 120.20 E
Dahlak Archipelago ❙❙ 102 15.45 N 40.30 E
Dahlonega 172 34.32 N 83.59 W
Dahra ✲ 50 36.25 N 1.00 E
Dahy, Nafūd ad- •8 84 22.20 N 45.35 E
Daimiel 50 39.04 N 3.37 W
Daingerfield 184 33.02 N 94.44 W
Dajianshan ▲ 80 26.42 N 103.34 E
Dakar 100 14.40 N 17.26 W
Dakhla 100 23.43 N 15.57 W
Đakovica 54 42.23 N 20.25 E
Dalälven ≃ 28 60.38 N 17.27 E
Dale Hollow Lake ⊜1 174 36.36 N 85.19 W
Daleville, Ala., U.S. 174 31.17 N 85.44 W
Daleville, Ind., U.S. 174 40.07 N 85.33 W
Dalhart 162 36.04 N 102.31 W
Dallas, N.C., U.S. 172 35.19 N 81.11 W
Dallas, Oreg., U.S. 180 44.55 N 123.19 W
Dallas, Pa., U.S. 166 41.20 N 75.58 W
Dallas, Tex., U.S. 162 32.47 N 96.48 W
Daloa 100 6.53 N 6.27 W
Dalton, Ga., U.S. 172 34.47 N 84.58 W
Dalton, Mass., U.S. 166 42.29 N 73.09 W
Daly City 184 37.42 N 122.29 W
Daly Waters 116 16.15 S 133.22 E
Damanhūr 102 31.02 N 30.28 E
Damascus → Dimashq, Sūrīy 84 33.30 N 36.18 E
Damascus, Md., U.S. 166 39.17 N 77.12 E
Damāvand, Qolleh-ye ▲ 84 35.56 N 52.08 E
Danakil Plain ⋍ 102 12.25 N 40.30 E
Da-nang 82 16.04 N 108.13 E
Danbury 166 41.23 N 73.27 W
Danby Lake ⊜ 184 34.14 N 115.07 W
Danger Point ➤ 104 34.40 S 19.17 E
Dania 172 26.03 N 80.09 W
Daniels Pass)(178 40.18 N 111.15 W
Dannemora 166 44.43 N 73.43 W
Dansville 166 42.34 N 77.42 W
Danube ≃ 20 45.20 N 29.40 E
Danube, Mouths of the ≃1 54 45.10 N 29.50 E
Danville, Ill., U.S. 174 40.08 N 87.37 W
Danville, Ind., U.S. 174 39.46 N 86.32 W
Danville, Ky., U.S. 174 37.39 N 84.46 W
Danville, Pa., U.S. 166 40.57 N 76.37 W
Danville, Va., U.S. 172 36.35 N 79.24 W
Danzig, Gulf of ⊂ 36 54.40 N 19.15 E
Dão ≃ 50 40.20 N 8.11 W
Daphne 174 30.36 N 87.54 W
Darabani 54 48.11 N 26.35 E
Darby 166 39.54 N 75.15 W
Darchan 80 49.28 N 105.56 E
Dardanelle 174 35.13 N 93.09 W
Dardanelle Lake ⊜1 174 35.25 N 93.20 W
Dardanelles → Çanakkale Boğazı ⋃ 54 40.15 N 26.25 E
Dar-el-Beida → Casablanca 100 33.39 N 7.35 W
Dar-es-Salaam 104 6.48 S 39.17 E
Darling ≃ 116 34.07 S 141.55 E
Darling Range ✲ 116 32.00 S 116.30 E
Darlington, Eng., U.K. 32 54.31 N 1.34 W
Darlington, S.C., U.S. 172 34.18 N 79.52 W
Darlington, Wis., U.S. 168 42.41 N 90.07 W
Darłowo 36 54.26 N 16.23 E
Darmstadt 36 49.53 N 8.40 E
Darnah 102 32.46 N 22.39 E
Darnétal 42 49.27 N 1.09 E
Darrington 180 48.15 N 121.36 W
Darsser Ort ➤ 36 54.29 N 12.31 E
Dartmoor ◆3 32 50.35 N 4.00 W
Dartmouth 160 44.40 N 63.34 W
Darwin 116 12.28 S 130.50 E
Dasht ≃ 84 25.10 N 61.40 E
Datong 80 40.08 N 113.13 E
Datu, Tandjung ➤ 82 2.05 N 109.39 E
Datu Piang 82 7.01 N 124.30 E
Daugava (Zapadnaja Dvina) ≃ 62 57.04 N 24.03 E
Daugavpils 26 55.53 N 26.32 E
Daule ≃ 144 2.10 S 79.52 W
Dauphin Island ❙ 174 30.14 N 88.12 W
Davao 82 7.04 N 125.36 E
Davao Gulf ⊂ 82 6.40 N 125.55 E
Davenport 168 41.32 N 90.41 W
David 130 8.26 N 82.26 W
Davidson 172 35.30 N 80.51 W
Davis 184 38.33 N 121.44 W
Davis, Mount ▲ 166 39.47 N 79.10 W
Davisson Lake ⊜1 180 46.30 N 122.20 W
Davis Strait ⋃ 160 67.00 N 57.00 W
Davos 42 46.48 N 9.50 E
Dawa (Daua) ≃ 102 4.11 N 42.06 E
Dawlish 32 50.35 N 3.28 W
Dawna Range ✲ 82 16.50 N 98.15 E
Dawson, Yukon, Can. 160 64.04 N 139.25 W
Dawson, Ga., U.S. 172 31.47 N 84.26 W
Dawson, Nebr., U.S. 174 40.08 N 95.50 W
Dawson Range ✲ 160 62.40 N 139.00 W
Dawson Springs 174 37.10 N 87.41 W
Dax 42 43.43 N 1.03 W
Daxing'anling-shanmai ✲ 80 49.40 N 122.00 E
Dayr az-Zawr 84 35.20 N 40.09 E
Dayrūt 102 27.33 N 30.49 E
Dayton, Ohio, U.S. 166 39.45 N 84.15 W
Dayton, Tenn., U.S. 174 35.30 N 85.00 W
Dayton, Wash., U.S. 180 46.19 N 117.59 W
Daytona Beach 172 29.12 N 81.00 W
De Aar 104 30.39 S 24.00 E
Dead Sea ⊜ 84 31.30 N 35.30 E
Deadwood 162 44.23 N 103.44 W
Deal 32 51.14 N 1.24 E
Dean Channel ⋃ 160 52.33 N 127.13 W
Dearborn 168 42.18 N 83.10 W
Dearg, Beinn ▲ 32 57.48 N 4.57 W
Dease ≃ 160 59.54 N 128.30 W
Death Valley ⋁ 184 36.30 N 117.00 W
Dębica 36 50.04 N 21.24 E
Dęblin 36 51.35 N 21.50 E
Debrecen 36 47.32 N 21.38 E
Debre Markos 102 10.20 N 37.45 E
Decatur, Ala., U.S. 174 34.36 N 86.59 W
Decatur, Ga., U.S. 172 33.46 N 84.18 W
Decatur, Ill., U.S. 174 39.51 N 89.32 W
Decatur, Ind., U.S. 174 40.50 N 84.56 W
Decazeville 42 44.34 N 2.15 E
Deccan ✲1 84 17.00 N 78.00 E
Deception Island ❙ 191 62.57 S 60.38 W
Decherd 174 35.13 N 86.05 W
Děčín 36 50.48 N 14.13 E
Decize 42 46.50 N 3.27 E
Decorah 168 43.18 N 91.48 W
Dee ≃ 32 51.20 N 4.00 W
Deerfield 168 42.10 N 87.51 W
Deerfield Beach 172 26.19 N 80.06 W
Deer Lodge 180 46.24 N 112.44 W
Deer Park 180 47.57 N 117.28 W
Deer River 168 47.20 N 93.48 W
Defiance 166 41.17 N 84.22 W
Deflotte, Cap ➤ 112 21.10 S 167.25 E
De Forest 168 43.15 N 89.20 W
De Funiak Springs 174 30.43 N 86.07 W
Deggendorf 36 48.51 N 12.59 E
De Gray Lake ⊜1 174 34.15 N 93.15 W
Dehiwala-Mount Lavinia 84 6.51 N 79.52 E
Dehra Dūn 84 30.20 N 78.02 E
Deinze 36 50.59 N 3.32 E
Dej 54 47.09 N 23.52 E
De Kalb 168 41.59 N 88.41 W
De Land 172 29.02 N 81.18 W
Delano, Calif., U.S. 184 35.41 N 119.15 W
Delano, Minn., U.S. 168 45.02 N 93.47 W
Delano Peak ▲ 178 38.22 N 112.23 W
Delaware, Ohio, U.S. 166 40.18 N 83.04 W
Delaware, Okla., U.S. 174 36.47 N 95.38 W
Delaware □3 162 39.10 N 75.30 W
Delaware ≃ 166 39.20 N 75.25 W
Delaware Bay ⊂ 166 39.05 N 75.15 W
Delaware City 166 39.34 N 75.36 W
Delcambre 174 29.57 N 91.57 W
Delémont 42 47.22 N 7.21 E
Delft 36 52.00 N 4.21 E
Delfzijl 36 53.19 N 6.46 E
Delgado, Cabo ➤ 104 10.40 S 40.35 E
Delhi, Bhārat 84 28.37 N 77.12 E
Delhi, La., U.S. 174 32.27 N 91.30 W
Delhi, N.Y., U.S. 166 42.17 N 74.55 W
Delicias 130 28.13 N 105.28 W
Delitzsch 36 51.31 N 12.20 E
Dellys 50 36.55 N 3.55 E
Delmenhorst 36 53.03 N 8.38 E
Delphi 174 40.36 N 86.41 W
Delphos 166 40.50 N 84.20 W
Delray Beach 172 26.28 N 80.04 W
Del Rio 162 29.22 N 100.54 W
Delta 178 38.44 N 108.04 W
Deming 178 32.16 N 107.45 W
Demirci 54 39.03 N 28.40 E
Demir Kapija ⋁ 54 41.24 N 22.15 E
Demmin 36 53.54 N 13.02 E
Demopolis 174 32.31 N 87.50 W
Dempo, Gunung ▲ 82 4.02 S 103.09 E
Denain 42 50.20 N 3.23 E
Dendermonde 36 51.02 N 4.07 E
Denham, Mount ▲ 130 18.13 N 77.32 W
Denham Springs 174 30.29 N 90.57 W
Den Helder 36 52.54 N 4.45 E
Denizli 54 37.46 N 29.06 E
Denmark 172 33.19 N 81.09 W
Denmark □1 28 56.00 N 10.00 E
Denmark Strait ⋃ 26a 67.00 N 25.00 W
Dennison 166 40.24 N 81.19 W
Denpasar 82 8.39 S 115.13 E
Denton 162 33.13 N 97.08 W
D'Entrecasteaux, Point ➤ 116 34.50 S 116.00 E
D'Entrecasteaux Islands ❙❙ 116a 9.30 S 150.40 E
Denver 178 39.43 N 105.01 W
De Pere 168 44.27 N 88.04 W
Depew 166 42.54 N 78.42 W
Deport 184 33.32 N 95.19 W
De Queen 174 34.02 N 94.21 W
De Quincy 174 30.27 N 93.26 W
Dera Ghāzi Khān 84 30.03 N 70.38 E
Dera Ismāīl Khān 84 31.50 N 70.54 E
Derby 32 52.55 N 1.29 W
Derbyshire □6 32 53.00 N 1.33 W
Derg, Lough ⊜ 32 53.00 N 8.20 W
De Ridder 174 30.51 N 93.17 W
Dermott 174 33.32 N 91.26 W
Derry 166 42.53 N 71.19 W
Derventa 54 44.58 N 17.55 E
Derwent ≃ 32 53.45 N 0.57 W
Desaguadero ≃, Arg. 146 34.13 S 66.47 W
Desaguadero ≃, Bol. 144 18.24 S 67.05 W
Des Allemands 174 29.50 N 90.28 W
Deschambault Lake ⊜ 160 54.40 N 103.35 W
Deschutes ≃ 180 45.38 N 120.54 W
Dese 102 11.05 N 39.41 E
Deseado ≃ 146 47.45 S 65.54 W
Desengaño, Punta ➤ 146 49.15 S 67.37 W
Desenzano del Garda 46 45.28 N 10.32 E
Deseret Peak ▲ 178 40.28 N 112.38 W
Desloge 174 37.53 N 90.33 W
Des Moines 168 41.35 N 93.37 W
Des Moines ≃ 162 40.22 N 91.26 W
Desna ≃ 62 50.33 N 30.32 E
De Soto 174 38.08 N 90.33 W
Despeñaperros, Desfiladero de)(50 38.24 N 3.30 W
Des Plaines 168 42.02 N 87.54 W
Dessau 36 51.50 N 12.14 E
Destin 174 30.24 N 86.30 W
Detmold 36 51.56 N 8.52 E
Detroit 168 42.20 N 83.03 W
Deutsche Bucht ⊂ 36 54.30 N 7.30 E
Deva 54 45.53 N 22.55 E
Dévaványa 36 47.02 N 20.58 E
Deventer 36 52.15 N 6.10 E
Devès, Monts du ✲ 42 45.00 N 3.45 E
Devils Lake 162 48.07 N 98.59 W
Devils Paw ▲ 162a 58.44 N 133.50 W
Devoll ≃ 54 40.49 N 19.51 E
Devon □6 32 50.45 N 3.50 W
Devon Island ❙ 160 75.00 N 87.00 W
Devonport 116 41.11 S 146.21 E
De Witt, Ark., U.S. 174 34.18 N 91.20 W
De Witt, Iowa, U.S. 168 41.49 N 90.33 W
De Witt, N.Y., U.S. 166 43.02 N 76.04 W
Dewsbury 32 53.42 N 1.37 W
Dexter, Maine, U.S. 166 45.01 N 69.18 W
Dexter, Mo., U.S. 174 36.48 N 89.57 W
Dezfūl 84 32.23 N 48.24 E
Dežneva, Mys ➤ 64 66.06 N 169.45 W
Dhamār 84 14.46 N 44.23 E
Dhaulāgiri ▲ 84 28.42 N 83.30 E
Dhodhekánisos (Dodecanese) ❙❙ 54 36.30 N 27.00 E
Diablo, Mount ▲ 184 37.53 N 121.55 W
Diablo Range ✲ 184 37.00 N 121.20 W
Diaka ≃1 100 15.13 N 4.14 W
Diamantina 144 18.15 S 43.36 W
Dibble Iceberg Tongue ⊼ 191 65.40 S 135.10 E
D'Iberville 174 30.26 N 88.54 W
Dickinson, N. Dak., U.S. 162 46.53 N 102.47 W
Dickinson, Tex., U.S. 174 29.28 N 95.03 W
Dickson 174 36.05 N 87.23 W
Diégo-Suarez 104 12.16 S 49.17 E
Diepholz 36 52.35 N 8.21 E
Dieppe 42 49.56 N 1.05 E
Digne 42 44.06 N 6.14 E
Digoin 42 46.29 N 3.59 E
Digul ≃ 82 7.07 S 138.42 E
Dijon 42 47.19 N 5.01 E
Dikhil 102 11.06 N 42.22 E
Dili 82 8.33 S 125.35 E
Dillon, Mont., U.S. 180 45.13 N 112.38 W
Dillon, S.C., U.S. 172 34.25 N 79.22 W
Dillon Lake ⊜1 166 40.02 N 82.10 W
Dimashq (Damascus) 84 33.30 N 36.18 E
Dimasse, Rass ➤ 46 35.37 N 11.03 E
Dîmbovița ≃ 54 44.14 N 26.27 E
Dimitrovgrad, Blg. 54 42.03 N 25.36 E
Dimitrovgrad, S.S.S.R. 26 54.14 N 49.39 E
Dimlang ▲ 100 8.24 N 11.47 E
Dinan 42 48.27 N 2.02 W
Dinant 36 50.16 N 4.55 E
Dinara ✲ 46 43.50 N 16.35 E
Dinard 42 48.38 N 2.04 W
Dingalan Bay ⊂ 82 15.18 N 121.25 E
Dingolfing 36 48.38 N 12.31 E
Dinkelsbühl 36 49.04 N 10.19 E
Dinosaur 178 40.15 N 109.01 W
Dinuba 184 36.32 N 119.23 W
Diourbel 100 14.40 N 16.15 W
Dire Dawa 102 9.37 N 41.52 E
Disappointment, Cape ➤ 146 54.53 S 36.07 W
Dishman 180 47.39 N 117.17 W
Disko ❙ 160 69.50 N 53.30 W
Disko Bugt ⊂ 160 69.15 N 52.00 W
Disney 174 36.29 N 95.01 W
District of Columbia □5 162 38.54 N 77.01 W
Disūq 102 31.08 N 30.39 E
Dithmarschen ◆1 36 54.05 N 9.00 E
Divinópolis 144 20.09 S 44.54 W
Divisor, Serra do ✲1 144 8.20 S 73.30 W
Dixfield 166 44.32 N 70.27 W
Dixon 168 41.50 N 89.29 W
Dixon Entrance ⋃ 162a 54.25 N 132.30 W
Diyarbakır 20 37.55 N 40.14 E
Dja ≃ 100 2.02 N 15.12 E
Djedi, Oued ⋁ 100 34.28 N 6.05 E
Djemmal 46 35.37 N 10.46 E
Djenné 100 13.54 N 4.33 W
Djerba, Île de ❙ 100 33.48 N 10.54 E
Djerem ≃ 100 5.20 N 13.24 E
Djerid, Chott ⩸ 100 33.42 N 8.26 E
Djibouti 102 11.36 N 43.09 E
Djibouti □1 102 11.30 N 43.00 E
Djidjelli 50 36.48 N 5.46 E
Djursholm 28 59.24 N 18.05 E
Dmitrija Lapteva, Proliv ⋃ 64 73.00 N 142.00 E
Dnepr ≃ 62 46.30 N 32.18 E
Dneprodzeržinsk 62 48.30 N 34.37 E
Dnepropetrovsk 62 48.27 N 34.59 E
Dnestr ≃ 62 46.18 N 30.17 E
Döbeln 36 51.07 N 13.07 E
Doberai, Jazirah ➤1 82 1.30 S 132.30 E
Doboj 54 44.44 N 18.06 E
Dobrudžansko plato ✲1 54 43.32 N 27.50 E
Dock Junction 172 31.11 N 81.31 W
Dodecanese → Dhodhekánisos ❙❙ 54 36.30 N 27.00 E
Dodge Center 168 44.02 N 92.51 W
Dodge City 162 37.45 N 100.01 W
Dodgeville 168 42.58 N 90.08 W
Dodman Point ➤ 32 50.13 N 4.48 W
Dodoma 104 6.11 S 35.45 E
Doetinchem 36 51.58 N 6.17 E
Doha → Ad-Dawhah 84 25.17 N 51.32 E
Doiran, Lake ⊜ 54 41.13 N 22.44 E
Dole 42 47.06 N 5.30 E
Dolisie 104 4.12 S 12.41 E
Dolomiti ✲ 46 46.25 N 11.50 E
Dolores ≃ 178 38.49 N 109.17 W
Dombes ◆1 42 46.00 N 5.03 E
Dombóvár 36 46.23 N 18.08 E
Domeyko, Cordillera ✲ 146 24.30 S 69.00 W
Dominica □1 130 15.30 N 61.20 W
Dominican Republic □1 130 19.00 N 70.40 W
Domodossola 46 46.07 N 8.17 E
Domuyo, Volcán ▲1 146 36.38 S 70.26 W
Don ≃ 62 47.04 N 39.18 E
Donaldsonville 174 30.06 N 90.59 W
Donalsonville 172 31.03 N 84.53 W
Donaueschingen 36 47.57 N 8.29 E
Don Benito 50 38.57 N 5.52 W
Doncaster 32 53.32 N 1.07 W
Dondra Head ➤ 84 5.55 N 80.35 E
Doneck 62 48.00 N 37.48 E
Donegal Bay ⊂ 32 54.30 N 8.30 W
Donga ≃ 100 8.19 N 9.58 E
Donghaidao ❙ 80 21.02 N 110.25 E
Dong-nai ≃ 82 10.45 N 106.46 E
Dongshaqundao (Pratas Islands) ❙❙ 80 20.42 N 116.43 E
Dongtinghu ⊜ 80 29.20 N 112.54 E
Doniphan 174 36.37 N 90.50 W
Donjek ≃ 160 62.35 N 140.00 W
Donner Pass)(184 39.19 N 120.20 W
Donora 166 40.11 N 79.52 W
Door Peninsula ➤1 168 44.55 N 87.20 W
Doraville 172 33.54 N 84.17 W
Dorchester 32 50.43 N 2.26 W
Dordogne ≃ 42 45.02 N 0.35 W
Dordrecht 36 51.49 N 4.40 E
Dore, Monts ✲ 42 45.30 N 2.45 E
Dornbirn 36 47.25 N 9.44 E
Dorohoi 54 47.57 N 26.24 E
Dorset □6 32 50.47 N 2.20 W
Dortmund 36 51.31 N 7.28 E
Dos Hermanas 50 37.17 N 5.55 W
Dothan 174 31.13 N 85.24 W
Douai 42 50.22 N 3.04 E
Douala 100 4.03 N 9.42 E
Douarnenez 42 48.06 N 4.20 W
Doubs ≃ 42 47.10 N 6.25 E
Doubtful Sound ⋃ 118 45.17 S 166.51 E
Douglas, I. of Man 32 54.09 N 4.28 W
Douglas, Ariz., U.S. 178 31.21 N 109.33 W
Douglas, Ga., U.S. 172 31.31 N 82.51 W
Douglas, Wyo., U.S. 178 42.45 N 105.24 W
Douglas Channel ⋃ 160 53.30 N 129.12 W
Douglas Lake ⊜1 172 36.00 N 83.22 W
Douglasville 172 33.45 N 84.45 W
Dourdou ≃ 42 44.00 N 2.41 E
Douro (Duero) ≃ 50 41.08 N 8.40 W
Douze ≃ 42 43.54 N 0.30 W
Dover, Eng., U.K. 32 51.08 N 1.19 E
Dover, Del., U.S. 166 39.10 N 75.32 W
Dover, N.H., U.S. 166 43.12 N 70.56 W
Dover, N.J., U.S. 166 40.53 N 74.34 W
Dover, Ohio, U.S. 166 40.32 N 81.29 W
Dover, Strait of (Pas de Calais) ⋃ 32 51.00 N 1.30 E
Dover-Foxcroft 166 45.11 N 69.13 W
Dowagiac 168 41.59 N 86.06 W
Downers Grove 174 41.48 N 88.01 W
Downingtown 166 40.00 N 75.42 W
Downs Mountain ▲ 180 43.18 N 109.40 W
Doylestown 166 40.19 N 75.08 W
Dra, Hamada du ◆2 100 29.00 N 6.45 W
Drâa, Oued ⋁ 100 28.43 N 11.09 W
Drachten 36 53.06 N 6.05 E
Dračie Jaskyně •5 36 49.05 N 19.35 E
Dracut 166 42.40 N 71.18 W
Drăgăşani 54 44.40 N 24.16 E
Dragonera, Isla ❙ 50 39.35 N 2.19 E
Draguignan 42 43.32 N 6.28 E
Drakensberg ✲ 104 27.00 S 30.00 E
Dráma 54 41.09 N 24.08 E
Drammen 28 59.44 N 10.15 E
Dranov, Ostrovul ❙ 54 44.52 N 29.15 E
Draper 178 40.32 N 111.52 W
Drau (Drava) (Dráva) ≃ 46 45.33 N 18.55 E
Drava (Drau) (Dráva) ≃ 46 45.33 N 18.55 E
Dravinja ≃ 46 46.22 N 15.57 E
Drawa ≃ 36 52.52 N 15.59 E
Dresden 36 51.03 N 13.44 E
Dreux 42 48.44 N 1.22 E
Drew 174 33.49 N 90.32 W
Drin ≃ 54 41.17 N 20.02 E
Drina ≃ 54 44.53 N 19.21 E
Drinit, Pellg i ⊂ 54 41.45 N 19.28 E
Driskill Mountain ▲2 174 32.25 N 92.54 W
Drobeta-Turnu-Severin 54 44.38 N 22.39 E
Drogheda 32 53.43 N 6.21 W
Dronne ≃ 42 45.02 N 0.09 W
Drummond Island ❙ 168 46.00 N 83.40 W
Drummondville 160 45.53 N 72.29 W
Drwęca ≃ 36 53.00 N 18.42 E
Duarte, Pico ▲ 130 19.02 N 70.59 W
Dubawnt Lake ⊜ 160 63.08 N 101.30 W
Dubayy 84 25.18 N 55.18 E
Dubbo 116 32.15 S 148.36 E
Dublin (Baile Átha Cliath), Eire 32 53.20 N 6.15 W
Dublin, Ga., U.S. 172 32.32 N 82.54 W
Dublin □6 32 53.20 N 6.15 W
Du Bois 166 41.07 N 78.46 W
Dubrovnik 54 42.38 N 18.07 E
Dubuque 168 42.30 N 90.41 W
Duck ≃ 174 36.02 N 87.52 W
Dudelange 36 49.28 N 6.05 E
Dudley 32 52.30 N 2.05 W
Dudweiler 36 49.17 N 7.02 E
Duero (Douro) ≃ 50 41.08 N 8.40 W
Dufourspitze ▲ 42 45.55 N 7.52 E
Dugi Otok ❙ 46 44.00 N 15.04 E
Du Gué ≃ 160 57.21 N 70.45 W
Duin Dui 112 15.24 S 167.46 E
Duisburg 36 51.25 N 6.46 E
Duitama 144 5.50 N 73.02 W
Dülmen 36 51.51 N 7.16 E
Duluth 168 46.47 N 92.06 W
Dumaguete 82 9.18 N 123.18 E
Dumas, Ark., U.S. 174 33.53 N 91.29 W
Dumbarton 32 55.57 N 4.35 W
Dumbier ▲ 36 48.57 N 19.37 E
Dumfries 32 55.04 N 3.37 W
Dumyāṭ 102 31.25 N 31.48 E
Dunajec ≃ 36 50.15 N 20.44 E
Dunărea Veche ≃ 54 45.17 N 28.02 E
Dunaújváros 36 46.58 N 18.57 E
Duna-völgyi-főcsatorna ⩸ 36 46.12 N 18.56 E
Dunbar 166 38.22 N 81.45 W
Duncan 162 34.30 N 97.57 W
Dundalk, Eire 32 54.01 N 6.25 W
Dundalk, Md., U.S. 166 39.15 N 76.31 W
Dundas 168 44.26 N 93.12 W
Dundee, Scot., U.K. 32 56.28 N 3.00 W
Dundee, Mich., U.S. 168 41.57 N 83.40 W
Dundrum Bay ⊂ 32 54.13 N 5.45 W
Dunedin, N.Z. 118 45.52 S 170.30 E
Dunedin, Fla., U.S. 172 28.00 N 82.47 W
Dunfermline 32 56.04 N 3.29 W
Dungeness ➤ 32 50.55 N 0.58 E
Dunkerque 42 51.03 N 2.22 E
Dunkirk, Ind., U.S. 174 40.23 N 85.13 W
Dunkirk, N.Y., U.S. 166 42.29 N 79.20 W
Dún Laoghaire 32 53.17 N 6.08 W
Dunn 172 35.19 N 78.37 W
Dunstable 32 51.53 N 0.32 W
DuQuoin 174 38.01 N 89.14 W
Durand, Mich., U.S. 168 42.55 N 83.59 W
Durand, Wis., U.S. 168 44.38 N 91.58 W
Durango, Esp. 50 43.10 N 2.37 W
Durango, Méx. 130 24.02 N 104.40 W
Durango, Colo., U.S. 178 37.16 N 107.53 W
Durant, Miss., U.S. 174 33.04 N 89.51 W
Durant, Okla., U.S. 162 34.00 N 96.23 W
Durazno 146 33.22 S 56.31 W
Durban 104 29.55 S 30.56 E
Düren 36 50.48 N 6.28 E
Durham, Eng., U.K. 32 54.47 N 1.34 W
Durham, N.H., U.S. 166 43.08 N 70.56 W
Durham, N.C., U.S. 172 35.59 N 78.54 W
Durham □6 32 54.45 N 1.45 W
Durmitor ▲ 54 43.08 N 19.01 E
Durrës 54 41.19 N 19.26 E
Dušanbe 62 38.35 N 68.48 E
Düsseldorf 36 51.12 N 6.47 E
Dvůr Králové [nad Labem] 36 50.26 N 15.48 E
Dwight 168 41.05 N 88.26 W
Dyer 174 36.04 N 88.59 W
Dyersburg 174 36.03 N 89.23 W
Dyersville 168 42.29 N 91.08 W
Dyfed □6 32 52.00 N 4.30 W
Dyje (Thaya) ≃ 36 48.37 N 16.56 E
Dyjsko-Svratecký Úval ⋁1 36 48.56 N 16.25 E
Džambul 62 42.54 N 71.22 E
Dzaoudzi 104 12.47 S 45.17 E
Dzavchan ≃ 80 48.54 N 93.23 E
Dzeržinsk 26 56.15 N 43.24 E
Dzierżoniów (Reichenbach) 36 50.44 N 16.39 E
Džugdžur, Chrebet ✲ 64 58.00 N 136.00 E

E

Name	Page	Lat ° ′	Long ° ′
Eagle Grove	168	42.40 N	93.54 W
Eagle Lake	184	40.39 N	120.44 W
Eagle Mountain	168	47.54 N	90.33 W
Eagle Pass	162	28.43 N	100.30 W
Eagleton Village	172	35.46 N	83.56 W
Earle	174	35.16 N	90.28 W
Earlington	174	37.16 N	87.30 W
Easley	172	34.50 N	82.36 W
East Alton	174	38.53 N	90.06 W
East Aurora	166	42.46 N	78.37 W
East-Berlin → Berlin (Ost)	36	52.30 N	13.25 E
Eastbourne	32	50.46 N	0.17 E
East Carbon	178	39.33 N	110.25 W
East Chicago	174	41.38 N	87.27 W
East China Sea	80	30.00 N	126.00 E
East Cote Blanche Bay	174	29.35 N	91.40 W
East Dereham	32	52.41 N	0.56 E
Eastern Ghāts	84	16.00 N	79.00 E
East Falkland	146	51.55 S	59.00 W
East Fayetteville	172	35.05 N	78.51 W
East Flat Rock	172	35.17 N	82.32 W
East Gaffney	172	35.05 N	81.42 W
East Grand Rapids	168	42.56 N	85.35 W
East Greenwich	166	41.40 N	71.27 W
East Grinstead	32	51.08 N	0.01 W
Easthampton	166	42.16 N	72.40 W
East Helena	180	46.35 N	111.56 W
East Kilbride	32	55.46 N	4.10 W
Eastlake	166	41.34 N	81.35 W
East Lansing	168	42.44 N	84.29 W
Eastleigh	32	50.58 N	1.22 W
East Liverpool	166	40.38 N	80.35 W
East London (Oos-Londen)	104	33.00 S	27.55 E
East Longmeadow	166	42.04 N	72.31 W
East Lynn Lake	166	38.05 N	82.20 W
Eastmain	160	52.15 N	78.35 W
Eastman	172	32.12 N	83.11 W
East Millinocket	166	45.37 N	68.35 W
East Moline	168	41.31 N	90.25 W
East Naples	172	26.08 N	81.46 W
Easton, Md., U.S.	166	38.46 N	76.04 W
Easton, Pa., U.S.	166	40.42 N	75.12 W
East Palestine	166	40.50 N	80.33 W
East Peoria	168	40.40 N	89.34 W
East Point	172	33.40 N	84.27 W
Eastport	166	44.54 N	67.00 W
East Porterville	184	36.04 N	118.56 W
East Prairie	174	36.47 N	89.23 W
East Retford	32	53.19 N	0.56 W
East Rockingham	172	34.57 N	79.45 W
East Saint Louis	174	38.38 N	90.09 W
East Spencer	172	35.41 N	80.26 W
East Stroudsburg	166	41.00 N	75.11 W
East Troy	168	42.47 N	88.24 W
Eaton	174	39.45 N	84.38 W
Eaton Rapids	168	42.36 N	84.39 W
Eatonton	172	33.20 N	83.23 W
Eau Claire	168	44.49 N	91.31 W
Eau-Claire, Lac à l'	160	56.10 N	74.25 W
Ebbw Vale	32	51.47 N	3.12 W
Ebensburg	166	40.29 N	78.44 W
Eberbach	36	49.28 N	8.59 E
Eberswalde	36	52.50 N	13.49 E
Ebingen	36	48.13 N	9.01 E
Ebola	102	3.20 N	20.57 E
Eboli	46	40.37 N	15.04 E
Ebro	50	40.43 N	0.54 E
Ebro, Delta del	50	40.43 N	0.54 E
Ebro, Embalse del	50	43.00 N	3.58 W
Écija	50	37.32 N	5.05 W
Eckernförde	36	54.28 N	9.50 E
Eckerö	28	60.14 N	19.35 E
Ecuador	144	2.00 S	77.30 W
Eddystone Rocks	32	50.12 N	4.15 W
Eddyville	174	37.03 N	88.04 W
Ede, Ned.	36	52.03 N	5.40 E
Ede, Nig.	100	7.44 N	4.27 E
Eden	180	42.03 N	109.26 W
Eden	32	54.57 N	3.01 W
Edenton	172	36.04 N	76.39 W
Eder	36	51.13 N	9.27 E
Edgefield	172	33.47 N	81.56 W
Edgemont	162	43.18 N	103.50 W
Edgerton	168	42.50 N	89.04 W
Edgewood	166	39.25 N	76.18 W
Édhessa	54	40.48 N	22.03 E
Edina, Minn., U.S.	168	44.55 N	93.20 W
Edina, Mo., U.S.	174	40.10 N	92.11 W
Edinboro	166	41.52 N	80.08 W
Edinburg, Ind., U.S.	174	39.21 N	85.58 W
Edinburg, Tex., U.S.	162	26.18 N	98.10 W
Edinburgh	32	55.57 N	3.13 W
Edirne	54	41.40 N	26.34 E
Edisto	172	32.39 N	80.24 W
Edisto Island	172	32.35 N	80.20 W
Edmonds	180	47.48 N	122.22 W
Edmonton	160	53.33 N	113.28 W
Edna	174	37.04 N	95.22 W
Edremit	54	39.35 N	27.01 E
Edremit Körfezi	54	39.30 N	26.45 E
Edrengijn Nuruu	80	44.15 N	97.45 E
Edward, Lake	104	0.25 S	29.30 E
Edwardsville	174	38.49 N	89.58 W
Eeklo	36	51.11 N	3.34 E
Eel	184	40.40 N	124.20 W
Eergu'nahe (Argun')	64	53.20 N	121.28 E
Effingham	174	39.07 N	88.33 W
Egadi, Isole	46	37.56 N	12.16 E
Egede og Rothes Fjord	160	66.00 N	38.00 W
Egedesminde	160	68.42 N	52.45 W
Eger	36	47.54 N	20.23 E
Egg Harbor City	166	39.32 N	74.39 W
Egypt	102	27.00 N	30.00 E
Eibar	50	43.11 N	2.28 W
Eichstätt	36	48.54 N	11.12 E
Eifel	36	50.15 N	6.45 E
Eilenburg	36	51.27 N	12.37 E
Einbeck	36	51.49 N	9.52 E
Eindhoven	36	51.26 N	5.28 E
Einsiedeln	42	47.08 N	8.45 E
Eisenach	36	50.59 N	10.19 E
Eisenberg	36	50.58 N	11.53 E
Eisenerz	36	47.33 N	14.53 E
Eisenerzer Alpen	36	47.28 N	14.45 E
Eisenhüttenstadt	36	52.10 N	14.39 E
Eisenstadt	36	47.51 N	16.32 E
Eisleben	36	51.31 N	11.32 E
Eislingen	36	48.42 N	9.42 E
Eitorf	36	50.46 N	7.26 E
Ejea de los Caballeros	50	42.08 N	1.08 W
Ekeren	36	51.17 N	4.25 E
Ekiatapskij Chrebet	64	68.30 N	179.00 E
El Aaiún	100	27.09 N	13.12 W
Elan	54	46.07 N	28.04 E
El Arahal	50	37.16 N	5.33 W
El Asnam	100	36.10 N	1.20 E
Elâzığ	20	38.41 N	39.14 E
Elba	174	31.25 N	86.04 W
Elba, Isola d'	46	42.46 N	10.17 E
El Banco	144	9.00 N	73.58 W
Elbasan	54	41.06 N	20.05 E
Elbe (Labe)	36	53.50 N	9.00 E
Elbe-Havel-Kanal	36	52.24 N	12.23 E
Elbert, Mount	178	39.07 N	106.27 W
Elberton	172	34.07 N	82.52 W
Elbeuf	42	49.17 N	1.00 E
Elbing → Elbląg	36	54.10 N	19.25 E
Elbląg (Elbing)	36	54.10 N	19.25 E
Elbląski, Kanał	36	53.43 N	19.53 E
El'brus, Gora	62	43.21 N	42.26 E
El Cajon	184	32.48 N	116.58 W
El Centro	184	32.48 N	115.34 W
Elche	50	38.15 N	0.42 W
Elda	50	38.29 N	0.47 W
El Djouf	100	20.30 N	8.00 W
Eldon	174	38.21 N	92.35 W
Eldora	168	42.19 N	93.26 W
El Dorado, Ark., U.S.	174	33.13 N	92.40 W
Eldorado, Ill., U.S.	174	37.49 N	88.26 W
El Dorado, Kans., U.S.	162	37.49 N	96.52 W
El Dorado Springs	174	37.52 N	94.01 W
Eldoret	104	0.31 N	35.17 E
Elektrostal'	62	55.47 N	38.28 E
Elephant Butte Reservoir	178	33.19 N	107.10 W
Elephant Island	191	61.10 S	55.14 W
Elephant Mountain	166	44.46 N	70.46 W
Eleuthera	130	25.10 N	76.14 W
Elevsís	54	38.02 N	23.32 E
El Ferrol del Caudillo	50	43.29 N	8.14 W
Elgin, Scot., U.K.	32	57.39 N	3.20 W
Elgin, Ill., U.S.	168	42.02 N	88.17 W
El Goléa	100	30.30 N	2.50 E
Elgon, Mount	104	1.08 N	34.33 E
El Hank	100	24.30 N	7.00 W
Elhovo	54	42.10 N	26.34 E
Elila	104	2.45 S	25.53 E
Eliot	166	43.09 N	70.48 W
Élisabethville → Lubumbashi	104	11.40 S	27.28 E
Elizabeth, Austl.	116	34.43 S	138.40 E
Elizabeth, N.J., U.S.	166	40.40 N	74.11 W
Elizabeth City	172	36.18 N	76.14 W
Elizabethton	172	36.21 N	82.13 W
Elizabethtown	174	37.42 N	85.52 W
El-Jadida	100	33.16 N	8.30 W
Ełk	36	53.50 N	22.22 E
Ełk, Pol.	36	53.31 N	22.47 E
Elk, W. Va., U.S.	166	38.21 N	81.38 W
El Kairouan	100	35.41 N	10.07 E
El Kala	46	36.50 N	8.30 E
El Kef	100	36.11 N	8.43 E
Elk Grove	184	38.25 N	121.22 W
Elkhart	174	41.41 N	85.58 W
Elkhorn	168	42.40 N	88.33 W
Elkin	172	36.16 N	80.51 W
Elkins	166	38.55 N	79.51 W
Elko	184	40.50 N	115.46 W
Elk River	168	45.18 N	93.35 W
Elkton	166	39.36 N	75.50 W
Ellendale, Minn., U.S.	168	43.52 N	93.18 W
Ellendale, N. Dak., U.S.	162	46.06 N	98.32 W
Ellensburg	180	47.00 N	120.32 W
Ellenville	166	41.43 N	74.28 W
Ellice	160	68.02 N	103.26 W
Ellicott City	166	39.16 N	76.48 W
Ellisville	174	31.36 N	89.12 W
Ellsworth, Maine, U.S.	166	44.33 N	68.26 W
Ellsworth, Wis., U.S.	168	44.44 N	92.29 W
Ellwangen	36	48.57 N	10.07 E
Ellwood City	166	40.50 N	80.17 W
Elma	180	47.00 N	123.25 W
El Mahdia	46	35.30 N	11.04 E
Elmhurst	168	41.53 N	87.56 W
Elmira	166	42.06 N	76.49 W
El Mirage	178	33.36 N	112.19 W
Elmira Heights	166	42.08 N	76.49 W
El Moknine	100	35.38 N	10.54 E
El Mreyyé	100	19.30 N	7.00 W
Elmshorn	36	53.45 N	9.39 E
El Nevado, Cerro, Arg.	146	35.35 S	68.30 W
El Nevado, Cerro, Col.	144	3.59 N	74.04 W
Elobey, Islas	104	0.59 N	9.30 E
El Oued	100	33.20 N	6.58 E
Eloy	178	32.45 N	111.33 W
El Paso	178	31.45 N	106.29 W
El Puerto de Santa María	50	36.36 N	6.13 W
El Reno	162	35.32 N	97.57 W
El Rio	184	34.14 N	119.10 W
Elroy	168	43.45 N	90.16 W
Elsa	160	63.55 N	135.28 W
El Salvador	130	13.50 N	88.55 W
Elsinore → Helsingør	28	56.02 N	12.37 E
Elsmere	166	39.44 N	75.36 W
Elsterwerda	36	51.28 N	13.31 E
El Tigre	144	8.55 N	64.15 W
Elvas	50	38.53 N	7.10 W
Elvins	174	37.50 N	90.34 W
Elwood, Ind., U.S.	174	40.17 N	85.50 W
Elwood, Kans., U.S.	174	39.45 N	94.52 W
Ely, Minn., U.S.	168	47.54 N	91.51 W
Ely, Nev., U.S.	184	39.15 N	114.53 W
Elyria	166	41.22 N	82.06 W
Embarras	174	38.39 N	87.37 W
Emden	36	53.22 N	7.12 E
Eminence	174	38.22 N	85.11 W
Emmaus	166	40.32 N	75.30 W
Emmen	36	52.47 N	7.00 E
Emmendingen	36	48.07 N	7.50 E
Emmerich	36	51.50 N	6.15 E
Emmett	180	43.52 N	116.30 W
Empalme	130	27.58 N	110.51 W
Emperor Range	114	5.45 S	154.55 E
Empoli	46	43.43 N	10.57 E
Emporia, Kans., U.S.	162	38.24 N	96.11 W
Emporia, Va., U.S.	172	36.41 N	77.32 W
Ems	36	53.30 N	7.00 E
Emsdetten	36	52.10 N	7.31 E
En (Inn)	42	48.35 N	13.28 E
Encampment	180	41.12 N	106.47 W
Encarnación	146	27.20 S	55.54 W
Encinitas	184	33.03 N	117.17 W
Encounter Bay	116	35.35 S	138.44 E
Enderby Land	191	67.30 S	53.00 E
Enfield	172	36.11 N	77.47 W
Engel's	62	51.30 N	46.07 E
England	174	34.33 N	91.58 W
England	32	52.30 N	1.30 W
Englewood, Colo., U.S.	178	39.39 N	104.59 W
Englewood, Fla., U.S.	172	26.58 N	82.21 W
English	160	50.12 N	95.00 W
English Channel (La Manche)	32	50.20 N	1.00 W
Enid	162	36.19 N	97.48 W
Enka	172	35.32 N	82.38 W
Enkhuizen	36	52.42 N	5.17 E
Enköping	28	59.38 N	17.04 E
Enna	46	37.34 N	14.17 E
Ennedi	102	17.15 N	22.00 E
Enns	36	48.13 N	14.29 E
Enns	36	48.14 N	14.32 E
Enosburg Falls	166	44.55 N	72.48 W
Enschede	36	52.12 N	6.53 E
Ensenada	130	31.52 N	116.37 W
Entebbe	104	0.04 N	32.28 E
Entenbühl	36	49.46 N	12.24 E
Enterprise, Ala., U.S.	174	31.19 N	85.51 W
Enterprise, Calif., U.S.	184	39.32 N	121.22 W
Entinas, Punta	50	36.41 N	2.46 W
Enugu	100	6.27 N	7.27 E
Enumclaw	180	47.12 N	121.59 W
Envalira, Port d'	50	42.35 N	1.45 E
Enza	46	44.54 N	10.31 E
Eo	50	43.28 N	7.03 W
Eolie, Isole	46	38.30 N	15.00 E
Épernay	42	49.03 N	3.57 E
Ephraim	178	39.22 N	111.35 W
Ephrata, Pa., U.S.	166	40.11 N	76.10 W
Ephrata, Wash., U.S.	180	47.19 N	119.33 W
Épinal	42	48.11 N	6.27 E
Epping	32	51.43 N	0.07 E
Epsom	32	51.20 N	0.16 W
Equatorial Guinea	100	2.00 N	9.00 E
Erath	174	29.58 N	92.02 W
Erba	46	45.48 N	9.15 E
Erciyeş Dağı	20	38.32 N	35.28 E
Érd	36	47.23 N	18.56 E
Erdek	54	40.24 N	27.48 E
Erding	36	48.18 N	11.54 E
Erebus, Mount	191	77.32 S	167.09 E
Erft	36	51.11 N	6.44 E
Erfurt	36	50.58 N	11.01 E
Ergene	54	41.01 N	26.22 E
Erges (Erjas)	50	39.40 N	7.01 E
Erice	46	38.02 N	12.36 E
Erie	166	42.08 N	80.04 W
Erie, Lake	162	42.15 N	81.00 W
Erímanthos	54	37.59 N	21.51 E
Erjas (Erges)	50	39.40 N	7.01 W
Erkelenz	36	51.05 N	9.19 E
Erlangen	36	49.36 N	11.01 E
Ermelo	104	26.34 S	29.58 E
Ermoúpolis	54	37.26 N	24.56 E
Erne, Lower Lough	32	54.10 N	7.30 W
Erne, Upper Lough	32	54.20 N	7.30 W
Eromanga	112	18.45 S	169.05 E
Errol Heights	180	45.29 N	122.33 W
Erwin	172	36.09 N	82.25 W
Erzgebirge (Krušné hory)	36	50.30 N	13.10 E
Erzincan	20	39.44 N	39.29 E
Erzurum	20	39.55 N	41.17 E
Esbjerg	28	55.28 N	8.27 E
Esbo → Espo	28	60.13 N	24.40 E
Esca	50	42.37 N	1.03 W
Escanaba	168	45.45 N	87.04 W
Escarpada Point	82	18.31 N	122.13 E
Escaut (Schelde)	36	51.22 N	4.15 E
Esch-sur-Alzette	36	49.30 N	5.59 E
Eschwege	36	51.11 N	10.04 E
Eschweiler	36	50.49 N	6.16 E
Escondido	184	33.07 N	117.05 W
Escuintla	130	14.18 N	90.47 W
Escurial, Serra do	144	10.04 S	41.05 W
Eşfahān	84	32.40 N	51.38 E
Eskilstuna	28	59.22 N	16.30 E
Eskişehir	20	39.46 N	30.32 E
Esmeraldas	144	0.59 N	79.42 W
Esmeraldas	144	0.58 N	79.38 W
Espanola	178	36.06 N	106.02 W
Espinhaço, Serra do	144	17.30 S	43.30 W
Espinho	50	41.00 N	8.39 W
Espíritu Santo	112	15.50 S	166.50 E
Espoo (Esbo)	28	60.13 N	24.40 E
Esquel	146	42.54 S	71.19 W
Essaouira	100	31.30 N	9.47 W
Essen	36	51.28 N	7.01 E
Essequibo	144	6.59 N	58.23 W
Essex	166	39.18 N	76.29 W
Essex Junction	166	44.29 N	73.07 W
Essexville	168	43.37 N	83.50 W
Esslingen	36	48.45 N	9.16 E
Est, Cap	104	15.16 S	50.29 E
Est, Pointe de l'	160	49.08 N	61.41 W
Estaca de Bares, Punta de la	50	43.46 N	7.42 W
Estacado, Llano	162	33.30 N	102.40 W
Estados, Isla de los	146	54.47 S	64.15 W
Estats, Pique d'	50	42.40 N	1.24 E
Este	46	45.14 N	11.39 E
Estelí	130	13.05 N	86.23 W
Estepona	50	36.26 N	5.08 W
Estes Park	178	40.23 N	105.31 W
Estrela	50	40.19 N	7.37 W
Estrela, Serra da	50	40.20 N	7.38 W
Estremadura	50	39.15 N	9.10 W
Esztergom	36	47.48 N	18.45 E
Étampes	42	48.26 N	2.09 E
Étaples	42	50.31 N	1.39 E
Ethiopia	102	9.00 N	39.00 E
Etna, Monte	46	37.46 N	15.00 E
Etoshapan	104	18.45 S	16.15 E
Etowah	172	35.20 N	84.32 W
Ettlingen	36	48.56 N	8.24 E
Ettrick	172	37.14 N	77.25 W
Eu	42	50.03 N	1.25 E
Euclid	166	41.34 N	81.32 W
Eudora, Ark., U.S.	174	33.07 N	91.16 W
Eudora, Kans., U.S.	174	38.57 N	95.06 W
Eufaula, Ala., U.S.	174	31.54 N	85.09 W
Eufaula, Okla., U.S.	174	35.17 N	95.35 W
Eufaula Lake	174	35.17 N	95.31 W
Eugene	180	44.02 N	123.05 W
Eugenia, Punta	130	27.50 N	115.05 W
Eume	50	43.25 N	8.08 W
Eunice	174	30.30 N	92.25 W
Eupen	36	50.38 N	6.02 E
Euphrates (Al-Furāt) (Fırat)	84	31.00 N	47.25 E
Eureka, Calif., U.S.	184	40.47 N	124.09 W
Europa, Picos de	50	43.12 N	4.48 W
Europa Point	50	36.10 N	5.22 W
Euskirchen	36	50.39 N	6.47 E
Eustis	172	28.51 N	81.41 W
Eutaw	174	32.50 N	87.53 W
Eutin	36	54.08 N	10.37 E
Eutsuk Lake	160	53.20 N	126.44 W
Evadale	184	30.21 N	94.04 W
Evans	178	40.22 N	104.40 W
Evans, Mount	178	39.35 N	105.38 W
Evansdale	168	42.30 N	92.17 W
Evanston, Ill., U.S.	168	42.03 N	87.42 W
Evanston, Wyo., U.S.	180	41.16 N	110.58 W
Evansville, Ind., U.S.	174	37.58 N	87.35 W
Evansville, Wis., U.S.	168	42.47 N	89.18 W
Eveleth	168	47.28 N	92.32 W
Everest	174	39.41 N	95.26 W
Everest, Mount (Zhumulangmafeng)	84	27.59 N	86.56 E
Everett	180	47.59 N	122.31 W
Evergem	36	51.07 N	3.42 E
Evergreen	174	31.26 N	86.57 W
Evergreen Park	174	41.43 W	87.42 W
Evesham	32	52.06 N	1.56 W
Évora	50	38.34 N	7.54 W
Évreux	42	49.01 N	1.09 E
Évros (Marica) (Meriç)	54	40.52 N	26.12 E
Évvoia	54	38.34 N	23.50 E
Excelsior Springs	174	39.20 N	94.13 W
Exe	32	50.37 N	3.25 W
Executive Committee Range	191	76.50 S	126.00 W
Exeter, Eng., U.K.	32	50.43 N	3.31 W
Exeter, Calif., U.S.	184	36.18 N	119.09 W
Exeter, N.H., U.S.	166	42.59 N	70.57 W
Exmouth	32	50.37 N	3.25 W
Experiment	172	33.16 N	84.17 W
Extremadura	50	39.00 N	6.00 W
Exuma Sound	130	24.15 N	76.00 W
Eyasi, Lake	104	3.40 S	35.05 E
Eyre North, Lake	116	28.40 S	137.10 E
Eyre South, Lake	116	29.30 S	137.20 E
Ezine	54	39.47 N	26.20 E

F

Name	Page	Lat ° ′	Long ° ′
Fabriano	46	43.20 N	12.54 E
Faddeja, Zaliv	62	76.40 N	107.20 E
Faenza	46	44.17 N	11.53 E
Faeroe Islands	20	62.00 N	7.00 W
Fafen	102	6.07 N	44.20 E
Făgăraş	54	45.51 N	24.58 E
Făgăraş, Munţii	54	45.35 N	25.00 E
Fagersta	28	60.00 N	15.47 E
Faguibine, Lac	100	16.45 N	3.54 W
Fairbanks	162a	64.51 N	147.43 W
Fairburn	172	33.34 N	84.35 W
Fairbury, Ill., U.S.	168	40.45 N	88.31 W
Fairbury, Nebr., U.S.	162	40.08 N	97.11 W
Fairfax, Ala., U.S.	174	32.48 N	85.11 W
Fairfax, Va., U.S.	166	38.51 N	77.18 W
Fairfield, Ala., U.S.	174	33.29 N	86.55 W
Fairfield, Calif., U.S.	184	38.15 N	122.03 W
Fairfield, Ill., U.S.	174	38.23 N	88.22 W
Fairfield, Iowa, U.S.	168	40.56 N	91.57 W
Fairfield, Maine, U.S.	166	44.35 N	69.36 W
Fairfield, Ohio, U.S.	166	39.20 N	84.33 W
Fairhaven, Mass., U.S.	166	41.39 N	70.54 W
Fair Haven, Vt., U.S.	166	43.36 N	73.16 W
Fair Head	32	55.13 N	6.09 W
Fairhope	174	30.31 N	87.54 W
Fair Isle	32	59.30 N	1.40 W
Fairland	174	36.45 N	94.51 W
Fairmont, Minn., U.S.	162	43.39 N	94.28 W
Fairmont, N.C., U.S.	172	34.30 N	79.07 W
Fairmont, W. Va., U.S.	166	39.29 N	80.09 W
Fairmount	174	40.25 N	85.39 W
Fair Oaks, Calif., U.S.	184	38.39 N	121.16 W
Fair Oaks, Ga., U.S.	172	33.55 N	84.32 W
Fair Plain	168	42.05 N	86.28 W
Fairport Harbor	166	41.45 N	81.17 W
Fairview	174	39.50 N	95.44 W
Fairweather, Mount	160	58.54 N	137.32 W
Falcon, Cap	50	35.46 N	0.48 W
Falconara Marittima	46	43.37 N	13.24 E
Falémé	100	14.46 N	12.14 W
Falkenberg	28	56.54 N	12.28 E
Falkensee	36	52.33 N	13.04 E
Falkenstein	36	50.29 N	12.22 E
Falkirk	32	56.00 N	3.48 W
Falkland Islands	146	51.45 S	59.00 W
Falkland Sound	146	51.45 S	59.25 W
Falköping	28	58.10 N	13.31 E
Fallbrook	184	33.23 N	117.15 W
Fallon	184	39.28 N	118.47 W
Fall River	166	41.43 N	71.08 W
Falls City	174	40.03 N	95.36 W
Falmouth, Eng., U.K.	32	50.08 N	5.04 W
Falmouth, Ky., U.S.	166	38.40 N	84.20 W
Falmouth, Maine, U.S.	166	43.39 N	70.16 W
False Divi Point	84	15.45 N	80.50 E
Falster	28	54.48 N	11.58 E
Fălticeni	54	47.28 N	26.18 E
Falun	28	60.36 N	15.38 E
Fano	46	43.50 N	13.01 E
Fan-si-pan	82	22.15 N	103.46 E
Faraān, Jazā'ir	84	16.48 N	41.54 E
Farafangana	104	22.49 S	47.50 E
Farah	84	31.29 N	61.24 E
Farcăul	54	47.56 N	24.27 E
Fareham	32	50.51 N	1.10 W
Farewell, Cape	118	40.30 S	172.41 E
Farewell Spit	118	40.31 S	172.52 E
Fargo	162	46.52 N	96.48 W
Faribault	168	44.18 N	93.16 W
Farilhões	50	39.28 N	9.34 W
Farmerville	174	32.47 N	92.24 W
Farmington, Ill., U.S.	168	40.42 N	90.00 W
Farmington, Maine, U.S.	166	44.40 N	70.09 W
Farmington, Minn., U.S.	168	44.38 N	93.08 W
Farmington, Mo., U.S.	174	37.47 N	90.25 W
Farmington, N.H., U.S.	166	43.24 N	71.04 W
Farmington, N. Mex., U.S.	178	36.44 N	108.12 W
Farmington, Utah, U.S.	178	40.59 N	111.53 W
Farmville, N.C., U.S.	172	35.36 N	77.35 W
Farmville, Va., U.S.	172	37.18 N	78.24 W
Farne Islands	32	55.38 N	1.38 W
Faro	50	37.01 N	7.56 W
Faro	100	9.21 N	12.55 E
Faro, Punta del	46	38.17 N	15.39 E
Fårön	28	57.56 N	19.08 E
Farquhar Group	104	10.10 S	51.10 E
Farrell	166	41.13 N	80.30 W
Fartak, Ra's	84	15.38 N	52.15 E
Farvel, Kap	160	59.45 N	44.00 W
Fasano	46	40.50 N	17.22 E
Favara	46	37.19 N	13.40 E
Favignana, Isola	46	37.56 N	12.19 E
Faxaflói	26a	64.25 N	23.00 W
Faxälven	28	63.13 N	17.13 E
Fayette, Ala., U.S.	174	33.42 N	87.50 W
Fayette, Iowa, U.S.	168	42.51 N	91.48 W
Fayette, Mo., U.S.	174	39.09 N	92.41 W
Fayetteville, Ark., U.S.	174	36.04 N	94.10 W
Fayetteville, Ga., U.S.	172	33.27 N	84.27 W
Fayetteville, N.C., U.S.	172	35.03 N	78.54 W
Fayetteville, Tenn., U.S.	174	35.09 N	86.35 W
Fazzān (Fezzan)	102	26.00 N	14.00 E
Fear, Cape	172	33.50 N	77.58 W
Feather	184	38.47 N	121.36 W
Fécamp	42	49.45 N	0.22 E
Federalsburg	166	38.42 N	75.47 W
Fedjadj, Chott el	100	33.55 N	9.10 E
Fehérgyarmat	36	47.58 N	22.32 E
Fehmarn	36	54.28 N	11.08 E
Fehmarn Belt	36	54.35 N	11.15 E
Feia, Lagoa	144	22.00 S	41.20 W
Feira de Santana	144	12.15 S	38.57 W
Feistritz	36	47.01 N	16.08 E
Feldkirch	36	47.14 N	9.36 E
Felixstowe	32	51.58 N	1.20 E
Fellbach	36	48.48 N	9.15 E
Feltre	46	46.01 N	11.54 E
Femunden	28	62.12 N	11.52 E
Fennimore	168	42.59 N	90.39 W
Fenton	168	42.48 N	83.42 W
Fergana	62	40.23 N	71.46 E
Fergus Falls	162	46.17 N	96.04 W
Ferguson	174	38.46 N	90.19 W
Ferlo, Vallée du	100	15.42 N	15.30 W
Fermo	46	43.09 N	13.43 E
Fernandina Beach	172	30.40 N	81.27 W
Fernán-Núñez	50	37.40 N	4.43 W
Ferndale, Mich., U.S.	166	42.28 N	83.08 W
Ferndale, Wash., U.S.	180	48.51 N	122.36 W
Fernley	184	39.36 N	119.15 W
Ferrara	46	44.50 N	11.35 E
Ferrat, Cap	50	35.54 N	0.23 W
Ferrato, Capo	46	39.18 N	9.38 E
Ferret, Cap	42	44.37 N	1.15 W
Ferriday	174	31.38 N	91.33 W
Fès	100	34.05 N	4.57 W
Festus	174	38.13 N	90.24 W
Feteşti	54	44.23 N	27.50 E
Fethiye	54	36.37 N	29.07 E
Feuilles, Rivière aux	160	58.47 N	70.04 W
Feyẕābād	84	35.01 N	58.46 E
Fianarantsoa	104	21.26 S	47.05 E
Fichtelberg	36	50.26 N	12.57 E
Fichtelgebirge	36	50.26 N	12.57 E
Fidenza	46	44.52 N	10.03 E
Fier	54	40.43 N	19.34 E
Figueira da Foz	50	40.09 N	8.52 W
Figueras	50	42.16 N	2.58 E
Figuig	100	32.10 N	1.15 W
Fiji	111	18.00 S	175.00 E
Filchner Ice Shelf	191	79.00 S	40.00 W
Filicudi, Isola	46	38.35 N	14.34 E
Fillmore	184	34.24 N	118.55 W
Fimi	104	3.01 S	16.58 E
Finale Ligure	46	44.10 N	8.20 E
Findlay	166	41.02 N	83.39 W
Finisterre, Cabo de	50	42.53 N	9.16 W
Finland	26	64.00 N	26.00 E
Finland, Gulf of	26	60.00 N	27.00 E
Finlay	160	57.00 N	125.05 W
Finn	32	54.50 N	7.29 W
Finspång	28	58.43 N	15.47 E
Finsterwalde	36	51.38 N	13.42 E
Fiora	46	42.20 N	11.34 E
Fırat → Euphrates	84	31.00 N	47.25 E
Firenze (Florence)	46	43.46 N	11.15 E
Firminy	42	45.23 N	4.18 E
Firth	162a	69.32 N	139.22 W
Fischbacher Alpen	36	47.28 N	15.30 E
Fish	104	28.07 S	17.45 E
Fitchburg	166	42.35 N	71.48 W
Fitzgerald	172	31.43 N	83.15 W
Five Points	178	35.04 N	106.41 W
Flagstaff	178	35.12 N	111.39 W
Flagstaff Lake	166	45.10 N	70.15 W
Flamborough Head	32	54.07 N	0.04 W
Fläming	36	52.00 N	12.30 E
Flaming Gorge Reservoir	178	41.15 N	109.30 W
Flathead Lake	180	47.52 N	114.08 W
Flat River	174	37.51 N	90.31 W
Flat Rock	166	42.06 N	83.18 W
Flattery, Cape	180	48.23 N	124.43 W
Flatwoods	166	38.31 N	82.43 W
Fleetwood	32	53.56 N	3.01 W
Flemingsburg	166	36.25 N	83.44 W
Flensburg	36	54.47 N	9.26 E
Flint, Wales, U.K.	32	53.15 N	3.07 W
Flint, Mich., U.S.	168	43.01 N	83.41 W
Flint	172	30.52 N	84.38 W
Flora	174	38.40 N	88.29 W
Florala	174	31.00 N	86.20 W
Florence → Firenze, It.	46	43.46 N	11.15 E
Florence, Ala., U.S.	174	34.49 N	87.40 W
Florence, Ariz., U.S.	178	33.02 N	111.23 W
Florence, Colo., U.S.	178	38.23 N	105.08 W
Florence, S.C., U.S.	172	34.12 N	79.46 W
Florencia	144	1.36 N	75.36 W
Flores	82	8.30 S	121.00 E
Floriano	144	6.47 S	43.01 W
Florida	162	28.00 N	82.00 W
Florida, Straits of	130	25.00 N	79.45 W
Florida Bay	172	25.00 N	80.45 W
Florida City	172	25.27 N	80.29 W
Florida Keys	172	24.45 N	81.00 W
Floridia	46	37.04 N	15.10 E
Flórina	54	40.47 N	21.24 E
Florissant	174	38.48 N	90.20 W
Flumen	50	41.43 N	0.09 W
Flumendosa	46	39.26 N	9.38 E
Flushing → Vlissingen, Ned.	36	51.26 N	3.35 E
Flushing, Mich., U.S.	168	43.04 N	83.51 W
Fluvia	50	42.12 N	3.07 E
Foča	54	43.31 N	18.46 E
Focşani	54	45.41 N	27.11 E
Foggia	46	41.27 N	15.34 E
Fogo Island	160	49.40 N	54.13 W
Fohnsdorf	36	47.13 N	14.41 E
Föhr	36	54.43 N	8.30 E
Foia	50	37.19 N	8.36 W
Foix	42	43.00 N	1.40 E
Foley, Ala., U.S.	174	30.25 N	87.41 W
Foley	168	45.40 N	93.55 W
Foligno	46	42.57 N	12.42 E
Folkestone	32	51.05 N	1.11 E
Folkston	172	30.50 N	82.01 W
Follonica, Golfo di	46	42.54 N	10.43 E
Folsom	184	38.41 N	121.15 W
Folsom Lake	184	38.43 N	121.08 W
Fond du Lac	168	43.47 N	88.27 W
Fondi	46	41.21 N	13.25 E
Fontainebleau	42	48.24 N	2.42 E
Fontana	184	34.06 N	117.26 W
Fontenay-le-Comte	42	46.28 N	0.48 W
Forbach	42	49.11 N	6.54 E
Forchheim	36	49.43 N	11.04 E
Ford City	166	40.46 N	79.32 W
Fordyce	174	33.49 N	92.25 W
Forel, Mont	160	67.00 N	37.00 W
Forest	174	32.22 N	89.28 W
Forest Acres	172	34.01 N	80.58 W
Forest City, Iowa, U.S.	168	43.16 N	93.39 W
Forest City, N.C., U.S.	172	35.20 N	81.52 W
Forest City, Pa., U.S.	166	41.39 N	75.28 W
Forest Lake	168	45.17 N	92.59 W
Forest Park	172	33.37 N	84.22 W
Forez, Monts du	42	45.35 N	3.48 E
Forggensee	36	47.36 N	10.44 E
Forks	180	47.57 N	124.23 W
Forlì	46	44.13 N	12.03 E
Formby Point	32	53.33 N	3.06 W
Formia	46	41.15 N	13.37 E
Formosa	146	26.11 S	58.11 W
Forrest City	174	35.01 N	90.47 W
Forst	36	51.44 N	14.39 E
Forsyth, Ga., U.S.	172	33.02 N	83.56 W
Forsyth, Mont., U.S.	180	46.16 N	106.41 W
Fortaleza	144	3.43 S	38.30 W
Fort Atkinson	168	42.56 N	88.50 W
Fort Benton	180	47.49 N	110.40 W
Fort Branch	174	38.15 N	87.35 W
Fort Bridger	180	41.19 N	110.23 W
Fort Collins	178	40.35 N	105.05 W
Fort-Dauphin	104	25.02 S	47.00 E
Fort-de-France	130	14.36 N	61.05 W
Fort Dodge	168	42.30 N	94.10 W
Fort Edward	166	43.16 N	73.35 W
Fort Garland	178	37.26 N	105.26 W
Fort Gibson	174	35.48 N	95.15 W
Fort Gibson Lake	174	36.00 N	95.18 W
Forth, Firth of	32	56.05 N	2.55 W
Fort-Lamy → Ndjamena	102	12.07 N	15.03 E
Fort Lauderdale	172	26.07 N	80.08 W
Fort Loudoun Lake	172	35.45 N	84.10 W
Fort Lupton	178	40.05 N	104.49 W
Fort Madison	168	40.38 N	91.27 W
Fort McPherson	160	67.27 N	134.53 W
Fort Meade	172	27.45 N	81.48 W
Fort Mill	172	35.01 N	80.57 W
Fort Morgan	162	40.15 N	103.48 W
Fort Myers	172	26.37 N	81.54 W
Fort Myers Beach	172	26.27 N	81.57 W
Fort Payne	174	34.27 N	85.43 W
Fort Peck Lake	180	47.45 N	106.50 W
Fort Pierce	172	27.27 N	80.20 W
Fort Plain	166	42.56 N	74.38 W
Fort Portal	104	0.40 N	30.17 E
Fort Scott	174	37.50 N	94.42 W
Fort Simpson	160	61.52 N	121.23 W
Fort Smith, N.W. Ter., Can.	160	60.00 N	111.53 W
Fort Smith, Ark., U.S.	174	35.23 N	94.25 W

Name	Page	Lat°′	Long°′
Fort Stockton	162	30.53 N	102.53 W
Fort Valley	172	32.33 N	83.53 W
Fort Victoria	104	20.05 S	30.50 E
Fortville	174	39.56 N	85.51 W
Fort Walton Beach	174	30.25 N	86.36 W
Fort Wayne	174	41.04 N	85.09 W
Fort Worth	162	32.45 N	97.20 W
Foshan	80	23.03 N	113.09 E
Fossano	46	44.33 N	7.43 E
Foster, Mount ∧	162a	59.48 N	135.29 W
Fostoria	166	41.09 N	83.25 W
Fougères	42	48.21 N	1.12 W
Foulness Island I	32	51.36 N	0.55 E
Foumban	100	5.43 N	10.55 E
Foumbouni	104	11.50 S	43.30 E
Fountain Inn	172	34.42 N	82.12 W
Fountain Place	174	30.31 N	91.09 W
Four Corners	180	44.56 N	123.02 W
Fourmies	42	50.00 N	4.03 E
Fouta Djallon [1]	100	11.30 N	12.30 W
Foveaux Strait	118	46.35 S	168.00 E
Fowler	174	40.37 N	87.19 W
Fox ≃, U.S.	168	41.21 N	88.50 W
Fox ≃, Wis., U.S.	168	44.32 N	88.01 W
Foxe Basin C	160	68.25 N	77.00 W
Foxe Channel	160	64.30 N	80.00 W
Foxen ⊜	28	59.23 N	11.52 E
Foxe Peninsula ≻[1]	160	65.00 N	76.00 W
Fox Lake	168	42.25 N	88.09 W
Foyle, Lough ⊜	32	55.07 N	7.08 W
Fraïn, Chott el ⊜	50	35.57 N	5.38 E
Framingham	166	42.17 N	71.25 W
Franca	144	20.32 S	47.24 W
Francavilla Fontana	46	40.31 N	17.35 E
France □[1]	42	46.00 N	2.00 E
Frances Lake ⊜	160	61.25 N	129.30 W
Francis Case, Lake ⊜[1]	162	43.15 N	99.00 W
Francistown	104	21.11 S	27.32 E
Francofonte	46	37.13 N	14.53 E
Francs Peak ∧	180	43.58 N	109.20 W
Frankenberg	36	50.54 N	13.01 E
Frankenmuth	168	43.20 N	83.44 W
Frankfort, Ind., U.S.	174	40.17 N	86.31 W
Frankfort, Ky., U.S.	174	38.12 N	84.52 W
Frankfort, N.Y., U.S.	166	43.02 N	75.04 W
Frankfurt am Main	36	50.07 N	8.40 E
Frankfurt an der Oder	36	52.20 N	14.33 E
Fränkische Alb	36	49.00 N	11.30 E
Franklin, Ind., U.S.	174	39.29 N	86.03 W
Franklin, Ky., U.S.	174	36.43 N	86.35 W
Franklin, La., U.S.	174	29.48 N	91.30 W
Franklin, Mass., U.S.	166	42.05 N	71.24 W
Franklin, N.H., U.S.	166	43.27 N	71.39 W
Franklin, N.J., U.S.	166	41.07 N	74.35 W
Franklin, N.C., U.S.	172	35.11 N	83.23 W
Franklin, Ohio, U.S.	166	39.34 N	84.18 W
Franklin, Pa., U.S.	166	41.24 N	79.50 W
Franklin, Tenn., U.S.	174	35.55 N	86.52 W
Franklin, Va., U.S.	172	36.41 N	76.55 W
Franklin, Wis., U.S.	168	42.54 N	88.03 W
Franklin Delano Roosevelt Lake ⊜[1]	180	48.20 N	118.10 W
Franklinton	174	30.51 N	90.09 W
Frascati	46	41.48 N	12.41 E
Fraser ≃	160	49.09 N	123.12 W
Fraserburgh	32	57.42 N	2.00 W
Frauenfeld	42	47.34 N	8.54 E
Fredericia	28	55.35 N	9.46 E
Frederick	166	39.25 N	77.25 W
Fredericksburg	166	38.18 N	77.29 W
Fredericktown	174	37.33 N	90.18 W
Fredericton	160	45.58 N	66.39 W
Frederikshavn	28	57.26 N	10.32 E
Fredonia, Kans., U.S.	174	37.32 N	95.49 W
Fredonia, N.Y., U.S.	166	42.27 N	79.20 W
Fredrikstad	28	59.13 N	10.57 E
Freehold	166	40.16 N	74.17 W
Freeland	166	41.01 N	75.47 W
Freeport, Ba.	130	26.30 N	78.45 W
Freeport, Ill., U.S.	168	42.17 N	89.36 W
Freeport, Maine, U.S.	166	43.51 N	70.06 W
Freeport, N.Y., U.S.	166	40.39 N	73.35 W
Freeport, Tex., U.S.	174	28.58 N	95.22 W
Freetown	100	8.30 N	13.15 W
Fregenal de la Sierra	50	38.10 N	6.39 W
Freiberg	36	50.54 N	13.20 E
Freiburg → Fribourg	42	46.48 N	7.09 E
Freiburg [im Breisgau]	36	47.59 N	7.51 E
Freising	36	48.23 N	11.44 E
Freital	36	51.00 N	13.39 E
Fréjus	42	43.26 N	6.44 E
Fremantle	116	32.03 S	115.45 E
Fremont, Calif., U.S.	184	37.34 N	122.01 W
Fremont	174	41.13 N	92.26 W
Fremont, Mich., U.S.	168	43.28 N	85.57 W
Fremont, Nebr., U.S.	162	41.26 N	96.30 W
Fremont, Ohio, U.S.	166	41.21 N	83.07 W
French Guiana □[2]	144	4.00 N	53.00 W
French Lick	174	38.33 N	86.37 W
Frenchman Bay C	166	44.25 N	68.10 W
Frenchman Flat ≃[1]	184	36.50 N	115.55 W
French Polynesia □[2]	10	15.00 S	140.00 W
Fresnillo	130	23.10 N	102.53 W
Fresno	184	36.45 N	119.45 W
Freudenstadt	36	48.28 N	8.25 E
Freycinet Peninsula ≻[1]	116	42.13 S	148.18 E
Fria, Cape ≻	104	18.30 S	12.01 E
Fribourg (Freiburg)	42	46.48 N	7.09 E
Fridley	168	45.06 N	93.15 W
Friedberg	36	50.20 N	8.45 E
Friedrichshafen	36	47.39 N	9.28 E
Frio, Cabo ≻	144	22.53 S	42.00 W
Frisian Islands II	28	53.30 N	6.40 E
Friza, Proliv	64	45.30 N	149.10 E
Frobisher Bay	160	63.44 N	68.28 W
Frome	32	51.14 N	2.20 W
Frome, Lake ⊜	116	30.48 S	139.48 E
Frontenac	174	37.29 N	94.44 W
Front Range	178	39.45 N	105.45 W
Front Royal	166	38.55 N	78.11 W
Frosinone	46	41.38 N	13.19 E
Frostburg	166	39.39 N	78.56 W
Fruita	178	39.09 N	108.44 W
Fruitland	166	38.19 N	75.37 W
Fruitvale	180	46.37 N	120.33 W
Frunze	62	42.54 N	74.36 E
Frýdek-Místek	36	49.41 N	18.22 E
Fucino, Conca del	46	42.01 N	13.31 E
Fuerte ≃	130	25.54 N	109.22 W
Fugløysund	26	70.12 N	20.20 E
Fuji	80	35.09 N	138.39 E
Fuji-san ∧[1]	80	35.22 N	138.44 E
Fukui	80	36.04 N	136.13 E
Fukuoka	80	33.35 N	130.24 E
Fukushima	80	37.45 N	140.28 E
Fūlādī, Kūh-e ∧	84	34.38 N	67.32 E
Fulda	36	50.33 N	9.41 E
Fulda ≃	36	51.25 N	9.39 E
Fullerton	184	33.52 N	117.55 W
Fulton, Ill., U.S.	168	41.52 N	90.11 W
Fulton, Kans., U.S.	174	38.01 N	94.43 W
Fulton, Ky., U.S.	174	36.30 N	88.53 W
Fulton, Miss., U.S.	174	34.16 N	88.31 W
Fulton, Mo., U.S.	174	38.52 N	91.57 W
Fulton, N.Y., U.S.	166	43.19 N	76.25 W
Fultondale	174	33.36 N	86.48 W
Funchal	100	32.38 N	16.54 W
Fundy, Bay of C	160	45.00 N	66.00 W
Fuquay-Varina	172	35.35 N	78.48 W
Furnas, Represa de ⊜[1]	144	20.45 S	46.00 W
Furneaux Group II	116	40.10 S	148.05 E
Fürstenfeldbruck	36	48.10 N	11.15 E
Fürstenwalde	36	52.21 N	14.04 E
Fürth	36	49.28 N	10.59 E
Fushun	80	41.52 N	123.53 E
Füssen	36	47.34 N	10.42 E
Fuxinshi	80	42.03 N	121.46 E
Fuzhou	80	26.06 N	119.17 E
Fyn I	28	55.20 N	10.30 E
G			
Gabas ≃	42	43.46 N	0.42 W
Gabès	100	33.53 N	10.07 E
Gabès, Golfe de C	100	34.00 N	10.25 E
Gabon □[1]	104	1.00 S	11.45 E
Gaborone	104	24.45 S	25.55 E
Gabrovo	54	42.52 N	25.19 E
Gadsden	174	34.02 N	86.02 W
Gaeta	46	41.12 N	13.35 E
Gaeta, Golfo di C	46	41.06 N	13.30 E
Gaffney	172	35.05 N	81.39 W
Gafsa	100	34.25 N	8.48 E
Gaggenau	36	48.48 N	8.19 E
Gagnoa	100	6.08 N	5.56 W
Gail ≃	36	46.36 N	13.53 E
Gainesville, Fla., U.S.	172	29.40 N	82.20 W
Gainesville, Ga., U.S.	172	34.18 N	83.50 W
Gainesville, Tex., U.S.	162	33.37 N	97.08 W
Gainsborough	32	53.24 N	0.46 W
Gairdner, Lake ⊜	116	31.35 S	136.00 E
Gaithersburg	166	39.09 N	77.12 W
Gal, Punta de ≻	50	39.10 N	1.05 E
Galán, Cerro ∧	146	25.55 S	66.52 W
Galana ≃	104	3.09 S	40.08 E
Galashiels	32	55.37 N	2.49 W
Galaţi	54	45.26 N	28.03 E
Galatina	46	40.10 N	18.10 E
Galax	172	36.40 N	80.56 W
Galena, Ill., U.S.	168	42.25 N	90.26 W
Galena, Kans., U.S.	174	37.04 N	94.38 W
Galena Park	174	29.44 N	95.14 W
Galera, Punta ≻, Chile	146	39.59 S	73.43 W
Galera, Punta ≻, Ec.	144	0.49 N	80.03 W
Galesburg	168	40.57 N	90.22 W
Galicia □[9]	50	43.00 N	8.00 W
Galion	166	40.44 N	82.47 W
Galite, Canal de la	46	37.20 N	9.00 E
Galka'yo	102	6.49 N	47.23 E
Gallarate	46	45.40 N	8.47 E
Gallatin, Mo., U.S.	174	39.55 N	93.58 W
Gallatin, Tenn., U.S.	174	36.24 N	86.27 W
Gallatin ≃	180	45.56 N	111.29 W
Galle	84	6.02 N	80.13 E
Galliano	174	29.26 N	90.20 W
Gallinas, Punta ≻	144	12.28 N	71.40 W
Gallipoli	46	40.03 N	17.58 E
Gallipolis	166	38.49 N	82.12 W
Gällivare	26	67.07 N	20.45 E
Gallo, Capo ≻	46	38.13 N	13.19 E
Gallup	178	35.32 N	108.44 W
Gallura [1]	46	41.05 N	9.15 E
Galva	168	41.10 N	90.03 W
Galveston	174	29.18 N	94.48 W
Galveston Bay C	174	29.36 N	94.57 W
Galveston Island I	174	29.13 N	94.55 W
Galway	32	53.16 N	9.03 W
Gambia □[1]	100	13.30 N	15.30 W
Gambia (Gambie) ≃	100	13.28 N	16.34 W
Gamlakarleby → Kokkola	28	63.50 N	23.07 E
Ganderkesee	36	53.02 N	8.32 E
Gandía	50	38.58 N	0.11 W
Gangdisishan ∧	80	31.29 N	80.45 E
Ganges (Ganga) (Padma) ≃	84	23.22 N	90.32 E
Gannett Peak ∧	180	43.11 N	109.39 W
Ganos Dağı ∧	54	40.47 N	27.16 E
Ganzhou	80	25.54 N	114.55 E
Gao	100	16.16 N	0.03 W
Gap	42	44.34 N	6.05 E
Garanhuns	144	8.54 S	36.29 W
García de Sola, Embalse de ⊜[1]	50	39.15 N	5.05 W
Garda, Lago di ⊜	46	45.40 N	10.41 E
Gardelegen	36	52.31 N	11.23 E
Garden City, Ga., U.S.	172	32.06 N	81.09 W
Garden City, Kans., U.S.	162	37.58 N	100.53 W
Gardendale	174	33.39 N	86.49 W
Garden Grove	184	33.46 N	117.57 W
Garden Lakes	172	34.17 N	85.16 W
Garden Peninsula ≻[1]	168	45.45 N	86.35 W
Gardiner	166	44.14 N	69.46 W
Gardiners Bay C	166	41.06 N	72.10 W
Gardner, Kans., U.S.	174	38.49 N	94.56 W
Gardner, Mass., U.S.	166	42.34 N	71.60 W
Gardnerville	184	38.56 N	119.45 W
Gardone Val Trompia	46	45.41 N	10.11 E
Gardunha, Serra da	50	40.05 N	7.31 W
Gargano, Testa del ≻	46	41.49 N	16.12 E
Garmisch-Partenkirchen	36	47.29 N	11.05 E
Garner, Iowa, U.S.	168	43.06 N	93.36 W
Garner, N.C., U.S.	172	35.43 N	78.37 W
Garnett	174	38.17 N	95.14 W
Garonne ≃	42	45.02 N	0.36 W
Garrett	174	41.21 N	85.08 W
Gartempe ≃	42	46.48 N	0.50 E
Gary, Ind., U.S.	174	41.36 N	87.20 W
Gary, Tex., U.S.	184	32.07 N	94.22 W
Gary, W. Va., U.S.	172	37.21 N	81.38 W
Gas City	174	40.29 N	85.37 W
Gasconade ≃	174	38.40 N	91.33 W
Gash (Al-Qash) ≃	102	16.48 N	35.51 E
Gaston, Lake ⊜[1]	172	36.35 N	78.00 W
Gastonia	172	35.16 N	81.11 W
Gatčina	26	59.34 N	30.08 E
Gateshead	32	54.58 N	1.37 W
Gâtine, Hauteurs de [2]	42	46.40 N	0.50 W
Gatineau ≃	160	45.27 N	75.40 W
Gatlinburg	172	35.43 N	83.31 W
Gatooma	104	18.21 S	29.55 E
Gausta ∧	28	59.50 N	8.35 E
Gavá	50	41.18 N	2.01 E
Gave d'Aspe ≃	42	43.12 N	0.36 W
Gävle	28	60.40 N	17.10 E
Gaya	84	24.48 N	85.03 E
Gaylord, Mich., U.S.	168	45.02 N	84.40 W
Gaylord, Minn., U.S.	168	44.33 N	94.13 W
Gaziantep	20	37.05 N	37.22 E
Gdańsk (Danzig)	36	54.23 N	18.40 E
Gdynia	36	54.32 N	18.33 E
Gêba ≃	100	11.46 N	15.36 W
Gebze	54	40.48 N	29.25 E
Gediz ≃	54	38.35 N	26.48 E
Geel	36	51.10 N	5.00 E
Geelong	116	38.08 S	144.21 E
Geesthacht	36	53.26 N	10.22 E
Geislingen	36	48.37 N	9.51 E
Geistown	166	40.17 N	78.52 W
Gejiu (Kokiu)	80	23.22 N	103.06 E
Gela	46	37.03 N	14.15 E
Gela, Golfo di C	46	37.00 N	14.10 E
Gelai ∧[1]	104	2.33 S	36.05 E
Geleen	36	50.58 N	5.52 E
Gelibolu	54	40.24 N	26.40 E
Gelibolu Yarımadası (Gallipoli Peninsula) ≻[1]	54	40.20 N	26.30 E
Gélise ≃	42	44.11 N	0.17 E
Gelsenkirchen	36	51.31 N	7.07 E
Gemlik	54	40.26 N	29.09 E
Genale ≃	102	5.43 N	40.53 E
General Carrera, Lago (Lago Buenos Aires) ⊜	146	46.35 S	72.00 W
General Roca	146	39.02 S	67.35 W
Genesee ≃	168	43.16 N	77.36 W
Geneseo, Ill., U.S.	168	41.27 N	90.09 W
Geneseo, N.Y., U.S.	166	42.48 N	77.49 W
Geneva, Ala., U.S.	174	31.02 N	85.52 W
Geneva, Ill., U.S.	168	41.53 N	88.18 W
Geneva, N.Y., U.S.	166	42.52 N	77.00 W
Geneva, Ohio, U.S.	166	41.48 N	80.57 W
Geneva, Lake ⊜	42	46.25 N	6.30 E
Genève	42	46.12 N	6.09 E
Genevia	174	34.43 N	92.13 W
Genil ≃	50	37.42 N	5.19 W
Genk	36	50.58 N	5.30 E
Gennargentu, Monti del	46	39.59 N	9.19 E
Genoa	168	42.06 N	88.42 W
Genova (Genoa)	46	44.25 N	8.57 E
Genova, Golfo di C	46	44.10 N	8.55 E
Gent (Gand)	36	51.03 N	3.43 E
Genthin	36	52.24 N	12.09 E
Geographe Bay C	116	33.35 S	115.15 E
George ≃	160	58.49 N	66.10 W
George, Lake ⊜, Ug.	104	0.02 N	30.12 E
George, Lake ⊜, Fla., U.S.	172	29.17 N	81.36 W
George, Lake ⊜, N.Y., U.S.	166	43.35 N	73.35 W
Georgetown, Cay. Is.	130	19.18 N	81.23 W
Georgetown, Gam.	100	13.30 N	14.47 W
Georgetown, Guy.	144	6.48 N	58.10 W
George Town → Pinang, Malay.	82	5.25 N	100.20 E
Georgetown, Del., U.S.	166	38.42 N	75.23 W
Georgetown, Ill., U.S.	174	39.59 N	87.38 W
Georgetown, Ky., U.S.	166	38.13 N	84.33 W
Georgetown, S.C., U.S.	172	33.23 N	79.17 W
Georgia □[3]	172	32.50 N	83.15 W
Georgian Bay C	160	45.15 N	80.50 W
Gera	36	50.52 N	12.04 E
Gerlachovský štít ∧	36	49.12 N	20.08 E
German Democratic Republic (Deutsche Demokratische Republik) □[1]	36	52.00 N	12.30 E
Germantown, Tenn., U.S.	174	35.05 N	89.49 W
Germantown, Wis., U.S.	168	43.14 N	88.06 W
Germany, Federal Republic of (Bundesrepublik Deutschland) □[1]	36	51.00 N	9.00 E
Germiston	104	26.15 S	28.05 E
Gerona	50	41.59 N	2.49 E
Gerrei [1]	46	39.28 N	9.20 E
Gers ≃	42	44.09 N	0.39 E
Getafe	50	40.18 N	3.43 W
Gettysburg	166	39.50 N	77.14 W
Gévora ≃	50	38.53 N	6.57 W
Geyser, Banc du [2]	104	12.25 S	46.25 E
Ghana □[1]	100	8.00 N	2.00 W
Ghardaïa	100	32.31 N	3.37 E
Ghawdex I	46	36.03 N	14.15 E
Ghazāl, Bahr al- ≃	102	9.31 N	30.25 E
Ghazal, Bahr el ≃	102	13.01 N	15.28 E
Ghazaouet	50	35.06 N	1.51 W
Ghaznī	84	33.33 N	68.26 E
Ghazzah	84	31.30 N	34.28 E
Gheorghe Gheorghiu-Dej	54	46.14 N	26.44 E
Gheorgheni	54	46.43 N	25.36 E
Gia-dinh	82	10.48 N	106.42 E
Giant Mountain ∧	166	44.10 N	73.44 W
Gibbon	168	44.32 N	94.31 W
Gibraltar	50	36.09 N	5.21 W
Gibraltar □[2]	50	36.11 N	5.22 W
Gibraltar, Strait of (Estrecho de Gibraltar)	50	35.57 N	5.36 W
Gibraltar Point ≻	32	53.05 N	0.19 E
Gibsonburg	166	41.23 N	83.19 W
Gibson City	168	40.28 N	88.22 W
Gien	42	47.42 N	2.38 E
Giessen	36	50.35 N	8.40 E
Gifford	172	27.41 N	80.25 W
Gifhorn	36	52.29 N	10.33 E
Gifu	80	35.25 N	136.45 E
Giglio, Isola del I	46	42.21 N	10.54 E
Gijón	50	43.32 N	5.40 W
Gila ≃	178	32.43 N	114.33 W
Gila Bend	178	32.57 N	112.43 W
Gilbert	168	47.29 N	92.28 W
Gilgit ≃	84	35.44 N	74.38 E
Gillespie	174	39.07 N	89.49 W
Gillette	162	44.18 N	105.30 W
Gillingham	32	51.24 N	0.33 E
Gilman	174	41.53 N	92.47 W
Gilmer	174	32.44 N	94.57 W
Gilo ≃	102	8.10 N	33.15 E
Gilroy	184	37.00 N	121.43 W
Giluwe, Mount ∧	116a	6.05 S	143.50 E
Gimone ≃	42	44.00 N	1.06 E
Ginosa	46	40.34 N	16.46 E
Gioia del Colle	46	40.48 N	16.56 E
Gioia Tauro	46	38.26 N	15.54 E
Girard, Kans., U.S.	174	37.31 N	94.51 W
Girard, Ohio, U.S.	166	41.10 N	80.42 W
Girardot	144	4.18 N	74.48 W
Gironde C[1]	42	45.20 N	0.45 W
Girou ≃	42	43.46 N	1.23 E
Gisborne	118	38.40 S	178.01 E
Gisenyi	104	1.42 S	29.15 E
Gitega	104	3.26 S	29.56 E
Giugliano [in Campania]	46	40.56 N	14.12 E
Giulianova	46	42.45 N	13.57 E
Giurgiu	54	43.53 N	25.57 E
Givors	42	45.35 N	4.46 E
Gizo	114	8.06 S	156.51 E
Giżycko	36	54.03 N	21.47 E
Gjelma	102	36.28 N	7.26 E
Gjirokastër	54	40.05 N	20.10 E
Gjøvik	28	60.48 N	10.42 E
Gjuhëzës, Kep i ≻	54	40.25 N	19.18 E
Glace Bay	160	46.12 N	59.57 W
Glacier Peak ∧	180	48.07 N	121.07 W
Gladbeck	36	51.34 N	6.59 E
Gladewater	174	32.33 N	94.56 W
Gladstone, Mich., U.S.	168	45.50 N	87.03 W
Gladstone, Mo., U.S.	174	39.13 N	94.34 W
Glåma ≃	28	59.12 N	10.57 E
Glarner Alpen	42	46.55 N	9.00 E
Glasgow, Scot., U.K.	32	55.53 N	4.15 W
Glasgow, Ky., U.S.	174	37.00 N	85.55 W
Glasgow, Mont., U.S.	180	48.12 N	106.38 W
Glas Maol ∧	32	56.52 N	3.22 W
Glassboro	166	39.42 N	75.07 W
Glauchau	36	50.49 N	12.32 E
Glazov	26	58.09 N	52.40 E
Gleinalpe	36	47.15 N	15.03 E
Glen Burnie	166	39.10 N	76.37 W
Glen Canyon V	178	37.10 N	110.50 W
Glencoe, Ala., U.S.	174	33.57 N	85.56 W
Glencoe, Ill., U.S.	168	42.08 N	87.45 W
Glencoe, Minn., U.S.	168	44.46 N	94.09 W
Glen Cove	166	40.52 N	73.37 W
Glendale, Ariz., U.S.	178	33.32 N	112.11 W
Glendale, Calif., U.S.	184	34.10 N	118.17 W
Glendale, Wis., U.S.	168	43.07 N	87.57 W
Glendive	162	47.06 N	104.43 W
Glen Lyon	166	41.10 N	76.05 W
Glennville	172	31.56 N	81.56 W
Glenrock	178	42.52 N	105.52 W
Glens Falls	166	43.19 N	73.39 W
Glenwood, Iowa, U.S.	174	41.03 N	95.45 W
Glenwood	178	33.19 N	108.53 W
Glenwood Springs	178	39.33 N	107.19 W
Glittertinden ∧	28	61.39 N	8.33 E
Gliwice (Gleiwitz)	36	50.17 N	18.40 E
Gliwicki, Kanał	36	50.22 N	18.05 E
Globe	178	33.24 N	110.47 W
Głogów	36	51.40 N	16.05 E
Gloucester, Eng., U.K.	32	51.53 N	2.14 W
Gloucester, Mass., U.S.	166	42.41 N	70.39 W
Gloucestershire □[6]	32	51.47 N	2.15 W
Gloversville	166	43.03 N	74.20 W
Głowno	36	51.58 N	19.44 E
Głuchołazy	36	50.20 N	17.22 E
Glückstadt	36	53.47 N	9.25 E
Gmunden	36	47.55 N	13.48 E
Gniezno	36	52.31 N	17.37 E
Gnjilane	54	42.28 N	21.29 E
Gobabis	104	22.30 S	18.58 E
Gobi [2]	80	43.00 N	105.00 E
Goce Delčev	54	41.34 N	23.44 E
Goch	36	51.41 N	6.10 E
Godāvari ≃	84	17.00 N	81.45 E
Gödöllő	36	47.36 N	19.22 E
Godoy Cruz	146	32.55 S	68.50 W
Gods ≃	160	56.22 N	92.51 W
Godthåb	160	64.11 N	51.44 W
Godwin Austen (K2) ∧	84	35.53 N	76.30 E
Goes	36	51.30 N	3.54 E
Goffstown	166	43.01 N	71.36 W
Gogebic, Lake ⊜	168	46.30 N	89.35 W
Goiana	144	7.33 S	34.59 W
Goiânia	144	16.40 S	49.16 W
Gökçeada I	54	40.10 N	25.50 E
Gölcük	54	40.44 N	29.48 E
Golden	178	39.46 N	105.13 W
Goldendale	180	45.49 N	120.50 W
Golden Meadow	174	29.23 N	90.16 W
Goldsboro	172	35.23 N	77.59 W
Goleniów	36	53.36 N	14.50 E
Goleta	184	34.27 N	119.50 W
Golfito	130	8.38 N	83.11 W
Goljama Kamčija ≃	54	43.03 N	27.29 E
Golo ≃	42	42.31 N	9.32 E
Gombe ≃	104	4.38 S	31.40 E
Gomel'	62	52.25 N	31.00 E
Gómez Palacio	130	25.34 N	103.30 W
Gonaïves	130	19.27 N	72.41 W
Gonâve, Île de la I	130	18.51 N	73.03 W
Gonder	102	12.40 N	37.30 E
Gondomar	50	41.09 N	8.32 W
Gönen	54	40.06 N	27.39 E
Gonggashan ∧	80	29.35 N	101.51 E
Gonggeershan ∧	80	38.37 N	75.20 E
Gongola ≃	100	9.30 N	12.04 E
Gonzales	174	30.14 N	90.55 W
Good Hope, Cape of ≻	104	34.24 S	18.30 E
Good Hope Mountain ∧	160	51.09 N	124.10 W
Gooding	180	42.56 N	114.43 W
Goodland	162	39.21 N	101.43 W
Goodview	168	44.04 N	91.41 W
Goodrich	184	30.36 N	94.57 W
Goodyear	178	33.26 N	112.21 W
Goole	32	53.42 N	0.52 W
Goose Creek	172	33.00 N	80.01 W
Goose Lake ⊜	184	41.57 N	120.25 W
Göppingen	36	48.42 N	9.40 E
Gorakhpur	84	26.45 N	83.22 E
Gorda, Punta ≻	130	22.24 N	82.10 W
Gordon	172	32.53 N	83.20 W
Gore	102	8.08 N	35.33 E
Gorham, Maine, U.S.	166	43.41 N	70.26 W
Gorham, N.H., U.S.	166	44.23 N	71.10 W
Gorinchem	36	51.50 N	5.00 E
Gorizia	46	45.57 N	13.38 E
Gorki → Gor'kij	26	56.20 N	44.00 E
Gor'kij (Gorky)	26	56.20 N	44.00 E
Gor'kovskoje Vodochranilišče ⊜[1]	62	57.00 N	43.10 E
Gorlice	36	49.40 N	21.10 E
Görlitz	36	53.24 N	13.54 E
Gorlovka	62	48.18 N	38.03 E
Gorna Orjahovica	54	43.07 N	25.41 E
Goro	112	22.16 S	167.02 E
Gorontalo	82	0.33 N	123.03 E
Gorul, Muntele ∧	54	45.48 N	26.25 E
Gorzów Wielkopolski (Landsberg an der Warthe)	36	52.44 N	15.15 E
Goshen, Ind., U.S.	174	41.35 N	85.50 W
Goshen, N.Y., U.S.	166	41.24 N	74.20 W
Goslar	36	51.54 N	10.25 E
Gostivar	54	41.47 N	20.54 E
Gostyń	36	51.53 N	17.00 E
Gostynin	36	52.26 N	19.29 E
Göta älv ≃	28	57.42 N	11.52 E
Göta kanal	28	58.50 N	13.58 E
Göteborg (Gothenburg)	28	57.43 N	11.58 E
Gotha	36	50.57 N	10.41 E
Gotland I	28	57.30 N	18.33 E
Gotska Sandön I	28	58.23 N	19.16 E
Göttingen	36	51.32 N	9.55 E
Gottwaldov	36	49.13 N	17.41 E
Gouda	36	52.01 N	4.43 E
Gouin, Réservoir ⊜[1]	160	48.38 N	74.54 W
Goulburn	116	34.45 S	149.43 E
Goulds	172	25.33 N	80.23 W
Goundam	100	16.25 N	3.40 W
Gouverneur	166	44.20 N	75.28 W
Governador Valadares	144	18.51 S	41.56 W
Gowanda	166	42.28 N	78.56 W
Goya	146	29.08 S	59.16 W
Graaff-Reinet	104	32.14 S	24.32 E
Gračanica	54	44.42 N	18.19 E
Grado	46	45.40 N	13.23 E
Grafton, Austl.	116	29.41 S	152.56 E
Grafton, N. Dak., U.S.	162	48.25 N	97.25 W
Grafton, W. Va., U.S.	166	39.20 N	80.01 W
Grafton, Wis., U.S.	168	43.19 N	87.56 W
Graham	172	36.05 N	79.25 W
Graham Island I	160	53.40 N	132.30 W
Grahamstown	104	33.19 S	26.31 E
Grajewo	36	53.39 N	22.27 E
Grambling	174	32.32 N	92.43 W
Grammichele	46	37.13 N	14.38 E
Grampian Mountains	32	56.45 N	4.00 W
Granada, Esp.	50	37.13 N	3.41 W
Granada, Nic.	130	11.56 N	85.57 W
Granby, Qué., Can.	160	45.24 N	72.44 W
Granby, Mo., U.S.	174	36.55 N	94.15 W
Gran Canaria I	100	28.00 N	15.36 W
Gran Chaco	146	23.00 S	60.00 W
Grand ≃, U.S.	174	39.23 N	93.06 W
Grand ≃, Mich., U.S.	168	42.40 N	84.40 W
Grand Bahama I	130	26.38 N	78.25 W
Grand Blanc	168	42.56 N	83.38 W
Grand Canal, Eire	32	53.21 N	6.14 W
Grand Canal → Yunhe, Zhg.	80	32.12 N	119.31 E
Grand Canyon	178	36.03 N	112.09 W
Grand Canyon V	178	36.10 N	112.45 W
Grand Cayman I	130	19.20 N	81.15 W
Grand Coulee	180	47.56 N	119.00 W
Grand Coulee V	180	47.45 N	119.15 W
Grande ≃, Bol.	144	15.51 S	64.39 W
Grande ≃, Esp.	50	39.07 N	0.44 W
Grande, Bahía C[3]	146	50.45 S	68.45 W
Grande, Boca ≃[1]	144	8.38 N	60.30 W
Grande, Rio (Bravo del Norte) ≃	162	25.55 N	97.09 W
Grande Comore I	104	11.35 S	43.20 E
Grande do Gurupá, Ilha I	144	1.00 S	51.30 W
Grand Erg de Bilma [2]	100	18.30 N	14.00 E
Grand Erg Occidental [2]	100	30.30 N	0.30 E
Grand Erg Oriental [2]	100	30.30 N	7.00 E
Grandes, Salinas	146	30.05 S	65.05 W
Grandfather Mountain ∧	172	36.07 N	81.48 W
Grand Forks	162	47.55 N	97.03 W
Grand Haven	168	43.04 N	86.13 W
Grand Hers ≃	42	43.47 N	1.20 E
Grand Island	162	40.55 N	98.21 W
Grand Island I	168	46.30 N	86.40 W
Grand Isle	174	29.14 N	90.00 W
Grand Junction	178	39.05 N	108.33 W
Grand Lake ⊜	174	29.55 N	92.47 W
Grand Ledge	168	42.45 N	84.45 W
Grand Lieu, Lac de ⊜	42	47.06 N	1.40 W
Grand Marais	168	47.45 N	90.20 W
Grand Rapids, Mich., U.S.	168	42.58 N	85.40 W
Grand Rapids, Minn., U.S.	168	47.14 N	93.31 W
Grand Teton ∧	180	43.44 N	110.48 W
Grand Traverse Bay C	168	45.02 N	85.30 W
Grand Turk	130	21.28 N	71.08 W
Grandview, Mo., U.S.	174	38.53 N	94.32 W
Grandview, Wash., U.S.	180	46.15 N	119.54 W
Granger, Utah, U.S.	178	40.42 N	111.57 W
Granger, Wash., U.S.	180	46.21 N	120.11 W
Grangeville	180	45.56 N	116.07 W
Granite City	174	38.42 N	90.09 W
Granite Falls	172	35.48 N	81.26 W
Granite Peak ∧	180	45.10 N	109.48 W
Graniteville	172	33.34 N	81.48 W
Granitola, Capo ≻	46	37.33 N	12.40 E
Granollers	50	41.37 N	2.18 E
Gran Paradiso ∧	46	45.32 N	7.16 E
Gran Sasso d'Italia	46	42.27 N	13.42 E
Grantham	32	52.55 N	0.39 W
Grants	178	35.09 N	107.52 W
Grants Pass	180	42.26 N	123.19 W
Grantsville	178	40.36 N	112.28 W
Granville, Fr.	42	48.50 N	1.36 W
Granville, Ohio, U.S.	166	40.04 N	82.31 W
Grass ≃	160	56.03 N	96.33 W
Grasse	42	43.40 N	6.55 E
Gravina in Puglia	46	40.49 N	16.25 E
Gray	172	33.01 N	83.32 W
Grays Harbor C	180	46.56 N	124.05 W
Grayson	166	38.20 N	82.57 W
Grays Peak ∧	178	39.37 N	105.45 W
Graz	36	47.05 N	15.27 E
Greaca, Lacul ⊜	54	44.05 N	26.23 E
Great Abaco I	130	26.28 N	77.05 W
Great Artesian Basin [1]	116	25.00 S	143.00 E
Great Astrolabe Reef [2]	111	18.52 S	178.31 E
Great Australian Bight C[3]	116	35.00 S	130.00 E
Great Barrier Reef [2]	116	18.00 S	145.50 E
Great Basin [1]	184	40.00 N	117.00 W
Great Bear Lake ⊜	160	66.00 N	120.00 W
Great Bend	162	38.22 N	98.46 W
Great Dismal Swamp	172	36.30 N	76.30 W
Great Divide Basin [1]	180	42.00 N	108.10 W
Great Dividing Range	116	25.00 S	147.00 E
Greater Antilles II	130	20.00 N	74.00 W
Greater Sunda Islands II	82	2.00 S	110.00 E
Great Exuma I	130	23.32 N	75.50 W
Great Falls, Mont., U.S.	180	47.30 N	111.17 W
Great Falls, S.C., U.S.	172	34.34 N	80.54 W
Great Inagua I	130	21.05 N	73.18 W
Great Indian Desert (Thar Desert) [2]	84	27.00 N	71.00 E
Great Karroo [1]	104	32.25 S	22.40 E
Great Malvern	32	52.07 N	2.19 W
Great Miami ≃	166	39.06 N	84.49 W
Great Ruaha ≃	104	7.56 S	37.52 E
Great Sacandaga Lake ⊜	166	43.08 N	74.10 W
Great Salt Lake ⊜	178	41.10 N	112.30 W
Great Salt Lake Desert [2]	178	40.40 N	113.30 W
Great Sandy Desert [2]	116	21.30 S	125.00 E
Great Slave Lake ⊜	160	61.30 N	114.00 W
Great Smoky Mountains	172	35.35 N	83.30 W
Great Victoria Desert [2]	116	28.30 S	127.45 E
Great Yarmouth	32	52.37 N	1.44 E
Gréboun, Mont ∧	100	20.00 N	8.35 E
Gredos, Sierra de	50	40.18 N	5.05 W
Greece	166	43.14 N	77.38 W
Greece (Ellás) □[1]	54	39.00 N	22.00 E
Greeley, Colo., U.S.	178	40.25 N	104.42 W
Greeley, Kans., U.S.	174	38.22 N	95.08 W
Green ≃, U.S.	178	38.11 N	109.53 W
Green ≃, Ky., U.S.	174	37.55 N	87.30 W
Greenacres	180	47.39 N	117.06 W
Green Bay	168	44.30 N	88.01 W
Green Bay C	168	45.00 N	87.30 W
Green Brier	174	36.27 N	86.49 W
Greencastle, Ind., U.S.	174	39.38 N	86.52 W
Greencastle, Pa., U.S.	166	39.47 N	77.44 W
Green Cove Springs	172	30.00 N	81.41 W
Greeneville	172	36.10 N	82.50 W
Greenfield, Iowa, U.S.	174	41.18 N	94.28 W
Greenfield, Mass., U.S.	166	42.36 N	72.36 W
Greenfield, Ohio, U.S.	166	39.21 N	83.23 W
Greenfield, Tenn., U.S.	174	36.09 N	88.48 W
Greenland □[2]	160	70.00 N	40.00 W
Green Mountains	166	43.45 N	72.45 W
Greenock	32	55.57 N	4.45 W
Green River	180	41.32 N	109.28 W
Greensboro, Ala., U.S.	174	32.42 N	87.36 W
Greensboro, Ga., U.S.	172	33.35 N	83.11 W
Greensboro, N.C., U.S.	172	36.04 N	79.47 W
Greensburg, Ind., U.S.	174	39.20 N	85.29 W
Greensburg, Ky., U.S.	174	37.16 N	85.30 W
Greensburg, Pa., U.S.	166	40.18 N	79.33 W
Green Valley	178	31.50 N	111.00 W
Greenville, Ala., U.S.	174	31.50 N	86.38 W
Greenville, Ill., U.S.	174	38.53 N	89.25 W
Greenville, Ky., U.S.	174	37.12 N	87.11 W
Greenville, Mich., U.S.	168	43.11 N	85.15 W
Greenville, Miss., U.S.	174	33.25 N	91.05 W
Greenville, N.C., U.S.	172	35.37 N	77.23 W
Greenville, Ohio, U.S.	166	40.06 N	84.38 W
Greenville, Pa., U.S.	166	41.24 N	80.23 W
Greenville, S.C., U.S.	172	34.51 N	82.23 W
Greenville, Tex., U.S.	162	33.08 N	96.07 W
Greenwich	166	41.01 N	73.38 W
Greenwood, Ark., U.S.	174	35.13 N	94.15 W
Greenwood, Ind., U.S.	174	39.37 N	86.07 W

Gree—Hung

Name	Page	Lat ° ′	Long ° ′
Greenwood, Miss., U.S.	174	33.31 N	90.11 W
Greenwood, S.C., U.S.	172	34.12 N	82.10 W
Greer	172	34.56 N	82.14 W
Greers Ferry Lake [1]	174	35.30 N	92.10 W
Greifswald	36	54.05 N	13.23 E
Greifswalder Bodden	36	54.15 N	13.35 E
Greiz	36	50.39 N	12.12 E
Grenada	174	33.47 N	89.55 W
Grenada [1]	130	12.07 N	61.40 W
Grenadine Islands	130	12.40 N	61.15 W
Grenchen	42	47.11 N	7.24 E
Grenoble	42	45.10 N	5.43 E
Gresham	180	45.30 N	122.26 W
Gresham Park	172	33.42 N	84.19 W
Gretna	174	29.55 N	90.03 W
Greven	36	52.05 N	7.36 E
Grevená	54	40.05 N	21.25 E
Grevenbroich	36	51.05 N	6.35 E
Grevesmühlen	36	53.51 N	11.10 E
Greybull	180	44.30 N	108.03 W
Greylock, Mount	166	42.38 N	73.10 W
Griesheim	36	49.50 N	8.34 E
Griffin	172	33.15 N	84.16 W
Grijalva	130	18.36 N	92.39 W
Grim, Cape	116	40.41 S	144.41 E
Grimma	36	51.14 N	12.43 E
Grimmen	36	54.07 N	13.02 E
Grimsby	32	53.35 N	0.05 W
Grimselpass	42	46.34 N	8.21 E
Grinnell	168	41.45 N	92.43 W
Grintavec	46	46.21 N	14.32 E
Griswold	174	41.14 N	95.08 W
Grodno	62	53.41 N	23.50 E
Grodzisk Mazowiecki	36	52.07 N	20.37 E
Groix, Île de	42	47.38 N	3.27 W
Grójec	36	51.52 N	20.52 E
Gronau	36	52.13 N	7.00 E
Groningen	36	53.13 N	6.33 E
Groot-Karasberge	104	27.20 S	18.40 E
Groot-Kei	104	32.41 S	28.22 E
Groot-Swartberge	104	33.22 S	22.20 E
Groot-Vis	104	33.30 S	27.08 E
Grootvloer	104	30.00 S	20.40 E
Grossenhain	36	51.17 N	13.31 E
Grosse Pointe	168	42.24 N	82.55 W
Grosser Arber	36	49.07 N	13.07 E
Grosser Beerberg	36	50.37 N	10.44 E
Grosser Feldberg	36	50.14 N	8.26 E
Grosser Priel	36	47.43 N	14.04 E
Grosseto	46	42.46 N	11.08 E
Grossglockner	36	47.04 N	12.42 E
Grottaglie	46	40.32 N	17.26 E
Grove	174	36.36 N	94.46 W
Grove City, Ohio, U.S.	166	39.53 N	83.06 W
Grove City, Pa., U.S.	166	41.10 N	80.05 W
Groves	174	29.57 N	93.55 W
Groveton, N.H., U.S.	166	44.36 N	71.31 W
Groveton, Tex., U.S.	184	31.03 N	95.08 W
Grovetown	172	33.27 N	82.12 W
Groznyj	62	43.20 N	45.42 E
Grudziądz	36	53.29 N	18.45 E
Grundy Center	168	42.22 N	92.47 W
Gryfice	36	53.56 N	15.12 E
Guacanayabo, Golfo de	130	20.28 N	77.30 W
Guadajira	50	38.52 N	6.41 W
Guadajoz	50	37.50 N	4.51 W
Guadalajara, Esp.	50	40.38 N	3.10 W
Guadalajara, Méx.	130	20.40 N	103.20 W
Guadalamar	50	38.05 N	3.06 W
Guadalaviar	50	40.21 N	1.08 W
Guadalcanal	114	9.32 S	160.12 E
Guadalén	50	38.05 N	3.32 W
Guadalén, Embalse de [1]	50	38.25 N	3.15 W
Guadalentín	50	37.59 N	1.04 W
Guadalmena	50	38.19 N	2.56 W
Guadalope	50	41.15 N	0.03 W
Guadalquivir	50	36.47 N	6.22 W
Guadalupe, Sierra de	50	39.26 N	5.25 W
Guadarrama, Puerto de	50	40.43 N	4.10 W
Guadarrama, Sierra de	50	40.55 N	4.00 W
Guadazaón	50	39.42 N	1.36 W
Guadeloupe [2]	130	16.15 N	61.35 W
Guadiana	50	37.14 N	7.22 W
Guadix	50	37.18 N	3.08 W
Gualdo Tadino	46	43.14 N	12.47 E
Gualeguaychú	146	33.01 S	58.31 W
Guam [2]	82	13.28 N	144.47 E
Guanajuato	130	21.01 N	101.15 W
Guane	130	22.12 N	84.05 W
Guangzhou (Canton)	80	23.06 N	113.16 E
Guantánamo	130	20.08 N	75.12 W
Guarda	50	40.32 N	7.16 W
Guardiato	50	38.20 N	5.22 W
Guareña	50	41.29 N	5.23 W
Guatemala	130	14.38 N	90.31 W
Guatemala [1]	130	15.30 N	90.15 W
Guaviare	144	4.03 N	67.44 W
Guayaquil	144	2.10 S	79.50 W
Guaymas	130	27.56 N	110.54 W
Gubbio	46	43.21 N	12.35 E
Gubin	36	51.56 N	14.45 E
Gúdar, Sierra de	50	40.27 N	0.42 W
Gudenå	28	56.29 N	10.13 E
Guebwiller	42	47.55 N	7.12 E
Guelma	100	36.28 N	7.26 E
Guelph	160	43.33 N	80.15 W
Güera	100	20.48 N	17.08 W
Guéret	42	46.10 N	1.52 E
Guernsey [2]	20	49.28 N	2.35 W
Guernsey	42	49.27 N	2.35 W
Guge	102	6.10 N	37.26 E
Guildford	32	51.14 N	0.35 W
Guilin	80	25.11 N	110.09 E
Guimarães	50	41.27 N	8.18 W
Guin	174	33.58 N	87.55 W
Guinea [1]	100	11.00 N	10.00 W
Guinea, Gulf	100	2.00 N	2.30 E
Guinea-Bissau [1]	100	12.00 N	15.00 W
Güines	130	22.50 N	82.02 W
Guingamp	42	48.33 N	3.11 W
Güira de Melena	130	22.48 N	82.30 W
Guiyang	80	26.35 N	106.43 E
Gujrānwāla	84	32.26 N	74.33 E
Gujrāt	84	32.34 N	74.05 E
Gulfport, Fla., U.S.	172	27.44 N	82.43 W
Gulfport, Miss., U.S.	174	30.22 N	89.06 W
Gulu	102	2.47 N	32.18 E
Gummersbach	36	51.02 N	7.34 E
Gunisao	160	53.54 N	97.58 W
Gunnison	178	39.03 N	108.35 W
Guntersville	174	34.21 N	86.18 W
Guntersville Lake [1]	174	34.45 N	86.03 W
Guntūr	84	16.18 N	80.27 E
Günzburg	36	48.27 N	10.16 E
Gurara	100	8.12 N	6.41 E
Gurdon	174	33.55 N	93.09 W
Gurghiului, Munții	54	46.41 N	25.12 E
Gurjev	62	47.07 N	51.56 E
Gurk	36	46.36 N	14.31 E
Gurvan Sajchan Uul	80	43.50 N	103.30 E
Gusau	100	12.12 N	6.40 E
Gus'-Chrustal'nyj	26	55.37 N	40.40 E
Gusev	26	54.36 N	22.12 E
Guspini	46	39.32 N	8.38 E
Gustav Holm, Kap	160	67.00 N	34.00 W
Güstrow	36	53.48 N	12.10 E
Gütersloh	36	51.54 N	8.23 E
Guthrie	162	35.53 N	97.25 W
Guthrie Center	174	41.41 N	94.30 W
Guttenberg	168	42.47 N	91.06 W
Guyana [1]	144	5.00 N	59.00 W
Guymon	162	36.41 N	101.29 W
Guyot, Mount	172	35.42 N	83.15 W
Gwda	36	53.04 N	16.44 E
Gwelo	104	19.27 S	29.49 E
Gwent [6]	32	51.43 N	2.57 W
Gwynedd [6]	32	53.00 N	4.00 W
Gyldenløves Fjord [2]	160	64.30 N	41.30 W
Gyöngyös	36	47.47 N	19.56 E
Győr	36	47.42 N	17.38 E
Gyula	36	46.39 N	21.17 E
H			
Haar	36	48.06 N	11.44 E
Haarlem	36	52.23 N	4.38 E
Habomai-shoto	64	43.30 N	146.10 E
Hachinohe	80	40.30 N	141.29 E
Hackensack	166	40.53 N	74.03 W
Hackettstown	166	40.51 N	74.50 W
Hadd, Ra's al-	84	22.32 N	59.48 E
Haderslev	28	55.15 N	9.30 E
Haḍramawt [1]	84	15.00 N	50.00 E
Hadūr Shu'ayb	102	15.18 N	43.59 E
Haeju	80	38.02 N	125.42 E
Haerbin	80	45.45 N	126.41 E
Hafnarfjördur	26a	64.03 N	21.56 W
Hafun, Ras	102	10.27 N	51.26 E
Hagen	36	51.22 N	7.28 E
Hagenow	36	53.26 N	11.11 E
Hagerstown, Ind., U.S.	174	39.55 N	85.10 W
Hagerstown, Md., U.S.	166	39.39 N	77.43 W
Hague, Cap de la	42	49.43 N	1.57 W
Haguenau	42	48.49 N	7.47 E
Haikou	80	20.06 N	110.21 E
Ḥā'il	84	27.33 N	41.42 E
Hailuoto	28	65.02 N	24.42 E
Hainandao	80	19.00 N	109.30 E
Haines City	172	28.07 N	81.37 W
Haines Junction	160	60.45 N	137.30 W
Hai-phong	82	20.52 N	106.41 E
Haiti [1]	130	19.00 N	72.25 W
Hajdúböszörmény	36	47.41 N	21.30 E
Hajdúnánás	36	47.51 N	21.26 E
Hajdúszoboszló	36	47.27 N	21.24 E
Hajnówka	36	52.45 N	23.36 E
Hakodate	80	41.45 N	140.43 E
Halab (Aleppo)	84	36.12 N	37.10 E
Halawa, Cape	162b	21.10 N	156.43 W
Halberstadt	36	51.54 N	11.02 E
Halden	28	59.09 N	11.23 E
Haldensleben	36	52.18 N	11.26 E
Haleakala Crater [6]	162b	20.43 N	156.13 W
Haleyville	174	34.14 N	87.37 W
Halfway	166	39.37 N	77.46 W
Halifax, N.S., Can.	160	44.39 N	63.36 W
Halifax, Eng., U.K.	32	53.44 N	1.52 W
Hallandale	172	25.59 N	80.09 W
Halla-san	80	33.22 N	126.32 E
Halle, Bel.	36	50.44 N	4.13 E
Halle, D.D.R.	36	51.29 N	11.58 E
Hallein	36	47.41 N	13.06 E
Halligen	36	54.35 N	8.35 E
Hallowell	166	44.17 N	69.48 W
Halls	174	35.53 N	89.24 W
Hallstahammar	28	59.37 N	16.13 E
Halmahera	82	1.00 N	128.00 E
Halmstad	28	56.39 N	12.50 E
Haltern	36	51.46 N	7.10 E
Haltiatunturi	26	69.18 N	21.16 E
Haltom City		32.48 N	97.16 W
Hamadān	84	34.48 N	48.30 E
Ḥamāh	84	35.08 N	36.45 E
Hamamatsu	80	34.42 N	137.44 E
Hamar	28	60.48 N	11.06 E
Hamburg, B.R.D.	36	53.33 N	9.59 E
Hamburg, Ark., U.S.	174	33.14 N	91.48 W
Hamburg, Iowa, U.S.	174	40.36 N	95.39 W
Hamburg, N.Y., U.S.	166	42.43 N	78.50 W
Hamburg, Pa., U.S.	166	40.34 N	75.59 W
Hamden	166	41.21 N	72.56 W
Hämeenlinna	28	61.00 N	24.27 E
Hameln	36	52.06 N	9.21 E
Hamhŭng	80	39.54 N	127.32 E
Hamilton, Ber.	130	32.17 N	64.46 W
Hamilton, Ont., Can.	160	43.15 N	79.51 W
Hamilton, N.Z.	118	37.47 S	175.17 E
Hamilton, Scot., U.K.	32	55.47 N	4.03 W
Hamilton, Ala., U.S.	174	34.09 N	88.06 W
Hamilton, Ill., U.S.	168	40.24 N	91.21 W
Hamilton, Mo., U.S.	174	39.45 N	94.01 W
Hamilton, Mont., U.S.	180	46.15 N	114.09 W
Hamilton, N.Y., U.S.	166	42.50 N	75.33 W
Hamilton, Ohio, U.S.	166	39.26 N	84.30 W
Hamilton, Mount	184	37.21 N	121.38 W
Hamilton Dome	180	43.46 N	108.34 W
Hamlet	172	34.53 N	79.42 W
Hamm	36	51.41 N	7.49 E
Hammamet	100	36.24 N	10.37 E
Hammamet, Golfe de	46	36.05 N	10.40 E
Hamm Lif	46	36.44 N	10.20 E
Hammār, Hawr al-	84	30.50 N	47.10 E
Hammerfest	26	70.40 N	23.42 E
Hammond, Ind., U.S.	174	41.36 N	87.30 W
Hammond, La., U.S.	174	30.30 N	90.28 W
Hammondsport	166	42.25 N	77.13 W
Hammonton	166	39.38 N	74.48 W
Hampshire [6]	32	51.05 N	1.15 W
Hampton, Iowa, U.S.	168	42.45 N	93.12 W
Hampton, N.H., U.S.	166	42.56 N	70.50 W
Hampton, S.C., U.S.	172	32.52 N	81.07 W
Hampton, Va., U.S.	172	37.01 N	76.22 W
Hampton Bays	166	40.53 N	72.31 W
Hamra, Saguia el	100	27.15 N	13.21 W
Hanahan	172	32.55 N	80.00 W
Hanang	104	4.26 S	35.24 E
Hanapepe	162b	21.55 N	159.35 W
Hanau	36	50.08 N	8.55 E
Hancock	168	47.07 N	88.35 W
Handan	80	36.37 N	114.29 E
Handen	28	59.10 N	18.08 E
Handlová	36	48.44 N	18.46 E
Hando	102	10.39 N	51.08 E
Hanford	184	36.20 N	119.39 W
Hangzhou	80	30.15 N	120.10 E
Hanīsh, Jazā'ir	84	13.45 N	42.45 E
Hannibal	174	39.42 N	91.22 W
Hannover	36	52.24 N	9.44 E
Ha-noi	82	21.02 N	105.51 E
Hanover, Ind., U.S.	174	38.43 N	85.28 W
Hanover, N.H., U.S.	166	43.42 N	72.18 W
Hanover, Pa., U.S.	166	39.48 N	76.59 W
Hanzhong	80	32.59 N	107.11 E
Hapeville	172	33.40 N	84.24 W
Harash, Bi'r al- [4]	102	25.30 N	22.12 E
Harbin → Haerbin	80	45.45 N	126.41 E
Hardangerfjorden [2]	28	60.10 N	6.00 E
Harderwijk	36	52.21 N	5.36 E
Hardin	180	45.44 N	107.37 W
Hardwick, Ga., U.S.	172	33.09 N	83.13 W
Hardwick, Vt., U.S.	166	44.30 N	72.22 W
Hareøen	160	70.25 N	54.50 W
Harer	102	9.18 N	42.08 E
Hargeysa	102	9.30 N	44.03 E
Harīrūd (Tedžen)	84	37.24 N	60.38 E
Harlan, Iowa, U.S.	174	41.39 N	95.19 W
Harlan, Ky., U.S.	172	36.51 N	83.19 W
Harlingen, Ned.	36	53.10 N	5.24 E
Harlingen, Tex., U.S.	162	26.11 N	97.42 W
Harlow	32	51.47 N	0.08 E
Harlowton	180	46.26 N	109.50 W
Harmanli	54	41.56 N	25.54 E
Harney Lake	180	43.14 N	119.07 W
Harney Peak	162	44.00 N	103.30 W
Härnösand	28	62.38 N	17.56 E
Harper, Liber.	100	4.25 N	7.43 W
Harriman	172	35.56 N	84.33 W
Harrington	166	38.56 N	75.35 W
Harrisburg, Ill., U.S.	174	37.44 N	88.33 W
Harrisburg, Pa., U.S.	166	40.16 N	76.52 W
Harrison	174	36.14 N	93.07 W
Harrison, Cape	160	54.55 N	57.55 W
Harrisonburg	166	38.34 N	78.58 W
Harrisonville	174	38.39 N	94.21 W
Harrodsburg	174	37.46 N	84.51 W
Harrogate	32	54.00 N	1.33 W
Harry S Truman Reservoir [1]	174	38.10 N	93.45 W
Harstad	26	68.46 N	16.30 E
Hart	160	65.51 N	137.22 W
Hartford, Ala., U.S.	174	31.06 N	85.42 W
Hartford, Conn., U.S.	166	41.46 N	72.41 W
Hartford, Mich., U.S.	168	42.12 N	86.10 W
Hartford, Wis., U.S.	168	43.19 N	88.22 W
Hartford City	174	40.27 N	85.22 W
Hartland Point	32	51.02 N	4.31 W
Hartlepool	32	54.42 N	1.11 W
Harts	104	28.24 S	24.17 E
Hartselle	174	34.27 N	86.56 W
Hartshorne	174	34.51 N	95.34 W
Hartsville, S.C., U.S.	172	34.23 N	80.04 W
Hartsville, Tenn., U.S.	174	36.24 N	86.10 W
Hartwell	172	34.21 N	82.56 W
Hartwell Lake [1]	172	34.30 N	82.55 W
Hārūt	84	31.35 N	61.18 E
Harvard	168	42.25 N	88.37 W
Harvey, Ill., U.S.	168	41.37 N	87.39 W
Harvey, N. Dak., U.S.	162	47.47 N	99.56 W
Harwich	32	51.57 N	1.17 E
Hase	36	52.41 N	7.18 E
Ḥashā, Jabal al-	84	13.43 N	44.31 E
Haskovo	54	41.56 N	25.33 E
Haslemere	32	51.06 N	0.43 W
Hasselt	36	50.56 N	5.20 E
Hassi el Ghella	50	35.28 N	1.03 W
Hässleholm	28	56.09 N	13.46 E
Hastings, N.Z.	118	39.38 S	176.51 E
Hastings, Eng., U.K.	32	50.51 N	0.36 E
Hastings, Mich., U.S.	168	42.39 N	85.17 W
Hastings, Minn., U.S.	168	44.44 N	92.51 W
Hastings, Nebr., U.S.	162	40.35 N	98.23 W
Hatchie	174	35.35 N	89.53 W
Hathob, Oued el	46	35.23 N	9.32 E
Hatteras, Cape	172	35.13 N	75.32 W
Hatteras Island	172	35.25 N	75.30 W
Hattiesburg	174	31.19 N	89.16 W
Hatvan	36	47.40 N	19.41 E
Hat Yai	82	7.01 N	100.28 E
Haugesund	28	59.25 N	5.18 E
Haukivesi	28	62.06 N	28.28 E
Haunstetten	36	48.18 N	10.54 E
Hauraki Gulf	118	36.20 S	175.05 E
Haut Atlas	100	31.30 N	6.00 W
Hautes Fagnes	36	50.30 N	6.05 E
Hautmont	42	50.15 N	3.56 E
Havana → La Habana, Cuba	130	23.08 N	82.22 W
Havana, Ill., U.S.	174	40.18 N	90.04 W
Havant	32	50.51 N	0.29 W
Havasu, Lake [1]	178	34.30 N	114.20 W
Havelland [1]	36	52.25 N	12.45 E
Havelock	172	34.53 N	76.54 W
Haverhill, Eng., U.K.	32	52.05 N	0.26 E
Haverhill, Mass., U.S.	166	42.47 N	71.05 W
Haverstraw	166	41.12 N	73.58 W
Havířov	36	49.47 N	18.27 E
Havlíčkův Brod	36	49.36 N	15.35 E
Havre	180	48.33 N	109.41 W
Havre de Grace	166	39.33 N	76.06 W
Hawaii [3]	162b	20.00 N	157.45 W
Hawaii	162b	19.30 N	155.30 W
Hawick	32	55.25 N	2.47 W
Hawke Bay	118	39.20 S	177.30 E
Hawkins	184	32.35 N	95.12 W
Hawkinsville	172	32.17 N	83.28 W
Haw Knob	172	35.19 N	84.02 W
Hawthorne	184	38.32 N	118.38 W
Hay, Mount	162a	59.15 N	137.37 W
Hayange	42	49.20 N	6.03 E
Hayes	160	57.03 N	92.09 W
Hayesville	180	44.59 N	122.58 W
Haynesville	174	32.58 N	93.08 W
Hayrabolu	54	41.12 N	27.06 E
Hay River	160	60.51 N	115.40 W
Hays	162	38.53 N	99.20 W
Hayti	174	36.14 N	89.44 W
Hayward	168	46.01 N	91.29 W
Hazard	172	37.15 N	83.12 W
Hazebrouck	42	50.43 N	2.32 E
Hazelwood	172	35.28 N	83.00 W
Hazlehurst, Ga., U.S.	172	31.52 N	82.36 W
Hazlehurst, Miss., U.S.	174	31.52 N	90.24 W
Hazleton	166	40.58 N	75.59 W
Headland	174	31.21 N	85.20 W
Heavener	174	34.53 N	94.36 W
Heber City	178	40.30 N	111.25 W
Heber Springs	174	35.30 N	92.02 W
Hebrides	32	57.00 N	6.30 W
Heerenveen	36	52.57 N	5.55 E
Heerlen	36	50.54 N	5.59 E
Hefa	84	32.49 N	35.00 E
Hefei	80	31.51 N	117.17 E
Heflin	174	33.39 N	85.35 W
Hegang	80	47.24 N	130.17 E
Heide	36	54.12 N	9.06 E
Heidelberg	36	49.25 N	8.43 E
Heidenheim	36	49.01 N	10.44 E
Heilbronn	36	49.08 N	9.13 E
Heiligenstadt	36	51.23 N	10.09 E
Heilongjiang (Amur)	64	52.56 N	141.10 E
Hekla [1]	26a	64.00 N	19.39 W
Helagsfjället	28	62.55 N	12.27 E
Helena, Ark., U.S.	174	34.32 N	90.35 W
Helena, Mont., U.S.	180	46.36 N	112.01 W
Helensburgh	32	56.01 N	4.44 W
Helgoland	36	54.12 N	7.53 E
Hellertown	166	40.35 N	75.21 W
Hellín	50	38.31 N	1.41 W
Hells Canyon	180	45.20 N	116.45 W
Hell-Ville	104	13.25 S	48.16 E
Helmond	36	51.29 N	5.40 E
Helmstedt	36	52.13 N	11.00 E
Helper	178	39.41 N	110.51 W
Helsingborg	28	56.03 N	12.42 E
Helsingfors → Helsinki	28	60.10 N	24.58 E
Helsingør (Elsinore)	28	56.02 N	12.37 E
Helsinki (Helsingfors)	28	60.10 N	24.58 E
Helska, Mierzeja [2]	36	54.45 N	18.39 E
Helston	32	50.05 N	5.16 W
Hemel Hempstead	32	51.46 N	0.28 W
Hemet	184	33.45 N	116.58 W
Henderson, Ky., U.S.	174	37.50 N	87.35 W
Henderson, Minn., U.S.	168	44.31 N	93.55 W
Henderson, Nev., U.S.	184	36.02 N	114.59 W
Henderson, N.C., U.S.	172	36.20 N	78.25 W
Henderson, Tenn., U.S.	174	35.27 N	88.38 W
Henderson, Tex., U.S.	174	32.09 N	94.48 W
Hendersonville, N.C., U.S.	172	35.19 N	82.28 W
Hendersonville, Tenn., U.S.	174	36.18 N	86.37 W
Hengelo	36	52.15 N	6.45 E
Hengyang	80	26.51 N	112.30 E
Henlopen, Cape	166	38.48 N	75.05 W
Hennebont	42	47.48 N	3.17 W
Hennef	36	50.46 N	7.16 E
Hennigsdorf	36	52.38 N	13.12 E
Henrietta Maria, Cape	160	55.09 N	82.20 W
Henry	168	41.07 N	89.41 W
Henry, Cape	172	36.55 N	76.01 W
Henzada	82	17.38 N	95.28 E
Herāt	84	34.20 N	62.07 E
Hérault	42	43.17 N	3.26 E
Herculaneum	174	38.16 N	90.23 W
Hereford	32	52.04 N	2.43 W
Hereford and Worcester [6]	32	52.10 N	2.30 W
Herford	36	52.06 N	8.40 E
Herisau	42	47.23 N	9.17 E
Herkimer	166	43.02 N	74.59 W
Hermann	174	38.42 N	91.27 W
Hermiston	180	45.51 N	119.17 W
Hermosillo	130	29.04 N	110.58 W
Hernád (Hornád)	36	47.56 N	21.08 E
Hernando	174	34.49 N	89.59 W
Herne	36	51.32 N	7.13 E
Herne Bay	32	51.23 N	1.08 E
Herning	28	56.08 N	8.59 E
Heroica Nogales	130	31.20 N	110.56 W
Herrin	174	37.48 N	89.02 W
Herschel Island	160	69.35 N	139.05 W
Hershey	166	40.17 N	76.39 W
Herstal	36	50.40 N	5.38 E
Hertford, Eng., U.K.	32	51.48 N	0.05 W
Hertford, N.C., U.S.	172	36.11 N	76.28 W
Hertfordshire [6]	32	51.50 N	0.10 W
Hess	160	63.34 N	133.57 W
Hetch Hetchy Aqueduct [1]	184	37.29 N	122.19 W
Hettstedt	36	51.38 N	11.30 E
Heves	36	47.36 N	20.17 E
Heysham	32	54.02 N	2.54 W
Hialeah	172	25.49 N	80.17 W
Hiawatha	174	39.51 N	95.32 W
Hibbing	168	47.25 N	92.56 W
Hickman	174	36.34 N	89.11 W
Hickory	172	35.44 N	81.21 W
Hicksville	166	41.18 N	84.46 W
Hidalgo del Parral	130	26.56 N	105.40 W
Hienghène	112	20.41 S	164.56 E
Higginsville	174	39.04 N	93.43 W
Highland, Calif., U.S.	184	34.08 N	117.12 W
Highland, Ill., U.S.	174	38.44 N	89.41 W
Highland, Ind., U.S.	174	41.33 N	87.27 W
Highland, Kans., U.S.	174	39.52 N	95.16 W
Highland Park, Ill., U.S.	168	42.11 N	87.48 W
Highland Park, Mich., U.S.	168	42.24 N	83.06 W
Highland Springs	172	37.33 N	77.20 W
High Point	172	35.58 N	80.01 W
High Point	166	41.19 N	74.40 W
Hightstown	166	40.16 N	74.31 W
Highwood	168	42.13 N	87.48 W
High Wycombe	32	51.38 N	0.46 W
Hiiumaa	62	58.52 N	22.40 E
Hijāz, Jabal al-	84	19.45 N	41.55 E
Hilden	36	51.10 N	6.56 E
Hildesheim	36	52.09 N	9.57 E
Hillcrest Center	184	35.23 N	118.57 W
Hillerød	28	55.56 N	12.19 E
Hillsboro, Ill., U.S.	174	39.09 N	89.29 W
Hillsboro, N.H., U.S.	166	43.07 N	71.54 W
Hillsboro, Ohio, U.S.	166	39.12 N	83.37 W
Hillsboro, Oreg., U.S.	180	45.31 N	122.59 W
Hillsdale	166	41.55 N	84.38 W
Hilo	162b	19.43 N	155.05 W
Hilton Head Island	172	32.12 N	80.45 W
Hilversum	36	52.14 N	5.10 E
Himalayas	84	28.00 N	84.00 E
Himeji	80	34.49 N	134.42 E
Ḥimṣ	84	34.44 N	36.43 E
Hindu Kush	84	36.00 N	71.30 E
Hinesville	172	31.51 N	81.36 W
Hingham	166	42.14 N	70.53 W
Hingol	84	25.23 N	65.28 E
Hinnøya	26	68.30 N	16.00 E
Hinojosa del Duque	50	38.30 N	5.09 W
Hinterrhein	42	46.49 N	9.25 E
Hinton	172	37.41 N	80.53 W
Hirosaki	80	40.35 N	140.28 E
Hiroshima	80	34.24 N	132.27 E
Hirschberg → Jelenia Gora	36	50.55 N	15.46 E
Hirson	42	49.55 N	4.05 E
Hispaniola	130	19.00 N	71.00 W
Hitachi	80	36.36 N	140.39 E
Hitchcock	174	29.21 N	95.01 W
Hitra	28	63.33 N	8.45 E
Hjälmaren	28	59.15 N	15.45 E
Hjørring	28	57.28 N	9.59 E
Hlohovec	36	48.25 N	17.47 E
Hnilec	36	48.53 N	21.01 E
Hobart	116	42.53 S	147.19 E
Hobbs	162	32.42 N	103.08 W
Hoboken, Bel.	36	51.10 N	4.21 E
Hoboken, N.J., U.S.	166	40.45 N	74.03 W
Hochalmspitze	36	47.01 N	13.19 E
Hochkönig	36	47.25 N	13.04 E
Hockenheim	36	49.19 N	8.33 E
Hodgenville	174	37.34 N	85.44 W
Hódmezővásárhely	36	46.25 N	20.20 E
Hodna, Chott el	100	35.25 N	4.45 E
Hodna, Monts du	50	35.50 N	4.50 E
Hodna, Plaine du	50	35.38 N	4.30 E
Hodonín	36	48.51 N	17.08 E
Hof	36	50.18 N	11.55 E
Hofheim in Unterfranken	36	50.08 N	10.31 E
Hofors	28	60.33 N	16.17 E
Hog, Tanjong	82	5.18 N	119.16 E
Hogansville	172	33.11 N	84.55 W
Hohe Acht	36	50.23 N	7.00 E
Hohenlimburg	36	51.21 N	7.35 E
Hohenwald	174	35.33 N	87.33 W
Hoher Dachstein	36	47.28 N	13.35 E
Hökensås [2]	28	58.11 N	14.08 E
Hokes Bluff	174	34.00 N	85.52 W
Hokkaidō	80	44.00 N	143.00 E
Holbæk	28	55.43 N	11.43 E
Holbrook	178	34.54 N	110.10 W
Holden	174	38.43 N	94.01 W
Hole in the Mountain Peak	184	40.55 N	115.05 W
Holguín	130	20.53 N	76.15 W
Holladay	178	40.40 N	111.49 W
Hollam's Bird Island	104	24.45 S	14.34 E
Holland	168	42.47 N	86.07 W
Hollandale	174	33.10 N	90.58 W
Hollidaysburg	166	40.26 N	78.23 W
Hollins	172	37.21 N	79.56 W
Hollister	184	36.51 N	121.24 W
Holly Hill	172	29.14 N	81.02 W
Holly Springs	174	34.41 N	89.26 W
Hollywood	172	26.00 N	80.09 W
Holmsjön	28	62.41 N	16.33 E
Holstebro	28	56.21 N	8.38 E
Holsteinsborg	160	66.55 N	53.40 W
Holston	172	35.57 N	83.51 W
Holston, North Fork	172	36.33 N	82.36 W
Holt, Ala., U.S.	174	33.15 N	87.29 W
Holt, Mich., U.S.	168	42.39 N	84.31 W
Holton	174	39.28 N	95.44 W
Holyhead	32	53.19 N	4.38 W
Holy Island, Eng., U.K.	32	55.41 N	1.48 W
Holy Island, Wales, U.K.	32	53.18 N	4.37 W
Holyoke	166	42.12 N	72.37 W
Holzminden	36	51.50 N	9.27 E
Hombori Tondo	100	15.16 N	1.40 W
Homburg	36	49.19 N	7.20 E
Homeland Park	172	34.27 N	82.41 W
Homer, La., U.S.	174	32.48 N	93.04 W
Homer, N.Y., U.S.	166	42.38 N	76.11 W
Homerville	172	31.02 N	82.45 W
Homestead	172	25.29 N	80.29 W
Homewood	174	33.29 N	86.48 W
Hondsrug [2]	36	52.55 N	6.50 E
Honduras [1]	130	15.00 N	86.30 W
Honea Path	172	34.27 N	82.24 W
Hønefoss	28	60.10 N	10.18 E
Honesdale	166	41.34 N	75.16 W
Honey Lake	184	40.16 N	120.19 W
Honfleur	42	49.25 N	0.14 E
Hon-gai	82	20.57 N	107.05 E
Hong Kong [2]	80	22.15 N	114.10 E
Honguedo, Détroit d'	160	49.15 N	64.00 W
Honiara	114	9.26 S	159.57 E
Honokaa	162b	20.05 N	155.28 W
Honolulu	162b	21.19 N	157.52 W
Honshū	80	36.00 N	138.00 E
Hood, Mount	180	45.23 N	121.41 W
Hood Canal	180	47.35 N	123.00 W
Hood River	180	45.43 N	121.31 W
Hoogeveen	36	52.43 N	6.29 E
Hooks	184	33.28 N	94.15 W
Hoopeston	168	40.28 N	87.40 W
Hoorn	36	52.38 N	5.04 E
Hoosick Falls	166	42.54 N	73.21 W
Hopatcong	166	40.56 N	74.39 W
Hope	174	33.40 N	93.36 W
Hope, Ben	32	58.24 N	4.36 W
Hope, Point	162a	68.21 N	166.50 W
Hopes Advance, Cap	160	61.04 N	69.34 W
Hope Valley	166	41.30 N	71.43 W
Hopewell	172	37.18 N	77.17 W
Hopkinsville	174	36.52 N	87.29 W
Hoquiam	180	46.59 N	123.53 W
Horgen	42	47.15 N	8.36 E
Horicon	168	43.27 N	88.38 W
Horn	26a	66.28 N	22.28 W
Hornád (Hernád)	36	47.56 N	21.08 E
Hornavan	26	66.10 N	17.30 E
Hornell	166	42.19 N	77.40 W
Hornomoravský úval	36	49.25 N	17.20 E
Hornos, Cabo de (Cape Horn)	146	55.59 S	67.16 W
Horse Cave	174	37.11 N	85.54 W
Horseheads	166	42.10 N	76.50 W
Horsens	28	55.52 N	9.52 E
Horsham	32	51.04 N	0.21 W
Hørsholm	28	55.53 N	12.30 E
Horten	28	59.25 N	10.30 E
Horton	174	39.40 N	95.32 W
Horton	160	70.00 N	126.53 W
Hortonville	168	44.20 N	88.38 W
Hosére Batandji	100	8.20 N	13.15 E
Hospitalet	50	41.22 N	2.08 E
Hoste, Isla	146	55.15 S	69.00 W
Hot Springs	162	43.26 N	103.29 W
Hot Springs National Park	174	34.30 N	93.03 W
Hot Sulphur Springs	178	40.04 N	106.06 W
Houghton	168	47.06 N	88.34 W
Houghton Lake	168	44.20 N	84.45 W
Houlton	166	46.08 N	67.51 W
Houma	174	29.36 N	90.43 W
Houston, Miss., U.S.	174	33.54 N	89.00 W
Houston, Mo., U.S.	174	37.22 N	91.58 W
Houston, Tex., U.S.	174	29.46 N	95.22 W
Hove	32	50.49 N	0.10 W
Howard	168	44.33 N	88.04 W
Howe, Cape	116	37.30 S	149.59 E
Howell	168	42.36 N	83.55 W
Howrah	84	22.35 N	88.20 E
Hoxie	174	36.03 N	90.58 W
Höxter	36	51.46 N	9.23 E
Hoyerswerda	36	51.26 N	14.14 E
Hoyt Lakes	168	47.31 N	92.08 W
Hradec Králové	36	50.12 N	15.50 E
Hranice	36	49.33 N	17.44 E
Hron	36	47.49 N	18.45 E
Hronov	36	50.29 N	16.12 E
Hrubieszów	36	50.49 N	23.55 E
Hrubý Jeseník	36	50.00 N	17.20 E
Hsinchu	80	24.48 N	120.58 E
Hsinkao Shan	80	23.28 N	120.57 E
Huacho	144	11.07 S	77.37 W
Huainan	80	32.40 N	117.00 E
Hualapai Peak	178	35.04 N	113.54 W
Hualien	80	23.58 N	121.36 E
Huallaga	144	5.10 S	75.32 W
Huambo	104	12.44 S	15.47 E
Huancayo	144	12.04 S	75.14 W
Huanghe	80	37.32 N	118.19 E
Huangshi	80	30.13 N	115.05 E
Huánuco	144	9.55 S	76.14 W
Huaras	144	9.32 S	77.32 W
Huascarán, Nevado	144	9.07 S	77.37 W
Hubli	84	15.20 N	75.08 E
Huddersfield	32	53.39 N	1.47 W
Huddinge	28	59.14 N	17.59 E
Hudiksvall	28	61.44 N	17.07 E
Hudson, Mass., U.S.	166	42.24 N	71.35 W
Hudson, Mich., U.S.	166	41.51 N	84.21 W
Hudson, N.H., U.S.	166	42.46 N	71.26 W
Hudson, N.C., U.S.	172	35.51 N	81.30 W
Hudson, N.Y., U.S.	166	42.15 N	73.47 W
Hudson, Ohio, U.S.	166	41.15 N	81.26 W
Hudson, Wis., U.S.	168	44.53 N	92.45 W
Hudson	166	40.42 N	74.02 W
Hudson Bay	160	60.00 N	86.00 W
Hudson Falls	166	43.18 N	73.35 W
Hudson Strait	160	62.30 N	72.00 W
Hudsonville	168	42.52 N	85.52 W
Hue	82	16.28 N	107.36 E
Huehuetenango	130	15.20 N	91.28 W
Huelva	50	37.16 N	6.57 W
Huelva, Río de	50	37.27 N	6.00 W
Huerva	50	41.39 N	0.52 W
Huesca	50	42.08 N	0.25 W
Hueytown	174	33.27 N	86.59 W
Hugo	162	34.01 N	95.31 W
Huhehaote	80	40.51 N	111.40 E
Huila, Nevado del	144	3.00 N	76.00 W
Ḥukayyim, Bi'r al- [4]	102	31.36 N	23.29 E
Hull	160	45.26 N	75.43 W
Hulunchi	80	49.01 N	117.32 E
Humbe, Serra do	104	12.13 S	15.25 E
Humber	32	53.40 N	0.10 W
Humberside [6]	32	53.50 N	0.30 W
Humboldt, Iowa, U.S.	168	42.44 N	94.13 W
Humboldt, Kans., U.S.	174	37.49 N	95.26 W
Humboldt, Tenn., U.S.	174	35.49 N	88.55 W
Humboldt	184	40.02 N	118.31 W
Humenné	36	48.56 N	21.55 E
Humeston	174	40.52 N	93.30 W
Humphreys, Mount	184	37.17 N	118.40 W
Humphreys Peak	178	35.20 N	111.40 W
Húnaflói	26a	65.50 N	20.50 W
Hunedoara	54	45.45 N	22.54 E
Hungary (Magyarország) [1]	36	47.00 N	20.00 E
Hŭngnam	80	39.50 N	127.38 E

Name	Page	Lat °′	Long °′
Hungry Horse Reservoir ◎[1]	180	48.15 N	113.50 W
Hunsberge ⛰	104	27.45 S	17.12 E
Hunsrück ⛰	36	49.50 N	6.40 E
Hunte ≃	36	52.30 N	8.19 E
Huntingburg	174	38.18 N	86.57 W
Huntingdon, Eng., U.K.	32	52.20 N	0.12 W
Huntingdon, Pa., U.S.	166	40.29 N	78.01 W
Huntingdon, Tenn., U.S.	174	36.00 N	88.26 W
Huntington, Ind., U.S.	174	40.53 N	85.30 W
Huntington, N.Y., U.S.	166	40.51 N	73.25 W
Huntington, W. Va., U.S.	166	38.25 N	82.26 W
Huntington Beach	184	33.39 N	117.60 W
Huntsville, Ala., U.S.	174	34.44 N	86.35 W
Huntsville, Tex., U.S.	162	30.43 N	95.33 W
Hunyani ≃	104	15.37 S	30.39 E
Huon Gulf ☾	116a	7.10 S	147.25 E
Hurley, N. Mex., U.S.	178	32.42 N	108.08 W
Hurley, Wis., U.S.	168	46.28 N	90.08 W
Huron, Ohio, U.S.	166	41.24 N	82.33 W
Huron, S. Dak., U.S.	162	44.22 N	98.13 W
Huron, Lake ◎	162	44.30 N	82.15 W
Hurricane	166	38.26 N	82.01 W
Hürth	36	50.52 N	6.51 E
Huși	54	46.40 N	28.04 E
Huskvarna	28	57.48 N	14.16 E
Husum	36	54.28 N	9.03 E
Hutchinson, Kans., U.S.	162	38.05 N	97.56 W
Hutchinson, Minn., U.S.	168	44.54 N	94.22 W
Hüttental	36	50.54 N	8.02 E
Huy	36	50.31 N	5.14 E
Hvannadalshnúkur ▲	26a	64.01 N	16.41 W
Hvar, Otok ▮	46	43.09 N	16.45 E
Hvarski Kanal ⋃	46	43.15 N	16.37 E
Hyannis	166	41.39 N	70.17 W
Hyde Park	166	41.47 N	73.56 W
Hyderābād, Bhārat	84	17.23 N	78.29 E
Hyderābād, Pāk.	84	25.22 N	68.22 E
Hyères	42	43.07 N	6.07 E
Hyndman	166	39.49 N	78.44 W
Hyndman Peak ▲	180	43.50 N	114.10 W
Hyrum	178	41.38 N	111.51 W
Hyvinkää	28	60.38 N	24.52 E

I

Ialomița ≃	54	44.42 N	27.51 E
Ialomiței, Balta ≋	54	44.30 N	28.00 E
Iași	54	47.10 N	27.35 E
Ibadan	100	7.17 N	3.30 E
Ibagué	144	4.27 N	75.14 W
Ibar ≃	54	43.44 N	20.45 E
Ibarra	144	0.21 N	78.07 W
Ibb	84	14.01 N	44.10 E
Ibbenbüren	36	52.16 N	7.43 E
Ibérico, Sistema ⛰	50	41.00 N	2.30 W
Ibiza	50	38.54 N	1.26 E
Ibiza ▮	50	39.00 N	1.25 E
Ibo	104	12.20 S	40.35 E
Iboundji, Mont ▲	104	1.08 S	11.48 E
Ica	144	14.04 S	75.42 W
Iceberg Pass)(	178	40.25 N	105.45 W
Iceland (Ísland) □[1]	26a	65.00 N	18.00 W
Ich Bogd Uul ⛰	80	44.55 N	100.20 E
Ichilo ≃	144	15.57 S	64.42 W
Ichkeul, Garaet ◎	46	37.10 N	9.40 E
Idabel	174	33.54 N	94.50 W
Idaho □[3]	162	45.00 N	115.00 W
Idaho Falls	180	43.30 N	112.02 W
Idaho Springs	178	39.45 N	105.31 W
Idar-Oberstein	36	49.42 N	7.19 E
Iderijn ≃	80	49.16 N	100.41 E
Idfū	102	24.58 N	32.52 E
Ídhi Óros ▲	54	35.18 N	24.43 E
Ídhra ▮	54	37.20 N	23.32 E
Ieper	36	50.51 N	2.53 E
Iesi	46	43.31 N	13.14 E
Ife	100	7.30 N	4.30 E
Iforas, Adrar des ⛰	100	20.00 N	2.00 E
Iglesias	46	39.19 N	8.32 E
Iglesiente ◆[1]	46	39.20 N	8.40 E
İğneada Burnu ≻	54	41.54 N	28.03 E
Iguaçu ≃	146	25.36 S	54.36 W
Iguaçu, Saltos do (Iguassu Falls) ⌊	146	25.41 S	54.26 W
Iguala	130	18.21 N	99.32 W
Igualada	50	41.35 N	1.38 E
Iguassu Falls → Iguaçu, Saltos do ⌊	146	25.41 S	54.26 W
Iguatu	144	6.22 S	39.18 W
Iguidi, Erg ∴[8]	100	26.35 N	5.40 W
Iijoki ≃	28	65.20 N	25.17 E
Iivaara ▲[2]	28	65.47 N	29.40 E
Ijebu-Ode	100	6.50 N	3.56 E
Ijill, Kediet ▲	100	22.38 N	12.33 W
IJmuiden	36	52.27 N	4.36 E
IJsselmeer (Zuiderzee) ▾[2]	36	52.45 N	5.25 E
Ikaría ▮	54	37.41 N	26.20 E
Ikerre	100	7.31 N	5.14 E
Ila	100	8.01 N	4.55 E
Ilan	80	24.45 N	121.44 E
Iława	36	53.37 N	19.33 E
Île-à-la-Crosse	160	55.27 N	107.53 W
Île-à-la-Crosse, Lac ◎	160	55.40 N	107.45 W
Île Desroches ▮	104	5.41 S	53.41 E
Ilesha	100	7.38 N	4.45 E
Ilhéus	144	14.49 S	39.02 W
Ilion	166	43.01 N	75.02 W
Illampu, Nevado ▲	144	15.50 S	68.34 W
Iller ≃	36	48.23 N	9.58 E
Illimani, Nevado ▲	144	16.39 S	67.48 W
Illinois □[3]	162	40.00 N	89.00 W
Illinois ≃	174	38.58 N	90.27 W
Il'men', Ozero ◎	62	58.17 N	31.20 E
Ilmenau	36	50.41 N	10.55 E
Iloilo	82	10.42 N	122.34 E
Ilorin	100	8.30 N	4.32 E
Imandra, Ozero ◎	62	67.30 N	33.00 E
Imatra	28	61.10 N	28.46 E
Immenstadt	36	47.33 N	10.13 E
Immokalee	172	26.25 N	81.25 W
Imola	46	44.21 N	11.42 E
Imperia	46	43.53 N	8.03 E
Imperial Beach	184	32.35 N	117.08 W
Imperial de Aragón, Canal ≍	50	42.02 N	1.33 W
Imperial Valley ∨	184	32.50 N	115.30 W
Inari ◎	26	69.00 N	28.00 E
Inca	50	39.43 N	2.54 E
Inch'ŏn	80	37.28 N	126.38 E
Incline Village	184	39.16 N	119.56 W
Indalsälven ≃	28	62.31 N	17.27 E
Independence, Iowa, U.S.	168	42.28 N	91.54 W
Independence, Kans., U.S.	174	37.13 N	95.42 W
Independence, Mo., U.S.	174	39.05 N	94.24 W
India □[1]	84	20.00 N	77.00 E
Indiana	166	40.37 N	79.09 W
Indiana □[3]	162	40.00 N	86.15 W
Indianapolis	174	39.46 N	86.09 W
Indianola, Iowa, U.S.	168	41.22 N	93.34 W
Indianola, Miss., U.S.	174	33.27 N	90.39 W
Indian River ☾	172	28.00 N	80.30 W
Indigirka ≃	64	70.48 N	148.54 E
Indio	184	33.43 N	116.13 W
Indispensable Strait ⋃	114	9.00 S	160.30 E
Indonesia □[1]	82	5.00 S	120.00 E
Indore	84	22.43 N	75.50 E
Indrāvati ≃	84	18.43 N	80.17 E
Indre ≃	42	47.16 N	0.19 E
Indus ≃	84	24.20 N	67.47 E
İnegöl	54	40.05 N	29.31 E
Infiernillo, Presa del ◎[1]	130	18.35 N	101.45 W
Ingelheim	36	49.59 N	8.05 E
Ingolstadt	36	48.46 N	11.27 E
Inhaca, Ilha da ▮	104	26.03 S	32.57 E
Inhambane	104	23.51 S	35.29 E
Inharrime	104	24.29 S	35.01 E
Inírida ≃	144	3.55 N	67.52 W
Inishtrahull ✣[2]	32	55.26 N	7.14 W
Injasuti ▲	104	29.09 S	29.23 E
Inle Lake ◎	82	20.32 N	96.55 E
Inn (En) ≃	42	48.35 N	13.28 E
Innsbruck	36	47.16 N	11.24 E
Innviertel ◆[1]	42	48.10 N	13.15 E
Inola	174	36.09 N	95.31 W
Inowrocław	36	52.48 N	18.15 E
In Salah	100	27.12 N	2.28 E
Inta	26	66.02 N	60.08 E
Interlaken	42	46.41 N	7.51 E
International Falls	168	48.36 N	93.25 W
Inthanon, Doi ▲	82	18.35 N	98.29 E
Inuvik	160	68.25 N	133.30 W
Invercargill	118	46.24 S	168.21 E
Inverness	32	57.27 N	4.15 W
Inyangani ▲	104	18.20 S	32.50 E
Ioánnina	54	39.40 N	20.50 E
Iola	174	37.55 N	95.24 W
Ione	184	38.21 N	120.56 W
Ionia	168	42.59 N	85.04 W
Ionian Sea ▾[2]	20	39.00 N	19.00 E
Iónioi Nísoi ▮▮	54	38.30 N	20.30 E
Íos ▮	54	36.42 N	25.24 E
Iowa	174	30.14 N	93.01 W
Iowa □[3]	162	42.15 N	93.15 W
Iowa ≃	168	41.10 N	91.02 W
Iowa City	168	41.40 N	91.32 W
Iowa Falls	168	42.31 N	93.16 W
Ípeiros ◆[1]	54	39.40 N	20.50 E
Ipel'(Ipoly) ≃	36	47.49 N	18.52 E
Ipiales	144	0.50 N	77.37 W
Ipoh	82	4.35 N	101.05 E
Ipswich, Austl.	116	27.36 S	152.46 E
Ipswich, Eng., U.K.	32	52.04 N	1.10 E
Ipswich, Mass., U.S.	166	42.41 N	70.50 W
Iquitos	144	3.46 S	73.15 W
Iráklion	54	35.20 N	25.09 E
Iran (Īrān) □[1]	84	32.00 N	53.00 E
Iran, Pegunungan ⛰	82	2.05 N	114.55 E
Irapuato	130	20.41 N	101.21 W
Iraq □[1]	84	33.00 N	44.00 E
Irazú, Volcán ▲[1]	130	9.58 N	83.53 W
Irbid	84	32.33 N	35.51 E
Irbīl	84	36.11 N	44.01 E
Ireland □[1]	32	53.00 N	8.00 W
Iri	80	35.56 N	126.57 E
Iringa	104	7.46 S	35.42 E
Irkutsk	64	52.16 N	104.20 E
Iroise ☾	42	48.15 N	4.55 W
Irondale	174	33.32 N	86.42 W
Irondequoit	166	43.12 N	77.36 W
Iron Gate ∨	54	44.41 N	22.31 E
Iron Gate Reservoir ◎[1]	54	44.30 N	22.00 E
Iron Mountain	168	45.49 N	88.04 W
Iron River	168	46.05 N	88.39 W
Ironton, Minn., U.S.	168	46.28 N	93.59 W
Ironton, Ohio, U.S.	166	38.31 N	82.40 W
Ironwood	168	46.27 N	90.10 W
Irrawaddy ≃	82	15.50 N	95.06 E
Irtyš ≃	62	61.04 N	68.52 E
Irún	50	43.21 N	1.47 W
Irvine, Scot., U.K.	32	55.37 N	4.40 W
Irvine, Ky., U.S.	172	37.42 N	83.58 W
Ísafjörđur	26a	66.08 N	23.13 W
Isar ≃	36	48.49 N	12.58 E
Ischia	46	40.44 N	13.57 E
Ischia, Isola d' ▮	46	40.43 N	13.54 E
Ise	80	34.29 N	136.42 E
Iserlohn	36	51.22 N	7.41 E
Isernia	46	41.36 N	14.14 E
Iseyin	100	7.58 N	3.36 E
Ishikari ≃	80	43.15 N	141.23 E
Ishinomaki	80	38.25 N	141.18 E
Ishpeming	168	46.30 N	87.40 W
Išimskaja Step' ≚	62	55.00 N	70.00 E
Isiro	102	2.47 N	27.37 E
Iskâr, Jazovir ◎[1]	54	43.23 N	27.29 E
İskenderun	20	36.37 N	36.07 E
İskenderun Körfezi ☾	20	36.30 N	35.40 E
Islāmābād	84	33.42 N	73.10 E
Island Pond	166	44.49 N	71.53 W
Islands, Bay of ☾	160	49.10 N	58.15 W
Isla Vista	184	34.25 N	119.53 W
Islay ▮	32	55.46 N	6.10 W
Isle ≃	42	44.55 N	0.15 W
Isle of Hope	172	31.58 N	81.05 W
Isle of Man □[2]	32	54.15 N	4.30 W
Isle of Palms	172	32.47 N	79.48 W
Isle of Wight □[6]	32	50.40 N	1.20 W
Isleta	178	34.55 N	106.42 W
Ismaning	36	48.14 N	11.41 E
Isola della Scala	46	45.16 N	11.00 E
Isola di Capo Rizzuto	46	38.58 N	17.06 E
Isosyöte ▲[2]	28	65.37 N	27.35 E
Isparta	20	37.46 N	30.33 E
Israel □[1]	84	31.30 N	35.00 E
Issoire	42	45.33 N	3.15 E
Issoudun	42	46.57 N	2.00 E
İstanbul	54	41.01 N	28.58 E
İstanbul Boğazı (Bosporus) ⋃	54	41.06 N	29.04 E
Istokpoga, Lake ◎	172	27.22 N	81.17 W
Istra ≻[1]	46	45.15 N	14.00 E
Istranca Dağları ⛰	54	41.50 N	27.30 E
Itabuna	144	14.48 S	39.16 W
Itagüí	144	6.10 N	75.36 W
Itajubá	144	22.26 S	45.27 W
Italy □[1]	46	42.50 N	12.50 E
Itapetininga	144	23.36 S	48.03 W
Ithaca, Mich., U.S.	168	43.18 N	84.36 W
Ithaca, N.Y., U.S.	166	42.27 N	76.30 W
Itháki ▮	54	38.24 N	20.42 E
Itta Bena	174	33.30 N	90.20 W
Ituiutaba	144	18.58 S	49.28 W
Ituri ≃	104	1.40 N	27.01 E
Itzehoe	36	53.55 N	9.31 E
Iuka	174	34.49 N	88.11 W
Ivangrad	54	42.50 N	19.52 E
Ivano-Frankovsk	62	48.55 N	24.43 E
Ivanovo	26	57.00 N	40.59 E
Ivory Coast □[1]	100	8.00 N	5.00 W
Ivrea	46	45.28 N	7.52 E
Iwaki	80	37.03 N	140.55 E
Iwo	100	7.38 N	4.11 E
Iza ≃	54	47.54 N	23.57 E
Izegem	36	50.55 N	3.12 E
Iževsk	26	56.51 N	53.14 E
Ižma ≃	62	65.19 N	52.54 E
İzmir	54	38.25 N	27.09 E
İzmit (Kocaeli)	54	40.46 N	29.55 E
Iznajar, Embalse de ◎[1]	50	37.15 N	4.30 W
İznik Gölü ◎	54	40.26 N	29.30 E
Izozog, Bañados de ≋	144	18.48 S	62.10 W
Izu-shotō ▮▮	80	32.00 N	140.00 E

J

Jabalón ≃	50	38.53 N	4.05 W
Jabalpur	84	23.10 N	79.57 E
Jablanica ≃	54	43.07 N	21.57 E
Jablonec nad Nisou	36	50.44 N	15.10 E
Jablonovyj Chrebet (Yablonovy Range) ⛰	64	53.30 N	115.00 E
Jaboatão	144	8.07 S	35.01 W
Jacareí	144	23.19 S	45.58 W
Jacinto City	174	29.46 N	95.16 W
Jackson, Ala., U.S.	174	31.31 N	87.53 W
Jackson, Calif., U.S.	184	38.21 N	120.46 W
Jackson, Ga., U.S.	172	33.18 N	83.58 W
Jackson, Ky., U.S.	172	37.33 N	83.23 W
Jackson, La., U.S.	174	30.50 N	91.13 W
Jackson, Mich., U.S.	168	42.15 N	84.24 W
Jackson, Miss., U.S.	174	32.18 N	90.12 W
Jackson, Mo., U.S.	174	37.23 N	89.40 W
Jackson, Ohio, U.S.	166	39.03 N	82.39 W
Jackson, S.C., U.S.	172	33.20 N	81.47 W
Jackson, Tenn., U.S.	174	35.37 N	88.49 W
Jackson, Wyo., U.S.	180	43.29 N	110.38 W
Jackson Lake ◎[1]	180	43.55 N	110.40 W
Jacksonville, Ala., U.S.	174	33.49 N	85.46 W
Jacksonville, Ark., U.S.	174	34.52 N	92.07 W
Jacksonville, Fla., U.S.	172	30.20 N	81.40 W
Jacksonville, Ill., U.S.	174	39.44 N	90.14 W
Jacksonville, N.C., U.S.	172	34.45 N	77.26 W
Jacksonville, Tex., U.S.	174	31.58 N	95.17 W
Jacmel	130	18.14 N	72.32 W
Jacob	104	4.11 S	13.17 E
Jacobābād	84	28.17 N	68.26 E
Jacques-Cartier, Mont ▲	160	48.59 N	65.57 W
Jadebusen ☾	36	53.30 N	8.10 E
J.A.D. Jensens Nunatakker ▲	160	62.45 N	48.00 W
Jaén	50	37.46 N	3.47 W
Jaffna	84	9.40 N	80.00 E
Jaffrey	166	42.50 N	72.04 W
Jagst ≃	36	49.14 N	9.11 E
Jaipur	84	26.56 N	75.50 E
Jajce	46	44.21 N	17.16 E
Jakarta	82	6.10 S	106.48 E
Jakobstad (Pietarsaari)	28	63.40 N	22.42 E
Jakupica ⛰	54	41.43 N	21.26 E
Jakutsk	64	62.13 N	129.49 E
Jalālābād	84	34.26 N	70.28 E
Jalapa Enríquez	130	19.32 N	96.55 W
Jalón ≃	50	41.47 N	1.04 W
Jamaica □[1]	130	18.15 N	77.30 W
Jamal, Poluostrov ≻[1]	64	70.00 N	70.00 E
Jamantau, Gora ▲	62	54.15 N	58.06 E
Jambes	36	50.28 N	4.52 E
Jambi	82	1.36 S	103.37 E
Jambol	54	42.29 N	26.30 E
Jambongan, Pulau ▮	82	6.40 N	117.27 E
James ≃, Va., U.S.	172	36.57 N	76.26 W
James Bay ☾	160	53.30 N	80.30 W
James Island	172	32.42 N	79.58 W
Jamestown, N. Dak., U.S.	162	46.54 N	98.42 W
Jamestown, N.Y., U.S.	166	42.06 N	79.14 W
Jammerbugten ☾	28	57.20 N	9.30 E
Jammu and Kashmir □[2]	84	35.00 N	76.00 E
Jāmnagar	84	22.28 N	70.04 E
Jamshedpur	84	22.48 N	86.11 E
Jamuna ≃	84	23.51 N	89.45 E
Janda, Laguna de la ◎	50	36.15 N	5.51 W
Janesville, Minn., U.S.	168	44.07 N	93.42 W
Janesville, Wis., U.S.	168	42.41 N	89.01 W
Janskij Zaliv ☾	64	71.50 N	136.00 E
Jantra ≃	54	43.38 N	25.34 E
Japan □[1]	80	36.00 N	138.00 E
Japan, Sea of ▾[2]	80	40.00 N	135.00 E
Jarama ≃	50	40.02 N	3.39 W
Jarocin	36	51.59 N	17.31 E
Jaroměř	36	50.21 N	15.55 E
Jaroslavl'	26	57.37 N	39.52 E
Jarosław	36	50.02 N	22.42 E
Järvenpää	28	60.28 N	25.06 E
Jasło	36	49.45 N	21.29 E
Jason Islands ▮▮	146	51.05 S	61.00 W
Jasonville	174	39.10 N	87.12 W
Jasper, Ala., U.S.	174	33.50 N	87.17 W
Jasper, Ind., U.S.	174	38.24 N	86.56 W
Jasper, Tex., U.S.	174	30.55 N	94.01 W
Jászapáti	36	47.31 N	20.09 E
Jat, Uad el ∨	100	26.45 N	13.03 W
Jataí	144	17.53 S	51.43 W
Játiva	50	38.59 N	0.31 W
Jaú	144	22.18 S	48.33 W
Javalambre ▲	50	40.06 N	1.03 W
Javari (Yavarí) ≃	144	4.21 S	70.02 W
Javor ⛰	54	44.05 N	18.55 E
Javorníky ⛰	36	49.20 N	18.20 E
Jawa (Java) ▮	82	7.30 S	110.00 E
Jawa, Laut (Java Sea) ▾[2]	82	5.00 S	110.00 E
Jawor	36	51.03 N	16.11 E
Jaworzno	36	50.13 N	19.15 E
Jay	174	36.25 N	94.48 W
Jaya, Puncak ▲	82	4.05 S	137.11 E
Jayapura (Sukarnapura)	82	2.32 S	140.42 E
Jay Peak ▲	166	44.55 N	72.32 W
Jaz Mūrīān, Hāmūn-e ◎	84	27.20 N	58.55 E
Jeanerette	174	29.55 N	91.40 W
Jędrzejów	36	50.39 N	20.18 E
Jefferson	168	43.01 N	88.48 W
Jefferson ≃	180	45.56 N	111.30 W
Jefferson, Mount ▲, Nev., U.S.	184	38.46 N	116.55 W
Jefferson, Mount ▲, Oreg., U.S.	180	44.40 N	121.47 W
Jefferson City, Mo., U.S.	174	38.34 N	92.10 W
Jefferson City, Tenn., U.S.	172	36.07 N	83.30 W
Jeffersontown	174	38.12 N	85.35 W
Jeffersonville	174	38.17 N	85.44 W
Jegorjevsk	26	55.23 N	39.02 E
Jekateriny, Proliv ⋃	64	53.53 N	140.25 E
Jelec	62	52.37 N	38.30 E
Jelenia Góra (Hirschberg)	36	50.55 N	15.46 E
Jelgava	26	56.39 N	23.42 E
Jelizavety, Mys ≻	64	54.24 N	142.42 E
Jellico	172	36.35 N	84.08 W
Jeloguj ≃	64	63.13 N	87.45 E
Jember	82	8.10 S	113.42 E
Jemez Springs	178	35.46 N	106.42 W
Jena, D.D.R.	36	50.56 N	11.35 E
Jena, La., U.S.	174	31.41 N	92.08 W
Jenisej ≃	62	71.50 N	82.40 E
Jenisejskij Kr'až ⛰	62	59.00 N	93.00 E
Jenisejskij Zaliv ☾	62	72.30 N	80.00 E
Jenkins	172	37.10 N	82.38 W
Jenkintown	166	40.06 N	75.08 W
Jennings	174	30.13 N	92.39 W
Jequié	144	13.51 S	40.05 W
Jérémie	130	18.39 N	74.07 W
Jerevan	62	40.11 N	44.30 E
Jerez de la Frontera	50	36.41 N	6.08 W
Jerez de los Caballeros	50	38.19 N	6.46 W
Jergeni ⛰[2]	62	47.00 N	44.00 E
Jerimoth Hill ▲[2]	166	41.52 N	71.47 W
Jerome	180	42.43 N	114.31 W
Jersey □[2]	32	49.15 N	2.10 W
Jersey City	166	40.44 N	74.02 W
Jersey Shore	166	41.12 N	77.16 W
Jerseyville	174	39.07 N	90.20 W
Jerte ≃	50	39.58 N	6.17 W
Jerusalem → Yerushalayim	84	31.46 N	35.14 E
Jesenice	46	46.27 N	14.04 E
Jesselton → Kota Kinabalu	82	5.59 N	116.04 E
Jessup	166	41.28 N	75.34 W
Jesup, Ga., U.S.	172	31.36 N	81.53 W
Jesup, Iowa, U.S.	168	42.29 N	92.04 W
Jevišovka ≃	36	48.48 N	16.28 E
Jezerce ▲	54	42.26 N	19.49 E
Jhang Maghiāna	84	31.16 N	72.19 E
Jhānsi	84	25.27 N	78.35 E
Jhelum	84	32.56 N	73.44 E
Jiamusi	80	46.50 N	130.21 E
Jiaozuo	80	35.15 N	113.18 E
Jičín	36	50.26 N	15.21 E
Jihlava	36	49.24 N	15.36 E
Jihlava ≃	36	48.55 N	16.37 E
Jijia ≃	54	46.54 N	28.05 E
Jilin	80	43.51 N	126.33 E
Jima	102	7.36 N	36.50 E
Jimbolia	54	45.47 N	20.43 E
Jinan (Tsinan)	80	36.40 N	116.57 E
Jindřichův Hradec	36	49.09 N	15.00 E
Jingdezhen	80	29.16 N	117.11 E
Jinja	104	0.26 N	33.12 E
Jinshajiang ≃	80	28.50 N	104.36 E
Jinzhou	80	41.07 N	121.08 E
Jirjā	102	26.20 N	31.53 E
Jiu ≃	54	43.47 N	23.48 E
Jixi	80	45.17 N	130.59 E
Jizera ≃	36	50.10 N	14.43 E
João Pessoa	144	7.07 S	34.52 W
Jódar	50	37.50 N	3.21 W
Jodhpur	84	26.17 N	73.01 E
Joensuu	28	62.36 N	29.46 E
Johannesburg	104	26.15 S	28.00 E
Johanngeorgenstadt	36	50.26 N	12.43 E
John Day ≃	180	45.44 N	120.39 W
Johnson	166	44.38 N	72.41 W
Johnsonburg	166	41.29 N	78.41 W
Johnson City, N.Y., U.S.	166	42.07 N	75.57 W
Johnson City, Tenn., U.S.	172	36.19 N	82.21 W
Johnston	172	33.50 N	81.48 W
Johnston City	174	37.49 N	88.56 W
Johnstown, N.Y., U.S.	166	43.00 N	74.22 W
Johnstown, Pa., U.S.	166	40.20 N	78.55 W
Johor Baharu	82	1.28 N	103.45 E
Joliet	168	41.32 N	88.05 W
Jolo	82	6.03 N	121.00 E
Jonesboro, Ark., U.S.	174	35.50 N	90.42 W
Jonesboro, Ga., U.S.	172	33.32 N	84.21 W
Jonesboro, Ind., U.S.	174	40.29 N	85.38 W
Jonesboro, La., U.S.	174	32.15 N	92.43 W
Jonesville	174	31.38 N	91.49 W
Jönköping	28	57.47 N	14.11 E
Jonquière	160	48.24 N	71.15 W
Joplin	174	37.06 N	94.31 W
Jordan	168	44.40 N	93.37 W
Jordan □[1]	84	31.00 N	36.00 E
Jordan ≃	178	40.49 N	112.08 W
Jos	100	9.55 N	8.53 E
Joshua Tree	184	34.08 N	116.19 W
Joškar-Ola	26	56.38 N	47.52 E
J. Percy Priest Lake ◎[1]	174	36.05 N	86.30 W
Juan Fernández, Archipiélago ▮▮	146	33.00 S	80.00 W
Juàzeiro	144	9.25 S	40.30 W
Juàzeiro do Norte	144	7.12 S	39.20 W
Jūbā	102	4.51 N	31.37 E
Juba ≃	104	0.12 N	42.40 E
Juby, Cap ≻	100	27.58 N	12.55 W
Júcar ≃	50	39.09 N	0.14 W
Juchitán	130	16.26 N	95.01 W
Juddah (Jidda)	84	21.30 N	39.12 E
Judenburg	36	47.10 N	14.40 E
Judith ≃	180	47.44 N	109.38 W
Judson	172	34.50 N	82.27 W
Jugorskij Šar, Proliv ⋃	62	69.45 N	60.35 E
Juigalpa	130	12.05 N	85.24 W
Juist ▮	36	53.40 N	7.00 E
Juiz de Fora	144	21.45 S	43.20 W
Jukagirskoje Ploskogorje ⛰[1]	64	66.00 N	155.00 E
Juliaca	144	15.30 S	70.08 W
Julian Alps ⛰	46	46.00 N	14.00 E
Juliana Top ▲	144	3.41 N	56.32 W
Julianehåb	160	60.43 N	46.01 W
Jülich	36	50.55 N	6.21 E
Jullundur	84	31.20 N	75.35 E
Jumentos Cays ▮▮	130	22.42 N	75.55 W
Jumet	36	50.26 N	4.25 E
Jumilla	50	38.29 N	1.17 W
Junction City	162	39.02 N	96.50 W
Jundiaí	144	23.11 S	46.52 W
Juneau, Alaska, U.S.	162a	58.20 N	134.27 W
Juneau, Wis., U.S.	168	43.24 N	88.42 W
Jungfrau ▲	42	46.32 N	7.58 E
Juniata ≃	166	40.24 N	77.01 W
Junín	146	34.35 S	60.57 W
Junín, Lago ◎	144	11.02 S	76.06 W
Jur ≃	102	8.39 N	29.18 E
Jura ⛰	42	46.45 N	6.30 E
Jūrmala	26	56.58 N	23.42 E
Juruá ≃	144	2.37 S	65.44 W
Jüterbog	36	51.59 N	13.04 E
Jutiapa	130	14.17 N	89.54 W
Juticalpa	130	14.42 N	86.15 W
Juventud, Isla de la ▮	130	21.40 N	82.50 W
Južno-Sachalinsk	64	46.58 N	142.42 E
Južnyj, Mys ≻	64	57.45 N	156.45 E
Južnyj Bug ≃	62	46.59 N	31.58 E
Jylland ≻[1]	28	56.00 N	9.15 E
Jyväskylä	28	62.14 N	25.44 E

K

Kaap Plato ⛰[1]	104	28.20 S	23.57 E
Kaapstad → Cape Town	104	33.55 S	18.22 E
Kabale	104	1.15 S	29.59 E
Kabetogama Lake ◎	168	48.28 N	92.59 W
Kab-hegy ▲	36	46.58 N	17.30 E
Kabīr Kūh ⛰	84	33.25 N	46.45 E
Kabompo ≃	104	14.10 S	23.11 E
Kābul	84	34.30 N	69.11 E
Kabwe (Broken Hill)	104	14.27 S	28.27 E
Kabylie ◆[1]	50	36.30 N	4.30 E
Kachovskoje Vodochranilišče ◎[1]	62	47.25 N	34.10 E
Kadan Kyun ▮	82	12.30 N	98.22 E
Kadeï ≃	102	3.31 N	16.05 E
Kadijevka	62	48.34 N	38.40 E
Kaduna	100	10.33 N	7.27 E
Kaduna ≃	100	8.45 N	5.45 E
Kaédi	100	16.09 N	13.30 W
Kaesŏng	80	37.59 N	126.33 E
Kafirévs, Ákra ≻	54	38.09 N	24.36 E
Kafu ≃	104	1.08 N	31.05 E
Kafue ≃	104	15.56 S	28.55 E
Kagera ≃	104	0.57 S	31.47 E
Kagoshima	80	31.36 N	130.33 E
Kahayan ≃	82	3.20 S	114.04 E
Kahiu Point ☾	162b	21.13 N	156.58 W
Kahler Asten ▲	36	51.11 N	8.29 E
Kahoka	174	40.25 N	91.43 W
Kahoolawe ▮	162b	20.33 N	156.37 W
Kahuku Point ≻	162b	21.43 N	157.59 W
Kahului	162b	20.54 N	156.28 W
Kaieteur Fall ⌊	144	5.10 N	59.28 W
Kaifeng	80	34.51 N	114.21 E
Kailua	162b	21.24 N	157.44 W
Kaïmakchalán ▲	54	40.58 N	21.48 E
Kaiserslautern	36	49.26 N	7.46 E
Kaiwi Channel ⋃	162b	21.15 N	157.30 W
Kajaani	28	64.14 N	27.41 E
Ka Lae ≻	162b	18.55 N	155.41 W
Kalahari Desert ◆[2]	104	24.00 S	21.30 E
Kalama	180	46.01 N	122.51 W
Kalámai	54	37.04 N	22.07 E
Kalamariá	54	40.35 N	22.58 E
Kalamazoo	168	42.17 N	85.32 W
Kalb, Ra's al- ≻	84	14.02 N	48.40 E
Kalemi (Albertville)	104	5.56 S	29.12 E
Kalgoorlie	116	30.45 S	121.28 E
Kaliakra, nos ≻	54	43.21 N	28.27 E
Kalimantan → Borneo ▮	82	0.30 N	114.00 E
Kálimnos	54	36.57 N	26.59 E
Kalinin	26	56.52 N	35.55 E
Kaliningrad (Königsberg), S.S.S.R.	26	54.43 N	20.30 E
Kaliningrad, S.S.S.R.	62	55.55 N	37.49 E
Kalispell	180	48.12 N	114.19 W
Kalisz	36	51.46 N	18.06 E
Kalixälven ≃	26	65.50 N	23.11 E
Kallavesi ◎	28	62.50 N	27.45 E
Kallsjön ◎	28	63.37 N	13.00 E
Kalmar	28	56.40 N	16.22 E
Kalmarsund ⋃	28	56.40 N	16.25 E
Kalničko Gorje ⛰	46	46.10 N	16.30 E
Kalocsa	36	46.32 N	18.59 E
Kalpeni Island ▮	84	10.05 N	73.38 E
Kalsūbai ▲	84	19.36 N	73.43 E
Kaluga	26	54.31 N	36.16 E
Kama ≃	62	55.45 N	52.00 E
Kamaishi	80	39.16 N	141.53 E
Kamarān ▮	84	15.21 N	42.34 E
Kamčatka, Poluostrov ≻[1]	64	56.00 N	160.00 E
Kamčatskij Zaliv ☾	64	55.35 N	162.21 E
Kamčija ≃	54	43.02 N	27.53 E
Kamensk-Ural'skij	62	56.28 N	61.54 E
Kamenz	36	51.16 N	14.06 E
Kamienna ≃	36	51.06 N	21.47 E
Kamienna Góra	36	50.47 N	16.01 E
Kamina	104	8.44 S	25.00 E
Kamloops	160	50.40 N	120.20 W
Kampala	104	0.19 N	32.25 E
Kampen	36	52.33 N	5.54 E
Kampinoska, Puszcza ◆[3]	36	52.20 N	20.30 E
Kâmpóng Cham	82	12.00 N	105.27 E
Kâmpóng Saôm, Chhâk ☾	82	10.50 N	103.32 E
Kâmpŭchéa □[1]	82	13.00 N	105.00 E
Kamskoje Vodochranilišče ◎[1]	62	58.52 N	56.15 E
Kamyšin	62	50.06 N	45.24 E
Kanaaupscow ≃	160	53.39 N	77.09 W
Kananga (Luluabourg)	104	5.54 S	22.25 E
Kanawha ≃	166	38.50 N	82.08 W
Kanazawa	80	36.34 N	136.39 E
Kandalakša	26	67.09 N	32.21 E
Kandik ≃	162a	65.24 N	142.34 W
Kandy	84	7.18 N	80.38 E
Kane	166	41.40 N	78.49 W
Kaneohe	162b	21.25 N	157.48 W
Kanggye	80	40.58 N	126.34 E
Kangnŭng	80	37.45 N	128.54 E
Kanin, Poluostrov ≻[1]	62	68.00 N	45.00 E
Kanin Nos, Mys ≻	62	68.39 N	43.16 E
Kanjiža	54	46.04 N	20.04 E
Kankakee	168	41.07 N	87.52 W
Kankakee ≃	168	41.23 N	88.16 W
Kankan	100	10.23 N	9.18 W
Kanmaw Kyun ▮	82	11.40 N	98.28 E
Kannapolis	172	35.30 N	80.37 W
Kano	100	12.00 N	8.30 E
Kānpur	84	28.28 N	80.21 E
Kansas □[3]	162	38.45 N	98.15 W
Kansas ≃	174	39.07 N	94.36 W
Kansas City, Kans., U.S.	174	39.07 N	94.39 W
Kansas City, Mo., U.S.	174	39.05 N	94.35 W
Kanye	104	24.59 S	25.19 E
Kaohsiung	80	22.38 N	120.17 E
Kaokoveld ⛰[1]	104	21.00 S	14.20 E
Kaolack	100	14.09 N	16.04 W
Kapaa	162b	22.05 N	159.19 W
Kapaonik ⛰	54	43.20 N	20.50 E
Kapfenberg	36	47.26 N	15.18 E
Kapıdağı Yarımadası ≻[1]	54	40.28 N	27.50 E
Kaplan	174	30.00 N	92.17 W
Kapos ≃	36	46.44 N	18.30 E
Kaposvár	36	46.22 N	17.47 E
Kapuas ≃	82	0.25 S	109.40 E
Kapuas Hulu, Pegunungan ⛰	82	1.25 N	113.15 E
Kapuskasing ≃	160	49.49 N	82.00 W
Kapuvár	36	47.36 N	17.02 E
Kara-Bogaz-Gol, Zaliv ☾	62	41.00 N	53.15 E
Karabük	20	41.12 N	32.37 E
Karacabey	54	40.13 N	28.21 E
Karāchi	84	24.52 N	67.03 E
Karaganda	62	49.50 N	73.10 E
Karaginskij Zaliv ☾	64	58.50 N	164.00 E
Karagoš, Gora ▲	64	51.44 N	89.24 E
Karakoram Range ⛰	84	35.30 N	77.00 E
Karakumskij Kanal ≍	62	37.35 N	61.50 E
Karakumy ◆[2]	62	39.00 N	60.00 E
Karamürsel	54	40.42 N	29.36 E
Kara Sea → Karskoje More ▾[2]	62	76.00 N	80.00 E
Karatau, Chrebet ⛰	62	43.50 N	68.30 E
Karawanken ⛰	46	46.30 N	14.25 E
Karbalā'	84	32.36 N	44.02 E
Karcag	36	47.19 N	20.56 E
Kardhítsa	54	39.21 N	21.55 E
Kârdžali	54	41.39 N	25.22 E
Karhula	28	60.31 N	26.57 E
Kariba, Lake ◎[1]	104	17.00 S	28.00 E
Karimata, Selat (Karimata Strait) ⋃	82	2.05 S	108.40 E
Karl-Marx-Stadt (Chemnitz)	36	50.50 N	12.55 E
Karlovac	46	45.29 N	15.34 E
Karlovo	54	42.38 N	24.48 E
Karlovy Vary	36	50.11 N	12.52 E
Karlshamn	28	56.10 N	14.51 E
Karlskoga	28	59.20 N	14.31 E
Karlskrona	28	56.10 N	15.35 E
Karlsöarna ▮▮	28	57.17 N	17.58 E
Karlsruhe	36	49.03 N	8.24 E
Karlstad	28	59.22 N	13.30 E
Karnack	184	32.40 N	94.10 W
Karnāli ≃	84	28.45 N	81.16 E
Karnobat	54	42.39 N	26.59 E
Kárpathos ▮	54	35.40 N	27.10 E
Karpenísion	54	38.55 N	21.40 E
Karrats Isfjord ☾[2]	160	71.20 N	54.00 W
Kars	20	40.36 N	43.05 E

Name	Page	Lat ° ′	Long ° ′
Karşıyaka	54	38.27 N	27.07 E
Karskije Vorota, Proliv ⋓	62	70.30 N	58.00 E
Karskoje More (Kara Sea) ⊤[2]	62	76.00 N	80.00 E
Kartal	54	40.53 N	29.10 E
Kartuzy	36	54.20 N	18.12 E
Karviná	36	49.50 N	18.30 E
Kasai (Cassai) ≃	104	3.06 S	16.57 E
Kashgar → Kashi	80	39.29 N	75.59 E
Kashi (Kashgar)	80	39.29 N	75.59 E
Kaskaskia ≃	174	37.59 N	89.56 W
Kásos I	54	35.22 N	26.56 E
Kasr, Ra's ≻	102	18.02 N	38.35 E
Kassalā	102	15.28 N	36.24 E
Kassel	36	51.19 N	9.29 E
Kasson	168	44.03 N	92.45 W
Kastoría	54	40.31 N	21.15 E
Kastrávion, Tekhnití Límni ⊜[1]	54	38.50 N	21.20 E
Kasūr	84	31.07 N	74.27 E
Kaszuby ◆[1]	36	54.10 N	18.15 E
Katahdin, Mount ∧	166	45.55 N	68.55 W
Katanga Plateau ⩕[1]	104	10.30 S	25.30 E
Kateríni	54	40.16 N	22.30 E
Kates Needle ∧	162a	57.03 N	132.03 W
Katherine	116	14.28 S	132.16 E
Kāthiāwār ≻[1]	84	21.58 N	70.30 E
Kātmāndu	84	27.43 N	85.19 E
Katowice	36	50.16 N	19.00 E
Katrīnah, Jabal ∧	102	28.31 N	33.57 E
Katrineholm	28	59.00 N	16.12 E
Katsina	100	13.00 N	7.32 E
Katsina Ala ≃	100	7.45 N	9.05 E
Kattegat ⋓	28	57.00 N	11.00 E
Katwijk aan Zee	36	52.13 N	4.24 E
Katzenbuckel ∧	36	49.28 N	9.02 E
Kauai I	162b	22.00 N	159.30 W
Kauai Channel ⋓	162b	21.45 N	158.50 W
Kaufbeuren	36	47.53 N	10.37 E
Kau Kau Bay C	114	9.42 S	160.40 E
Kaukauna	168	44.17 N	88.17 W
Kaukauveld ⩕[1]	104	20.00 S	20.30 E
Kaunakakai	162b	21.06 N	157.01 W
Kaunas	26	54.54 N	23.54 E
Kavajë	54	41.11 N	19.33 E
Kavála	54	40.56 N	24.25 E
Kavieng	116a	2.35 S	150.50 E
Kavīr, Dasht-e ◆[2]	84	34.40 N	54.30 E
Kawasaki	80	35.32 N	139.43 E
Kawm Umbū	102	24.28 N	32.57 E
Kayes	100	14.27 N	11.26 W
Kayseri	20	38.43 N	35.30 E
Kaysville	178	41.02 N	111.56 W
Kazachskij Melkosopočnik ⩕[2]	62	49.00 N	72.00 E
Kazan'	26	55.49 N	49.08 E
Kazanlâk	54	42.38 N	25.21 E
Kazbek, Gora ∧	62	42.42 N	44.31 E
Kazincbarcika	36	48.16 N	20.37 E
Kéa I	54	37.34 N	24.22 E
Kearney	162	40.42 N	99.05 W
Kearns	178	40.39 N	111.59 W
Kearny	178	33.03 N	110.55 W
Kebnekaise ∧	26	67.53 N	18.33 E
Kecel	36	46.32 N	19.16 E
Kech ≃	84	26.00 N	62.44 E
Kecskemét	36	46.54 N	19.42 E
Kediri	82	7.49 S	112.01 E
Kędzierzyn	36	50.20 N	18.12 E
Keele Peak ∧	160	63.26 N	130.19 W
Keene	166	42.56 N	72.17 W
Keeseville	166	44.30 N	73.29 W
Keetmanshoop	104	26.36 S	18.08 E
Kefallinía I	54	38.15 N	20.35 E
Keflavík	26a	64.02 N	22.36 W
Ke-ga, Mui ≻	82	12.53 N	109.28 E
Keglo, Baie C	160	59.10 N	65.50 W
Kehl	36	48.35 N	7.50 E
Keizer	180	44.57 N	123.01 W
Kékes ∧	36	47.55 N	20.02 E
Kelamayi	80	45.37 N	84.53 E
Kelang	82	3.02 N	101.27 E
Kelantan ≃	82	6.11 N	102.15 E
Kelbia, Sebkra ⊜	46	35.51 N	10.16 E
Keleti-főcsatorna ≚	36	48.01 N	21.20 E
Kelheim	36	48.55 N	11.52 E
Kelibia	46	36.51 N	11.06 E
Kellogg	180	47.32 N	116.07 W
Kelso	180	46.09 N	122.54 W
Keluang	82	2.02 N	103.19 E
Kem'	26	64.57 N	34.36 E
Kemah	184	29.30 N	95.01 W
Kemerovo	64	55.20 N	86.05 E
Kemi	28	65.49 N	24.32 E
Kemijärvi	26	66.40 N	27.25 E
Kemijoki ≃	28	65.47 N	24.30 E
Kemmerer	180	41.48 N	110.32 W
Kemmuna I	46	36.00 N	14.20 E
Kempen	36	51.22 N	6.25 E
Kempten [allgäu]	36	47.43 N	10.19 E
Kemul, Kong ∧	82	1.52 N	116.11 E
Kenbridge	172	36.58 N	78.08 W
Kendal	32	54.20 N	2.45 W
Kendall	172	25.41 N	80.19 W
Kendallville	174	41.27 N	85.16 W
Kenema	100	7.52 N	11.12 W
Kenitra	100	34.16 N	6.40 W
Kenmare	162	48.40 N	102.05 W
Kennebec ≃	166	44.00 N	69.50 W
Kennebunk	166	43.23 N	70.33 W
Kennedy, Mount ∧	160	60.30 N	139.00 W
Kenner	174	29.59 N	90.15 W
Kennett	174	36.14 N	90.03 W
Kennett Square	166	39.51 N	75.43 W
Kennewick	180	46.12 N	119.07 W
Kenogami ≃	160	51.06 N	84.28 W
Kenosha	168	42.35 N	87.49 W
Kenova	166	38.24 N	82.35 W
Kent, Ohio, U.S.	166	41.09 N	81.22 W
Kent, Wash., U.S.	180	47.23 N	122.14 W
Kent □[6]	32	51.15 N	0.40 E
Kenton	166	40.39 N	83.36 W
Kentucky □[3]	162	37.30 N	85.15 W
Kentucky ≃	172	38.41 N	85.11 W
Kentucky Lake ⊜[1]	174	36.25 N	88.05 W
Kentwood	174	30.56 N	90.31 W
Kenya □[1]	104	1.00 N	38.00 E
Kenya, Mount ∧	104	0.10 S	37.20 E
Kenyon	168	44.16 N	92.59 W
Keokuk	168	40.24 N	91.24 W
Keosauqua	174	40.44 N	91.58 W
Keota	174	35.15 N	94.55 W
Keowee, Lake ⊜[1]	172	34.45 N	82.55 W
Kępno	36	51.17 N	17.59 E
Kerava	28	60.24 N	25.07 E
Kerč'	62	45.22 N	36.27 E
Kerinci, Gunung ∧	82	1.42 S	101.16 E
Kerkenna, Îles II	100	34.44 N	11.12 E
Kérkira (Corfu)	54	39.36 N	19.56 E
Kérkira I	54	39.40 N	19.42 E
Kerkrade	36	50.52 N	6.04 E
Kerkrade [-Holz]	36	50.52 N	6.04 E
Kermān, Īrān	84	30.17 N	57.05 E
Kerman, Calif., U.S.	184	36.43 N	120.04 W
Kermānshāh	84	34.19 N	47.04 E
Kerme Körfezi C	54	36.50 N	28.00 E
Kern ≃	184	35.13 N	119.17 W
Kernersville	172	36.07 N	80.04 W
Kerr Reservoir ⊜[1]	172	36.35 N	70.28 W
Kerulen (Cherlen) (Kelulunhe) ≃	80	48.48 N	117.00 E
Keşan	54	40.51 N	26.37 E
Keszthely	36	46.46 N	17.15 E
Ketchikan	162a	55.21 N	131.35 W
Kętrzyn (Rastenburg)	36	54.06 N	21.23 E
Kettering, Eng., U.K.	32	52.24 N	0.44 W
Kettering, Ohio, U.S.	166	39.41 N	84.10 W
Kevelaer	36	51.35 N	6.15 E
Kewanee	168	41.14 N	89.56 W
Kewaunee	168	44.27 N	87.30 W
Keweenaw Bay C	168	46.56 N	88.23 W
Keweenaw Peninsula ≻[1]	168	47.12 N	88.25 W
Keweenaw Point ≻	168	47.30 N	87.50 W
Key Largo I	172	25.16 N	80.19 W
Keyser	166	39.26 N	78.59 W
Key West	172	24.33 N	81.48 W
Kežmarok	36	49.08 N	20.25 E
Khalkís	54	38.28 N	23.36 E
Khambhāt, Gulf of C	84	21.00 N	72.30 E
Khānewāl	84	30.18 N	71.56 E
Khanh-hung	82	9.36 N	105.58 E
Khaniá	54	35.31 N	24.02 E
Khark, Jazīreh-ye I	84	29.15 N	50.20 E
Kharkov → Char'kov	62	50.00 N	36.15 E
Khartoum → Al-Khurṭūm	102	15.36 N	32.32 E
Khāsh ≃	84	31.11 N	62.05 E
Khersan ≃	84	31.33 N	50.22 E
Khíos	54	38.22 N	26.08 E
Khíos I	54	38.22 N	26.00 E
Khon Kaen	82	16.26 N	102.50 E
Khorramshahr	84	30.25 N	48.11 E
Khouribga	100	32.54 N	6.57 W
Khulna	84	22.48 N	89.33 E
Khūryān Mūryān II	84	17.30 N	56.00 E
Khyber Pass)(	84	34.05 N	71.10 E
Kičevo	54	41.31 N	20.57 E
Kiel, B.R.D.	36	54.20 N	10.08 E
Kiel, Wis., U.S.	168	43.55 N	88.02 W
Kielce	36	50.52 N	20.37 E
Kieler Bucht C	36	54.35 N	10.35 E
Kiev → Kijev	62	50.26 N	30.31 E
Kiffa	100	16.37 N	11.24 W
Kifisiá	54	38.04 N	23.48 E
Kigali	104	1.57 S	30.04 E
Kii-suidō ⋓	80	33.55 N	134.55 E
Kijev	62	50.26 N	30.31 E
Kikinda	54	45.50 N	20.28 E
Kikládhes II	54	37.30 N	25.00 E
Kikwit	104	5.02 S	18.49 E
Kilauea Crater •[6]	162b	19.25 N	155.17 W
Kilgore	174	32.23 N	94.53 W
Kilimanjaro ∧	104	3.04 S	37.22 E
Kilkenny	32	52.39 N	7.15 W
Kilkís	54	41.00 N	22.53 E
Killeen	162	31.08 N	97.44 W
Kilmarnock	32	55.36 N	4.30 W
Kilombero ≃	104	8.31 S	37.22 E
Kiltān I	84	11.29 N	73.00 E
Kim ≃	100	5.28 N	11.07 E
Kimberley	104	28.43 S	24.46 E
Kimberly	168	44.17 N	88.20 W
Kimch'aek	80	40.41 N	129.12 E
Kimry	26	56.52 N	37.21 E
Kinabalu, Gunong ∧	82	6.05 N	116.33 E
Kinder	174	30.29 N	92.51 W
Kindia	100	10.04 N	12.51 W
Kindu-Port-Empain	104	2.57 S	25.56 E
Kinel'	26	53.14 N	50.39 E
Kinešma	26	57.26 N	42.09 E
King City	184	36.13 N	121.08 W
Kingman, Ariz., U.S.	178	35.12 N	114.04 W
Kings Beach	184	39.14 N	120.01 W
Kingsburg	184	36.31 N	119.33 W
Kingsford	168	45.48 N	88.04 W
King's Lynn	32	52.45 N	0.24 E
Kings Mountain	172	35.15 N	81.20 W
Kings Peak ∧	178	40.46 N	110.22 W
Kingsport	172	36.32 N	82.33 W
Kingston, Jam.	130	18.00 N	76.48 W
Kingston, Norf. I.	113	29.03 S	167.58 E
Kingston, Mass., U.S.	166	41.59 N	70.43 W
Kingston, N.Y., U.S.	166	41.56 N	74.00 W
Kingston, Pa., U.S.	166	41.16 N	75.54 W
Kingston, Tenn., U.S.	172	35.52 N	84.31 W
Kingston upon Hull	32	53.45 N	0.20 W
Kingstown	130	13.09 N	61.14 W
Kingstree	172	33.40 N	79.50 W
Kingsville	162	27.31 N	97.52 W
King William's Town	104	32.51 S	27.22 E
Kingwood	166	39.28 N	79.41 W
Kinkony, Lac ⊜	104	16.08 S	45.50 E
Kinnairds Head ≻	32	57.42 N	2.00 W
Kinshasa (Léopoldville)	104	4.18 S	15.18 E
Kinston	172	35.16 N	77.35 W
Kintyre ≻[1]	32	55.32 N	5.35 W
Kinyeti ∧	102	3.57 N	32.54 E
Kipengere Range ⩕	104	9.10 S	34.15 E
Kipushi	104	11.46 N	27.14 E
Kira Kira	114	10.27 S	161.55 E
Kirchheim	36	48.10 N	10.30 E
Kirgizskij Chrebet ⩕	62	42.30 N	74.00 E
Kiribati □[1]	10	4.00 S	175.00 E
Kırıkkale	20	39.50 N	33.31 E
Kırkağaç	54	39.06 N	27.40 E
Kirkcaldy	32	56.07 N	3.10 W
Kirkland	180	47.41 N	122.12 W
Kirkland Lake	160	48.09 N	80.02 W
Kırklareli	54	41.44 N	27.12 E
Kirksville	174	40.12 N	92.35 W
Kirkūk	84	35.28 N	44.28 E
Kirkwall	32	58.59 N	2.58 W
Kirkwood	174	38.35 N	90.24 W
Kirov	26	58.38 N	49.42 E
Kirovabad	62	40.40 N	46.22 E
Kirovakan	62	40.48 N	44.30 E
Kirovograd	62	48.30 N	32.18 E
Kirovsk	26	67.37 N	33.35 E
Kīrthar Range ⩕	84	27.00 N	67.10 E
Kirtland	178	36.44 N	108.21 W
Kiruna	26	67.51 N	20.16 E
Kisangani (Stanleyville)	104	0.30 N	25.12 E
Kisel'ovsk	64	54.00 N	86.39 E
Kišin'ov	62	47.00 N	28.50 E
Kiskőrös	36	46.38 N	19.17 E
Kiskunfélegyháza	36	46.43 N	19.52 E
Kiskunhalas	36	46.26 N	19.30 E
Kissimmee	172	28.18 N	81.24 W
Kissimmee, Lake ⊜	172	27.55 N	81.16 W
Kisújszállás	36	47.13 N	20.46 E
Kisumu	104	0.06 S	34.45 E
Kisvárda	36	48.13 N	22.05 E
Kita	100	13.03 N	9.29 W
Kitakyūshū	80	33.53 N	130.50 E
Kitami	80	43.48 N	143.54 E
Kitchener	160	43.27 N	80.29 W
Kíthira I	54	36.20 N	22.58 E
Kíthnos I	54	37.25 N	24.28 E
Kitimat	160	54.03 N	128.33 W
Kittanning	166	40.49 N	79.32 W
Kittery	166	43.05 N	70.45 W
Kitwe	104	12.49 S	28.13 E
Kitzbühel	36	47.27 N	12.23 E
Kitzingen	36	49.44 N	10.09 E
Kivu, Lac ⊜	104	2.00 S	29.10 E
Kızıl ≃	20	41.44 N	35.58 E
Kjustendil	54	42.17 N	22.41 E
Kladno	36	50.08 N	14.05 E
Klagenfurt	36	46.38 N	14.18 E
Klaipėda (Memel)	26	55.43 N	21.07 E
Klamath ≃	184	41.33 N	124.04 W
Klamath Falls	180	42.13 N	121.46 W
Klamath Mountains ⩕	180	41.40 N	123.20 W
Klarälven (Trysilelva) ≃	28	59.23 N	13.32 E
Klatovy	36	49.24 N	13.18 E
Klerksdorp	104	26.58 S	26.39 E
Klet' ∧	36	48.52 N	14.17 E
Kleve	36	51.48 N	6.09 E
Klin	26	56.20 N	36.44 E
Klingenthal	36	50.21 N	12.28 E
Klínovec ∧	36	50.24 N	12.58 E
Kłobuck	36	50.55 N	18.57 E
Kłodzko	36	50.27 N	16.39 E
Klondike □[9]	160	63.30 N	139.00 W
Klosterneuburg	36	48.18 N	16.20 E
Klosterwappen ∧	36	47.46 N	15.48 E
Kluane Lake ⊜	160	61.15 N	138.40 W
Kl'učevskaja Sopka, Vulkan ∧[1]	64	56.04 N	160.38 E
Kluczbork	36	50.59 N	18.13 E
Knaresborough	32	54.00 N	1.27 W
Kneža	54	43.30 N	24.05 E
Knightstown	174	39.48 N	85.32 W
Knin	46	44.02 N	16.12 E
Knittelfeld	36	47.14 N	14.50 E
Knob Noster	174	38.46 N	93.33 W
Knokke	36	51.21 N	3.17 E
Knox	174	41.18 N	86.37 W
Knox, Cape ≻	160	54.11 N	133.04 W
Knoxville, Ill., U.S.	168	40.55 N	90.17 W
Knoxville, Iowa, U.S.	168	41.19 N	93.06 W
Knoxville, Tenn., U.S.	172	35.58 N	83.56 W
Kobar Sink •[7]	102	14.00 N	40.30 E
Kōbe	80	34.41 N	135.10 E
København (Copenhagen)	28	55.40 N	12.35 E
Koblenz	36	50.21 N	7.35 E
Kocaeli → İzmit	54	40.46 N	29.55 E
Kočani	54	41.55 N	22.25 E
Kocher ≃	36	49.14 N	9.12 E
Kōchi	80	33.33 N	133.33 E
Kodiak Island I	162a	57.30 N	153.30 W
Köflach	36	47.04 N	15.05 E
Koforidua	100	6.03 N	0.17 W
Kōfu	80	35.39 N	138.35 E
Kogaluc ≃	160	59.40 N	77.35 W
Kogaluc, Baie C	160	59.20 N	77.50 W
Køge	28	55.27 N	12.11 E
Køge Bugt C, Dan.	28	55.30 N	12.20 E
Køge Bugt C, Grn.	160	65.00 N	40.30 W
Kohāt	84	33.35 N	71.26 E
Kohler	168	43.44 N	87.46 W
Kohtla-Järve	26	59.24 N	27.15 E
Kokand	62	40.33 N	70.57 E
Kokemäenjoki ≃	28	61.33 N	21.42 E
Kokkola (Gamlakarleby)	28	63.50 N	23.07 E
Kokomo	174	40.29 N	86.08 W
Kokopo	116a	4.20 S	152.15 E
Kokšaalatau, Chrebet ⩕	62	41.00 N	78.00 E
Kolárovo	36	47.52 N	18.02 E
Kolding	28	55.31 N	9.29 E
Kolea	50	36.38 N	2.46 E
Kolgujev, Ostrov I	62	69.05 N	49.15 E
Kolhāpur	84	16.42 N	74.13 E
Kolín	36	50.01 N	15.13 E
Köln (Cologne)	36	50.56 N	6.59 E
Koło	36	52.12 N	18.38 E
Kołobrzeg	36	54.12 N	15.33 E
Kolomna	26	55.05 N	38.49 E
Kolovrat, Mount ∧	114	9.10 S	161.05 E
Kolpino	26	59.45 N	30.36 E
Kol'skij Poluostrov (Kola Peninsula) ≻[1]	62	67.30 N	37.00 E
Kolubara ≃	54	44.40 N	20.15 E
Kolwezi	104	10.43 S	25.28 E
Kolyma ≃	64	69.30 N	161.00 E
Kolymskaja Nizmennost' ⊻	64	68.30 N	154.00 E
Kom ∧	54	43.10 N	23.03 E
Komadugu Gana ≃	100	13.05 N	12.24 E
Komadugu Yobe ≃	100	13.43 N	13.20 E
Komandorskije Ostrova II	64	55.00 N	167.00 E
Komárno	36	47.45 N	18.09 E
Komárom	36	47.44 N	18.08 E
Komló	36	46.12 N	18.16 E
Kommunarsk	62	48.30 N	38.47 E
Kommunizma, Pik ∧	62	38.57 N	72.01 E
Komoé ≃	100	5.12 N	3.44 W
Komotiní	54	41.08 N	25.25 E
Komovi ⩕	54	42.40 N	19.40 E
Kompasberg ∧	104	31.45 S	24.32 E
Komsomol'sk-na-Amure	64	50.35 N	137.02 E
Komsomol'skoj Pravdy, Ostrova II	64	77.20 N	107.40 E
Kona Coast •[2]	162b	19.25 N	155.55 W
Koné	112	21.04 S	164.52 E
Königssee ⊜	36	47.36 N	12.59 E
Konin	36	52.13 N	18.16 E
Könkämäälv ≃	26	68.29 N	22.17 E
Konkouré ≃	100	9.58 N	13.42 W
Końskie	36	51.12 N	20.26 E
Konstantinovka	26	56.41 N	50.53 E
Konstanz	36	47.40 N	9.10 E
Konya	20	37.52 N	32.31 E
Konžakovskij Kamen', Gora ∧	62	59.38 N	59.08 E
Kópavogur	26a	64.06 N	21.50 W
Kopejsk	62	55.07 N	61.37 E
Koper	42	45.33 N	13.44 E
Köping	28	59.31 N	16.00 E
Koppány ≃	36	46.35 N	18.26 E
Koprivnica	46	46.10 N	16.50 E
Korab ⩕	54	41.47 N	20.34 E
Kor'akskoje Nagorje ⩕	64	62.30 N	172.00 E
Koralpe ⩕	36	46.50 N	14.58 E
Korbach	36	51.16 N	8.52 E
Korçë	54	40.37 N	20.46 E
Korčula, Otok I	46	42.57 N	16.50 E
Korčulanski Kanal ⋓	46	43.03 N	16.40 E
Korea, North □[1]	80	40.00 N	127.00 E
Korea, South □[1]	80	36.30 N	128.00 E
Korea Bay C	80	39.00 N	124.00 E
Korea Strait ⋓	80	34.00 N	129.00 E
Korhogo	100	9.27 N	5.38 W
Korinthiakós Kólpos C	54	38.19 N	22.04 E
Kórinthos (Corinth)	54	37.56 N	22.56 E
Korínthou, Dhiórix ≚	54	37.57 N	22.56 E
Kőris-hegy ∧	36	47.18 N	17.45 E
Kōriyama	80	37.24 N	140.23 E
Korneuburg	36	48.21 N	16.20 E
Korónia, Límni ⊜	54	40.41 N	23.05 E
Körös ≃	36	46.43 N	20.12 E
Korso	28	60.21 N	25.06 E
Korsør	28	55.20 N	11.09 E
Kortrijk (Courtrai)	36	50.50 N	3.16 E
Kos I	54	36.50 N	27.10 E
Kościan	36	52.06 N	16.38 E
Kościerzyna	36	54.08 N	18.00 E
Kosciusko	174	32.58 N	89.35 W
Kosciusko, Mount ∧	116	36.27 S	148.16 E
Košice	36	48.43 N	21.15 E
Köslin → Koszalin	36	54.12 N	16.09 E
Kosovska Mitrovica	54	42.53 N	20.52 E
Kosteröarna I	28	58.54 N	11.02 E
Kostroma	26	57.46 N	40.55 E
Kostrzyn	36	52.37 N	14.39 E
Koszalin (Köslin)	36	54.12 N	16.09 E
Kőszeg	36	47.23 N	16.33 E
Kota Baharu	82	6.08 N	102.15 E
Kota Kinabalu (Jesselton)	82	5.59 N	116.04 E
Kotel'nyj, Ostrov I	64	75.45 N	138.44 E
Köthen	36	51.45 N	11.58 E
Kotka	28	60.28 N	26.55 E
Kotlas	26	61.16 N	46.35 E
Kotlenski prohod)(	54	42.53 N	26.27 E
Kotto ≃	102	4.14 N	22.02 E
Koudougou	100	12.15 N	2.22 W
Koulikoro	100	12.53 N	7.33 W
Koumac	112	20.33 S	164.17 E
Koussi, Emi ∧	102	19.50 N	18.30 E
Koutiala	100	12.23 N	5.28 W
Kouvola	28	60.52 N	26.42 E
Kovrov	26	56.22 N	41.18 E
Kowkcheh ≃	84	37.10 N	69.23 E
Kowloon (Jiulong)	80	22.18 N	114.10 E
Kozáni	54	40.18 N	21.47 E
Koźle	36	50.20 N	18.08 E
Kra, Isthmus of •[3]	82	10.20 N	99.00 E
Kragujevac	54	44.01 N	20.55 E
Kraków	36	50.03 N	19.58 E
Kralendijk	130	12.10 N	68.17 W
Kraljevo	54	43.43 N	20.41 E
Kralupy nad Vltavou	36	50.11 N	14.18 E
Kramatorsk	62	48.43 N	37.32 E
Kranj	46	46.15 N	14.21 E
Kraśnik	36	50.56 N	22.13 E
Kraśnik Fabryczny	36	50.58 N	22.12 E
Krasnodar	62	45.02 N	39.00 E
Krasnoj Armii, Proliv ⋓	62	80.00 N	94.35 E
Krasnojarsk	64	56.01 N	92.50 E
Krasnyj Luč	26	57.04 N	30.05 E
Krasnystaw	36	50.59 N	23.10 E
Kraszna (Crasna) ≃	54	48.09 N	22.20 E
Krbava ◆[1]	46	44.40 N	15.35 E
Krefeld	36	51.20 N	6.34 E
Kremenčug	62	49.04 N	33.25 E
Krems an der Donau	36	48.25 N	15.36 E
Krishna ≃	84	15.43 N	80.55 E
Kristiansand	28	58.10 N	8.00 E
Kristianstad	28	56.02 N	14.08 E
Kristiansund	28	63.07 N	7.45 E
Kristinehamn	28	59.20 N	14.07 E
Kríti I	54	35.29 N	24.42 E
Kritikón Pélagos ⊤[2]	54	35.46 N	23.54 E
Krivaja ≃	54	44.27 N	18.09 E
Krivoj Rog	62	47.55 N	33.21 E
Krk, Otok I	46	45.05 N	14.35 E
Krn ∧	42	46.16 N	13.40 E
Krnov	36	50.05 N	17.41 E
Krokodil ≃	104	24.12 S	26.52 E
Kroměříž	36	49.18 N	17.24 E
Kronach	36	50.14 N	11.20 E
Kronockij Zaliv C	64	54.12 N	160.36 E
Kronštadt	26	59.59 N	29.45 E
Kroonstad	104	27.46 S	27.12 E
Kroppefjäll ∧[2]	28	58.40 N	12.13 E
Krosno	36	49.42 N	21.46 E
Krotoszyn	36	51.42 N	17.26 E
Krugersdorp	104	26.05 S	27.35 E
Krung Thep (Bangkok)	82	13.45 N	100.31 E
Kruševac	54	43.35 N	21.20 E
Krymskij Poluostrov ≻[1]	62	45.00 N	34.00 E
Krynica	36	49.25 N	20.56 E
Krzna ≃	36	52.08 N	23.31 E
Ksar el Boukhari	50	35.51 N	2.52 E
Ksar-el-Kebir	100	35.01 N	5.54 W
Ksar Hellal	46	35.39 N	10.54 E
Ksour Essaf	46	35.25 N	11.00 E
Kuala Lumpur	82	3.10 N	101.42 E
Kuala Terengganu	82	5.20 N	103.08 E
Kuantan	82	3.48 N	103.20 E
Kuban' ≃	62	45.20 N	37.30 E
Kuching	82	1.33 N	110.20 E
Kudymkar	26	59.01 N	54.37 E
Kufstein	36	47.35 N	12.10 E
Kujawy ◆[1]	36	52.45 N	18.30 E
Kujbyšev	26	53.12 N	50.09 E
Kujbyševskoje Vodochranilišče ⊜[1]	62	53.40 N	49.00 E
Kujū-san ∧	80	33.05 N	131.15 E
Kula, Jugo.	54	45.36 N	19.32 E
Kula, Tür.	54	38.32 N	28.40 E
Kula Kangri ∧	84	28.03 N	90.27 E
Kulmbach	36	50.06 N	11.27 E
Kulundinskaja Step' ⊻	62	53.00 N	79.00 E
Kuma ≃	62	44.56 N	47.00 E
Kumamoto	80	32.48 N	130.43 E
Kumanovo	54	42.08 N	21.43 E
Kumasi	100	6.41 N	1.35 W
Kumla	28	59.08 N	15.08 E
Kummerower See ⊜	36	53.49 N	12.52 E
Kumo	100	10.03 N	11.13 E
Kumukahi, Cape ≻	162b	19.31 N	154.49 W
Kungwe Mount ∧	104	6.07 S	29.48 E
Kunhegyes	36	47.22 N	20.38 E
Kunlunshanmai ⩕	80	36.30 N	88.00 E
Kunming	80	25.05 N	102.40 E
Kunsan	80	35.58 N	126.41 E
Kuopio	28	62.54 N	27.41 E
Kupang	82	10.10 S	123.35 E
Kurashiki	80	34.35 N	133.46 E
Kure	80	34.14 N	132.34 E
Kurgan	62	55.26 N	65.18 E
Kuril'skije Ostrova (Kuril Islands) II	64	46.10 N	152.00 E
Kursk	62	51.42 N	36.12 E
Kurume	80	33.19 N	130.31 E
Kuşadası Körfezi C	54	37.50 N	27.08 E
Kusawa Lake ⊜	160	60.20 N	136.15 W
Kuş Gölü ⊜	54	40.10 N	27.57 E
Kushiro	80	42.58 N	144.23 E
Kuskokwim ≃	162a	60.17 N	162.27 W
Kustanaj	62	53.10 N	63.35 E
Kūstī	102	13.10 N	32.40 E
Kut, Ko I	82	11.40 N	102.35 E
Kütahya	20	39.25 N	29.59 E
Kutaisi	62	42.15 N	42.40 E
Kutch, Gulf of C	84	22.36 N	69.30 E
Kutina	46	45.29 N	16.46 E
Kutná Hora	36	49.57 N	15.16 E
Kutno	36	52.15 N	19.23 E
Kutztown	166	40.31 N	75.47 W
Kuusankoski	28	60.54 N	26.38 E
Kuwait □[1]	84	29.30 N	47.45 E
Kuybyshev → Kujbyšev	26	53.12 N	50.09 E
Kuzneck	26	53.07 N	46.36 E
Kuzneckij Alatau ⩕	62	54.45 N	88.00 E
Kvænangen C[2]	26	70.05 N	21.13 E
Kvarner C	46	44.45 N	14.15 E
Kwando (Cuando) ≃	104	18.27 S	23.32 E
Kwangju	80	35.09 N	126.54 E
Kwango (Cuango) ≃	104	3.14 S	17.23 E
Kwenge ≃	104	4.50 S	18.42 E
Kwidzyn	36	53.45 N	18.56 E
Kwilu (Cuilo) ≃	104	3.22 S	17.22 E
Kwisa ≃	36	51.35 N	15.25 E
Kymijoki ≃	28	60.30 N	26.52 E
Kyoga, Lake ⊜	104	1.30 N	33.00 E
Kyŏngju	80	35.51 N	129.14 E
Kyōto	80	35.00 N	135.45 E
Kyūshū I	80	33.00 N	131.00 E
Kyzylkum ◆[2]	62	42.00 N	64.00 E
Kzyl-Orda	62	44.48 N	65.28 E
L			
La Alcarria ◆[1]	50	40.30 N	2.45 W
La Barge	180	42.16 N	110.12 W
La Baule	42	47.17 N	2.24 W
Labé	100	11.19 N	12.17 W
Labe (Elbe) ≃	36	53.50 N	9.00 E
Laberge, Lake ⊜	160	61.11 N	135.12 W
Laborec ≃	36	48.31 N	21.54 E
Labrador ◆[1]	160	54.00 N	62.00 W
Labrador Sea ⊤[2]	160	57.00 N	53.00 W
Labuan, Pulau I	82	5.21 N	115.13 E
Labuk ≃	82	5.54 N	117.30 E
Lacanau, Étang de C	42	44.58 N	1.07 E
La Carolina	50	38.15 N	3.37 W
Laccadive Islands II	84	10.00 N	73.00 E
La Ceiba	130	15.47 N	86.50 W
Lacey	180	47.07 N	122.49 W
Lac-giao	82	12.40 N	108.03 E
La Chaux-de-Fonds	42	47.06 N	6.50 E
La Chorrera	130	8.53 N	79.47 W
L'achovskije Ostrova II	64	73.30 N	141.00 E
La Ciotat	42	43.10 N	5.36 E
Lackawanna	166	42.49 N	78.50 W
Lacombe	174	30.19 N	89.58 W
Laconia	166	43.31 N	71.29 W
La Coruña	50	43.22 N	8.23 W
La Crescent	168	43.50 N	91.19 W
La Crosse, Wis., U.S.	168	43.49 N	91.15 W
Ladākh ◆[1]	84	34.45 N	76.30 E
La Dorada	144	5.27 N	74.40 W
Ladožskoje Ozero (Lake Ladoga) ⊜	62	61.00 N	31.30 E
Ladson	172	32.59 N	80.09 W
Ladue ≃	162a	63.09 N	140.25 W
Ladysmith, S. Afr.	104	28.34 S	29.45 E
Ladysmith, Wis., U.S.	168	45.28 N	91.12 W
Lae	116a	6.45 S	147.00 E
La Encantada, Cerro de ∧	130	31.00 N	115.24 W
Læsø I	28	57.16 N	11.01 E
Lafayette, Ala., U.S.	174	32.54 N	85.24 W
Lafayette, Calif., U.S.	184	37.54 N	122.07 W
Lafayette, Colo., U.S.	178	40.00 N	105.05 W
Lafayette, Ga., U.S.	172	34.42 N	85.17 W
Lafayette, Ind., U.S.	174	40.25 N	86.53 W
Lafayette, La., U.S.	174	30.14 N	92.01 W
Lafayette, Tenn., U.S.	174	36.32 N	86.01 W
Lafayette Southwest	174	30.11 N	92.03 W
Lafia	100	8.30 N	8.30 E
La Flèche	42	47.42 N	0.05 W
Lafnitz ≃	36	46.57 N	16.16 E
La Follette	172	36.23 N	84.07 W
La Galite I	100	37.32 N	8.56 E
Lagan ≃	28	56.33 N	12.56 E
Lågen ≃	28	61.08 N	10.25 E
Laghouat	100	33.50 N	2.59 E
Lagny	42	49.37 N	2.55 E
Lagos	100	6.27 N	3.24 E
La Goulette	46	36.49 N	10.18 E
La Grand'Combe	42	44.13 N	4.02 E
La Grande	180	45.20 N	118.05 W
La Grande ≃	160	53.50 N	79.00 W
La Grange, Ga., U.S.	172	33.02 N	85.02 W
Lagrange, Ind., U.S.	174	41.39 N	85.25 W
La Grange, Ky., U.S.	174	38.24 N	85.23 W
La Grange, N.C., U.S.	172	35.19 N	77.47 W
La Gran Sabana ⊻	144	5.30 N	61.30 W
La Guaira	144	10.36 N	66.56 W
Laguna Beach	184	33.33 N	117.51 W
La Habana (Havana)	130	23.08 N	82.22 W
Lahaina	162b	20.52 N	156.41 W
La Harpe	174	37.55 N	95.18 W
Lahore	84	31.35 N	74.18 E
Lahr	36	48.20 N	7.52 E
Lahti	28	60.58 N	25.40 E
Lainioälven ≃	26	67.22 N	23.39 E
Laizhouwan C	80	37.36 N	119.30 E
La Jara ◆[1]	50	39.42 N	4.54 W
Lajosmizse	36	47.02 N	19.34 E
La Junta	162	37.59 N	103.33 W
Lake Arthur	174	30.05 N	92.41 W
Lake Carmel	166	41.27 N	73.40 W
Lake Charles	174	30.13 N	93.12 W
Lake City, Fla., U.S.	172	30.12 N	82.38 W
Lake City, Minn., U.S.	168	44.27 N	92.16 W
Lake City, S.C., U.S.	172	33.52 N	79.45 W
Lake Crystal	168	44.06 N	94.13 W
Lake Forest, Fla., U.S.	172	30.24 N	81.41 W
Lake Forest, Ill., U.S.	168	42.15 N	87.50 W
Lake Geneva	168	42.36 N	88.26 W
Lake Havasu City	178	34.27 N	114.22 W
Lake Jackson	174	29.02 N	95.27 W
Lakeland, Fla., U.S.	172	28.03 N	81.57 W
Lakeland, Ga., U.S.	172	31.02 N	83.04 W
Lake Mills, Iowa, U.S.	168	43.25 N	93.32 W
Lake Mills, Wis., U.S.	168	43.05 N	88.55 W
Lake Oswego	180	45.26 N	122.39 W
Lake Park	172	26.49 N	80.04 W
Lake Providence	174	32.48 N	91.11 W
Lake Stevens	180	48.01 N	122.04 W
Lakeview, Ga., U.S.	172	34.59 N	85.16 W
Lakeview, Mich., U.S.	168	42.18 N	85.12 W
Lake View, N.Y., U.S.	166	42.43 N	78.56 W
Lake Village	174	33.20 N	91.17 W
Lakeville	168	44.39 N	93.14 W
Lake Wales	172	27.54 N	81.35 W
Lakewood, Colo., U.S.	178	39.44 N	105.06 W
Lakewood, N.J., U.S.	166	40.06 N	74.13 W
Lakewood, N.Y., U.S.	166	42.06 N	79.20 W
Lakewood, Ohio, U.S.	166	41.29 N	81.48 W
Lakewood Center	180	47.10 N	122.31 W
Lake Worth	172	26.37 N	80.03 W
Laksefjorden C[2]	26	70.58 N	27.00 E
La Libertad	130	16.47 N	90.07 W
La Línea	50	36.10 N	5.19 W
Lalla Khedidja, Tamgout de ∧	50	36.27 N	4.15 E
La Maddalena	46	41.13 N	9.24 E
La Mancha ◆[1]	50	39.05 N	3.00 W
La Manche (English Channel) ⋓	32	50.20 N	1.00 W
Lamap	112	16.26 S	167.43 E
Lamar, Colo., U.S.	162	38.05 N	102.37 W
Lamar, Mo., U.S.	174	37.29 N	94.17 W
La Marque	174	29.22 N	94.58 W
Lambaréné	104	0.42 S	10.13 E
Lambasa	111	16.26 S	179.24 E
Lambay Island I	32	53.29 N	6.01 W
Lambert Glacier ⊠	191	71.00 S	70.00 E
Lambertville	166	40.22 N	74.57 W
Lamenu	112	16.34 S	168.11 E
La Mesa, Calif., U.S.	184	32.46 N	117.01 W
La Mesa, N. Mex., U.S.	178	32.07 N	106.42 W
Lamesa, Tex., U.S.	162	32.44 N	101.57 W
Lamía	54	38.54 N	22.26 E
Lamoni	168	40.37 N	93.56 W
Lamont	184	35.15 N	118.55 W
Lampang	82	18.18 N	99.31 E
Lampedusa, Isola di I	46	35.31 N	12.35 E
Lampertheim	36	49.35 N	8.28 E
Lanai I	162b	20.50 N	156.55 W
Lanai City	162b	20.50 N	156.55 W
Lancashire □[6]	32	53.45 N	2.40 W
Lancaster, Eng., U.K.	32	54.03 N	2.48 W
Lancaster, Calif., U.S.	184	34.42 N	118.08 W
Lancaster, Ky., U.S.	172	37.37 N	84.35 W
Lancaster, N.H., U.S.	166	44.29 N	71.34 W
Lancaster, N.Y., U.S.	166	42.54 N	78.40 W
Lancaster, Ohio, U.S.	166	39.43 N	82.36 W
Lancaster, Pa., U.S.	166	40.02 N	76.19 W
Lancaster, S.C., U.S.	172	34.43 N	80.46 W

Name	Page	Lat	Long
Lancaster, Wis., U.S.	168	42.51 N	90.43 W
Lancaster Sound ധ	160	74.13 N	84.00 W
Lanciano	46	42.14 N	14.23 E
Lańcut	36	50.05 N	22.13 E
Landau	36	49.12 N	8.07 E
Lander	180	42.50 N	108.44 W
Landerneau	42	48.27 N	4.15 W
Landis	172	35.33 N	80.37 W
Landösjön	28	63.35 N	14.04 E
Land's End ⟩	32	50.03 N	5.44 W
Landshut	36	48.33 N	12.09 E
Landskrona	28	55.52 N	12.50 E
Lanesboro	168	43.43 N	91.59 W
Lanett	174	32.57 N	85.12 W
Langano, Lake ⬭	102	7.35 N	38.48 E
Langdon	162	48.46 N	98.22 W
Langeberg 𐤀	104	34.00 S	20.40 E
Langeland ⎮	28	55.00 N	10.50 E
Langenfeld	36	51.07 N	6.56 E
Langenhagen	36	52.27 N	9.44 E
Langenthal	42	47.13 N	7.47 E
Langeoog ⎮	36	53.46 N	7.32 E
Langjökull 🞋	26a	64.42 N	20.12 W
Langkawi, Pulau ⎮	82	6.22 N	99.50 E
Langnau	42	46.57 N	7.47 E
Langøya ⎮	26	68.44 N	14.50 E
Langres	42	47.52 N	5.20 W
Lang-son	82	21.50 N	106.44 E
Lannion	42	48.44 N	3.28 W
L'Anse	168	46.45 N	88.27 W
Lansing	168	42.43 N	84.34 W
Lantana	172	26.35 N	80.03 W
Lanzhou	80	36.03 N	103.41 E
Laoag	82	18.12 N	120.36 E
Laon	42	49.34 N	3.40 E
La Oroya	144	11.32 S	75.54 W
Laos ◻¹	82	18.00 N	105.00 E
Laou, Oued ≃	50	35.29 N	5.04 W
La Palma	130	8.25 N	78.09 W
La Paz, Bol.	144	16.30 S	68.09 W
La Paz, Méx.	130	24.10 N	110.18 W
Lapeer	168	43.03 N	83.19 W
Lapland ♦¹	26	68.00 N	25.00 E
La Plata	146	34.55 S	57.57 W
La Plata Peak 𐤀	178	39.02 N	106.28 W
La Porte	174	41.36 N	86.43 W
La Porte City	168	42.19 N	92.12 W
Lappeenranta	28	61.04 N	28.11 E
Laptev Sea → Laptevych,more ▽²	64	76.00 N	126.00 E
Laptevych, More (Laptev Sea) ▽²	64	76.00 N	126.00 E
L'Aquila	46	42.22 N	13.22 E
Larache	100	35.12 N	6.10 W
Laramie	178	41.19 N	105.35 W
Laramie Mountains 𐤀	178	42.00 N	105.40 W
Larche, Col de ⟩(	42	44.25 N	6.53 E
Laredo	162	27.31 N	99.30 W
Largo	172	27.55 N	82.47 W
La Rioja	146	29.26 S	66.51 W
La Rioja ♦¹	50	42.20 N	0.22 W
Lárisa	54	39.38 N	22.25 E
Lārkāna	84	27.33 N	68.13 E
Larne	32	54.51 N	5.49 W
La Rochelle	42	46.10 N	1.10 W
La Roche-sur-Yon	42	46.40 N	1.26 W
La Roda	50	39.13 N	2.09 W
Larose	174	29.35 N	90.23 W
Larvik	28	59.04 N	10.00 E
Larzac, Causse du ♦¹	42	44.00 N	3.15 E
Lasa (Lhasa)	80	29.40 N	91.09 E
La Sagra 𐤀	50	37.57 N	2.34 W
La Salle	168	41.20 N	89.06 W
Las Casitas, Cerro 𐤀	130	23.32 N	109.59 W
Lascaux, Grotte de •⁵	42	45.01 N	1.08 E
Las Cruces	178	32.18 N	106.29 W
La Serena	146	29.54 S	71.16 W
La Serena ♦¹	50	38.45 N	5.30 W
La Seyne	42	43.06 N	5.53 E
La Sila 𐤀	46	39.15 N	16.30 E
Las Marismas ⬳	50	37.00 N	6.15 W
Las Minas, Cerro 𐤀	130	14.33 N	88.39 W
La Solana	50	38.56 N	3.14 W
Las Palmas de Gran Canaria	100	28.06 N	15.24 W
La Spezia	46	44.07 N	9.50 E
Las Piedras	146	34.44 S	56.13 W
Lassen Peak 𐤀¹	184	40.29 N	121.31 W
Las Tablas	130	7.46 N	80.17 W
Lastovski Kanal ധ	46	42.50 N	16.59 E
Las Vegas, Nev., U.S.	184	36.11 N	115.08 W
Las Vegas, N. Mex., U.S.	178	35.36 N	105.13 W
Lata 𐤀	113	14.14 S	169.29 W
La Teste-de-Buch	42	44.38 N	1.09 W
Latina	46	41.28 N	12.52 E
Latorica ≃	36	48.28 N	21.50 E
La Tortuga, Isla ⎮	144	10.56 N	65.20 W
Latrobe	166	40.19 N	79.23 W
Lauchhammer	36	51.30 N	13.47 E
Lauf an der Pegnitz	36	49.30 N	11.17 E
Lau Group ⎮⎮	112	18.20 S	178.30 W
Launceston	116	41.26 S	147.08 E
La Unión, El Sal.	130	13.20 N	87.51 W
La Unión, Esp.	50	37.37 N	0.52 W
Laurel, Del., U.S.	166	38.33 N	75.34 W
Laurel, Md., U.S.	166	39.06 N	76.51 W
Laurel, Miss., U.S.	174	31.42 N	89.08 W
Laurel, Mont., U.S.	180	45.40 N	108.46 W
Laurel Bay	172	32.27 N	80.48 W
Laureldale	166	40.23 N	75.55 W
Laurens	172	34.30 N	82.01 W
Laurie Island ⎮	191	60.45 S	44.35 W
Laurinburg	172	34.47 N	79.27 W
Lauritsala	28	61.04 N	28.16 E
Laurium	168	47.14 N	88.26 W
Lausanne	42	46.31 N	6.38 E
Laut, Pulau ⎮	82	4.43 N	107.59 E
Lautoka	111	17.37 S	177.27 E
Lava, Nosy ⎮	104	14.33 S	47.36 E
Laval, Qué., Can.	160	45.33 N	73.44 W
Laval, Fr.	42	48.04 N	0.46 W
Lavant ≃	36	46.36 N	14.57 E
Lavapié, Punta ⟩	146	37.09 S	73.35 W
La Vega	130	19.13 N	70.31 W
Lavello	46	41.03 N	15.48 E
La Vergne ♦¹	50	45.00 N	5.30 W
La Vera ♦¹	50	40.07 N	5.30 W
Lavonia	172	34.26 N	83.06 W
Lawers, Ben 𐤀	32	56.33 N	4.15 W
Lawrence, Ind., U.S.	174	39.50 N	86.02 W
Lawrence, Kans., U.S.	162	38.57 N	95.14 W
Lawrence, Mass., U.S.	166	42.42 N	71.09 W
Lawrenceburg, Ind., U.S.	174	39.06 N	84.51 W
Lawrenceburg, Ky., U.S.	174	38.02 N	84.54 W
Lawrenceburg, Tenn., U.S.	174	35.15 N	87.20 W
Lawrenceville	172	33.57 N	83.59 W
Lawton	162	34.37 N	98.25 W
Lawz, Jabal al- 𐤀	84	28.40 N	35.18 E
Layton	178	41.04 N	111.58 W
Lead	162	44.21 N	103.46 W
Leadville	178	39.15 N	106.20 W
League City	174	29.31 N	95.05 W
Lealman	172	27.50 N	82.41 W
Leatherman Peak 𐤀	180	44.05 N	113.44 W
Leavenworth, Kans., U.S.	174	39.19 N	94.55 W

Name	Page	Lat	Long
Leavenworth, Wash., U.S.	180	47.36 N	120.40 W
Łeba ≃	36	54.47 N	17.33 E
Lebanon, Ind., U.S.	174	40.03 N	86.28 W
Lebanon, Ky., U.S.	174	37.34 N	85.15 W
Lebanon, Mo., U.S.	174	37.41 N	92.40 W
Lebanon, N.H., U.S.	166	43.38 N	72.15 W
Lebanon, Ohio, U.S.	166	39.26 N	84.13 W
Lebanon, Oreg., U.S.	180	44.32 N	122.54 W
Lebanon, Pa., U.S.	166	40.20 N	76.25 W
Lebanon, Tenn., U.S.	174	36.12 N	86.18 W
Lebanon ◻¹	84	33.50 N	35.50 E
Lebork	36	54.33 N	17.44 E
Lebrija	50	36.55 N	6.04 W
Łebsko, Jezioro ⊂	36	54.44 N	17.24 E
Le Cateau	42	50.06 N	3.33 E
Lecce	46	40.23 N	18.11 E
Lecco	46	45.51 N	9.23 E
Lech ≃	36	48.44 N	10.56 E
Lechtaler Alpen 𐤀	36	47.15 N	10.30 E
Le Claire	168	41.36 N	90.21 W
Le Creusot	42	46.48 N	4.26 E
Łęczyca	36	52.04 N	19.13 E
Led'anaja, Gora 𐤀	64	61.53 N	171.09 W
Leech Lake ⬭	168	47.09 N	94.23 W
Leeds, Eng., U.K.	32	53.50 N	1.35 W
Leeds, Ala., U.S.	174	33.33 N	86.33 W
Leer	36	53.14 N	7.26 E
Leesburg, Fla., U.S.	172	28.49 N	81.53 W
Leesburg, Va., U.S.	166	39.07 N	77.34 W
Lees Summit	174	38.55 N	94.23 W
Leesville	174	31.08 N	93.16 W
Leeuwarden	36	53.12 N	5.46 E
Leeward Islands ⎮⎮	130	17.00 N	63.00 W
Legazpi	82	13.08 N	123.44 E
Leghorn → Livorno	46	43.33 N	10.19 E
Legionowo	36	52.25 N	20.56 E
Legnago	46	45.11 N	11.18 E
Legnano	46	45.36 N	8.54 E
Legnica (Liegnitz)	36	51.13 N	16.09 E
Le Havre	42	49.30 N	0.08 E
Lehi	178	40.24 N	111.51 W
Lehigh Acres	172	26.36 N	81.39 W
Lehighton	166	40.49 N	75.45 W
Lehrte	36	52.22 N	9.59 E
Leicester	32	52.38 N	1.05 W
Leicestershire ◻⁶	32	52.40 N	1.10 W
Leiden	36	52.09 N	4.30 E
Leighton Buzzard	32	51.55 N	0.40 W
Leinster ◻⁹	32	53.05 N	7.00 W
Leipzig	36	51.19 N	12.20 E
Leitchfield	174	37.29 N	86.18 W
Leitha (Lajta) ≃	36	47.54 N	17.17 E
Leizhoubandao ⟩¹	80	21.15 N	110.09 E
Lekkous, Oued ≃	50	34.58 N	5.52 W
Leland	174	33.24 N	90.54 W
Lelishan 𐤀	80	33.26 N	81.42 E
Le Locle	42	47.03 N	6.45 E
Le Madonie 𐤀	46	37.55 N	14.00 E
Le Maire, Estrecho de ധ	146	54.50 S	65.00 W
Le Mans	42	48.00 N	0.12 E
Lemay	174	38.32 N	90.17 W
Lemberg 𐤀	36	48.09 N	8.45 E
Lemesós	84	34.40 N	33.02 E
Lemgo	36	52.02 N	8.54 E
Lemhi Range 𐤀	180	44.30 N	113.25 W
Lemitar	178	34.09 N	106.55 W
Lemmon	162	45.56 N	102.10 W
Lemon Grove	184	32.44 N	117.02 W
Le Murge 𐤀¹	46	40.52 N	16.42 E
Lena ≃	64	72.25 N	126.40 E
Lenakel	112	19.32 S	169.16 E
Lenina, Pik 𐤀	62	39.20 N	72.55 E
Leninabad	62	40.17 N	69.37 E
Leninakan	62	40.48 N	43.50 E
Leningrad	26	59.55 N	30.15 E
Leninogorsk	26	54.36 N	52.30 E
Leninsk-Kuzneckij	64	54.38 N	86.10 E
Lenoir	172	35.55 N	81.32 W
Lenoir City	172	35.48 N	84.16 W
Lens	42	50.26 N	2.50 E
Lentini	46	37.17 N	15.00 E
Leoben	36	47.23 N	15.06 E
Leominster	166	42.31 N	71.45 W
León, Esp.	50	42.36 N	5.34 W
León, Méx.	130	21.07 N	101.40 W
León, Nic.	130	12.26 N	86.53 W
León, Iowa, U.S.	168	40.44 N	93.45 W
León ◻⁹	50	42.00 N	6.00 W
León, Montes de 𐤀	50	42.30 N	6.18 W
Leonberg	36	48.48 N	9.01 E
Leonforte	46	37.39 N	14.24 E
Léopoldville → Kinshasa	104	4.18 S	15.18 E
Lepe	50	37.15 N	7.12 W
Lepontine, Alpi 𐤀	42	46.25 N	8.40 E
Le Port	104	20.55 S	55.18 E
Le Puy	42	45.02 N	3.53 E
Lerici	46	44.04 N	9.55 E
Lérida	50	41.37 N	0.37 E
Le Roy, Kans., U.S.	174	38.05 N	95.38 W
Le Roy, N.Y., U.S.	166	42.59 N	77.59 W
Lerwick	32	60.09 N	1.09 W
Les Cayes	130	18.12 N	73.45 W
Leskovac	54	42.59 N	21.57 E
Lesotho ◻¹	104	29.30 S	28.30 E
Les Sables-d'Olonne	42	46.30 N	1.47 W
Lesser Antilles ⎮⎮	130	15.00 N	61.00 W
Lesser Slave Lake ⬭	160	55.25 N	115.30 W
Le Sueur	168	44.27 N	93.54 W
Lésvos ⎮	54	39.10 N	26.20 E
Leszno	36	51.51 N	16.35 E
Letea, Ostrovul ⎮	54	45.19 N	29.20 E
Letsôk-aw Kyun ⎮	82	11.37 N	98.15 E
Leucadia	184	33.04 N	117.18 W
Leucate, Étang de ⊂	42	42.51 N	3.00 E
Leuna	36	51.19 N	12.01 E
Leuven	36	50.53 N	4.42 E
Levádhia	54	38.26 N	22.54 E
Levante, Riviera di ≃²	46	45.15 N	9.30 E
Leverkusen	36	51.03 N	6.59 E
Levice	36	48.13 N	18.37 E
Levitha ⎮	54	37.00 N	26.28 E
Levittown, N.Y., U.S.	166	40.41 N	73.31 W
Levittown, Pa., U.S.	166	40.09 N	74.50 W
Lévka Óri 𐤀	54	35.18 N	24.01 E
Levkás	54	38.50 N	20.41 E
Levkósia	54	38.39 N	20.27 E
Levuka	111	17.41 S	178.50 E
Lewes, Eng., U.K.	32	50.52 N	0.01 E
Lewes, Del., U.S.	166	38.47 N	75.08 W
Lewis, Isle of ⎮	32	58.10 N	6.40 W
Lewisburg, Pa., U.S.	166	40.58 N	76.53 W
Lewisburg, W. Va., U.S.	174	35.27 N	86.48 W
Lewis Smith Lake ⬭¹	174	34.05 N	87.07 W
Lewiston, Idaho, U.S.	180	46.25 N	117.01 W
Lewiston, Maine, U.S.	166	44.06 N	70.13 W
Lewistown, Ill., U.S.	168	40.23 N	90.09 W
Lewistown, Mont., U.S.	180	47.04 N	109.26 W
Lewistown, Pa., U.S.	166	40.36 N	77.31 W
Lexington, Ky., U.S.	174	38.03 N	84.30 W
Lexington, Mass., U.S.	166	42.27 N	71.14 W
Lexington, Miss., U.S.	174	33.07 N	90.03 W
Lexington, N.C., U.S.	172	35.49 N	80.15 W
Lexington, Tenn., U.S.	174	35.39 N	88.24 W
Lexington, Va., U.S.	172	37.47 N	79.27 W
Lexington Park	166	38.16 N	76.27 W

Name	Page	Lat	Long
Leyre ≃	42	44.39 N	1.01 W
Lhasa → Lasa	80	29.40 N	91.09 E
Lhut ≃	102	10.25 N	51.05 E
Liaodongbandao ⟩¹	80	40.00 N	122.20 E
Liaodongwan ⊂	80	40.30 N	121.30 E
Liaoyang	80	41.17 N	123.11 E
Liaoyuan	80	42.54 N	125.07 E
Liard ≃	160	61.52 N	121.18 W
Libby	180	48.23 N	115.33 W
Liberal	162	37.02 N	100.55 W
Liberec	36	50.46 N	15.03 E
Liberia	130	10.38 N	85.27 W
Liberia ◻¹	100	6.00 N	10.00 W
Liberty, Ky., U.S.	174	37.19 N	84.56 W
Liberty, Mo., U.S.	174	39.15 N	94.25 W
Liberty, N.C., U.S.	172	35.51 N	79.34 W
Liberty, N.Y., U.S.	166	41.48 N	74.45 W
Liberty, S.C., U.S.	172	34.48 N	82.42 W
Liberty, Tex., U.S.	174	30.03 N	94.47 W
Libertyville	168	42.17 N	87.57 W
Libourne	42	44.55 N	0.14 W
Libreville	104	0.23 N	9.27 E
Libya ◻¹	102	27.00 N	17.00 E
Libyan Desert → Aṣ-Ṣaḥrā' al-Lībīyah ♦²	102	24.00 N	25.00 E
Licata	46	37.05 N	13.56 E
Lichfield	32	52.42 N	1.48 W
Lichtenfels	36	50.09 N	11.04 E
Licking ≃	166	39.06 N	84.30 W
Lidingö	28	59.22 N	18.08 E
Lidköping	28	58.30 N	13.10 E
Lidzbark	36	53.16 N	19.49 E
Lidzbark Warmiński	36	54.09 N	20.35 E
Liechtenstein ◻¹	20	47.09 N	9.35 E
Liège	36	50.38 N	5.34 E
Liegnitz → Legnica	36	51.13 N	16.09 E
Lienz	46	46.50 N	12.47 E
Liepāja	26	56.31 N	21.01 E
Lier	36	51.08 N	4.34 E
Liestal	42	47.29 N	7.44 E
Liévin	42	50.25 N	2.46 E
Lifou, Île ⎮	112	20.53 S	167.13 E
Lighthouse Point	172	26.17 N	80.07 W
Lighthouse Point ⟩	168	45.13 N	85.32 W
Ligonier	174	41.28 N	85.35 W
Ligurian Sea ▽²	46	43.30 N	9.00 E
Lihue	162b	21.59 N	159.22 W
Likasi (Jadotville)	104	10.59 S	26.44 E
Likoma Island ⎮	104	12.05 S	34.45 E
Likouala	104	0.50 S	17.11 E
Lille	42	50.38 N	3.04 E
Lillestrøm	28	59.57 N	11.05 E
Lilongwe	104	13.59 S	33.44 E
Lim ≃	54	43.45 N	19.13 E
Lima, Perú	144	12.03 S	77.03 W
Lima, Ohio, U.S.	166	40.44 N	84.06 W
Lima (Limia) ≃	50	41.41 N	8.50 W
Limburg an der Lahn	36	50.23 N	8.04 E
Limeira	144	22.34 S	47.24 W
Limerick	32	52.40 N	8.38 W
Limfjorden ധ	28	56.55 N	9.10 E
Limia (Lima) ≃	50	41.41 N	8.50 W
Límnos ⎮	54	39.54 N	25.21 E
Limoges	42	45.50 N	1.16 E
Limón	130	10.00 N	83.02 W
Limousins, Plateau du 𐤀¹	42	45.30 N	1.15 E
Limoux	42	43.04 N	2.14 E
Limpopo ≃	104	25.15 S	33.30 E
Linares, Chile	146	35.51 S	71.36 W
Linares, Esp.	50	38.05 N	3.38 W
Linch	180	43.37 N	106.12 W
Lincoln, Eng., U.K.	32	53.14 N	0.33 W
Lincoln, Ill., U.S.	174	40.09 N	89.22 W
Lincoln, Maine, U.S.	166	45.22 N	68.30 W
Lincoln, Nebr., U.S.	162	40.48 N	96.42 W
Lincoln, Mount 𐤀	178	39.21 N	106.07 W
Lincoln City	180	44.59 N	123.59 W
Lincoln Park, Colo., U.S.	178	37.35 N	104.12 W
Lincoln Park, Mich., U.S.	168	42.14 N	83.09 W
Lincolnshire ◻⁶	32	52.55 N	0.22 W
Lincolnton	172	35.29 N	81.14 W
Lincoln Village	184	38.01 N	121.19 W
Linda	184	39.08 N	121.34 W
Lindale, Ala., U.S.	172	34.11 N	85.11 W
Lindau	36	47.33 N	9.41 E
Linden, Ala., U.S.	174	32.18 N	87.47 W
Linden, Tex., U.S.	184	33.01 N	94.22 W
Lindenows Fjord ⊂²	160	60.45 N	43.30 W
Linderödsåsen 𐤀²	28	55.53 N	13.56 E
Lindesnes ⟩	28	58.00 N	7.02 E
Lindi	104	10.00 S	39.43 E
Lindi ≃	104	0.33 N	25.05 E
Lingayen Gulf ⊂	82	16.15 N	120.14 E
Lingen	36	52.31 N	7.19 E
Lingga, Kepulauan ⎮⎮	82	0.05 S	104.35 E
Linh, Ngoc 𐤀	82	15.04 N	107.59 E
Linköping	28	58.25 N	15.37 E
Linlithgow	32	55.59 N	3.37 W
Linnhe, Loch ⊂	32	56.37 N	5.25 W
Linosa, Isola di ⎮	46	35.52 N	12.52 E
Lins	144	21.40 S	49.45 W
Linton, Ind., U.S.	174	39.02 N	87.10 W
Linton, N. Dak., U.S.	162	46.16 N	100.14 W
Linz	36	48.18 N	14.18 E
Lion, Golfe du ⊂	42	43.00 N	4.00 E
Lipa	82	13.57 N	121.10 E
Lipari, Isola ⎮	46	38.30 N	14.57 E
Lipeck	26	52.37 N	39.35 E
Lipenská přehrada ⬭¹	36	48.43 N	14.04 E
Lipez, Cerro 𐤀	144	21.53 S	66.52 W
Lipno	36	52.51 N	19.10 E
Lipova	54	46.05 N	21.40 E
Lippe ≃	36	51.39 N	6.38 E
Lippstadt	36	51.40 N	8.19 E
Liptovský Mikuláš	36	49.06 N	19.37 E
Lisboa (Lisbon)	50	38.43 N	9.08 W
Lisbon → Lisboa, Port.	50	38.43 N	9.08 W
Lisbon, Ohio, U.S.	166	40.47 N	80.46 W
Lisbon Falls	166	44.00 N	70.03 W
Lisburn	32	54.31 N	6.03 W
Lisburne, Cape ⟩	112	15.40 S	166.43 E
Liscia ≃	46	41.11 N	9.19 E
Lisičansk	26	48.55 N	38.26 E
Lisieux	42	49.09 N	0.14 E
Lismore	116	28.48 S	153.17 E
Lora del Rio	50	37.39 N	5.32 W
Lorain	166	41.28 N	82.10 W
Lorca	50	37.40 N	1.42 W
Lordsburg	178	32.21 N	108.43 W
Lorestān ♦⁸	84	33.30 N	48.30 E
Loreto	130	26.01 N	111.21 W
Lorica	144	9.14 N	75.49 W
Lorient	42	47.45 N	3.22 W
Lörrach	36	47.37 N	7.40 E
Los Alamos	178	35.53 N	106.19 W
Los Angeles, Chile	146	37.28 S	72.21 W
Los Angeles, Calif., U.S.	184	34.03 N	118.15 W
Los Angeles Aqueduct ⬳	184	35.22 N	118.05 W
Los Banos	184	37.03 N	120.51 W
Los Gatos	184	37.13 N	121.58 W
Los Mochis	130	25.45 N	108.57 W
Los Padillas	178	34.57 N	106.43 W
Los Palacios y Villafranca	50	37.10 N	5.56 W
Los Roques, Islas ⎮⎮	144	11.50 N	66.45 W
Lost Nation	174	41.58 N	90.49 W
Lost River Range 𐤀	180	44.10 N	113.30 W
Lost Trail Pass)(	180	45.41 N	113.57 W
Lot ≃	42	44.18 N	0.20 E

Name	Page	Lat	Long
Lota	146	37.05 S	73.10 W
Lotrului, Munţii 𐤀	54	45.30 N	23.52 E
Lotsane ≃	104	22.41 S	28.11 E
Lotta ≃	26	68.36 N	31.06 E
Louangphrabang	82	19.52 N	102.08 E
L'Ouarsenis, Massif de 𐤀	50	35.40 N	1.50 E
Loudon	172	35.44 N	84.20 W
Loudonville	166	40.38 N	82.14 W
Louga	100	15.37 N	16.13 W
Louge ≃	42	43.27 N	1.20 E
Loughborough	32	52.47 N	1.11 W
Louisa	172	38.07 N	82.36 W
Louisburg, Kans., U.S.	174	38.37 N	94.41 W
Louisburg, N.C., U.S.	172	36.06 N	78.18 W
Louisiana	174	39.27 N	91.03 W
Louisiana ◻³	162	31.15 N	92.15 W
Louis Trichardt	104	23.01 S	29.43 E
Louisville, Ga., U.S.	172	33.00 N	82.24 W
Louisville, Ky., U.S.	174	38.16 N	85.45 W
Louisville, Miss., U.S.	174	33.07 N	89.03 W
Louisville, Ohio, U.S.	166	40.50 N	81.16 W
Louny	36	50.19 N	13.46 E
Lourdes	42	43.06 N	0.03 W
Lourenço Marques → Maputo	104	25.58 S	32.35 E
Louth	32	53.22 N	0.01 W
Louviers	42	49.13 N	1.10 E
Lovat' ≃	62	58.14 N	31.28 E
Loveč	54	43.08 N	24.43 E
Loveland	178	40.24 N	105.05 W
Lovell	180	44.50 N	108.24 W
Lovelock	184	40.11 N	118.28 W
Loves Park	168	42.19 N	89.03 W
Lowell, Ind., U.S.	174	41.18 N	87.25 W
Lowell, Mass., U.S.	166	42.39 N	71.18 W
Lowell, Mich., U.S.	168	42.56 N	85.20 W
Lower Hutt	118	41.13 S	174.55 E
Lower Red Lake ⬭	168	48.00 N	94.50 W
Lowestoft	32	52.29 N	1.45 E
Manderson	180	44.16 N	107.58 W
Lowville	166	43.47 N	75.29 W
Loyality Islands → Loyauté, Îles ⎮⎮	112	21.00 S	167.00 E
Loyauté, Îles (Loyality Islands) ⎮⎮	112	21.00 S	167.00 E
Lozère, Mont 𐤀	42	44.25 N	3.45 E
Loznica	54	44.32 N	19.13 E
Lua ≃	102	2.46 N	18.26 E
Lualaba ≃	104	0.26 N	25.20 E
Luanda	104	8.48 S	13.14 E
Luando ≃	104	10.19 S	16.40 E
Luanginga ≃	104	4.17 S	20.02 E
Luangwa (Aruángua) ≃	104	15.11 S	22.56 E
Luanshya	104	13.08 S	28.24 E
Luapula ≃	104	9.26 S	28.33 E
Lubań	36	51.08 N	15.18 E
Lubango	104	14.55 S	13.30 E
Lübben	36	51.56 N	13.53 E
Lübbenau	36	51.52 N	13.57 E
Lubbock	162	33.35 N	101.51 W
Lübeck	36	53.52 N	10.40 E
Lübecker Bucht ⊂	36	54.00 N	10.55 E
Lubelska, Wyżyna 𐤀²	36	51.00 N	23.00 E
L'ubercy	26	55.41 N	37.53 E
Lubilash ≃	104	6.02 S	23.45 E
Lubin	36	51.24 N	16.13 E
Lublin	36	51.15 N	22.35 E
Lubliniec	36	50.40 N	18.41 E
Lubsko	36	51.46 N	14.59 E
Lubudi	104	6.51 S	21.18 E
Lubudi ≃	104	9.13 S	25.38 E
Lubumbashi (Élisabethville)	104	11.40 S	27.28 E
Lucania 𐤀	46	40.30 N	16.00 E
Lucania, Mount 𐤀	160	61.01 N	140.28 W
Lucca	46	43.50 N	10.29 E
Luce Bay ⊂	32	54.47 N	4.50 W
Lucedale	174	30.55 N	88.35 W
Lucena, Esp.	50	37.24 N	4.29 W
Lučenec	36	48.20 N	19.40 E
Lucena, Pil.	82	13.56 N	121.37 E
Lucera	46	41.30 N	15.20 E
Luck	62	50.44 N	25.20 E
Luckenwalde	36	52.05 N	13.10 E
Lucknow	84	26.50 N	80.55 E
Luçon	42	46.27 N	1.10 W
Lüda (Dairen)	80	38.53 N	121.35 E
Luda Kamčija ≃	54	43.03 N	27.29 E
Lüdenscheid	36	51.13 N	7.38 E
Lüderitz	104	26.38 S	15.10 E
Ludhiāna	84	30.55 N	75.51 E
Ludington	168	43.57 N	86.27 W
Ludlow, Mass., U.S.	166	42.10 N	72.29 W
Ludlow, Vt., U.S.	166	43.24 N	72.42 W
Ludvika	28	60.09 N	15.11 E
Ludwigsburg	36	48.53 N	9.11 E
Ludwigsfelde	36	52.17 N	13.16 E
Ludwigshafen	36	49.29 N	8.26 E
Ludwigslust	36	53.19 N	11.30 E
Luena	104	12.31 S	22.34 E
Lufkin	174	31.20 N	94.44 W
Lugano	42	46.01 N	8.58 E
Lugano, Lago di ⬭	42	46.00 N	9.00 E
Luganville	112	15.32 S	167.08 E
Lugenda ≃	104	11.25 S	38.33 E
Lugo, Esp.	50	43.00 N	7.34 W
Lugo, It.	46	44.25 N	11.54 E
Lugoj	54	45.41 N	21.54 E
Luino	42	46.00 N	8.44 E
Lukanga Swamp ⬳	104	14.25 S	27.45 E
Łuków	36	51.56 N	22.23 E
Lula ≃	102	1.27 N	20.00 E
Luleå	26	65.35 N	22.10 E
Luleälven ≃	26	65.35 N	22.03 E
Lüleburgaz	54	41.24 N	27.21 E
Luluabourg → Kananga	104	5.54 S	22.25 E
Luma	113	14.14 S	169.32 W
Lumberton, Miss., U.S.	174	31.00 N	89.27 W
Lumberton, N.C., U.S.	172	34.37 N	79.00 W
Lund	28	55.42 N	13.11 E
Lundi ≃	104	21.43 S	32.34 E
Lundy ⎮	32	51.10 N	4.40 W
Lune ≃	32	54.02 N	2.50 W
Lüneburg	36	53.15 N	10.23 E
Lüneburger Heide ♦¹	36	53.10 N	10.10 E
Lunéville	42	48.36 N	6.30 E
Lungué-Bungo ≃	104	14.19 S	23.14 E
Luning	184	38.30 N	118.11 W
Luoyang	80	34.41 N	112.28 E
Luray	166	38.40 N	78.28 W
Lúrio ≃	104	13.35 S	40.32 E
Lusaka	104	15.25 S	28.17 E
Lusambo	104	4.58 S	23.27 E
Lushnje	54	40.56 N	19.42 E
Lüshun (Port Arthur)	80	38.47 N	121.13 E
Lusk	162	42.45 N	104.27 W
Lüt, Dasht-e ♦²	84	33.00 N	57.00 E
Lutcher	174	30.02 N	90.42 W
Luton	32	51.53 N	0.25 W
Luverne	174	31.43 N	86.16 W
Luvua ≃	104	8.31 S	37.23 E
Luxembourg	42	49.36 N	6.09 E
Luxembourg ◻¹	20	49.45 N	6.05 E

Meze—Naum

Name	Page	Lat°	Long°
Mezen' ≃	62	66.11 N	43.59 E
Mezőberény	36	46.50 N	21.02 E
Mezőkövesd	36	47.50 N	20.34 E
Mezőtúr	36	47.00 N	20.38 E
M'goun, Irhil ▲	100	31.31 N	6.25 W
Miami, Ariz., U.S.	178	33.24 N	110.52 W
Miami, Fla., U.S.	172	25.46 N	80.12 W
Miami, Okla., U.S.	174	36.53 N	94.53 W
Miami Beach	172	25.47 N	80.08 W
Miami Canal ☰	172	25.47 N	80.15 W
Miamisburg	166	39.38 N	84.17 W
Miami Springs	172	25.49 N	80.17 W
Miass	62	54.59 N	60.06 E
Michalovce	36	48.45 N	21.55 E
Michigan □3	162	44.00 N	85.00 W
Michigan, Lake ⊜	168	44.00 N	87.00 W
Michigan Center	168	42.14 N	84.20 W
Michigan City	174	41.43 N	86.54 W
Michikamau Lake ⊜	160	54.00 N	64.00 W
Michipicoten Island I	160	47.45 N	85.45 W
Mičurinsk	62	52.54 N	40.30 E
Middelburg	36	51.30 N	3.37 E
Middle Andaman I	84	12.30 N	92.50 E
Middleboro	166	41.49 N	70.55 W
Middlebury	166	44.01 N	73.10 W
Middlesboro	172	36.36 N	83.43 W
Middlesbrough	32	54.35 N	1.14 W
Middleton	168	43.06 N	89.30 W
Middletown, Conn., U.S.	166	41.33 N	72.39 W
Middletown, Del., U.S.	166	39.25 N	75.47 W
Middletown, Ind., U.S.	174	40.03 N	85.32 W
Middletown, Ky., U.S.	174	38.15 N	85.32 W
Middletown, Md., U.S.	166	39.27 N	77.33 W
Middletown, N.Y., U.S.	166	41.27 N	74.25 W
Middletown, Ohio, U.S.	166	39.29 N	84.25 W
Middletown, R.I., U.S.	166	41.32 N	71.17 W
Mid Glamorgan □6	32	51.40 N	3.30 W
Midi, Canal du ☰	42	43.26 N	1.58 E
Midi de Bigorre, Pic du ▲	42	42.56 N	0.08 E
Midland, Mich., U.S.	168	43.37 N	84.14 W
Midland, Pa., U.S.	168	40.15 N	80.13 W
Midland, Tex., U.S.	162	32.00 N	102.05 W
Midway Islands □2	10	28.13 N	177.22 W
Międzyrzec Podlaski	36	52.00 N	22.47 E
Międzyrzecz	36	52.28 N	15.35 E
Mielec	36	50.18 N	21.25 E
Mieres	50	43.15 N	5.46 W
Miguel Alemán, Presa ⊜1	130	18.13 N	96.32 W
Mihajlovgrad	54	43.25 N	23.13 E
Mikkeli	28	61.41 N	27.15 E
Mikkwa ≃	160	58.25 N	114.45 W
Mikołów	36	50.11 N	18.55 E
Milaca	168	45.45 N	93.29 W
Milagro	144	2.07 S	79.36 W
Milan → Milano, It.	46	45.28 N	9.12 E
Milan, Mich., U.S.	168	42.05 N	83.40 W
Milan, Mo., U.S.	174	40.12 N	93.07 W
Milan, N. Mex., U.S.	178	35.09 N	107.54 W
Milan, Tenn., U.S.	174	35.55 N	88.46 W
Milano (Milan)	46	45.28 N	9.12 E
Milâs	54	37.19 N	27.47 E
Milazzo	46	38.14 N	15.15 E
Milbank	162	45.13 N	96.38 W
Miles City	180	46.25 N	105.51 W
Miletto, Monte ▲	46	41.27 N	14.22 E
Milford, Conn., U.S.	166	41.13 N	73.04 W
Milford, Del., U.S.	166	38.55 N	75.25 W
Milford, Mass., U.S.	166	42.08 N	71.32 W
Milford, Mich., U.S.	168	42.35 N	83.36 W
Milford, N.H., U.S.	166	42.50 N	71.39 W
Milford Haven	32	51.40 N	5.02 W
Millau	42	44.06 N	3.05 E
Millbury	166	42.11 N	71.46 W
Millcreek	178	40.43 N	111.51 W
Millcreek Township	166	42.05 N	80.10 W
Milledgeville	172	33.04 N	83.14 W
Mille Lacs Lake ⊜	168	46.15 N	93.40 W
Millen	172	32.48 N	81.57 W
Miller	162	44.31 N	98.59 W
Millersburg	166	40.33 N	76.58 W
Millersville	166	40.00 N	76.22 W
Millevaches, Plateau de ⋀1	42	45.30 N	2.10 E
Millington	174	35.21 N	89.54 W
Millinocket	166	45.39 N	68.43 W
Mills	180	42.50 N	106.22 W
Mill Valley	184	37.54 N	122.32 W
Millville	166	39.24 N	75.02 W
Millwood Lake ⊜1	174	33.45 N	94.00 W
Mílos I	54	36.41 N	24.15 E
Milpitas	184	37.26 N	121.54 W
Milton, Del., U.S.	166	38.47 N	75.19 W
Milton, Fla., U.S.	174	30.38 N	87.03 W
Milton, Pa., U.S.	166	41.01 N	76.51 W
Milton, Vt., U.S.	166	44.38 N	73.07 W
Milton, Wis., U.S.	168	42.47 N	88.56 W
Milton-Freewater	180	45.56 N	118.23 W
Milwaukee	168	43.02 N	87.55 W
Milwaukie	180	45.27 N	122.38 W
Mims	172	28.40 N	80.51 W
Minas	146	34.23 S	55.14 W
Minatitlán	130	17.59 N	94.31 W
Mindanao I	82	8.00 N	125.00 E
Mindanao Sea ▾2	82	9.10 N	124.25 E
Mindelo	100	16.53 N	25.00 W
Minden, B.R.D.	36	52.17 N	8.55 E
Minden, La., U.S.	174	32.37 N	93.17 W
Minden, Nev., U.S.	184	38.57 N	119.45 W
Mindoro I	82	12.50 N	121.05 E
Mindoro Strait ⋃	82	12.20 N	120.40 E
Mineral Point	168	42.52 N	90.11 W
Mineral Wells	162	32.48 N	98.07 W
Minersville	166	40.41 N	76.16 W
Minerva	166	40.44 N	81.06 W
Minervino Murge	46	41.05 N	16.05 E
Mingo Junction	166	40.19 N	80.37 W
Minho □9	50	41.40 N	8.30 W
Minho (Miño) ≃	50	41.52 N	8.51 W
Minna	100	9.37 N	6.33 E
Minneapolis	168	44.59 N	93.13 W
Minnehaha	180	45.39 N	122.37 W
Minnesota □3	162	46.00 N	94.15 W
Minnesota ≃	168	44.54 N	93.10 W
Miño (Minho) ≃	50	41.52 N	8.51 W
Minot	162	48.14 N	101.18 W
Minsk	62	53.54 N	27.34 E
Mińsk Mazowiecki	36	52.11 N	21.34 E
Minto, Lac ⊜	160	51.00 N	73.37 W
Minturno	46	41.15 N	13.45 E
Mira	46	45.26 N	12.08 E
Mira ≃	50	37.43 N	8.47 W
Miramichi Bay C	160	47.08 N	65.08 W
Miranda de Ebro	50	42.41 N	2.57 W
Mirandola	46	44.53 N	11.04 E
Miri	82	4.23 N	113.59 E
Mīrpur Khās	84	25.32 N	69.00 E
Misāḥah, Bi'r ▾4	102	22.12 N	27.57 E
Mishawaka	174	41.40 N	86.11 W
Mishmi Hills ⋀2	84	29.00 N	96.00 E
Misilmeri	46	38.01 N	13.27 E
Miskitos, Cayos II	130	14.23 N	82.46 W
Miskolc	36	48.06 N	20.47 E
Misrātah	102	32.23 N	15.06 E
Mississippi □3	162	32.50 N	89.30 W
Mississippi ≃	162	29.00 N	89.15 W
Mississippi Delta ⌣2	174	29.10 N	89.15 W
Mississippi Sound ⋃	174	30.15 N	88.40 W
Missoula	180	46.52 N	114.01 W
Missouri □3	162	38.30 N	93.30 W
Missouri ≃	162	38.50 N	90.08 W
Missouri Valley	174	41.33 N	95.53 W
Misterbianco	46	37.31 N	15.01 E
Misti, Volcán ▲1	144	16.18 S	71.24 W
Mistretta	46	37.56 N	14.22 E
Mita, Punta ≻	130	20.47 N	105.33 W
Mitchell, Ind., U.S.	174	38.44 N	86.28 W
Mitchell, S. Dak., U.S.	162	43.43 N	104.01 W
Mitchell, Mount ▲	172	35.46 N	82.16 W
Mitilíni	54	39.06 N	26.32 E
Mito	80	36.22 N	140.28 E
Mitsio, Nosy I	104	12.54 S	48.36 E
Mittellandkanal ☰	36	52.16 N	11.41 E
Mittweida	36	50.59 N	12.59 E
Mitumba, Monts ⋀	104	6.00 S	29.00 E
Miyakonojō	80	31.44 N	131.04 E
Miyazaki	80	31.54 N	131.26 E
Mizen Head ≻	32	51.27 N	9.49 W
Mjölby	28	58.19 N	15.08 E
Mjøsa ⊜	28	60.40 N	11.00 E
Mladá Boleslav	36	50.23 N	14.59 E
Mława	36	53.06 N	20.23 E
Mljet, Otok I	46	42.45 N	17.30 E
Mljetski Kanal ⋃	46	42.48 N	17.35 E
Moa ≃	100	6.59 N	11.36 W
Moab	178	38.35 N	109.33 W
Moberly	174	39.25 N	92.26 W
Mobile	174	30.42 N	88.05 W
Mobile Bay C	174	30.25 N	88.00 W
Mobridge	162	45.32 N	100.26 W
Moçambique	104	15.03 S	40.42 E
Moçâmedes	104	15.10 S	12.09 E
Mochudi	104	24.28 S	26.05 E
Möckeln ⊜	28	56.40 N	14.10 E
Mocksville	172	35.54 N	80.34 W
Móco, Serra ▲	104	12.28 S	15.10 E
Močurica ≃	54	42.31 N	26.32 E
Modder ≃	104	29.02 S	24.37 E
Modena	46	44.40 N	10.55 E
Modesto	184	37.39 N	120.60 W
Modica	46	36.51 N	14.47 E
Mödling	36	48.05 N	16.17 E
Modra Špilja ⁕5	46	43.00 N	16.02 E
Moe	116	38.10 S	146.15 E
Moers	36	51.27 N	6.37 E
Mogadisho	102	2.01 N	45.20 E
Mogi das Cruzes	144	23.31 S	46.11 W
Mogil'ov	62	53.54 N	30.21 E
Mogliano Veneto	46	45.33 N	12.14 E
Mogollon Rim ⁕4	178	32.30 N	111.00 W
Mohács	36	45.59 N	18.42 E
Mohammedia	100	33.44 N	7.24 W
Mohave, Lake ⊜1	184	35.25 N	114.38 W
Mohawk ≃	166	42.47 N	73.42 W
Moheli I	104	12.15 S	43.45 E
Mohicanville Reservoir ⊜1	166	40.45 N	82.00 W
Moinești	54	46.28 N	26.29 E
Mojave ≃	184	35.06 N	116.04 W
Mojave Desert ◆2	184	35.00 N	117.00 W
Mokp'o	80	34.48 N	126.22 E
Mokrisset	50	34.59 N	5.20 W
Mokša ≃	62	54.44 N	41.53 E
Mol	36	51.11 N	5.06 E
Mola di Bari	46	41.04 N	17.05 E
Moldova ≃	54	46.54 N	26.58 E
Moldoveanu ▲	54	45.36 N	24.44 E
Molepolole	104	24.25 S	25.30 E
Molfetta	46	41.12 N	16.36 E
Molina de Segura	50	38.03 N	1.12 W
Moline	168	41.30 N	90.31 W
Molins de Rey	50	41.25 N	2.01 E
Mollendo	144	17.02 S	72.01 W
Mölln	36	53.37 N	10.41 E
Mölndal	28	57.39 N	12.01 E
Molokai I	162b	21.07 N	157.00 W
Molopo ≃	104	28.30 S	20.13 E
Molucca Sea → Maluku, Laut ▾2	82	0.02 S	125.00 E
Mombasa	104	4.03 S	39.40 E
Momence	168	41.10 N	87.40 W
Momskij Chrebet ⋀	64	66.00 N	146.00 E
Møn I	28	55.00 N	12.20 E
Mona, Isla de I	130	18.05 N	67.54 W
Monaca	166	40.41 N	80.17 W
Monaco	42	43.42 N	7.23 E
Monaco □1	20	43.45 N	7.25 E
Monadhliath Mountains ⋀	32	57.15 N	4.10 W
Monadnock, Mount ▲	166	42.52 N	72.07 W
Monarch Pass)(	178	38.30 N	106.19 W
Monastir	46	35.47 N	10.50 E
Moncalieri	46	45.00 N	7.41 E
Mončegorsk	26	67.54 N	32.58 E
Mönchengladbach	36	51.12 N	6.28 E
Monclova	130	26.54 N	101.25 W
Moncton	160	46.06 N	64.47 W
Mondovi, It.	46	44.23 N	7.49 E
Mondovi, Wis., U.S.	168	44.34 N	91.40 W
Mondragone	46	41.07 N	13.53 E
Monessen	166	40.09 N	79.53 W
Monett	174	36.55 N	93.55 W
Monfalcone	46	45.49 N	13.32 E
Monferrato ◆1	46	44.55 N	8.05 E
Monforte de Lemos	50	42.31 N	7.30 W
Mongol Altajn Nuruu ⋀	80	47.00 N	92.00 E
Mongolia □1	80	46.00 N	105.00 E
Monico	168	45.35 N	89.09 W
Monida Pass)(	180	44.33 N	112.18 W
Monitor Range ⋀	184	38.45 N	116.30 W
Monmouth, Ill., U.S.	168	40.55 N	90.39 W
Monmouth, Oreg., U.S.	180	44.51 N	123.14 W
Mono ≃	100	6.17 N	1.51 E
Mono Lake ⊜	184	38.00 N	119.00 W
Monongahela	166	40.11 N	79.56 W
Monopoli	46	40.57 N	17.19 E
Monor	36	47.21 N	19.27 E
Monreale	46	38.05 N	13.17 E
Monroe, Ga., U.S.	172	33.47 N	83.43 W
Monroe, Iowa, U.S.	174	41.31 N	93.06 W
Monroe, La., U.S.	174	32.33 N	92.07 W
Monroe, Mich., U.S.	168	41.55 N	83.24 W
Monroe, N.C., U.S.	172	34.59 N	80.33 W
Monroe, N.Y., U.S.	166	41.20 N	74.11 W
Monroe, Wash., U.S.	180	47.51 N	121.58 W
Monroe, Wis., U.S.	168	42.36 N	89.38 W
Monroe, Lake ⊜1	174	39.05 N	86.25 W
Monroe City	174	39.39 N	91.44 W
Monroeville, Ala., U.S.	174	31.31 N	87.20 W
Monroeville, Pa., U.S.	166	40.26 N	79.47 W
Monrovia	100	6.18 N	10.47 W
Mons	36	50.27 N	3.56 E
Montalto ▲	46	38.10 N	15.55 E
Montana □3	162	47.00 N	110.00 W
Montargis	42	48.00 N	2.45 E
Montauban	42	44.01 N	1.21 E
Montauk Point ≻	166	41.04 N	71.52 W
Montbéliard	42	47.31 N	6.48 E
Mont Belvieu	184	29.51 N	94.54 W
Montbrison	42	45.36 N	4.03 E
Montceau [-les-Mines]	42	46.40 N	4.22 E
Montclair, Calif., U.S.	184	34.06 N	117.41 W
Montclair, N.J., U.S.	166	40.49 N	74.13 W
Mont-de-Marsan	42	43.53 N	0.30 W
Montecatini Terme	46	43.53 N	10.46 E
Montecito	184	34.26 N	119.39 W
Monte Cristo, Cerro ▲	130	14.25 N	89.21 W
Montecristo, Isola di I	46	42.20 N	10.19 E
Montego Bay	130	18.28 N	77.55 W
Montélimar	42	44.34 N	4.45 E
Montelindo ≃	146	23.56 S	57.12 W
Montereau-faut-Yonne	42	48.23 N	2.57 E
Monterey, Calif., U.S.	184	36.37 N	121.55 W
Monterey, Tenn., U.S.	174	36.09 N	85.16 W
Monterey Bay C	184	36.45 N	121.55 W
Montería	144	8.46 N	75.53 W
Monterotondo	46	42.03 N	12.37 E
Monterrey	130	25.40 N	100.19 W
Montesano	180	46.59 N	123.36 W
Monte Sant'Angelo	46	41.42 N	15.57 E
Monte Santu, Capo di ≻	46	40.05 N	9.44 E
Montes Claros	144	16.43 S	43.52 W
Montevallo	174	33.06 N	86.52 W
Montevarchi	46	43.31 N	11.34 E
Montevideo	146	34.53 S	56.11 W
Monte Vista	178	37.35 N	106.09 W
Montezuma	172	32.18 N	84.02 W
Montgomery, Ala., U.S.	174	32.23 N	86.18 W
Montgomery, Minn., U.S.	168	44.26 N	93.35 W
Montgomery, W. Va., U.S.	166	38.11 N	81.19 W
Montgomery City	174	38.59 N	91.30 W
Monticello, Ark., U.S.	174	33.38 N	91.47 W
Monticello, Ga., U.S.	172	33.18 N	83.40 W
Monticello, Ill., U.S.	174	40.01 N	88.34 W
Monticello, Ind., U.S.	174	40.45 N	86.46 W
Monticello, Iowa, U.S.	168	42.15 N	91.12 W
Monticello, Ky., U.S.	174	36.50 N	84.51 W
Monticello, N.Y., U.S.	166	41.39 N	74.42 W
Montichiari	46	45.25 N	10.23 E
Montiel, Campo de ≚	50	38.46 N	2.44 W
Montijo, Esp.	50	38.55 N	6.37 W
Montijo, Port.	50	38.42 N	8.58 W
Montilla	50	37.35 N	4.38 W
Montluçon	42	46.21 N	2.36 E
Montoro	50	38.01 N	4.23 W
Montoursville	166	41.15 N	76.55 W
Montpelier, Idaho, U.S.	180	42.19 N	111.18 W
Montpelier, Ind., U.S.	174	40.33 N	85.17 W
Montpelier, Ohio, U.S.	166	41.35 N	84.36 W
Montpelier, Vt., U.S.	166	44.16 N	72.35 W
Montpellier	42	43.36 N	3.53 E
Montréal	160	45.31 N	73.34 W
Montreal Lake ⊜	160	54.20 N	105.40 W
Montreux	42	46.26 N	6.55 E
Montrose, Scot., U.K.	32	56.43 N	2.29 W
Montrose, Colo., U.S.	178	38.29 N	107.53 W
Montserrat □2	130	16.45 N	62.12 W
Monument Valley V	178	37.05 N	110.20 W
Monywa	82	22.05 N	95.08 E
Monza	46	45.35 N	9.16 E
Moorefield	166	39.04 N	78.58 W
Mooresville, Ind., U.S.	174	39.37 N	86.22 W
Mooresville, N.C., U.S.	172	35.35 N	80.48 W
Moosburg	36	48.29 N	11.57 E
Moosehead Lake ⊜	166	45.40 N	69.40 W
Moose Jaw	160	50.23 N	105.32 W
Mooselookmeguntic Lake ⊜	166	44.53 N	70.48 W
Mopti	100	14.30 N	4.12 W
Mór	36	47.23 N	18.12 E
Mora, Esp.	50	39.41 N	3.46 W
Mora, Minn., U.S.	168	45.53 N	93.18 W
Morādābād	84	28.50 N	78.47 E
Mórahalom	36	46.13 N	19.54 E
Moraleda, Canal de ⋃	146	44.30 S	73.30 W
Moran	174	37.55 N	95.10 W
Morant Cays II	130	17.24 N	75.59 W
Moratalla	50	38.12 N	1.53 W
Moratuwa	84	6.46 N	79.53 E
Morava (March) ≃	36	48.10 N	16.59 E
Moray Firth C1	32	57.50 N	3.30 W
More, Ben ▲	32	56.23 N	4.31 W
Moreau ≃	162	45.18 N	100.43 W
Morecambe	32	54.04 N	2.53 W
Morehead	166	38.11 N	83.25 W
Morehead City	172	34.43 N	76.43 W
Morelia	130	19.42 N	101.07 W
Morena, Sierra ⋀	50	38.00 N	5.00 W
Morgan City	174	29.42 N	91.12 W
Morganfield	174	37.41 N	87.55 W
Morganton	172	35.45 N	81.41 W
Morgantown	166	39.38 N	79.57 W
Morghāb (Murgab) ≃	84	38.18 N	61.12 E
Moriarty	178	34.59 N	106.03 W
Morioka	80	39.42 N	141.09 E
Morlaix	42	48.35 N	3.50 W
Morocco □1	100	32.00 N	5.00 W
Morogoro	104	6.49 S	37.40 E
Moro Gulf C	82	6.51 N	123.00 E
Morón	130	22.06 N	78.38 W
Morondava	104	20.17 S	44.17 E
Morón de la Frontera	50	37.08 N	5.27 W
Moroni	104	11.41 S	43.16 E
Morpeth	32	55.10 N	1.41 W
Morrilton	174	35.09 N	92.45 W
Morris	168	41.22 N	88.26 W
Morrison	168	41.49 N	89.58 W
Morristown, N.J., U.S.	166	40.48 N	74.29 W
Morristown, Tenn., U.S.	172	36.13 N	83.18 W
Morrisville, Pa., U.S.	166	40.13 N	74.47 W
Morrisville, Vt., U.S.	166	44.34 N	72.44 W
Morro, Punta ≻	146	27.07 S	70.57 W
Morro Bay	184	35.22 N	120.51 W
Mortara	46	45.15 N	8.44 E
Morton, Ill., U.S.	168	40.37 N	89.28 W
Morton, Miss., U.S.	174	32.21 N	89.40 W
Morvan ⋀	42	47.05 N	4.00 E
Mosbach	36	49.21 N	9.08 E
Moscow → Moskva, S.S.S.R.	26	55.45 N	37.35 E
Moscow, Idaho, U.S.	180	46.44 N	117.00 W
Mosel (Moselle) ≃	42	50.22 N	7.36 E
Moses Lake	180	47.08 N	119.17 W
Moshi	104	3.21 S	37.20 E
Mosinee	168	44.47 N	89.43 W
Moskenesøya I	26	67.59 N	13.00 E
Moskva (Moscow)	26	55.45 N	37.35 E
Mosonmagyaróvár	36	47.51 N	17.17 E
Mosquitos, Golfo de los C	130	9.00 N	81.15 W
Moss	28	59.26 N	10.42 E
Mosselbaai	104	34.11 S	22.08 E
Mossoró	144	5.11 S	37.20 W
Moss Point	174	30.25 N	88.29 W
Most	36	50.32 N	13.39 E
Mostaganem	100	35.51 N	0.07 E
Mostar	46	43.20 N	17.49 E
Møsting, Kap ≻	160	64.00 N	41.00 W
Motala	28	58.33 N	15.03 E
Motherwell	32	55.48 N	4.00 W
Motril	50	36.45 N	3.31 W
Motru	54	44.50 N	23.00 E
Motutapu I	114	21.15 S	159.43 W
Mouila	104	1.52 S	11.01 E
Moulins	42	46.34 N	3.20 E
Moulmein	82	16.30 N	97.38 E
Moulouya, Oued ≃	100	35.05 N	2.25 W
Moulton	174	34.29 N	87.18 W
Moultrie	172	31.11 N	83.47 W
Moultrie, Lake ⊜1	172	33.20 N	80.05 W
Mound Bayou	174	33.54 N	90.44 W
Mound City	174	38.08 N	94.49 W
Moundou	102	8.34 N	16.05 E
Moundsville	166	39.55 N	80.44 W
Mounier, Mont ▲	42	44.09 N	6.58 E
Mountainair	178	34.31 N	106.15 W
Mountain Brook	174	33.29 N	86.46 W
Mountain Grove	174	37.08 N	92.16 W
Mountain Home, Ark., U.S.	174	36.20 N	92.23 W
Mountain Home, Idaho, U.S.	180	43.08 N	115.41 W
Mountain Nile (Baḥr al-Jabal) ≃	102	9.30 N	30.30 E
Mountain View, Ark., U.S.	174	35.52 N	92.07 W
Mountain View, Calif., U.S.	184	37.23 N	122.04 W
Mountain View, Wyo., U.S.	180	42.52 N	106.55 W
Mount Airy	172	36.31 N	80.37 W
Mount Ayr	174	40.43 N	94.14 W
Mount Carmel, Ill., U.S.	174	38.25 N	87.46 W
Mount Carmel, Pa., U.S.	166	40.48 N	76.25 W
Mount Clemens	168	42.36 N	82.53 W
Mount Dora	172	28.48 N	81.38 W
Mount Gambier	116	37.50 S	140.46 E
Mount Holly	172	35.18 N	81.01 W
Mount Horeb	168	43.00 N	89.44 W
Mount Isa	116	20.44 S	139.30 E
Mount Kisco	166	41.12 N	73.44 W
Mount Lebanon	166	40.23 N	80.03 W
Mount Morris, Ill., U.S.	168	42.03 N	89.26 W
Mount Morris, Mich., U.S.	168	43.07 N	83.42 W
Mount Morris, N.Y., U.S.	166	42.44 N	77.53 W
Mount Olive	172	35.12 N	78.04 W
Mount Pleasant, Iowa, U.S.	168	40.58 N	91.33 W
Mount Pleasant, Mich., U.S.	168	43.35 N	84.47 W
Mount Pleasant, Pa., U.S.	166	40.09 N	79.33 W
Mount Pleasant, S.C., U.S.	172	32.47 N	79.52 W
Mount Pleasant, Tenn., U.S.	174	35.32 N	87.13 W
Mount Pleasant, Tex., U.S.	174	33.09 N	94.58 W
Mount Roskill	118	36.55 S	174.45 E
Mount Savage	166	39.42 N	78.53 W
Mount's Bay C	32	50.03 N	5.25 W
Mount Sterling, Ky., U.S.	172	38.04 N	83.56 W
Mount Sterling, Ohio, U.S.	166	39.43 N	83.16 W
Mount Union	166	40.23 N	77.53 W
Mount Vernon, Ill., U.S.	174	38.19 N	88.55 W
Mount Vernon, Ind., U.S.	174	37.56 N	87.54 W
Mount Vernon, Iowa, U.S.	168	41.55 N	91.23 W
Mount Vernon, Mo., U.S.	174	37.06 N	93.49 W
Mount Vernon, Ohio, U.S.	166	40.23 N	82.29 W
Mount Vernon, Wash., U.S.	180	48.25 N	122.20 W
Mount Wellington	118	36.54 S	174.51 E
Mourdi, Dépression du ⁕7	102	18.10 N	23.00 E
Mourne Mountains ⋀	32	54.10 N	6.04 W
Moyen Atlas ⋀	100	33.30 N	5.00 W
Moyeuvre-Grande	42	49.15 N	6.02 E
Mozambique □1	104	18.15 S	35.00 E
Mozambique Channel ⋃	104	19.00 S	41.00 E
Možga	26	56.23 N	52.17 E
Mrągowo	36	53.52 N	21.19 E
Mrhila, Djebel ▲	46	35.25 N	9.14 E
Msaken	46	35.44 N	10.35 E
M'Sila	50	35.46 N	4.31 E
Mtwara	104	10.16 S	40.11 E
Muar	82	2.02 N	102.34 E
Muchinga Mountains ⋀	104	12.00 S	31.45 E
Mudanjiang	80	44.35 N	129.36 E
Mufulira	104	12.33 S	28.14 E
Mugello V	46	43.55 N	11.30 E
Muğla	54	37.12 N	28.22 E
Mugodžary ⋀2	62	49.00 N	58.40 E
Mühlacker	36	48.57 N	8.50 E
Mühldorf	36	48.15 N	12.32 E
Mühlhausen	36	51.12 N	10.27 E
Mühlviertel ◆1	36	48.25 N	14.10 E
Mukačevo	54	48.27 N	22.45 E
Mukden → Shenyang	80	41.48 N	123.27 E
Mukilteo	180	47.57 N	122.18 W
Mukwonago	168	42.52 N	88.20 W
Mulde ≃	36	51.10 N	12.48 E
Muldraugh	174	37.56 N	85.59 W
Muldrow	174	35.24 N	94.36 W
Mulhacén ▲	50	37.03 N	3.19 W
Mulhouse	42	47.45 N	7.20 E
Mull, Island of I	32	56.27 N	6.00 W
Mullens	172	37.35 N	81.23 W
Mullett Lake ⊜	168	45.30 N	84.30 W
Mullins	172	34.12 N	79.15 W
Multān	84	30.11 N	71.29 E
Mun ≃	82	15.19 N	105.30 E
Muna, Pulau I	82	5.00 S	122.30 E
München (Munich)	36	48.08 N	11.34 E
Muncie	174	40.11 N	85.23 W
Mundelein	168	42.16 N	88.00 W
Münden	36	51.25 N	9.39 E
Mundo ≃	50	38.19 N	1.40 W
Munich → München	36	48.08 N	11.34 E
Munising	168	46.25 N	86.40 W
Münster, B.R.D.	36	51.57 N	7.37 E
Munster, B.R.D.	36	52.59 N	10.05 E
Munster □9	32	52.25 N	8.20 W
Muoro	46	40.20 N	9.20 E
Muqayshiṭ I	84	24.12 N	53.42 E
Mura (Mur) ≃	36	46.18 N	16.53 E
Muradiye	54	38.39 N	27.21 E
Murchison ≃	116	27.42 S	114.09 E
Murchison Falls ↳	102	2.17 N	31.41 E
Murcia	50	37.59 N	1.07 W
Murcia □9	50	38.30 N	1.45 W
Murfreesboro, Ark., U.S.	174	34.04 N	93.41 W
Murfreesboro, N.C., U.S.	172	36.27 N	77.06 W
Murfreesboro, Tenn., U.S.	174	35.51 N	86.23 W
Murgab (Morghāb) ≃	84	38.18 N	61.12 E
Muri	114	21.14 S	159.43 W
Müritz ⊜	36	53.25 N	12.43 E
Murmansk	26	68.58 N	33.05 E
Murom	26	55.34 N	42.02 E
Muroran	80	42.18 N	140.59 E
Murphy	172	35.05 N	84.01 W
Murphysboro	174	37.46 N	89.20 W
Murray, Ky., U.S.	174	36.37 N	88.19 W
Murray, Utah, U.S.	178	40.40 N	111.53 W
Murray, Lake ⊜1	172	34.04 N	81.23 W
Murrumbidgee ≃	116	34.43 S	143.12 E
Murter, Otok I	46	43.48 N	15.37 E
Murud, Gunong ▲	82	3.52 N	115.30 E
Mürzzuschlag	36	47.36 N	15.41 E
Musala ▲	54	42.11 N	23.34 E
Muscatine	174	41.25 N	91.03 W
Mus-Chaja, Gora ▲	64	62.35 N	140.50 E
Muscle Shoals	174	34.45 N	87.40 W
Mushin	100	6.32 N	3.22 E
Musishan ▲	80	36.03 N	80.07 E
Muskegon	168	43.14 N	86.16 W
Muskegon ≃	168	43.14 N	86.20 W
Muskegon Heights	168	43.12 N	86.12 W
Muskogee	174	35.45 N	95.22 W
Musselshell ≃	180	47.21 N	107.58 W
Mussomeli	46	37.35 N	13.46 E
Mustafakemalpaşa	54	40.02 N	28.24 E
Mustafa Kemalpaşa ≃	54	40.07 N	28.33 E
Mutsamudu	104	12.09 S	44.25 E
Mwanza	104	2.31 S	32.54 E
Mweru, Lake ⊜	104	9.00 S	28.45 E
Myaungmya	82	16.36 N	94.56 E
Myerstown	166	40.22 N	76.19 W
Myingyan	82	21.28 N	95.23 E
Myitkyinā	80	25.23 N	97.24 E
Myjava	36	48.45 N	17.34 E
Mymensingh	84	24.45 N	90.24 E
Myrtle Beach	172	33.42 N	78.52 W
Myrtle Grove	174	30.25 N	87.18 W
Myślenice	36	49.51 N	19.56 E
Mysłowice	36	50.15 N	19.07 E
Mysore	84	12.18 N	76.39 E
Mystic	174	40.47 N	92.57 W
Myszków	36	50.36 N	19.20 E
My-tho	82	10.21 N	106.21 E
Mytišči	26	55.55 N	37.46 E
Mže ≃	36	49.46 N	13.24 E
Mzuzu	104	11.27 S	33.55 E
N			
Naab ≃	36	49.01 N	12.02 E
Naach, Jbel ▲	50	34.53 N	3.22 W
Naalehu	162b	19.04 N	155.35 W
Nabeul	100	36.27 N	10.44 E
Nabī Shu'ayb, Jabal an- ▲	84	15.18 N	43.59 E
Nābulus	84	32.13 N	35.15 E
Náchod	36	50.25 N	16.10 E
Nachodka	64	42.48 N	132.52 E
Nacka	28	59.18 N	18.10 E
Nacogdoches	174	31.36 N	94.39 W
Nădlac	54	46.10 N	20.45 E
Nador	50	35.12 N	2.55 W
Næstved	28	55.14 N	11.46 E
Naga	82	13.37 N	123.11 E
Nagano	80	36.39 N	138.11 E
Nagaoka	80	37.27 N	138.51 E
Nagasaki	80	32.48 N	129.55 E
Nagoya	80	35.10 N	136.55 E
Nāgpur	84	21.08 N	79.04 E
Nagykanizsa	36	46.27 N	17.00 E
Nagykáta	36	47.25 N	19.45 E
Nagykőrös	36	47.02 N	19.43 E
Naha	80	26.13 N	127.40 E
Nahe ≃	36	49.58 N	7.57 E
Nairobi	104	1.17 S	36.49 E
Najin	80	42.15 N	130.18 E
Najramdal Uul ▲	80	49.10 N	87.52 W
Nakhon Pathom	82	13.49 N	100.03 E
Nakhon Ratchasima	82	14.58 N	102.07 E
Nakhon Sawan	82	15.41 N	100.07 E
Nakhon Si Thammarat	82	8.26 N	99.58 E
Nakło nad Notecią	36	53.08 N	17.35 E
Nakskov	28	54.50 N	11.09 E
Nakuru	104	0.17 S	36.04 E
Nal'čik	62	43.29 N	43.37 E
Namangan	62	41.00 N	71.40 E
Nam-dinh	82	20.25 N	106.10 E
Namib Desert ◆2	104	23.00 S	15.00 E
Namibia □2	104	22.00 S	17.00 E
Nampa	180	43.34 N	116.34 W
Namp'o	80	38.45 N	125.23 E
Nampula	104	15.07 S	39.15 E
Namsen ≃	26	64.27 N	11.28 E
Namuchabawashan ▲	80	29.38 N	95.04 E
Namuhu ⊜	80	30.42 N	90.30 E
Namur	36	50.28 N	4.52 E
Namysłów	36	51.05 N	17.42 E
Nan ≃	82	15.42 N	100.09 E
Nanaimo	160	49.10 N	123.56 W
Nanchang	80	28.41 N	115.53 E
Nanchong	80	30.48 N	106.04 E
Nancy	42	48.41 N	6.12 E
Nanda Devi ▲	84	30.23 N	79.59 E
Nandi	111	17.48 S	177.25 E
Nandi Bay C	111	17.44 S	177.25 E
N'andoma	26	61.40 N	40.12 E
Nanga Parbat ▲	84	35.15 N	74.36 E
Nanjing	80	32.03 N	118.47 E
Nanling ⋀	80	25.00 N	112.00 E
Nanning	80	22.48 N	108.20 E
Nansa ≃	50	43.22 N	4.29 W
Nansei-shotō (Ryukyu Islands) II	80	26.30 N	128.00 E
Nanshan → Qilianshanmai ⋀	80	39.06 N	98.40 E
Nantes	42	47.13 N	1.33 W
Nanticoke	166	41.12 N	76.00 W
Nantong	80	32.02 N	120.53 E
Nantucket Island I	166	41.16 N	70.03 W
Nantucket Sound ⋃	166	41.30 N	70.15 W
Nanty Glo	166	40.28 N	78.50 W
Nanuque	144	17.50 S	40.21 W
Nanyang	80	33.00 N	112.32 E
Nanyuki	104	0.01 N	37.04 E
Nao, Cabo de la ≻	50	38.44 N	0.14 E
Náousa	54	40.37 N	22.05 E
Napa	184	38.18 N	122.17 W
Naperville	168	41.48 N	88.09 W
Napier	118	39.29 S	176.55 E
Naples → Napoli, It.	46	40.51 N	14.17 E
Naples, Fla., U.S.	172	26.08 N	81.48 W
Napoleon	166	41.23 N	84.08 W
Napoli (Naples)	46	40.51 N	14.17 E
Napoli, Golfo di C	46	40.43 N	14.10 E
Nappanee	174	41.27 N	86.00 W
Nara	80	34.41 N	135.50 E
Nārāyanganj	84	23.37 N	90.30 E
Narbonne	42	43.11 N	3.00 E
Nardò	46	40.11 N	18.02 E
Narew ≃	36	52.26 N	20.42 E
Narinda, Baie de C	104	14.55 S	47.30 E
Narni	46	42.31 N	12.31 E
Naro	46	37.17 N	13.48 E
Narodnaja, Gora ▲	62	65.04 N	60.09 E
Narovorovo	112	15.13 S	168.09 E
Narva	26	59.23 N	28.12 E
Narvik	26	68.26 N	17.25 E
Nashua, Iowa, U.S.	168	42.57 N	92.32 W
Nashua, N.H., U.S.	166	42.46 N	71.27 W
Nashville, Ark., U.S.	174	33.57 N	93.51 W
Nashville, Ga., U.S.	172	31.12 N	83.15 W
Nashville, Ill., U.S.	174	38.21 N	89.23 W
Nashville, Tenn., U.S.	174	36.09 N	86.48 W
Näsijärvi ⊜	28	61.37 N	23.42 E
Nāsik	84	19.59 N	73.47 E
Nassau	130	25.05 N	77.21 W
Nasser, Lake ⊜1	100	22.40 N	32.00 E
Nässjö	28	57.39 N	14.41 E
Natal	144	5.47 S	35.13 W
Natchez	174	31.34 N	91.23 W
Natchitoches	174	31.46 N	93.05 W
Natewa Bay C	111	16.35 S	179.40 E
Natick	166	42.17 N	71.21 W
National City	184	32.40 N	117.06 W
Natron, Lake ⊜	104	2.25 S	36.00 E
Nattastunturit ▲	26	68.12 N	27.20 E
Nauen	36	52.36 N	12.52 E
Naugatuck	166	41.30 N	73.04 W
Naumburg	36	51.09 N	11.48 E

Name	Page	Lat°′	Long°′
Nauru □[1]	10	0.32 S	166.55 E
Nausori	111	18.02 S	175.32 E
Navajo Reservoir ⊜[1]	178	36.55 N	107.30 W
Navarra □[4]	50	42.40 N	1.30 W
Navia ≃	50	43.33 N	6.44 W
Navojoa	130	27.06 N	109.26 W
Návpaktos	54	38.23 N	21.50 E
Návplion	54	37.34 N	22.48 E
Nawābshāh	84	26.15 N	68.25 E
Náxos I	54	37.02 N	25.35 E
Nazareth	166	40.44 N	75.19 W
Naze	80	28.23 N	129.30 E
Nazilli	54	37.55 N	28.21 E
Ndjamena (Fort-Lamy)	102	12.07 N	15.03 E
Ndola	104	12.58 S	28.38 E
Ndreketi ≃	111	16.34 S	178.53 E
Neagh, Lough ⊜	32	54.38 N	6.24 W
Neajlov ≃	54	44.11 N	26.12 E
Neath	32	51.40 N	3.48 W
Nebo, Mount ▲	178	39.49 N	111.46 W
Nebraska □[3]	162	41.30 N	100.00 W
Nebraska City	162	40.41 N	95.52 W
Nebrodi ⋀	46	37.55 N	14.35 E
Necedah	168	44.02 N	90.05 W
Neches ≃	174	29.55 N	93.52 W
Neckar ≃	36	49.31 N	8.26 E
Neckarsulm	36	49.12 N	9.13 E
Nederland	174	29.58 N	93.60 W
Nédroma	50	35.01 N	1.45 W
Negaunee	168	46.30 N	87.36 W
Negombo	84	7.13 N	79.50 E
Negra, Punta ≻	144	6.06 S	81.09 W
Negro ≃, Arg.	146	41.02 S	62.47 W
Negro ≃, S.A.	144	3.08 S	59.55 W
Negros I	82	10.00 N	123.00 E
Nehawka	174	40.50 N	95.59 W
Neheim-Hüsten	36	51.27 N	7.57 E
Neiges, Piton des ▲	104	21.05 S	55.29 E
Neijiang	80	29.35 N	105.03 E
Neillsville	168	44.34 N	90.36 W
Neisse (Nysa Łużycka) (Nisa) ≃	36	52.04 N	14.46 E
Neiva	144	2.56 N	75.18 W
Nekoosa	168	44.19 N	89.54 W
Nelson	118	41.17 S	173.17 E
Nelson ≃	160	57.04 N	92.30 W
Nelsonville	166	39.27 N	82.14 W
Nelspruit	104	25.30 S	30.58 E
Nëma	100	16.37 N	7.15 W
Nemaha	174	40.20 N	95.40 W
Neman (Nemunas) ≃	62	55.18 N	21.23 E
Nemuna, Bjeshkët e ⋀	54	42.27 N	19.47 E
Nemunas (Neman) ≃	62	55.18 N	21.23 E
Nemuro	80	43.20 N	145.35 E
Neodesha	174	37.25 N	95.41 W
Neosho	174	36.52 N	94.22 W
Neosho ≃	174	35.48 N	95.18 W
Nepal (Nepāl) □[1]	84	28.00 N	84.00 E
Nephi	178	39.43 N	111.50 W
Neptune	166	40.12 N	74.02 W
Nera ≃	46	42.26 N	12.24 E
Nerastro, Sarīr ◆[2]	102	24.20 N	20.37 E
Neretva ≃	54	43.40 N	17.59 E
Nerva	50	37.42 N	6.32 W
Ness, Loch ⊜	32	57.15 N	4.30 W
Nesselrode, Mount ▲	162a	58.58 N	134.18 W
Netanya	84	32.20 N	34.51 E
Netherlands □[1]	36	52.15 N	5.30 E
Netherlands Antilles □[2]	130	12.15 N	69.00 W
Nettuno	46	39.13 N	17.08 E
Nettilling Lake ⊜	160	66.30 N	70.40 W
Nettuno	46	41.27 N	12.39 E
Neubrandenburg	36	53.33 N	13.15 E
Neuburg an der Donau	36	48.44 N	11.11 E
Neuchâtel	42	46.59 N	6.56 E
Neuchâtel, Lac de ⊜	42	46.52 N	6.50 E
Neu-Isenburg	36	50.03 N	8.41 E
Neumarkt in der Oberpfalz	36	49.16 N	11.28 E
Neumünster	36	54.04 N	9.59 E
Neunkirchen	36	47.43 N	16.05 E
Neunkirchen / saar	36	49.20 N	7.10 E
Neuquén	146	38.57 S	68.04 W
Neuruppin	36	52.55 N	12.48 E
Neuse ≃	172	35.06 N	76.30 W
Neusiedler See ⊜	36	47.50 N	16.46 E
Neuss	36	51.12 N	6.41 E
Neustadt an der Weinstrasse	36	49.21 N	8.08 E
Neustadt in Holstein	36	54.06 N	10.48 E
Neustrelitz	36	53.21 N	13.04 E
Neutral Zone □[2]	84	29.10 N	45.30 E
Neu-Ulm	36	48.23 N	10.01 E
Neuwied	36	50.25 N	7.27 E
Nevada, Iowa, U.S.	168	42.01 N	93.27 W
Nevada, Mo., U.S.	174	37.51 N	94.22 W
Nevada □[3]	162	39.00 N	117.00 W
Nevada, Sierra ⋀, Esp.	50	37.05 N	3.10 W
Nevada, Sierra ⋀, Calif., U.S.	184	38.00 N	119.15 W
Nevers	42	47.00 N	3.09 E
Nevinnomyssk	62	44.38 N	41.56 E
Nevis I	130	17.10 N	62.34 W
Nevis, Ben ▲	32	56.48 N	5.01 W
New ≃	172	38.10 N	81.12 W
New Albany, Ind., U.S.	174	38.18 N	85.49 W
New Albany, Miss., U.S.	174	34.29 N	89.00 W
New Amsterdam	144	6.15 N	57.31 W
Newark, Del., U.S.	166	39.41 N	75.45 W
Newark, N.J., U.S.	166	40.44 N	74.10 W
Newark, N.Y., U.S.	166	43.03 N	77.06 W
Newark, Ohio, U.S.	166	40.04 N	82.24 W
Newark Lake ⊜	184	39.41 N	115.44 W
Newark-upon-Trent	32	53.05 N	0.49 W
New Baltimore	168	42.41 N	82.44 W
New Bedford	166	41.38 N	70.56 W
Newberg	180	45.18 N	122.58 W
New Berlin	168	42.58 N	88.07 W
New Bern	172	35.07 N	77.03 W
Newberry	172	34.17 N	81.37 W
New Boston	174	33.28 N	94.25 W
New Britain	166	41.40 N	72.47 W
New Britain I	116a	6.00 S	150.00 E
New Brunswick	166	40.29 N	74.27 W
New Brunswick □[4]	160	46.30 N	66.15 W
New Buffalo	168	41.47 N	86.45 W
Newburgh, Ind., U.S.	174	37.57 N	87.24 W
Newburgh, N.Y., U.S.	166	41.30 N	74.01 W
Newbury	32	51.25 N	1.20 W
Newburyport	166	42.49 N	70.53 W
New Caledonia □[2]	112	21.30 S	165.30 E
New Carlisle	166	39.56 N	84.02 W
Newcastle, Austl.	116	32.56 S	151.46 E
Newcastle, S. Afr.	104	27.49 S	29.55 E
New Castle, Del., U.S.	166	39.40 N	75.34 W
New Castle, Ind., U.S.	174	39.55 N	85.22 W
New Castle, Pa., U.S.	166	41.00 N	80.20 W
Newcastle-under-Lyme	32	53.00 N	2.14 W
Newcastle upon Tyne	32	54.59 N	1.35 W
Newcastle Waters	116	17.24 S	133.24 E
New City	166	41.09 N	73.59 W
Newcomerstown	166	40.16 N	81.36 W
New Delhi	84	28.36 N	77.15 E
New Ellenton	172	33.24 N	81.42 W
Newfound Gap)(	172	35.37 N	83.25 W
Newfoundland □[4]	160	52.00 N	56.00 W
New Georgia I	114	8.15 S	157.30 E
New Georgia Group II	114	8.30 S	157.20 E
New Glarus	168	42.49 N	89.38 W
New Glasgow	160	45.35 N	62.39 W
Newhall	184	34.23 N	118.31 W
New Hampshire □[3]	162	43.35 N	71.40 W
New Hampton	168	43.03 N	92.19 W
New Hanover I	116a	2.30 S	150.15 E
New Haven, Conn., U.S.	166	41.18 N	72.56 W
New Haven, Ind., U.S.	166	41.04 N	85.01 W
New Hebrides □[2]	112	16.00 S	167.00 E
New Hebrides (Nouvelles-Hébrides) II	112	16.00 S	167.00 E
New Holland	166	40.06 N	76.05 W
New Holstein	168	43.57 N	88.05 W
New Iberia	174	30.00 N	91.49 W
New Ireland I	116a	3.20 S	152.00 E
New Jersey □[3]	162	40.15 N	74.30 W
New Kensington	166	40.34 N	79.46 W
New Lexington	166	39.43 N	82.13 W
New London, Conn., U.S.	166	41.21 N	72.07 W
New London, Iowa, U.S.	168	40.55 N	91.24 W
New London, Wis., U.S.	168	44.23 N	88.45 W
New Madrid	174	36.36 N	89.32 W
Newmarket, Eng., U.K.	32	52.15 N	0.25 E
Newmarket, N.H., U.S.	166	43.05 N	70.56 W
New Martinsville	166	39.39 N	80.52 W
New Mexico □[3]	162	34.30 N	106.00 W
Newnan	172	33.23 N	84.48 W
New Orleans	174	29.58 N	90.07 W
New Paltz	166	41.45 N	74.05 W
New Philadelphia	166	40.30 N	81.27 W
New Plymouth	118	39.04 S	174.05 E
Newport, Eng., U.K.	32	50.42 N	1.18 W
Newport, Wales, U.K.	32	52.01 N	4.51 W
Newport, Ark., U.S.	174	35.37 N	91.17 W
Newport, Ky., U.S.	166	39.06 N	84.29 W
Newport, Maine, U.S.	166	44.50 N	69.17 W
Newport, N.H., U.S.	166	43.21 N	72.09 W
Newport, Oreg., U.S.	180	44.38 N	124.03 W
Newport, R.I., U.S.	166	41.13 N	71.18 W
Newport, Tenn., U.S.	172	35.58 N	83.11 W
Newport, Vt., U.S.	166	44.57 N	72.12 W
Newport, Wash., U.S.	180	48.11 N	117.03 W
Newport Beach	184	33.37 N	117.56 W
Newport News	172	37.04 N	76.28 W
New Port Richey	172	28.16 N	82.43 W
New Prague	168	44.32 N	93.34 W
New Providence I	130	25.02 N	77.24 W
Newquay	32	50.25 N	5.05 W
New Richmond	168	45.07 N	92.32 W
New Roads	174	30.42 N	91.26 W
New Rochelle	166	40.55 N	73.47 W
Newry	32	54.11 N	6.20 W
New Smyrna Beach	172	29.02 N	80.56 W
Newton, Ill., U.S.	174	38.59 N	88.10 W
Newton, Iowa, U.S.	168	41.42 N	93.03 W
Newton, Kans., U.S.	162	38.03 N	97.21 W
Newton, Mass., U.S.	166	42.21 N	71.11 W
Newton, Miss., U.S.	174	32.19 N	89.10 W
Newton, N.J., U.S.	166	41.03 N	74.45 W
Newton, N.C., U.S.	172	35.40 N	81.13 W
Newton Abbot	32	50.32 N	3.36 W
Newton Falls	166	41.11 N	80.59 W
Newtownabbey	32	54.42 N	5.54 W
Newtownards	32	54.36 N	5.41 W
New Ulm	168	44.19 N	94.28 W
New Westminster	160	49.12 N	122.55 W
New Whiteland	174	39.33 N	86.05 W
New York	166	40.43 N	74.01 W
New York □[3]	162	43.00 N	75.00 W
New York State Barge Canal ≅	166	43.05 N	78.43 W
New Zealand □[1]	118	41.00 S	174.00 E
Ngami, Lake ⊜	104	20.37 S	22.40 E
Ngatangiia	114	21.14 S	159.43 W
Ng'iro, Ewaso ≃	104	0.28 N	39.55 E
Ngoko ≃	104	1.40 N	16.03 E
Nguru	100	12.52 N	10.27 E
Nha-trang	82	12.15 N	109.11 E
Niagara	168	45.46 N	88.02 W
Niagara Falls, Ont., Can.	160	43.06 N	79.04 W
Niagara Falls, N.Y., U.S.	166	43.06 N	79.02 W
Niamey	100	13.31 N	2.07 E
Nias, Pulau I	82	1.05 N	97.35 E
Nicaragua □[1]	130	13.00 N	85.00 W
Nicaragua, Lago de ⊜	130	11.30 N	85.30 W
Nicastro (Lamezia Terme)	46	38.59 N	16.20 E
Nice	42	43.42 N	7.15 E
Niceville	174	30.31 N	86.29 W
Nicholasville	172	37.53 N	84.34 W
Nicobar Islands II	82	8.00 N	93.30 E
Nicolet, Lake ⊜	168	50.10 N	120.25 W
Nicollet	168	44.17 N	94.11 W
Nicosia, It.	46	37.45 N	14.24 E
Nicosia → Levkosia, Kípros	84	35.10 N	33.22 E
Nicoya, Peninsula de ≻[1]	130	10.00 N	85.25 W
Nida ≃	36	50.18 N	20.52 E
Nidd ≃	32	54.01 N	1.12 W
Nidzica	36	53.22 N	20.26 E
Niedere Tauern ⋀	36	47.18 N	14.00 E
Nienburg	36	52.38 N	9.13 E
Niger □[1]	100	16.00 N	8.00 E
Niger ≃	100	5.33 N	6.33 E
Nigeria □[1]	100	10.00 N	8.00 E
Nigrita	54	40.55 N	23.30 E
Niigata	80	37.55 N	139.03 E
Niihau I	162b	21.55 N	160.10 W
Nijmegen	36	51.50 N	5.50 E
Nikolajev	62	46.58 N	32.00 E
Nikopol'	62	47.35 N	34.25 E
Nikšić	54	42.46 N	18.56 E
Nile (Nahr an-Nīl) ≃	102	30.10 N	31.06 E
Niles, Ill., U.S.	168	42.01 N	87.49 W
Niles, Mich., U.S.	168	41.50 N	86.15 W
Niles, Ohio, U.S.	166	41.11 N	80.45 W
Nimba, Mont ▲	100	7.37 N	8.25 W
Nimba Mountains ⋀	100	7.30 N	8.30 W
Nîmes	42	43.50 N	4.21 E
Nine Degree Channel ⊔	84	9.00 N	72.50 E
Ninety Mile Beach •[2]	116	38.13 S	147.23 E
Ningbo	80	29.52 N	121.31 E
Niobrara ≃	162	42.45 N	98.00 W
Nioro du Sahel	100	15.15 N	9.35 W
Niort	42	46.19 N	0.27 W
Nipigon, Lake ⊜	160	49.50 N	88.30 W
Nipissing, Lake ⊜	160	46.17 N	80.00 W
Niš	54	43.19 N	21.54 E
Nišava ≃	54	43.22 N	21.46 E
Niscemi	46	37.08 N	14.24 E
Nisling ≃	160	62.27 N	139.30 W
Nissan ≃	28	56.40 N	12.51 E
Niterói	144	22.53 S	43.07 W
Nitra	36	48.20 N	18.05 E
Nitra ≃	36	47.46 N	18.10 E
Nitro	166	38.25 N	81.50 W
Niue □[2]	10	19.02 S	169.52 W
Nive ≃	42	43.30 N	1.29 W
Nivelles	36	50.36 N	4.20 E
Nixa	174	37.03 N	93.18 W
Nizke Beskydy ⋀	36	49.20 N	21.30 E
Nizke Tatry ⋀	36	48.54 N	19.40 E
Nižnekamsk	26	55.32 N	51.58 E
Nižnij Tagil	62	57.55 N	59.57 E
Njombe ≃	104	6.56 S	35.06 E
Nkongsamba	100	4.57 N	9.56 E
Nmai ≃	80	25.42 N	97.30 E
Nobeoka	80	32.35 N	131.40 E
Noblesville	174	40.03 N	86.01 W
Noce ≃	46	46.09 N	11.04 E
Nocera [Inferiore]	46	40.44 N	14.38 E
Nogales	178	31.20 N	110.56 W
Nogent-le-Rotrou	42	48.19 N	0.50 E
Noginsk	26	55.51 N	38.27 E
Noir, Causse ⋀[1]	42	44.10 N	3.15 E
Noirmoutier, Île de I	42	47.00 N	2.15 W
Nokia	28	61.28 N	23.30 E
Nokomis	174	39.18 N	89.18 W
Nola	46	40.55 N	14.33 E
Nolin Lake ⊜[1]	174	37.20 N	86.10 W
Nome	162a	64.30 N	165.24 W
Nong Khai	82	17.52 N	102.44 E
Noordoost Polder ◆[1]	36	52.42 N	5.45 E
Norsena Islands II	102	16.02 N	39.58 E
Norcross	172	33.57 N	84.13 W
Norden	36	53.36 N	7.12 E
Nordenham	36	53.29 N	8.28 E
Nordenšel'da, Archipelag II	64	76.45 N	96.00 E
Norderney I	36	53.42 N	7.10 E
Nordhausen	36	51.30 N	10.47 E
Nordhorn	36	52.27 N	7.05 E
Nordkapp ≻	26	71.11 N	25.48 E
Nördlingen	36	48.51 N	10.30 E
Nord-Ostsee-Kanal ≅	36	53.53 N	9.08 E
Nordpfälzer Bergland ⋀	36	49.40 N	7.40 E
Nordre Strømfjord C[2]	160	67.50 N	52.00 W
Nordstrand I	36	54.30 N	8.53 E
Norfolk, Nebr., U.S.	162	42.02 N	97.25 W
Norfolk, Va., U.S.	172	36.40 N	76.14 W
Norfolk □[6]	32	52.35 N	1.00 E
Norfolk Island □[2]	113	29.02 S	167.57 E
Norfork Lake ⊜[1]	174	36.25 N	92.10 W
Noril'sk	64	69.20 N	88.06 E
Normal, Ala., U.S.	174	34.47 N	86.34 W
Normal, Ill., U.S.	168	40.31 N	88.59 W
Norman	162	35.13 N	97.26 W
Norman, Lake ⊜[1]	172	35.35 N	80.55 W
Normanton	116	17.40 S	141.05 E
Norra Storfjället ▲	26	65.52 N	15.18 E
Nørresundby	28	57.04 N	9.55 E
Norris Lake ⊜[1]	172	36.20 N	83.55 W
Norristown	166	40.07 N	75.21 W
Norrköping	28	58.36 N	16.11 E
Norrtälje	28	59.46 N	18.42 E
Norte, Canal do ⊔	144	0.30 N	50.30 W
North, Cape ≻[2]	160	47.02 N	60.25 W
North Adams	166	42.42 N	73.07 W
Northampton, Eng., U.K.	32	52.14 N	0.54 W
Northampton, Mass., U.S.	166	42.19 N	72.38 W
Northampton, Pa., U.S.	166	40.41 N	75.30 W
Northamptonshire □[6]	32	52.20 N	0.50 W
North Andaman I	84	13.15 N	92.55 E
North Atlanta	172	33.51 N	84.21 W
North Augusta	172	33.30 N	81.58 W
North Bay	160	46.19 N	79.28 W
North Bend	180	43.24 N	124.14 W
North Canton	166	40.53 N	81.24 W
North Carolina □[3]	162	35.30 N	80.00 W
North Channel ⊔, Ont., Can.	160	46.02 N	82.50 W
North Channel ⊔, U.K.	32	55.10 N	5.40 W
North Charleston	172	32.53 N	80.00 W
North Chicago	168	42.20 N	87.51 W
North College Hill	166	39.12 N	84.32 W
North Conway	166	44.03 N	71.08 W
North Crossett	174	33.11 N	91.57 W
North Dakota □[3]	162	47.30 N	100.15 W
North Downs ⋀[1]	32	51.20 N	0.10 E
North East, Md., U.S.	166	39.36 N	75.56 W
North East, Pa., U.S.	166	42.13 N	79.50 W
Northeim	36	51.42 N	10.00 E
Northern Indian Lake ⊜	160	57.20 N	97.20 W
Northern Ireland □[8]	32	54.40 N	6.45 W
Northfield, Minn., U.S.	168	44.27 N	93.09 W
Northfield, Vt., U.S.	166	44.09 N	72.40 W
North Fond du Lac	168	43.38 N	88.28 W
North Foreland ≻	32	51.23 N	1.27 E
North Fort Myers	172	26.40 N	81.54 W
North Frisian Islands II	26	54.50 N	8.12 E
Northglenn	178	39.54 N	104.58 W
North Gulfport	174	30.25 N	89.06 W
North Haven	166	41.23 N	72.52 W
North Henderson	172	36.21 N	78.22 W
North Highlands	184	38.40 N	121.23 W
North Hudson	168	44.59 N	92.46 W
North Island I	118	39.00 S	176.00 E
North Las Vegas	184	36.12 N	115.07 W
North La Veta Pass)(	178	37.37 N	105.11 W
North Little Rock	174	34.46 N	92.14 W
North Manchester	174	41.00 N	85.46 W
North Manitou Island I	168	45.06 N	86.01 W
North Mankato	168	44.10 N	94.00 W
North Miami	172	25.54 N	80.11 W
North Miami Beach	172	25.56 N	80.09 W
North Muskegon	168	43.15 N	86.17 W
North Ogden	178	41.18 N	112.00 W
North Palisade ▲	184	37.06 N	118.31 W
North Palm Beach	172	26.49 N	80.04 W
North Park	168	42.20 N	89.02 W
North Platte	162	41.08 N	100.46 W
North Platte ≃	162	41.15 N	100.45 W
Northport	174	33.14 N	87.35 W
North Salt Lake	178	40.50 N	111.55 W
North Saskatchewan ≃	160	53.15 N	105.06 W
North Sea ▼[2]	20	55.20 N	3.00 E
Northumberland □[6]	32	55.15 N	2.05 W
North Vernon	174	39.00 N	85.38 W
Northwest Territories □[4]	160	70.00 N	100.00 W
North Wilkesboro	172	36.10 N	81.09 W
Northwood	168	43.27 N	93.13 W
North Yorkshire □[6]	32	54.15 N	1.30 W
Norton	172	36.56 N	82.38 W
Norton Sound ⊔	162a	63.50 N	164.00 W
Nortonville	174	39.25 N	95.20 W
Norwalk, Conn., U.S.	166	41.07 N	73.27 W
Norwalk, Iowa, U.S.	168	41.29 N	93.41 W
Norwalk, Ohio, U.S.	166	41.15 N	82.37 W
Norway, Maine, U.S.	166	44.13 N	70.32 W
Norway, Mich., U.S.	168	45.47 N	87.55 W
Norway □[1]	26	62.00 N	10.00 E
Norwegian Sea ▼[2]	26	70.00 N	2.00 E
Norwich, Eng., U.K.	32	52.38 N	1.18 E
Norwich, Conn., U.S.	166	41.32 N	72.05 W
Norwich, N.Y., U.S.	166	42.32 N	75.31 W
Norwood, Mass., U.S.	166	42.11 N	71.12 W
Norwood, Minn., U.S.	168	44.46 N	93.55 W
Norwood, N.C., U.S.	172	35.14 N	80.07 W
Norwood, Ohio, U.S.	166	39.10 N	84.28 W
Norwoodville	168	41.39 N	93.33 W
Nossi-Bé I	104	13.20 S	48.15 E
Nossob (Nossop) ≃	104	26.55 S	20.37 E
Noteć ≃	36	52.44 N	15.26 E
Notikewin ≃	160	57.15 N	117.05 W
Noto	46	36.53 N	15.05 E
Noto, Golfo di C	46	36.50 N	15.15 E
Noto-hantō ≻[1]	80	37.20 N	137.00 E
Notre Dame, Monts ⋀	160	48.10 N	68.00 W
Nottingham	32	52.58 N	1.10 W
Nottinghamshire □[6]	32	53.00 N	1.00 W
Nouadhibou	100	20.54 N	17.04 W
Nouakchott	100	18.06 N	15.57 W
Nouméa	112	22.16 S	166.27 E
Nouveau-Québec, Cratère du •[6]	160	61.17 N	73.40 W
Nouvelle-Calédonie I	112	21.30 S	165.30 E
Nova Friburgo	144	22.16 S	42.32 W
Novaja Zeml'a II	62	74.00 N	57.00 E
Novara	46	45.28 N	8.38 E
Nova Scotia □[4]	160	45.00 N	63.00 W
Novato	184	38.06 N	122.34 W
Nova Zagora	54	42.29 N	26.01 E
Novelda	50	38.23 N	0.46 W
Nové Město nad Váhom	36	48.46 N	17.49 E
Nové Zámky	36	47.59 N	18.11 E
Novgorod	26	58.31 N	31.17 E
Novi Bečej	54	45.36 N	20.08 E
Novi Ligure	46	44.46 N	8.47 E
Novi Pazar, Blg.	54	43.21 N	27.12 E
Novi Pazar, Jugo.	54	43.08 N	20.31 E
Novi Sad	54	45.15 N	19.50 E
Novočerkassk	62	47.25 N	40.06 E
Novokujbyševsk	26	53.07 N	49.58 E
Novokuzneck	64	53.45 N	87.06 E
Novomoskovsk	62	54.05 N	38.13 E
Novorossijsk	62	44.45 N	37.45 E
Novošachtinsk	62	47.47 N	39.56 E
Novosibirsk	64	55.02 N	82.55 E
Novosibirskije Ostrova II	64	75.00 N	142.00 E
Novosibirskoje Vodochranilišče ⊜[1]	62	54.35 N	82.35 E
Nový Bohumín	36	49.56 N	18.20 E
Nový Jičín	36	49.36 N	18.00 E
Nowa Ruda	36	50.35 N	16.31 E
Nowa Sól (Neusalz)	36	51.48 N	15.44 E
Nowata	174	36.42 N	95.38 W
Nowshāk ▲	84	36.26 N	71.50 E
Nowshera	84	34.01 N	71.59 E
Nowy Dwór Mazowiecki	36	52.26 N	20.43 E
Nowy Sącz	36	49.38 N	20.42 E
Nowy Targ	36	49.29 N	20.02 E
Noya ≃	50	41.28 N	1.56 E
Noyon	42	49.35 N	3.00 E
Nsawam	100	5.50 N	0.20 W
Ntem ≃	100	2.15 N	9.45 E
Nūbah, Jibāl an- ⋀	102	12.00 N	30.45 E
Nubian Desert ◆[2]	102	20.30 N	33.00 E
Nueces ≃	162	27.50 N	97.30 W
Nueva, Isla I	146	55.13 S	66.30 W
Nueva Gerona	130	21.53 N	82.48 W
Nueva Rosita	130	27.57 N	101.13 W
Nuevitas	130	21.33 N	77.16 W
Nuevo Laredo	130	27.30 N	99.31 W
Nûgssuaq ≻[1]	160	71.45 N	53.00 W
Nullarbor Plain ≚	116	31.00 S	129.00 E
Numazu	80	35.06 N	138.52 E
Nuneaton	32	52.32 N	1.28 W
Nunivak Island I	162a	60.00 N	166.30 W
Nuoro	46	40.19 N	9.20 E
Nürnberg	36	49.27 N	11.04 E
Nurra ◆[1]	46	40.45 N	8.15 E
Nürtingen	36	48.38 N	9.20 E
Nusa Tenggara (Lesser Sunda Islands) II	82	9.00 S	120.00 E
Nushan ≃	80	26.50 N	99.03 E
Nutter Fort	166	39.20 N	80.19 W
Nuweveldberge ⋀	104	32.13 S	21.40 E
Nyack	166	41.05 N	73.55 W
Nyala	102	12.03 N	24.53 E
Nyanza	104	2.21 S	29.45 E
Nyasa, Lake ⊜	104	12.00 S	34.30 E
Nyborg	28	55.19 N	10.48 E
Nybro	28	56.45 N	15.54 E
Nyíregyháza	36	47.59 N	21.43 E
Nykøbing	28	54.46 N	11.53 E
Nyköping	28	58.45 N	17.00 E
Nymburk	36	50.11 N	15.03 E
Nynäshamn	28	58.54 N	17.57 E
Nyon	42	46.23 N	6.14 E
Nyong ≃	100	3.17 N	9.54 E
Nysa	36	50.29 N	17.20 E
Nysa Kłodzka ≃	36	50.49 N	17.50 E
Nzérékoré	100	7.45 N	8.49 W
Nzi ≃	100	5.57 N	4.50 W
O			
Oahe, Lake ⊜[1]	162	45.30 N	100.25 W
Oahu I	162b	21.30 N	158.00 W
Oakdale	174	30.49 N	92.40 W
Oak Grove	174	32.52 N	91.23 W
Oak Harbor	180	48.18 N	122.39 W
Oak Hill	166	37.59 N	81.09 W
Oak Knolls	184	34.51 N	120.27 W
Oakland, Calif., U.S.	184	37.47 N	122.13 W
Oakland, Iowa, U.S.	174	41.19 N	95.23 W
Oakland, Maine, U.S.	166	44.33 N	69.43 W
Oakland City	174	38.20 N	87.21 W
Oakland Park	172	26.12 N	80.07 W
Oak Lawn	168	41.43 N	87.45 W
Oak Park	168	41.53 N	87.48 W
Oakridge, Oreg., U.S.	180	43.45 N	122.28 W
Oak Ridge, Tenn., U.S.	172	36.01 N	84.16 W
Oamaru	118	45.06 S	170.58 E
Oaxaca	130	17.00 N	96.30 W
Ob' ≃	62	66.45 N	69.30 E
Ober Ennstal V	36	47.28 N	14.10 E
Oberhausen	36	51.28 N	6.50 E
Oberlin	166	41.18 N	82.13 W
Oberursel	36	50.11 N	8.35 E
Obihiro	80	42.55 N	143.12 E
Obock	102	11.59 N	43.16 E
Obra ≃	36	52.36 N	15.28 E
Obščij Syrt ▲	62	52.00 N	51.30 E
Obskaja Guba C	62	69.00 N	73.00 E
Obuasi	100	6.14 N	1.39 W
Ocala	172	29.11 N	82.07 W
Ocaña	144	8.15 N	73.20 W
Occidental, Cordillera ⋀, Col.	144	5.00 N	76.00 W
Occidental, Cordillera ⋀, Perú	144	10.00 S	77.00 W
Ocean City, Md., U.S.	166	38.20 N	75.05 W
Ocean City, N.J., U.S.	166	39.16 N	74.36 W
Oceanside	184	33.12 N	117.23 W
Ocean Springs	174	30.25 N	88.50 W
Ochlockonee ≃	172	29.58 N	84.21 W
Ochtrup	36	52.13 N	7.11 E
Ocilla	172	31.36 N	83.15 W
Ocklawaha, Lake ⊜[1]	172	29.30 N	81.50 W
Ocmulgee ≃	172	31.58 N	82.32 W
Ocoee	172	28.35 N	81.33 W
Oconee ≃	172	31.58 N	82.32 W
Oconomowoc	168	43.07 N	88.30 W
Oconto	168	44.43 N	87.52 W
Oconto Falls	168	44.52 N	88.08 W
Ocotal	130	13.38 N	86.29 W
Ocotlán	130	20.21 N	102.46 W
Ocracoke Island I	172	35.09 N	75.53 W
Ocreza, Ribeira da ≃	50	39.32 N	7.50 W
Oda	100	5.55 N	0.59 W
Oda, Jabal ▲	102	20.21 N	36.39 E
Ödemiş	54	38.13 N	27.59 E
Odendaalsrus	104	27.48 S	26.45 E
Odense	28	55.24 N	10.23 E
Odenwald ⋀	36	49.40 N	9.00 E
Oder (Odra) ≃	36	53.32 N	14.38 E
Oderbruch ◆[1]	36	52.40 N	14.15 E
Odessa, S.S.S.R.	62	46.28 N	30.44 E
Odessa, Mo., U.S.	174	39.00 N	93.57 W
Odessa, Tex., U.S.	162	31.51 N	102.22 W
Odessa, Wash., U.S.	180	47.20 N	118.41 W
Odorheiu Secuiesc	54	46.18 N	25.18 E
Oelde	36	51.49 N	8.08 E
Oelsnitz	36	50.24 N	12.10 E
Oelwein	168	42.41 N	91.55 W
O'Fallon	174	38.49 N	90.42 W
Ofanto ≃	46	41.22 N	16.13 E
Offenbach	36	50.08 N	8.47 E
Offenburg	36	48.28 N	7.57 E
Ogallala	162	41.08 N	101.43 W
Ogbomosho	100	8.08 N	4.15 E
Ogden, Iowa, U.S.	168	42.02 N	94.02 W
Ogden, Utah, U.S.	178	41.14 N	111.58 W
Ogden, Mount ▲	162a	58.26 N	133.23 W
Ogdensburg	166	44.42 N	75.29 W
Ogeechee ≃	172	31.51 N	81.06 W
Ogilvie Mountains ⋀	160	65.00 N	139.30 W
Oglesby	168	41.18 N	89.04 W
Ogliastra ◆[1]	46	40.00 N	9.30 E
Oglio ≃	46	45.02 N	10.39 E
Ogooué ≃	104	0.49 S	9.00 E
O'Higgins, Lago (Lago San Martín) ⊜	146	49.00 S	72.40 W
Ohio □[3]	162	40.15 N	82.45 W
Ohio ≃	162	36.59 N	89.08 W
Ohrid	54	41.07 N	20.47 E
Ohrid, Lake ⊜	54	41.02 N	20.43 E
Oil City	166	41.26 N	79.42 W
Oildale	184	35.25 N	119.01 W
Oise ≃	42	49.00 N	2.04 E
Ōita	80	33.14 N	131.36 E
Ojos del Salado, Nevado ▲	146	27.06 S	68.32 W
Oka ≃	62	56.20 N	43.59 E
Okanogan	180	48.22 N	119.35 W
Okanogan ≃	162	48.06 N	119.43 W
Okāra	84	30.49 N	73.27 E
Okavango (Cubango) ≃	104	18.50 S	22.25 E
Okavango Swamp ☷	104	18.45 S	22.45 E
Okayama	80	34.39 N	133.55 E
Okeechobee	172	27.15 N	80.50 W
Okeechobee, Lake ⊜	172	26.55 N	80.45 W
Okefenokee Swamp ☷	172	30.42 N	82.20 W
Okemos	168	42.43 N	84.26 W
Okhotsk, Sea of (Ochotskoje More) ▼[2]	64	53.00 N	150.00 E
Okinawa-jima I	80	26.30 N	128.00 E
Oklahoma □[3]	162	35.30 N	98.00 W
Oklahoma City	162	35.28 N	97.32 W
Okmulgee	162	35.37 N	95.58 W
Okolona, Ky., U.S.	174	38.08 N	85.41 W
Okolona, Miss., U.S.	174	34.00 N	88.45 W
Oksskolten ▲	26	65.59 N	14.15 E
Okt'abr'skoj Revol'ucii, Ostrov I	64	79.30 N	97.00 E
Olanchito	130	15.30 N	86.35 W
Öland I	28	56.45 N	16.38 E
Olathe	174	38.53 N	94.49 W
Olavarría	146	36.54 S	60.17 W
Oława	36	50.57 N	17.17 E
Olbia	46	40.55 N	9.29 E
Old Crow	162a	67.35 N	139.50 W
Old Crow ≃	162a	67.35 N	139.50 W
Oldenburg	36	53.08 N	8.13 E
Oldenburg [in Holstein]	36	54.17 N	10.52 E
Oldenzaal	36	52.19 N	6.56 E
Old Faithful Geyser ▾[4]	180	44.30 N	110.45 W
Old Forge	166	41.22 N	75.44 W
Oldham	32	53.33 N	2.07 W
Old Orchard Beach	166	43.31 N	70.23 W
Old Speck Mountain ▲	166	44.34 N	70.57 W
Old Town	166	44.56 N	68.39 W
Old Wives Lake ⊜	160	50.06 N	106.00 W
Olean	166	42.05 N	78.26 W
Olen'okskij Zaliv C	64	73.20 N	121.00 E
Oléron, Île d' I	42	45.56 N	1.15 W
Oleśnica	36	51.13 N	17.23 E
Olhão	50	37.02 N	8.50 W
Olib, Otok I	46	44.22 N	14.48 E
Ólimbos ▲, Ellás	54	40.05 N	22.21 E
Ólimbos ▲, Kípros	84	34.56 N	32.52 E
Olinda	144	8.01 S	34.51 W
Oliva	50	38.55 N	0.07 W
Oliva de la Frontera	50	38.16 N	6.55 W
Olivehurst	184	39.06 N	121.34 W
Oliver Springs	172	36.03 N	84.20 W
Olney	174	38.44 N	88.05 W
Olomouc	36	49.36 N	17.16 E
Olongapo	82	14.50 N	120.16 E
Oloron-Sainte-Marie	42	43.12 N	0.36 W
Olot	50	42.11 N	2.29 E
Olpe	36	51.02 N	7.52 E
Olsztyn (Allenstein)	36	53.48 N	20.29 E
Olt ≃	54	43.43 N	24.51 E
Olten	42	47.21 N	7.54 E
Olteniţa	54	44.05 N	26.39 E
Oluan Pi ≻	80	21.54 N	120.51 E
Ol'utorskij, Mys ≻	64	59.55 N	170.27 E
Olympia	180	47.03 N	122.53 W
Olympic Mountains ⋀	180	47.50 N	123.45 W
Olympus, Mount ▲	180	47.48 N	123.43 W
Omagh	32	54.36 N	7.18 W
Omaha	174	41.16 N	95.57 W
Omak	180	48.24 N	119.31 W
Oman □[1]	84	22.00 N	58.00 E
Oman, Gulf of C	84	24.30 N	58.30 E
Omegna	46	45.53 N	8.24 E
Ometepe, Isla de I	130	11.30 N	85.35 W
Omineca ≃	160	56.05 N	124.30 W
Omo ≃	102	4.32 N	36.04 E
Omro	168	44.02 N	88.44 W
Omsk	64	55.00 N	73.24 E
Omul ▲	54	45.26 N	25.26 E
Omulew ≃	36	53.05 N	21.32 E
Ōmuta	80	33.02 N	130.27 E
Onalaska	168	43.53 N	91.14 W
Onda	50	39.58 N	0.15 W
Ondava ≃	36	48.27 N	21.48 E
Ondo	100	7.04 N	4.47 E
Oneco	172	27.27 N	82.33 W
Onega ≃	62	63.58 N	37.55 E
Oneida, N.Y., U.S.	166	43.06 N	75.39 W
Oneida, Tenn., U.S.	172	36.30 N	84.31 W
Oneida Lake ⊜	166	43.13 N	76.00 W
O'Neill	162	42.27 N	98.39 W
Oneonta, Ala., U.S.	174	33.57 N	86.29 W
Oneonta, N.Y., U.S.	166	42.27 N	75.04 W
Onežskoje Ozero ⊜	62	61.30 N	35.45 E
Onitsha	100	6.09 N	6.47 E
Onon ≃	64	51.42 N	115.50 E
Onslow Bay C	172	34.20 N	77.20 W
Ontario, Calif., U.S.	184	34.04 N	117.39 W
Ontario, Ohio, U.S.	166	40.46 N	82.35 W
Ontario, Oreg., U.S.	180	44.02 N	116.58 W
Ontario □[4]	160	51.00 N	85.00 W
Ontario, Lake ⊜	162	43.45 N	78.00 W
Onteniente	50	38.49 N	0.37 W
Ontonagon	168	46.52 N	89.19 W
Oologah Lake ⊜[1]	174	36.33 N	95.36 W

Name	Page	Lat	Long
Oostelijk Flevoland ↜¹	36	52.30 N	5.45 E
Oostende (Ostende)	36	51.13 N	2.55 E
Oosterhout	36	51.38 N	4.51 E
Opava	36	49.56 N	17.54 E
Opelika	174	32.39 N	85.23 W
Opelousas	174	30.32 N	92.05 W
Opladen	36	51.04 N	7.00 E
Opoczno	36	51.23 N	20.17 E
Opole (Oppeln)	36	50.41 N	17.55 E
Opp	174	31.17 N	86.22 W
Oppeln → Opole	36	50.41 N	17.55 E
Opportunity	180	47.39 N	117.15 W
Oracle	178	32.37 N	110.46 W
Oradea	54	47.03 N	21.57 E
Oran	100	35.43 N	0.43 W
Orange, Austl.	116	33.17 S	149.06 E
Orange, Fr.	42	44.08 N	4.48 E
Orange, Tex., U.S.	184	30.01 N	93.44 W
Orange, Va., U.S.	166	38.15 N	78.07 W
Orange (Oranje) ≃	104	28.41 S	16.28 E
Orange, Cabo �‾	144	4.24 N	51.33 W
Orangeburg	172	33.30 N	80.52 W
Orange Park	172	30.10 N	81.42 W
Oranienburg	36	52.45 N	13.14 E
Oranjestad	130	12.33 N	70.06 W
Orăştie	54	45.50 N	23.12 E
Orb ≃	42	43.15 N	3.18 E
Orbetello	46	42.27 N	11.13 E
Orbieu ≃	42	43.14 N	2.54 E
Orce ≃	50	37.44 N	2.28 W
Orchard Homes	180	46.55 N	114.04 W
Orchard Mesa	178	39.01 N	108.30 W
Orchard Park	166	42.43 N	78.45 W
Orchila, Isla l	144	11.48 N	66.09 W
Orchon ≃	80	50.21 N	106.05 E
Ordžonikidze	62	43.03 N	44.40 E
Örebro	28	59.17 N	15.13 E
Orechovo-Zujevo	26	55.49 N	38.59 E
Oregon, Ill., U.S.	168	42.01 N	89.20 W
Oregon, Ohio, U.S.	166	41.38 N	83.28 W
Oregon □³	162	44.00 N	121.00 W
Oregon City	180	45.21 N	122.36 W
Orem	178	40.19 N	111.42 W
Orenburg	62	51.54 N	55.06 E
Orense	50	42.20 N	7.51 W
Orestiás	54	41.30 N	26.31 E
Orford Ness �‾	32	52.05 N	1.34 E
Orient	174	41.12 N	94.25 W
Oriental, Cordillera ⱄ, Col.	144	6.00 N	73.00 W
Oriental, Cordillera ⱄ, Perú	144	11.00 S	74.00 W
Orihuela	50	38.05 N	0.57 W
Orillia	160	44.37 N	79.25 W
Orinoco ≃	144	8.37 N	62.15 W
Oristano	46	40.00 N	8.40 E
Orizaba	130	18.51 N	97.06 W
Orkney Islands □⁴	32	59.00 N	3.00 W
Orlando	172	28.32 N	81.23 W
Orléanais □⁹	42	47.50 N	2.00 E
Orléans, Fr.	42	47.55 N	1.54 E
Orleans, Vt., U.S.	166	44.49 N	72.12 W
Orléans, Canal d' ⁼	42	47.54 N	1.55 E
Orlová	36	49.50 N	18.24 E
Ormoc	82	11.00 N	124.37 E
Ormond Beach	172	29.17 N	81.02 W
Örnsköldsvik	28	63.18 N	18.43 E
Orofino	180	46.29 N	116.15 W
Or'ol	62	52.59 N	36.05 E
Orono	166	44.53 N	68.40 W
Orosei, Golfo di ⊂	46	40.10 N	9.50 E
Orosháza	36	46.34 N	20.40 E
Oroszlány	36	47.30 N	18.19 E
Oroville, Calif., U.S.	184	39.31 N	121.33 W
Oroville, Wash., U.S.	180	48.56 N	119.26 W
Oroville, Lake ⊜¹	184	39.32 N	121.25 W
Orrville	166	40.50 N	81.46 W
Orša	26	54.30 N	30.24 E
Orsasjön ⊜	28	61.07 N	14.34 E
Orta Nova	46	41.19 N	15.42 E
Ortegal, Cabo ↾	50	43.45 N	7.53 W
Orthon ≃	144	10.50 S	66.04 W
Ortigueira, Ría de ⊂¹	50	43.42 N	7.51 W
Orting	180	47.06 N	122.12 W
Ortles ⋀	46	46.31 N	10.33 E
Ortona	46	42.21 N	14.24 E
Orvieto	46	42.43 N	12.07 E
Orzyc ≃	36	52.47 N	21.13 E
Oš	62	40.33 N	72.48 E
Osa, Península de ↾¹	130	8.34 N	83.31 W
Osage	168	43.17 N	92.49 W
Osage ≃	174	38.35 N	91.57 W
Osage City	174	38.38 N	95.50 W
Ōsaka	80	34.40 N	135.30 E
Osâm ≃	54	43.42 N	24.51 E
Osawatomie	174	38.31 N	94.57 W
Osburn	180	47.30 N	116.00 W
Osceola, Ark., U.S.	174	35.42 N	89.58 W
Osceola, Iowa, U.S.	168	41.02 N	93.46 W
Oschatz	36	51.17 N	13.07 E
Oschersleben	36	52.01 N	11.13 E
Oshawa	160	43.54 N	78.51 W
Oshkosh	168	44.01 N	88.33 W
Oshogbo	100	7.47 N	4.34 E
Osijek	54	45.33 N	18.41 E
Osimo	46	43.29 N	13.29 E
Oskaloosa, Iowa, U.S.	168	41.17 N	92.39 W
Oskaloosa, Kans., U.S.	174	39.13 N	95.19 W
Oskarshamn	28	57.16 N	16.26 E
Oslo	28	59.55 N	10.45 E
Oslofjorden ⊂²	28	59.20 N	10.35 E
Osnabrück	36	52.16 N	8.02 E
Osorno	146	40.34 S	73.09 W
Oss	36	51.46 N	5.31 E
Ossa, Mount ⋀	116	41.54 S	146.01 E
Osse ≃, Fr.	42	44.07 N	0.17 E
Osse ≃, Nig.	100	6.10 N	5.20 E
Osseo	168	44.35 N	91.12 W
Ossining	166	41.10 N	73.52 W
Ostende → Oostende	36	51.13 N	2.55 E
Osterholz-Scharmbeck	36	53.14 N	8.47 E
Osterode	36	51.44 N	10.11 E
Östersund	28	63.11 N	14.39 E
Ostrava	36	49.50 N	18.17 E
Ostredok ⋀	36	48.55 N	19.04 E
Ostróda	36	53.43 N	19.59 E
Ostrołęka	36	53.06 N	21.34 E
Ostrov ≃¹	36	50.17 N	12.57 E
Ostrov ↜¹	36	47.55 N	17.35 E
Ostrowiec Świętokrzyski	36	50.57 N	21.23 E
Ostrów Mazowiecka	36	52.49 N	21.54 E
Ostrów Wielkopolski	36	51.39 N	17.49 E
Osum ≃	54	40.44 N	17.35 E
Osumi ≃	54	40.48 N	19.52 E
Ōsumi-shotō ‖	80	30.30 N	130.00 E
Osuna	50	37.14 N	5.07 W
Oswego, Kans., U.S.	174	37.10 N	95.06 W
Oswego, N.Y., U.S.	166	43.27 N	76.31 W
Oswestry	32	52.52 N	3.04 W
Oświęcim	36	50.03 N	19.12 E
Otaru	80	43.13 N	141.00 E
Othello	180	46.50 N	119.10 W
Oti ≃	100	8.40 N	0.13 E
Otjiwarongo	104	20.29 S	16.36 E
Otoskwin ≃	160	52.13 N	88.06 W
Otra ≃	28	58.09 N	8.00 E
Otradnyj	26	53.22 N	51.21 E
Otranto, Strait of ≃¹	54	40.00 N	19.00 E
Otrokovice	36	49.13 N	17.31 E
Otsego	168	42.27 N	85.42 W
Ōtsu	80	35.00 N	135.52 E
Ottawa, Ont., Can.	160	45.25 N	75.42 W
Ottawa, Ill., U.S.	168	41.21 N	88.51 W
Ottawa, Kans., U.S.	174	38.37 N	95.16 W
Ottawa, Ohio, U.S.	166	41.01 N	84.03 W
Ottawa ≃	160	45.20 N	73.58 W
Ottumwa	168	41.01 N	92.25 W
Otwock	36	52.07 N	21.16 E
Ötztaler Alpen ⱄ	46	46.45 N	10.55 E
Ou ≃, Afr.	102	9.18 N	18.14 E
Ou ≃, Lao	82	20.04 N	102.13 E
Ouachita ≃	174	31.38 N	91.49 W
Ouachita, Lake ⊜¹	174	34.40 N	93.25 W
Ouachita Mountains ⱄ	174	34.40 N	94.25 W
Ouagadougou	100	12.22 N	1.31 W
Ouahigouya	100	13.35 N	2.25 W
Ouaka ≃	102	4.59 N	19.56 E
Ouarane ◂¹	100	21.00 N	10.30 W
Ouargla	100	31.59 N	5.25 E
Oubangui (Ubangi) ≃	100	1.15 N	17.50 E
Oudenaarde	36	50.51 N	3.36 E
Oudtshoorn	104	33.35 S	22.14 E
Ouémé ≃	100	6.29 N	2.32 E
Ouenza	46	35.57 N	8.04 E
Ouessant, Île d' l	42	48.28 N	5.05 W
Ouezzane	100	34.52 N	5.35 W
Ouidah	100	6.22 N	2.05 E
Oujda	100	34.41 N	1.45 W
Oulu	28	65.01 N	25.28 E
Oulujärvi ⊜	28	64.20 N	27.15 E
Oulujoki ≃	28	65.01 N	25.25 E
Oum er Rbia, Oued ≃	100	33.19 N	8.21 W
Ouro Prêto	144	20.23 S	43.30 W
Ourthe ≃	36	50.38 N	5.35 E
Ouse ≃	32	53.42 N	0.41 W
Oust ≃	42	47.39 N	2.06 W
Ovalle	146	30.36 S	71.12 W
Overflakkee l	36	51.45 N	4.10 E
Overland Park	174	38.59 N	94.40 W
Overton	184	36.33 N	114.27 W
Oviedo	50	43.22 N	5.50 W
Oviksfjällen ⱄ	28	63.00 N	13.51 E
Owatonna	168	44.05 N	93.14 W
Owego	166	42.06 N	76.16 W
Owens ≃	184	36.31 N	117.57 W
Owensboro	174	37.46 N	87.07 W
Owens Lake ⊜	184	36.25 N	117.56 W
Owen Sound	160	44.34 N	80.56 W
Owen Stanley Range ⱄ	116a	9.20 S	147.55 E
Owensville	174	38.21 N	91.29 W
Owl ≃	160	57.51 N	92.44 W
Owo	100	7.15 N	5.37 E
Owosso	168	43.00 N	84.10 W
Owyhee ≃	180	43.46 N	117.02 W
Oxelösund	28	58.40 N	17.06 E
Oxford, Eng., U.K.	32	51.46 N	1.15 W
Oxford, Ala., U.S.	174	33.37 N	85.50 W
Oxford, Mich., U.S.	168	42.49 N	83.16 W
Oxford, Miss., U.S.	174	34.22 N	89.32 W
Oxford, N.C., U.S.	172	36.19 N	78.35 W
Oxford, Ohio, U.S.	166	39.30 N	84.44 W
Oxford, Pa., U.S.	166	39.47 N	75.59 W
Oxfordshire □⁶	32	51.50 N	1.15 W
Oxnard	184	34.12 N	119.11 W
Oyo	100	7.51 N	3.56 E
Oyonnax	42	46.15 N	5.40 E
Ozamiz	82	8.08 N	123.50 E
Ozark, Ala., U.S.	174	31.28 N	85.38 W
Ozark, Ark., U.S.	174	35.29 N	93.50 W
Ozark, Mo., U.S.	174	37.01 N	93.12 W
Ozark Reservoir ⊜¹	174	35.35 N	94.00 W
Ozarks, Lake of the ⊜¹	174	38.10 N	92.50 W
Ózd	36	48.14 N	20.18 E
Ozieri	46	40.35 N	9.00 E
Ozorków	36	51.58 N	19.19 E

Name	Page	Lat	Long
P			
Paarl	104	33.45 S	18.56 E
Pabianice	36	51.40 N	19.22 E
Pachino	46	36.42 N	15.06 E
Pachuca	130	20.07 N	98.44 W
Pacific	174	38.29 N	90.45 W
Pacifica	184	37.38 N	122.29 W
Pacific Grove	184	36.38 N	121.56 W
Pacific Islands Trust Territory □²	82	10.00 N	143.00 E
Padang	82	0.57 S	100.21 E
Paden City	166	39.36 N	80.56 W
Paderborn	36	51.43 N	8.45 E
Padirac, Gouffre de ⁵	42	44.44 N	1.27 E
Padma → Ganges ≃	84	23.22 N	90.32 E
Padova	46	45.25 N	11.53 E
Paducah	174	37.05 N	88.36 W
Pădurea Craiului, Munţii ⱄ	54	46.55 N	22.20 E
Paektu-san ⋀	80	42.00 N	128.03 E
Pagalu l	104	1.25 S	5.36 E
Paget, Mount ⋀	113	54.26 S	36.33 W
Pago Pago	113	14.16 S	170.42 W
Pago Pago Harbor ⊂	113	14.17 S	170.40 W
Pagosa Spring	178	37.16 N	107.01 W
Pahala	162b	19.12 N	155.29 W
Pahang ≃	82	3.32 N	103.28 E
Pahokee	172	26.49 N	80.40 W
Paignton	32	50.26 N	3.34 W
Päijänne ⊜	28	61.35 N	25.30 E
Painesville	166	41.43 N	81.15 W
Painted Desert ◂²	178	36.00 N	111.20 W
Painted Rock Reservoir ⊜¹	178	33.00 N	112.50 W
Paintsville	172	37.49 N	82.48 W
Paisley	32	55.50 N	4.26 W
Paj-Choj ⱄ²	62	69.00 N	63.00 E
Pajjer, Gora ⋀	62	66.42 N	64.25 E
Pakanbaru	82	0.32 N	101.27 E
Pakaraima Mountains ⱄ	144	5.30 N	60.40 W
Pakistan (Pākistān) □¹	84	30.00 N	70.00 E
Pakokku	82	21.20 N	95.05 E
Paks	36	46.39 N	18.53 E
Palagonia	46	37.19 N	14.45 E
Palagruža, Otoci ‖	46	42.24 N	16.15 E
Palapye	104	22.37 S	27.06 E
Palatka	172	29.39 N	81.38 W
Palau Islands ‖	82	7.30 N	134.30 E
Palawan l	82	9.30 N	118.30 E
Palembang	82	2.55 S	104.45 E
Palencia	50	42.01 N	4.32 W
Palermo, Golfo di ⊂	46	38.07 N	13.21 E
Palestine, Ill., U.S.	174	39.00 N	87.37 W
Palestine, Tex., U.S.	162	31.46 N	95.38 W
Palisades Reservoir ⊜¹	180	43.20 N	111.05 W
Palk Strait ⋃	84	10.00 N	79.45 E
Pallastunturi ⋀	26	68.06 N	24.00 E
Pallier	112	14.53 S	166.35 E
Palma, Bahía de ⊂	50	39.27 N	2.35 E
Palma [de Mallorca]	50	39.34 N	2.39 E
Palma di Montechiaro	46	37.11 N	13.46 E
Palmas, Cape ↾	100	4.22 N	7.44 W
Palmas, Golfo di ⊂	46	39.00 N	8.30 E
Palma Soriano	130	20.13 N	76.00 W
Palm Bay	172	28.02 N	80.35 W
Palm Beach	172	26.42 N	80.02 W
Palmdale	184	34.35 N	118.07 W
Palmerston North	118	40.21 S	175.37 E
Palmerton	166	40.48 N	75.37 W
Palmetto, Fla., U.S.	172	27.31 N	82.35 W
Palmetto, Ga., U.S.	172	33.31 N	84.40 W
Palmi	46	38.21 N	15.51 E
Palmira	144	3.32 N	76.16 W
Palm Springs	184	33.50 N	116.33 W
Palmyra, Mo., U.S.	174	39.48 N	91.31 W
Palmyra, N.Y., U.S.	166	43.04 N	77.14 W
Palmyra, Pa., U.S.	166	40.18 N	76.36 W
Palo Alto	184	37.27 N	122.09 W
Palomar Mountain ⋀	184	33.22 N	116.50 W
Palos, Cabo de ↾	50	37.38 N	0.41 W
Pamiers	42	43.07 N	1.36 E
Pamir ⱄ, As.	62	38.00 N	73.00 E
Pamir ⱄ, S.S.S.R.	62	38.00 N	73.00 E
Pamlico Sound ⋃	172	35.20 N	75.55 W
Pampa	162	35.32 N	100.58 W
Pamplona, Col.	144	7.23 N	72.39 W
Pamplona, Esp.	50	42.49 N	1.38 W
Pana	174	39.23 N	89.05 W
Panama, Okla., U.S.	174	35.10 N	94.40 W
Panamá, Pan.	130	8.58 N	79.32 W
Panama □¹	130	9.00 N	80.00 W
Panama City	174	30.10 N	85.41 W
Panamint Range ⱄ	184	36.30 N	117.20 W
Panaro ≃	46	44.55 N	11.25 E
Pancevo	54	44.52 N	20.39 E
P'andž (Panj) ≃	84	37.06 N	68.20 E
Panevėžys	26	55.44 N	24.21 E
Pangani ≃	104	5.26 S	38.58 E
Pangkalpinang	82	2.08 S	106.08 E
Pangnirtung	160	66.08 N	65.44 W
Panié, Mont ⋀	112	20.36 S	164.46 E
Panj (P'andž) ≃	84	37.06 N	68.20 E
Pantelleria, Isola di l	46	36.47 N	12.00 E
Paola, It.	46	39.22 N	16.03 E
Paola, Kans., U.S.	174	38.35 N	94.53 W
Paoli	168	38.33 N	86.28 W
Pápa	36	47.19 N	17.28 E
Papantla	130	20.27 N	97.19 W
Papatoetoe	118	36.58 S	174.52 E
Papenburg	36	53.05 N	7.23 E
Papua, Gulf of ⊂	116a	8.30 S	145.00 E
Papua New Guinea □¹	116a	6.00 S	150.00 E
Pará ≃	144	1.30 S	48.55 W
Paracel Islands ‖	82	16.30 N	112.15 E
Paraćin	54	43.52 N	21.24 E
Paradise, Calif., U.S.	184	39.45 N	121.37 W
Paradise, Nev., U.S.	184	36.06 N	115.10 W
Paradise Valley	178	33.32 N	111.57 W
Paragould	174	36.03 N	90.29 W
Paraguá ≃, Bol.	144	13.34 S	61.53 W
Paragua ≃, Ven.	144	6.55 N	62.55 W
Paraguaná, Península de ↾¹	144	11.55 N	70.00 W
Paraguay □¹	146	23.00 S	58.00 W
Paramaribo	144	5.50 N	55.10 W
Paramillo, Nudo de ⋀	144	7.04 N	75.55 W
Paramus	166	40.57 N	74.04 W
Paraná	146	31.44 S	60.32 W
Paraná ≃, Bra.	144	12.30 S	48.14 W
Paraná ≃, S.A.	146	33.43 S	59.15 W
Paray-le-Monial	42	46.27 N	4.07 E
Parchim	36	53.25 N	11.51 E
Pardeeville	168	43.32 N	89.18 W
Pardubice	36	50.02 N	15.47 E
Parecis, Chapada dos ⱄ¹	144	13.00 S	60.00 W
Pareloup, Lac de ⊜	42	44.15 N	2.45 E
Parepare	82	4.01 S	119.38 E
Pariñas, Punta ↾	144	4.40 S	81.20 W
Paringul ⋀	54	45.22 N	23.33 E
Paris, Fr.	42	48.52 N	2.20 E
Paris, Ark., U.S.	174	35.18 N	93.44 W
Paris, Ill., U.S.	174	39.36 N	87.42 W
Paris, Ky., U.S.	166	38.13 N	84.14 W
Paris, Tenn., U.S.	174	36.19 N	88.20 W
Paris, Tex., U.S.	162	33.40 N	95.33 W
Parkersburg, Iowa, U.S.	168	42.35 N	92.47 W
Parkersburg, W. Va., U.S.	166	39.17 N	81.32 W
Park Falls	168	45.56 N	90.32 W
Park Forest	168	41.28 N	87.38 W
Parkland	180	47.09 N	122.26 W
Parkrose	180	45.34 N	122.33 W
Parkville	180	47.40 N	117.18 W
Parma, It.	46	44.48 N	10.20 E
Parma, Ohio, U.S.	166	41.22 N	81.43 W
Parma ≃	46	44.56 N	10.26 E
Parnaíba	144	2.54 S	41.47 W
Parnassós ⋀	54	38.32 N	22.35 E
Pärnu	26	58.24 N	24.32 E
Paro	84	27.26 N	89.25 E
Páros l	54	37.08 N	25.12 E
Parpaillon ⱄ	42	44.30 N	6.40 E
Parramatta	116	33.49 S	151.00 E
Parrett ≃	32	51.13 N	3.01 W
Parrsta ≃	54	54.12 N	15.33 E
Parsons, Kans., U.S.	174	37.20 N	95.16 W
Parsons, Tenn., U.S.	174	35.39 N	88.07 W
Parthenay	42	46.39 N	0.15 W
Partille	28	57.44 N	12.07 E
Partinico	46	38.03 N	13.07 E
Pasadena, Calif., U.S.	184	34.09 N	118.09 W
Pasadena, Tex., U.S.	174	29.42 N	95.13 W
Pa Sak ≃	82	14.21 N	100.35 E
Pascagoula	174	30.21 N	88.31 W
Paşcani	54	47.15 N	26.44 E
Pasco	180	46.14 N	119.06 W
Pasewalk	36	53.30 N	14.00 E
P'asinskij Zaliv ⊂	62	73.00 N	86.00 E
Pasłęka ≃	36	54.26 N	19.46 E
Paso Robles	184	35.38 N	120.41 W
Passaic	166	40.51 N	74.08 W
Passau	36	48.35 N	13.28 E
Passero, Capo ↾	46	36.41 N	15.08 E
Passos	144	20.43 S	46.37 W
Pastaza ≃	144	4.50 S	76.25 W
Pasto	144	1.13 N	77.17 W
Patagonia ◂¹	146	44.00 S	68.00 W
Pate Island l	104	2.07 S	41.03 E
Paternò	46	37.34 N	14.54 E
Paterson	166	40.55 N	74.10 W
Pathfinder Reservoir ⊜¹	178	42.30 N	106.50 W
Patiāla	84	30.19 N	76.23 E
P'atigorsk	62	44.03 N	43.04 E
Patna	84	25.36 N	85.07 E
Patos	144	7.01 S	37.16 W
Patos, Lagoa dos ⊂	146	31.06 S	51.15 W
Patos de Minas	144	18.35 S	46.32 W
Patrai	54	38.15 N	21.44 E
Patterson, Calif., U.S.	184	37.28 N	121.07 W
Patterson, La., U.S.	174	29.42 N	91.18 W
Patterson, Mount ⋀	160	64.04 N	134.39 W
Patti, Golfo di ⊂	46	38.12 N	15.05 E
Patuca ≃	130	15.50 N	84.17 W
Patuxent ≃	166	38.18 N	76.25 W
Pau	42	43.18 N	0.22 W
Pau, Gave de ≃	42	43.33 N	1.12 W
Paulo Afonso	144	9.21 S	38.14 W
Pausania	46	40.55 N	9.06 E
Pavia	46	45.10 N	9.10 E
Pavillion	180	43.15 N	108.42 W
Pavlodar	62	52.18 N	76.57 E
Pavlovo	26	55.58 N	43.04 E
Paw Paw	168	42.13 N	85.53 W
Paw Paw Lake	168	42.12 N	86.15 W
Pawtucket	166	41.53 N	71.23 W
Paxton	168	40.27 N	88.06 W
Payette	180	44.05 N	116.56 W
Paysandú	146	32.19 S	58.05 W
Payson, Ariz., U.S.	178	34.14 N	111.20 W
Payson, Utah, U.S.	178	40.03 N	111.44 W
Pazardžik	54	42.12 N	24.20 E
Peabody	166	42.32 N	70.55 W
Peace ≃	160	59.00 N	111.25 W
Peach Orchard	172	33.22 N	82.03 W
Peald̄oaivi ⋀	26	69.11 N	26.36 E
Peale, Mount ⋀	178	38.26 N	109.14 W
Pearl ≃	174	32.18 N	90.12 W
Pearl ≃	174	30.11 N	89.32 W
Pearland	174	29.34 N	95.17 W
Pearl Harbor ⊂	162b	21.22 N	157.58 W
Pearl River	166	41.04 N	74.02 W
Peć	54	42.40 N	20.19 E
Pečora	26	65.10 N	57.11 E
Pečora ≃	62	68.13 N	54.15 E
Pečorskaja Guba ⊂	62	68.40 N	54.45 E
Pečorskoje More ≃²	62	70.00 N	54.00 E
Pecos, N. Mex., U.S.	178	35.29 N	105.41 W
Pecos, Tex., U.S.	162	31.25 N	103.30 W
Pecos ≃	162	29.42 N	101.22 W
Pécs	36	46.05 N	18.13 E
Pee Dee ≃	172	33.21 N	79.16 W
Peekskill	166	41.17 N	73.55 W
Peel	32	54.13 N	4.40 W
Peene ≃	36	54.09 N	13.46 E
Pegnitz ≃	36	49.29 N	11.00 E
Pegu	82	17.20 N	96.29 E
Pegu Yoma ⱄ	80	19.00 N	95.50 E
Peine	36	52.19 N	10.13 E
Pek ≃	54	44.46 N	21.33 E
Pekin	168	40.35 N	89.40 W
Peking → Beijing	80	39.55 N	116.25 E
Pelagie, Isole ‖	46	35.40 N	12.40 E
Pelat, Mont ⋀	42	44.16 N	6.42 E
Peleaga, Vîrful ⋀	54	45.22 N	22.54 E
Pelham	172	31.08 N	84.09 W
Pelhřimov	36	49.26 N	15.13 E
Pella	168	41.25 N	92.55 W
Pell City	174	33.35 N	86.17 W
Pellegrino, Cozzo ⋀	46	39.45 N	16.03 E
Pellworm l	36	54.31 N	8.38 E
Pelly ≃	160	62.47 N	137.19 W
Pelly Crossing	160	62.50 N	136.35 W
Pelly Mountains ⱄ	160	62.00 N	133.00 W
Pelopónnisos ⱄ¹	54	37.30 N	22.00 E
Peloritani, Monti ⱄ	46	38.05 N	15.25 E
Pelvoux, Massif du ⱄ¹	42	44.55 N	6.20 E
Pemadumcook Lake ⊜	166	45.40 N	68.55 W
Pematangsiantar	82	2.57 N	99.03 E
Pemba Island l	104	7.31 S	39.25 E
Pembroke, N.C., U.S.	172	34.41 N	79.12 W
Pembroke, Wales, U.K.	32	51.41 N	4.55 W
Pen Argyl	166	40.52 N	75.16 W
Peñalara ⋀	50	40.51 N	3.57 W
Pen̄arroya-Pueblonuevo	50	38.18 N	5.16 W
Penas, Golfo de ⊂	146	47.22 S	74.50 W
Pendjari ≃	100	10.54 N	0.51 E
Pendleton, Ind., U.S.	174	40.01 N	85.45 W
Pendleton, Oreg., U.S.	180	45.40 N	118.47 W
Pendleton, S.C., U.S.	172	34.39 N	82.47 W
Pend Oreille, Lake ⊜	180	48.10 N	116.11 W
P'enghu Liehtao ‖	80	23.30 N	119.30 E
Peniche	50	39.21 N	9.23 W
Penmarc'h, Pointe de ↾	42	47.48 N	4.22 W
Penn Hills	166	40.28 N	79.53 W
Pennines ⱄ	32	54.10 N	2.05 W
Pennines, Alpes ⱄ	42	46.05 N	7.50 E
Penns Grove	166	39.43 N	75.28 W
Pennsauken	166	39.58 N	75.04 W
Pennsville	166	39.39 N	75.30 W
Penn Yan	166	42.40 N	77.03 W
Penobscot ≃	166	44.30 N	68.50 W
Penobscot Bay ⊂	166	44.15 N	68.52 W
Penonomé	130	8.31 N	80.22 W
Penrith	32	54.40 N	2.44 W
Pensacola	174	30.25 N	87.13 W
Pensacola Bay ⊂	174	30.25 N	87.06 W
Penticton	160	49.30 N	119.35 W
Pentland Firth ⋃	32	58.44 N	3.13 W
Penza	62	53.13 N	45.00 E
Penzance	32	50.07 N	5.33 W
Peoria, Ariz., U.S.	178	33.35 N	112.14 W
Peoria, Ill., U.S.	168	40.42 N	89.36 W
Peoria Heights	168	40.45 N	89.34 W
Pequot Lakes	168	46.36 N	94.19 W
Perak ≃	82	3.58 N	100.53 E
Perdido, Monte ⋀	50	42.40 N	0.05 E
Perdido ≃	174	30.29 N	87.26 W
Pereira	144	4.49 N	75.43 W
Pergamino	146	33.53 S	60.35 W
Pergine Valsugana	46	46.04 N	11.14 E
Périgueux	42	45.11 N	0.43 E
Perkasie	166	40.22 N	75.17 W
Perleberg	36	53.04 N	11.51 E
Pernik	54	42.36 N	23.02 E
Perpignan	42	42.41 N	2.53 E
Perrine	172	25.36 N	80.21 W
Perry, Fla., U.S.	172	30.07 N	83.35 W
Perry, Ga., U.S.	172	32.27 N	83.44 W
Perry, Iowa, U.S.	168	41.50 N	94.06 W
Perry, Kans., U.S.	174	39.05 N	95.24 W
Perryton	162	36.24 N	100.48 W
Perryville	174	37.43 N	89.52 W
Persian Gulf ⊂	84	27.00 N	51.00 E
Perth, Austl.	116	31.56 S	115.50 E
Perth, Scot., U.K.	32	56.24 N	3.28 W
Perth Amboy	166	40.30 N	74.16 W
Peru, Ill., U.S.	168	41.20 N	89.08 W
Peru, Ind., U.S.	174	40.45 N	86.04 W
Peru □¹	144	10.00 S	76.00 W
Perugia	46	43.08 N	12.22 E
Pervoural'sk	62	56.54 N	59.58 E
Pesaro	46	43.54 N	12.55 E
Pescara	46	42.28 N	14.13 E
Pescia	46	43.54 N	10.41 E
Peshāwar	84	34.01 N	71.33 E
Peshtigo	168	45.03 N	87.45 W
Peštera	54	42.02 N	24.18 E
Petah Tiqwa	84	32.05 N	34.53 E
Petaluma	184	38.14 N	122.39 W
Petatlán	130	17.31 N	101.16 W
Petenwell Lake ⊜¹	168	44.10 N	89.57 W
Peterborough, Ont., Can.	160	44.18 N	78.19 W
Peterborough, Eng., U.K.	32	52.35 N	0.15 W
Peterborough, N.H., U.S.	166	42.53 N	71.57 W
Peterhead	32	57.30 N	1.49 W
Peterlee	32	54.46 N	1.19 W
Peter Pond Lake ⊜	160	55.55 N	108.44 W
Petersburg, Ill., U.S.	174	40.01 N	89.51 W
Petersburg, Ind., U.S.	174	38.30 N	87.17 W
Petersburg, Va., U.S.	172	37.13 N	77.24 W
Petersburg, W. Va., U.S.	166	39.00 N	79.07 W
Petilia Policastro	46	39.07 N	16.47 E
Petite Rivière de La Baleine ≃	160	56.00 N	76.45 W
Petit-Saint-Bernard, Col du ⋈	42	45.41 N	6.53 E
Petoskey	168	45.22 N	84.57 W
Petrič	54	41.24 N	23.13 E
Petrila	54	45.27 N	23.25 E
Petrinja	46	45.26 N	16.17 E
Petrohanski prohod ⋈	54	43.08 N	23.08 E
Petrolina	144	9.24 S	40.30 W
Petropavlovsk	62	54.54 N	69.06 E
Petropavlovsk-Kamčatskij	64	53.01 N	158.39 E
Petrópolis	144	22.31 S	43.10 W
Petroşani	54	45.25 N	23.22 E
Petrozavodsk	26	61.47 N	34.20 E
Pezinok	36	48.18 N	17.17 E
Pforzheim	36	48.54 N	8.42 E
Pfungstadt	36	49.48 N	8.36 E
Phangan, Ko l	82	9.45 N	100.04 E
Phan-rang	82	11.34 N	108.59 E
Phan-thiet	82	10.56 N	108.06 E
Phenix City	172	32.29 N	85.01 W
Phetchabun, Thiu Khao ⱄ	82	16.20 N	100.55 E
Philadelphia, Miss., U.S.	174	32.46 N	89.07 W
Philadelphia, Pa., U.S.	166	39.57 N	75.07 W
Philippi	166	39.09 N	80.02 W
Philippines □¹	82	13.00 N	122.00 E
Philipsburg	166	40.53 N	78.05 W
Phillips	168	45.41 N	90.24 W
Phillipsburg, Ga., U.S.	172	31.34 N	83.31 W
Phillipsburg, N.J., U.S.	166	40.42 N	75.12 W
Phitsanulok	82	16.50 N	100.15 E
Phnum Pénh	82	11.33 N	104.55 E
Phoenix	178	33.27 N	112.05 W
Phoenixville	166	40.08 N	75.31 W
Phrae	82	18.09 N	100.08 E
Phra Nakhon Si Ayutthaya	82	14.21 N	100.33 E
Phuket	82	7.53 N	98.24 E
Phuket, Ko l	82	8.00 N	98.22 E
Phu-quoc, Dao l	82	10.12 N	104.00 E
Piacenza	46	45.01 N	9.40 E
Pianosa, Isola l	46	42.35 N	10.04 E
Piaseczno	36	52.05 N	21.01 E
Piatra-Neamţ	54	46.56 N	26.22 E
Piave ≃	46	45.32 N	12.44 E
Piazza Armerina	46	37.23 N	14.22 E
Pibor ≃	102	8.26 N	33.13 E
Picayune	174	30.26 N	89.41 W
Picher	174	36.59 N	94.50 W
Pickens	172	34.53 N	82.42 W
Pickwick Lake ⊜¹	174	34.55 N	88.10 W
Picton, Isla l	146	55.02 S	66.57 W
Pidurutalagala ⋀	84	7.00 N	80.46 E
Piedmont, Ala., U.S.	174	33.55 N	85.37 W
Piedmont, Mo., U.S.	174	37.09 N	90.42 W
Piedras Negras	130	28.42 N	100.31 W
Pieksämäki	28	62.18 N	27.08 E
Pielinen ⊜	28	63.15 N	29.40 E
Pierre	162	44.22 N	100.21 W
Piešt'any	36	48.36 N	17.50 E
Pietermaritzburg	104	29.37 S	30.16 E
Pietersburg	104	23.54 S	29.25 E
Pietrasanta	46	43.57 N	10.14 E
Pietrosu, Vîrful ⋀	54	47.36 N	24.38 E
Pietrosul ⋀	54	47.08 N	25.11 E
Piggott	174	36.22 N	90.11 W
Pikes Peak ⋀	178	38.51 N	105.03 W
Pikesville	166	39.23 N	76.44 W
Piketon	166	39.04 N	83.01 W
Pikeville	172	37.29 N	82.31 W
Piła (Schneidemühl)	36	53.10 N	16.44 E
Pilbarra Point ↾	112	18.59 S	169.14 E
Pilcomayo ≃	146	25.21 S	57.42 W
Pilica ≃	36	51.52 N	21.17 E
Pinang (George Town)	82	5.25 N	100.19 E
Pinang, Pulau l	82	5.24 N	100.19 E
Pinar del Río	130	22.25 N	83.42 W
Pinardville	166	42.59 N	71.33 W
Pinckneyville	174	38.05 N	89.23 W
Pindhos Óros ⱄ	54	39.49 N	21.14 E
Pine Bluff	174	34.13 N	92.01 W
Pine City	168	45.50 N	92.59 W
Pine Creek	168	13.49 S	131.49 E
Pine Creek ≃	166	41.10 N	77.16 W
Pine Creek Lake ⊜¹	174	34.05 N	95.05 W
Pinega ≃	62	64.08 N	41.54 E
Pine Hills	172	28.35 N	81.27 W
Pinehouse Lake ⊜	160	55.32 N	106.35 W
Pinehurst	172	35.11 N	79.27 W
Pine Island l	172	26.35 N	82.06 W
Pineland	184	31.15 N	93.58 W
Pinellas Park	172	27.51 N	82.43 W
Pine Point	160	61.01 N	114.15 W
Pinerolo	46	44.53 N	7.21 E
Pineville, Ky., U.S.	172	36.46 N	83.42 W
Pineville, La., U.S.	174	31.19 N	92.26 W
Pineville, N.C., U.S.	172	35.05 N	80.53 W
Ping ≃	82	15.42 N	100.09 E
Pingtung	80	22.40 N	120.29 E
Pinneberg	36	53.40 N	9.47 E
Pins, Île des ‖	112	22.37 S	167.30 E
Piombino	46	42.55 N	10.32 E
Pionki	36	51.30 N	21.27 E
Piotrków Trybunalski	36	51.25 N	19.42 E
Pipestone	168	44.00 N	96.19 W
Piqua	168	40.09 N	84.15 W
Piracicaba	144	22.43 S	47.38 W
Piraeus → Piraiévs	54	37.57 N	23.38 E
Piraiévs (Piraeus)	54	37.57 N	23.38 E
Pirapora	144	17.21 S	44.56 W
Pirin ⱄ	54	41.40 N	23.30 E
Pirmasens	36	49.12 N	7.36 E
Pirna	36	50.58 N	13.56 E
Pirón ≃	50	41.23 N	4.31 W
Pirot	54	43.09 N	22.35 E
Pisa	46	43.43 N	10.23 E
Pisco	144	13.42 S	76.13 W
Písek	36	49.19 N	14.10 E
Pisticci	46	40.23 N	16.34 E
Pistoia	46	43.55 N	10.55 E
Pit ≃	184	40.45 N	122.22 W
Pitcairn □²	25	25.04 S	130.06 W
Piteå	28	65.20 N	21.30 E
Piteälven ≃	28	65.14 N	21.32 E
Piteşti	54	44.52 N	24.52 E
Pittsboro	172	35.43 N	79.11 W
Pittsburg	174	37.25 N	94.42 W
Pittsburgh	166	40.26 N	80.00 W
Pittsfield, Ill., U.S.	174	39.36 N	90.48 W
Pittsfield, Maine, U.S.	166	44.47 N	69.23 W
Pittsfield, Mass., U.S.	166	42.27 N	73.15 W
Pittsfield, N.H., U.S.	166	43.18 N	71.19 W
Pittston	166	41.19 N	75.47 W
Piura	144	5.12 S	80.38 W
Piva ≃	54	43.21 N	18.51 E
Placentia Bay ⊂	160	47.15 N	54.30 W
Placetas	130	22.19 N	79.40 W

Name	Page	Lat° ′	Long° ′
Țarābulus (Tripoli), Lubnān	84	34.26 N	35.51 E
Țarābulus (Tripolitania) ◆[1]	102	31.00 N	15.00 E
Taramakau ≃	118	42.34 S	171.08 E
Taranto	46	40.28 N	17.15 E
Taranto, Golfo di C	46	40.10 N	17.20 E
Tarare	42	45.54 N	4.26 E
Tarbes	42	43.14 N	0.05 E
Tarboro	172	35.54 N	77.32 W
Tardoki-Jani, Gora ∧	64	48.55 N	138.04 E
Tarentum	166	40.36 N	79.45 W
Targhee Pass)(	180	44.41 N	111.17 W
Târgovište	54	43.15 N	26.34 E
Tarifa, Punta de ➤	50	36.00 N	5.37 W
Tarija	144	21.31 S	64.45 W
Tarkio	174	40.27 N	95.23 W
Tarkwa	100	5.19 N	1.59 W
Tarlac	82	15.29 N	120.35 E
Tarn ≃	42	44.05 N	1.06 E
Tarna ≃	36	47.31 N	19.59 E
Tarnica ∧	36	49.05 N	22.42 E
Tarnobrzeg	36	50.35 N	21.41 E
Tarnów	36	50.01 N	21.00 E
Tarnowskie Góry	36	50.27 N	18.52 E
Taro ≃	46	45.00 N	10.15 E
Tarpon Springs	172	28.09 N	82.45 W
Tarragona	50	41.07 N	1.15 E
Tarrakoski L	26	68.10 N	20.00 E
Tarrant	174	33.34 N	86.46 W
Tarrasa	50	41.34 N	2.01 E
Tarsus	20	36.55 N	34.53 E
Tartagal	146	22.32 S	63.49 W
Tartu	26	58.23 N	26.43 E
Tashk, Daryācheh-ye ⊜	84	29.20 N	54.05 E
Tashkent → **Taškent**	62	41.20 N	69.18 E
Tasikmalaya	82	7.20 S	108.12 E
Tåsinge I	28	55.00 N	10.36 E
Taškent	62	41.20 N	69.18 E
Tasman, Mount ∧	118	43.34 S	170.09 E
Tasman Bay C	118	41.00 S	173.20 E
Tasmania I	116	42.00 S	147.00 E
Tasman Sea ⊤[2]	118	39.00 S	170.00 E
Tata	36	47.39 N	18.18 E
Tatabánya	36	47.34 N	18.26 E
Tatarskij Proliv ⊔	64	50.00 N	141.15 E
Tatnam, Cape ➤	160	57.16 N	91.00 W
Tauber ≃	36	49.46 N	9.31 E
Taum Sauk Mountain ∧	174	37.34 N	90.44 W
Taunton, Eng., U.K.	32	51.01 N	3.06 W
Taunton, Mass., U.S.	166	41.54 N	71.06 W
Taupo, Lake ⊜	118	38.49 S	175.55 E
Tauranga	118	37.42 S	176.10 E
Taurianova	46	38.21 N	16.01 E
Tavares	172	28.48 N	81.44 W
Taveuni I	111	16.51 S	179.58 W
Tavoliere ◆[1]	46	41.35 N	15.25 E
Távora ≃	50	41.09 N	7.35 W
Tavoy	82	14.05 N	98.12 E
Tavşanlı	54	39.33 N	29.30 E
Taw ≃	32	51.04 N	4.11 W
Ṭawkar	102	18.26 N	37.44 E
Taxco de Alarcón	130	18.33 N	99.36 W
Tay, Loch ⊜	32	56.30 N	4.10 W
Taylor, Mount ∧	178	35.14 N	107.37 W
Taylors	172	34.55 N	82.18 W
Taza	100	34.16 N	4.01 W
Tazewell	172	37.07 N	81.31 W
Tazin Lake ⊜	160	59.47 N	109.03 W
Tbilisi	62	41.43 N	44.49 E
Tczew	36	54.06 N	18.47 E
Te Anau, Lake ⊜	118	45.12 S	167.48 E
Teano	46	41.15 N	14.04 E
Tébessa	100	35.28 N	8.09 E
Téboursouk, Monts de ∧∧	46	36.30 N	9.10 E
Tech ≃	42	42.36 N	3.03 E
Tecuci	54	45.50 N	27.26 E
Tecumseh	168	42.00 N	83.57 W
Tedžen (Harīrūd) ≃	84	37.24 N	60.38 E
Tees ≃	32	54.34 N	1.16 W
Tegucigalpa	130	14.06 N	87.13 W
Tehachapi Pass)(	184	35.06 N	118.18 W
Tehrān	84	35.40 N	51.26 E
Tehuacán	130	18.27 N	97.23 W
Tehuantepec, Golfo de C	130	16.00 N	94.50 W
Teifi ≃	32	52.07 N	4.42 W
Teignmouth	32	50.33 N	3.30 W
Tejo → Tagus ≃	50	38.40 N	9.24 W
Tejon Pass)(	184	34.48 N	118.52 W
Teke Burnu ➤	54	40.02 N	26.10 E
Tekeze ≃	102	14.20 N	35.50 E
Tela	130	15.44 N	87.27 W
Tel Aviv-Yafo	84	32.03 N	34.46 E
Teleño ∧	50	42.21 N	6.23 W
Teleorman ≃	54	43.52 N	25.26 E
Telertheba, Djebel ∧	100	24.10 N	6.51 E
Telescope Peak ∧	184	36.10 N	117.05 W
Tell City	174	37.57 N	86.46 W
Telok Anson	82	4.02 N	101.01 E
Teltow	36	52.23 N	13.16 E
Telukbetung	82	5.27 S	105.16 E
Te Manga ∧	114	21.13 S	159.45 W
Temirtau	62	50.05 N	72.56 E
Tempe	178	33.25 N	111.56 W
Temperance	168	41.47 N	83.34 W
Tempio Pausania	46	40.54 N	9.07 E
Temple	162	31.06 N	97.21 W
Templin	36	53.07 N	13.30 E
Temuco	146	38.44 S	72.36 W
Tenaha	184	31.57 N	94.15 W
Tende, Col de)(	42	44.09 N	7.34 E
Ténès, Cap ➤	50	36.33 N	1.21 E
Tenkiller Ferry Lake ⊜[1]	174	35.43 N	95.00 W
Tennessee □[3]	162	35.50 N	85.30 W
Tennessee ≃	162	37.04 N	88.33 W
Ten Thousand Islands II	172	25.50 N	81.33 W
Tepic	130	21.30 N	104.54 W
Teplice	36	50.39 N	13.48 E
Tera ≃	50	41.54 N	5.44 W
Teramo	46	42.39 N	13.42 E
Terek ≃	62	43.44 N	46.33 E
Teresina	144	5.05 S	42.49 W
Teresópolis	144	22.26 S	42.59 W
Terkos Gölü ⊜	54	41.20 N	28.35 E
Termini Imerese	46	37.59 N	13.42 E
Termini Imerese, Golfo di C	46	38.05 N	13.50 E
Terminillo, Monte ∧	46	42.28 N	13.00 E
Términos, Laguna de C	130	18.37 N	91.33 W
Termoli	46	42.00 N	15.00 E
Terneuzen	36	51.20 N	3.50 E
Terni	46	42.34 N	12.37 E
Ternitz	36	47.44 N	16.03 E
Ternopol'	62	49.34 N	25.36 E
Terracina	46	41.17 N	13.15 E
Terra di Bari ◆[1]	46	41.10 N	16.50 E
Terralba	46	39.43 N	8.38 E
Terre Haute	174	39.28 N	87.24 W
Terschelling I	36	53.24 N	5.20 E
Teruel	50	40.21 N	1.06 W
Teslin	160	60.09 N	132.45 W
Teslin ≃	160	61.34 N	134.54 W
Teslin Lake ⊜	160	60.15 N	132.57 W
Test ≃	32	50.55 N	1.29 W
Testa, Capo ➤	46	41.14 N	9.09 E
Têt ≃	42	42.44 N	3.02 E
Tete	104	16.13 S	33.35 E
Teterow	36	53.46 N	12.34 E
Teton ≃	180	47.56 N	110.31 W
Tétouan	100	35.34 N	5.23 W
Tetovo	54	42.01 N	20.58 E
Teulada, Capo ➤	46	38.52 N	8.39 E
Teutoburger Wald ◆[3]	36	52.10 N	8.15 E
Teutopolis	174	39.08 N	88.29 W
Tevere (Tiber) ≃	46	41.44 N	12.14 E
Texarkana, Ark., U.S.	174	33.26 N	94.02 W
Texarkana, Tex., U.S.	174	33.26 N	94.03 W
Texas □[3]	162	31.30 N	99.00 W
Texas City	174	29.23 N	94.54 W
Texel I	36	53.05 N	4.45 E
Texoma, Lake ⊜[1]	162	33.55 N	96.37 W
Thabana Ntlenyana ∧	104	29.28 S	29.16 E
Thailand □[1]	82	15.00 N	100.00 E
Thailand, Gulf of C	82	10.00 N	101.00 E
Thai-nguyen	82	21.36 N	105.50 E
Thale	36	51.45 N	11.02 E
Thames ≃	32	51.28 N	0.43 E
Thames, Firth Of C	118	37.00 S	175.25 E
Thāmir, Jabal ∧	102	13.53 N	45.30 E
Thanh-hoa	82	19.48 N	105.46 E
Thanh-pho Ho Chi Minh (Sai-gon)	82	10.45 N	106.40 E
Thásos I	54	40.41 N	24.47 E
Thatcher	178	32.51 N	109.46 W
Thau, Bassin de C	42	43.23 N	3.36 E
Thayer, Kans., U.S.	174	37.30 N	95.28 W
Thayer, Mo., U.S.	174	36.31 N	91.33 W
The Brothers II	84	12.09 N	53.12 E
The Cheviot ∧	32	55.28 N	2.09 W
The Dalles	180	45.36 N	121.10 W
The Everglades ≋	172	26.00 N	80.40 W
The Father ∧	116a	5.03 S	151.20 E
The Fens ≋	32	52.38 N	0.02 E
The Hague → 's-Gravenhage	36	52.06 N	4.18 E
The Minch ⊔	32	58.05 N	5.55 W
The Naze ➤	32	51.53 N	1.16 E
The Needles ➤	32	50.39 N	1.34 W
Theodore Roosevelt Lake ⊜[1]	178	33.42 N	111.07 W
Thermaïkós Kólpos C	54	40.23 N	22.47 E
Thermopolis	180	43.39 N	108.13 W
The Slot ⊔	114	8.00 S	158.10 E
The Sound ⊔	28	55.50 N	12.40 E
Thessaloníki (Salonika)	54	40.38 N	22.56 E
Thetford	32	52.25 N	0.45 E
The Wash C	32	52.55 N	0.15 E
The Weald ◆[1]	32	51.05 N	0.05 E
Thibodaux	174	29.48 N	90.49 W
Thief River Falls	162	48.07 N	96.10 W
Thiene	46	45.42 N	11.29 E
Thiensville	168	43.14 N	87.58 W
Thiers	42	45.51 N	3.34 E
Thiès	100	14.48 N	16.56 W
Thika	104	1.03 S	37.05 E
Thimbu	84	27.28 N	89.39 E
Thingvallavatn ⊜	26a	64.12 N	21.10 W
Thio	112	21.37 S	166.14 E
Thionville	42	49.22 N	6.10 E
Thíra I	54	36.24 N	25.29 E
Thirsk	32	54.14 N	1.20 W
Thívai (Thebes)	54	38.21 N	23.19 E
Thjórsá ≃	26a	63.47 N	20.48 W
Thomaston, Ga., U.S.	172	32.54 N	84.20 W
Thomaston, Maine, U.S.	166	44.05 N	69.10 W
Thomasville, Ala., U.S.	174	31.55 N	87.51 W
Thomasville, Ga., U.S.	172	30.50 N	83.59 W
Thomasville, N.C., U.S.	172	35.53 N	80.05 W
Thompson ≃	174	39.45 N	93.36 W
Thompson Peak ∧	184	41.00 N	123.03 W
Thomson	172	33.28 N	82.30 W
Thonon-les-Bains	42	46.22 N	6.29 E
Thornton	178	39.51 N	104.59 W
Thorp	168	44.58 N	90.48 W
Thouars	42	46.59 N	0.13 W
Thousand Oaks	184	34.10 N	118.50 W
Thrace □[9]	20	41.20 N	26.45 E
Three Points, Cape ➤	100	4.45 N	2.06 W
Three Rivers	168	41.57 N	85.38 W
Three Sisters ∧	180	44.10 N	121.46 W
Thun	42	46.45 N	7.37 E
Thunder Bay	160	48.23 N	89.15 W
Thunderbolt	172	32.03 N	81.04 W
Thunersee ⊜	42	46.40 N	7.45 E
Thurmont	166	39.37 N	77.25 W
Tianjin (Tientsin)	80	39.08 N	117.12 E
Tianmushan ∧∧	80	30.25 N	119.30 E
Tiaret	100	35.28 N	1.21 E
Tibasti, Sarīr ◆[2]	102	24.15 N	17.15 E
Tiber Reservoir ⊜[1]	180	48.22 N	111.17 W
Tibesti ∧∧	102	21.30 N	17.30 E
Țibleș, Munții ∧∧	54	47.38 N	24.05 E
Tiburón, Isla I	130	29.00 N	112.23 W
Tice	172	26.41 N	81.49 W
Ticino ≃	46	45.09 N	9.14 E
Ticonderoga	166	43.51 N	73.26 W
Tidirhine, Jbel ∧	50	34.50 N	4.30 W
Tidra, Île I	100	19.44 N	16.24 W
Tiel	36	51.54 N	5.25 E
Tielelihu ⊜	80	44.30 N	85.15 E
Tienen	36	50.48 N	4.57 E
Tien Shan ∧∧	80	42.00 N	80.00 E
Tientsin → **Tianjin**	80	39.08 N	117.12 E
Tierra de Campos ◆[1]	50	42.10 N	4.50 W
Tierra del Fuego, Isla Grande de I	146	54.00 S	69.00 W
Tiffin	166	41.07 N	83.11 W
Tifton	172	31.27 N	83.31 W
Tigris (Dicle) (Dijlah) ≃	84	31.00 N	47.25 E
Tijuana	130	32.32 N	117.01 W
Tilburg	36	51.34 N	5.05 E
Tilemsi, Vallée du ∨	100	16.15 N	0.02 E
Tillamook	180	45.27 N	123.51 W
Tillmans Corner	174	30.46 N	88.08 W
Tilton	166	43.27 N	71.35 W
Timanskij Kr'až ∧	62	65.00 N	51.00 E
Timaru	118	44.24 S	171.15 E
Timimoun	100	29.14 N	0.16 E
Timiris, Cap ➤	100	19.23 N	16.32 W
Timișoara	54	45.45 N	21.13 E
Timmins	160	48.28 N	81.20 W
Timms Hill ∧[2]	168	45.27 N	90.11 W
Timok ≃	54	44.13 N	22.40 E
Timor I	82	9.00 S	125.00 E
Timor Sea ⊤[2]	82	10.00 S	128.00 E
Tims Ford Lake ⊜[1]	174	35.15 N	86.10 W
Tinaca Point ➤	82	5.33 N	125.20 E
Tinian I	82	15.00 N	145.38 E
Tinkisso ≃	100	11.21 N	9.10 W
Tínos I	54	37.38 N	25.10 E
Tinrhert, Plateau du ∧∧[1]	100	29.00 N	9.00 E
Tioman, Pulau I	82	2.48 N	104.10 E
Tippecanoe ≃	174	40.31 N	86.47 W
Tipperary	32	52.29 N	8.10 W
Tipperary □[6]	32	52.40 N	8.20 W
Tipton, Ind., U.S.	174	40.17 N	86.02 W
Tipton, Iowa, U.S.	168	41.46 N	91.08 W
Tipton, Mo., U.S.	174	38.39 N	92.47 W
Tiptonville	174	36.23 N	89.29 W
Tip Top Mountain ∧	160	48.16 N	85.59 W
Tīrān, Jazīrat I	102	27.56 N	34.34 E
Tiranë	54	41.20 N	19.50 E
Tiraspol'	62	46.51 N	29.38 E
Tire	54	38.04 N	27.45 E
Tiree I	32	56.31 N	6.49 W
Tîrgoviște	54	44.56 N	25.27 E
Tîrgu-Jiu	54	45.02 N	23.17 E
Tîrgu Mureș	54	46.33 N	24.33 E
Tîrgu-Neamț	54	47.12 N	26.22 E
Tîrgu-Ocna	54	46.15 N	26.37 E
Tirich Mīr ∧	84	36.15 N	71.50 E
Tîrnava Mare ≃	54	46.09 N	23.42 E
Tîrnava Mică ≃	54	46.11 N	23.55 E
Tîrnăveni	54	46.20 N	24.17 E
Tírnavos	54	39.45 N	22.17 E
Tirso ≃	46	39.52 N	8.33 E
Tiruchchirāppalli	84	10.49 N	78.41 E
Tirunelveli	84	8.44 N	77.41 E
Tisa (Tisza) ≃	54	45.15 N	20.17 E
Tissemsilt	50	35.35 N	1.50 E
Tiszavasvári	36	47.58 N	21.22 E
Titicaca, Lago ⊜	144	15.50 S	69.20 W
Titikaveka	114	21.15 S	159.45 W
Titograd	54	42.26 N	19.14 E
Titovo Užice	54	43.51 N	19.51 E
Titov Veles	54	41.41 N	21.48 E
Titov vrh ∧	54	42.00 N	20.51 E
Titteri ∧∧	50	36.00 N	3.30 E
Titusville, Fla., U.S.	172	28.37 N	80.49 W
Titusville, Pa., U.S.	166	41.38 N	79.41 W
Tiverton	32	50.55 N	3.29 W
Tivoli	46	41.58 N	12.48 E
Tizimín	130	21.10 N	88.10 W
Tizi-Ouzou	100	36.48 N	4.02 E
Tjörn I	28	58.00 N	11.38 E
Tlemcen	100	34.52 N	1.15 W
Toast	172	36.30 N	80.38 W
Toba, Danau ⊜	82	2.35 N	98.50 E
Tobago I	130	11.15 N	60.40 W
Toba Kākar Range ∧∧	84	31.15 N	68.00 E
Tobol ≃	62	58.10 N	68.12 E
Tocantins ≃	144	1.45 S	49.10 W
Toccoa	172	34.35 N	83.19 W
Tocopilla	146	22.05 S	70.12 W
Togo □[1]	100	8.00 N	1.10 E
Togwotee Pass)(	180	43.45 N	110.04 W
Toiyabe Range ∧∧	184	39.10 N	117.10 W
Tokat	20	40.19 N	36.34 E
Tokushima	80	34.04 N	134.34 E
Tōkyō	80	35.42 N	139.46 E
Tolbuhin	54	43.34 N	27.50 E
Toledo, Esp.	50	39.52 N	4.01 W
Toledo, Iowa, U.S.	168	42.00 N	92.35 W
Toledo, Ohio, U.S.	166	41.39 N	83.32 W
Toledo, Montes de ∧∧	50	39.33 N	4.20 W
Toledo Bend Reservoir ⊜[1]	174	31.30 N	93.45 W
Tolima, Nevado del ∧	144	4.40 N	75.19 W
Toljatti	26	53.31 N	49.26 E
Tollense ≃	36	53.54 N	13.02 E
Tolleson	178	33.27 N	112.16 W
Tolmezzo	46	46.24 N	13.01 E
Tolosa	50	43.08 N	2.04 W
Tolstoj, Mys ➤	64	59.10 N	155.12 E
Toluca	130	19.17 N	99.40 W
Tomah	168	43.59 N	90.30 W
Tomahawk	168	45.28 N	89.44 W
Tomakomai	80	42.38 N	141.36 E
Tomaniivi, Mount ∧	111	17.37 S	178.01 E
Tomaszów Lubelski	36	50.28 N	23.25 E
Tomaszów Mazowiecki	36	51.32 N	20.01 E
Tombigbee ≃	174	31.04 N	87.58 W
Tombouctou (Timbuktu)	100	16.46 N	3.01 W
Tombstone	178	31.43 N	110.04 W
Tombstone Mountain ∧	160	64.25 N	138.30 W
Tomelloso	50	39.10 N	3.01 W
Tomini, Teluk C	82	0.20 S	121.00 E
Tompkinsville	174	36.42 N	85.41 W
Tomsk	64	56.30 N	84.58 E
Toms River	166	39.58 N	74.12 W
Tonawanda	166	43.01 N	78.53 W
Tonbridge	32	51.12 N	0.16 E
Tonga □[1]	10	20.00 S	175.00 W
Tongeren	36	50.47 N	5.28 E
Tonghua	80	41.50 N	125.55 E
Tongjosŏn-man C	80	39.30 N	128.00 E
Tongue ≃	180	46.24 N	105.52 W
Tonkin, Gulf of C	82	20.00 N	108.00 E
Tonopah	184	38.04 N	117.14 W
Tønsberg	28	59.17 N	10.25 E
Tooele	178	40.32 N	112.18 W
Toowoomba	116	27.33 S	151.57 E
Topeka	174	39.03 N	95.41 W
Topl'a ≃	36	48.45 N	21.45 E
Toplica ≃	54	43.13 N	21.49 E
Topol'čany	36	48.34 N	18.10 E
Topolnica ≃	54	42.11 N	24.18 E
Toppenish	180	46.23 N	120.19 W
Topsham	166	43.56 N	69.58 W
Torari	112	17.39 S	168.32 E
Torbalı	54	38.10 N	27.21 E
Torch ≃	160	53.50 N	103.05 W
Torch Lake ⊜	168	45.00 N	85.19 W
Torgau	36	51.34 N	13.00 E
Torgelow	36	53.37 N	14.00 E
Torhout	36	51.04 N	3.06 E
Torino (Turin)	46	45.03 N	7.40 E
Torneälven ≃	26	65.48 N	24.08 E
Torneträsk ⊜	26	68.20 N	19.10 E
Toro	50	41.31 N	5.24 W
Törökszentmiklós	36	47.11 N	20.25 E
Toronto, Ont., Can.	160	43.39 N	79.23 W
Toronto, Ohio, U.S.	166	40.28 N	80.36 W
Tororo	104	0.42 N	34.11 E
Toros Dağları ∧∧	20	37.00 N	33.00 E
Torquay (Torbay)	32	50.28 N	3.30 W
Torrance	184	33.50 N	118.19 W
Torre Annunziata	46	40.45 N	14.27 E
Torredonjimeno	50	37.46 N	3.57 W
Torrejón, Embalse de ⊜[1]	50	39.50 N	5.50 W
Torrejón de Ardoz	50	40.27 N	3.29 W
Torrelavega	50	43.21 N	4.03 W
Torremaggiore	46	41.41 N	15.17 E
Torrens, Lake ⊜	116	31.00 S	137.50 E
Torrente	50	39.26 N	0.28 W
Torreón	130	25.33 N	103.26 W
Torres Strait ⊔	116	10.25 S	142.10 E
Torridge ≃	32	51.03 N	4.11 W
Torrington, Conn., U.S.	166	41.48 N	73.08 W
Torrington, Wyo., U.S.	162	42.04 N	104.11 W
Tórshavn	20	62.01 N	6.46 W
Tortona	46	44.54 N	8.52 E
Tortosa	50	40.48 N	0.31 E
Tortosa, Cabo de ➤	50	40.43 N	0.55 E
Tortue, Île de la I	130	20.04 N	72.49 W
Toruń	36	53.02 N	18.35 E
Toržok	26	57.03 N	34.58 E
Tosas, Puerto de)(	50	42.19 N	2.01 E
Tottori	80	35.30 N	134.14 E
Toubkal, Jbel ∧	100	31.05 N	7.55 W
Touggourt	100	33.10 N	6.00 E
Toul	42	48.41 N	5.54 E
Toulnustouc ≃	160	49.35 N	68.24 W
Toulon	42	43.07 N	5.56 E
Toulouse	42	43.36 N	1.26 E
Toungoo	82	18.56 N	96.26 E
Tourcoing	42	50.43 N	3.09 E
Tournai	36	50.36 N	3.23 E
Tours	42	47.23 N	0.41 E
Touside, Pic ∧	102	21.02 N	16.25 E
Towanda	166	41.46 N	76.26 W
Towcester	32	52.08 N	1.00 W
Tower	168	47.48 N	92.17 W
Townsend	180	46.19 N	111.31 W
Townsville	116	19.16 S	146.48 E
Towson	166	39.24 N	76.36 W
Towuti, Danau ⊜	82	2.45 S	121.32 E
Toyama	80	36.41 N	137.13 E
Toyohashi	80	34.46 N	137.23 E
Trabzon	84	41.00 N	39.43 E
Tracy	184	37.44 N	121.25 W
Traer	168	42.12 N	92.28 W
Trafalgar, Cabo ➤	50	36.11 N	6.02 W
Tralee	32	52.16 N	9.42 W
Tranås	28	58.03 N	14.59 E
Trang	82	7.33 N	99.36 E
Trangan, Pulau I	82	6.35 S	134.20 E
Trani	46	41.17 N	16.26 E
Trapani	46	38.01 N	12.31 E
Trasimeno, Lago ⊜	46	43.08 N	12.06 E
Trás-os-Montes □[9]	50	41.30 N	7.15 W
Traun	36	48.13 N	14.14 E
Traunstein	36	47.52 N	12.38 E
Traverse City	168	44.46 N	85.37 W
Travnik	46	44.14 N	17.40 E
Trbovlje	46	46.10 N	15.03 E
Trebbia ≃	46	45.04 N	9.41 E
Třebíč	36	49.13 N	15.53 E
Trebišov	36	48.40 N	21.47 E
Třeboňská pánev ≚[1]	36	49.00 N	14.50 E
Treene ≃	36	54.22 N	9.05 E
Treinta y Tres	146	33.14 S	54.23 W
Trélazé	42	47.27 N	0.28 W
Trelew	146	43.15 S	65.18 W
Trelleborg	28	55.22 N	13.10 E
Tremblant, Mont ∧	160	46.16 N	74.35 W
Tremonton	178	41.43 N	112.10 W
Trenčín	36	48.54 N	18.04 E
Trent ≃	32	53.42 N	0.41 W
Trento	46	46.04 N	11.08 E
Trenton, Mo., U.S.	174	40.05 N	93.37 W
Trenton, N.J., U.S.	166	40.13 N	74.45 W
Trenton, Tenn., U.S.	174	35.59 N	88.56 W
Trentwood	180	47.42 N	117.13 W
Tres Arroyos	146	38.23 S	60.17 W
Três Lagoas	144	20.48 S	51.43 W
Três Marias, Represa ⊜[1]	144	18.12 S	45.15 W
Treviglio	46	45.31 N	9.35 E
Treviso	46	45.40 N	12.15 E
Trevose	166	40.09 N	74.59 W
Trevose Head ➤	32	50.33 N	5.01 W
Trier	36	49.45 N	6.38 E
Trieste	46	45.40 N	13.46 E
Triglav ∧	46	46.23 N	13.50 E
Tríkala	54	39.34 N	21.46 E
Trikora, Puncak ∧	82	4.15 S	138.45 E
Trincomalee	84	8.34 N	81.14 E
Třinec	36	49.41 N	18.40 E
Trinidad, Bol.	144	14.47 S	64.47 W
Trinidad, Cuba	130	21.48 N	79.59 W
Trinidad, Colo., U.S.	162	37.10 N	104.31 W
Trinidad I	130	10.30 N	61.15 W
Trinidad and Tobago □[1]	130	11.00 N	61.00 W
Trinity ≃	174	29.47 N	94.42 W
Trinity Bay C	174	29.40 N	94.45 W
Trion	172	34.33 N	85.19 W
Tripoli → Țarābulus	102	32.54 N	13.11 E
Trípolis	54	37.31 N	22.21 E
Triton Island I	82	15.47 N	111.12 E
Trivandrum	84	8.28 N	76.57 E
Trnava	36	48.23 N	17.35 E
Trobriand Islands II	116a	8.35 S	151.05 E
Troina	46	37.47 N	14.37 E
Troisdorf	36	50.49 N	7.08 E
Trois Fourches, Cap des ➤	50	35.26 N	2.58 W
Trois-Rivières	160	46.21 N	72.33 W
Trojan	54	42.51 N	24.43 E
Trollhättan	28	58.16 N	12.18 E
Tromelin I	104	15.52 S	54.25 E
Tromsø	26	69.40 N	18.58 E
Tronador, Monte ∧	146	41.10 S	71.54 W
Trondheim	28	63.25 N	10.25 E
Trotuș ≃	54	46.03 N	27.14 E
Trotwood	166	39.48 N	84.18 W
Troup	184	32.09 N	95.07 W
Trout Lake ⊜	160	51.13 N	93.20 W
Trowbridge	32	51.20 N	2.13 W
Troy, Ala., U.S.	174	31.48 N	85.58 W
Troy, Kans., U.S.	174	39.49 N	95.05 W
Troy, Mo., U.S.	174	38.59 N	90.59 W
Troy, N.C., U.S.	172	35.22 N	79.53 W
Troy, N.Y., U.S.	166	42.43 N	73.40 W
Troy, Ohio, U.S.	166	40.02 N	84.13 W
Troyes	42	48.18 N	4.05 E
Truchas Peak ∧	178	35.58 N	105.39 W
Trujillo, Esp.	50	39.28 N	5.53 W
Trujillo, Hond.	130	15.55 N	86.00 W
Trujillo, Perú	144	8.07 S	79.02 W
Trumann	174	35.41 N	90.31 W
Trumbull	166	41.15 N	73.12 W
Truro	32	50.16 N	5.03 W
Truth or Consequences (Hot Springs)	178	33.08 N	107.15 W
Trutnov	36	50.34 N	15.55 E
Truyère ≃	42	44.39 N	2.34 E
Tryon	172	35.13 N	82.14 W
Trzcianka	36	53.03 N	16.28 E
Trzebinia	36	50.10 N	19.18 E
Tsaratanana, Massif du ∧∧	104	14.00 S	49.00 E
Tshangalele, Lac ⊜	104	10.55 S	27.03 E
Tsiafajavona ∧	104	19.21 S	47.15 E
Tsiribihina ≃	104	19.42 S	44.31 E
Tsitsihar → Qiqihaer	80	47.19 N	123.55 E
Tsu	80	34.43 N	136.31 E
Tsugaru-kaikyō ⊔	80	41.35 N	141.00 E
Tsumeb	104	19.13 S	17.42 E
Tsuruga	80	35.39 N	136.04 E
Tsuruoka	80	38.44 N	139.50 E
Tua ≃	50	41.13 N	7.26 W
Tual	82	5.40 S	132.45 E
Tuba City	178	36.08 N	111.14 W
Tübingen	36	48.31 N	9.02 E
Țubruq	102	32.05 N	23.59 E
Tucson	178	32.13 N	110.58 W
Tucumcari	162	35.10 N	103.44 W
Tudela	50	42.05 N	1.36 W
Tuela ≃	50	41.30 N	7.12 W
Tugela ≃	104	29.14 S	31.30 E
Tuguegarao	82	17.37 N	121.44 E
Tuktoyaktuk	160	69.27 N	133.02 W
Tula	26	54.12 N	37.37 E
Tulancingo	130	20.05 N	98.22 W
Tulare	184	36.13 N	119.21 W
Tularosa	178	33.04 N	106.01 W
Tularosa Valley ≚[1]	178	32.45 N	106.10 W
Tulcán	144	0.48 N	77.43 W
Tulcea	54	45.11 N	28.48 E
Tuléar	104	23.21 S	43.40 E
Tullahoma	174	35.22 N	86.11 W
Tulle	42	45.16 N	1.46 E
Tulsa	162	36.09 N	95.58 W
Tuluá	144	4.06 N	76.11 W
Tumaco	144	1.49 N	78.46 W
Tuman-gang ≃	80	42.18 N	130.41 E
Tumba	28	59.12 N	17.49 E
Tumba, Lac ⊜	104	0.48 S	18.03 E
Tumbes	144	3.34 S	80.28 W
T'umen'	62	57.09 N	65.32 E
Tumuc-Humac Mountains ∧∧	144	2.20 N	55.00 W
Tumwater	180	47.01 N	122.54 W
Tunbridge Wells	32	51.08 N	0.16 E
Tunca (Tundža) ≃	54	41.40 N	26.34 E
Tunis	100	36.48 N	10.11 E
Tunis, Golfe de C	100	37.00 N	10.30 E
Tunisia □[1]	100	34.00 N	9.00 E
Tunja	144	5.31 N	73.22 W
Tuokusidawanling ∧	80	37.14 N	85.47 E
Tupã	144	21.56 S	50.30 W
Tupelo	174	34.16 N	88.43 W
Tupper Lake	166	44.13 N	74.29 W
Tupungato, Cerro ∧	146	33.22 S	69.47 W
Turano ≃	46	42.26 N	12.47 E
Turbacz ∧	36	49.33 N	20.08 E
Turda	54	46.34 N	23.47 E
Turek	36	52.02 N	18.30 E
Turgajskaja Dolina ∨	62	51.00 N	64.30 E
Turgutlu	54	38.30 N	27.43 E
Turia ≃	50	39.27 N	0.19 W
Turin → Torino	46	45.03 N	7.40 E
Túrkeve	36	47.06 N	20.45 E
Turkey □[1], As.	20	39.00 N	35.00 E
Turkey □[1], Eur.	20	39.00 N	35.00 E
Turks and Caicos Islands □[2]	130	21.45 N	71.35 W
Turks Islands II	130	21.24 N	71.07 W
Turku (Åbo)	28	60.27 N	22.17 E
Turkwel ≃	102	3.06 N	36.06 E
Turlock	184	37.30 N	120.51 W
Turneffe Islands II	130	17.22 N	87.51 W
Turners Falls	166	42.36 N	72.33 W
Turnhout	36	51.19 N	4.57 E
Turnor Lake ⊜	160	56.32 N	108.38 W
Turnov	36	50.35 N	15.10 E
Turnu-Măgurele	54	43.45 N	24.53 E
Turopolje ≚	46	45.40 N	16.05 E
Turquino, Pico ∧	130	19.59 N	76.50 W
Turritano ◆[1]	46	40.48 N	8.30 E
Turtle Lake	168	45.24 N	92.08 W
Tuscaloosa	174	33.13 N	87.33 W
Tuscarora Mountain ∧	166	40.10 N	77.45 W
Tuscola	174	39.48 N	88.17 W
Tuscumbia	174	34.44 N	87.42 W
Tuskegee	174	32.26 N	85.42 W
Tutova ≃	54	46.06 N	27.32 E
Tutrakan	54	44.03 N	26.37 E
Tutuila I	113	14.18 S	170.42 W
Tutupaca, Volcán ∧[1]	144	17.01 S	70.22 W
Tuvalu □[1]	10	8.00 S	178.00 E
Țuwayq, Jabal ∧∧	84	23.00 N	46.00 E
Tuxpan	130	21.57 N	105.18 W
Tuxtla Gutiérrez	130	16.45 N	93.07 W
Tuzla	54	44.32 N	18.41 E
Twentynine Palms	184	34.08 N	116.03 W
Twin Falls	180	42.34 N	114.28 W
Twin Lakes	168	42.32 N	88.15 W
Twinsburg	166	41.19 N	81.27 W
Two Harbors	168	47.01 N	91.40 W
Tychy	36	50.09 N	18.59 E
Tyler	174	32.21 N	95.18 W
Tyne ≃	32	55.01 N	1.26 W
Tynemouth	32	55.01 N	1.24 W
Tyrone	166	40.40 N	78.14 W
Tyrrhenian Sea (Mare Tirreno) ⊤[2]	46	40.00 N	12.00 E
Tywi ≃	32	51.46 N	4.22 W
U			
Ubangi (Oubangui) ≃	100	1.15 N	17.50 E
Ube	80	33.56 N	131.15 E
Úbeda	50	38.01 N	3.22 W
Uberaba	144	19.45 S	47.55 W
Uberlândia	144	18.56 S	48.18 W
Ubon Ratchathani	82	15.14 N	104.54 E
Ubundi	104	0.21 S	25.29 E
Ucayali ≃	144	4.30 S	73.27 W
Uchiura-wan C	80	42.20 N	140.40 E
Uchta	26	63.33 N	53.38 E
Uddevalla	28	58.21 N	11.55 E
Uddjaur ⊜	26	65.55 N	17.49 E
Udine	46	46.03 N	13.14 E
Udon Thani	82	17.26 N	102.46 E
Ueckermünde	36	53.44 N	14.03 E
Uele ≃	102	4.09 N	22.26 E
Uelzen	36	52.58 N	10.33 E
Uere ≃	102	3.42 N	25.24 E
Uetersen	36	53.41 N	9.39 E
Ufa	62	54.44 N	55.56 E
Ugalla ≃	104	5.08 S	30.42 E
Uganda □[1]	104	1.00 N	32.00 E
Ugoma ∧	104	4.00 S	28.45 E
Uherské Hradiště	36	49.05 N	17.28 E
Uhrichsville	166	40.24 N	81.20 W
Uinta Mountains ∧∧	178	40.45 N	110.05 W
Uitenhage	104	33.40 S	25.28 E
Újfehértó	36	47.48 N	21.40 E
Ujiji	104	4.55 S	29.41 E
Ujjain	84	23.12 N	75.46 E
Ujung Pandang (Makasar)	82	5.07 S	119.24 E
Ukerewe Island I	104	2.03 S	33.00 E
Ukiah	184	39.09 N	123.13 W
Ukrina ≃	46	45.05 N	17.56 E
Ulaanbaatar	80	47.55 N	106.53 E
Ulan Bator → **Ulaanbaatar**	80	47.55 N	106.53 E
Ulan-Ude	64	51.50 N	107.37 E
Ulcinj	54	41.55 N	19.11 E
Uljanovsk	26	54.20 N	48.24 E
Ullŭng-do I	80	37.29 N	130.52 E
Ulm	36	48.24 N	10.00 E
Ulsan	80	35.34 N	129.19 E
Ulster □[9]	32	54.35 N	7.00 W
Ulubat Gölü ⊜	54	40.10 N	28.35 E
Ulu Dağ ∧	54	40.04 N	29.13 E
Uluguru Mountains ∧∧	104	7.10 S	37.40 E
Umanak Fjord C[2]	160	70.55 N	53.00 W
Umeå	28	63.50 N	20.15 E
Umeälven ≃	28	63.47 N	20.16 E
Umfuli ≃	104	17.30 S	29.23 E
Umm Durmān (Omdurman)	102	15.38 N	32.30 E
'Umrān	84	15.50 N	43.56 E
Umtali	104	18.58 S	32.40 E
Umtata	104	31.35 S	28.47 E
Unac ≃	46	44.30 N	16.09 E
'Unayzah	84	26.06 N	43.56 E
Uncompahgre Peak ∧	178	38.04 N	107.28 W
Undu Cape ➤	111	16.08 S	179.57 W
Ungava, Péninsule d' ➤[1]	160	60.00 N	74.00 W
Ungava Bay C	160	59.30 N	67.30 W
Unije, Otok I	46	44.38 N	14.15 E
Unimak Island I	162a	54.50 N	164.00 W
Union, Miss., U.S.	174	32.34 N	89.14 W
Union, Mo., U.S.	174	38.27 N	91.00 W
Union, N.J., U.S.	166	40.42 N	74.16 W
Union, S.C., U.S.	172	34.43 N	81.37 W
Union City, Ga., U.S.	172	33.35 N	84.33 W
Union City, Ind., U.S.	174	40.12 N	84.49 W
Union City, Pa., U.S.	166	41.54 N	79.51 W
Union City, Tenn., U.S.	174	36.26 N	89.03 W
Union Gap	180	46.34 N	120.34 W
Union Grove	168	42.41 N	88.03 W

Name	Page	Lat °′	Long °′
Union of Soviet Socialist Republics □¹, As.	62	60.00 N	80.00 E
Union of Soviet Socialist Republics □¹, Eur.	62	60.00 N	80.00 E
Union Park	172	28.30 N	81.15 W
Union Springs, Ala., U.S.	174	32.09 N	85.49 W
Union Springs, N.Y., U.S.	166	42.50 N	76.42 W
Uniontown	166	39.54 N	79.44 W
Unionville	174	40.29 N	93.01 W
United Arab Emirates □¹	84	24.00 N	54.00 E
United Kingdom □¹	32	54.00 N	2.00 W
United States □¹	162	38.00 N	97.00 W
University City	174	38.39 N	90.19 W
University Park	178	32.17 N	106.45 W
Unna	36	51.32 N	7.41 E
Unstrut ≃	36	51.10 N	11.48 E
Unža ≃	62	57.20 N	43.08 E
Upemba, Lac ⊜	104	8.36 S	26.26 E
Upington	104	28.25 S	21.15 E
Upolu I	113	13.55 S	171.45 W
Upolu Point ≻	162b	20.16 N	155.51 W
Upper Arlington	166	40.00 N	83.03 W
Upper Arrow Lake ⊜	160	50.30 N	117.55 W
Upper Hutt	118	41.08 S	175.04 E
Upper Klamath Lake ⊜	180	42.23 N	122.55 W
Upper Red Lake ⊜	168	48.10 N	94.40 W
Upper Sandusky	166	40.50 N	83.17 W
Upper Volta □¹	100	13.00 N	2.00 W
Uppsala	28	59.52 N	17.38 E
Ural ≃	62	47.00 N	51.48 E
Ural Mountains → Ural'skije Gory ⋀	62	60.00 N	60.00 E
Ural'sk	62	51.14 N	51.22 E
Ural'skije Gory (Ural Mountains) ⋀	62	60.00 N	60.00 E
Urbana, Ill., U.S.	174	40.07 N	88.12 W
Urbana, Ohio, U.S.	166	40.07 N	83.45 W
Urbandale	168	41.38 N	93.48 W
Urbiña, Peña ▲	50	43.01 N	5.57 W
Urbino	46	43.43 N	12.38 E
Ure ≃	32	54.01 N	1.12 W
Urfa	20	37.08 N	38.46 E
Ursus	36	52.12 N	20.53 E
Uruapan	130	19.25 N	102.04 W
Uruguay □¹	146	33.00 S	56.00 W
Urunchi → Wulumuqi	80	43.48 N	87.35 E
Usa ≃	62	65.57 N	56.55 E
Uşak	54	38.41 N	29.25 E
Usk ≃	32	51.36 N	2.58 W
Üsküdar	54	41.01 N	29.01 E
Usolje-Sibirskoje	64	52.47 N	103.38 E
Ussuri (Wusulijiang) ≃	64	48.27 N	135.04 E
Ussurijsk	64	43.48 N	131.59 E
Uster	42	47.21 N	8.43 E
Ustica, Isola di I	46	38.42 N	13.10 E
Ústí nad Labem	36	50.40 N	14.02 E
Ústí nad Orlicí	36	49.58 N	16.24 E
Ustka	36	54.35 N	16.50 E
Ust'-Kamenogorsk	64	49.58 N	82.38 E
Ust'urt, Plato ⋀¹	62	43.00 N	56.00 E
Utah □³	162	39.30 N	111.30 W
Utah Lake ⊜	178	40.13 N	111.49 W
Utembo ≃	104	17.06 S	22.01 E
Utica, Mich., U.S.	168	42.38 N	83.02 W
Utica, N.Y., U.S.	166	43.05 N	75.14 W
Utrecht	36	52.05 N	5.08 E
Utrera	50	37.11 N	5.47 W
Utsunomiya	80	36.33 N	139.52 E
Uusimaa ◆¹	28	60.30 N	25.00 E
Uvalde	162	29.13 N	99.47 W
Uvéa	112	20.27 S	166.36 E
Uvs Nuur ⊜	64	50.20 N	92.45 E
Uwajima	80	33.13 N	132.34 E
'Uwaynāt, Jabal al- ▲	102	21.54 N	24.58 E
Uyuni, Salar de ≚	144	20.20 S	67.42 W
Užgorod	54	48.37 N	22.18 E
Uzunköprü	54	41.16 N	26.41 E
V			
Vaal ≃	104	29.04 S	23.38 E
Vaalserberg ▲	36	50.46 N	6.01 E
Vaasa (Vasa)	28	63.06 N	21.36 E
Vác	36	47.47 N	19.08 E
Vacaville	184	38.21 N	121.59 W
Vaccarès, Étang de C	42	43.32 N	4.34 E
Vadsø	26	70.05 N	29.46 E
Vaduz	42	47.09 N	9.31 E
Vaga ≃	62	62.48 N	42.56 E
Váh ≃	36	47.55 N	18.00 E
Vajgač, Ostrov I	62	70.00 N	59.30 E
Vākhān ◆¹	84	37.00 N	73.00 E
Valaisannes, Alpes ⋀	42	46.00 N	7.30 E
Valašské Meziříčí	36	49.28 N	17.58 E
Valdagno	46	45.39 N	11.18 E
Valdajskaja Vozvyšennost' ⋀²	62	57.00 N	33.30 E
Valdavia ≃	50	42.24 N	4.16 W
Valdecañas, Embalse de ⊜¹	50	39.45 N	5.30 W
Valdepeñas	50	38.46 N	3.23 W
Valderaduey ≃	50	41.31 N	5.42 W
Valders	168	44.09 N	87.53 W
Valdés, Peninsula ≻¹	146	42.30 S	64.00 W
Valdese	172	35.44 N	81.34 W
Val di Mazara ◆¹	46	37.50 N	13.00 E
Val di Noto ◆¹	46	37.05 N	14.40 E
Valdivia	146	39.48 S	73.14 W
Valdobbiadene	46	45.54 N	12.00 E
Valdosta	172	30.50 N	83.17 W
Valence	42	44.56 N	4.54 E
Valencia, Esp.	50	39.28 N	0.22 W
Valencia, Ven.	144	10.11 N	68.00 W
Valencia □⁹	50	39.30 N	0.40 W
Valencia, Golfo de C	50	39.50 N	0.30 E
Valencia de Alcántata	50	39.25 N	7.14 W
Valenciennes	42	50.21 N	3.32 E
Valentine	162	42.52 N	100.33 W
Valenza	46	45.01 N	8.38 E
Valera	144	9.19 N	70.37 W
Valjevo	54	44.16 N	19.53 E
Valkeakoski	28	61.16 N	24.02 E
Valkenswaard	36	51.21 N	5.28 E
Valladolid	50	41.39 N	4.43 W
Vall de Uxó	50	39.49 N	0.14 W
Valle de la Pascua	144	9.13 N	66.00 W
Valledupar	144	10.29 N	73.15 W
Vallejo	184	38.07 N	122.14 W
Vallenar	146	28.35 S	70.46 W
Valletta	46	35.54 N	14.31 E
Valley City	162	46.55 N	97.59 W
Valley Station	174	38.06 N	85.52 W
Vallgrund I	28	63.12 N	21.14 E
Valls	50	41.17 N	1.15 E
Valparaiso, Chile	146	33.02 S	71.38 W
Valparaiso, Fla., U.S.	174	30.29 N	86.30 W
Valparaiso, Ind., U.S.	174	41.28 N	87.03 W
Vals, Tanjung ≻	82	8.26 S	137.38 E
Valsbaai C	104	34.12 S	18.40 E
Valverde del Camino	50	37.34 N	6.45 W
Van	20	38.28 N	43.20 E
Van Buren	174	35.26 N	94.21 W
Vancouver, B.C., Can.	160	49.16 N	123.07 W
Vancouver, Wash., U.S.	180	45.39 N	122.40 W
Vancouver, Mount ▲	162a	60.20 N	139.40 W
Vancouver Island I	160	49.45 N	126.00 W
Vandalia, Ill., U.S.	174	38.58 N	89.06 W
Vandalia, Mo., U.S.	174	39.19 N	91.29 W
Vandalia, Ohio, U.S.	166	39.53 N	84.12 W
Vanderbijlpark	104	26.42 S	27.54 E
Vandergrift	166	40.36 N	79.34 W
Vänern ⊜	28	58.55 N	13.30 E
Vänersborg	28	58.22 N	12.19 E
Van Gölü ⊜	20	38.33 N	42.46 E
Vannes	42	47.39 N	2.46 W
Vanoise, Massif de la ⋀	42	45.20 N	6.40 E
Vantaa ≃	28	60.13 N	24.59 E
Vanua Levu I	111	16.33 S	179.15 E
Van Wert	166	40.52 N	84.35 W
Vārānasi (Benares)	84	25.20 N	83.00 E
Varaždin	46	46.19 N	16.20 E
Varazze	46	44.22 N	8.34 E
Varberg	28	57.06 N	12.15 E
Vardar (Axiós) ≃	54	40.31 N	22.43 E
Vardø	26	70.21 N	31.02 E
Varel	36	53.22 N	8.10 E
Vareš	54	44.09 N	18.19 E
Varese	46	45.48 N	8.48 E
Varkaus	28	62.19 N	27.55 E
Varna	54	43.13 N	27.55 E
Värnamo	28	57.11 N	14.02 E
Varnenski zaliv C	54	43.11 N	27.56 E
Varnsdorf	36	50.52 N	14.40 E
Várpalota	36	47.12 N	18.09 E
Varsinais-Suomi ◆¹	28	60.40 N	22.30 E
Vascongadas □⁹	50	43.00 N	2.45 W
Vashon Island I	180	47.24 N	122.27 W
Vaslui	54	46.38 N	27.44 E
Vassar	168	43.22 N	83.35 W
Västerås	28	59.37 N	16.33 E
Västervik	28	57.45 N	16.38 E
Vasto	46	42.07 N	14.42 E
Vas'uganje ≣	62	58.00 N	77.00 E
Vathí	54	37.45 N	26.59 E
Vatican City (Città del Vaticano) □¹	46	41.54 N	12.27 E
Vaticano, Capo ≻	46	38.38 N	15.50 E
V'atka ≃	62	55.36 N	51.30 E
Vatnajökull ⊠	26a	64.25 N	16.50 W
Vatra Dornei	54	47.21 N	25.21 E
Vättern ⊜	28	58.24 N	14.36 E
Vatu-i-Ra Channel Ʋ	111	17.17 S	178.31 E
Vatukoula	111	17.31 S	177.51 E
Växjö	28	56.52 N	14.49 E
Veazie	166	44.51 N	68.42 W
Vechta	36	52.43 N	8.16 E
Vecsés	36	47.25 N	19.16 E
Vedea ≃	54	43.53 N	25.59 E
Veedersburg	174	40.07 N	87.16 W
Veendam	36	53.06 N	6.58 E
Veenendaal	36	52.02 N	5.34 E
Vega I	26	65.39 N	11.50 E
Vejer de la Frontera	50	36.15 N	5.58 W
Vejle	28	55.42 N	9.32 E
Velbert	36	51.20 N	7.02 E
Velebitski Kanal Ʋ	46	45.00 N	14.50 E
Velencei-tó ⊜	36	47.12 N	18.35 E
Velez de la Gomera, Peñón de I	50	35.11 N	4.21 W
Vélez-Málaga	50	36.47 N	4.06 W
Velikaja ≃	62	57.48 N	28.20 E
Velika Morava ≃	54	44.43 N	21.03 E
Velikije Luki	26	56.20 N	30.32 E
Velikij-ust'ug	26	60.48 N	46.18 E
Veliki kanal ≣	54	45.45 N	18.50 E
Veliki Vitorog ▲	46	44.07 N	17.03 E
Veliko Tărnovo	54	43.04 N	25.39 E
Velino, Monte ▲	46	42.09 N	13.23 E
Velká Deštná ▲	36	50.18 N	16.24 E
Veľká Fatra ⋀	36	49.00 N	19.05 E
Velletri	46	41.41 N	12.47 E
Venado Tuerto	146	33.45 S	61.58 W
Vendée ◆¹	42	46.40 N	1.10 W
Vendôme	42	47.48 N	1.04 E
Venezia (Venice)	46	45.27 N	12.21 E
Venezuela □¹	144	8.00 N	66.00 W
Venezuela, Golfo de C	144	11.30 N	71.00 W
Venice → Venezia, It.	46	45.27 N	12.21 E
Venice, Fla., U.S.	172	27.06 N	82.27 W
Venice, Gulf of C	46	45.15 N	13.00 E
Vénissieux	42	45.41 N	4.53 E
Venlo	36	51.24 N	6.10 E
Venosa	46	40.57 N	15.49 E
Ventimiglia	46	43.47 N	7.36 E
Ventura	184	34.17 N	119.18 W
Ver	112	14.11 S	167.34 E
Veracruz	130	19.12 N	96.08 W
Vercelli	46	45.19 N	8.25 E
Verchojanskij Chrebet ⋀	64	67.00 N	129.00 E
Verde ≃	178	33.33 N	111.40 W
Verden	36	52.55 N	9.13 E
Verdon ≃	42	43.43 N	5.46 E
Verdun	42	49.10 N	5.23 E
Vereeniging	104	26.38 S	27.57 E
Vergara	50	43.07 N	2.25 W
Vergennes	166	44.10 N	73.15 W
Vermilion	166	41.25 N	82.22 W
Vermilion Bay C	174	29.40 N	92.00 W
Vermilion Lake ⊜	168	47.53 N	92.25 W
Vermillion	162	42.47 N	96.56 W
Vermont □³	162	43.50 N	72.45 W
Vernal	178	40.27 N	109.32 W
Verneukpan ≚	104	30.00 S	21.10 E
Vernon, Fr.	42	47.48 N	1.38 E
Vernon, Ala., U.S.	174	33.45 N	88.07 W
Vernon, Conn., U.S.	166	41.52 N	72.27 W
Vero Beach	172	27.38 N	80.24 W
Véroia	54	40.31 N	22.12 E
Verona, It.	46	45.27 N	11.00 E
Verona, Miss., U.S.	174	34.12 N	88.43 W
Versailles, Fr.	42	48.48 N	2.08 E
Versailles, Ky., U.S.	174	38.03 N	84.44 W
Versailles, Mo., U.S.	174	38.26 N	92.51 W
Vert, Cap ≻	100	14.43 N	17.30 W
Vertou	42	47.10 N	1.29 W
Verviers	36	50.35 N	5.52 E
Vesoul	42	47.38 N	6.10 E
Vestavia Hills	174	33.27 N	86.47 W
Vestfjorden C²	26	68.08 N	15.00 E
Vestmannaeyjar	26a	63.26 N	20.12 W
Vesuvio ▲¹	46	40.49 N	14.26 E
Veszprém	36	47.06 N	17.55 E
Vésztő	36	46.55 N	21.16 E
Vetlanda	28	57.26 N	15.04 E
Vettore, Monte ▲	46	42.49 N	13.16 E
Vevey	42	46.28 N	6.51 E
Vézère ≃	42	44.53 N	0.53 E
Viadana	46	44.56 N	10.31 E
Vian	174	35.30 N	94.58 W
Viana do Castelo	50	41.42 N	8.50 W
Viangchan (Vientiane)	82	17.58 N	102.36 E
Viareggio	46	43.52 N	10.14 E
Viaur ≃	42	44.08 N	2.23 E
Viborg	28	56.26 N	9.24 E
Vibo Valentia	46	38.40 N	16.06 E
Vicenza	46	45.33 N	11.33 E
Vich	50	41.56 N	2.15 E
Vichy	42	46.08 N	3.26 E
Vicksburg	174	32.14 N	90.56 W
Victoria, Cam.	100	4.01 N	9.12 E
Victoria, B.C., Can.	160	48.25 N	123.22 W
Victoria (Xianggang), H.K.	80	22.17 N	114.09 E
Victoria, Sey.	104	4.38 S	55.27 E
Victoria, Tex., U.S.	162	28.48 N	97.00 W
Victoria, Lake ⊜	104	1.00 S	33.00 E
Victoria, Mount ▲, Austl.	116	8.55 S	147.35 E
Victoria, Mount ▲, Mya.	82	21.14 N	93.55 E
Victoria de las Tunas	130	20.58 N	76.57 W
Victoria Falls ⊾	104	17.55 S	25.51 E
Victoria Island I	160	71.00 N	114.00 W
Victoria Nile ≃	102	2.14 N	31.26 E
Victoria Peak ▲	130	16.48 N	88.37 W
Victorville	184	34.32 N	117.18 W
Vičuga	26	57.13 N	41.56 E
Vidalia, Ga., U.S.	172	32.13 N	82.25 W
Vidalia, La., U.S.	174	31.34 N	91.26 W
Vidin	54	43.59 N	22.52 E
Vidor	174	30.07 N	94.01 W
Viedma, Lago ⊜	146	49.35 S	72.35 W
Vienna → Wien, Öst.	36	48.13 N	16.20 E
Vienna, Ga., U.S.	172	32.06 N	83.47 W
Vienna, W. Va., U.S.	166	39.20 N	81.26 W
Vienne	42	45.31 N	4.52 E
Vienne ≃	42	47.13 N	0.05 E
Vieques, Isla de I	130	18.08 N	65.25 W
Viersen	36	51.15 N	6.23 E
Vierwaldstätter See ⊜	42	47.00 N	8.28 E
Vierzon	42	47.13 N	2.05 E
Vieste	46	41.53 N	16.10 E
Vietnam □¹	82	16.00 N	108.00 E
Vigevano	46	45.19 N	8.51 E
Vignola	46	44.29 N	11.00 E
Vigo	50	42.14 N	8.43 W
Vigo, Ría de C¹	50	42.15 N	8.45 W
Vihorlat ⋀	36	48.55 N	22.10 E
Vihren ▲	54	41.46 N	23.24 E
Vijayawāda	84	16.31 N	80.37 E
Vila	112	17.44 S	168.19 E
Vila do Conde	50	41.21 N	8.45 W
Vilafranca del Panadés	50	41.21 N	1.42 E
Vila Franca de Xira	50	38.57 N	8.59 W
Vilaine ≃	42	47.30 N	2.27 W
Vila Nova de Gaia	50	41.08 N	8.37 W
Vila Real	50	41.18 N	7.45 W
Vila Velha	144	20.20 S	40.17 W
Vil'kickogo, Proliv Ʋ	64	77.55 N	103.00 E
Villacañas	50	39.38 N	3.20 W
Villacarrillo	50	38.07 N	3.05 W
Villach	36	46.36 N	13.50 E
Villacidro	46	39.27 N	8.44 E
Villafranca di Verona	46	45.21 N	10.50 E
Villa Grove	174	39.52 N	88.10 W
Villahermosa	130	17.59 N	92.55 W
Villa María	146	32.25 S	63.15 W
Villa Nueva, Arg.	146	32.54 S	68.47 W
Villanueva, N. Mex., U.S.	178	35.17 N	105.23 W
Villanueva de Córdoba	50	38.20 N	4.37 W
Villanueva de la Serena	50	38.58 N	5.48 W
Villanueva del Rio y Minas	50	37.39 N	5.42 W
Villanueva y Geltrú	50	41.14 N	1.44 E
Villa Rica	172	33.44 N	84.55 W
Villarrica	146	25.45 S	56.26 W
Villarrobledo	50	39.16 N	2.36 W
Villas	166	39.02 N	74.56 W
Villavicencio	144	4.09 N	73.37 W
Villefranche	42	45.59 N	4.43 E
Villefranche-de-Rouergue	42	44.21 N	2.02 E
Villena	50	38.38 N	0.51 W
Villeneuve-Saint-Georges	42	48.44 N	2.27 E
Villeneuve-sur-Lot	42	44.25 N	0.42 E
Ville Platte	174	30.42 N	92.16 W
Villerupt	42	49.28 N	5.56 E
Villeurbanne	42	45.46 N	4.53 E
Villingen-Schwenningen	36	48.04 N	8.28 E
Vilnius	26	54.41 N	25.19 E
Vilvoorde	36	50.56 N	4.26 E
Vina ≃	100	7.45 N	15.36 E
Viña del Mar	146	33.02 S	71.34 W
Vinaroz	50	40.28 N	0.29 E
Vincennes	174	38.41 N	87.32 W
Vincent	174	33.23 N	86.25 W
Vincent, Point ≻	113	29.00 S	167.55 E
Vindelälven ≃	28	63.54 N	19.52 E
Vindhya Range ⋀	84	23.00 N	77.00 E
Vine Grove	174	37.49 N	85.59 W
Vineland	166	39.29 N	75.02 W
Vineyard Sound Ʋ	166	41.25 N	70.46 W
Vinh	82	18.40 N	105.40 E
Vinh-long	82	10.15 N	105.58 E
Vinita	174	36.39 N	95.09 W
Vinkovci	54	45.17 N	18.49 E
Vinnica	62	49.14 N	28.29 E
Vinson Massif ▲	191	78.35 S	85.25 W
Vinton, Iowa, U.S.	168	42.10 N	92.01 W
Vinton, La., U.S.	174	30.11 N	93.35 W
Vinton, Va., U.S.	172	37.17 N	80.01 W
Virden	174	39.30 N	89.46 W
Vire	42	48.50 N	0.53 W
Vire ≃	42	49.20 N	1.07 W
Virgin ≃	178	36.31 N	114.20 W
Virginia, S. Afr.	104	28.12 S	26.49 E
Virginia, Minn., U.S.	168	47.31 N	92.32 W
Virginia □³	162	37.30 N	78.45 W
Virginia Beach	172	36.51 N	75.58 W
Virihaure ⊜	26	67.20 N	16.35 E
Viroqua	168	43.34 N	90.53 W
Virovitica	54	45.50 N	17.23 E
Vis, Otok I	46	43.02 N	16.11 E
Visalia	184	36.20 N	119.18 W
Viseu	50	40.39 N	7.55 W
Vișeu ≃	54	46.55 N	23.47 E
Vishākhapatnam	84	17.43 N	83.19 E
Viso, Monte ▲	46	44.40 N	7.07 E
Visoko	54	43.59 N	18.11 E
Vista	184	33.12 N	117.15 W
Vitarte	144	12.02 S	76.56 W
Vitebsk	26	55.12 N	30.11 E
Viterbo	46	42.25 N	12.06 E
Viti Levu I	111	18.00 S	178.00 E
Vitória, Bra.	144	20.19 S	40.21 W
Vitoria, Esp.	50	42.51 N	2.40 W
Vitória da Conquista	144	14.51 S	40.51 W
Vitré	42	48.08 N	1.12 W
Vitry-le-François	42	48.44 N	4.35 E
Vittoria	46	36.57 N	14.32 E
Vittorio Veneto	46	45.59 N	12.18 E
Vivian	174	32.53 N	93.59 W
Vizcaya □⁴	50	43.20 N	2.45 W
Vlaardingen	36	51.54 N	4.21 E
Vlădeasa ▲	54	46.45 N	22.48 E
Vladimir	26	56.10 N	40.25 E
Vladivostok	64	43.10 N	131.56 E
Vlasinsko Jezero ⊜	54	42.42 N	22.22 E
Vlieland I	36	53.15 N	5.00 E
Vlissingen (Flushing)	36	51.26 N	3.35 E
Vlorë	54	40.27 N	19.30 E
Vlorës, Gji i C	54	40.25 N	19.25 E
Vltava ≃	36	50.21 N	14.30 E
Vogelsberg ⋀	36	50.30 N	9.15 E
Voghera	46	44.59 N	9.01 E
Voiron	42	45.22 N	5.35 E
Vojmsjön ⊜	28	64.55 N	16.40 E
Volchov	26	59.55 N	32.20 E
Volchov ≃	62	60.08 N	32.20 E
Volga ≃	62	45.55 N	47.52 E
Volgograd (Stalingrad)	62	48.44 N	44.25 E
Volgogradskoje Vodochranilišče ⊜¹	62	49.20 N	45.00 E
Völklingen	36	49.15 N	6.50 E
Vologda	26	59.12 N	39.55 E
Vólos	54	39.21 N	22.56 E
Volta, Lake ⊜¹	100	7.30 N	0.15 E
Volta Blanche (White Volta) ≃	100	9.10 N	1.15 W
Volta Noire (Black Volta) ≃	100	8.41 N	1.33 E
Volta Redonda	144	22.32 S	44.07 W
Volterra	46	43.24 N	10.51 E
Volturno ≃	46	41.01 N	13.55 E
Volžsk	26	55.53 N	48.21 E
Volžskij	62	48.50 N	44.44 E
Vorderrhein ≃	42	46.49 N	9.25 E
Vordingborg	28	55.01 N	11.55 E
Voriai Sporádhes II	54	39.17 N	23.23 E
Vorkuta	26	67.27 N	63.58 E
Voronež	62	51.40 N	39.10 E
Vorošilovgrad	62	48.34 N	39.20 E
Voskresensk	26	55.19 N	38.42 E
Vostočno-Sibirskoje More (East Siberian Sea) ₸²	64	74.00 N	166.00 E
Votkinsk	26	57.03 N	53.59 E
Vouga ≃	50	40.41 N	8.40 W
Vraca	54	43.12 N	23.33 E
Vrancei, Munții ⋀	54	46.00 N	26.30 E
Vrangel'a, Ostrov I	64	71.00 N	179.30 W
Vranje	54	42.33 N	21.54 E
Vrbas	54	45.35 N	19.39 E
Vrbas ≃	46	45.06 N	17.31 E
Vrchlabí	36	50.38 N	15.37 E
Vršac	54	45.07 N	21.18 E
Vryburg	104	26.55 S	24.45 E
Vsetín	36	49.21 N	17.59 E
Vught	36	51.40 N	5.17 E
Vukovar	54	45.21 N	19.00 E
Vulcan	54	45.23 N	23.17 E
Vulcano, Isola I	46	38.27 N	14.58 E
Vunmarama	112	15.29 S	168.10 E
Vuoksenniska	28	61.13 N	28.49 E
Vyborg	26	60.42 N	28.45 E
Vyčegda ≃	62	61.18 N	46.36 E
Vygozero, Ozero ⊜	62	63.35 N	34.42 E
Vyškov	36	49.16 N	17.00 E
W			
Wa	100	10.04 N	2.29 W
Waal ≃	36	51.55 N	4.30 E
Waalwijk	36	51.42 N	5.04 E
Wabasca ≃	160	58.22 N	115.20 W
Wabash	174	40.48 N	85.49 W
Wabash ≃	174	37.46 N	88.02 W
Wabasha	168	44.23 N	92.02 W
Wąbrzeźno	36	53.17 N	18.57 E
Wachau ◆¹	36	48.18 N	15.24 E
Waco	162	31.55 N	97.08 W
Waconia	168	44.51 N	93.47 W
Waddeneilanden II	36	53.26 N	5.30 E
Waddenzee ₸²	36	53.15 N	5.15 E
Waddington, Mount ▲	160	51.23 N	125.15 W
Wadesboro	172	34.58 N	80.04 W
Wādī Halfā'	102	21.56 N	31.20 E
Wadley	172	32.52 N	82.24 W
Wad Madanī	102	13.25 N	33.28 E
Wadsworth	166	41.02 N	81.44 W
Wageningen	36	51.58 N	5.40 E
Wagga Wagga	116	35.07 S	147.22 E
Wagoner	174	35.58 N	95.22 W
Wagrien ◆¹	36	54.15 N	10.45 E
Wągrowiec	36	52.49 N	17.11 E
Wahiawa	162b	21.30 N	158.01 W
Wahpeton	162	46.16 N	96.36 W
Waialua	162b	21.34 N	158.08 W
Waianae	162b	21.27 N	158.11 W
Waiblingen	36	48.50 N	9.19 E
Wailuku	162b	20.53 N	156.30 W
Wainganga ≃	84	18.50 N	79.55 E
Waitato ≃	118	37.43 S	176.14 E
Waitemata	118	36.56 S	174.42 E
Waite Park	168	45.33 N	94.14 W
Wakatipu, Lake ⊜	118	45.05 S	168.34 E
Wakayama	80	34.13 N	135.11 E
Wakefield, Eng., U.K.	32	53.42 N	1.29 W
Wakefield, R.I., U.S.	166	41.26 N	71.30 W
Wake Forest	172	35.59 N	78.30 W
Wake Island □²	10	19.17 N	166.36 E
Wake Village	184	33.26 N	94.07 W
Wakkanai	80	45.25 N	141.40 E
Wałbrzych (Waldenburg)	36	50.46 N	16.17 E
Walcheren I	36	51.33 N	3.35 E
Walcott	174	41.35 N	90.47 W
Wałcz	36	53.17 N	16.28 E
Waldbröl	36	50.53 N	7.37 E
Walden	166	41.34 N	74.11 W
Walden Ridge ▲	172	35.30 N	85.15 W
Waldorf	166	38.37 N	76.54 W
Waldron	174	34.54 N	94.05 W
Waldviertel ◆¹	36	48.40 N	15.40 E
Wales □⁸	32	52.30 N	3.30 W
Walhalla, N. Dak., U.S.	162	48.55 N	97.55 W
Walhalla, S.C., U.S.	172	34.46 N	83.04 W
Walker	168	47.06 N	94.35 W
Walker ≃	184	38.54 N	118.47 W
Walkertown	172	36.10 N	80.10 W
Wallace, Idaho, U.S.	180	47.28 N	115.56 W
Wallace, N.C., U.S.	172	34.44 N	77.59 W
Walla Walla	180	46.08 N	118.20 W
Wallingford	166	41.27 N	72.50 W
Wallis and Futuna □²	10	14.00 N	177.00 W
Wallula, Lake ⊜¹	180	46.07 N	119.58 W
Walnut Ridge	174	36.04 N	90.57 W
Walsall	32	52.35 N	1.58 W
Walsenburg	178	37.37 N	104.47 W
Walsrode	36	52.52 N	9.35 E
Walterboro	172	32.55 N	80.39 W
Walter F. George Lake ⊜¹	172	31.49 N	85.08 W
Waltershausen	36	50.53 N	10.33 E
Waltham	166	42.23 N	71.14 W
Walton, Ky., U.S.	166	38.52 N	84.37 W
Walton, N.Y., U.S.	166	42.10 N	75.08 W
Walurigi	112	15.21 S	167.50 E
Walvisbaai (Walvis Bay)	104	22.59 S	14.31 E
Walworth	168	42.32 N	88.36 W
Wamba ≃	104	3.56 S	17.12 E
Wami ≃	104	6.08 S	38.49 E
Wamsutter	180	41.40 N	107.58 W
Wanganui	118	39.56 S	175.03 E
Wangen [im Allgäu]	36	47.41 N	9.50 E
Wangerooge I	36	53.46 N	7.55 E
Wankie	104	18.22 S	26.29 E
Wanne-Eickel	36	51.32 N	7.09 E
Wansbeck ≃	32	55.08 N	1.35 W
Wapakoneta	166	40.34 N	84.12 W
Wapato	180	46.27 N	120.25 W
Wapello	168	41.11 N	91.11 W
Wappingers Falls	166	41.36 N	73.55 W
Wapsipinicon ≃	168	41.44 N	90.20 W
Warangal	84	18.00 N	79.35 E
Warden	180	46.58 N	119.02 W
Ware	166	42.16 N	72.15 W
Waren	36	53.31 N	12.40 E
Warendorf	36	51.57 N	7.59 E
Ware Shoals	172	34.24 N	82.15 W
Warminster, Eng., U.K.	32	51.13 N	2.12 W
Warminster, Pa., U.S.	166	40.12 N	75.06 W
Warner Mountains ⋀	184	41.40 N	120.20 W
Warner Robins	172	32.37 N	83.36 W
Warnow ≃	36	54.06 N	12.09 E
Warren, Ark., U.S.	174	33.37 N	92.04 W
Warren, Mich., U.S.	168	42.28 N	83.01 W
Warren, Ohio, U.S.	166	41.14 N	80.52 W
Warren, Pa., U.S.	166	41.51 N	79.08 W
Warrensburg, Mo., U.S.	174	38.46 N	93.44 W
Warrensburg, N.Y., U.S.	166	43.30 N	73.46 W
Warrenton, Ga., U.S.	172	33.24 N	82.40 W
Warrenton, Va., U.S.	166	38.43 N	77.48 W
Warri	100	5.31 N	5.45 E
Warrington, Eng., U.K.	32	53.24 N	2.37 W
Warrington, Fla., U.S.	174	30.23 N	87.16 W
Warrior	174	33.49 N	86.49 W
Warrnambool	116	38.23 S	142.29 E
Warsaw → Warszawa, Pol.	36	52.15 N	21.00 E
Warsaw, Ind., U.S.	174	41.14 N	85.51 W
Warsaw, N.C., U.S.	172	35.00 N	78.05 W
Warsaw, N.Y., U.S.	166	42.44 N	78.08 W
Warszawa (Warsaw)	36	52.15 N	21.00 E
Warta ≃	36	52.35 N	14.39 E
Warwick, Eng., U.K.	32	52.17 N	1.34 W
Warwick, R.I., U.S.	166	41.43 N	71.28 W
Warwickshire □⁶	32	52.13 N	1.37 W
Wasatch Range ⋀	178	41.15 N	111.30 W
Wasco	184	35.36 N	119.20 W
Waseca	168	44.05 N	93.30 W
Washburn	168	46.41 N	90.52 W
Washington, D.C., U.S.	166	38.54 N	77.01 W
Washington, Ga., U.S.	172	33.44 N	82.44 W
Washington, Ill., U.S.	168	40.42 N	89.24 W
Washington, Ind., U.S.	174	38.40 N	87.10 W
Washington, Iowa, U.S.	168	41.18 N	91.42 W
Washington, Mo., U.S.	174	38.33 N	91.01 W
Washington, N.C., U.S.	172	35.33 N	77.03 W
Washington, Pa., U.S.	166	40.10 N	80.15 W
Washington □³	162	47.30 N	120.30 W
Washington, Mount ▲	166	44.15 N	71.15 W
Washington Court House	166	39.32 N	83.26 W
Washington Island I	168	45.23 N	86.55 W
Washington Terrace	178	41.12 N	111.59 W
Wasserkuppe ▲	36	50.30 N	9.56 E
Waterbury, Conn., U.S.	166	41.33 N	73.02 W
Waterbury, Vt., U.S.	166	44.20 N	72.46 W
Wateree ≃	172	33.45 N	80.37 W
Waterford, Eire	32	52.15 N	7.06 W
Waterford, Wis., U.S.	168	42.46 N	88.13 W
Waterloo, Bel.	36	50.43 N	4.23 E
Waterloo, Ill., U.S.	174	38.20 N	90.09 W
Waterloo, Iowa, U.S.	168	42.30 N	92.20 W
Waterloo, N.Y., U.S.	166	42.54 N	76.52 W
Waterloo, Wis., U.S.	168	43.11 N	88.59 W
Watertown, N.Y., U.S.	166	43.59 N	75.55 W
Watertown, S. Dak., U.S.	162	44.54 N	97.07 W
Watertown, Wis., U.S.	168	43.12 N	88.43 W
Water Valley	174	34.09 N	89.38 W
Waterville	166	44.33 N	69.38 W
Watervliet	166	42.44 N	73.42 W
Watford	32	51.40 N	0.25 W
Watford City	162	47.48 N	103.17 W
Wathaman ≃	160	57.16 N	102.52 W
Watseka	168	40.47 N	87.44 W
Watson Lake	160	60.07 N	128.48 W
Watsonville	184	36.55 N	121.45 W
Wattenscheid	36	51.29 N	7.08 E
Watts Bar Lake ⊜¹	172	35.48 N	84.39 W
Watzmann ▲	36	47.33 N	12.55 E
Waukegan	168	42.22 N	87.50 W
Waukesha	168	43.01 N	88.14 W
Waukon	168	43.16 N	91.29 W
Waunakee	168	43.11 N	89.27 W
Waupaca	168	44.21 N	89.05 W
Waupun	168	43.38 N	88.44 W
Wausau	168	44.59 N	89.39 W
Wauseon	166	41.33 N	84.09 W
Wautoma	168	44.04 N	89.17 W
Wauwatosa	168	43.03 N	88.00 W
Waveland	174	30.16 N	89.29 W
Waveney ≃	32	52.28 N	1.45 E
Waverly, Iowa, U.S.	168	42.44 N	92.29 W
Waverly, N.Y., U.S.	166	42.00 N	76.32 W
Waverly, Ohio, U.S.	166	39.07 N	82.59 W
Waverly, Tenn., U.S.	174	36.05 N	87.48 W
Waycross	172	31.13 N	82.21 W
Waylyn	172	32.51 N	80.00 W
Wayne, Mich., U.S.	168	42.17 N	83.23 W
Wayne, Nebr., U.S.	162	42.14 N	97.01 W
Wayne, N.J., U.S.	166	40.55 N	74.17 W
Waynesboro, Ga., U.S.	172	33.06 N	82.01 W
Waynesboro, Miss., U.S.	174	31.40 N	88.39 W
Waynesboro, Pa., U.S.	166	39.45 N	77.35 W
Waynesboro, Va., U.S.	172	38.04 N	78.53 W
Waynesburg	166	39.54 N	80.11 W
Waynesville, Mo., U.S.	174	37.50 N	92.12 W
Waynesville, N.C., U.S.	172	35.29 N	83.00 W
Wda ≃	36	53.25 N	18.29 E
Wear ≃	32	54.55 N	1.22 W
Weatherford	162	35.32 N	98.42 W
Weaver	174	33.45 N	85.49 W
Webb City	174	37.09 N	94.28 W
Webster	166	42.03 N	71.53 W
Webster City	168	42.28 N	93.49 W
Weddell Sea ₸²	191	72.00 S	45.00 W
Wedel	36	53.35 N	9.41 E
Weert	36	51.15 N	5.43 E
Weiden in der Oberpfalz	36	49.41 N	12.10 E
Weifang	80	36.42 N	19.04 E
Weilheim	36	47.50 N	11.08 E
Weimar	36	50.59 N	11.19 E
Weinheim	36	49.33 N	8.39 E
Weir	174	37.19 N	94.46 W
Weirton	166	40.25 N	80.35 W
Weiser	180	44.15 N	116.58 W
Weissenburg in Bayern	36	49.01 N	10.58 E
Weissenfels	36	51.12 N	11.58 E
Weiss Lake ⊜¹	172	34.15 N	85.35 W
Weisswasser	36	51.30 N	14.38 E
Weiz	36	47.13 N	15.37 E
Wejherowo	36	54.37 N	18.15 E
Welch, Okla., U.S.	174	36.52 N	95.06 W
Welch, W. Va., U.S.	172	37.25 N	81.31 W
Welcome	172	34.49 N	82.26 W
Weldon	172	36.25 N	77.36 W
Welkom	104	27.59 S	26.45 E
Welland	160	42.59 N	79.15 W
Wellingborough	32	52.19 N	0.42 W
Wellington, N.Z.	118	41.18 S	174.47 E
Wellington, Eng., U.K.	32	52.43 N	2.31 W
Wellington, Ohio, U.S.	166	41.10 N	82.13 W
Wells, Minn., U.S.	168	43.44 N	93.44 W
Wells, Nev., U.S.	184	41.07 N	114.58 W
Wellsboro	166	41.45 N	77.18 W
Wellsburg	166	40.16 N	80.37 W
Wellston	166	39.07 N	82.32 W
Wellsville	174	38.43 N	95.05 W
Wellsville, Mo., U.S.	174	39.04 N	91.34 W
Wellsville, N.Y., U.S.	166	42.07 N	77.57 W
Wellsville, Ohio, U.S.	166	40.36 N	80.39 W
Wels	36	48.10 N	14.02 E

Name	Page	Lat °′	Long °′
Welsh	174	30.14 N	92.49 W
Wembere ≃	104	4.10 S	34.11 E
Wenatchee	180	47.25 N	120.19 W
Wendell	172	35.47 N	78.22 W
Wenzhou	80	28.01 N	120.39 E
Werdau	36	50.44 N	12.22 E
Werder	36	52.23 N	12.56 E
Werdohl	36	51.16 N	7.46 E
Werl	36	51.33 N	7.54 E
Werne [an der Lippe]	36	51.40 N	7.38 E
Wernigerode	36	51.50 N	10.47 E
Werra ≃	36	51.26 N	9.39 E
Wesel	36	51.40 N	6.38 E
Weser ≃	36	53.32 N	8.34 E
Wesleyville	166	42.08 N	80.01 W
West Allis	168	43.01 N	88.00 W
West Bend	168	43.25 N	88.11 W
West-Berlin → Berlin (West)	36	52.31 N	13.24 E
West Bridgford	32	52.56 N	1.08 W
Westbrook	166	43.41 N	70.21 W
West Burlington	168	40.49 N	91.09 W
Westby	168	43.39 N	90.51 W
West Chester	166	39.58 N	75.36 W
Westcliffe	178	38.08 N	105.28 W
West Columbia, S.C., U.S.	172	34.00 N	81.04 W
West Columbia, Tex., U.S.	174	29.09 N	95.39 W
West Cote Blanche Bay C	174	29.40 N	91.45 W
West Des Moines	168	41.35 N	93.43 W
Westerly	166	41.22 N	71.50 W
Western Ghāts ⋏	84	14.00 N	75.00 E
Western Isles Islands □4	32	57.40 N	7.00 W
Westernport	166	39.29 N	79.03 W
Western Sahara □2	100	24.30 N	13.00 W
Western Samoa □1	113	13.55 S	172.00 W
Westerstede	36	53.15 N	7.55 E
Westerville	166	40.08 N	82.56 W
Westerwald ⋏	36	50.40 N	7.55 E
West Falkland I	146	51.50 S	60.00 W
Westfield, Mass., U.S.	166	42.08 N	72.45 W
Westfield, N.J., U.S.	166	40.39 N	74.21 W
Westfield, N.Y., U.S.	166	42.19 N	79.35 W
West Frankfort	174	37.54 N	88.55 W
West Glamorgan □6	32	51.35 N	3.35 W
West Hartford	166	41.46 N	72.45 W
West Haven	166	41.16 N	72.57 W
West Helena	174	34.33 N	90.39 W
West Indies II	130	19.00 N	70.00 W
West Jefferson	166	39.57 N	83.16 W
West Jordan	178	40.36 N	111.58 W
West Lafayette	174	40.27 N	86.55 W
Westlake	174	30.15 N	93.15 W
West Laramie	178	41.17 N	105.40 W
West Liberty	168	41.34 N	91.16 W
West Memphis	174	35.08 N	90.11 W
West Mifflin	166	40.22 N	79.52 W
Westminster, Colo., U.S.	178	39.50 N	105.02 W
Westminster, Md., U.S.	166	39.35 N	77.00 W
Westminster, S.C., U.S.	172	34.40 N	83.06 W
West Monroe	174	32.31 N	92.09 W
Westmont	166	40.19 N	78.57 W
Weston	166	39.02 N	80.28 W
Weston-super-Mare	32	51.21 N	2.59 W
West Orange	174	30.05 N	93.46 W
Westover	166	39.38 N	79.58 W
West Palm Beach	172	26.43 N	80.04 W
West Pensacola	174	30.27 N	87.15 W
West Plains	174	36.44 N	91.51 W
West Point, Ga., U.S.	172	32.52 N	85.10 W
West Point, Miss., U.S.	174	33.36 N	88.39 W
West Point, N.Y., U.S.	166	41.23 N	73.57 W
West Point Lake ⊜1	172	33.00 N	85.10 W
Westport, N.Z.	118	41.45 S	171.36 E
Westport, Conn., U.S.	166	41.09 N	73.22 W
Westport, Wash., U.S.	180	46.53 N	124.06 W
West Richland	180	46.18 N	119.20 W
West Rutland	166	43.36 N	73.03 W
West Sacramento	184	38.34 N	121.32 W
West Salem	168	43.54 N	91.05 W
West Slope	180	45.31 N	122.46 W
West Sussex □6	32	50.55 N	0.35 W
West Terre Haute	174	39.28 N	87.27 W
West Union	168	42.57 N	91.49 W
West Valley	180	46.08 N	113.01 W
Westville, Ind., U.S.	174	41.33 N	86.54 W
Westville, Okla., U.S.	174	35.59 N	94.34 W
West Virginia □3	162	38.45 N	80.30 W
West Warwick	166	41.42 N	71.32 W
West Webster	166	43.12 N	77.30 W
Westwego	174	29.55 N	90.09 W
Westwood Lakes	172	25.44 N	80.22 W
Wetar, Pulau I	82	7.48 S	126.18 E
Wethersfield	166	41.43 N	72.40 W
Wetumpka	174	32.27 N	86.13 W
Wetzlar	36	50.33 N	8.29 E
Wewak	116a	3.35 S	143.40 E
Wexford	32	52.20 N	6.27 W
Weyib ≃	102	4.11 N	42.09 E
Weymouth, Eng., U.K.	32	50.36 N	2.28 W
Weymouth, Mass., U.S.	166	42.13 N	70.58 W
Whalsay I	32	60.22 N	0.59 W
Whangaehu ≃	118	40.03 S	175.06 E
Whangarei	118	35.43 S	174.19 E
Wheatland	178	42.03 N	104.57 W
Wheaton, Ill., U.S.	174	41.52 N	88.06 W
Wheaton, Md., U.S.	166	39.03 N	77.03 W
Wheat Ridge	178	39.46 N	105.07 W
Wheeler ≃	160	57.02 N	67.13 W
Wheeler Lake ⊜1	174	34.40 N	87.05 W
Wheeler Peak ∧, Nev., U.S.	184	38.59 N	114.19 W
Wheeler Peak ∧, N. Mex., U.S.	178	36.34 N	105.25 W
Wheeling	166	40.05 N	80.42 W
Whidbey Island I	180	48.15 N	122.40 W
Whitby	32	54.29 N	0.37 W
White ≃, U.S.	162	43.45 N	99.30 W
White ≃, U.S.	174	33.53 N	91.03 W
White ≃, U.S.	178	40.04 N	109.41 W
White ≃, Ind., U.S.	174	38.25 N	87.44 W
White ≃, Nev., U.S.	184	37.42 N	115.10 W
White Bay C	160	50.00 N	56.30 W
White Bear Lake	168	45.05 N	93.01 W
White Cap Mountain ∧	166	45.35 N	69.13 W
White Castle	174	30.10 N	91.09 W
Whiteface, Mount ∧	166	44.22 N	73.54 W
Whitefish	180	48.25 N	114.20 W
Whitefish ≃	168	45.55 N	86.57 W
Whitefish Bay	168	43.07 N	87.55 W
White Hall, Ill., U.S.	174	39.26 N	90.24 W
Whitehall, Mich., U.S.	168	43.24 N	86.21 W
Whitehall, N.Y., U.S.	166	43.33 N	73.25 W
Whitehaven	32	54.33 N	3.35 W
Whitehorse	160	60.43 N	135.03 W
Whitehouse	184	32.13 N	95.14 W
White Lake ⊜	174	29.45 N	92.30 W
White Mountain Peak ∧	184	37.38 N	118.15 W
White Mountains ⋏, U.S.	184	37.30 N	118.15 W
White Mountains ⋏, N.H., U.S.	166	44.10 N	71.35 W
White Nile (Al-Bahr al-Abyad) ≃	102	15.38 N	32.31 E
White Oak	184	32.32 N	94.52 W
White Plains	166	41.02 N	73.46 W
White River Junction	166	43.39 N	72.19 W
White Salmon	180	45.44 N	121.29 W
Whitesands	112	19.28 S	169.25 E
White Sulphur Springs	172	37.48 N	80.18 W
Whiteville	172	34.20 N	78.42 W
White Volta (Volta Blanche) ≃	100	9.10 N	1.15 W
Whitewater	168	42.50 N	88.44 W
Whitewater Baldy ∧	178	33.20 N	108.39 W
Whiting	168	44.29 N	89.33 W
Whitman	166	42.05 N	70.56 W
Whitney, Mount ∧	184	36.35 N	118.18 W
Whittle, Cap >	160	50.11 N	60.08 W
Wichita	162	37.41 N	97.20 W
Wichita Falls	162	33.54 N	98.30 W
Wickenburg	178	33.58 N	112.44 W
Wicklow Mountains ⋏	32	53.02 N	6.24 W
Widawa ≃	36	51.13 N	16.55 E
Widnes	32	53.22 N	2.44 W
Wieliczka	36	49.59 N	20.04 E
Wielkopolska ◆1	36	51.50 N	17.20 E
Wieluń	36	51.14 N	18.34 E
Wien (Vienna)	36	48.13 N	16.20 E
Wiener Neustadt	36	47.49 N	16.15 E
Wienerwald ⋏	36	48.10 N	16.00 E
Wieprz ≃	36	51.34 N	21.49 E
Wieprza ≃	36	54.26 N	16.22 E
Wieprz-Krzna, Kanał ≅	36	51.56 N	22.56 E
Wierzyca ≃	36	53.51 N	18.50 E
Wiesbaden	36	50.05 N	8.14 E
Wiesloch	36	49.17 N	8.42 E
Wigan	32	53.33 N	2.38 W
Wiggins	174	30.51 N	89.08 W
Wilbur	180	47.46 N	118.42 W
Wilburton	174	34.55 N	95.19 W
Wildspitze ∧	36	46.53 N	10.52 E
Wildwood	166	38.59 N	74.49 W
Wilhelm, Mount ∧	116a	5.45 S	145.05 E
Wilhelm-Pieck-Stadt Guben	36	51.57 N	14.43 E
Wilhelmshaven	36	53.31 N	8.08 E
Wilkes-Barre	166	41.14 N	75.53 W
Wilkesboro	172	36.09 N	81.09 W
Wilkes Land ◆1	191	69.00 S	120.00 E
Willamette ≃	180	45.39 N	122.46 W
Willapa Bay C	180	46.37 N	124.00 W
Willard	166	41.03 N	82.44 W
Willcox	178	32.15 N	109.50 W
Willemstad	130	12.06 N	68.56 W
William "bill" Dannelly Reservoir ⊜1	174	32.10 N	87.10 W
Williams	178	35.15 N	112.11 W
Williamsburg, Ky., U.S.	172	36.44 N	84.10 W
Williamsburg, Va., U.S.	172	37.16 N	76.43 W
Williamson	172	37.41 N	82.17 W
Williamsport	166	41.14 N	77.00 W
Williamston, Mich., U.S.	168	42.41 N	84.17 W
Williamston, N.C., U.S.	172	35.51 N	77.04 W
Williamston, S.C., U.S.	172	34.37 N	82.29 W
Williamstown, Ky., U.S.	166	38.38 N	84.34 W
Williamstown, Mass., U.S.	166	42.43 N	73.12 W
Williamstown, N.J., U.S.	166	39.41 N	74.60 W
Williamstown, W. Va., U.S.	166	39.24 N	81.27 W
Willimantic	166	41.43 N	72.13 W
Willingboro	166	40.03 N	74.53 W
Williston, N. Dak., U.S.	162	48.09 N	103.37 W
Williston, S.C., U.S.	172	33.24 N	81.25 W
Williston Lake ⊜1	160	55.40 N	123.40 W
Willoughby	166	41.38 N	81.25 W
Willowick	166	41.38 N	81.28 W
Willow Springs	174	36.59 N	91.58 W
Wilmette	168	42.04 N	87.43 W
Wilmington, Del., U.S.	166	39.44 N	75.33 W
Wilmington, Ill., U.S.	168	41.18 N	88.09 W
Wilmington, N.C., U.S.	172	34.13 N	77.55 W
Wilmington, Ohio, U.S.	166	39.27 N	83.50 W
Wilmore	172	37.52 N	84.40 W
Wilson	172	35.44 N	77.55 W
Wilson, Mount ∧, Calif., U.S.	184	34.13 N	118.04 W
Wilson, Mount ∧, Colo., U.S.	178	37.51 N	107.59 W
Wilson Lake ⊜1	174	34.49 N	87.30 W
Wilsons Promontory >	116	38.55 S	146.20 E
Wilton	166	44.35 N	70.14 W
Wilton Manors	172	26.10 N	80.07 W
Wiltshire □6	32	51.15 N	1.50 W
Winamac	174	41.03 N	86.36 W
Winchendon	166	42.41 N	72.03 W
Winchester, Eng., U.K.	32	51.04 N	1.19 W
Winchester, Ind., U.S.	174	40.10 N	84.59 W
Winchester, Ky., U.S.	172	37.59 N	84.11 W
Winchester, Tenn., U.S.	174	35.10 N	86.01 W
Winchester, Va., U.S.	166	39.11 N	78.10 W
Wind ≃, Yukon, Can.	160	65.49 N	135.18 W
Wind ≃, Wyo., U.S.	180	43.35 N	108.13 W
Windber	166	40.14 N	78.50 W
Winder	172	32.59 N	83.43 W
Windhoek	104	22.34 S	17.06 E
Wind Lake	168	42.50 N	88.09 W
Wind River Peak ∧	180	42.42 N	109.07 W
Wind River Range ⋏	180	43.05 N	109.25 W
Windsor, Ont., Can.	168	42.18 N	83.01 W
Windsor, Eng., U.K.	32	51.29 N	0.38 W
Windsor, Conn., U.S.	166	41.51 N	72.39 W
Windsor, Mo., U.S.	174	38.32 N	93.31 W
Windsor, N.C., U.S.	172	36.00 N	76.57 W
Windsor, Vt., U.S.	166	43.29 N	72.23 W
Windsor Forest	172	32.56 N	81.11 W
Windsor Locks	166	41.56 N	72.38 W
Windward Islands II	130	13.00 N	61.00 W
Windward Passage ꓘ	130	20.00 N	73.50 W
Winfield, Ala., U.S.	174	33.56 N	87.49 W
Winfield, Kans., U.S.	162	37.15 N	96.59 W
Wingate	172	34.59 N	80.27 W
Winisk ≃	160	55.17 N	85.05 W
Winisk Lake ⊜	160	52.55 N	87.22 W
Winneba	100	5.25 N	0.36 W
Winnebago, Lake ⊜	168	44.00 N	88.25 W
Winneconne	168	44.07 N	88.43 W
Winnemucca	184	40.58 N	117.44 W
Winnemucca Lake ⊜	184	40.09 N	119.20 W
Winnetka	168	42.07 N	87.44 W
Winnfield	174	31.55 N	92.38 W
Winnibigoshish, Lake ⊜	168	47.27 N	94.12 W
Winnipeg	160	49.53 N	97.09 W
Winnipeg ≃	160	50.38 N	96.19 W
Winnipeg, Lake ⊜	160	52.00 N	97.00 W
Winnipegosis, Lake ⊜	160	52.30 N	100.00 W
Winnipesaukee, Lake ⊜	166	43.35 N	71.20 W
Winnsboro, La., U.S.	174	32.10 N	91.43 W
Winnsboro, S.C., U.S.	172	34.22 N	81.05 W
Winnsboro Mills	172	34.22 N	81.06 W
Winona, Minn., U.S.	168	44.03 N	91.39 W
Winona, Miss., U.S.	174	33.29 N	89.44 W
Winona Lake	174	41.14 N	85.49 W
Winooski	166	44.29 N	73.11 W
Winschoten	36	53.08 N	7.02 E
Winslow, Ariz., U.S.	178	35.01 N	110.42 W
Winslow, Maine, U.S.	166	44.32 N	69.38 W
Winsted	168	44.58 N	94.03 W
Winston	172	28.02 N	82.01 W
Winston-Salem	172	36.06 N	80.15 W
Winter Garden	172	28.34 N	81.35 W
Winter Haven	172	28.01 N	81.44 W
Winter Park, Fla., U.S.	172	28.36 N	81.20 W
Winter Park, N.C., U.S.	172	34.11 N	77.56 W
Winterset	168	41.20 N	94.01 W
Winterswijk	36	51.58 N	6.44 E
Winterthur	42	47.30 N	8.43 E
Winthrop	166	44.18 N	69.59 W
Winthrop Harbor	168	42.29 N	87.49 W
Wipperfürth	36	51.07 N	7.23 E
Wirral >1	32	53.20 N	3.03 W
Wisbech	32	52.40 N	0.10 E
Wisconsin □3	162	44.45 N	89.30 W
Wisconsin ≃	168	43.00 N	91.15 W
Wisconsin, Lake ⊜1	168	43.24 N	89.43 W
Wisconsin Dells	168	43.38 N	89.46 W
Wisconsin Rapids	168	44.23 N	89.49 W
Wise	172	36.59 N	82.34 W
Wisła ≃	36	54.22 N	18.55 E
Wisłok ≃	36	50.13 N	22.32 E
Wisłoka ≃	36	50.27 N	21.23 E
Wismar	36	53.53 N	11.28 E
Wister	174	34.58 N	94.43 W
Witbank	104	25.56 S	29.07 E
Witney	32	51.48 N	1.29 W
Witten	36	51.26 N	7.20 E
Wittenberg	36	51.52 N	12.39 E
Wittenberge	36	53.00 N	11.44 E
Wittstock	36	53.10 N	12.29 E
Witwatersrand ◆1	104	26.00 S	27.00 E
W. J. van Blommestein Meer ⊜1	144	4.45 N	55.00 W
Wkra ≃	36	52.27 N	20.44 E
Włocławek	36	52.39 N	19.02 E
Woburn	166	42.29 N	71.09 W
Woking	32	51.20 N	0.34 W
Wolf ≃	168	44.11 N	88.48 W
Wolf Creek ≃	178	40.12 N	108.29 W
Wolfeboro	166	43.35 N	71.12 W
Wolfen	36	51.40 N	12.16 E
Wolfenbüttel	36	52.10 N	10.32 E
Wolf Lake	168	43.14 N	86.10 W
Wolf Point	180	48.05 N	105.39 W
Wolf Rock I2	32	49.57 N	5.49 W
Wolfsberg	36	46.51 N	14.51 E
Wolfsburg	36	52.25 N	10.47 E
Wolgast	36	54.03 N	13.46 E
Wolin I	36	53.55 N	14.31 E
Wollaston, Islas II	146	55.40 S	67.30 W
Wollaston Lake ⊜	160	58.15 N	103.20 W
Wollongong	116	34.25 S	150.54 E
Wołomin	36	52.21 N	21.14 E
Wolverhampton	32	52.36 N	2.08 W
Wŏnju	80	37.22 N	127.58 E
Wŏnsan	80	39.09 N	127.25 E
Wood, Mount ∧	180	45.17 N	109.49 W
Woodall Mountain ∧2	174	34.45 N	88.11 W
Woodbridge	166	38.39 N	77.15 W
Woodburn	180	45.09 N	122.51 W
Woodbury	166	39.50 N	75.10 W
Woodland	184	38.41 N	121.46 W
Woodlark Island I	116a	9.05 S	152.50 E
Wood River	174	38.52 N	90.05 W
Woodruff	172	34.45 N	82.02 W
Woods, Lake of the ⊜	160	49.15 N	94.45 W
Woodstock, N.B., Can.	160	46.09 N	67.34 W
Woodstock, Ill., U.S.	168	42.19 N	88.27 W
Woodstock, Vt., U.S.	166	43.37 N	72.31 W
Woodward	162	36.26 N	99.24 W
Woonsocket	166	42.00 N	71.31 W
Wooster	166	40.48 N	81.56 W
Worcester, S. Afr.	104	33.39 S	19.27 E
Worcester, Eng., U.K.	32	52.11 N	2.13 W
Worcester, Mass., U.S.	166	42.16 N	71.48 W
Workington	32	54.39 N	3.35 W
Worksop	32	53.18 N	1.07 W
Worland	180	44.01 N	107.57 W
Worms	36	49.38 N	8.22 E
Wörther See ⊜	36	46.37 N	14.10 E
Worthing	32	50.48 N	0.23 W
Worthington, Ohio, U.S.	166	40.05 N	83.01 W
Wowoni, Pulau I	82	4.08 S	123.06 E
Wrangell Mountains ⋏	162a	62.00 N	143.00 W
Wrath, Cape >	32	58.37 N	5.01 W
Wrens	172	33.12 N	82.23 W
Wrexham	32	53.03 N	3.00 W
Wright City	174	34.03 N	95.01 W
Wright Patman Lake ⊜1	174	33.16 N	94.14 W
Wrightsville	172	32.44 N	82.43 W
Wrocław (Breslau)	36	51.06 N	17.00 E
Września	36	52.20 N	17.34 E
Wugongshan ⋏	80	27.21 N	113.50 E
Wuhan	80	30.36 N	114.17 E
Wuhu	80	31.21 N	118.22 E
Wulumuqi (Urumchi)	80	43.48 N	87.35 E
Wunnummin Lake ⊜	160	52.55 N	89.10 W
Wunstorf	36	52.25 N	9.26 E
Wuppertal	36	51.16 N	7.11 E
Würzburg	36	49.48 N	9.56 E
Wurzen	36	51.22 N	12.44 E
Wusulijiang (Ussuri) ≃	64	48.27 N	135.04 E
Wutongqiao	80	29.26 N	103.51 E
Wuxi	80	31.35 N	120.18 E
Wuzhou	80	23.30 N	111.27 E
Wyandotte	168	42.12 N	83.10 W
Wykoff	168	43.42 N	92.16 W
Wyndham	116	15.28 S	128.06 E
Wynne	174	35.14 N	90.47 W
Wyoming	168	42.54 N	85.42 W
Wyoming □3	162	43.00 N	107.30 W
Wyszków	36	52.36 N	21.28 E
Wytheville	172	36.57 N	81.05 W
X			
Xánthi	54	41.08 N	24.53 E
Xarrama ≃	50	38.14 N	8.20 W
Xau, Lake ⊜	104	21.15 S	24.38 E
Xenia	166	39.41 N	83.56 W
Xiamen (Amoy)	80	24.28 N	118.07 E
Xi'an (Sian)	80	34.15 N	108.52 E
Xiangtan	80	27.51 N	112.54 E
Xiaoxing'anling-shanmai ⋏	80	48.45 N	127.00 E
Xingkathu (Ozero Chanka) ⊜	80	45.00 N	132.24 E
Xingu ≃	144	1.30 S	51.53 W
Xinhailian	80	34.39 N	119.16 E
Xinxiang	80	35.20 N	113.51 E
Xuzhou	80	34.16 N	117.11 E
Y			
Yadkin ≃	172	35.23 N	80.03 W
Yadkinville	172	36.08 N	80.39 W
Yaheladazeshan ∧	80	35.12 N	95.20 E
Yakima	180	46.36 N	120.31 W
Yakima ≃	180	46.15 N	119.02 W
Yale, Mount ∧	178	38.51 N	106.18 W
Yalujiang (Amnok-kang) ≃	80	39.55 N	124.22 E
Yamagata	80	38.15 N	140.15 E
Yamaguchi	80	34.10 N	131.29 E
Yamdena, Pulau I	82	7.36 S	131.25 E
Yampa	178	40.09 N	106.55 W
Yampa ≃	178	40.32 N	108.59 W
Yanbu'	84	24.05 N	38.03 E
Yangquan	80	37.52 N	113.36 E
Yangtze → Changjiang ≃	80	31.48 N	121.10 E
Yangzhou	80	32.24 N	119.26 E
Yankton	162	42.53 N	97.23 W
Yantai (Chefoo)	80	37.33 N	121.20 E
Yaoundé	100	3.52 N	11.31 E
Yap I	82	9.31 N	138.06 E
Yapen, Pulau I	82	1.45 S	136.15 E
Yaqui ≃	130	27.37 N	110.39 W
Yare ≃	32	52.35 N	1.44 E
Yarīm	84	14.29 N	44.21 E
Yarmouth	166	43.48 N	70.12 W
Yasawa Group II	111	17.00 S	177.23 E
Yata ≃	144	10.29 S	65.26 W
Yates Center	174	37.53 N	95.44 W
Yatsushiro	80	32.30 N	130.36 E
Yatta Plateau ◆1	104	2.00 S	38.00 E
Yavarí (Javari) ≃	144	4.21 S	70.02 W
Yaví, Cerro ∧	144	5.32 N	65.59 W
Yazd	84	31.53 N	54.25 E
Yazoo ≃	174	32.22 N	91.00 W
Yazoo City	174	32.51 N	90.28 W
Yding Skovhøj ∧2	28	56.00 N	9.48 E
Yecla	50	38.37 N	1.07 W
Yellowhead Pass)(	160	52.53 N	118.28 W
Yellowknife	160	62.27 N	114.21 W
Yellowknife ≃	160	62.31 N	114.19 W
Yellow Sea ▾2	80	36.00 N	123.00 E
Yellowstone ≃	162	47.58 N	103.59 W
Yellowstone Falls ⱶ	180	44.43 N	110.30 W
Yellowstone Lake ⊜	180	44.25 N	110.22 W
Yellowstone National Park	180	44.58 N	110.42 W
Yemen □1	84	15.00 N	44.00 E
Yemen, People's Democratic Republic of □1	84	15.00 N	48.00 E
Yenangyaung	82	20.28 N	94.52 E
Yendi	100	9.26 N	0.01 W
Yenişehir	54	40.16 N	29.39 E
Yeovil	32	50.57 N	2.39 W
Yerevan → Jerevan	62	40.11 N	44.30 E
Yerington	184	38.59 N	119.10 W
Yerupaja, Nevado ∧	144	10.16 S	76.54 W
Yerushalayim (Jerusalem)	84	31.46 N	35.13 E
Yesa, Embalse de ⊜1	50	42.36 N	1.09 W
Yeu, Île d' I	42	46.42 N	2.20 W
Yiannitsá	54	40.48 N	22.25 E
Yibin	80	28.47 N	104.38 E
Yichang	80	30.42 N	111.11 E
Yichun	80	47.42 N	128.55 E
Yinchuan	80	38.30 N	106.18 E
Yingkou	80	40.40 N	122.14 E
Yining (Kuldja)	80	43.55 N	81.14 E
Yogyakarta	82	7.48 S	110.22 E
Yokkaichi	80	34.58 N	136.37 E
Yokohama	80	35.27 N	139.39 E
Yokosuka	80	35.18 N	139.40 E
Yom ≃	82	15.52 N	100.16 E
Yonago	80	35.26 N	133.20 E
Yonezawa	80	37.55 N	140.07 E
Yonkers	166	41.00 N	73.52 W
York, Eng., U.K.	32	53.58 N	1.05 W
York, Ala., U.S.	174	32.29 N	88.18 W
York, Pa., U.S.	166	39.58 N	76.44 W
York, S.C., U.S.	172	35.00 N	81.14 W
York ≃	172	37.15 N	76.23 W
York, Cape >	116	10.42 S	142.31 E
Yorkville	166	43.07 N	75.16 W
Yoro	130	15.09 N	87.07 W
Yŏsu	80	34.46 N	127.44 E
Youngstown, N.Y., U.S.	166	43.15 N	79.03 W
Youngstown, Ohio, U.S.	166	41.06 N	80.39 W
Youssoufia	100	32.16 N	8.33 W
Ypsilanti	168	42.15 N	83.36 W
Yreka	184	41.44 N	122.38 W
Ystad	28	55.25 N	13.49 E
Ystwyth ≃	32	52.24 N	4.05 W
Yuba City	184	39.08 N	121.37 W
Yūbari	80	43.04 N	141.59 E
Yucaipa	184	34.02 N	117.02 W
Yucatan Channel ꓘ	130	21.45 N	85.45 W
Yucatan Peninsula >1	130	19.30 N	89.00 W
Yucca Valley	184	34.07 N	116.35 W
Yugoslavia □1	20	44.00 N	19.00 E
Yukon □4	160	64.00 N	135.00 W
Yukon ≃	162a	62.33 N	163.59 W
Yuma	178	32.43 N	114.37 W
Yumen	80	39.56 N	97.51 E
Yunhe (Grand Canal) ≅	80	32.12 N	119.31 E
Yurimaguas	144	5.54 S	76.05 W
Yverdon	42	46.47 N	6.39 E
Z			
Zaandam	36	52.26 N	4.49 E
Zăbala ≃	54	45.51 N	26.46 E
Zabarjad, Jazīrat I	102	23.37 N	36.12 E
Ząbkowice Śląskie	36	50.36 N	16.53 E
Zabrze	36	50.18 N	18.46 E
Zacapa	130	14.58 N	89.32 W
Zacatecas	130	22.47 N	102.35 W
Zachary	174	30.39 N	91.09 W
Zadar	46	44.07 N	15.14 E
Zadetkyi Kyun I	82	9.58 N	98.13 E
Zadorra ≃	50	42.40 N	2.54 W
Zafra	50	38.25 N	6.25 W
Żagań	36	51.37 N	15.19 E
Zaghouan, Djebel ∧	46	36.21 N	10.08 E
Zagora ⋏	46	43.40 N	16.15 E
Zagorsk	26	56.18 N	38.08 E
Zagreb	46	45.48 N	15.58 E
Zāgros, Kūhhā-ye ⋏	84	33.40 N	47.00 E
Zagyva ≃	36	47.10 N	20.13 E
Zahlah	84	33.51 N	35.53 E
Zaire □1	104	4.00 S	25.00 E
Zaïre → Congo ≃	104	6.04 S	12.24 E
Zaječar	54	43.54 N	22.17 E
Zajsan, Ozero ⊜	62	48.00 N	84.00 E
Zákinthos	54	37.47 N	20.53 E
Zákinthos I	54	37.52 N	20.44 E
Zakopane	36	49.19 N	19.57 E
Zala ≃	36	46.43 N	17.16 E
Zalaegerszeg	36	46.51 N	16.51 E
Zalău	54	47.11 N	23.03 E
Zambezi (Zambeze) ≃	104	18.55 S	36.04 E
Zambia □1	104	15.00 S	30.00 E
Zamboanga	82	6.54 N	122.04 E
Zambrów	36	53.00 N	22.15 E
Zamfara ≃	100	12.05 N	4.02 E
Zamora	50	41.30 N	5.45 W
Zamora de Hidalgo	130	19.59 N	102.16 W
Zamość	36	50.44 N	23.15 E
Zandvoort	36	52.22 N	4.32 E
Zanesville	166	39.56 N	82.01 W
Zanzibar	104	6.10 S	39.11 E
Zanzibar Island I	104	6.10 S	39.20 E
Zapadnaja Dvina (Daugava) ≃	62	57.04 N	24.03 E
Zapadna Morava ≃	54	43.42 N	21.23 E
Zapadno-Sibirskaja Nizmennost' ≚	62	60.00 N	75.00 E
Zapadnyj Sajan ⋏	62	53.00 N	94.00 E
Zaporožje	62	47.50 N	35.10 E
Zaragoza	50	41.38 N	0.53 W
Zārate	146	34.06 S	59.02 W
Zard Kūh ∧	84	32.22 N	50.04 E
Zaria	100	11.07 N	7.44 E
Żary (Sorau)	36	51.38 N	15.09 E
Zāskār Mountains ⋏	84	33.00 N	78.00 E
Žatec	36	50.18 N	13.32 E
Zavalla	184	31.09 N	94.26 W
Zawiercie	36	50.30 N	19.25 E
Zāwiyat al-Baydā'	102	32.46 N	21.43 E
Ždanov	62	47.06 N	37.33 E
Zduńska Wola	36	51.36 N	18.57 E
Zebulon	172	35.49 N	78.19 W
Zeeland	168	42.49 N	86.01 W
Zehdenick	36	52.59 N	13.20 E
Zeist	36	52.05 N	5.15 E
Zeitz	36	51.03 N	12.08 E
Zele	36	51.04 N	4.02 E
Zelengora ⋏	54	43.15 N	18.45 E
Zeletin ≃	54	46.03 N	27.23 E
Zella-Mehlis	36	50.39 N	10.39 E
Zel'onodol'sk	26	55.51 N	48.33 E
Zembra, Île I	46	37.08 N	10.48 E
Zenica	54	44.12 N	17.55 E
Zephyrhills	172	28.14 N	82.11 W
Zerbst	36	51.58 N	12.04 E
Zereh, Gowd-e ⊜	84	29.45 N	61.50 E
Zerga, Merja C	50	34.51 N	6.17 W
Zeroud, Oued V	46	35.50 N	10.13 E
Zeulenroda	36	50.39 N	11.58 E
Zevenaar	36	51.56 N	6.05 E
Zêzere ≃	50	39.28 N	8.20 W
Zgierz	36	51.52 N	19.25 E
Zhalinghu ⊜	80	34.53 N	97.58 E
Zhangjiakou (Kalgan)	80	40.50 N	114.53 E
Zhangzhou	80	24.33 N	117.39 E
Zhanjiang	80	21.16 N	110.28 E
Zhengzhou	80	34.48 N	113.39 E
Zhenjiang	80	32.13 N	119.26 E
Zhob ≃	84	32.04 N	69.50 E
Zhujiangkou C	80	23.36 N	113.44 E
Zhuzhou	80	27.50 N	113.09 E
Žiar nad Hronom	36	48.36 N	18.52 E
Zibo	80	36.47 N	118.01 E
Zielona Góra (Grünberg)	36	51.56 N	15.31 E
Zigana Dağları ⋏	84	40.37 N	39.30 E
Zigong	80	29.24 N	104.47 E
Ziguinchor	100	12.35 N	16.16 W
Žigulevsk	26	53.25 N	49.27 E
Žilina	36	49.14 N	18.46 E
Zillah	180	46.24 N	120.16 W
Zillertaler Alpen ⋏	36	47.00 N	11.55 E
Zimbabwe □1	104	20.00 S	30.00 E
Zimnicea	54	43.39 N	25.21 E
Zinder	100	13.48 N	8.59 E
Zion	168	42.27 N	87.50 W
Žitomir	62	50.16 N	28.40 E
Zittau	36	50.54 N	14.47 E
Ziway, Lake ⊜	102	8.00 N	38.50 E
Zlatoust	62	55.10 N	59.40 E
Złotoryja	36	51.08 N	15.55 E
Złotów	36	53.22 N	17.02 E
Znojmo	36	48.52 N	16.02 E
Zomba	104	15.23 S	35.18 E
Zonguldak	20	41.27 N	31.49 E
Zrenjanin	54	45.23 N	20.24 E
Zrmanja ≃	46	44.15 N	15.32 E
Zuckerhütl ∧	36	46.58 N	11.09 E
Zug	42	47.10 N	8.31 E
Zugspitze ∧	36	47.25 N	10.59 E
Zuiderzee → IJsselmeer ▾2	36	52.45 N	5.25 E
Zumbrota	168	44.17 N	92.40 W
Zuni	178	35.04 N	108.51 W
Zunyi	80	27.39 N	106.57 E
Zuqar, Jazīrat I	84	14.00 N	42.45 E
Zürich	42	47.23 N	8.32 E
Zürichsee ⊜	42	47.13 N	8.45 E
Zutphen	36	52.08 N	6.12 E
Zvolen	36	48.35 N	19.08 E
Zweibrücken	36	49.15 N	7.21 E
Zwickau	36	50.44 N	12.29 E
Zwischenahn	36	53.11 N	8.00 E
Zwolle, Ned.	36	52.30 N	6.05 E
Zwolle, La., U.S.	174	31.38 N	93.38 W
Żyrardów	36	52.04 N	20.25 E
Żywiec	36	49.41 N	19.12 E